T0178572

Lecture Notes in Computer Science   14551

Founding Editors

Gerhard Goos
Juris Hartmanis

Editorial Board Members

The series Lecture Notes in Computer Science (LNCS), including its subseries Lecture Notes in Artificial Intelligence (LNAI) and Lecture Notes in Bioinformatics (LNBI), has established itself as a medium for the publication of new developments in computer science and information technology research, teaching, and education.

LNCS enjoys close cooperation with the computer science R & D community, the series counts many renowned academics among its volume editors and paper authors, and collaborates with prestigious societies. Its mission is to serve this international community by providing an invaluable service, mainly focused on the publication of conference and workshop proceedings and postproceedings. LNCS commenced publication in 1973.

Mohamed Mosbah · Florence Sèdes ·
Nadia Tawbi · Toufik Ahmed ·
Nora Boulahia-Cuppens · Joaquin Garcia-Alfaro
Editors

Foundations and Practice of Security

16th International Symposium, FPS 2023
Bordeaux, France, December 11–13, 2023
Revised Selected Papers, Part I

Springer

Editors
Mohamed Mosbah (iD)
University of Bordeaux
Bordeaux, France

Nadia Tawbi (iD)
Université Laval
Québec, QC, Canada

Nora Boulahia-Cuppens (iD)
Polytechnique Montréal
Montreal, QC, Canada

Florence Sèdes (iD)
Toulouse III - Paul Sabatier University
Toulouse, France

Toufik Ahmed (iD)
University of Bordeaux
Bordeaux, France

Joaquin Garcia-Alfaro (iD)
Telecom SudParis
Palaiseau, France

ISSN 0302-9743   ISSN 1611-3349 (electronic)
Lecture Notes in Computer Science
ISBN 978-3-031-57536-5   ISBN 978-3-031-57537-2 (eBook)
https://doi.org/10.1007/978-3-031-57537-2

Foreword Message from the Chairs

The 16th International Symposium on Foundations and Practice of Security (FPS 2023) was hosted by the Bordeaux Institute of Technology (Bordeaux INP), in Bordeaux, France, from December 11 to December 13, 2023.

FPS's aim was to discuss and exchange theoretical and practical ideas that address security issues in interconnected systems. It allowed scientists to present their work and establish links and promote scientific collaboration, joint research programs, and student exchanges between institutions involved in this important and fast-moving research field.

The call for papers welcomed submissions spanning the full range of theoretical and applied work including user research, methods, tools, simulations, demos, and practical evaluations. We also invited researchers and practitioners working in privacy, security, resiliency, trustworthy data systems, and related areas to submit their original papers. This year, special care was given to enhancing Cybersecurity and Resiliency with Artificial Intelligence.

FPS 2023 received 80 submissions from countries all over the world. On average, each paper was reviewed (single blind) by three program committee members, and there were several online discussions in case of divergent evaluations. The Program Committee selected 27 regular papers and 8 short papers for presentation. An invited paper was also selected for publication in this book. The selected papers have been organized in the following sections: Artificial Intelligence and Cybersecurity; Security Analysis; Phishing and Social Networks; Vulnerabilities, Exploits and Threats; Malware Analysis; Security Design and Short Papers.

December 2023

Nadia Tawbi
Florence Sèdes
Mohamed Mosbah
Nora Boulahia-Cuppens
Toufik Ahmed

Organization

General Chairs

Toufik Ahmed   Bordeaux INP, France
Nora Cuppens   École Polytechnique de Montréal, Canada

Program Committee Chairs

Mohamed Mosbah   Bordeaux INP, France
Florence Sèdes   Université Toulouse III Paul Sabatier, France
Nadia Tawbi   Université Laval, Canada

Keynote Chair

Guy-Vincent Jourdan   University of Ottawa, Canada

Local Organization Chair

Léo Mendiboure   Université Gustave Eiffel, France

Publications Chair

Joaquin Garcia-Alfaro   Institut Polytechnique de Paris, France

Publicity Chairs

Raphaël Khoury   Université du Québec en Outaouais, Canada
Paria Shirani   University of Ottawa, Canada
Reda Yaich   IRT SystemX, France

Program Committee

Carlisle Adams	University of Ottawa, Canada
Esma Aïmeur	Université de Montréal, Canada
Furkan Alaca	Queen's University, Canada
Abdelmalek Benzekri	Université Toulouse 3 Paul Sabatier, France
Anis Bkakria	IRT SystemX, France
Guillaume Bonfante	LORIA – Université de Lorraine, France
Ana Rosa Cavalli	Institut Polytechnique de Paris, France
Xihui Chen	University of Luxembourg, Luxembourg
Kimberly A. Cornell	University at Albany, USA
Frédéric Cuppens	Polytechnique Montréal, Canada
Nora Cuppens-Boulahia	Polytechnique Montréal, Canada
Xavier de Carné de Carnavalet	Hong Kong Polytechnic University, China
Benoit Dupont	Université de Montréal, Canada
Latifa El Bargui	University of Ottawa, Canada
Sebastien Gambs	Université du Québec à Montréal, Canada
Joaquin Garcia-Alfaro	Institut Polytechnique de Paris, France
Talal Halabi	Université Laval, Canada
Sylvain Hallé	Université du Québec à Chicoutimi, Canada
Abdessamad Imine	LORIA-Inria Lorraine, France
Jason Jaskolka	Carleton University, Canada
Mathieu Jaume	Sorbonne Université, France
Houda Jmila	Commissariat à l'Energie Atomique, France
Guy-Vincent Jourdan	University of Ottawa, Canada
Raphaël Khoury	Université du Québec en Outaouais, Canada
Hyoungshick Kim	Sungkyunkwan University, South Korea
Hyungjoon Koo	Sungkyunkwan University, South Korea
Evangelos Kranakis	Carleton University, Canada
Romain Laborde	University Paul Sabatier Toulouse III, France
Pascal Lafourcade	University Clermont Auvergne, France
Maryline Laurent	Institut Polytechnique de Paris, France
Mounier Laurent	Laboratoire Vérimag, France
Olivier Levillain	Institut Polytechnique de Paris, France
Luigi Logrippo	Université du Québec en Outaouais, Canada
Taous Madi	King Abdullah University of Science and Technology, Saudi Arabia
Jean-Yves Marion	Université de Lorraine, France
Andrew M. Marshall	University of Mary Washington, USA
Daiki Miyahara	University of Electro-Communications, Japan
Mohamed Mosbah	LaBRI – University of Bordeaux, France
Djedjiga Mouheb	University of Sharjah, United Arab Emirates

Paliath Narendran	University at Albany, USA
Omer Landry Nguena Timo	Université du Québec en Outaouais, Canada
Marie-Laure Potet	Laboratoire Vérimag, France
Isabel Praça	Instituto Superior de Engenharia do Porto, Portugal
Silvio Ranise	University of Trento and Fondazione Bruno Kessler, Italy
Jean-Marc Robert	École de technologie supérieure, Canada
Michael Rusinowitch	LORIA – Inria Nancy, France
Kazuo Sakiyama	University of Electro-Communications, Japan
Khosro Salmani	Mount Royal University, Canada
Giada Sciarretta	Fondazione Bruno Kessler, Italy
Florence Sèdes	Université Toulouse III Paul Sabatier, France
Paria Shirani	University of Ottawa, Canada
Renaud Sirdey	Commissariat à l'Energie Atomique, France
Natalia Stakhanova	University of Saskatchewan, Canada
Nadia Tawbi	Université Laval, Canada
Sadegh Torabi	Concordia University, Canada
Jun Yan	Concordia University, Canada
Nicola Zannone	Eindhoven University of Technology, The Netherlands

Steering Committee

Frédéric Cuppens	École Polytechnique de Montréal, Canada
Nora Cuppens-Boulahia	École Polytechnique de Montréal, Canada
Mourad Debbabi	University of Concordia, Canada
Joaquin Garcia-Alfaro	Institut Polytechnique de Paris, France
Evangelos Kranakis	Carleton University, Canada
Pascal Lafourcade	University of Clermont Auvergne, France
Jean-Yves Marion	Mines de Nancy, France
Ali Miri	Toronto Metropolitan University, Canada
Rei Safavi-Naini	Calgary University, Canada
Nadia Tawbi	Université Laval, Canada

Additional Reviewers

Shashank Arora	Guillaume Gagnon
Pradeep K. Atrey	Asmaa Hailane
Stefano Berlato	Frédéric Hayek
Josee Desharnais	Li Huang

Padmavathi Iyer

Nerys Jimenez-Pichardo

Mohamed Ali Kandi

Youcef Korichi

Vinh Hoa La

Abir Laraba

Wissam Mallouli

Gael Marcadet

Majid Mollaeefar

Manh-Dung Nguyen

Huu Nghia Nguyen

Charles Olivier-Anclin

Sankita Patel

Josue Ruiz

Amir Sharif

Valeria Valdés

Badreddine Yacine Yacheur

Atefeh Zareh Chahoki

Formal Verification of Security Protocols: the Squirrel Prover (Keynote)

Stéphanie Delaune

Univ Rennes, CNRS, IRISA, France

Abstract. Security protocols are widely used today to secure transactions that take place through public channels like the Internet. Common applications involve the secure transfer of sensitive information like credit card numbers or user authentication on a system. Because of their increasing ubiquity in many important applications (e.g. electronic commerce, government-issued ID), a very important research challenge consists in developing methods and verification tools to increase our trust on security protocols, and so on the applications that rely on them.

Formal methods have introduced various approaches to prove that security protocols indeed guarantee the expected security properties. Tools like ProVerif [5] and Tamarin [6] analyse protocols in the symbolic model, leveraging techniques from model-checking, automated reasoning, and concurrency theory. However, it's essential to note that security in the symbolic model doesn't necessarily imply security in the cryptographer's standard model—the computational model—where attackers operate as probabilistic polynomial time Turing machines. Verification techniques for the computational model, though crucial, often exhibit less flexibility or automation compared to tools in the symbolic model.

In recent collaborative efforts, my colleagues and I have proposed a novel approach [1], building upon the Computationally Complete Symbolic Attacker (CCSA) logic introduced by Gergei Bana and Hubert Comon a few years ago [3, 4]. This approach has been implemented in a new proof assistant called SQUIRREL, and the effectiveness of the SQUIRREL prover has been validated across various case studies. The SQUIRREL tool, a user-friendly manual, as well as an online platform to experiment SQUIRREL without installing it, are now available: https://squirrel-prover.github.io.

This work received funding from the France 2030 program managed by the French National Research Agency under grant agreement No. ANR-22-PECY-0006.

Figure 1 shows a screenshot of the SQUIRREL prover. On the left, a description of the Basic Hash protocol written in the input language of SQUIRREL is depicted. The scenario under study features several reader sessions with access to a database, and several tags where each tag can play multiple sessions. The exists instruction encodes the database lookup performed by the reader.

Fig. 1. Screenshot of the SQUIRREL prover on the Basic Hash protocol.

Then, an authentication property on the Basic Hash protocol is expressed. Here cond@R1(j) is a macro which stands for the condition of action R1(j) – the condition for executing the then branch of the reader. The authentication lemma expresses that, whenever this condition holds, there must be some session k of tag i (the one using key(i)) that has been executed before R1(j). Moreover, the output of the tag's action should coincide with the input of the reader's action. Finally, this authentication goal is proved using a succession of six tactics.

On the right, the status of the proof after the execution of the three first tactics is shown. The hypotheses are written above the horizontal line, and the goal that remains to be proved is written below the horizontal line. At this stage of the proof, we can see that some hypotheses have been introduced (intro tactic), and the macro cond@R1(j) has been expanded (expand tactic). The next step of the proof consists of applying the euf tactic (unforgeability of h). Roughly, if snd(input@R1(j) is a valid hash of fst(input@R1(j)), thus the term fst(input@R1(j)) must be equal to a message that has previously been hashed. As the only application of the h function is in the action performed by the tag and is applied on the nonce nT, after applying the euf tactic, we obtain:

```
[goal> Focused goal (1/1):
System: BasicHash
Variables: i0,j:index[const]
HEq: snd (input@R1(j)) = h (fst (input@R1(j)), key i0)
Hap: happens(R1(j))
------------------------------------------------
(exists (k:index), T(i0, k) < R1(j) && fst (input@R1(j)) = nT (i0, k)) =>
exists (i,k:index),
  T(i, k) < R1(j) &&
  fst (output@T(i, k)) = fst (input@R1(j)) &&
  snd (output@T(i, k)) = snd (input@R1(j))
```

In Fig. 2, some results that have been obtained with the SQUIRREL prover are summarised. The number of LoC mentioned includes both the model and the proof script. The cryptographic assumptions on which the proof relies on are also indicated, as well as the security properties under study.

Protocol name	LoC	Assumptions	Security Properties
Basic Hash	100	PRF, EUF	authentication & unlinkability
Hash Lock	130	PRF, EUF	authentication & unlinkability
LAK (with pairs)	250	PRF, EUF	authentication & unlinkability
MW	300	PRF, EUF, XOR	authentication & unlinkability
Feldhofer	270	ENC-KP, INT-CTXT	authentication & unlinkability
Private authentication	100	CCA$_1$, ENC-KP	anonymity
Signed DDH [ISO 9798-3]	240	EUF, DDH	authentication & strong secrecy
CANAuth	450	EUF	authentication
SLK06	80	EUF	authentication
YPLRK05	160	EUF	authentication

Fig. 2. Some results obtained with the SQUIRREL prover on various protocols [1, 2].

References

1. Baelde, D., Delaune, S., Jacomme, C., Koutsos, A., Moreau, S.: An interactive prover for protocol verification in the computational model. In: Proceedings of the 42nd IEEE Symposium on Security and Privacy (S&P'21), San Fransisco/Virtual, USA (May 2021)
2. Baelde, D., Delaune, S., Koutsos, A., Moreau, S.: Cracking the stateful nut: computational proofs of stateful security protocols using the SQUIRREL proof assistant. In: Proceedings of the 35th IEEE Computer Security Foundations Symposium (CSF'22), pp. 289–304, Haifa, Israel. IEEE Computer Society Press (Aug 2022)
3. Bana, G., Comon-Lundh, H.: Towards unconditional soundness: computationally complete symbolic attacker. In: Degano, P., Guttman, J.D. (eds.) Principles of Security and Trust. POST 2012. Lecture Notes in Computer Science, vol. 7215, pp. 189–208. Springer, Berlin (2012). https://doi.org/10.1007/978-3-642-28641-4_11
4. Bana, G., Comon-Lundh, H.: A computationally complete symbolic attacker for equivalence properties. In Proceedings of the 21st Conference on Computer and Communications Security (CCS'14), pp. 609–620. ACM (2014)

5. Blanchet, B.: An efficient cryptographic protocol verifier based on prolog rules. In: Proceedings of the 14th IEEE Computer Security Foundations Workshop (CSFW'01), pp. 82–96. IEEE Computer Society (2001)
6. Meier, S., Schmidt, B., Cremers, C., Basin, D.: The TAMARIN prover for the symbolic analysis of security protocols. In: Sharygina, N., Veith, H. (eds.) Computer Aided Verification. CAV 2013. Lecture Notes in Computer Science, vol. 8044, pp. 696–701. Springer, Berlin (2013). https://doi.org/10.1007/978-3-642-39799-8_48

Contents – Part I

Phishing and Social Network

Vulnerabilities and Exploits

Network and System Threat

Malware Analysis

Security Design

Contents – Part II

AI and Cybersecurity

An Adversarial Robustness Benchmark
for Enterprise Network Intrusion Detection

João Vitorino$^{(\boxtimes)}$ ⓘ, Miguel Silva ⓘ, Eva Maia ⓘ, and Isabel Praça ⓘ

Research Group on Intelligent Engineering and Computing for Advanced Innovation and
Development (GECAD), School of Engineering, Polytechnic of Porto (ISEP/IPP),
4249-015 Porto, Portugal
`{jpmvo,mdgsa,egm,icp}@isep.ipp.pt`

Abstract. As cyber-attacks become more sophisticated, improving the robustness of Machine Learning (ML) models must be a priority for enterprises of all sizes. To reliably compare the robustness of different ML models for cyber-attack detection in enterprise computer networks, they must be evaluated in standardized conditions. This work presents a methodical adversarial robustness benchmark of multiple decision tree ensembles with constrained adversarial examples generated from standard datasets. The robustness of regularly and adversarially trained RF, XGB, LGBM, and EBM models was evaluated on the original CICIDS2017 dataset, a corrected version of it designated as NewCICIDS, and the HIKARI dataset, which contains more recent network traffic. NewCICIDS led to models with a better performance, especially XGB and EBM, but RF and LGBM were less robust against the more recent cyber-attacks of HIKARI. Overall, the robustness of the models to adversarial cyber-attack examples was improved without their generalization to regular traffic being affected, enabling a reliable detection of suspicious activity without costly increases of false alarms.

Keywords: machine learning · enterprise networks · adversarial attacks · adversarial training · cybersecurity

1 Introduction

Protecting digital assets and business processes is a priority for enterprises of all sizes. As cyber-attacks become more sophisticated, network intrusion detection systems stand out as a critical security component to monitor network traffic and identify suspicious activity [1]. Artificial Intelligence (AI), and more specifically Machine Learning (ML), has become significantly valuable to strengthen enterprise network security. ML models can be used to tackle the growing number of threats by performing anomaly detection and even classifying the cyber-attacks targeting an enterprise [2].

In the network intrusion detection domain, ML models based on ensembles of decision trees are very well-established. Bagging ensembles like Random Forest (RF) and boosting ensembles like Extreme Gradient Boosting (XGB) are reliable and computationally efficient models that are commonly used to detect and classify cyber-attacks in enterprise-scale computer networks [3, 4].

M. Mosbah et al. (Eds.): FPS 2023, LNCS 14551, pp. 3–17, 2024.
https://doi.org/10.1007/978-3-031-57537-2_1

However, an attacker may craft an adversarial cyber-attack example with specialized inputs capable of evading detection and disrupting the confidentiality, integrity, and availability of the data and business processes of an enterprise. Adversarial ML is a rapidly growing research field that addresses these disruptions by studying the adversarial attacks that attempt to exploit the vulnerabilities of ML models and the possible defense strategies to improve robustness against such attacks [5, 6].

Even though there are several studies that use standard benchmark datasets to compare the performance of ML models for network intrusion detection, there is still a lack of consistency in the studies that analyze their robustness [7, 8]. Different studies follow distinct approaches to evaluate robustness, preventing researchers from knowing which models are the most suitable for their specific computer networks, and which adversarial attacks could be used against them in a real scenario [9, 10]. Therefore, to reliably compare the robustness of different types of ML models with different datasets, they must be evaluated in standardized conditions.

This work presents a methodical adversarial robustness benchmark of multiple decision tree ensembles with constrained adversarial examples generated from standard datasets for network intrusion detection. The robustness of regularly and adversarially trained RF, XGB, Light Gradient Boosting Machine (LGBM), and Explainable Boosting Machine (EBM) models is evaluated on the original CICIDS2017 dataset, a corrected version of it designated as NewCICIDS, and the HIKARI dataset, which contains more recent network traffic. The results obtained in each dataset are compared to analyze their suitability for network intrusion detection tasks, and the robustness of the models to adversarial cyber-attack examples is assessed, to verify if it can be improved without their generalization to regular network traffic being affected.

The present paper is organized into multiple sections, meant to enable researchers to replicate this benchmark and perform trustworthy comparisons with the results of future studies. Section 2 provides a survey of previous work on the use of ML for enterprise network intrusion detection and the standard datasets. Section 3 describes the data preprocessing and selected features, the benchmark methodology, and the fine-tuning of the models. Section 4 presents an analysis of the obtained results for each dataset. Finally, Sect. 5 addresses the main conclusions and future research topics.

2 Related Work

To perform a reliable benchmark of RF, XGB, LGBM, and EBM, it is important to understand the results and conclusions of previous work on the use of ML for network intrusion detection in enterprise computer networks.

Recent studies [11–13] mostly evaluate ML models using the publicly available CICIDS2017 dataset, which is very well-established across the scientific community. Despite not being very recent, it continues to be used to compare the performance of novel models with the state-of-the-art results of previous models of the previous years. Since this dataset is so widely used, researchers have also carefully analyzed it and performed corrections to some of the network traffic flows it contains, publishing a corrected version designated as NewCICIDS [14, 15]. Despite the limited use of this newer version, it was used in [16] to evaluate the robustness of decision tree ensembles when confronted with adversarial attacks. The results exhibited a lack of robustness in these ensembles, so it is essential to further improve their training processes.

As new cyber-attacks and adversarial methods are encountered, it is essential to train ML models with the most up-to-date datasets containing high-quality data recordings [17]. To develop more robust cybersecurity solutions, recent studies start to use other datasets like HIKARI because there are new types of attacks that are starting to be used against modern enterprises [18, 19].

In a recent study addressing botnet detection [20], the researchers trained lightweight models using both the HIKARI dataset and the CTU-13 dataset. The authors experimented dimensionality reduction techniques, and the models reached an accuracy of 99% with all the features and 96% with a reduced number of features. Expanding to other types of cyber-attacks, in [21], the CICIDS2017 and HIKARI datasets were combined to improve data quality. This study compared various models, including RF, XGB, Logistic Regression, Deep Neural Network, and Long Short-Term Memory, and the best precision was 99% and the accuracy 86%. These results are substantially lower than in the previous study that only used the HIKARI dataset, so they may be caused by the increased diversity of cyber-attacks of the combined datasets.

To choose the best models capable of dealing with the unbalanced data of these datasets, in [22], the HIKARI dataset was used for training RF, XGB, Multilayer Perceptron, and Convolutional Neural Network. The authors concluded that these models may not effectively detect zero-day attacks, so it is necessary to improve their training processes to make them more robust. Additionally, in [23], the HIKARI dataset was also used to develop classifiers capable of detecting out-of-distribution data, which presents similarities to zero-day attacks. Several tree ensembles, such as RF and Gradient Boosted Decision Trees (GDBT), were evaluated. The authors' version of GBDT reached the highest accuracy, 99.57%, and area under the ROC curve, 90.30%. On the other hand, RF achieved the higher area under the precision and recall curve, 83.35%, denoting that, in some evaluation metrics, the lightweight ensembles can reach better results than the more complex ensembles that perform gradient boosting.

Overall, the recent studies on network intrusion have demonstrated that using tree ensembles is a promising approach to detect suspicious activity in enterprise computer networks. The commonly used models include stacking and bagging ensembles, as well as gradient boosting ensembles, which can have very good results against regular network traffic flows [19]. However, to the best of our knowledge, no previous work has analyzed how the time-related characteristics of the three considered datasets affect the robustness of RF, XGB, LGBM, and EBM against perturbed network traffic flows.

3   Methods

This section describes the considered datasets, the data preprocessing stage, and the utilized models and adversarial method. The work was carried out on a common machine with 16 GB of RAM, a 6-core CPU and a 4 GB GPU. The implementation relied on the Python programming language and the following libraries: *numpy* and *pandas* for general data manipulation, *scikit-learn* for the implementation of RF, *xgboost* for XGB, *lightgbm* for LGBM, and *interpret* for EBM.

3.1 Datasets and Data Preprocessing

Due to their use across several studies, three standard datasets for binary network traffic classification were considered for the benchmark: CICIDS2017, NewCICIDS, and HIKARI. The main characteristics of these datasets are briefly described below.

CICIDS2017 [24] is a very highly used dataset that contains common cyber-attacks performed in an enterprise computer network. It includes multiple captures of benign activity and several types of probing, brute-force, and DoS attacks, which were recorded in 2017 in an heterogenous testbed environment with 12 interacting machines. The network traffic flows were converted to a tabular data format using the CICFlowMeter [25] tool, provided by the Canadian Institute for Cybersecurity. This process resulted in 872105 data samples of the benign class and 266507 of the malicious class, in the combined dataset of the Tuesday and Wednesday captures.

Even though CICIDS2017 continues to be used as a standard benchmark dataset to compare the performance of novel ML models with baseline models from previous studies, some discrepancies have been noticed on a portion of the attack vectors it contains. A corrected version of this dataset has been created to address this issue and provide more realistic network traffic flows, being designated as NewCICIDS [14, 15]. It includes the same types of cyber-attacks as the original dataset, but it has a reduced size, with 638432 benign samples and 106538 malicious samples.

A more recent dataset, HIKARI [26], is starting to be used in various studies because it includes cyber-attacks that have started to be performed in more recent years. It contains probing and brute-force attacks, as well as benign background traffic of the normal operation of an enterprise network that uses the HTTPS communication protocol to encrypt network traffic. The data was recorded in 2021 to tackle the lack of datasets containing application-layer attacks on encrypted traffic, using similar features to those utilized in CICIDS2017 and NewCICIDS. The resulting network traffic flows correspond to 214904 benign samples and 13349 malicious samples, so HIKARI has a higher data imbalance than the previous two datasets, representing more realistic conditions for enterprise-scale network intrusion detection.

Before the three datasets could be used, a data preprocessing phase was required to create stratified training and holdout sets with 70% and 30% of the data, respectively. In addition to removing rows with missing data, it was necessary to select relevant and unbiased features. A study [27] has analyzed the feature importance rankings of the more than 80 features of the HIKARI dataset, observing that the most impactful ones represented time-related characteristics. By only using these features, the training and inference time of multiple ML models were greatly reduced without a significant decrease in their performance in a holdout evaluation. Therefore, it is possible to select only these features and still achieve a good generalization.

Table 1 provides an overview of the selected time-related characteristics of network traffic flows. From 7 main characteristics, 24 features were selected, based on the feature importance rankings of the considered study. In the three datasets, the forward part of a flow corresponds to a client machine that opens a connection with the server, sending network packets. Likewise, the backward part corresponds to the packets sent by the server back to the client within that connection. The full connection will be classified as either a benign flow that is part of the normal operation of the network or a malicious flow in which the client sent ill-intentioned packets. Regarding the IAT keyword, it corresponds to the Inter-Arrival Time, the elapsed time between the arrival of two subsequent network packets within a flow.

Table 1. Main characteristics of the utilized datasets.

Characteristic	Description	Selected Features				
		Total	Mean	Std	Max	Min
Flow Packet IAT	Packet IAT of the full connection	No	Yes	Yes	Yes	Yes
Forward Packet IAT	Packet IAT of the client	Yes	Yes	Yes	Yes	Yes
Backward Packet IAT	Packet IAT of the server	Yes	Yes	Yes	Yes	Yes
Forward Bulk Rate	Transmission rate of the client	No	Yes	No	No	No
Backward Bulk Rate	Transmission rate of the server	No	Yes	No	No	No
Flow Active Time	Transmission time of the full connection	No	Yes	Yes	Yes	Yes
Flow Idle Time	Inactive time of the full connection	No	Yes	Yes	Yes	Yes

3.2 Benchmark Methodology

The robustness analysis methodology introduced in [28] was followed to ensure an unbiased benchmark of the considered ML models. It includes both a regular training process and an adversarial training process, which is a well-established adversarial defense strategy. In the former, the original training set of a certain dataset is used to train, fine-tune, and validate an ML model. In the latter, data augmentation is performed by creating simple perturbations in the original training set, resulting in an adversarial training set that contains both original data samples and slightly perturbed data samples.

Afterwards, the considered methodology establishes a performance evaluation in both normal conditions and during a direct attack to the models. In the former, the models perform predictions of the data samples in the regular holdout set of a certain dataset, and several standard evaluation metrics are computed. In the latter, a full adversarial evasion attack is performed against each model, with specialized perturbations to deceive that specific model. Since different models are susceptible to different perturbations, the attacks result in model-specific adversarial holdout sets. In the case of network intrusion detection, these attacks are targeted, attempting to cause misclassifications from the malicious class to the target benign class.

The adversarial examples were generated using the Adaptive Perturbation Pattern Method (A2PM) [29]. It relies on pattern sequences that learn the characteristics of each class and create constrained data perturbations, according to the provided information about the feature set, which corresponds to a gray-box setting. The patterns record the value intervals of different feature subsets, which are then used to ensure that the perturbations take the correlations of the features into account, generating realistic adversarial examples. Therefore, when applied to network intrusion detection, the patterns iteratively optimize the perturbations that are performed on each feature of a network traffic flow according to the constraints of a computer network.

For adversarial training, a simple function provided by the method was used to create a perturbation in each malicious sample of a training set, performing data augmentation. Hence, a model was able to learn not only from a sample, but also from a simple variation of it. Figure 1 provides an overview of the creation of an adversarial training set that is common to all models. Starting from a regular training set with 70% of a dataset, another set of the same size can be obtained, with a perturbation in each sample.

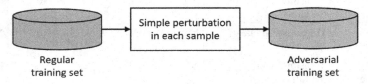

Fig. 1. Creation of a simple adversarial training set.

To perform adversarial evasion attacks specific to each model, the full A2PM attack created as many data perturbations as necessary in a holdout set until every malicious sample was misclassified as benign or a total of 15 attack iterations were performed. No more iterations were allowed because a high number of requests to a specific server would increase the risk of the anomalous behavior being noticed by the security practitioners overseeing the networking infrastructure of an enterprise network [10]. Figure 2 provides an overview of the creation of model-specific adversarial holdout sets that are used for the benchmark. Starting from a regular holdout set with 30% of a dataset, several other sets of the same size can be obtained, with many specialized data perturbations to cause misclassifications in a certain ML model.

3.3 Models and Fine-Tuning

Due to their well-established performance in enterprise network intrusion detection and the good results obtained in the surveyed studies, four supervised tree ensembles were considered for the benchmark: RF, XGB, LGBM, and EBM.

The optimal configuration for each model and each dataset were obtained via a grid search with well-established hyperparameter combinations for binary network traffic classification, and the best hyperparameters were determined through a 5-fold cross-validation. Five stratified subsets were created, each with 20% of a training set. Then, five distinct iterations were performed, each training a model with four subsets and validating

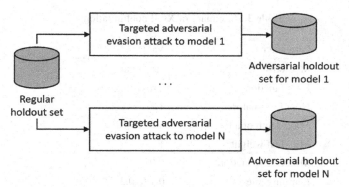

Fig. 2. Creation of model-specific adversarial holdout sets.

it with the remaining one. Due to its adequacy for unbalanced data and consolidation of precision and recall, the F1-score was selected as the validation metric. After the fine-tuning process, each model was retrained with a complete training set, so it was ready for the benchmark with the regular and adversarial holdout sets, which also included other evaluation metrics, such as accuracy and false positive rate.

Random Forest. RF [30] is a supervised ensemble created through bagging and using the Gini Impurity criterion to calculate the best node splits. Each individual tree performs a prediction according to a feature subset, and the most common vote is chosen. RF is based on the concept that the collective decisions of many trees will be better than the decisions of just one. Table 2 summarizes the fine-tuned configuration.

Table 2. Summary of RF configuration.

Parameter	Value
Criterion	Gini Impurity
No. of estimators	100
Max. features	4
Max. depth of a tree	8 to 16
Min. samples in a leaf	2

Extreme Gradient Boosting. XGB [31] performs gradient boosting using a supervised ensemble with a level-wise growth strategy. The nodes within each tree are split level by level, using the Histogram method to compute fast histogram-based approximations and seeking to minimize the Cross-Entropy loss function during its training. Table 3 summarizes the fine-tuned configuration.

Table 3. Summary of XGB configuration.

Parameter	Value
Method	Histogram
Loss function	Cross-Entropy
No. of estimators	100
Max. depth of a tree	4 to 16
Min. leaf weight	1
Min. loss reduction	0.01
Learning rate	0.1 to 0.3
Feature subsample	0.7 to 0.8

Light Gradient Boosting Machine. LGBM [32] also uses a supervised ensemble to perform gradient boosting. The nodes are split using a leaf-wise strategy for a best-first approach, performing the split with the higher loss reduction. LGBM uses Gradient-based One-Side Sampling (GOSS) to build the decision trees, which is computationally lighter than previous methods and therefore provides a faster training process. Table 4 summarizes the fine-tuned configuration.

Table 4. Summary of LGBM configuration.

Parameter	Value
Method	GOSS
Loss function	Cross-Entropy
No. of estimators	100
Max. leaves in a tree	15
Min. samples in a leaf	20
Min. loss reduction	0.01
Learning rate	0.1 to 0.2
Feature subsample	0.7 to 0.8

Explainable Boosting Machine. EBM [33] is a generalized additive model that performs cyclic gradient boosting with a tree ensemble. Unlike the other three black-box models, EBM is a glass-box model that remains explainable and interpretable during the inference phase [34]. Each feature contributes to a prediction in an additive manner that enables their individual contribution to be measured and explained. Table 5 summarizes the fine-tuned configuration.

Table 5. Summary of EBM configuration.

Parameter	Value
Loss function	Cross-Entropy
No. of estimators	100
Max. number of bins	256
Max. leaves in a tree	7 to 15
Min. samples in a leaf	2
Learning rate	0.1

4 Results and Discussion

This section presents and discusses the results obtained by evaluating the performance of the ML models created through regular and adversarial training. The evaluation considers the regular holdout set of the CICIDS2017, NewCICIDS, and HIKARI datasets, as well as the model-specific adversarial holdout sets.

4.1 CICIDS2017

The models trained with the CICIDS2017 dataset obtained very high results across several standard evaluation metrics. Despite only using 24 time-related features of the dataset, they enabled all four models to detect the anomalous behavior of most malicious flows, distinguishing cyber-attacks from benign activity and reaching F1-scores over 89%. Nonetheless, when adversarial attacks were performed against these models, their precision and recall exhibited significant declines that resulted in F1-scores lower than 0.1% after the attack iterations were complete. This failure to detect adversarial examples suggests that tree ensembles are inherently vulnerable to modifications of the time-related characteristics of network traffic flows.

On the other hand, the models created through adversarial training had substantially lower declines, preserving their precision above 97%. Even though the recall of EBM was only approximately 60% when attacked, RF, XGB, and LGBM all retained a higher recall above 73%. Hence, by training with a simple perturbation per malicious sample, the robustness of the models was improved, and most malicious flows could not evade detection. Regarding benign flows, it is important to note that the false positive rates were decreased to below 0.40%, which indicates that deploying these models in a real computer network could lead to less false alarms and therefore less unnecessary mitigation measures that would be costly for an enterprise.

Table 6 provides the obtained results for the models trained with the CICIDS2017 dataset, considering standard evaluation metrics for binary network traffic classification. The ACC, PRC, RCL, F1S, and FPR columns correspond to accuracy, precision, recall, F1-score, and false positive rate. The optimal result would be 100% for all metrics except the false positive rate, which should be as close to 0% as possible. Additionally, the results achieved by the adversarially trained models on the adversarial holdout sets are highlighted in bold.

Table 6. Obtained results for the CICIDS2017 dataset.

Model	Training	Attacked	Evaluation Metrics (%)				
			ACC	PRC	RCL	F1S	FPR
RF	Regular	No	95.21	90.74	88.59	89.65	2.76
		Yes	74.48	0.03	0.01	0.01	2.76
	Adversarial	No	93.84	99.20	74.30	84.96	0.18
		Yes	**93.80**	**99.19**	**74.12**	**84.84**	**0.18**
XGB	Regular	No	95.29	90.73	88.94	89.83	2.78
		Yes	74.48	0.36	0.03	0.06	2.78
	Adversarial	No	94.67	98.93	78.07	87.27	0.26
		Yes	**94.30**	**98.91**	**76.5**	**86.28**	**0.26**
LGBM	Regular	No	94.95	90.12	88.09	89.09	2.95
		Yes	74.35	0.57	0.05	0.09	2.95
	Adversarial	No	94.19	98.93	76.01	85.97	0.25
		Yes	**93.50**	**98.89**	**73.05**	**84.03**	**0.25**
EBM	Regular	No	94.98	90.43	87.86	89.13	2.84
		Yes	74.42	0.08	0.01	0.01	2.84
	Adversarial	No	94.4	98.43	77.31	86.6	0.38
		Yes	**90.13**	**97.96**	**60.08**	**74.48**	**0.38**

4.2 NewCICIDS

The models trained with the corrected version of CICIDS2017 exhibited much better results than those of the original dataset. Training with the corrected network traffic flows of NewCICIDS led all four models to achieve F1-scores higher than 99% on the regular holdout set, and their false positive rates did not exceed 0.20%. Despite the performance of the models being significantly decreased in the model-specific adversarial holdout sets, it was still slightly better than the decline observed in the original dataset. It is pertinent to highlight the better robustness of the regularly trained EBM, which retained a precision of over 31% throughout the adversarial evasion attack just by training with the corrected flows of NewCICIDS.

As before, performing adversarial training led to a great improvement in the robustness of the models. This defense strategy enabled the detection of most adversarial cyber-attack examples, reducing the number of misclassifications that would be harmful for an enterprise. Even though the recall of the adversarially trained RF and XGB was slightly decreased, they preserved their precision of 99.88% and 99.90%, without this metric being decreased by the attack. Since only very few of the perturbed malicious flows were misclassified, the functionality of those cyber-attacks would be prevented in a real enterprise communication network. Furthermore, RF and XGB achieved the best false positive rates, 0.06% and 0.05%, respectively, which indicates that the corrected dataset also led to models with better generalization.

Table 7 provides the obtained results for the models trained with the NewCICIDS dataset, highlighting the precision of the regularly trained EBM and the results of all the adversarially trained models.

Table 7. Obtained results for the NewCICIDS dataset.

Model	Training	Attacked	Evaluation Metrics (%)				
			ACC	PRC	RCL	F1S	FPR
RF	Regular	No	99.90	99.81	99.92	99.87	0.11
		Yes	64.19	0.01	0.01	0.01	0.11
	Adversarial	No	99.67	99.88	99.20	99.54	0.06
		Yes	**99.63**	**99.88**	**99.08**	**99.48**	**0.06**
XGB	Regular	No	99.94	99.89	99.94	99.92	0.06
		Yes	64.22	2.59	0.01	0.01	0.06
	Adversarial	No	99.93	99.90	99.89	99.90	0.05
		Yes	**99.84**	**99.90**	**99.64**	**99.77**	**0.05**
LGBM	Regular	No	99.79	99.63	99.79	99.71	0.20
		Yes	64.14	7.36	0.03	0.06	0.20
	Adversarial	No	99.72	99.67	99.54	99.60	0.19
		Yes	**94.91**	**99.61**	**86.10**	**92.36**	**0.19**
EBM	Regular	No	99.86	99.76	99.84	99.80	0.14
		Yes	64.21	**31.48**	0.11	0.22	0.14
	Adversarial	No	99.80	99.74	99.71	99.72	0.15
		Yes	**98.13**	**99.72**	**95.02**	**97.32**	**0.15**

4.3 HIKARI

The models trained with the more recent HIKARI dataset obtained F1-scores between 83% and 84%, which are lower than those of the previous datasets, but are still reasonably high for a binary network traffic classification task. The targeted adversarial evasion attack caused the recall and precision of all four models to decrease, but XGB was able to retain a precision of over 58% and EBM of over 98%. Since their false positive rates were near 0.01%, the results denote that more than half of the adversarial examples were detected and there were very benign flows mistakenly predicted as malicious, which is very important for an enterprise-scale computer network.

Despite also having equivalent false positive rates, the adversarially trained models did not exhibit high increases in their robustness. When attacked, the F1-scores of RF, XGB, LGBM, and EBM, were approximately 82%, 62%, 27%, and 63%, respectively. These results are substantially lower than those obtained in the previous datasets, suggesting that the greater complexity of the more recent cyber-attacks makes it more difficult to distinguish them from benign flows that are part of the normal operation of an enterprise network. Therefore, adversarial training is not always guaranteed to help ML models achieve an adversarially robust generalization. It is pertinent to carefully evaluate their performance, assessing if they exhibit a good generalization to regular traffic and a good robustness to adversarially perturbed traffic.

Table 8 provides the obtained results for the models trained with the HIKARI dataset, highlighting the precision of the regularly trained XGB and EBM and the results of all the adversarially trained models.

Table 8. Obtained results for the HIKARI dataset.

Model	Training	Attacked	Evaluation Metrics (%)				
			ACC	PRC	RCL	F1S	FPR
RF	Regular	No	98.34	99.79	71.84	83.54	0.01
		Yes	94.14	0.01	0.01	0.01	0.01
	Adversarial	No	98.33	99.90	71.59	83.40	0.01
		Yes	**98.21**	**99.89**	**69.46**	**81.94**	**0.01**
XGB	Regular	No	98.35	99.83	71.91	83.60	0.01
		Yes	94.15	**58.33**	0.17	0.35	0.01
	Adversarial	No	98.36	99.86	72.01	83.68	0.01
		Yes	**96.76**	**99.78**	**44.72**	**61.76**	**0.01**
LGBM	Regular	No	98.36	99.86	72.13	83.76	0.01
		Yes	94.15	0.01	0.01	0.01	0.01
	Adversarial	No	98.35	99.72	72.01	83.63	0.01
		Yes	**95.05**	**98.74**	**15.63**	**26.99**	**0.01**
EBM	Regular	No	98.35	99.76	72.01	83.64	0.01
		Yes	95.01	**98.84**	14.86	25.83	0.01
	Adversarial	No	98.35	99.69	71.94	83.57	0.01
		Yes	**96.84**	**99.52**	**46.14**	**63.05**	**0.01**

5   Conclusions

This work benchmarked the robustness of multiple decision tree ensembles for enterprise network intrusion detection. Regularly and adversarially trained RF, XGB, LGBM, and EBM models were fine-tuned and evaluated on the original CICIDS2017 dataset, the corrected NewCICIDS dataset, and the HIKARI dataset with more recent network traffic. Targeted adversarial evasion attacks were performed using A2PM, and the results obtained in the adversarial holdout sets were compared to those of the regular holdout sets, assessing if the models correctly classified perturbed data samples and preserved high evaluation metrics, indicating a good robustness.

The best results across several evaluation metrics were achieved in the corrected version of CICIDS2017, which provided substantial improvements in both regular samples and perturbed samples, in comparison with the original dataset. Even though the recall of the adversarially trained RF and XGB was slightly decreased, these models were able to preserve best precision, 99.88% and 99.90%. Hence, the adversarially trained models were able to detect most of the perturbed malicious flows, which would prevent the functionality of those cyber-attacks in a real enterprise network.

However, when facing the more recent network traffic of the HIKARI dataset, the ML models were less robust. XGB and EBM preserved a reasonably good precision when attacked, but RF and LGBM exhibited numerous misclassifications. Despite the best false positive rates being achieved in HIKARI, these worse results suggest that the greater complexity of the more recent cyber-attacks makes it more difficult to distinguish them from benign flows. Therefore, in addition to an adversarial training process, other adversarial defense strategies may be needed.

Overall, the robustness of the four ML models to adversarial cyber-attack examples was improved without their generalization to regular traffic being affected, enabling a reliable detection of suspicious activity in enterprise networks without costly increases of false alarms. In the future, it could be valuable to explore the intrinsic explainability capabilities of EBM and apply ad-hoc and post-hoc explainability methods to RF, XGB, and LGBM, enabling a better understanding of the reasoning behind their misclassifications. To further contribute to adversarial ML research, it is important to also benchmark the adversarial robustness of these tree ensembles for multi-class classification and compare them with other types of ML models, including deep learning models.

Acknowledgments. This work has been supported by the UIDB/00760/2020 and UIDP/00760/2020 projects.

References

1. European Union Agency for Cybersecurity, Christoforatos, N., Lella, I., Rekleitis, E., Van Heurck, C., Zacharis, A.: Cyber Europe 2022: After Action Report (2022). https://doi.org/10.2824/397622
2. European Union Agency for Cybersecurity, et al.: ENISA Threat Landscape 2022 (2022). https://doi.org/10.2824/764318
3. Liu, H., Lang, Bo.: Machine learning and deep learning methods for intrusion detection systems: a survey. Appl. Sci. **9**(20), 4396 (2019). https://doi.org/10.3390/app9204396
4. Vitorino, J., Andrade, R., Praça, I., Sousa, O., Maia, E.: A comparative analysis of machine learning techniques for IoT intrusion detection. In: Aïmeur, E., Laurent, M., Yaich, R., Dupont, B., Garcia-Alfaro, J. (eds.) Foundations and Practice of Security: 14th International Symposium, FPS 2021, Paris, France, December 7–10, 2021, Revised Selected Papers, pp. 191–207. Springer, Cham (2022). https://doi.org/10.1007/978-3-031-08147-7_13

5. Alotaibi, A., Rassam, M.A.: Adversarial machine learning attacks against intrusion detection systems: a survey on strategies and defense. Fut. Internet **15**(2), 62 (2023). https://doi.org/10.3390/fi15020062
6. Rosenberg, I., Shabtai, A., Elovici, Y., Rokach, L.: Adversarial machine learning attacks and defense methods in the cyber security domain. ACM Comput. Surv. **54**(5), 1–36 (2021). https://doi.org/10.1145/3453158
7. Martins, N., Cruz, J.M., Cruz, T., Abreu, P.H.: Adversarial machine learning applied to intrusion and malware scenarios: a systematic review. IEEE Access **8**, 35403–35419 (2020). https://doi.org/10.1109/ACCESS.2020.2974752
8. Vitorino, J., Dias, T., Fonseca, T., Maia, E., Praça, I.: Constrained adversarial learning and its applicability to automated software testing: a systematic review. arXiv (2023). https://doi.org/10.48550/arXiv.2303.07546
9. Apruzzese, G., Andreolini, M., Ferretti, L., Marchetti, M., Colajanni, M.: Modeling realistic adversarial attacks against network intrusion detection systems. Digit. Threats Res. Pract. **3**(3), 1–19 (2022). https://doi.org/10.1145/3469659
10. Vitorino, J., Praça, I., Maia, E.: SoK: realistic adversarial attacks and defenses for intelligent network intrusion detection. Comput. Secur. **134**, 103433 (2023). https://doi.org/10.1016/j.cose.2023.103433
11. Ho, S., Jufout, S.A., Dajani, K., Mozumdar, M.: A novel intrusion detection model for detecting known and innovative cyberattacks using convolutional neural network. IEEE Open J. Comput. Soc. **2**, 14–25 (2021). https://doi.org/10.1109/OJCS.2021.3050917
12. Rodríguez, M., Alesanco, Á., Mehavilla, L., García, J.: Evaluation of machine learning techniques for traffic flow-based intrusion detection. Sensors **22**(23), 9326 (2022). https://doi.org/10.3390/s22239326
13. Abdulhammed, R., Musafer, H., Alessa, A., Faezipour, M., Abuzneid, A.: Features dimensionality reduction approaches for machine learning based network intrusion detection. Electronics **8**(3), 322 (2019). https://doi.org/10.3390/electronics8030322
14. Lanvin, M., Gimenez, P.-F., Han, Y., Majorczyk, F., Mé, L., Totel, É.: Errors in the CICIDS2017 dataset and the significant differences in detection performances it makes. In: Kallel, S., Jmaiel, M., Zulkernine, M., Kacem, A.H., Cuppens, F., Cuppens, N. (eds.) Risks and Security of Internet and Systems: 17th International Conference, CRiSIS 2022, Sousse, Tunisia, December 7–9, 2022, Revised Selected Papers, pp. 18–33. Springer, Cham (2023). https://doi.org/10.1007/978-3-031-31108-6_2
15. Liu, L., Engelen, G., Lynar, T., Essam, D., Joosen, W.: Error prevalence in NIDS datasets: a case study on CIC-IDS-2017 and CSE-CIC-IDS-2018. In: 2022 IEEE Conference on Communications and Network Security (CNS), IEEE, October 2022, pp. 254–262 (2022). https://doi.org/10.1109/CNS56114.2022.9947235
16. Catillo, M., Del Vecchio, A., Pecchia, A., Villano, U.: A case study with CICIDS2017 on the robustness of machine learning against adversarial attacks in intrusion detection. In: Proceedings of the 18th International Conference on Availability, Reliability and Security, pp. 1–8 (2023)
17. McCarthy, A., Ghadafi, E., Andriotis, P., Legg, P.: Functionality-preserving adversarial machine learning for robust classification in cybersecurity and intrusion detection domains: a survey. J. Cybersecur. Priv. **2**(1), 154–190 (2022). https://doi.org/10.3390/jcp2010010
18. Fernandes, R., Lopes, N.: Network intrusion detection packet classification with the HIKARI-2021 dataset: a study on ML algorithms. In: 10th International Symposium on Digital Forensics and Security, ISDFS 2022, Institute of Electrical and Electronics Engineers Inc. (2022). https://doi.org/10.1109/ISDFS55398.2022.9800807
19. Louk, M.H.L., Tama, B.A.: Dual-IDS: A bagging-based gradient boosting decision tree model for network anomaly intrusion detection system. Exp. Syst. Appl. **213**, 119030 (2023). https://doi.org/10.1016/j.eswa.2022.119030

20. Kabla, A.H.H., Thamrin, A.H., Anbar, M., Manickam, S., Karuppayah, S.: PeerAmbush: multi-layer perceptron to detect peer-to-peer botnet. Symmetry **14**(12), 2483 (2022). https://doi.org/10.3390/sym14122483
21. Wang, L., Cheng, Z., Lv, Q., Wang, Y., Zhang, S., Huang, W.: ACG: attack classification on encrypted network traffic using graph convolution attention networks. Institute of Electrical and Electronics Engineers (IEEE), June 2023, pp. 47–52 (2023). https://doi.org/10.1109/cscwd57460.2023.10152599
22. Kwon, D., Neagu, R.M., Rasakonda, P., Ryu, J.T., Kim, J.: Evaluating unbalanced network data for attack detection. In: Proceedings of the 2023 on Systems and Network Telemetry and Analytics, SNTA 2023, July 2023, pp. 23–26. Association for Computing Machinery, Inc. (2023). https://doi.org/10.1145/3589012.3594898
23. Koda, S., Morikawa, I.: OOD-robust boosting tree for intrusion detection systems. In: Proceedings of the International Joint Conference on Neural Networks. Institute of Electrical and Electronics Engineers Inc. (2023). https://doi.org/10.1109/IJCNN54540.2023.10191603
24. Sharafaldin, I., Lashkari, A.H., Ghorbani, A.A.: Toward generating a new intrusion detection dataset and intrusion traffic characterization. In: Proceedings of the 4th International Conference on Information Systems Security and Privacy, SciTePress, 2018, pp. 108–116 (2018). https://doi.org/10.5220/0006639801080116
25. CICFlowMeter Canadian Institute for Cybersecurity. https://www.unb.ca/cic/research/applications.html#CICFlowMeter. Accessed 09 Dec 2022
26. Ferriyan, A., Thamrin, A.H., Takeda, K., Murai, J.: Generating network intrusion detection dataset based on real and encrypted synthetic attack traffic. Appl. Sci. **11**(17), 7868 (2021). https://doi.org/10.3390/app11177868
27. Fernandes, R., Silva, J., Ribeiro, O., Portela, I., Lopes, N.: The impact of identifiable features in ML classification algorithms with the HIKARI-2021 dataset. In: 11th International Symposium on Digital Forensics and Security, ISDFS 2023. Institute of Electrical and Electronics Engineers Inc. (2023). https://doi.org/10.1109/ISDFS58141.2023.10131864
28. Vitorino, J., Praça, I., Maia, E.: Towards adversarial realism and robust learning for IoT intrusion detection and classification. Ann. Telecommun. **78**(7–8), 401–412 (2023). https://doi.org/10.1007/s12243-023-00953-y
29. Vitorino, J., Oliveira, N., Praça, I.: Adaptative perturbation patterns: realistic adversarial learning for robust intrusion detection. Fut. Internet **14**(4), 108 (2022). https://doi.org/10.3390/fi14040108
30. Breiman, L.: Random forests. Mach. Learn. **45**(1), 5–32 (2001). https://doi.org/10.1023/A:1010933404324
31. Chen, T., Guestrin, C.: XGBoost: a scalable tree boosting system. In: Proceedings of the ACM SIGKDD International Conference on Knowledge Discovery and Data Mining, 13–17 August, pp. 785–794 (2016). https://doi.org/10.1145/2939672.2939785
32. Ke, G., et al.: LightGBM: a highly efficient gradient boosting decision tree. In: Advances in Neural Information Processing Systems (NIPS), 2017 December, pp. 3147–3155 (2017)
33. Lou, Y., Caruana, R., Gehrke, J.: Intelligible models for classification and regression. In: Proceedings of the 18th ACM SIGKDD International Conference on Knowledge Discovery and Data Mining, KDD 2012, pp. 150–158. Association for Computing Machinery, New York (2012). https://doi.org/10.1145/2339530.2339556
34. Nori, H., Jenkins, S., Koch, P., Caruana, R.: InterpretML: a unified framework for machine learning interpretability (2019)

Securing Smart Vehicles Through Federated Learning

Sadaf MD Halim[1]($\boxtimes$), Md Delwar Hossain[2], Latifur Khan[1], Anoop Singhal[3], Hiroyuki Inoue[4], Hideya Ochiai[5], Kevin W. Hamlen[1], and Youki Kadobayashi[2]

[1] The University of Texas at Dallas, Richardson, TX, USA
sxh190015@utdallas.edu
[2] Nara Institute of Science and Technology, Nara, Ikoma, Japan
[3] National Institute of Standards and Technology, Gaithersburg, Maryland, USA
[4] Kyoto Sangyo University, Kyoto, Japan
[5] The University of Tokyo, Tokyo, Japan

Abstract. As cars evolve to be smarter than ever, they also become susceptible to attack. Malicious entities can attempt to override automated functions by sending a series of attack signals to the smart vehicle. It is thus imperative that we create systems to detect these attacks on the fly, so that they may be discarded. Machine learning approaches are a natural choice for detecting such attacks based on the payload information. However, machine learning models typically require a large dataset for training, in order to attain good performance. With manufacturers independently gathering this data based on their own cars, it is unlikely that all this data will be available in one place. To address this issue, we explore federated solutions that learn in a distributed manner for increased smart vehicle security. We explore challenging scenarios in which we do not assume an independent and identically distributed (IID) setting for the data, which is typical in many federated learning environments. We investigate various degrees of such heterogeneity in the attack data distribution between different manufacturers, and study the effectiveness of detection systems under them. Furthermore, with a combination of techniques including triplet-mixup based augmentation and a data exchange scheme involving synthetically generated samples, we show that we can attain strong performance in the most challenging label distribution scenarios. We perform our experiments on a publicly available dataset and on a proprietary attack dataset developed for this project.

Keywords: Smart Vehicle Security · Federated Learning · Augmentation · Synthetic Data Generation · Non-IID Data

1 Introduction

With cars becoming increasingly connected, they have become both smarter and more susceptible to attack [14]. These smart cars are connected cyber-physical systems with a wide range of automated functionality. These cars feature a

M. Mosbah et al. (Eds.): FPS 2023, LNCS 14551, pp. 18–35, 2024.
https://doi.org/10.1007/978-3-031-57537-2_2

large number of Electronic Control Units (ECUs), and these ECUs communicate amongst themselves through the aid of a Controller Area Network (CAN) bus system. While the CAN Bus serves a crucial role for a smart car, it is nonetheless vulnerable to a variety of attacks from malicious entities.

As the central communication system in a smart car, detecting any potential attacks on the CAN Bus is of utmost importance. The CAN Bus receives messages through CAN Frames. Figure 1 shows the breakdown of a CAN message.

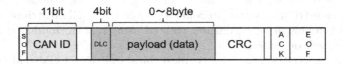

Fig. 1. A CAN Message Frame [7]

Standard CAN frames in vehicles lack encryption or authentication, making them vulnerable to various attacks. Attackers can exploit these vulnerabilities through external connections like OBD-II diagnostics ports, telematics units, or in-vehicle infotainment systems. To address this, Intrusion Detection Systems (IDS) are essential. Placed between external input and the CAN Bus, IDS filters malicious signals, allowing only benign ones. Machine learning models, particularly Deep Neural Networks, are popular choices for IDS design [1,12]. A robust model requires a large, diverse dataset of various attacks. In reality, car manufacturers collect their own data independently. This data often includes sensitive information, such as CAN IDs, making manufacturers reluctant to share it. Consequently, a centralized model relying on a single local dataset would miss valuable training data from other sources, due to privacy concerns.

Federated Learning (FL) provides an effective solution. In FL, multiple client devices have their own local data and train individual local models. These local models are then aggregated at a central server to create a global model. We adopt a "cross-silo" FL setting, where we have a limited number of clients, each representing a car manufacturer. Since data is collected independently by each manufacturer, it is reasonable to assume that not all manufacturers are exposed to the same distribution of attacks. For example, a manufacturer may encounter many spoofing attacks but few Denial-of-Service attacks, while another may experience the opposite. These manufacturers, acting as clients, train local models that are aggregated to create a global model. This can detect a broader range of threats compared to a model trained on a single manufacturer's data.

A well-studied challenge in Federated Learning is dealing with non independent and identically distributed (non-IID) data [23]. A realistic implementation of our Federated Learning set up will meet the same challenge, because the distribution of attacks experienced by different manufacturers will vary widely. In the most challenging cases, the set of attacks that one manufacturer sees may be completely disjoint from the set of attacks seen by another. One objective of this study is to investigate these scenarios to see how Federated Learning fares.

To tackle all these challenges, we propose **FAST-SV: F**ederated **A**ugmented **S**ynthetic **T**raining for **S**mart **V**ehicles. FAST-SV generates synthetic CAN-attack data on the client side and redistributes this in a systematic way to achieve optimal performance in the most challenging non-IID data distribution scenarios. Finally, we developed an in-house dataset called the NAIST CAN Attack Dataset using four real car models. This dataset was built to complement an existing Car-Hacking Dataset [18,20]. Our contributions are summarized as:

1. We investigate a variety of non-IID distribution scenarios for CAN-Bus attacks, and examine how performance varies.
2. We propose FAST-SV, a technique which generates synthetic CAN-attack data and redistributes them, to combat extreme non-IID distributions.
3. We develop a new in-house dataset created using real car models that can be used for attack detection.
4. We run additional studies that explore how well FAST-SV scales to large numbers of clients, and we investigate important privacy considerations.

2   Background and Related Work

2.1   Related Work on CAN-Based Attacks

There has been extensive research on attacks via the CAN Bus. This includes successful attack creation, like the Spoofing attack in [8], which exploits CAN protocol vulnerabilities, and attack detection, including general Deep learning (DL) techniques [1], and unsupervised intrusion detection methods [6]. Our focus lies in Federated Learning for CAN Bus attack detection, particularly in the non-IID setting, mirroring real-world scenarios with data generated in diverse locations and distributions. While [19] and [21] explore similar themes, the inherent non-IID nature of CAN Bus attack data in a federated setting remains unaddressed in existing literature. This challenge arises from varying attack exposure across car manufacturers, making standard Federated Learning techniques less effective. Solving the non-IID issue in this context is crucial for developing practical intrusion detection solutions.

2.2   Federated Learning, Non-IID Challenges and Synthetic Data

Federated Learning (FL) [16] addresses the challenge of learning from data distributed across multiple locations instead of a centralized dataset. FL finds applications in various domains [13], including ours, where sensitive vehicle data may not be shared by manufacturers. In FL, a central server coordinates multiple client machines. Each client typically possesses its own neural network with local weights. The FL process occurs in rounds: the central server sends global weights to all clients, clients update their local weights using their data, and sends back the updated local weights. Aggregation methods, like Federated Averaging (FedAvg) proposed in [16], combine these weights, often by averaging, to produce an updated global set of weights. FedAvg takes a weighted average of the client weights, weighted by the number of local data points at each client.

Non-IID Data. Learning with non-IID data poses a major challenge. Previous work [23,24] showed that non-IID data causes the model weights to diverge, and this divergence was captured by tracking the earth mover's distance (EMD) between the distribution over classes on each device. Since the standard FedAvg technique often suffers in non-IID scenarios, certain FL models have been built to address this. For instance, SCAFFOLD [9] is one of the most popular models that addresses non-IID data by correcting the client-drift in local updates.

Synthetic Sample Generation via Augmentation Techniques. Data Augmentation is a means of increasing the variety and diversity in a dataset [4] to increase performance. In popular domains such as images, augmentation has been extensively explored. For tabular datasets, there are several approaches, including SMOTE [2], which uses a combination of K-nearest-neighbours (KNN) and interpolation to construct minority class data. Another simple solution involves a mixup of feature values of data instances [22]. We use Triplet Mixup [10] to generate a new instance from three existing instances, detailed in Sect. 4.3.

Sharing Synthetic Samples to Tackle Non-IID Distributions. Sharing a small set of data across clients is one solution for tackling non-IID distributions [23]. While effective, it contradicts a key motivation behind FL, which is that the sensitive data cannot be shared. To address privacy concerns, one can generate synthetic data based on the sensitive data, and distribute **only** the synthetically generated data to clients. This alleviates privacy concerns since the data shared is artificial. Thus, we adapt this approach, where we utilize simple triplet mixup techniques to generate artificial tabular data instances that are shared to address the non-IID setting. In a similar vein, SDA-FL [11] uses locally trained Generative Adversarial Networks (GAN) [5] at the client side to create synthetic images to share. However, training a GAN to generate images at each client is computationally expensive. Instead, our solution, tailored for CAN-based car security datasets, involves simple augmentation techniques to generate the artificial tabular data, making the system lightweight and practical.

2.3 Car Hacking Dataset

Detecting CAN attacks has garnered substantial research attention, leading to the creation of datasets like the Car-Hacking Dataset [18,20]. This dataset captures CAN Traffic through the OBD-II port of an actual automobile while it is actively subjected to message injection attacks. It comprises 30 to 40 min of CAN Traffic, including 300 intrusions where message injections occurred, each lasting 3 to 5 s. The dataset encompasses four key attack types (as described in Sect. 3), which we extensively explore in the paper. Notably, this dataset is highly imbalanced, with 85.9% of the samples being benign, while the remaining samples correspond to the four different attacks.

3   An In-House Dataset and its Attacks

In addition to the publicly available Car Hacking Dataset [7], we created our
own CAN bus attack dataset for experimentation, shown in Table 1. This dataset
comprises four distinct real-car models to which we injected DoS, Fuzzing, and
two types of Spoofing attacks. This dataset is intentionally imbalanced to mimic
real-world scenarios where normal traffic predominates over anomalous traffic.

DoS Attack. Attackers can inject flooding attacks into the CAN bus communication when compromising a car. This involves sending continuous arbitrary messages with high-priority bits. According to CAN message characteristics, messages with high priority bits must be given precedence. Consequently,
high-frequency and high-priority CAN messages flood the communication system, occupying it with artificial/fake messages. This disrupts the transmission
of legitimate messages and disables some ECU functions.

Fuzzing Attack. In a fuzzing attack, an attacker injects random CAN IDs,
DLC, and data fields that mimic legitimate traffic into the CAN bus network
system. Due to the lack of basic security mechanisms in the CAN bus communication system, an attacker can easily inject a fuzzing attack. Fuzzing attacks can
lead to malfunctions in the entire CAN bus network, causing effects like shaking
of the steering wheel, erratic signal light behavior and automatic gear shifts.

Spoofing Attack (RPM/Gear). In a spoofing attack, an attacker injects a
modified CAN message with a specific CAN ID. If the attacker's CAN IDs are
present in the real system's CAN ID list, the ECUs can be deceived. This makes
it challenging to differentiate between legitimate and malicious messages. We
deal with two types of spoofing attacks. In *Spoofing Attack (RPM)*, messages of
certain CAN ID's related to RPM information are injected to deceive the RPM
Gauge. In *Spoofing Attack (Gear)*, messages of certain CAN ID's related to Gear
information are injected to fool the drive gear indication.

3.1   Data Collection Setup and Process

To create the dataset, we first collected attack-free traffic from real cars by using
CAN analyzers, such as the Vehicle Spy 3 Professional and the OBD-II interface,
This was done for four real-car models: Toyota, Subaru, Mitsubishi, and Suzuki.
Next, attacks were performed on each of them. We inject DoS, Fuzzing, RPM,
and Gear Spoofing attacks. The injection of messages for each attack scenario is
depicted in Fig. 2. [7] In this section, we describe how each of the attacks were
performed to create the NAIST CAN Attack Dataset.

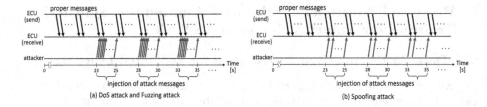

Fig. 2. Injection of Messages

Table 1. NAIST CAN attack Datasets - Benign and Attack Instances

Attack	Toyota	Subaru	Suzuki	Mitsubishi
Benign	20059084 (83.84%)	12317789 (90.44%)	38755172 (95.83%)	17296650 (93.60%)
DoS	2550773 (10.66%)	849444 (6.24%)	1117074 (2.76%)	784535 (4.25%)
Fuzzing	1087504 (4.55%)	340282 (2.50%)	296252 (0.73%)	296294 (1.60%)
RPM	118103 (0.49%)	65697 (0.48%)	149458 (0.37%)	52764 (0.29%)
Gear	110227 (0.46%)	46926 (0.34%)	124548 (0.31%)	49247 (0.27%)

DoS Attack. For the DoS dataset, a large number of messages were injected with CAN ID 00, DLC 8, and data 00, starting at 20 s. The attack spanned 5 s, with a 2-second duration and a 0.5 ms interval time.

Fuzzing Attack. In fuzzing attacks, attackers inject numerous CAN messages with arbitrary CAN IDs. Random numbers were generated using the *randint* function. The attacks used random CAN IDs between 0×000 and $0 \times 7FF$, varied lengths, and data for 5 s, with a 2-second duration, and a 1ms interval time. The attack commenced at 20 s.

Spoofing Injection Attack (for Gear and RPM). Spoofing attacks were conducted on RPM and Gear data. These attacks lasted for 5 s with a 2-second duration, starting at 10 s. The spoofed data is detailed below, with xx and yy representing spoofed values, and CS as a checksum value.

- *Toyota:* RPM data - CAN ID 1C4, DLC 8, data xx, yy, 00, 00, 00, 00, 00, CS, with a 23 ms interval. Gear data - CAN ID 3BC, DLC 8, data 00, xx, 00, 00, 00, 00, 00, 00, with a 100 ms interval.
- *Subaru:* RPM data - CAN ID 141, DLC 8, data 00, 00, 00, 00, yy, xx, 02, with a 10 ms interval. Gear data - CAN ID 148, DLC 8, data xx, 00, 00, 01, 00, 00, yy, 01, with a 10 ms interval.
- *Suzuki:* RPM data - CAN ID 13F, DLC 8, data xx, yy, 00, 00, 00, 00, 00, 00, with a 20 ms interval. Gear data - CAN ID 381, DLC 5, data 00, xx, 00, 00, 00, with a 100 ms interval.
- *Mitsubishi*: RPM data - CAN ID 338, DLC 8, 00, 00, 00, 00, 00, 00, data xx, yy, with a 10 ms interval. Gear data - CAN ID 218, DLC 8, data 00, 00, xx, 00, 00, 00, 00, 00, with a 120 ms interval.

4   Proposed Approach: Federated Augmented Synthetic Training for Smart Vehicles (FAST-SV)

4.1   Data Partitioning and Distribution for Federated Learning

We leverage Federated Learning (FL) because it is unlikely that car manufacturers would share large in-house datasets to collaboratively train an attack detection system. In the FL setting, manufacturers are required to only train a local model and share their parameters in order to train collaboratively. Manufacturers encounter diverse attacks, leading to non-independent and non-identically distributed (non-IID) data. Each manufacturer independently trains a local model with their dataset. Subsequently, they share their model parameters with a central aggregator, which averages and sends them back to the manufacturers. This process occurs over several rounds. To study various federated scenarios, we partition existing datasets into disjoint datasets which we provide to individual clients, each representing a manufacturer. Data partitioning is performed in several ways to skew attack label distributions, to simulate the real-world:

1. Approximately Uniform Attack Distribution: This is the simplest partitioning scheme where all client datasets are created with approximately the same label distribution, by sampling from the original dataset randomly and creating partitions for each client.
2. One Attack Removed: In this setting, each client's dataset is created by first partitioning randomly and then removing one attack type entirely from the client's dataset. The attack type which will be removed varies in each client.
3. Half of the Attacks Removed: Here, we remove half of the attack types from each client's dataset. Therefore, in the Car-Hacking Dataset where there are initially 4 attack types, each client will see any 2 out of the 4 attack classes.
4. Only One Attack Present: This is the most extreme setting, where each client only sees one of the attack types and nothing else.

4.2   Sharing Synthetic Samples

In order to combat dramatic shifts in attack distribution from one client to another, we utilize the following pipeline illustrated in Fig. 3:

1. At the start of FL training, each client generates synthetic examples using its local dataset and an augmentation technique (Sect. 4.3)
2. These artificial examples are shared with the server.
3. The server creates a *balanced set* of synthetic samples from all the samples it receives. To create this balanced set, the server simply pools together all synthetic samples that it received, and then creates a new set where each attack class is present in equal counts, choosing the instances of each attack type at random until the desired count is reached.
4. The server distributes the balanced set of synthetic examples to all clients
5. The *Federated Averaging* process begins.

This pipeline summarizes our overall method, called FAST-SV. This is detailed in Algorithm 1. FAST-SV is essentially a series of procedures built on top of the simple Federated Averaging process. One could replace the Federated Averaging technique with more advanced aggregation methods such as

---

Algorithm 1. FAST-SV

1: **Input: clients, attack_types**
2: # Step 1: Synthetic Data Generation on Client Devices
3: **for** each client in clients **do**
4:     local_data = load_local_data(client)
5:     Initialize **synthetic_data_local**
6:     **for** each attack_type in attack_types **do**
7:         filtered_data = filter(local_data, attack_type)   ▷ Client-side
8:         synthetic_data = triplet_mixup*(filtered_data)   ▷ Client-side
9:         Push synthetic_data to **synthetic_data_local**   ▷ Client-side
10:    **end for**
11:    send_to_server(synthetic_data_local)   ▷ Client-side
12: **end for**
13: # Step 2: Server Receives and Combines All Synthetic Data
14: all_synthetic_data = combine_synthetic_data()   ▷ Server-side
15: # Step 3: Server Balances Synthetic Data
16: balanced_data = BALANCE_SYNTHETIC_DATA(all_synthetic_data)   ▷ Server-side
17: # Step 4: Distribute Balanced Data to Clients
18: **for** each client in clients **do**
19:    send_to_client(client, balanced_data)   ▷ Server-side
20: **end for**
21: **for** each client in clients **do**
22:    Add balanced_data to **local_data**   ▷ Client-side
23: **end for**
24: # Step 5: Federated Averaging for desired number of rounds
25: FedAvg*(clients)
26:
27: **function** BALANCE_SYNTHETIC_DATA(all_synthetic_data)
28:    Initialize an empty dictionary **attack_counts** for each attack
29:    Initialize an empty list **balanced_samples**
30:    **for** each sample in all_synthetic_data **do**
31:        attack_label = get_attack_label(sample)
32:        Add sample to **attack_counts[attack_label]**
33:    **end for**
34:    Find the minimum count **min_count** among attack_counts
35:    **for** each attack_label in attack_counts **do**
36:        Randomly select **min_count** samples from attack_counts[attack_label]
37:        Add these samples to **balanced_samples**
38:    **end for**
39:    **return balanced_samples**
40: **end function**

---

* Due to space constraints, these functions are not explicitly defined. You can find the full triplet_mixup() in [10], and FedAvg() in [16]

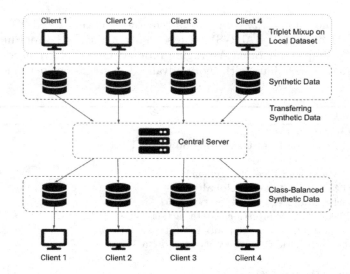

Fig. 3. An overview of synthetic data sharing pipeline.

SCAFFOLD, but we chose to build on top of Federated Averaging because it is the most simple and lightweight (no extra overhead is incurred beyond simple weighted averaging), and yet provides near-perfect accuracy when used with the techniques in FAST-SV. This makes more advanced aggregation methods redundant.

4.3   Generating Samples via Triplet Mixup at the Client Level

Here, we detail triplet-mixup, the technique we use to generate synthetic attacks. Traditional Mixup [22] augments data between a data pair:

$$\hat{x} = \lambda x_i + (1 - \lambda)x_j \qquad \hat{y} = \lambda y_i + (1 - \lambda)y_j \qquad (1)$$

where $\lambda \sim Beta(\alpha, \alpha)$ for $\alpha \in (0, \infty)$. In contrast, we follow [10] and use a triplet based mixup strategy which creates a more diverse set of augmented samples:

$$\hat{x} = \lambda_i x_i + \lambda_j x_j + (1 - \lambda_i - \lambda_j)x_k \qquad (2)$$

where $\lambda_i, \lambda_j \sim Uniform(0, \alpha)$ with $\alpha \in (0, 0.5]$. Additionally, data points x_i, x_j, and x_k are from the same class.

This technique limits sensitive information from being leaked because each value in the synthetic instances is some *combination* of existing samples, and therefore produces values that do not necessarily exist in "parent" samples. For instance, we verified experimentally that it generates an entirely new set of CAN IDs in the resulting samples through combining triplets of existing CAN IDs.

4.4   The Machine Learning Backbone

For the machine-learning model, we use a simple Multi-Layer-Perceptron (MLP). The MLP used had 2 dense layers with 200 neurons each, with ReLU activation functions and a final softmax layer for classification. We used the NAdam optimizer with a learning rate of 0.0001. For all experiments, we split the data into train-test splits, using 80% to train and the rest for testing. We trained our clients for 50 FL rounds. In conventional, non-federated ML settings, where all data is in one place, our basic MLP network achieves excellent accuracy (over 99%), showcasing its proficiency in discerning attacks. This aligns with related work in Sect. 2.1, where similar accuracy levels were achieved with simple models when the data is centrally located, or distributed among clients uniformly.

Our main focus is federated learning, particularly in strongly non-IID distributions. Traditional FL methods like FedAvg [16] struggle in such cases, regardless of the model complexity. On the other hand, in FL settings with uniform data distributions, a basic MLP works well, indicating complex ML backbones may not be needed. Our aim is to excel in strongly non-IID scenarios by tailoring the FL method for this application, to make practical systems for the real world.

5   Experiments and Results

5.1   Results on CAN Attack Datasets

Section 4.1 outlined several ways in which attacks can be distributed to clients. Now we provide a simpler naming scheme for them, which follows the format *A-B*: *A* denotes the number of attacks that the client has in its local dataset, and *B* denotes the number of attacks missing. With 4 attacks in all our datasets, we get 4 different scenarios where clients have at least 1 attack to learn from.

1. **4-0**: This setting corresponds to the *Approximately Uniform Attack Distribution* setting described in 4.1. All 4 attack types are present in all clients.
2. **3-1**: This corresponds to the *One Attack Removed* setting from 4.1. Here, 3 of the 4 attacks (randomly chosen) are available to a client, with 1 unseen.
3. **2-2**: This corresponds to *Half of the Attacks Removed* from Sect. 4.1, i.e. any 2 of the attacks are seen by each client and 2 remain unseen.
4. **1-3**: This corresponds to the *Only One Attack Present* scenario where only 1 of the attacks (chosen at random) is seen by a client and 3 are unseen.

We conduct our experiments with 4 FL clients, trained for 50 FL rounds, and each client conceptually represents a manufacturer. All client datasets have examples from the benign class in all settings. In all experiments with FAST-SV, a client shares only 100 synthetic samples of each attack type in its local dataset.

Baselines. To the best of our knowledge, no work in the literature specifically conducts non-IID experiments on CAN Attack Datasets. Nonetheless, we create certain baselines to compare to our approach. We use the following FL systems:

- FedAvg: This is the standard Federated Learning algorithm [16], which has proven surprisingly effective in various datasets.
- SCAFFOLD: This [9] is one of the most popular FL algorithms, specifically designed to tackle non-IID distributions by correcting drifts in client weights.
- FAST-SV: This represents our method.

Table 2 shows the overall results on the Car Hacking Dataset. While the Accuracy and Weighted-F1 metrics appear high across all settings and FL Models, this is primarily because the dataset is severely imbalanced, with a vast majority being Benign samples which are correctly classified. Therefore, the important metric is the Macro-F1, which is a non-weighted average F1 score. This metric captures whether all types of attacks are actually being recognized. For instance, the FedAvg model achieves a high accuracy of 90.1% in the 1-3 setting, but has a macro-F1 score of only 41.6%. This is because, in this setting, FedAvg actually recognizes 2 out of the 5 labels. To see this, refer to Table 3, which shows the per-class precision and recall for FedAvg in the Car Hacking Dataset. Similarly, Table 4 and Table 5 show the per-class metrics for SCAFFOLD and FAST-SV, respectively. Across all metrics and settings, FAST-SV performs the best. This difference is more notable when one looks at the more relevant metrics in the strongly non-IID settings (1-3, 2-2), where it achieves near-perfect Macro-F1 scores as well as per-class metrics, unlike the other 2 baselines. The impact of the synthetically generated samples is thus clear. Among baselines, we see that SCAFFOLD overall outperforms FedAvg in the Car-Hacking Dataset.

The NAIST CAN dataset comprises 4 sub-datasets created on 4 different cars (Toyota, Subaru, Suzuki, and Mitsubishi). Table 6 shows the results on this dataset. The pattern remains largely the same overall, with FAST-SV significantly outperforming the baselines, guided by its synthetically generated samples. We leave out per-class metrics for the NAIST dataset for space constraints.

Table 2. Performance on the Car Hacking Dataset

Setting	FL Model	Performance (%)		
		Accuracy	Weighted-F1	Macro-F1
4-0	FedAvg	99.9	99.9	99.9
	SCAFFOLD	99.9	99.9	99.9
	FAST-SV	99.9	99.9	99.9
3-1	FedAvg	99.9	99.9	99.9
	SCAFFOLD	99.9	99.9	99.9
	FAST-SV	99.9	99.9	99.9
2-2	FedAvg	96.4	94.6	79.3
	SCAFFOLD	96.1	95.0	79.0
	FAST-SV	99.9	99.9	99.9
1-3	FedAvg	90.1	85.6	41.6
	SCAFFOLD	92.1	89.0	56.2
	FAST-SV	99.7	99.7	99.0

Table 3. Per-Class Results for *FedAvg* on the Car-Hacking Dataset.

Setting	Precision (%)					Recall (%)				
	Benign	DoS	Fuzzing	Gear	RPM	Benign	DoS	Fuzzing	Gear	RPM
4-0	100	100	99.9	100	100	99.9	100	99.8	100	100
3-1	99.9	100	99.9	100	99.9	99.9	100	99.7	100	100
2-2	95.9	100	100	100	99.9	100	0.06	96.7	100	100
1-3	89.6	0.00	100	0.00	99.9	100	0.00	7.15	0	100

Table 4. Per-Class Results for *SCAFFOLD* on the Car-Hacking Dataset.

Setting	Precision (%)					Recall (%)				
	Benign	DoS	Fuzzing	Gear	RPM	Benign	DoS	Fuzzing	Gear	RPM
4-0	100	99.9	100	100	100	99.9	100	99.9	100	100
3-1	99.9	100	100	99.8	99.9	100	100	99.3	100	100
2-2	96.0	89.1	100	100	100	100	0.00	97.0	100	100
1-3	92.1	0.00	100	0.00	94.1	100	0.00	75.0	0	100

Table 5. Per-Class Results for *FAST-SV* on the Car-Hacking Dataset.

Setting	Precision (%)					Recall (%)				
	Benign	DoS	Fuzzing	Gear	RPM	Benign	DoS	Fuzzing	Gear	RPM
4-0	100	100	99.9	100	100	99.9	100	100	100	100
3-1	99.9	100	99.9	99.9	99.9	100	100	99.6	100	100
2-2	99.9	100	99.9	100	99.9	100	100	99.1	100	100
1-3	99.7	100	100	99.9	99.9	100	100	91.5	100	100

Table 6. Performance on the NAIST Dataset

Model	Setting	FL Model	Performance (%)		
			Accuracy	Weighted-F1	Macro-F1
Toyota	4-0	FedAvg	99.9	99.9	99.9
		SCAFFOLD	99.1	99.1	78.9
		FAST-SV	99.9	99.9	99.9
	3-1	FedAvg	98.5	98.1	58.7
		SCAFFOLD	99.1	99.0	79.0
		FAST-SV	99.9	99.9	99.9
	2-2	FedAvg	98.4	98.0	58.6
		SCAFFOLD	95.0	93.1	59.2
		FAST-SV	99.9	99.9	99.8
	1-3	FedAvg	98.1	97.6	57.6
		SCAFFOLD	95.0	93.1	59.0
		FAST-SV	99.8	99.8	99.6
Subaru	4-0	FedAvg	99.9	99.9	99.9
		SCAFFOLD	97.1	95.0	40.1
		FAST-SV	99.9	99.9	99.9
	3-1	FedAvg	98.9	98.5	58.8
		SCAFFOLD	97.5	96.2	60.0
		FAST-SV	99.9	99.9	99.9
	2-2	FedAvg	98.9	98.5	58.9
		SCAFFOLD	97.0	95.0	40.0
		FAST-SV	99.9	99.9	99.9
	1-3	FedAvg	98.8	98.3	58.1
		SCAFFOLD	97.1	96.0	44.4
		FAST-SV	99.8	99.8	99.5
Suzuki	4-0	FedAvg	99.9	99.9	99.9
		SCAFFOLD	99.1	98.0	60.1
		FAST-SV	99.9	99.9	99.9
	3-1	FedAvg	99.3	98.9	58.9
		SCAFFOLD	99.1	98.0	60.1
		FAST-SV	99.9	99.9	99.9
	2-2	FedAvg	99.2	98.9	58.3
		SCAFFOLD	99.1	98.0	60.1
		FAST-SV	99.9	99.9	99.9
	1-3	FedAvg	99.2	98.8	57.2
		SCAFFOLD	96.0	94.1	20.1
		FAST-SV	99.9	99.9	99.7

(continued)

Table 6. (*continued*)

Mitsubishi	4-0	FedAvg	99.9	99.9	99.9
		SCAFFOLD	98.0	97.0	40.40
		FAST-SV	99.9	99.9	99.9
	3-1	FedAvg	98.9	98.6	56.0
		SCAFFOLD	99.1	99.0	58.3
		FAST-SV	99.9	99.9	99.9
	2-2	FedAvg	99.3	98.9	58.6
		SCAFFOLD	98.0	97.1	40.0
		FAST-SV	99.9	99.9	99.7
	1-3	FedAvg	99.1	98.8	57.4
		SCAFFOLD	94.2	91.1	19.0
		FAST-SV	99.7	99.7	98.0

5.2   Investigating the Specific IID Challenge

A major disadvantage that FedAvg and SCAFFOLD face in most non-IID settings is that they have no exposure to certain attacks at all. Furthermore, the feature spaces that these attack types occupy are very distinct. To visualize this, we utilize a technique called t-SNE [15], which can reduce high-dimensional feature spaces (such as a CAN payload), into 2 dimensions. Figure 4 shows a t-SNE plot where 2500 samples from each of the 5 classes(4 attacks and 1 benign) were plotted after reducing dimensions. Each point is colored by its label. Other than the benign class, we see that the 4 attacks have little feature space overlap. This is why sharing synthetic samples is so effective in FAST-SV; the artificial samples familiarize the clients with the distinct feature space of the missing attacks.

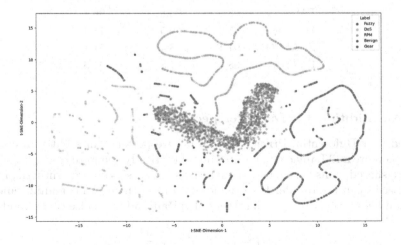

Fig. 4. A 2D t-SNE representation of the feature space of each attack.

Alternative Augmentation Approaches. Other augmentation methods like SMOTE, or pair mix-up can be used in FAST-SV. However, SMOTE involves computing K-nearest-neighbors and is slower than mix-up, which selects minority class triplets randomly. Secondly, [10] shows that triplet mixup performs better than mixing pairs. Thus, triplet mixup provides a simple yet powerful solution.

5.3   Scaling FAST-SV

In this experiment, we scale our setup by changing the client entity from "manufacturer" to smaller-scale entities like "car dealerships" or individual vehicles. Accordingly, we increase the client count from 4 to 1000 clients. For space constraints, we present the results for this experiment only on the publicly available Car-Hacking Dataset in Table 7. We observe a consistent pattern in this 1000-client experiment, where FAST-SV rapidly adapts to extreme non-IID settings, demonstrating superior performance, especially in terms of Macro-F1.

Table 7. Performance with 1000 clients on the Car Hacking Dataset

Setting	FL Model	Performance (%)		
		Accuracy	Weighted-F1	Macro-F1
4-0	FedAvg	99.1	99.1	97.5
	SCAFFOLD	99.2	99.2	97.2
	FAST-SV	99.7	99.7	99.9
3-1	FedAvg	99.1	99.1	97.4
	SCAFFOLD	99.0	99.0	96.9
	FAST-SV	99.4	99.4	97.9
2-2	FedAvg	93.9	91.5	65.2
	SCAFFOLD	92.0	89.1	57.0
	FAST-SV	98.9	98.8	96.1
1-3	FedAvg	85.9	79.5	18.4
	SCAFFOLD	91.1	88.4	51.1
	FAST-SV	98.1	97.8	91.5

5.4   An Additional Privacy Perspective

Inspired by ϵ-Differential Privacy (ϵ-DP) [3], we perform an additional experiment where we add Laplacian noise to the synthetically generated samples before they are shared. This is because, though the samples shared are synthetic, inference attacks can try to infer the original data from them. Thus adding random noise can help protect from such attacks. Typically, adding noise corresponds to:

$$f_\varepsilon(D) = f(D) + Lap\left(\frac{\Delta f}{\varepsilon}\right) \qquad (3)$$

Here, $f(D)$ is the output of a function f on dataset D without privacy mechanisms, $f_\varepsilon(D)$ is the differentially private output, and $Lap\left(\frac{\Delta f}{\varepsilon}\right)$ is the added noise from the Laplace distribution, where Δf is the function's sensitivity and ε is the privacy parameter. Different from the standard ϵ-DP setting where noise is added to the output of a function, we add noise *to the synthetic samples* based on several ϵ-values from a range recommended by [17]. We fix the *sensitivity*, Δf, to 1. Table 8 shows results. For space constraints, we report results from the Car Hacking Dataset, on only the most difficult distribution settings: 1-3, and 2-2. We see that for all ϵ-values, FAST-SV performs well despite adding substantial noise. Lower ϵ-values imply more added noise. Comparing with the 1-3 and 2-2 settings from Table 2 shows that FAST-SV with significant Laplacian noise still beats baselines. Finally, adversaries may still attempt inferences from noisy data, by filtering out noise. However, the perturbation for each sample is drawn independently from a Laplace distribution, limiting individual-level inferences. Nonetheless, the effectiveness of such methods varies based on many factors. Thus, we do not provide formal privacy guarantees, leaving it to future work. Instead, we empirically show FAST-SV's ability to tolerate noisy synthetic data.

Table 8. FAST-SV with noisy synthetic data, on Car Hacking Dataset.

Setting	Epsilon	Accuracy (%)	Weighted-F1 (%)	Macro-F1 (%)
2-2	0.1	99.9	99.9	99.9
	1	99.9	99.9	99.9
	5	99.9	99.9	99.9
1–3	0.1	96.3	94.5	78.9
	1	99.5	98.2	99.5
	5	99.6	98.6	99.7

6   Conclusion

This work investigates federated methods for enhancing smart vehicle security, in the context of non-IID data distributions. We introduce FAST-SV, a technique that generates synthetic CAN attack data and redistributes it systematically to address extreme non-IID distributions. We conducted evaluations using a substantial in-house dataset involving four real car models and an existing dataset. Our findings reveal that standard FL algorithms falter when multiple classes are missing from clients. FAST-SV effectively tackles this issue, achieving near-optimal performance in non-IID scenarios. We initially assume clients represent car manufacturers but demonstrate scalability to scenarios with many smaller clients. Finally, we explore enhanced security through the addition of noise.

Disclaimer. Commercial products are identified in order to adequately specify certain procedures. In no case does such identification imply recommendation or endorsement by the National Institute of Standards and Technology, nor does it imply that the identified products are necessarily the best available for the purpose.

Acknowledgement. For the authors in Japan, the research was supported by the ICSCoE Core Human Resources Development Program and JSPS KAKENHI Grant Number 22H03572, Japan.

For the authors in the US, the research was supported in part by the National Center for Transportation Cybersecurity and Resiliency (TraCR) (a U.S. Department of Transportation National University Transportation Center) headquartered at Clemson University, Clemson, South Carolina, USA. Any opinions, findings, conclusions, and recommendations expressed in this material are those of the author(s) and do not necessarily reflect the views of TraCR, and the U.S. Government assumes no liability for the contents or use thereof.

Other support was provided in part by the following: NIST Award # 60NANB23D007, NSF awards DMS-1737978, DGE-2039542, OAC-1828467, OAC-1931541, and DGE-1906630, ONR awards N00014-17-1-2995 and N00014-20-1-2738.

References

1. Amato, F., Coppolino, L., Mercaldo, F., Moscato, F., Nardone, R., Santone, A.: Can-bus attack detection with deep learning. IEEE Trans. Intell. Transp. Syst. **22**(8), 5081–5090 (2021)
2. Chawla, N.V., Bowyer, K.W., Hall, L.O., Kegelmeyer, W.P.: Smote: synthetic minority over-sampling technique. J. Artif. Intell. Res. **16**, 321–357 (2002)
3. Dwork, C.: Differential privacy. In: Bugliesi, M., Preneel, B., Sassone, V., Wegener, I. (eds.) ICALP 2006. LNCS, vol. 4052, pp. 1–12. Springer, Heidelberg (2006). https://doi.org/10.1007/11787006_1
4. Feng, S.Y., Gangal, V., Wei, J., Chandar, S., Vosoughi, S., Mitamura, T., Hovy, E.: A survey of data augmentation approaches for NLP. arXiv Preprint arXiv:2105.03075 (2021)
5. Goodfellow, I., Pouget-Abadie, J., Mirza, M., Xu, B., Warde-Farley, D., Ozair, S., Courville, A., Bengio, Y.: Generative adversarial networks. Commun. ACM **63**(11), 139–144 (2020)
6. Hanselmann, M., Strauss, T., Dormann, K., Ulmer, H.: Canet: an unsupervised intrusion detection system for high dimensional can bus data. IEEE Access **8**, 58194–58205 (2020)
7. Hossain, M.D., Inoue, H., Ochiai, H., Fall, D., Kadobayashi, Y.: An effective in-vehicle can bus intrusion detection system using cnn deep learning approach. In: 2020 IEEE Global Communications Conference, pp. 1–6. IEEE (2020)
8. Iehira, K., Inoue, H., Ishida, K.: Spoofing attack using bus-off attacks against a specific ecu of the can bus. In: 2018 15th IEEE Annual Consumer Communications and Networking Conference (CCNC), pp. 1–4 (2018). https://doi.org/10.1109/CCNC.2018.8319180
9. Karimireddy, S.P., Kale, S., Mohri, M., Reddi, S., Stich, S., Suresh, A.T.: Scaffold: stochastic controlled averaging for federated learning. In: International Conference on Machine Learning, pp. 5132–5143. PMLR (2020)

10. Li, X., Khan, L., Zamani, M., Wickramasuriya, S., Hamlen, K.W., Thuraisingham, B.: Mcom: a semi-supervised method for imbalanced tabular security data. In: Sural, S., Lu, H. (eds.) Data and Applications Security and Privacy XXXVI, pp. 48–67. Springer International Publishing, Cham (2022)
11. Li, Z., Shao, J., Mao, Y., Wang, J.H., Zhang, J.: Federated learning with gan-based data synthesis for non-iid clients. In: Goebel, R., Yu, H., Faltings, B., Fan, L., Xiong, Z. (eds.) Trustworthy Federated Learning, pp. 17–32. Springer International Publishing, Cham (2023)
12. Lin, Y., Chen, C., Xiao, F., Avatefipour, O., Alsubhi, K., Yunianta, A.: An evolutionary deep learning anomaly detection framework for in-vehicle networks - can bus. IEEE Transactions on Industry Applications, pp. 1–1 (2020). https://doi.org/10.1109/TIA.2020.3009906
13. Liu, M., Ho, S., Wang, M., Gao, L., Jin, Y., Zhang, H.: Federated learning meets natural language processing: a survey. CoRR **abs/2107.12603** (2021). https://arxiv.org/abs/2107.12603
14. Lokman, S.F., Othman, A.T., Abu-Bakar, M.H.: Intrusion detection system for automotive controller area network (can) bus system: a review. EURASIP J. Wirel. Commun. Netw. **2019**, 1–17 (2019)
15. Van der Maaten, L., Hinton, G.: Visualizing data using t-sne. J. Mach. Learn. Res. **9**(11) (2008)
16. McMahan, B., Moore, E., Ramage, D., Hampson, S., Arcas, B.A.y.: Communication-efficient learning of deep networks from decentralized data. In: Singh, A., Zhu, J. (eds.) Proceedings of the 20th International Conference on Artificial Intelligence and Statistics. Proceedings of Machine Learning Research, PMLR (2017)
17. NIST: Differential privacy: Future work and open challenges (March 2023). https://www.nist.gov/blogs/cybersecurity-insights/differential-privacy-future-work-open-challenges
18. Seo, E., Song, H.M., Kim, H.K.: Gids: Gan based intrusion detection system for in-vehicle network. In: 2018 16th Annual Conference on Privacy, Security and Trust (PST), pp. 1–6 (Aug 2018)
19. Shibly, K.H., Hossain, M.D., Inoue, H., Taenaka, Y., Kadobayashi, Y.: Personalized federated learning for automotive intrusion detection systems. In: 2022 IEEE Future Networks World Forum (FNWF), pp. 544–549 (2022)
20. Song, H.M., Woo, J., Kim, H.K.: In-vehicle network intrusion detection using deep convolutional neural network. Vehicular Commun. **21**, 100198 (2020)
21. Zhang, H., Zeng, K., Lin, S.: Federated graph neural network for fast anomaly detection in controller area networks. IEEE Trans. Inform. Forens. Security **18**, 1566–1579 (2023)
22. Zhang, H., Cisse, M., Dauphin, Y.N., Lopez-Paz, D.: Mixup: beyond empirical risk minimization. arXiv Preprint arXiv:1710.09412 (2017)
23. Zhao, Y., Li, M., Lai, L., Suda, N., Civin, D., Chandra, V.: Federated learning with non-iid data. CoRR **abs/1806.00582** (2018)
24. Zhu, H., Xu, J., Liu, S., Jin, Y.: Federated learning on non-iid data: a survey. Neurocomputing **465**, 371–390 (2021)

Using Reed-Muller Codes for Classification with Rejection and Recovery

Daniel Fentham[1]([✉]) [iD], David Parker[2] [iD], and Mark Ryan[1] [iD]

[1] School of Computer Science, University of Birmingham, Birmingham, UK
dxf209@student.bham.ac.uk, m.d.ryan@cs.bham.ac.uk
[2] Department of Computer Science, University of Oxford, Oxford, UK
david.parker@cs.ox.ac.uk

Abstract. When deploying classifiers in the real world, users expect them to respond to inputs appropriately. However, traditional classifiers are not equipped to handle inputs which lie far from the distribution they were trained on. Malicious actors can exploit this defect by making adversarial perturbations designed to cause the classifier to give an incorrect output. Classification-with-rejection methods attempt to solve this problem by allowing networks to refuse to classify an input in which they have low confidence. This works well for strongly adversarial examples, but also leads to the rejection of weakly perturbed images, which intuitively could be correctly classified. To address these issues, we propose Reed-Muller Aggregation Networks (RMAggNet), a classifier inspired by Reed-Muller error-correction codes which can correct and reject inputs. This paper shows that RMAggNet can minimise incorrectness while maintaining good correctness over multiple adversarial attacks at different perturbation budgets by leveraging the ability to correct errors in the classification process. This provides an alternative classification-with-rejection method which can reduce the amount of additional processing in situations where a small number of incorrect classifications are permissible.

Keywords: Deep Neural Networks · Adversarial Examples · Classification-with-rejection · Error-correction codes · ML Security

1 Introduction

Deep Neural Networks (DNNs) have shown incredible performance in numerous classification tasks, including image classification [1], medical diagnosis [2] and malware detection [3]. However, a fundamental shortcoming is that they pass judgement beyond their expertise. When presented with data outside of the distribution they were trained on, DNNs will attempt to classify that data by selecting from one of the finite labels available, often reporting high confidence in the classifications they have made. The most egregious examples of this occur when a DNN is presented with an input which is far outside of the domain it has been trained on (for example, presenting an image of a cat to a text classification

M. Mosbah et al. (Eds.): FPS 2023, LNCS 14551, pp. 36–52, 2024.
https://doi.org/10.1007/978-3-031-57537-2_3

model), which it will confidently assign a class to. This behaviour is also present in adversarial examples, which were introduced in the seminal paper by Szegedy et al. in 2018 [4], where an (almost) invisible perturbation pushes an input far from the training distribution, leading to a confident misclassification [5]. Since then, extensive research has been conducted exploring new, more sophisticated, attacks on networks of different architectures [6–8] and defences that attempt to mitigate their effectiveness [9–11]. This results in hesitation when applying DNN models to safety- and security-critical applications where there is a high cost of misclassification.

Classification-with-rejection (CWR) methods [11–14] attempt to address this limitation by refusing to assign a label to an input when the confidence in the classification is low. In this paper, we present an approach to CWR that parallels ideas from Error-Correcting Output Codes (ECOCs) [11,14], where an ensemble of networks perform classification by generating binary strings, extending them with a reject option. ECOC methods have received little attention as a defence mechanism against adversarial attacks, even though the independence of the individual networks offers a natural defence. A notable property of adversarial attacks is that they are highly transferable between models, meaning an adversarial attack crafted for one network will likely deceive another with high probability, provided the networks perform a similar task [15]. Since ECOC methods promote diversity in the constituent network's tasks, an adversarial attack crafted to change the output reported by one network is less likely to fool another in a way which would result in further misclassification. Moreover, due to the aggregated nature of the resulting classification, an adversary would need to create a perturbation which can fool multiple networks simultaneously, necessitating precise bit-flipping strategies which lead to a valid target class.

In this paper, we introduce Reed-Muller Aggregation Networks (RMAggNet), which apply error correcting codes to the correction and rejection of classifications, ultimately producing a new kind of ECOC classifier. Similar to existing ECOCs, these consist of multiple DNNs, each performing a simple classification task which determines if an input belongs to a defined subset of the classes, resulting in a binary answer. The results of these networks are aggregated together into a binary string which we compare to class binary strings which represent each of the classes from the dataset. If the resulting binary string is the same as a class binary string, we return the associated label as a result, otherwise we attempt to correct the result (if we have a small enough Hamming distance), or reject the result and refuse to classify the input. Thus, unlike existing CWR methods our approach has the ability to both correct and reject inputs.

We evaluate the effectiveness of RMAggNet by comparing it to two other CWR approaches: an ensemble of networks (with a voting-based rejection process) and Confidence Calibrated Adversarial Training (CCAT) [16]. After performing tests using the EMNIST and CIFAR-10 datasets with open-box PGD L_∞ and PGD L_2 adversarial attacks, we conclude that RMAggNet can greatly reduce the amount of rejected inputs in certain circumstances, making it a viable alternative to methods such as CCAT if some incorrectness is acceptable. We expand on this finding using the MNIST dataset, along with closed-box adversarial attacks, in an extended version of this paper [17].

In summary, this paper makes the following contributions:

- We introduce RMAggNet, a novel ECOC classification method which leverages the power of Reed-Muller codes to create a classifier which can both correct and reject inputs (Sect. 3)[1].
- We show the effectiveness of RMAggNet on the EMNIST and CIFAR-10 datasets with open-box gradient-based adversarial attacks (Sects. 4 & 5).
- We discuss the application of RMAggNet to classification tasks, providing guidance on when it may be a strong alternative to other CWR methods (Sect. 6).

2 Related Work

2.1 Error Correcting Output Codes

Verma and Swami defined an error-correcting output code (ECOC) classification method which uses an ensemble of models, each trained to perform a subset of the classification [11]. Their model uses Hadamard matrices to construct binary codes, which are assigned to classes from the dataset. Multiple DNNs are then defined to generate a set amount of bits from each code for each class, essentially following a set membership classification approach. When an input is passed to the multiple networks, a vector of real numbers is generated, and the similarity between this vector and the class vectors is calculated, with the most similar vector being returned as the final classification.

The authors argue that this classification method has greater resilience to adversarial attacks than traditional ensemble methods due to the independence of the models, encouraged by the diverse classification tasks. This reduces the chance of multiple coordinated bit-flips occurring due to a single perturbation as a result of the transferability of adversarial attacks. Verma and Swami focus their attention on multi-bit outputs, where four networks produce a combined total of 16, 32, or 64 bits, encoding the input into 4, 8 or 16 bits, respectively. This approach to ECOC classification leads to similar networks being trained, where, in many cases, the entire set of classes is being used by all networks. This results in each network learning similar features, reducing independence and lowering resilience to transfer attacks.

Song et al., proposed a method which extends the work by Verma and Swami, introducing Error Correcting Neural Networks (ECNN) [14]. This paper improves ECOCs by increasing the number of networks to one per output bit and optimising the codeword matrix using simulated annealing [18] which encourages each classifier to learn unique features, enhancing robustness against direct and transfer adversarial attacks. However, in practice, the ECNN implementation trains a single network with each classifier having a unique top layer. This

---

[1] Code available at: https://github.com/dfenth/RMAggNet.

reduces the independence between networks since each of them share the same low level features which can be used by adversaries.

These approaches are similar to the method proposed in this paper; however, there are a few key differences. While Verma and Swami [11] and Song et al. [14] discuss the use of error correction, it is not actively utilised in the classification process. In addition, error correction provides a natural implementation of CWR where outputs which deviate significantly from existing classes can trigger a *reject* option where the classifier refuses to return a result. This paper aims to address these gaps by exploring the application of error correction and classification-with-rejection approaches to ECOC methods. We hope to provide insights into the effectiveness, practicality and benefits of these strategies.

2.2 Confidence Calibrated Adversarial Training

Many CWR methods have been proposed over the years [12,13,16]. We focus on the Confidence Calibrated Adversarial Training (CCAT) CWR method which was introduced by Stutz et al. in 2020 [16]. CCAT attempts to produce a model which is robust to unseen threat models which use different L_p norms or larger perturbations when generating adversarial examples. CCAT achieves good rejection performance through adversarial training where the model is trained to predict the classes of clean data with high confidence and produce a uniform distribution for adversarial examples within an ϵ-ball of the true image.

3 Reed-Muller Aggregation Networks (RMAggNet)

3.1 Reed-Muller Codes

We begin with some brief background on Reed-Muller codes, which are multi-error detecting and correcting codes [19,20]. This extends earlier work on Hamming codes [21] and generalise many other error correction methods.

Reed-Muller is often represented with the notation $[2^m, k, 2^{m-r}]_q$. We set q, the number of elements in the finite field, to 2, meaning any codes we create will be binary. In the low-degree polynomial interpretation, m denotes the number of variables and r denotes the highest degree of the polynomial both of which influence the properties of the Reed-Muller code. The first element of the tuple (2^m) represents the length of the codewords we will use. The second element (k) represents the length of the message we can encode and is calculated as

$$k = \sum_{i=0}^{r} \binom{m}{i} \tag{1}$$

The final element (2^{m-r}) is the minimum Hamming distance between any two codes we generate, and influences the amount of error correction that can be applied. For simplicity, we set $n = 2^m$ and $d = 2^{m-r}$ condensing the notation to $[n, k, d]_2$.

A key advantage of Reed-Muller codes is that they allow us to unambiguously correct a number of bits equal to the Hamming bound t:

$$t = \left\lfloor \frac{(d-1)}{2} \right\rfloor \qquad (2)$$

due to the guaranteed Hamming distance between any two codewords. This can be thought of as an open Hamming sphere around each codeword with a radius of 2^{m-r-1} which does not intersect any other sphere.

To build Reed-Muller codes with pre-determined Hamming distances, we start by selecting values for m and r which fit our use case, i.e., we can generate codewords of appropriate length with a desired amount of correction. Once we have chosen m and r, we can calculate k (see Eq. 1) and we can define the low-degree polynomial, which will have k coefficients, m variables and a maximum degree of r. This allows us to generate the codewords with a minimal Hamming distance of d between any two of the codes.

We specify the coefficients of the polynomial in k different ways where a single coefficient is set to one, and all others are zero. This gives us k polynomials with fixed coefficients and m free variables. We can then define the basis vectors of the space by instantiating every possible combination of variables for each of the fixed coefficient polynomials. This creates k codewords of length 2^m all of which have a guaranteed Hamming distance of at least d. We can have up to 2^k valid codewords which satisfy the Hamming distance guarantee. These additional codewords can be generated by performing an XOR operation on all possible combinations of the basis vectors generating a closed set. We refer to these binary vectors as *codewords*.

3.2   Reed-Muller Aggregation Networks

We can now define a Reed-Muller Aggregation Network (RMAggNet) which uses multiple networks, trained on separate tasks, to create a binary vector which we can classify, correct, or reject. To create an RMAggNet we start by defining Reed-Muller codes which act as class codewords for the dataset classes we intend to recognise. To define appropriate Reed-Muller codes, we have to consider a number of factors related to the problem we are solving.

The first is the number of classes in the dataset ($|C|$). We must make sure that the message length k is adequate for the number of classes, such that, $|C| \leq 2^k$. From the definition of k (Eq. 1) we can see that it depends on both m and r, therefore these values are influenced by $|C|$ and must be considered early on in the design process. The number of classes in the dataset is the primary point to consider when deciding on values for m and r, because if we do not satisfy $|C| \leq 2^k$ then we will not have an effective classifier.

The second factor we must consider, is whether we have appropriate error correction for the problem. The maximum number of errors we can correct is represented by the Hamming bound t (Eq. 2) which relies on d which is 2^{m-r}, so we also need to take this into account when deciding on m and r.

The third factor is that we must have a low probability of assigning a valid codeword to a random noise image. A fundamental flaw with traditional DNNs is that they will assign a class to any input, even if the input is far from the distribution they have been trained on. The probability of assigning a random noise image a valid class is $|C|/2^n$ where we have no error correction, however, with error correction, the probability increases to $(|C| \cdot \sum_{i=0}^{t} \binom{n}{i}))/2^n$. This means that it is advantageous to only use the amount of error correction that is necessary for the problem at hand, even if that means we are not correcting the maximum number of bits theoretically possible.

Once we have a set of codewords which fit the problem specification, the length of the codewords (n) determines the number of networks included in the aggregation. We can assign each network a unique index value corresponding to an index within the class codeword binary strings. The values at the index positions define a set partition which determines which classes a network is trained to return a 1 for and which it returns a 0 for (i.e., the network returns a 1 for all classes with a 1 at the index and 0 otherwise). We can also view the class codewords as a matrix, with each network assigned to a column with 1s and 0s indicating the partition between sets. By randomly shuffling the class codewords, each network is trained to recognise a set of approximately half of the classes.

With the classification task for each network defined, we can move on to training. The training process requires us to adjust the true labels of each input with each network having a unique set of true labels for the training data, where the true labels correspond to the set partition label. Once the dataset has been adjusted each network is trained independently.

During inference we pass the same input to the n networks which produces n real values $\mathbf{v} \in \mathbb{R}^n$. We select a threshold value τ which acts as a bias, with a large τ leading to codewords consisting of more 0 bits. We compare each of the n real values of $\mathbf{v}$ to τ with the following rule:

$$v_i = \begin{cases} 1 & \text{if } v_i \geq \tau \\ 0 & \text{otherwise} \end{cases}$$

This produces a binary string which we can compare to the class codewords. If any of the class codewords match the predicted binary string exactly, we can return the label associated with it as the result; however, if none match, we calculate the Hamming distance between the prediction and the class codewords. If we find a Hamming distance less than or equal to t, then we can unambiguously correct to, and return, that class codeword due to the properties of Reed-Muller codes. Otherwise, we refuse to classify the input and return a rejection.

4   Evaluation Methodology

4.1   Threat Model

We begin by establishing the threat model under which we expect the RMAggNet defence to operate effectively as per the recommendations made by Carlini et al. [22]. Our assumptions consider an adversary who knows the purpose of the model (i.e., the classes the model can output) and is capable of providing the model with inputs. The actions of the adversary are constrained by a limited perturbation cost, where the L_p-norm between the original (x) and perturbed ($\tilde{x}$) image must be below some threshold ϵ, i.e., ($|x - \tilde{x}|_p \leq \epsilon$), where p is either 2 or ∞ depending on the attack used. The norm used for an attack changes the focus of the adversarial perturbation. The L_2 attacks encourage small changes across all input dimensions, which distributes the perturbation across multiple features, whereas the L_∞ attack encourages perturbations which focus on a single feature, maximising this as much as the budget (ϵ) allows. The ultimate aim of the adversary is to generate perturbed images which are not noticeable to a time constrained human.

The level of access to the model granted to the adversary depends on the specific adversarial attack being employed. In the case of open-box attacks, the adversary has full access to the target model and can generate adversarial perturbations tailored to deceive that particular network. This represents the worst-case scenario. On the other hand, closed-box attacks represent a more realistic setting where the adversary does not have access to the model parameters. In this case it is necessary to train a surrogate model which performs the same classification task as the target model. Adversarial examples are then generated for this surrogate model, which leverage transferability to create adversarial examples for the target model. In this paper we focus on the more challenging open-box attacks. Experiments using closed-box attacks can be found in the extended version of this paper [17].

We employ two attacks to generate adversarial examples, focusing on the gradient-based Projected Gradient Descent (PGD) attack [23], using both the L_2- and L_∞-norm. In the extended paper we also include the gradient-free Boundary attack in the L_2-norm [24], and transfer attacks to demonstrate the adversarial robustness of these approaches in a closed-box setting. The use of both gradient and gradient-free attacks allows us to more thoroughly evaluate the robustness of the models. While gradient based attacks tend to produce stronger adversarial examples, they can fail to produce effective perturbations if the target model performs any kind of gradient masking. To ensure that we have a fair and reliable evaluation of the robustness we include gradient-free attacks to eliminate the possibility that any results are solely due to masking the model gradients.

4.2 Comparison Methods

To evaluate the classification and rejection ability of RMAggNet we have implemented two other comparison methods.

The first is a traditional ensemble method which consists of n networks (where n is the same number of networks used for RMAggNet) each of which are trained to perform the full classification task, as opposed to RMAggNet where each network is trained to perform set membership over two partitions. To aggregate the ensemble method results from the multiple networks, we have set up a simple voting system with an associated threshold (σ). When an input is passed to the ensemble, each network classifies the data producing a predicted class. If we exceed the threshold with the percentage of networks that agree on a single class, that class is returned as the most likely answer, otherwise, the input is rejected and no class is returned.

The second is the CCAT method (see Sect. 2.2) which uses adversarial training as per the original paper [16] using the original code which is slightly modified[2]. The adversarial training process allows CCAT to reject adversarial inputs within an ϵ-ball by learning to return a uniform distribution over all of the classes. This is then extrapolated beyond the ϵ-ball to larger perturbations. A threshold (τ) is specified which represents the confidence bound that must be exceeded so that the result is not rejected. Unlike the original paper where an optimal τ is calculated based on performance on the clean dataset, we vary τ to determine the effect on the rejection ability.

4.3   Datasets

We use multiple datasets to evaluate the effectiveness of RMAggNet on a variety of classification tasks. We focus on the EMNIST (balanced) [25] and CIFAR-10 datasets. The EMNIST dataset provides us with a simple classification task which consists of 131,600 grey-scale images of size 28×28, with 47 balanced classes including handwritten digits, upper- and lower-case letters (with some lower case classes excluded). Since we have 47 classes, the number of networks in RMAggNet is expanded to 32, with the same amount used for the Ensemble method. CIFAR-10 represents a more challenging classification task, increasing the image complexity with full colour images of size 32×32 over 10 possible classes which uses 16 networks for RMAggNet and Ensemble.

4.4   Generation of Adversarial Examples

To generate adversarial images from the selected datasets we use the FoolBox library [26,27]. We generate adversarial images using PGD L_2 and PGD L_∞ attacks. Due to the complex nature of some of the networks, adjustments needed to be made to generate adversarial examples.

RMAggNet: Due to the non-differentiable nature of RMAggNet from thresholding, direct attacks are difficult to generate. Following approaches such as BPDA [28] we implement a hybrid RMAggNet which replaces the final mapping from a binary string to class (or reject) with a Neural Network. This allows us to backpropagate through the entire model to produce effective adversarial examples.

Ensemble: We implement an ensemble via logits method [29] where the result of each network is weighted. Due to the voting system for the rejection we set equal weights over all networks. This approach allows us to have an ensemble method which mimics the voting output, except it is differentiable, therefore we can generate adversarial examples using the multiple networks directly.

---

[2] https://github.com/davidstutz/confidence-calibrated-adversarial-training.

CCAT: Since CCAT is a standard Network which has undergone specific adversarial training, the generation of adversarial attacks is simple. Many attacks in the FoolBox library are able to generate adversarial examples without any modification of the network.

5 Results

5.1 EMNIST Dataset

Results for the EMNIST dataset use RMAggNet with $m = 5$, $r = 1$ which gives us 32 networks with 7 bits of error correction (EC). We also use 32 networks for the Ensemble method for parity. All methods use ResNet-18 models [30]. Table 1 shows the results on the clean EMNIST dataset where we expect to maximise correctness. All three models perform similarly, with Ensemble achieving the highest correctness, closely followed by RMAggNet and CCAT. However, all models come close to state-of-the-art performance (91.06%) [31], with minimal negative impacts from the adversarial defence.

Table 1. Results for the clean EMNIST dataset showing the percentage of classifications that are correct, rejected and incorrect. Bold text indicates the metric of interest. Higher correctness is better.

CCAT

τ	Correct	Rejected	Incorrect
0	**88.68**	0.00	11.32
0.10	**88.60**	0.15	11.24
0.20	**87.54**	2.41	10.05
0.30	**85.46**	6.45	8.09
0.40	**83.16**	10.29	6.55
0.50	**80.70**	14.22	5.08
0.60	**77.95**	18.03	4.02
0.70	**74.23**	22.71	3.06
0.80	**69.48**	28.46	2.06
0.90	**60.74**	38.05	1.20
1.0	**0.00**	100.00	0.00

Ensemble

σ	Correct	Rejected	Incorrect
0	**89.78**	0.00	10.22
0.10	**89.78**	0.00	10.22
0.20	**89.78**	0.01	10.21
0.30	**89.76**	0.05	10.19
0.40	**89.70**	0.28	10.03
0.50	**89.20**	1.41	9.39
0.60	**87.76**	4.45	7.79
0.70	**85.94**	7.68	6.38
0.80	**83.89**	11.05	5.06
0.90	**80.60**	15.60	3.80
1.0	**68.34**	30.15	1.51

RMAggNet $[32, 6, 16]_2$

EC	Correct	Rejected	Incorrect
7	**89.16**	2.14	8.70
6	**87.93**	4.59	7.48
5	**86.54**	6.98	6.48
4	**84.99**	9.49	5.52
3	**83.29**	12.03	4.68
2	**80.85**	15.15	4.00
1	**77.19**	19.59	3.23
0	**70.02**	27.72	2.26

The performance on adversarial datasets generated with open-box attacks is shown in Tables 2 and 3. For both of these experiments we aim to minimise incorrectness, either by correctly classifying or rejecting the data. Correctly classifying the data is preferred since it reduces the reliance on downstream rejection handling.

Table 2 shows the results of the PGD L_∞ attack at varying perturbation budgets (ϵ). The CCAT results demonstrate strong performance with 0% incorrectness for $\tau > 0$ for all ϵ. At $\tau = 0$ we effectively disable the confidence threshold of CCAT and see 100% incorrectness as it is trained to return a uniform distribution for adversarial inputs. It is worth noting that the 0% incorrectness of CCAT is achieved through the rejection of all of the inputs, even at lower ϵ where both Ensemble and RMAggNet show that correct classifications can be recovered. This points towards a disadvantage of the conservative nature of CCAT. In situations where we want the option to reject, but can tolerate some incorrectness, CCAT often becomes ineffective for classification. Comparing Ensemble and RMAggNet, RMAggNet can achieve significantly lower incorrectness over all ϵ, translating the incorrectness into correct or rejected classifications depending on the amount of EC. This leads to RMAggNet being able to achieve higher correctness than both Ensemble and CCAT.

The results of the PGD L_2 attacks are in Table 3. The results are similar to those in Table 2, with CCAT reducing incorrectness to 0% through rejection alone. RMAggNet outperforms Ensemble in both maximum correctness and minimum incorrectness for $\epsilon = 0.30$ and $\epsilon = 1.0$. However, Ensemble can achieve higher correctness for $\epsilon = 3.0$ at the cost of incorrectness, which remains significantly higher than RMAggNet's.

From these results, we can conclude that RMAggNet provides more flexibility where small amounts of incorrectness is tolerable. The error correction process allows us to make trade-offs between maximising correctness and minimising incorrectness, with RMAggNet outperforming Ensemble in both of these metrics. RMAggNet comes close to CCAT in minimising incorrectness with the added advantage that, for small ϵ, we can recover and correctly classify many of the inputs, reducing pressure on downstream rejection handling.

Table 2. Results of PGD L_∞ adversaries generated using open-box attacks on EMNIST images with percentages of correct, rejected and incorrect classifications. Lower incorrectness is better.

PGD(L_∞)

CCAT

τ	ϵ	Correct	Rejected	Incorrect	ϵ	Correct	Rejected	Incorrect	ϵ	Correct	Rejected	Incorrect
0.00	0.05	0.00	0.00	100.00	0.10	0.00	0.00	100.00	0.30	0.00	0.00	100.00
0.30		0.00	100.00	0.00		0.00	100.00	0.00		0.00	100.00	0.00
0.70		0.00	100.00	0.00		0.00	100.00	0.00		0.00	100.00	0.00
0.90		0.00	100.00	0.00		0.00	100.00	0.00		0.00	100.00	0.00

Ensemble

σ	ϵ	Correct	Rejected	Incorrect	ϵ	Correct	Rejected	Incorrect	ϵ	Correct	Rejected	Incorrect
0.00	0.05	71.70	0.00	28.30	0.10	29.40	0.00	70.60	0.30	0.00	0.00	100.00
0.30		71.70	0.00	28.30		29.40	0.00	70.60		0.00	0.00	100.00
0.70		64.10	15.20	20.70		20.80	22.60	56.60		0.00	0.00	100.00
1.00		31.40	60.10	8.50		3.20	73.70	23.10		0.00	4.60	95.40

RMAggNet

EC	ϵ	Correct	Rejected	Incorrect	ϵ	Correct	Rejected	Incorrect	ϵ	Correct	Rejected	Incorrect
7	0.05	80.70	3.60	15.70	0.10	62.90	8.70	28.40	0.30	0.50	39.50	60.00
6		78.00	8.50	13.50		59.30	15.60	25.10		0.40	54.00	45.60
5		75.00	13.70	11.30		54.10	23.40	22.50		0.30	68.30	31.40
4		71.90	17.90	10.20		48.20	31.50	20.30		0.10	77.80	22.10
3		68.90	22.20	8.90		41.40	41.50	17.10		0.10	87.90	12.00
2		63.20	29.10	7.70		29.30	56.70	14.00		0.00	94.40	5.60
1		54.30	39.60	6.10		16.80	72.40	10.80		0.00	98.50	1.50
0		28.50	67.10	4.40		2.30	92.00	5.70		0.00	100.00	0.00

Table 3. Results of PGD L_2 adversaries generated using open-box attacks on EMNIST images with percentages of correct, rejected and incorrect classifications. Lower incorrectness is better.

PGD(L_2)

CCAT

τ	ϵ	Correct	Rejected	Incorrect	ϵ	Correct	Rejected	Incorrect	ϵ	Correct	Rejected	Incorrect
0.00	0.30	0.20	0.00	99.80	1.0	0.00	0.00	100.00	3.0	0.00	0.00	100.00
0.30		0.00	100.00	0.00		0.00	100.00	0.00		0.00	100.00	0.00
0.70		0.00	100.00	0.00		0.00	100.00	0.00		0.00	100.00	0.00
0.90		0.00	100.00	0.00		0.00	100.00	0.00		0.00	100.00	0.00

Ensemble

σ	ϵ	Correct	Rejected	Incorrect	ϵ	Correct	Rejected	Incorrect	ϵ	Correct	Rejected	Incorrect
0.00	0.30	84.80	0.00	15.20	1.0	62.40	0.00	37.60	3.0	19.60	0.00	80.40
0.30		84.80	0.00	15.20		62.40	0.00	37.60		19.60	0.00	80.40
0.70		79.50	9.10	11.40		57.10	13.00	29.90		19.50	0.20	80.30
1.00		60.60	35.90	3.50		47.40	39.80	12.80		18.50	9.80	71.70

RMAggNet

EC	ϵ	Correct	Rejected	Incorrect	ϵ	Correct	Rejected	Incorrect	ϵ	Correct	Rejected	Incorrect
7	0.30	86.00	3.10	10.90	1.0	70.40	6.60	23.00	3.0	9.20	25.70	65.10
6		84.40	6.20	9.40		67.60	12.20	20.20		6.40	37.60	56.00
5		82.70	9.10	8.20		65.20	17.40	17.40		5.00	45.60	49.40
4		80.70	12.40	6.90		61.70	23.40	14.90		3.10	55.60	41.30
3		77.70	16.40	5.90		57.40	29.30	13.30		2.00	65.00	33.00
2		74.10	20.90	5.00		50.30	38.10	11.60		1.00	75.60	23.40
1		68.00	28.20	3.80		39.10	51.50	9.40		0.70	86.10	13.20
0		56.00	41.30	2.70		15.10	78.60	6.30		0.00	94.60	5.40

5.2 CIFAR-10 Dataset

Results for the CIFAR-10 dataset use RMAggNet with $m = 4$, $r = 1$ which gives us 16 networks with 3 bits of error correction. We use 16 networks in the Ensemble method for parity. All networks use an architecture outlined in the extended paper.

Table 4 shows the results on the clean CIFAR-10 dataset where we aim to maximise correctness. Ensemble reports the highest correctness, followed by RMAggNet, then CCAT. All models report correctness within 3% of one another, so, we can conclude that all are equally capable in terms of classification ability.

Table 5 shows the results for the L_∞ attacks on CIFAR-10, with Table 5a reporting the results of the open-box attack on the surrogate model. This indicates that the attack on the surrogate model is very effective, leading to low accuracy of the model at all $\epsilon > 0$. The L_∞ closed-box transfer attacks on the CIFAR-10 models can be seen in Table 5b, where we aim to reduce incorrectness. The results show a strong adversarial attack due to low correctness from Ensemble and RMAggNet, even for low values of ϵ. The CCAT model is able to reliably reject all adversarial inputs for all non-zero confidence thresholds. The Ensemble method classifies significantly more inputs correctly compared to RMAggNet for all values of ϵ that we tested, however, the percentage of correct classifications are still low, leading to an ineffective classifier. This result shows that CCAT is an effective method for avoiding adversarial results when strong

Table 4. Results for the clean CIFAR-10 dataset showing the percentage of classifications that are correct, rejected and incorrect. Bold text indicates the metric of interest. Higher correctness is better.

CCAT					Ensemble			
τ	Correct	Rejected	Incorrect		σ	Correct	Rejected	Incorrect
0	**76.41**	0.00	23.59		0	**79.34**	0.00	20.66
0.10	**76.41**	0.00	23.59		0.10	**79.54**	0.00	20.46
0.20	**76.21**	0.68	23.11		0.20	**79.35**	0.00	20.65
0.30	**75.10**	3.76	21.14		0.30	**79.53**	0.02	20.45
0.40	**72.62**	9.38	18.00		0.40	**79.24**	1.05	19.71
0.50	**68.59**	17.41	14.00		0.50	**77.14**	6.73	16.13
0.60	**64.04**	25.55	10.41		0.60	**75.31**	11.23	13.46
0.70	**58.81**	33.72	7.47		0.70	**68.79**	22.62	8.59
0.80	**52.81**	42.39	4.80		0.80	**65.38**	28.00	6.62
0.90	**44.64**	52.54	2.82		0.90	**56.57**	40.23	3.20
1.0	**1.09**	98.91	0.00		1.0	**39.21**	59.83	0.96

RMAggNet $[16, 5, 8]_2$			
EC	Correct	Rejected	Incorrect
3	**77.11**	12.76	10.13
2	**68.32**	27.23	4.45
1	**57.90**	40.09	2.01
0	**42.46**	59.96	0.58

attacks are used. Further results from closed-box transfer attacks can be found in the full paper [17].

The performance on the CIFAR-10 datasets using open-box attacks is shown in Tables 6 and 7. We, again, aim to minimise incorrectness.

The PGD L_∞ results in Table 6 show low correctness for both Ensemble and RMAggNet for all ϵ which indicates that this is a strong adversarial attack, which is reduced to unrecognisable images at $\epsilon = 0.3$. With this in mind, it is better to compare the methods focusing on incorrectness and rejection performance. Ensemble struggles to reject inputs, leading to nearly 100% incorrectness across all ϵ which indicates that the adversarial examples are able to fool the multiple networks that form this method. RMAggNet shows slightly better performance, with much higher rejection for $EC = 0$. CCAT can achieve the lowest incorrectness scores, which are significantly lower for $\epsilon = 0.75$ and $\epsilon = 2.5$. This indicates that when we expect strong adversaries with little chance of recovery, CCAT is the best-performing model.

Table 7 shows the results for PGD L_2 on CIFAR-10. Interestingly, RMAggNet can outperform both Ensemble and CCAT at $\epsilon = 0.30$ with a lower incorrectness and higher correctness than both methods. For $\epsilon = 0.75$ and $\epsilon = 2.5$ CCAT can report the lowest incorrectness by a significant margin. Over all ϵ values RMAggNet reports lower incorrectness than Ensemble, achieving higher correctness at $\epsilon = \{0.30, 0.75\}$.

These results show the effect that strong adversaries have on the classification ability of these models. In this circumstance, CCAT is the better model, rejecting most adversaries, while Ensemble struggles to reject the inputs, and RMAggNet has varying performance when attempting to correct the images. However, this is a worst-case scenario.

6   Discussion

The results from Sect. 5 allow us to determine how RMAggNet can be used, and when it may have advantages over competing methods.

Table 5. Results for the transfer attacks using PGD L_∞. Table 5a shows the accuracy of the surrogate model on the PGD L_∞ adversarial datasets. Table 5b shows the results of the adversarial datasets on the CCAT, Ensemble and RMAggNet models.

(a) Accuracy of the surrogate CIFAR-10 classifier on the adversarial datasets generated using PGD L_∞ with different perturbation budgets (ϵ).

ϵ	Accuracy (%)
0.00	81.21
0.05	0.10
0.10	0.10
0.30	0.00

(b) Percentage of correct, rejected and incorrect classifications of the models using transfer attacks on a surrogate CIFAR-10 classifier using the PGD L_∞ attack. Lower incorrectness is better.

PGD(L_∞)

CCAT

τ	ϵ	Correct	Rejected	Incorrect	ϵ	Correct	Rejected	Incorrect	ϵ	Correct	Rejected	Incorrect
0.00	0.05	14.80	0.00	85.20	0.10	9.50	0.00	90.50	0.30	11.20	0.00	88.80
0.30		0.00	100.00	0.00		0.00	100.00	0.00		0.00	100.00	0.00
0.70		0.00	100.00	0.00		0.00	100.00	0.00		0.00	100.00	0.00
1.00		0.00	100.00	0.00		0.00	100.00	0.00		0.00	100.00	0.00

Ensemble

σ	ϵ	Correct	Rejected	Incorrect	ϵ	Correct	Rejected	Incorrect	ϵ	Correct	Rejected	Incorrect
0.00	0.05	57.30	0.00	42.70	0.10	37.70	0.00	62.30	0.30	16.60	0.00	83.40
0.30		56.80	0.00	43.20		38.50	0.10	61.40		16.90	0.00	83.10
0.70		42.30	32.70	25.00		26.80	29.50	43.70		7.90	38.20	53.90
1.00		16.80	77.90	5.30		10.00	75.60	14.40		0.50	83.80	15.70

RMAggNet

EC	ϵ	Correct	Rejected	Incorrect	ϵ	Correct	Rejected	Incorrect	ϵ	Correct	Rejected	Incorrect
3	0.05	44.90	15.30	39.80	0.10	21.70	12.90	65.40	0.30	2.10	5.20	92.70
2		34.20	39.20	26.60		16.10	29.70	54.20		1.10	11.10	87.80
1		24.80	58.30	16.90		9.30	48.30	42.40		0.50	23.20	76.30
0		16.20	75.60	8.20		4.40	70.10	25.50		0.30	49.40	50.30

Table 6. Results of PGD L_∞ adversaries generated using open-box attacks on CIFAR-10 images with percentages of correct, rejected and incorrect classifications. Lower incorrectness is better.

PGD(L_∞)

CCAT

τ	ϵ	Correct	Rejected	Incorrect	ϵ	Correct	Rejected	Incorrect	ϵ	Correct	Rejected	Incorrect
0.00	0.05	9.00	0.00	91.00	0.10	7.10	0.00	92.90	0.30	5.40	0.00	94.60
0.30		0.00	99.00	1.00		0.00	97.50	2.50		0.20	83.00	16.80
0.70		0.00	99.50	0.50		0.00	98.50	1.50		0.00	86.40	13.60
0.90		0.00	99.70	0.30		0.00	98.80	1.20		0.00	89.50	10.50

Ensemble

σ	ϵ	Correct	Rejected	Incorrect	ϵ	Correct	Rejected	Incorrect	ϵ	Correct	Rejected	Incorrect
0.00	0.05	1.10	0.00	98.90	0.10	0.00	0.00	100.00	0.30	0.00	0.00	100.00
0.30		0.90	0.00	99.10		0.00	0.00	100.00		0.00	0.00	100.00
0.70		0.50	2.70	96.80		0.00	0.10	99.90		0.00	0.00	100.00
1.00		0.20	14.80	85.00		0.00	1.60	98.40		0.00	0.10	99.90

RMAggNet

EC	ϵ	Correct	Rejected	Incorrect	ϵ	Correct	Rejected	Incorrect	ϵ	Correct	Rejected	Incorrect
3	0.05	18.50	12.90	68.60	0.10	6.40	9.50	84.10	0.30	0.20	11.10	88.70
2		15.60	27.20	57.20		5.00	24.10	70.90		0.20	26.20	73.60
1		12.80	43.70	43.50		4.00	44.90	51.10		0.00	50.80	49.20
0		9.50	65.20	25.30		3.10	67.60	29.30		0.00	82.30	17.70

Table 7. Results of PGD L_2 adversaries generated using open-box attacks on CIFAR-10 images with percentages of correct, rejected and incorrect classifications. Lower incorrectness is better.

PGD(L_2)

CCAT

τ	ϵ	Correct	Rejected	Incorrect	ϵ	Correct	Rejected	Incorrect	ϵ	Correct	Rejected	Incorrect
0.00	0.30	29.20	0.00	**70.80**	0.75	12.50	0.00	**87.50**	2.5	10.20	0.00	**89.80**
0.30		0.50	92.10	**7.40**		0.00	97.50	**2.50**		0.00	99.50	**0.50**
0.70		0.00	96.00	**4.00**		0.00	99.20	**0.80**		0.00	99.80	**0.20**
0.90		0.00	97.40	**2.60**		0.00	99.70	**0.30**		0.00	99.80	**0.20**

Ensemble

σ	ϵ	Correct	Rejected	Incorrect	ϵ	Correct	Rejected	Incorrect	ϵ	Correct	Rejected	Incorrect
0.00	0.30	54.30	0.00	**45.70**	0.75	26.70	0.00	**73.30**	2.5	13.40	0.00	**86.60**
0.30		53.30	0.00	**46.70**		26.50	0.00	**73.50**		13.30	0.00	**86.70**
0.70		42.00	28.60	**29.40**		23.30	12.90	**63.80**		13.00	0.90	**86.10**
1.00		23.10	70.20	**6.70**		16.20	54.70	**29.10**		12.20	6.30	**81.50**

RMAggNet

EC	ϵ	Correct	Rejected	Incorrect	ϵ	Correct	Rejected	Incorrect	ϵ	Correct	Rejected	Incorrect
3	0.30	64.00	15.30	**20.70**	0.75	39.80	17.00	**43.20**	2.5	11.10	10.80	**78.10**
2		52.40	36.30	**11.30**		32.90	37.90	**29.20**		9.60	23.20	**67.20**
1		41.20	52.10	**6.70**		25.60	54.90	**19.50**		8.20	41.80	**50.00**
0		28.70	69.10	**2.20**		19.40	71.70	**8.90**		5.60	63.00	**31.40**

We start by discussing the hyperparameters of RMAggNet (see extended paper [17], Sect. 5.1). The selection of hyperparameters is dependent on the problem, with the most important aspect being the number of classes the dataset has. If a dataset has $|C|$ classes, then we require at least $\lceil \log_2 |C| \rceil$ networks to generate a unique encoding for each class. This works well for datasets such as MNIST or CIFAR-10, with ten classes each, which requires at least four networks, however, this approach is less optimal for datasets with a small number of classes. For datasets with few classes we are only able to produce $\binom{|C|}{s}$ unique networks (where s is the number of classes we allow in the partitioned set) which limits the number of networks we can use and increases the probability that a random noise input will be assigned a valid class, which decreases adversarial defence.

When deciding on the number of networks to aggregate over (n), we have two constraints. The number of networks must be a power of 2, and we must ensure that $|C| \leq 2^k$, (i.e. we have enough class codewords for the number of classes in the dataset). Since $n = 2^m$, and the value of k is influenced by both m and r, we must balance n with the amount of error correction we need and the probability of a random noise input being assigned a valid class. The results presented in this paper have focused on datasets with 10 and 47 classes, requiring 16 and 32 networks respectively. If we consider extending this approach to ImageNet with 1000 classes, we can see the effect of scaling on RMAggNet. For 1000 classes we have the restriction that $1000 \leq 2^k$, therefore $k \geq 10$. If we use 32 networks ($m = 5$, $r = 2$) we get $k = 16$ with 3 errors corrected ($t = 3$) with a probability of a random noise input being assigned a valid class of 1.28×10^{-3}. This indicates that scaling to datasets with more classes is feasible using RMAggNet.

The comparisons between RMAggNet, Ensemble and CCAT over the EMNIST and CIFAR-10 datasets on clean and adversarial inputs allow us to place RMAggNet in context with the other methods. The results for these tests are in sections 5.1, and 5.2 (more results available in the extended paper [17]).

Results on the clean testing data (Tables 1 and 4) show that RMAggNet is able to train models which are competitive with the other architectures, equalling Ensemble for some datasets. This result shows that the RMAggNet method has minimal impact on clean dataset performance.

Across the adversarial tests CCAT is able to reject the most adversarial inputs leading to nearly 0 incorrect classifications. However, CCAT does not attempt correction of any inputs which leads to 0 correct classifications at most confidence thresholds. This even occurs when both Ensemble and RMAggNet recover over 80% of the labels from an adversarial attack (Table 3). This approach to rejection means that CCAT is ideal for situations where any uncertainty in the correctness of a result cannot be tolerated. However, if we can allow some incorrectness, and want the option to reject, then Ensemble and RMAggNet allow us to classify many inputs correctly, greatly reducing the reliance on downstream rejection handling, at the risk of small amounts of incorrectness. If we compare the Ensemble method with RMAggNet, over many of the datasets RMAggNet is able to outperform Ensemble with a slightly higher (or equal) number of correct classifications, and lower incorrectness for comparable correctness as it uses the reject option more effectively. This becomes more pronounced at higher ϵ. The application of RMAggNet to datasets with many more classes, such as ImageNet, would be interesting future work since we have stated that $|C| \leq 2^k$ (Sect. 3.2), and this can be achieved by either adding more networks (increasing m) or increasing the polynomial degree (r) which decreases error correction ability and increases the probability of assigning random noise a class. Striking this balance would lead to interesting results regarding the applicability of RMAggNet to larger datasets.

7 Conclusion

In this paper we have seen how an architecture leveraging Reed-Muller codes can be used to create an effective CWR method which (to our knowledge) is the first approach combining its rejection and correction ability. The experimental results show the advantages of RMAggNet and allow us to determine situations where it can be beneficial to a system. Comparing the results of RMAggNet to CCAT, shows that CCAT is able to reject nearly 100% of the adversarial images over all attacks and datasets we tested. However, this comes at the cost of rejecting inputs that could otherwise be classified correctly. The sensitive approach of CCAT could be detrimental to a system where the rejected inputs still need to be processed, either using more computationally expensive processes, or reviewed by a human. RMAggNet is able to achieve low incorrectness, often with higher correctness, meaning that, provided the system can accept small amounts of incorrectness, we can reduce the reliance on downstream rejection handling. From the results, we can see that this can be a significant improvement for small perturbations on the EMNIST dataset. Comparing the results of RMAggNet to Ensemble, the results show that RMAggNet appears to be more resilient to adversarial attacks, particularly open-box attacks, often achieving lower incorrectness than Ensemble by having higher correctness for small ϵ, or higher rejection for larger ϵ. This means that we can expect RMAggNet to be a better choice in situations where adversaries are present.

References

1. Chen, X., et al.: Symbolic discovery of optimization algorithms. arXiv:2302.06675 (2023)
2. Tragakis, A., Kaul, C., Murray-Smith, R., Husmeier, D.: The fully convolutional transformer for medical image segmentation. In: Proceedings of the IEEE/CVF Winter Conference on Applications of Computer Vision, pp. 3660–3669 (2023)
3. Pierazzi, F., Pendlebury, F., Cortellazzi, J., Cavallaro, L.: Intriguing properties of adversarial ml attacks in the problem space. In: 2020 IEEE Symposium on Security and Privacy (SP), 2020, pp. 1332–1349 (2020)
4. Szegedy, C., et al.: Intriguing properties of neural networks. arXiv:1312.6199 (2013)
5. Smith, L., Gal, Y.: Understanding measures of uncertainty for adversarial example detection. In: 34th Conference on Uncertainty in Artificial Intelligence 2018, UAI 2018, vol. 2, mar 2018, pp. 560–569 (2018)
6. Zou, A., Wang, Z., Kolter, J.Z., Fredrikson, M.: Universal and transferable adversarial attacks on aligned language models (2023)
7. Morris, J.X., Lifland, E., Yoo, J.Y., Grigsby, J., Jin, D., Qi, Y.: TextAttack: a framework for adversarial attacks, data augmentation, and adversarial training in nlp. In: Proceedings of the 2020 Conference on Empirical Methods in Natural Language Processing: System Demonstrations, pp. 119–126 (2020)
8. Chen, S.-T., Cornelius, C., Martin, J., Chau, D.H.P.: ShapeShifter: robust physical adversarial attack on faster R-CNN object detector. In: Berlingerio, M., Bonchi, F., Gärtner, T., Hurley, N., Ifrim, G. (eds.) ECML PKDD 2018. LNCS (LNAI), vol. 11051, pp. 52–68. Springer, Cham (2019). https://doi.org/10.1007/978-3-030-10925-7_4
9. Papernot, N., McDaniel, P., Wu, X., Jha, S., Swami, A.: Distillation as a defense to adversarial perturbations against deep neural networks. In: 2016 IEEE Symposium on Security and Privacy (SP). IEEE, 2016, pp. 582–597 (2016)
10. Goodfellow, I.J., Shlens, J., Szegedy, C.: Explaining and harnessing adversarial examples. arXiv:1412.6572 (2014)
11. Verma, G., Swami, A.: Error correcting output codes improve probability estimation and adversarial robustness of deep neural networks. In: Advances in Neural Information Processing Systems, vol. 32 (2019)
12. Cortes, C., DeSalvo, G., Mohri, M.: Learning with rejection. In: Ortner, R., Simon, H.U., Zilles, S. (eds.) ALT 2016. LNCS (LNAI), vol. 9925, pp. 67–82. Springer, Cham (2016). https://doi.org/10.1007/978-3-319-46379-7_5
13. Charoenphakdee, N., Cui, Z., Zhang, Y., Sugiyama, M. In: International Conference on Machine Learning, PMLR, 2021, pp. 1507–1517 (2021)
14. Song, Y., Kang, Q., Tay, W.P.: Error-correcting output codes with ensemble diversity for robust learning in neural networks. Proc. AAAI Conf. Artif. Intell. **35**(11), 9722–9729 (2021)

15. Papernot, N., McDaniel, P., Goodfellow, I.: Transferability in machine learning: from phenomena to black-box attacks using adversarial samples. arXiv:1605.07277 (2016)
16. Stutz, D., Hein, M., Schiele, B.: Confidence-calibrated adversarial training: generalizing to unseen attacks. In: Proceedings of the International Conference on Machine Learning ICML (2020)
17. Fentham, D., Parker, D., Ryan, M.: Using Reed-Muller codes for classification with rejection and recovery. arXiv:2309.06359 (2023)
18. Gamal, A., Hemachandra, L., Shperling, I., Wei, V.: Using simulated annealing to design good codes. IEEE Trans. Inf. Theory **33**(1), 116–123 (1987)
19. Muller, D.E.: Application of boolean algebra to switching circuit design and to error detection. In: Transactions of the I.R.E. Professional Group on Electronic Computers, vol. EC-3, no. 3, pp. 6–12 (1954)
20. Reed, I.: A class of multiple-error-correcting codes and the decoding scheme. Trans. IRE Profess. Group Inform. Theory **4**(4), 38–49 (1954)
21. Hamming, R.W.: Error detecting and error correcting codes. Bell System Tech. J. **29**(2), 147–160 (1950)
22. Carlini, N., et al.: On evaluating adversarial robustness. arXiv:1902.06705 (2019)
23. Madry, A., Makelov, A., Schmidt, L., Tsipras, D., Vladu, A.: Towards deep learning models resistant to adversarial attacks. arXiv:1706.06083 (2017)
24. Brendel, W., Rauber, J., Bethge, M.: Decision-based adversarial attacks: Reliable attacks against black-box machine learning models. In: International Conference on Learning Representations (2018)
25. Cohen, G., Afshar, S., Tapson, J., Van Schaik, A.: Emnist: extending mnist to handwritten letters. In: 2017 International Joint Conference on Neural Networks (IJCNN), IEEE, 2017, pp. 2921–2926 (2017)
26. Rauber, J., Zimmermann, R., Bethge, M., Brendel, W.: Foolbox native: fast adversarial attacks to benchmark the robustness of machine learning models in pytorch, tensorflow, and jax. *Journal of Open Source Software*, vol. 5, no. 53, p. 2607, 2020. https://doi.org/10.21105/joss.02607
27. Rauber, J., Brendel, W., Bethge, M.: Foolbox: a python toolbox to benchmark the robustness of machine learning models. In: Reliable Machine Learning in the Wild Workshop, 34th International Conference on Machine Learning (2017)
28. Athalye, A., Carlini, N., Wagner, D.: Obfuscated gradients give a false sense of security: Circumventing defenses to adversarial examples. In: International Conference on Machine Learning. PMLR, 2018, pp. 274–283 (2018)
29. Dong, Y., et al.: Boosting adversarial attacks with momentum. In: Proceedings of the IEEE Conference on Computer Vision and Pattern Recognition, 2018, pp. 9185–9193 (2018)
30. He, K., Zhang, X., Ren, S., Sun, J.: Deep residual learning for image recognition. In: Proceedings of the IEEE Conference on Computer Vision and Pattern Recognition, 2016, pp. 770–778 (2016)
31. Jeevan, P., Viswanathan, K., Sethi, A.: Wavemix-lite: a resource-efficient neural network for image analysis. arXiv:2205.14375 (2022)

Unsupervised Clustering of Honeypot Attacks by Deep HTTP Packet Inspection

Victor Aurora[1], Christopher Neal[1,2]([✉]), Alexandre Proulx[1,3],
Nora Boulahia Cuppens[1], and Frédéric Cuppens[1]

[1] Polytechnique Montreal, Montreal, Canada
{victor.aurora,christopher.neal,alexandre-2.proulx,
nora.boulahia-cuppens,frederic.cuppens}@polymtl.ca
[2] IRT SystemX, Palaiseau, France
[3] Thales Research and Technology, Quebec City, Canada

Abstract. The increasing complexity of cyberattacks has prompted researchers to keep pace with this trend by proposing automated cyberattack classification methods. Current research directions favor supervised learning detection methods; however, they are limited by the fact that they must be continually trained on vast labelled datasets and cannot generalize to unseen events. We propose a novel unsupervised learning detection approach that performs deep packet inspection on HTTP-specific features, contrary to other works that work with generic numerical network-based features. Our method is divided into three phases: pre-processing, dimension reduction and clustering. By analyzing the content of each HTTP packet, we achieve the perfect isolation of each web attack in the CIC-IDS2017 dataset in separate clusters. Further, we run our method on real-world data collected from a honeypot platform to demonstrate its classification abilities. For future work, the proposed method could be applied to other protocols and extended with more correlation techniques to classify complex attacks.

Keywords: Cyberattack Classification · Unsupervised Learning · Deep Packet Inspection · Honeypot · HTTP

1 Introduction

The information networks that support society's economic, industrial, and political activities are threatened daily by malicious actors conducting a wide range of cyberattacks. Detection of these malicious events from within an amalgam of legitimate network traffic is at the forefront of network defence. Where traditional techniques have used hard-coded detection rules to identify violations from genuine traffic, recent advancements are looking at Machine Learning (ML) to automate classification tasks and streamline the work of security personnel. Nevertheless, many recently proposed solutions rely on supervised learning methods, thus restricting their ability to generalize to unseen events.

This research was supported by Thales Research and Technology (TRT) Canada.

This paper proposes a novel unsupervised learning approach to automate cyberattack classification. The unsupervised learning method can classify attacks never encountered in training, making it uniquely advantageous in the context of defensive mechanisms, such as honeypots, which indiscriminately capture raw data from unsuspecting attackers. We build and test our unsupervised classification model using an unlabelled dataset collected by an internet-facing honeypot. This dataset contains 1,369,692 Hypertext Transfer Protocol (HTTP) entries that exhibit a range of activities, including, but not limited to, port scanning, data scraping, web crawling, and vulnerability testing.

Our model employs a novel approach that combines a pre-processing method, an dimensionality reduction algorithm, and an efficient clustering technique to classify malicious data. To validate our approach, we apply it to HTTP attacks on the well-known CIC-IDS2017 dataset [31], which includes four different web attacks and has been used to benchmark several supervised classification techniques. We further evaluate our method on an unlabelled dataset of honeypot entries. Although we focus on the HTTP protocol, our approach has the potential to be extended to any communication protocol. To summarize, our main contributions are the following:

- Develop a novel approach for attack classification on the HTTP protocol by performing deep inspection of packets.
- Create a new unsupervised model for attack classification by combining several state-of-the-art algorithms.
- Validate our approach on the CIC-IDS2017 dataset, where labeled data is present.
- Analyze the result of our method on an unlabelled dataset collected by an internet-facing honeypot platform.

The remainder of the paper is organized as follows. Section 2 provides an overview of influential works that perform attack classification under supervised and unsupervised learning paradigms. The description of our method is provided in Sect. 3, where we outline the method for reducing the data's feature space and determining the clusters of data samples. In Sects. 4 and 5, we evaluate our classification approach on the labelled CIC-IDS2017 and unlabelled honeypot datasets, respectively. We provide a discussion and look at future work in Sect. 6. Lastly, Sect. 7 concludes the paper.

2 Background and Related Work

Honeypots attract malicious behaviour representing real-world computer network attacks [29]. The data collected by honeypots is unlabelled; therefore, supervised learning detection approaches are inappropriate for identifying attacks [21,27]. Owezarski [30] proposes an unsupervised method to classify attacks in a honeypot environment; however, it is limited to detecting Denial-of-Service (DoS) and port scan attacks. Boukela et al. [23] present another unsupervised method for detecting attacks against honeypots, yet they are limited to identifying outliers without giving details about the attack. To address these limitations, we develop our classification method to classify events based on the unique properties of their HTTP packets.

We select CIC-IDS2017 as the validation dataset for our method through consulting influential surveys [25,33,37]. This dataset represents a computer network of a small business with several employees performing work tasks, where malicious traffic is generated through several attacks, such as Denial of Service, Brute Force, and Port Scans. Panigrahi and Borah [31] conclude that using CIC-IDS2017 is challenging since it is a scattered and large dataset. Nevertheless, it is a complete dataset with various attacks relevant to our case, including web attacks. Numerous works apply supervised learning techniques to CIC-IDS2017 to detect the attacks with a high-success rate [24,32,39].

Next, we discuss some unsupervised methods and their pre-processing steps used on other datasets since they are relevant to this work. An interesting starting point is the survey of Wu et al. [36] on network attack detection methods based on deep learning techniques. They divide the unsupervised techniques into three categories: autoencoder-based methods, deep belief network-based methods, and generative adversarial network-based methods. Yet, other methods not based on deep learning techniques also exist. For example, Takyi et al. [35] provide a review of clustering techniques for traffic classification. Despite not being applied to attack classification, it is relevant to our work since both use network data. Takyi et al. [35] compare different techniques by describing the features used and each method's objectives, limitations, and results. We notice that K-Means is the most commonly used algorithm. Moreover, none of these techniques use a protocol's categorical or specific features. In addition, we observe that hierarchical clustering techniques are often too complex and too slow for large datasets.

Another interesting example not cited in these two surveys is the work of Zanero and Savaresi [38]. They build a two-stage model to perform detection on the DARPA99 dataset [26]. The first stage uses an unsupervised algorithm to cluster packet payloads to have a tractable size. In the second stage, Principal Direction Algorithm, K-Means, and Self-Organizing Map algorithm (SOM) are comparatively used to have the best results. Then, they show that with the SOM algorithm, they can easily detect malicious traffic from benign traffic. Meira et al. [28] compare different clustering techniques for cyberattack anomaly detection. They use other pre-processing techniques (Z-score and Equal frequency + min-max) with Isolation Forests, K-Means, 1-Nearest Neighbour, Autoencoder, Scaled Convex Hull, and Support Vector Machines. Again, the authors use numerical features not specific to a particular protocol.

In analyzing these related works we come to the following conclusions for creating an attack classifier for honeypot, and more generally for IDS attack, data. Attacks generated in the real-world are not labelled, therefore the legitimacy of supervised learning-based classification method is put into question and we choose to investigate unsupervised approaches. There is extensive work that establishes MCA as a suitable method to perform dimension reduction and

K-Means to perform clustering tasks. We therefore use these methods in our approach and investigate its effectiveness in classifying malicious data packets. Additionally, previous works tend to analyze meta-data related to packets when performing classification, while we use the presumption that performing deep packet inspection may provide more precise attack classification.

3   Description of Method

We work with a single protocol, namely HTTP, to be able to perform deep packet inspection. Applying this process to other protocols is left as future work. This work only considers malicious data since our purpose is to classify attacks and not to detect whether an entry is an attack. Hence, we consider honeypot data or alerts generated from an Intrusion Detection System. Our proposed method leverages several existing techniques that are executed over three phases, outlined as follows:

1. **Pre-processing.** We tokenize and then inspect the payload, the Uniform Resource Locator (URL), and the user-agent of each packet to make equal the values of these very similar attributes. To do so, we develop a new algorithm with existing Python libraries.
2. **Dimension reduction.** We transform the data into a reduced 3-dimensional representation. The categorical features are processed into three numerical features by applying Multiple Correspondence Analysis (MCA) [20].
3. **Clustering.** We use K-Means [34] to assign a cluster label to each point. Our model, by using three different clustering metrics, suggests one or more ideal numbers of clusters.

We hypothesise that a classification that inspects each packet deeply will be more accurate than a classification that only relies on numerical packet meta-data. Thus, we must have access to each data packet. This is an important constraint since many datasets propose only extracted features, not the whole network packet capture (i.e. PCAP). Moreover, to apply our model to raw network captures, we consider only HTTP packets of each dataset and write an algorithm which extracts the features from the raw network capture. As the time when each attack occurs is given, we label these HTTP packets by using timestamps. We are then able to apply our 3-phase model.

3.1   Pre-processing Phase

The pre-processing phase begins with extracting HTTP features from the network traffic data. To realize our deep packet inspection, we choose the features that are the most significant to describe an HTTP packet: *Method, URL, Payload*, and *User-Agent*. These features represent almost an entire packet and provide important information for each packet.

The general objective for the pre-processing phase is to analyze, for each feature, if there are similar entries in the dataset (except for Method since it can take only a few values). For example, the payload "username=admin&password =12345" and the payload "username=admin&password=pass" are considered as equal by the algorithm. Failing to pre-process these values would result in considering these two payloads as completely different in the next phase. However, both of these payloads are login attempts.

To pre-process the data, we first tokenize each URL, payload, and user agent with a custom-made tokenizer that outperforms existing tokenizers on our data. Our two previous payload examples become "username, admin, password, 12345" and "username, admin, password, pass", respectively. Then, we build a dictionary for each feature within the entirety of the vocabulary and the occurrence of each word. Afterwards, we delete all the rare words: the minimal occurrence for a word to be kept in one of the model's hyperparameters. This gives our first hyperparameter, *count_threshold*. This enables us to standardize the meaning of each value for each feature by keeping only the most common words, which helps to find which values are similar.

Then, for each value, we calculate the similarity with each other for a given feature. The similarity is computed with the difflib Python library [4]. The similarity is a score between 0 and 1, where a value of 1 indicates that the features are identical. For each feature, we set a similarity threshold; if two values reach this threshold, we consider that these two values are equal. This is our second hyperparameter, *similarity_threshold*. The pre-processing phase identifies when two values are considered equal by the algorithm using the similarity score. We determine the values for our hyperparameters through a manual inspection of which values are considered equal while considering the number of unique values before and after pre-processing.

3.2 Feature Reduction Phase

The second phase of our model transforms the representation of each entry and its four categorical features into a 3-dimensional vector. Thus, our 4-categorical space becomes a 3-numerical space. We choose a 3-numerical space since it enables having a graphical representation of our data and can be readily interpreted. This dimension reduction is achieved using MCA. MCA is an extension of Correspondence Analysis (CA), a common algorithm that analyses the dependencies between two categorical variables. MCA is used when there are more than two categorical variables to analyze. To do so, a one-hot encoded version of our dataset is computed, and CA is applied.

PyPi provides a library named Prince [9] to apply MCA, as well as other dimension reduction techniques like Principal Component Analysis (PCA) and Factor Analysis of Mixed Data (FAMD). We use this library to perform our dimension reduction.

3.3 Clustering Phase

After the second phase, the data comprises only three numerical features. Thus, we can now apply classical clustering algorithms. In this study, we apply K-

Means to our datasets due to its widespread acceptance and straightforward implementation. We estimate the ideal number of clusters to classify our feature-reduced data samples using three commonly used existing metrics: the Within-Cluster Sum of Squares Score (WCSS), the Davies-Bouldin score, and the Silhouette score. Each scoring method indicates the ideal number of clusters for a particular set of input points. We estimate the ideal number of clusters for our data by comparing the results from the different scoring methods. Note that WCSS is directly related to the Elbow method. These methods suggest several clusters for a particular clustering model. The Silhouette Score has to be as close as possible to 1, and the Davies-Bouldin Score as close as possible to 0. By comparing the results of the Elbow method and the two other scores for the number of clusters, the choice of the cluster number is straightforward because these metrics converge to a unique choice.

Within-Cluster Sum of Squares Score and Elbow Method. This is a commonly used method in the scientific literature for determining the number of clusters. The WCSS score must be computed for different cluster numbers to use the Elbow method. WCSS is the sum of the squared distance between each point and the centroid in a cluster. The WCSS calculation is provided in Eq. 1:

$$WCSS = \sum_{C_k \in C} \sum_{d_i \in C_k} distance(d_i, C_k)^2 \tag{1}$$

where C is the set of cluster centroids, d_i is a data point in a cluster C_k, and n is the number of clusters.

In our case, we compute WCSS from 2 to 20 clusters. Then, we plot the graph of the WCSS evolution depending on the number of clusters. The ideal number of clusters is located at the Elbow point. The Elbow point is where diminishing returns are no longer worth the additional cost, which means that adding another cluster no longer helps represent the data. Graphically, we obtain an elbow-shaped visualization in which the optimal number of clusters represents the tip of the elbow, i.e. the point corresponding to the number of clusters from which the variance no longer decreases significantly.

Davies-Bouldin Score. The Davis-Boulding score is the average similarity measure of each cluster with its most similar cluster. The similarity is the ratio of intra-cluster distances to inter-cluster distances. The minimum score is zero, with lower values indicating better clustering. The formula for the Davies-Bouldin score is provided in Eq. 2:

$$DB = \frac{1}{n} \sum_{k=1}^{n} \max_{k' \neq k}(\frac{\delta_k + \delta_{k'}}{d(\mu_k, \mu_{k'})}) \tag{2}$$

where, $\mu_k = \frac{1}{|C_k|} \sum_{i \in C_k} d_i$ and $\delta_k = \frac{1}{|C_k|} \sum_{i \in C_k} d(d_i, \mu_k)$. d is the euclidean distance.

Silhouette Score. For each point, the Silhouette coefficient is the difference between the average distance to points in the same group (cohesion) and the average distance to points in other neighbouring groups (separation). If this difference is negative, the point is, on average closer to the neighbouring group than its own and thus poorly ranked. Conversely, if this difference is positive, the point is, on average closer to its group than to the neighbouring group, and it is therefore well ranked. The Silhouette score is the average of the silhouette coefficient for all points. The Silhouette score (and coefficient) varies between 1 (best classification) and -1 (worst classification). The silhouette score calculation is shown in Eq. 3:

$$S_{sil} = \frac{1}{n} \sum_{k=1}^{n} \frac{1}{|C_k|} \sum_{i \in C_k} s_{sil}(i) \tag{3}$$

The silhouette coefficient is: $s_{sil}(i) = \frac{b(i)-a(i)}{\max(a(i),b(i))}$. $a(i)$ is the average distance of the point to its group: $a(i) = \frac{1}{|C_k|-1} \sum_{j \in C_k, j \neq i} d(d_i, d_j)$. $b(i)$ is the average distance of the point to its neighbouring group: $b(i) = \min_{k' \neq k} \frac{1}{|C'_k|} \sum_{i' \in C_{k'}} d(d_i, d_{i'})$.

K-Means. K-Means [34] is a commonly used clustering algorithm. With K-Means, we consider the distance of a point to the average of the points of its cluster. Thus, the function to be minimized is the sum of the squares of these distances. Thus, K-Means is an algorithm to address an optimization problem where we want to find: $\arg\min_C \sum_{k=1}^{n} \sum_{d_i \in C_k} \|d_i - \mu_k\|^2$, where μ_k are the barycenters of the points in C_k.

4   Evaluation of Method on CIC-IDS2017 Dataset

4.1   Overview of CIC-IDS2017 Dataset

The CIC-IDS2017 dataset is a valuable resource for cybersecurity researchers, as it provides a diverse and extensive collection of network traffic data, allowing for the development and evaluation of intrusion detection systems. The data has been generated to provide the behavior of 25 users of the course of 5 days with the occurrence of several attacks. A particularly noteworthy feature of this dataset is that it accurately portrays real-world PCAPs.

The CIC-IDS2017 dataset is very imbalanced; however, it is important to note that our method is not sensitive to imbalanced data. This dataset contains 2,830,540 instances in total. 2,359,087 instances are benign traffic, and 471,453 instances are from 14 different attacks. We consider only the four attacks relevant to the HTTP protocol, thus reducing the total entries to 130,855. The label and number of instances for each episode are as follows: Botnet (`botnet`, 118,765 instances), Brute Force (`brute-web`, 6,548 instances), XSS (`brute-xss`, 5,505 instances) and SQL Injection (`sql-inj`, 37 instances).

4.2 Pre-processing of CIC-IDS2017 Dataset

In this section, we discuss the selection of the chosen hyperparameters to be used on the CIC-IDS2017 dataset and how it affects the performance of the clustering procedure. The number of unique values for each feature greatly influences the choice of hyperparameter values. The dimension reduction algorithm gives worse results if the number of unique values is too high because these methods are based on one-hot encoding. Making semantic links between data is extremely complicated if entries do not share enough common values. Hence, this high number of unique values for each feature, named high cardinality, leads to overfitting because the model cannot generalize information. In addition to an overfitted model, high cardinality leads to problems in computational time. After several attempts and manual inspection of similar values, we set $count\_threshold = 1$ and $similarity\_threshold = 0.5$ for the hyperparameter values. Thus, Table 1 shows the number of unique values for each feature for CIC-IDS2017 (130,855 entries) before and after pre-processing.

Table 1. Number of unique values for each features of CIC-IDS2017 before and after pre-processing

Feature	Unique values before pre-pro.	Unique values after pre-pro.
Payload	7,086	27
URL	5,548	39
User-Agent	3	3
Method	2	2

We observe that User-Agent, in this particular case, does not need to be pre-processed because of its very low number of unique values (i.e. 3). It is the same case for the value of Method, but this is expected since Method cannot have a high number of different values by definition.

4.3 Clustering Results on CIC-IDS2017 Dataset

We use three cluster scoring methods and demonstrate the results in Fig. 1. We identify the ideal number of clusters to be 4, where the Silhouette score is highest, the Davies Bouldin score is lowest, and there is an elbow for the WCSS score. Often, these methods will produce slightly different values for the number of clusters, and a process is required to find a compromise between the values. In this case, each scoring method determines that the number of clusters should be 4; we thus use this value. This is an ideal result since there are, in fact, four different attacks.

To evaluate our method, we assign a label for each cluster by inspecting its content. Then, we use precision, recall and F1-score to evaluate our classification.

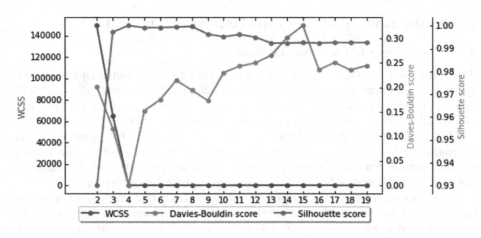

Fig. 1. Results of clustering scoring for CIC-IDS2017 dataset

Table 2. Number of entries and labels assigned to each of the clusters for CIC-IDS2017

Cluster	# botnet	# brute-xss	# brute-web	# sql-inj	label assigned
1	118, 765	0	0	0	botnet
2	0	5, 505	0	0	brute-xss
3	0	0	6, 548	0	brute-web
4	0	0	0	37	sql-inj

The number of entries and the label assigned to each of our clusters are shown in Table 2.

Different metrics can be used for multi-class classification evaluation. The micro-average is relevant to our case: it computes a global average F1-score by counting the sums of the True Positives (TP), False Negatives (FN), and False Positives (FP). Micro-averaging computes the proportion of correctly classified observations out of all observations. In a multi-class classification with a single label per observation, the precision, recall and f1-score share the same value. This value is given by F1-score = recall = precision = $\frac{TP}{TP+\frac{1}{2}(FP+FN)}$.

With this metric, we can claim that 100% of the CIC-IDS2017 data has been correctly classified using our method. We use these results to offer legitimacy to our clustering method for identifying different attacks. We recognize that this is not a definitive analysis and we can't claim that our method will make correct classification predictions across all datasets. Nonetheless, we feel this is an encouraging result and it validates that our method can effectively classify real-world attacks. In the next section, we apply our method to the Honeypot data, where the attack data is not labelled, which is the intended purpose of this method.

5   Evaluation of Method on Honeypot Dataset

5.1   Overview of Honeypot Dataset

The data used for this work has been collected from an industrial honeypot software product over several months. For confidentiality reasons, the complete details of the data collection process have been deliberately omitted. The honeypot collects data from several protocols, but we focus on HTTP for this work.

The honeypot for HTTP data consists of a login portal that prompts for a username and password without the real possibility of connecting. Therefore, the interactions with this portal are somewhat limited, resulting in the collected data being composed of botnets or automated vulnerability testing tools.

The entirety of the HTTP dataset contains 1,369,692 entries, wherein we select a randomized subset of 100,000 entries for our experimental analysis. We choose to work with this subset due to the computational limitations of our setup since performing our analysis on 100,000 entries takes about 2.5 days to complete. We justify this decision through the fact that other studies have shown that it is possible to obtain very close precision (when assigning new labels) by working on a subset of data with K-Means [22].

5.2   Pre-processing of Honeypot Data

Table 3 shows the number of unique values in the Honeypot dataset before and after the pre-processing procedure. Here we set the hyperparameters to $count\_threshold = 1$ and $similarity\_threshold = 0.5$.

In Table 3, we note that the number of unique values for Payload is initially almost twice as high as the number of unique values for URL, whereas, after the pre-processing, it is more than ten times lower. Our algorithm found more similarity between the payloads than between URLs. This is entirely consistent since payloads often contain very similar values. For example, a brute force attack attempt will generate nearly identical payloads. It should also be noted that pre-processing has not been applied to the Method attribute. Indeed, this attribute contains only very few unique values, making distinguishing certain attacks possible. Since the number of unique values is already low, it would not be relevant to decrease it further and lose information.

Table 3. Number of unique values for each feature of the Honeypot data before and after pre-processing

Feature	Unique values before pre-pro.	Unique values after pre-pro.
Payload	66,671	139
URL	37,279	1,519
User-Agent	1,284	169
Method	52	52

5.3   Clustering Results on Honeypot Dataset

We demonstrate the results of the clustering scoring metrics in Fig. 2. Here, we notice that the Silhouette score is high for the number of clusters ranging from 2 to 11 (inclusive), then it decreases slightly before decreasing considerably from 16 clusters. The Silhouette score, therefore, informs us that the ideal number of clusters is between 2 and 11. The Davies-Bouldin score gives us more information because it presents a minimum of 11 clusters. The WCSS score does not particularly show a bend, so it isn't easy to use in this case. Finally, it is relevant to choose 11 as the ideal number of clusters since it is at this number that the Davies-Bouldin score reaches its minimum and the Silhouette score is very close to its maximum.

Since the latter is bounded, we recall that the only metric directly interpretable is the Silhouette score. Thus, for a given point, a score of -1 represents the worst classification and one the best, and a score of 0 indicates that the point is perfect between the different clusters. Here, the silhouette score is 0.9748, which is encouraging for the quality of our classification.

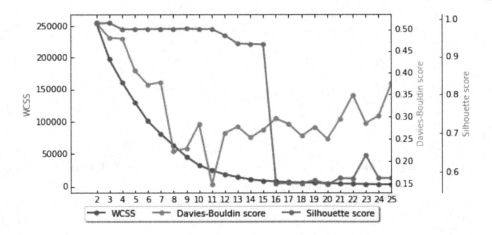

Fig. 2. Results of clustering scoring for Honeypot dataset

5.4   Analysis of Honeypot Data Clusters

Our proposed method offers security analysts a method to classify malicious events to understand the threats they face. Here we demonstrate the information we are able to uncover about the attacks using our unsupervised approach. We present the distribution of the data clusters and a description of the attacks they represent in Table 4. In Fig. 3, we show the 3D visualization of the clustering procedure.

Table 4. Distribution of clusters in Honeypot data

Cluster	# Entries	Description
0	178,619	Connection tests, multiple vulnerability tests
1	1	Unique large User-Agent
2	96	Exploit CVE-2018-10561
3	14	User-Agent XTC Botnet
4	1	User-Agent ApiTool
5	6	Unique large User-Agent
6	439	Exploit Netlink 1.0.11 router, unique User-Agent
7	215	Exploit CWE-912
8	276	Exploit Netlink 1.0.11 router, unique User-Agent
9	21	Exploit CVE-2017-9248
10	80	Exploit CVE-2020-28036

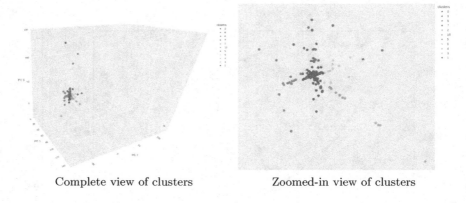

Complete view of clusters   Zoomed-in view of clusters

Fig. 3. 3D Visualization of Clusters in Honeypot Data

Note that cluster 0 contains the majority of the data (99.36%). We see that a third of the data in this cluster has no payload or URL, likely corresponding to testing if the host is available and accepts a connection on port 80. For the other two-thirds, many vulnerabilities are tested and often many times.

For example, the most popular payload consists of the keywords "admin", "die", "md5", "S3pt3mb3r", returns 20,383 times, and is present only in this cluster. This corresponds to an attack on the proprietary software vBulletin [16], which suffered from the Common Vulnerability and Exposure (CVE)-2019-16759 [3] vulnerability, which affected, on the day of its discovery, more than 100,000 websites. This vulnerability allows an unauthenticated user to take control of the server fairly quickly, which is why automated test tools have widely used it. It would not be relevant to expose each of the vulnerabilities tested in this cluster, since dozens of them exist. The previous example only shows that the same vulnerability can have many entries in the same cluster. Also, this example was chosen because it is a good example of what attackers are looking for. In order to have a more macroscopic description of the main cluster, it is interesting to analyze the user-agents. Indeed, these can sometimes directly give the identity of the software or botnet that is used. In other cases, random user-agents are chosen, which is why we cannot rely solely on user-agents to interpret our clusters. However, here are the different user-agents and their categories for cluster 0:

- **Explorers blindly testing vulnerabilities**: ZmEu [19] or l9explore [5]
- **Port scanners**: CensysInspect [1], ProjectDiscovery [11], Masscan [13], Nessus, MercuryBoard [10], zGrab [18]
- **Homemade scripts**: Curl [2], Python Request [14], OKhttp [8], PyCurl [12], UrlLib [15], GoHttp [6], jndi/ldap [7], AIOhttp [17]
- **Indexing robots used by search engines**: Google Bot, Baidu Spider

The clusters appearing very far from the others (i.e. 1, 3, 4, and 5) each have a distinct user-agent. Cluster 4 has ApiTool as the user-agent, which tests for a very particular Internet-of-Things (IoT) exploit. Cluster 3 has the user-agent XTC Botnet (it is encouraging that a botnet has been isolated in a cluster). Clusters 1 and 5 both have a unique user-agent of a considerable length. To explain this, we must note that if an attribute exceeds a predefined size of 100,000 characters, we assign it a fixed unique identifier. This prevents our algorithm from processing excessive data, which aims to impact the availability of the attacked system (a user-agent of several gigabytes can only have this objective). Thus, all saturation attempts with long attribute values will have the same unique identifier. Clusters 1 and 5 have the same identifier. However, they differ by their URL, payload, and method.

Clusters 2, 6, 7, 8, 9 and 10 are closer together and are centred around the main cluster (0). These clusters have a few common values with cluster 0 yet are different enough to be isolated in their own cluster. Each cluster isolates a different attempted vulnerability exploit, making this a promising result. Cluster 2 attempts CVE-2018-10561, cluster 7 attempts Common Weakness Enumeration (CWE)-912, cluster 9 attempts CVE-2017-9248, and cluster 10 attempts CVE-2020-28036. Both clusters 6 and 8 attempt to exploit Netlink 1.0.11 routers and differ by their user-agent.

6 Discussion

The fact that we achieved a perfect clustering of the CIC-IDS2017 is a promising result for our method, particularly since the dataset is heavily unbalanced. We do recognize that this is still an initial result and there is more to done to further validate this method, such as performing classification on several labelled datasets and comparing the results to other methods. It is important to mention that this result is aided by the fact that the CIC-IDS2017 does not contain complex and multi-step attacks. For example, for an XSS attack, each entry corresponds to an XSS tentative and has a similar Payload, URL, Method, and User-Agent.

When applying our method to the unlabelled Honeypot dataset, we get promising results in that we can cluster several attacks by their attempted vulnerability exploit and identify a botnet. However, the fact that a disproportionate number of attack instances were clustered into a single group is something that needs to be addressed. Performing the clustering on a reduced 3-dimensional space allows for more straightforward computations and visualization; however, increasing the number of dimensions may potentially resolve the issue, as mentioned earlier.

An intended goal is to perform our method on other communication protocols with categorical and numerical features. In this case, we could use FAMD, which applies classical PCA on numerical variables and MCA on categorical variables. With our approach, we would have no limitation in feature selection (i.e. PCA for numerical features, MCA for categorical features, and FAMD for both numerical and categorical features).

The primary goal of this work is to classify unlabelled attack packets in order to aid a security analyst in prioritizing remediation tasks. Our method leverages existing unsupervised learning techniques and we are able to form clusters that represent different types of attacks. However, the assessment of the correctness of the clusters is subjective in this work as we use manual inspection of these clusters to confirm that they are reasonable. Ultimately, a detailed comparison with other classification methods is needed to give more insights into the validity of these clusters. Nonetheless, this work demonstrates a viable approach to classifying unlabelled attack packets, highlights challenges that we're overcome, and provides areas for improvement.

7 Conclusion

To conclude, we propose a new method for automated web attack detection based on deep inspection of HTTP packets for unlabelled data by focusing on the content of packets and not on the metadata. The method comprises three phases: tokenising packets' contents, reducing the categorical feature space into numerical features using MCA, and clustering using K-Means. The method is verified on the CIC-IDS2017 dataset, where it can classify all attacks perfectly. The method is then applied to unlabelled honeypot data, where it can isolate several attack types. Future work involves extending this method to other protocols and refining the clustering approach to better isolate attacks within large clusters.

References

1. Censys—industry-leading cloud and internet asset discovery solutions. https://censys.io/
2. curl. https://curl.se/
3. CVE - CVE-2019-16759. https://cve.mitre.org/cgi-bin/cvename.cgi?name=CVE-2019-16759
4. difflib - Helpers for computing deltas - Python 3.10.6 documentation. https://docs.python.org/3/library/difflib.html
5. "l9explore," original-date: 2020-12-15T00:39:15Z. https://github.com/LeakIX/l9explore
6. Azhar, N.B.: "gohttp," original-date: 2017-11-08T15:28:32Z. https://github.com/nahid/gohttp
7. NDI/LDAP service provider. https://docs.oracle.com/javase/8/docs/technotes/guides/jndi/jndi-ldap.html
8. Overview - OkHttp. https://square.github.io/okhttp/
9. Prince · PyPI. https://pypi.org/project/prince/
10. Product catalog—mercury security access control hardware & solutions. https://mercury-security.com/portal/
11. Projectdiscovery.io. https://projectdiscovery.io/#/
12. PycURL home page. http://pycurl.io/
13. Graham, R.D.: "MASSCAN: Mass IP port scanner," original-date: 2013-07-28T05:35:33Z. https://github.com/robertdavidgraham/masscan
14. Requests · PyPI. https://pypi.org/project/requests/
15. urllib - URL handling modules - python 3.11.0 documentation. https://docs.python.org/3/library/urllib.html
16. vBulletin 5 connect, the world's leading community software. https://www.vbulletin.com/
17. Welcome to AIOHTTP - aiohttp 3.8.3 documentation. https://docs.aiohttp.org/en/stable/
18. "ZGrab 2.0," original-date: 2016-08-19T23:22:02Z. https://github.com/zmap/zgrab2
19. ZmEu, "Zmeubot - module for ZNC (v0.1)," original-date: 2016-01-22T12:00:27Z. https://github.com/happyhater/zmeubot-znc
20. Abdi, H., Valentin, D.: Multiple correspondence analysis, p. 13 (2007)
21. Ahmetoglu, H., Das, R.: A comprehensive review on detection of cyber-attacks: data sets, methods, challenges, and future research directions. Internet of Things **20**, 100615 (2022). https://doi.org/10.1016/j.iot.2022.100615, https://www.sciencedirect.com/science/article/pii/S254266052200097X
22. Bejarano, J., et al.: Sampling within k-means algorithm to cluster large datasets. UMBC Student Collection (2011)
23. Boukela, L., Zhang, G., Bouzefrane, S., Zhou, J.: An outlier ensemble for unsupervised anomaly detection in honeypots data. Intell. Data Anal. **24**(4), 743–758 (2020)
24. Faker, O., Dogdu, E.: Intrusion detection using big data and deep learning techniques. In: Proceedings of the 2019 ACM Southeast Conference, ACM SE 2019, pp. 86–93. Association for Computing Machinery (2019)
25. Ghurab, M., Gaphari, G., Alshami, F., Alshamy, R., Othman, S.: A detailed analysis of benchmark datasets for network intrusion detection system (2021)

26. Lippmann, R., Haines, J.W., Fried, D.J., Korba, J., Das, K.: The 1999 DARPA off-line intrusion detection evaluation. Comput. Netw. **34**(4), 579–595 (2000)
27. Matin, I.M.M., Rahardjo, B.: Malware detection using honeypot and machine learning. In: 2019 7th International Conference on Cyber and IT Service Management (CITSM), vol. 7, pp. 1–4. IEEE (2019)
28. Meira, J., et al.: Performance evaluation of unsupervised techniques in cyber-attack anomaly detection. J. Ambient Intell. Human Comput. **11**(11), 4477–4489 (2020)
29. Mokube, I., Adams, M.: Honeypots: concepts, approaches, and challenges. In: Proceedings of the 45th Annual Southeast Regional Conference, pp. 321–326 (2007)
30. Owezarski, P.: Unsupervised classification and characterization of honeypot attacks. In: 10th International Conference on Network and Service Management (CNSM) and Workshop, pp. 10–18. IEEE (2014)
31. Panigrahi, R., Borah, S.: A detailed analysis of CICIDS2017 dataset for designing intrusion detection systems. Int. J. Eng. Technol. **7**, 479–482 (2018)
32. Pelletier, Z., Abualkibash, M.: Evaluating the CIC IDS-2017 dataset using machine learning methods and creating multiple predictive models in the statistical computing language R. Int. Res. J. Adv. Eng. Sci. **5**(2), 5 (2020)
33. Ring, M., Wunderlich, S., Scheuring, D., Landes, D., Hotho, A.: A survey of network-based intrusion detection data sets. Comput. Secur. **86**, 147–167 (2019)
34. Sinaga, K.P., Yang, M.S.: Unsupervised k-means clustering algorithm. IEEE Access **8**, 80716–80727 (2020)
35. Takyi, K., Bagga, A., Goopta, P.: Clustering techniques for traffic classification: a comprehensive review. In: 2018 7th International Conference on Reliability, Infocom Technologies and Optimization (Trends and Future Directions) (ICRITO), pp. 224–230 (2018)
36. Wu, Y., Wei, D., Feng, J.: Network attacks detection methods based on deep learning techniques: a survey. Secur. Commun. Netw. **2020**, e8872923 (2020)
37. Yavanoglu, O., Aydos, M.: A review on cyber security datasets for machine learning algorithms. In: 2017 IEEE International Conference on Big Data (Big Data), pp. 2186–2193 (2017)
38. Zanero, S., Savaresi, S.M.: Unsupervised learning techniques for an intrusion detection system. In: Proceedings of the 2004 ACM Symposium on Applied Computing, SAC 2004, pp. 412–419. Association for Computing Machinery (2004)
39. Zhang, X., Chen, J., Zhou, Y., Han, L., Lin, J.: A multiple-layer representation learning model for network-based attack detection. IEEE Access **7**, 91992–92008 (2019)

Security Analysis

Practices for Assessing the Security Level of Solidity Smart Contracts

Mohamed Mekkouri[ID] and Christine Hennebert[(✉)][ID]

Univ. Grenoble Alpes, CEA, LETI, DSYS, 38000 Grenoble, France
mohamed.mekkouri@student-cs.fr, christine.hennebert@cea.fr

Abstract. In 2022, the Ethereum Entreprise Alliance (EEA) published a first version of EthTrust [2], a document that aims to certify the security level of smart contracts written in the Solidity language. A smart contract is a computer code whose execution is triggered by a transaction issued by a peer on a distributed network. Once deployed in a blockchain, the contract is immutable and no security flaw can be corrected. In order to provide an uninitiated user with the means to check the security level of the targeted contract before sending a transaction, it would be desirable to have a tool capable of certifying the security level of smart contracts. With this objective in mind, the work presented in this paper aims to qualify the existing tools for detecting vulnerabilities in contracts, as well as advances based on the use of AI to analyse the Solidity language. Finally, the needs and a methodology are discussed to build a tool for systematically certifying the security level of open source smart contracts.

Keywords: Security Level · Vulnerability · Smart Contract · Solidity · Static Analysis Tool · Classifier · AI-based detection

1 Introduction

The first blockchain to be deployed on a global scale began in January 2009, creating Bitcoin. The crypto-currency held by users is hosted on the ledger, shared and replicated among the network peers. To spend their currency, users send a transaction to the blockchain attesting that they are the owner, thereby unlocking the cryptographic padlock protecting their currency within the ledger. In Bitcoin, this padlock is called a "lock script". Bitcoin includes five lock scripts for different uses. They are coded using a stack-oriented programming language, with a limited number of instructions executed at low level, with a good level of security.

In early 2014, Ethereum was launched, introducing a new protocol based on the Solidity language. This Turing-Complete language enables in addition to

This work is a collaborative research action that is supported by the French National Research Agency (ANR) in the framework of the "investissements d'avenir" program ANR-10-AIRT-05, irtnanoelec.

© The Author(s), under exclusive license to Springer Nature Switzerland AG 2024
M. Mosbah et al. (Eds.): FPS 2023, LNCS 14551, pp. 71–86, 2024.
https://doi.org/10.1007/978-3-031-57537-2_5

build decentralized applications (dApp) introducing a new paradigm. By introducing smart contracts, the creators of Ethereum extracted Bitcoin's hard-coded scripts from the infrastructure and offered a tool chain enabling developers to write a contract (i.e. a small piece of code resembling a script) dedicated to their use, then compile it before deploying the resulting bytecode in the ledger. Execution of the contract will be triggered by incoming transactions and run within an Ethereum Virtual Machine (EVM) by the network peers, who must agree on the result of the execution. The fact that everyone may write, deploy and/or use a smart contract in the blockchain comes at a cost: the security.

One approach could be to use a formally proven language, but this option is still being explored, notably through research based on Why3 [4] or OCaml with the Michelson[1] language. Solidity is still the most widely used language, and is becoming standard for many uses, although it includes vulnerabilities and has suffered high-impact attacks such as TheDAO[2] in 2016 or Parity[3] in 2017.

The strength of the Solidity language lies in the fact that it is widely used and that the source code of contracts is available on-chain, allowing anyone to conduct an audit. In 2022, the Ethereum Enterprise Alliance (EEA) introduced a first draft of the EthTrust document [2], which introduces criteria for establishing the security level of smart contract. However, to perform this audit, one needs to be expert in the field. Since one of the main advantages of blockchain technology is to be user-centric, it would be desirable to have an automatic smart contract analysis tool available to everyone. A user could then know the level of security of a contract before choosing to use it (i.e. sending a transaction).

This paper explores this idea by following this organisation: in Sect. 2, existing vulnerabilities are collected and a set of snippets is developed to reproduce and exploit each one. Existing contract analysis tools are then tested on our snippets in the Sect. 3. The Sect. 4 presents the state of the art in the use of Artificial Intelligence (AI) to detect vulnerabilities in the code of smart contracts. This study is explored in Sect. 5 to propose a classification of vulnerabilities and a methodology for progressing towards the construction of a tool providing the security level of Solidity contracts.

2   Vulnerabilities of Solidity

Solidity is a formally unproven language and therefore vulnerable, but very accessible. It is the main language used on Ethereum, and many smart contracts developed in Solidity are becoming standards, such as ERC20. Its use requires a deep experience of decentralized programming, as well as knowledge of the best coding practices and known vulnerabilities.

---

[1] https://tezos.gitlab.io/active/michelson.html.
[2] https://blog.chain.link/reentrancy-attacks-and-the-dao-hack/.
[3] https://hackingdistributed.com/2017/07/22/deep-dive-parity-bug/.

2.1   Knowledge Base of Vulnerabilities

Identifying vulnerabilities in Solidity smart contracts is laborious, because there are numerous and they can take various forms. Several works list best practices and vulnerabilities. These include scientific papers as the didactic study [5], recommendations as the Consensys best practice guide[4], practical libraries as *not-so-smart-contracts*[5] which allows to practice, or also the contests database[6]. To the best of our knowledge, this is the classification *swc-registry*[7] that maintains the most comprehensive and up-to-date list of vulnerabilities, and that are used as a reference for our study. Each entry of the Smart contract Weakness Classification (SWC) is labeled with the Common Weakness Enumeration (CWE) that serves as a common language, measuring stick for security tools.

Once deployed in the blockchain, the smart contract is not modifiable and the potential vulnerabilities it contains are no longer patchable. They may include bugs, unintended behaviors, or be exploited to create loss of asset for their owner (i.e. gas, token, ether, access right), or denial of service. Vulnerabilities may arise from a lack of knowledge of best practices in the use of Solidity, inconsistent tool versions in the development chain (language, compiler, EVM as runtime environment), or the limitations of blockchain use. While the development of secure smart contract remains the domain of experienced developers, anyone should be able to check its level of security.

2.2   Implementing Vulnerabilities

The first phase of our study involved establishing a complete set of vulnerabilities based on the SWC registry. For each SWC entry, a faulty smart contract is implemented, as well as a decentralized application (dApp) to exploit the vulnerability. The tests have been performed in the Ethereum brownie environment. Once achieved our snippets of contracts, ad-hoc countermeasures are implemented. An example of this work is illustrated below with the vulnerability swc-132 named *Unexpected Ether balance.*

Swc-132 is about contracts that exhibit faulty behavior when they make unwavering assumptions about a particular Ether balance. There exists means to deliberately transfer Ether to a contract, bypassing its fallback function, either through the use of *selfdestruct()* function or by directing mining rewards to the targeted account, or by sending Ether to an address that does not yet exist. In the most serious circumstances, this vulnerability could potentially give rise to Denial of Service (DOS) situations, effectively incapacitating the contract functionality as illustrated in Fig. 1.

For example in the function *lock*, the strict check of the balance of the newly created contract can be exploited. The dApp leveraging this vulnerability is presented in Fig. 2. At start, some Ether are locked for *accounts[1]* to verify

---

[4] https://consensys.github.io/smart-contract-best-practices/attacks/.

[5] https://github.com/crytic/not-so-smart-contracts.

[6] https://github.com/ethereum/solidity-underhanded-contest.

[7] https://swcregistry.io/.

```
function lock(Term term, bytes calldata edgewareAddr, bool isValidator)
        external
        payable
        didStart
        didNotEnd
    {
        uint256 eth = msg.value;
        address owner = msg.sender;
        uint256 unlockTime = unlockTimeForTerm(term);
        // Create ETH lock contract
        Swc132_Lock lockAddr = (new Swc132_Lock).value(eth)(owner, unlockTime);
        // ensure lock contract has all ETH, or fail
        require(address(lockAddr).balance == msg.value,"where the hell did the money come from");
        emit Locked(owner, eth, lockAddr, term, edgewareAddr, isValidator, now);
    }
```

Fig. 1. Smart contract implementing swc-132 vulnerability (see footnote 7).

```
def exploit(contract):
    my_bytes = b'\x00\x01\x02'
    edgerkey = encode_abi(['bytes'], [my_bytes])
    tx = contract.lock(contract.getTerm(0), edgerkey, False,{'from':accounts[1],'amount':1000000000000000000})
    # we try to identify the address of the next Lock contract
    next_lock_address = contract.addressFrom(contract.address,web3.eth.getTransactionCount(contract.address))
    # now that we have the address we can transfer some wei to make the verification fail
    accounts[2].transfer(to=next_lock_address,amount=10)
    # this should be reverted
    contract.lock(contract.getTerm(1), edgerkey, False,{'from':accounts[2],'amount':1000000000000000000})
    contract.lock(contract.getTerm(2), edgerkey, False,{'from':accounts[3],'amount':1000000000000000000})
    contract.lock(contract.getTerm(0), edgerkey, False,{'from':accounts[4],'amount':1000000000000000000})
```

Fig. 2. dApp exploiting swc-132 vulnerability.

that it works. After that, the aim is to guess the address of the next *lock* contract using the function *addressFrom* provided for illustrative purposes. It takes the address and transaction count of the deploying contract, and generates the address. Then, some Ether is sent to this address that does not exist yet. Consequently, when another user wants to lock Ether, the transaction is always reverted, because whenever a user executes the function *lock* the strict equality included in the *require* command leads to reversion, and the transaction count is not incremented so the address generated by *addressFrom* is always the same. This illustrates an example of a DoS attack against a smart contract exploiting the strict balance check.

To avoid this exploitation, strict equality checks on Ether balances must be avoided in a contract. If exact values of deposited Ether are required, a self-defined variable should be used that gets incremented in payable functions, to safely track the deposited Ether. This variable will not be influenced by the forced Ether sent via a *selfdestruct()* call.

The vulnerabilities considered for our study are listed in Table 1, with an ad-hoc countermeasure for each.

2.3   Classification and Certification

EEA recently introduces a draft of security level specifications in order to quote the security level of Solidity smart contracts. The current version of the document EthTrust is dated of 11 august 2023 [2], and based on the vulnerabilities known at this date. EthTrust is organised in requirements related to thematic possibly grouping several exploited vulnerabilities. Each requirement is quoted with a security level [S], [M] or [Q].

The security level [S] is intended to allow an unguided automated tool to analyze the source code, as well as the bytecode of smart contracts. The tool should determine whether the contract meets all the requirements quoted [S]. However, for the ambiguous situations that are difficult to verify automatically, the associated requirements are overriding to higher level security quotation. The security level [M] means that the code of the smart contract has been carefully reviewed and approved by human auditors, doing a manual analysis. The security level [Q] implies that the intended functionalities of the smart contract are well documented, and that the code and documentation has been thoroughly reviewed by human auditors to ensure that security flaws cannot come from functional or safety drawbacks.

These criteria show that (1) many requirements require human analysis, (2) the rating is not linked to the severity or the impact of the exploit but to the ability to detect the vulnerability.

The synthesis presented in Table 1 shows that many vulnerabilities of the *swc-registry* are not quoted in EthTrust. The second phase of our study therefore consists of testing existing automatic Solidity analysis tools on our snippets of vulnerable contracts. According to the criteria outlined in EthTrust, vulnerabilities that can be detected automatically would be classified as [S].

3   Detection of Vulnerabilities Using Non-AI Approaches

This section presents the tools tested on our snippets of vulnerable contracts. The detection principle used by each tool is detailed, to enable a more refined interpretation of the results presented in Table 2.

3.1   Definitions

Symbolic execution: Symbolic execution is a technique used in computer science and software analysis to reason about the behavior of a program by tracking the possible values of variables and expressions symbolically, rather than using concrete values. It is a method to explore all possible execution paths of a program without actually running it.

SMT solving: Satisfiability Modulo Theories (SMT) solvers help to identify vulnerabilities by analysing the feasibility of different conditions and constraints that could potentially lead to security issues. Many software vulnerabilities arise due to specific conditions being met during program execution. For

Table 1. Knowledge base of vulnerabilities and their countermeasures.

ID	Title	Countermeasure
EthTrust Security Level [S]		
swc-101	Integer Overflow and Underflow	Use a compiler version posterior to 0.8.0 or Use SafeMath library (OpenZeppelin)
swc-104	Unchecked Call Return Value	Check the return
swc-106	Unprotected SELFDESTRUCT Instruction	Remove the self-destruct functionality
swc-109	Uninitialized Storage Pointer	Use a compiler version posterior to 0.5.0
swc-115	Authorization through tx.origin	Should be avoided
swc-117	Signature Malleability	Do not include a signature into a signed message hash
swc-118	Incorrect Constructor Name	Solidity version 0.4.22 introduces a new constructor keyword
swc-132	Unexpected Ether balance	Avoid strict equality checks for the Ether balance
EthTrust Security Level [M]		
swc-116	Block values as a proxy for time	Use oracles instead
swc-122	Lack of Proper Signature Verification	.
swc-124	Write to Arbitrary Storage Location	.
swc-127	Arbitrary Jump with Function Type Variable	The use of assembly should be minimal. Don't allow users to assign arbitrary values to func. type variables
EthTrust Security Level [Q]		
swc-105	Unprotected Ether Withdrawal	Implement controls so withdrawals can only be triggered by authorized parties
swc-123	Requirement Violation	Weaken the condition, or make sure no invalid inputs provided
swc-126	Insufficient Gas Griefing	Only allow trusted users to relay transactions Require that the forwarder provides enough gas
swc-128	DoS With Block Gas Limit	Actions that require looping across the entire data structure should be avoided If needed, plan for it to require multiple transactions
not classified in EthTrust		
swc-100	Function Default Visibility	Set visibility for all functions and use a recent compiler
swc-102	Outdated Compiler Version	Use a recent version of Solidity
swc-103	Floating Pragma	Use a unique version of Solidity
swc-107	Reentrancy	Make sure all internal state changes are performed before the call is executed, or Use a reentrancy lock e.g. OpenZeppelin's ReentrancyGuard
swc-108	State Variable Default Visibility	Explicitly define visibility for all state variables
swc-110	Assert Violation	If the condition is not invariant, replace with require
swc-111	Use of Deprecated Solidity Functions	Use alternatives to the deprecated constructions
swc-112	Delegatecall to Untrusted Callee	Never call delegatecall into untrusted contracts
swc-113	DoS with Failed Call	Delegates only to trusted contracts
swc-114	Transaction Order Dependence	Use of commit reveal hash scheme

(continued)

Table 1. (*continued*)

SWC-119	Shadowing State Variables	Check for compiler warnings
SWC-120	Weak Sources of Randomness from Chain Attributes	Use external sources of randomness
SWC-121	Missing Protection against Signature Replay Attacks	.
SWC-125	Incorrect Inheritance Order	When inheriting multiple contracts, especially if they have identical functions, a developer should carefully specify inheritance in the correct order
SWC-129	Typographical Error	Use SafeMath Library
SWC-130	Right-To-Left-Override control character (U+202E)	Should not appear in the source code
SWC-131	Presence of unused variables	Remove all unused variables from the code
SWC-133	Hash Collisions	When using abi.encodePacked(), use length fixed array
SWC-134	Message call with hardcoded gas amount	Use .call.value(...)("")
SWC-135	Code With No Effects	Write unit tests to verify correct behaviour of the code
SWC-136	Unencrypted Private Data On-Chain	Any private data should preferably be stored off-chain

example, a buffer overflow vulnerability occurs when an attacker can input more data than a buffer can handle. Vulnerabilities like this depend on certain conditions, such as the length of input data exceeding the buffer size, you can express these conditions as logical constraints involving program variables and inputs. For instance, you could express the buffer overflow vulnerability as a constraint like *input_ length > buffer_ size*. These constraints describe scenario where vulnerabilities might occur.

Taint analysis: Taint analysis is a technique used in computer security to track and understand how certain information, often referred to as "taint", spreads or influences different parts of a program. Imagine taint as a color that can spread from one place to another in a computer program. Taint analysis helps to understand how potentially unsafe or sensitive data spreads through the program, highlighting areas where this data could have unintended or risky effects.

3.2   The Tools Considered

Slither is an open-source python-based static analysis framework for the Solidity programming language. It converts the Solidity Abstract Syntax Tree (AST) generated by the Solidity compiler into an intermediary language called "SlithIR" which facilitates vulnerability and optimization detection.

Solhint is a Solidity linter based on a powerful parser generator ANTLR (ANother Tool for Language Recognition).

Mythril uses symbolic execution, SMT solving and taint analysis to detect a variety of security vulnerabilities.

Securify2.0 implements context-sensitive static analysis, which means it takes into account the context in which various program elements are used.

solidityScan is a close source and pay-per-use solidity scanner designed to detect vulnerabilities.

MythX includes static analysis, dynamic analysis, symbolic execution and fuzzing in a pay-per-use software.

Oyente is a symbolic execution tool that works directly with EVM bytecode without access to source code written in Solidity.

3.3   Vulnerabilities Detected

To qualify the results obtained and compare scanning tools and techniques, the following notation key are used:

◇ : detects tautology
◇◇ : notifies Warning or INFO
◇◇◇ : detects a consequence of the vulnerability
✦ : Detected
✦✦ : Detected by compiler
✦✦✦ : Detected with Precision
. : Not detected

This summary shows that the automatic contract scanning tools are complementary. Oyente is particularly good at detecting underflow/overflow (swc-101), transaction order dependence (swc-114) and code with no effect (swc-135). Among the tools tested, Mythril detects the most vulnerabilities. Securify and solidityScan can be used to track down vulnerabilities beyond swc-128. SolidityScan also provides a wealth of information for optimising gas consumption.

The swc-117 and swc-118 vulnerabilities are rated [S] in EthTrust, although no tool considered can reliably automatically detect them. Swc-118 is fixed using a version of compiler (*solc*) higher than 0.4.22.

Swc-117 concerns the malleability property of the transaction signature. The digital signature of a transaction could correspond to the correct address of the issuing account, whereas the content of the transaction would have been falsified (wrong hash). This attack is not so easy to reproduce with Ethereum, because the ethereum digital signature does not use a random number as a nonce, but an unpredictable fixed number, which avoids disclosing the public key to verify the address of the issuing account. The digital signature has three components (r, v, s), r being a point on an elliptical curve. By transmitting the two coordinates of r(x, y), the malleability of the signature is no longer possible when contracts are operated on Ethereum.

Other vulnerabilities are not automatically detected and require human expertise, in particular swc-122 quoted [M], swc-123 and swc-126 quoted [Q] in EthTrust.

Table 2. Results of the smart contract scanning.

ID	Slither	Solhint	Mythril	Securify2.0	solidityScan	MythX	Oyente
swc-100	◇◇	♦	♦♦♦	♦♦	♦♦	.	.
swc-101	◇	.	.	.	.	.	♦♦♦
swc-102	♦	♦	.	♦♦♦	♦	.	.
swc-103	♦	♦	.	.	♦♦♦	♦	♦
swc-104	♦	♦♦	♦	♦	♦	♦	.
swc-105	.	.	.	.	.	.	.
swc-106	♦	♦	♦	♦	♦	.	.
swc-107	♦	♦	♦	♦	.	.	♦
swc-108	.	♦	.	♦	♦	♦	.
swc-109	♦	♦♦	.	♦♦	♦♦	.	.
swc-110	♦	♦♦♦	♦	.	.	.	.
swc-111	♦	♦♦	.	♦♦	♦♦	.	.
swc-112	♦	♦	♦♦♦	♦	.	.	.
swc-113	.	.	.	◇◇◇	.	.	.
swc-114	.	.	.	♦	.	.	♦♦♦
swc-115	◇◇	♦	♦	♦	♦	♦	.
swc-116	◇◇	♦	♦♦♦	♦	♦	.	♦
swc-117	.	.	.	.	◇◇◇	.	.
swc-118	.	.	.	.	.	.	.
swc-119	◇◇ or ♦♦	♦♦	.	.	.	.	.
swc-120	◇◇◇	◇◇◇	♦♦♦	♦	.	♦	.
swc-121	.	.	.	.	.	.	.
swc-122	.	.	.	.	.	.	.
swc-123	.	.	.	.	.	.	.
swc-124	◇	.	♦♦♦	♦	.	.	.
swc-125	.	.	.	.	.	.	.
swc-126	.	.	.	.	.	.	.
swc-127	◇◇◇	◇◇◇	♦♦♦	.	◇◇◇	.	.
swc-128	♦	.	.	.	♦	.	♦
swc-129	♦	♦♦	.	♦♦	♦♦	.	.
swc-130	♦	◇◇	.	♦	♦♦	.	.
swc-131	♦	.	.	♦	♦	.	.
swc-132	♦	.	.	♦	♦	.	.
swc-133	♦	.	.	.	.	.	.
swc-134	♦	♦	.	.	◇◇	.	.
swc-135	◇◇◇	.	.	.	.	.	♦♦♦
swc-136	.	.	.	.	.	.	.

4   Related Work on AI-Based Detection

Tests carried out with detection tools show that none of them can reliably detect all vulnerabilities. Other approaches have therefore been explored, based on the use of AI. This section summarises the state of the art in this area.

4.1   Deep Learning Model

Momeni *et al.* introduce in [11] the idea of using machine learning techniques to reduce contract analysis time, which is rather long when using static analysis tools. To extract the features presented as input to the AI, an Abstract Syntax Tree (AST) is generated from the parsed code and a Control Flow Graph (CFG) is formed. Then, the works consist in testing four classifiers on each considered vulnerability, namely Support Vector Machine (SVM), Neural Network (NN), Random Forest (RF) and Decision Tree (DT). The training is supervised with a dataset that has been labelled using the Mythril and Slither tools. As result, the authors show that the contract scanning is 20.000 times faster than with static analysis tools.

Learning AI from the natural flow of code leads to inaccuracies and even classification errors, because there are many ways of writing code that lead to the same bug. The Eth2Vec [6] paper looks at a deep learning technique called Paragraph Vector-Distributed Memory (PV-DM) that is adapted to recognise patterns in compiled code. To do this, the authors assume that the *solc* compiler translates the different ways of writing the same bug into a more restricted subset of patterns at the bytecode level. The AI learns from the bytecode and/or assembly code, and the resulting classifier takes the bytecode and/or assembly code as input. The analysis is performed with unsupervised settings, leading to less reliable detection than supervised techniques as illustrated in Table 3.

To go further, the authors of EtherGIS [10] use the Graph Neural Network (GNN) on contract Control Flow Graph (CFG). CFG consists in transforming bytecode to graph features composed of nodes and edges attributes used as inputs of the GNN classifier. At this stage, the question arises of how to represent the input data, as well as the choice of the classifier model in order to obtain the best reliability in detecting the targeted vulnerability.

The paper CBGRU [3] tackles this question and introduces a deep analysis considering two word embedding approaches for features extraction from contracts, entitled *Word2Vec* and *FastText*. Five known text classifiers are tested, namely: Gated Recurrent Unit (GRU), Convolutional Neural Network (CNN), Long Short Term Memory (LSTM), Bidirectional LSTM (Bi-LSTM) and Bidirectional Long Short Term Memory (Bi-GRU). As result, an hybrid model taking the advantages of each technique is proposed to detect vulnerabilities in contracts with a high level of reliability.

4.2   Training

To train an AI in order to perform a supervised detection that targets given vulnerabilities, a carefully labelled dataset is needed.

There are three main techniques for labelling data: (1) using scanning tools, (2) injection of vulnerabilities, (3) manually.

The smartBugs[8] [13] and scrawlD[9] [8] projects have built up a database of labelled contracts using automatic scanning tools. The smartBugs dataset contains 47,000 contracts covering the following vulnerabilities: access control (swc-105, swc-106, swc-112), arithmetic (swc-101), denial of service (swc-113, swc-128), front running (swc-114), reentrancy (swc-107), time manipulation (swc-116) and unchecked low calls (swc-104). The scrawlD dataset contains 6,780 contracts referenced by address and available for consultation on the Ethereum public blockchain. Although this work is significant, the use of these datasets will not train an AI to detect vulnerabilities other than those already found by the tools used to perform the labelling. Their objective is to improve performance, i.e. scanning speed.

The authors of solidiFI[10] [12] have built a dataset by faults injection in valid contracts. For that, they develop full code snippet covering the following vulnerabilities: time manipulation (swc-116), arithmetic (swc-101), use of tx.origin (swc-115), reentrancy (swc-107), unauthorised Ether control (swc-105, swc-106, swc-112) and transaction order dependency (swc-114). Their goal is not to train an AI with this dataset, but rather to qualify statically the reliability of the contract scanning tools. For the same purpose, the authors of smartBugs have shared a set of 69 manually labelled contracts. This manual labelling should be pursued with two objectives: (1) statistical qualification of the contract scanning tools for vulnerabilities quoted [S], (2) building a dataset usable to train AI to detect vulnerabilities quoted [M] or even [Q].

4.3   Reliability of the Detection

In order to evaluate the relevance of the machine learning models, the following criteria are considered. In summary, a higher F1-score results in a more effective detection of the targeted vulnerability.

Accuracy: percentage of samples correctly classified

$$Accuracy = \frac{1}{total\ samples} \sum_{k=0}^{total\ samples} 1\ (if\ sample\ is\ correctly\ detected)$$

Precision: performance of the classifier to predict the correct values

$$Precision = \frac{true\ positives}{false\ positives\ +\ true\ positives}$$

Recall: performance of a learning model to predict the classes of interest

$$Recall = \frac{true\ positives}{true\ positives + false\ negatives}$$

F1-score: measure of the incorrectly predicted labels

$$F1 - Score = 2 * \frac{Precision\ *\ Recall}{Precision\ +\ Recall}$$

---

[8] https://github.com/smartbugs/smartbugs.
[9] https://github.com/sujeetc/ScrawlD.
[10] https://github.com/DependableSystemsLab/SolidiFI/tree/master/contracts.

The Table 3 resumes the reliability of the *Reentrancy* (swc-107) detection for several machine learning techniques in the related work. With the same feature extraction method, Momeni *et al.* [11] applies NN and DT for *Reentrancy* detection leading to interesting results. The use of DT leads to a better *Accurancy* for the same *Precision*, whereas NN is largely better on *Recall* leading to a higher *F1-score*. *Precision* and *Recall* are a trade-off where *Precision* detects only the samples positive without any doubt, and *Recall* is more lax in detecting the samples that appear positive. An ideal classifier would maximize both *Precision* and *Recall*, to get the highest *F1-score*. As Eth2Vec [6] is an unsupervised classifier, the *Accuracy* is not evaluated. The *Precision* obtained is very good but the *F1-score* is finally damaged due to a poor *Recall*. However, the unsupervised technique does not make any assumptions about the coding of vulnerability, nor about labelling, which introduces a bias depending on how it is done, and on the quantity of labelled data. In the following, EtherGIS [10] improves *F1-score* by improving *Accuracy* thanks to the use of GNN, while *Recall* remains fairly low. To significantly improve *Recall*, the authors suggest working on feature extractions, which is the subject of the work presented in CBGRU [3], leading to the highest *Recall* and an excellent *F1-score*.

Table 3. Score of several Deep Learning models to detect *Reentrancy* (swc-107).

Feature Extraction	Machine Learning Model	Accuracy	Precision	Recall	F1-Score
AST and CFG	NN (Momeni [11])	90%	69%	79%	73%
AST and CFG	DT (Momeni [11])	93%	69%	61%	65%
bytecode or assembly	PV-DM (Eth2Vec [6])		86.6%	54.8%	61.5%
CFG	GNN (EtherGIS [10])	95.6%	91%	72.1%	80.5%
Word2Vec or FastText	CNN (CBGRU [3])	93.30%	96.30%	85.95%	90.92%

5   Classification

The Sect. 4 reports on advances in the field of vulnerabilities detection for Solidity smart contracts based on the use of AI. The work highlights that the choice of the feature extraction technique and the choice of the machine learning model have a major impact on the quality of the detection. Additionally, a feature extraction/AI-model combination can lead to reliable detection for a given vulnerability, and be less relevant for another vulnerability. Furthermore, state-of-the-art studies on the subject consider vulnerabilities quoted [S] in EthTrust, i.e. detected by automatic analysis tools. However, our objective is not to save analysis time, but to detect new vulnerabilities that are not detected by automatic analysis tools, in particular the vulnerabilities quoted [M].

5.1 Suggested Classification

Based on the detection results of the automatic analysis tools presented in Sect. 3, the classification of vulnerabilities presented in Table 4 is introduced, according to the [S], [M] and [Q] security level from EthTrust, defined in Sect. 2.

With the aim of developing a rating tool available to everyone, the idea is that [S]-quoted vulnerabilities can be detected using automatic analysis tools, while the detection of [M]-quoted vulnerabilities is reliable using AI-based techniques. The next step will be to deal with the [Q] vulnerabilities, for which knowledge of the use case and functionalities are required.

In Table 4, some SWC vulnerabilities are followed by the letter "G" for "Generalised", meaning that they cover all problems of the same type as the reference SWC. As example, swc-104 *"Unchecked Call Return Value"* is a precaution designed to check the value returned by the function called, in order to prevent bugs. The vulnerability may arise when a contract makes an external call but does not properly check the return value of the call. However, in the Solidity language, you can also omit to set a return value without the compilation or execution being affected. This behavior is included in swc-104 G.

The comments indicate the differences in assessment when compared to the EthTrust classification [2] (EEA Editor's Draft, 11 August 2023).

5.2 Needs for an Enhanced Detection Tool

The development of a tool for automatic certification of the security level of smart contracts requires different needs depending on the security level targeted.

For security level [S], there are already automatic analysis tools capable of detecting vulnerabilities, but no tool detects all of them. It would therefore be desirable to develop an additional tool that combines the advantages of several tools with complementary results. For instance, this tool could leverage the strengths of Mythril, solidityScan, and Oyente.

For security level [M], no automatic analysis tool is available today. AI-based detection techniques seem promising and could be applied to this category. But to perform supervised learning, a labelled dataset is required, containing a significant number of samples for each of the classified vulnerabilities [M]. This is a long and tedious task. So the question arises as to how to build it.

Initially, one possibility would be to follow the vulnerability injection technique introduced in solidiFI [12]. Our snippets of vulnerable contracts could be used for fault injection (see Sect. 2), as well as other existing works. The labelled dataset should be open source and even become a reference for the scientific community. It should be systematically used by all learning projects, enabling the results obtained with this or that feature extraction and AI-model to be compared and verified. Another way of feeding the dataset is to manually label existing contracts, especially in Ethereum[11,12]. To do this, a challenge could be systematically proposed during hackathons in this field.

---

[11] https://etherscan.io/.

[12] https://library.dedaub.com/transactions/ethereum.

Table 4. Suggested classification.

ID	Title	Comments
Security Level [S]		
swc-100	Function Default Visibility	in EthTrust [Q]
swc-101	Integer Overflow and Underflow	
swc-102	Outdated Compiler Version	
swc-104	Unchecked Call Return Value	
swc-106	Unprotected SELFDESTRUCT Instruction	
swc-107	Re-entrancy	
swc-108	State Variable Default Visibility	in EthTrust [Q]
swc-109	Uninitialized Storage Pointer	
swc-111	Use of Deprecated Solidity Functions	
swc-112	Delegatecall to Untrusted Callee	
swc-115	Authorization through tx.origin	
swc-116	Block values as a proxy for time	
swc-119	Shadowing State Variables	
swc-129	Typographical Error	
swc-130	Right-To-Left-Override control character	
swc-131	Presence of unused variables	in EthTrust [Q]
swc-132	Unexpected Ether balance	
swc-134	Message call with hardcoded gas amount	
swc-135	Code With No Effects	in EthTrust [Q]
Security Level [M]		
swc-101	Integer Overflow and Underflow	in EthTrust [S]
swc-104 G	Handle External Call Returns	in EthTrust [S]
swc-103	Floating Pragma	
swc-105	Unprotected Ether Withdrawal	
swc-110	Assert Violation	
swc-112	Delegatecall to Untrusted Callee	
swc-117	Signature Malleability	
swc-118	Incorrect Constructor Name	in EthTrust [Q]
swc-120	Weak Sources of Randomness from Chain	
swc-121	Missing Protection against Signature Replay	
swc-122	Lack of Proper Signature Verification	
swc-124	Write to Arbitrary Storage Location	
swc-126	Insufficient Gas Griefing	in EthTrust [Q]
swc-127	Arbitrary Jump with Function Type Variable	
swc-128	DoS With Block Gas Limit	in EthTrust [Q]
swc-133	Hash Collisions	in EthTrust [S]
Security Level [Q]		
swc-100	Function Default Visibility	
swc-106	Unprotected SELFDESTRUCT Instruction	in EthTrust [S]
swc-108	State Variable Default Visibility	
swc-112 G	Delegatecall to Untrusted Callee	in EthTrust [S]
swc-114	Transaction Order Dependence	
swc-114 G	Protect Against MEV Attacks	
swc-115 G	Authorization through tx.origin	in EthTrust [S]
swc-116 G	Block values as a proxy for time	
swc-118	Incorrect Constructor Name	
swc-123	Requirement Violation	
swc-125	Incorrect Inheritance Order	in EthTrust [S]
swc-130 G	Unicode Control and Homoglyph Character	in EthTrust [S]
swc-131	Presence of unused variables	
swc-135	Code With No Effects	
swc-136	Unencrypted Private Data On-Chain	

For security level [Q], a methodology for dealing with residual vulnerabilities could be considered in the light of the results obtained for rated vulnerabilities [M]. For example, it would be necessary to assess the degree to which the presentation of information on usage and functionalities could be standardised or systematised, in order to provide a framework for exploiting them.

6 Conclusion

In this paper, the feasibility of creating a tool that automatically certifies the security level of Solidity smart contracts is explored with the aim of making it available to end-users. The introduction in EthTrust [2] of criteria and requirements for classifying vulnerabilities gives consistency to this work.

To do this, a set of snippets exploiting all the vulnerabilities in the *swc-registry* is built. Then, the existing analysis tools are tested and evaluated on our snippets in order to qualify them. To reduce the analysis time of these tools, machine learning techniques were reviewed. A summary of the state-of-the-art in this field is presented and discussed in this paper, highlighting (1) the difficulty of labelling a dataset, ideally manually, (2) the importance of extracting features, and (3) the complexity of selecting the AI model leading to the most reliable detection, as each vulnerability is singular. In the light of this analysis and the EthTrust criteria, a classification of vulnerabilities is suggested: detected by automatic tools for the [S] rating, which we believe can be detected by an AI for the [M] rating, and residual vulnerabilities rated [Q] for which knowledge of usage and functionalities is required.

As perspectives, the needs are outlined for progress in the construction of a certification tool for security level [S] based on automatic analysis tools, and security level [M] based on the use of AI.

References

1. Wood, G.: Ethereum: a secure decentralised generalised transaction ledger. Ethereum Yellow Paper (2014). https://ethereum.github.io/yellowpaper/paper. pdf
2. Ethereum Entreprise Alliance: EEA EthTrust Security Levels Specification v-after-1 (Editor's Draft). EEA Editor's Draft, 27 August 2023. https://entethalliance. github.io/eta-registry/security-levels-spec.html
3. Zhang, L., et al.: CBGRU: a detection method of smart contract vulnerability based on a hybrid model. MDPI Sensors **22**(9), 3577 (2022). https://dl.acm.org/ doi/abs/10.1145/3457337.3457841
4. Nehaï, Z., Bobot, F.: Deductive proof of industrial smart contracts using Why3. In: Sekerinski, E., et al. (eds.) FM 2019. LNCS, vol. 12232, pp. 299–311. Springer, Cham (2020). https://doi.org/10.1007/978-3-030-54994-7_22
5. Atzei, N., Bartoletti, M., Cimoli, T.: A survey of attacks on Ethereum smart contracts (SoK). In: Maffei, M., Ryan, M. (eds.) POST 2017. LNCS, vol. 10204, pp. 164–186. Springer, Heidelberg (2017). https://doi.org/10.1007/978-3-662-54455-6_8

6. Ashizawa, N., Yanai, N., Cruz, J.P., Okamura, S.: Eth2Vec: learning contract-wide code representations for vulnerability detection on Ethereum smart contracts. arXiv:2101.02377v2 [cs.CR], 8 January 2021. https://arxiv.org/pdf/2101.02377.pdf

7. Goswami, S., Singh, R., Saikia, N., Bora, K.K., Sharma, U.: TokenCheck: towards deep learning based security vulnerability detection in ERC-20 tokens. In: 2021 IEEE Region 10 Symposium (TENSYMP), Jeju, Republic of Korea, pp. 1–8 (2021). https://doi.org/10.1109/TENSYMP52854.2021.9550913

8. Yashavant, C.S., Kumar, S., Karkare, A.: ScrawlD: a dataset of real world Ethereum smart contracts labelled with vulnerabilities. arXiv:2202.11409v3 [cs.CR], 25 February 2022. https://arxiv.org/pdf/2202.11409.pdf

9. Hao, X., Ren, W., Zheng, W., Zhu, T.: SCScan: a SVM-based scanning system for vulnerabilities in blockchain smart contracts. In: 2020 IEEE 19th International Conference on Trust, Security and Privacy in Computing and Communications (TrustCom), Guangzhou, China, pp. 1598–1605 (2020). https://doi.org/10.1109/TrustCom50675.2020.00221

10. Zeng, Q., et al.: EtherGIS: a vulnerability detection framework for Ethereum smart contracts based on graph learning features. In: 2022 IEEE 46th Annual Computers, Software, and Applications Conference (COMPSAC), Los Alamitos, CA, USA, pp. 1742–1749 (2022). https://doi.org/10.1109/COMPSAC54236.2022.00277

11. Momeni, P., Wang, Y., Samavi, R.: Machine learning model for smart contracts security analysis. In: IEEE Proceeding of PST 2019, pp. 1–6 (2019)

12. Ghaleb, A., Pattabiraman, K.: How effective are smart contract analysis tools? Evaluating smart contract static analysis tools using bug injection. arXiv:2005.11613v1 [cs.SE], 23 May 2020. https://arxiv.org/pdf/2005.11613.pdf

13. Durieux, T., Ferreira, J.F., Abreu, R., Cruz, P.: Empirical review of automated analysis tools ethereum smart contracts. arXiv:1910.10601v2 [cs.SE], 9 February 2020. https://arxiv.org/pdf/1910.10601.pdf

14. Luu, L., Chu, D.-H., Olickel, H., Saxena, P., Hobor, A.: Making smart contracts smarter. In: Proceedings of the 2016 ACM SIGSAC Conference on Computer and Communications Security, pp. 254–269 (2016)

15. Tsankov, P., Dan, A., Drachsler-Cohen, D., Gervais, A., Buenzli, F., Vechev, M.: Securify: practical security analysis of smart contracts. In: Proceedings of the 2018 ACM SIGSAC Conference on Computer and Communications Security, pp. 67–82 (2018)

16. Mueller, B.: Smashing Ethereum smart contracts for fun and real profit, HITB SECCONF Amsterdam (2018)

17. Feist, J., Grieco, G., Groce, A.: Slither: a static analysis framework for smart contracts. In: 2019 IEEE/ACM 2nd International Workshop on Emerging Trends in Software Engineering for Blockchain (WETSEB), pp. 8–15 (2019)

Effectiveness of Binary-Level CFI Techniques

Ruturaj K. Vaidya and Prasad A. Kulkarni$^{(\boxtimes)}$

University of Kansas, 2900 Bob Bilings PKWY H12, Lawrence, KS 66045, USA
{ruturajkvaidya,prasadk}@ku.edu

Abstract. Memory corruption is an important class of vulnerability that can be leveraged to craft control flow hijacking attacks. *Control Flow Integrity (CFI)* provides protection against such attacks. Application of type-based CFI policies requires information regarding the number and type of function arguments. Binary-level type recovery is inherently speculative, which motivates the need for an evaluation framework to assess the effectiveness of binary-level CFI techniques. In this work, we develop a novel and extensible framework to assess how the program analysis information we get from advanced binary analysis tools affects the efficacy of type-based CFI techniques. We introduce new and insightful metrics to quantitatively compare source independent CFI policies with their *ground truth* source aware counterparts. We leverage our framework to evaluate binary-level CFI policies implemented using program analysis information extracted from the IDA Pro binary analyzer and compared with the ground truth information obtained from the LLVM compiler.

1 Introduction

Software written in memory unsafe languages like C and C++ is vulnerable to *Code-Reuse Attacks (CRA)* such as return-into-libc (full function reuse attack) [4], ROP (Return Oriented Programming) [3,18] and COOP (Counterfeit Object-oriented Programming) [9,10,17]. *Control flow integrity (CFI)* [1] is a popular technique to prevent such control flow hijacking attacks. CFI aims to ensure that the control flow of the program stays within the legitimate targets desired by the programmer. Usually, this is achieved by computing the user intended control flow targets using a static analysis phase to insert security checks into the generated binary code. The inserted security checks monitor and enforce the control flow of the program to stay within the desired target locations at run-time.

Various CFI techniques have been proposed after the introduction of an exemplary CFI model by Abadi et al. [1]. CFI techniques could be source-code aware — implemented at source or compiler-level, or source-code independent — implemented at the binary level. Binary-level CFI techniques are necessary to secure *unprotected* and *untrusted* programs and third-party libraries that are typically shipped without their corresponding high-level source codes.

© The Author(s), under exclusive license to Springer Nature Switzerland AG 2024
M. Mosbah et al. (Eds.): FPS 2023, LNCS 14551, pp. 87–103, 2024.
https://doi.org/10.1007/978-3-031-57537-2_6

CFI techniques typically require the accurate recovery of function call-site and function signature information, including argument counts and all argument types. Lack of accurate program analysis information at the binary-level makes it extremely challenging to build a precise function call-graph for large binary software. In turn, the effectiveness of binary-level CFI techniques depend and suffer from the inaccuracies of the program information extracted by the adopted binary analysis framework. Over- or under-approximation of reachable call-targets by CFI techniques can result in false negatives (attacks go undetected) or false positives (correct control flow tagged), which can dent the usability of CFI.

Our goal is to study and quantify the correctness of binary-level CFI techniques and how they are impacted by the inaccuracies in program analysis information recovered by binary analyzers. We focus on *type-based* CFI techniques that use the number and type of arguments to match each call-site to the set of *potential* call-targets. Source-level CFI techniques have access to precise program and type information, and are therefore most likely to achieve their *design* objective. We use the output of each source-level CFI technique as the *ground truth* to assess the accuracy of the corresponding binary-level CFI technique.

In this work, we develop a novel framework, called *β-CFI*, to study and quantify the effectiveness of different binary-level CFI techniques. Our framework supports the integration of different source (compilers) based and binary-level analysis modules to gather program information required to model different CFI techniques, each at the source and binary levels. To validate our framework, we develop a source-level analysis module using the LLVM compiler [13] and a binary-level analysis module using the IDA Pro and Hex-Rays software reverse engineering (SRE) tools [8]. The analysis modules statically recover program information, including call-site and call-target argument counts, argument types, and the function return type. We also model four different CFI techniques that employ the analysis information gathered by the source/binary-level analysis modules to impose the call-target constraints.

Next, we introduce new and insightful metrics to quantitatively compare the effectiveness of CFI policies instituted at the binary level with the *ground truth* provided by their source-aware counterparts. Unlike most existing CFI metrics that only measure the *number* of call-targets reached without regards to their *correctness* compared to the ground truth set of call-targets [2,6,7,15,20,25], our approach provides a more correct metric for evaluating the accuracy of binary-level CFI techniques.

We make the following contributions in this paper:

- We develop a modular and extensible framework[1] along with a common language to compare the accuracy and effectiveness of binary-level type-based CFI techniques.
- We develop a mechanism to model multiple different type-based CFI techniques using program information obtained from different sources.

---

[1] Our framework is available online - https://github.com/Ruturaj4/B-CFI.

- We develop metrics to quantitatively measure the accuracy of binary-level CFI techniques compared to *ground truth* results obtained with access to the source code.
- We employ our framework, models, metrics and mechanisms to recover program information from IDA Pro binary analyzer, and LLVM compiler, and employ that information to quantitatively assess the accuracy of four binary-level CFI techniques compared to their source-level equivalents.

2 Background and Related Work

2.1 Control Flow Integrity (CFI)

Code-Reuse Attacks (CRA) [3,4,9,10,17,18] allow attackers to exploit spacial and temporal memory safety violations to alter the control flow of the program. CFI provides protection against such arbitrary control flow subversion. CFI techniques use static or dynamic analysis to compute the program control flow graph (CFG) and then check at run-time if the program execution follows the CFG computed in the previous analysis stage. Thus, CFI maintains program integrity by only allowing legitimate control transfers during execution.

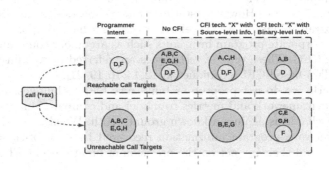

Fig. 1. High-level overview of CFI techniques

We use Fig. 1 to describe, at a high-level, how CFI techniques work and also to explain our goals in this work. When coding, the developers may intend the control-flow at each *indirect call-site* to only reach a few potential function *targets* during program execution. For instance, the programmer *intent* in our example (as illustrated in Fig. 1-(A)) is for the indirect call-site to only reach targets 'D' and 'F'. Unfortunately, this programmer intent is not explicitly encoded in the source-code, and is lost before it reaches the compiler. Without any CFI check, an attacker may be able to subvert the call-site to reach *any* reachable function target ('A', 'B', 'C', 'D', 'E', 'F', 'G', and 'H' in our example, Fig. 1-(B)).

Different CFI techniques use various *safe* approaches that constrict the set of spurious reachable targets, while ensuring that the technique does not inadvertently disallow any correct (but, unknown) programmer-intended targets. If a correct target is not in the set of reachable targets, then the CFI check may trigger a *false positive* alarm for correct program flow during execution. At the same time, if the set of reachable targets is overly broad, then the CFI technique may leave the program more vulnerable to attacks. In our example, the source-level CFI technique partitions the targets into reachable and unreachable sets, as illustrated in Fig. 1-(C). For the CFI policies that employ types to determine the set of "valid" targets, these results obtained from employing a program representation with perfect type information (like the source-code) presents the best case result they can achieve.

Unfortunately, program analysis information recovered by binary-level SRE tools may be imprecise, which can cause the *same* CFI algorithm to produce different and incorrect reachable and unreachable target function sets at the binary-level for each call-site (as illustrated in Fig. 1-(D)). Our goal in this work is simply to measure and study this imprecision in the output of binary-level CFI techniques as compared to their source-level counterparts.[2]

Abadi et al. introduced the idea of CFI by statically computing the CFG and restricting control flow of the program to the valid targets during runtime [1]. Since then, researchers have developed many CFI policies and algorithms that differ in their implementation, precision and cost. Several CFI approaches employ pointer analysis to construct the CFG that is needed by the algorithm [20,22,24,25]. However, static points-to-analysis is imprecise, especially for program binaries [5]. Therefore, researchers have proposed CFI techniques that incorporate program invariants such as argument count and types to construct the CFG. These type of techniques are referred to as Run-time Type Checking (RTC) based CFI techniques [5,12,14,16,19–21].

In this work, we do not propose or build new CFI techniques. Instead, we develop a new framework and metrics to model and compare binary-level RTC based CFI mechanisms against a known ground-truth. We also assess the accuracy of the relevant program information recovered by state-of-the-art binary analysis tools, and their impact on the precision of binary-level CFI policies.

2.2   CFI Security Policy Comparison Metrics

Researchers have developed several mechanisms and metrics to evaluate and compare the protection provided by different CFI policies. *Average Indirect target Reduction (AIR)* [25] measures the reduction of permitted call-targets. *AIA* [7] computes the average number of call-targets per function call. Similarly, *fAIR* [20] and *fAIA* [6] are forward-edge variations of the previous metrics. The *CTR (Call-Target Reduction)* metric provides absolute values (rather than

---

[2] It is important to realize that even if the binary-level CFI technique produces a more desirable outcome (for example, by allowing all programmer-intended targets and a smaller spurious set in the reachable set), it is still considered erroneous in this work, if it does not match the output of the corresponding source-level approach, since the technique did not function as algorithmically designed (due to imprecise analysis data), and any observed *"improvement"* is merely coincidental.

averaged results) of reachable call-targets at every indirect call-site [15]. Most of these metrics use a relative measure, such as reduction in the average number of reachable *targets* from each call-site, or reduction in the number potential gadgets, etc. to assess the accuracy and benefit of the CFI technique.

Burow et al. propose a metric called *QuantitativeSecurity* that computes the number of equivalence classes and the inverse of the size of the largest class, to quantify the security of CFI techniques [2]. Frassetto et al. develop the *BLOCK-Insulation* and *CFGInsulation* metrics to calculate the distance between a vulnerable instruction to system call at basic-block granularity [6].

None of these existing CFI metrics incorporate the notion of obtaining the actual accuracy of any CFI technique as compared to some known ground truth, and determining the false positive and false negative call-targets at each call-site. In this work, we show why such earlier CFI metrics are ill-suited for comparing the performance of binary-level CFI policies. We introduce new metrics that can quantitatively compare the accurate call-targets in each equivalence class identified by binary-level policy with that of call-targets recuperated in the corresponding equivalence class using a source aware ground truth policy.

2.3 CFI Frameworks

It is difficult to compare and assess the performance of different CFI policies as they use different settings, including compilers, operating systems and machines. Therefore, researchers have built detailed frameworks, mechanisms, and metrics to compare and assess CFI techniques uniformly.

Farkhani et al. develop a framework to analyze the ability of RTC CFI mechanisms, and compare them with a points-to analysis based CFI mechanism [5]. Li et al. introduce CScan — a framework to compute actual feasible targets using run-time checks and CBench — an extensive set of vulnerable programs to assess the effectiveness of CFI techniques [11]. *ConFIRM* [23] analytically compares various CFI policies in terms of compatibility issues in contrast to focusing on performance or security.

Our framework to evaluate binary-level CFI policies is inspired by a compiler-level CFI policy comparison framework, called LLVM-CFI [15]. This framework provides a LLVM-Clang based unified framework for statically modelling and systematically assessing various CFI techniques. LLVM-CFI leverages a link time optimization (*LTO*) pass in the LLVM compiler to impose constraints on invariants collected during compilation to implement CFI policies. The CFI policies in our current work also adhere to much of the formalization described by this earlier work. However, our goals, implementation machinery and metrics used differ considerably from LLVM-CFI.

The CFI policies in LLVM-CFI are modelled based on their idealized representation, which means that they do not consider the effect of loss in high-level information whilst modelling source insentient CFI techniques. In other words, the binary-level CFI policies in LLVM-CFI are established on the premise that the analysis primitives are all recovered correctly at the binary level. Instead, our goal in this work, which is to compare the precision of binary-level CFI policies,

92   R. K. Vaidya and P. A. Kulkarni

requires us to gather the necessary program information from both binary-level and source-level analysis tools.

None of these earlier CFI policy comparison frameworks and metrics attempt to study and assess how the loss of program information at the binary-level affects the efficacy of different binary-level CFI policies compared to some ground truth, which we do in this work. Furthermore, we also develop a new set of metrics that can more accurately determine the accuracy of binary-level CFI policies compared to a ground truth, which was not attempted by earlier CFI policy comparison frameworks.

3 Implementation

In this section we describe the design and implementation of the CFI policy comparison framework and the CFI models that we build and use for this work.

3.1 Design Overview

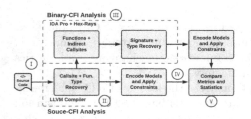

Fig. 2. Block Diagram of β-CFI

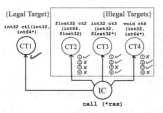

Fig. 3. Indirect call-site targeting functions in binary hardened with four different policies— ① TypeArmor, ② IFCC, ③ MCFI and ④ τCFI

In this paper, we introduce *β-CFI*—a binary level CFI comparison framework. To assess and analyze the precision of type-based binary-level CFI techniques, we design and construct an evaluator framework that is capable of comparing the results achieved by different CFI techniques at both the source-sentient and insentient levels. Figure 2 shows the high-level block diagram of our evaluation technique. The technique can be broadly classified into two stages. Firstly, relevant program analysis information is collected from both source-level (LLVM) and binary-level (IDA Pro) means and secondly, this information is fed into the CFI models, and the results are computed, compared and analyzed.

In further detail, our technique performs the following steps: ① First, the source code to be analyzed is compiled (using the LLVM compiler, in this work). ② During compilation, we collect various program analysis information, including function argument counts, and argument and function types at each call-site and at every call-target using a dynamically loadable *LLVM LTO* (Link Time Optimization) pass that we built for this work. This pass makes separate compilation of source files possible providing flexibility. These source-level analysis statistics are used to drive an idealized representation (or ground truth) of our type-based CFI policies. (III) The output binary is then employed for β-CFI statistics collection. In this work we leverage IDA Pro [8] — a popular reverse engineering framework to statically analyze the binaries and recuperate static analysis information, including indirect calls and program functions accompanied by their type signatures i.e. function return type, function argument counts and their types at each call-target and call-site. We also leverage Hex-Rays decompiler to refine the type information generated by IDA Pro. The advanced type inference in the decompiler assists us to model robust run-time type checking (RTC) policies at the binary level.

We invoke our LLVM LTO pass after full link time optimizations to ensure the accurate source to binary function matching. We do not consider any unmatched functions if they aren't identified correctly by IDA tool. Although we employ LLVM and IDA Pro for this work, our framework is modular and evaluators can use any other source- and binary-level static analysis tools to extract function and call-site related program analysis information.

(IV) After the recovery of these analysis primitives at both the source level and binary-level, type-based policy constraints are applied corresponding to each deployed CFI policy. At this stage, evaluators can select and encode any CFI policy of their choice by setting various type-based constraints. Thus, this extensible and convenient framework will enable analysts to implement and verify new type-based CFI policies at the binary level without doing repetitive compilation and analysis. To validate our framework, we implement and deploy four type-based policies (explained in details in 3.2) for evaluation. (V) Finally, the output of the CFI models using source-level and binary-level program information is compared and the final results are displayed to the evaluator.

3.2   Type-Based CFI Policies

In this section we describe the four type-based CFI policies we model by applying different type-based constraints. Some of these were also used and compared in the LLVM-CFI work [15]. Figure 3 displays an indirect call-site targeting four different functions in a binary hardened by modeling four different type-based CFI policies. The function shown on the far-left (CT1) is the only legal call-target intended to be called from indirect call (IC) instruction call (*rax). Besides, three other functions (CT2-CT4) are illegal call-targets and should ideally be unreachable during correct program execution. We assume that the attacker controls the value of register rax.

We now discuss constraints and type collisions imposed by the four CFI policies we employ. However, our technique is adaptable and evaluators can introduce and model other policies with various levels of type-based precision.

① **TypeArmor** [21] was originally implemented at the binary level by using coarse-grained type invariants. The policy considers the number of arguments without explicit types. At each call-site the call is allowed only if the number of arguments at the call-target are equal or less than that at the call-site (maximum up to six). Additionally, void and non-void functions are differentiated i.e. call-sites which expect a return value must only target functions with non-void return type. Note that such assumptions can not be made on the contrary, i.e. if a call-site doesn't expect a return value, then it can call void as well as non-void functions. This relaxed policy is practical at the binary level, as it is often difficult to infer whether the function is going to return a value or not. Thus, at the example call-site in Fig. 3, the TypeArmor CFI policy allows the `call (*rax)` instruction to reach `CT1`, `CT2` and `CT3` functions, which includes two illegal targets.

② **IFCC** [20] is implemented similar to the encoding explained in [15]. IFCC takes into account the argument and parameter counts, along with their basic types to match call-sites to call-targets. However, base pointers types are not considered, i.e. `void*` and `int*` are considered equivalent. Therefore, functions `CT3` and `CT4` in Fig. 3 are allowed (in addition to `CT1`). Return type is not taken into consideration. Note that the types are not over-approximated i.e. they are not considered as upper bound, but are matched according to the exact type.

③ **MCFI** [16] is a CFI policy that is stricter than IFCC in terms of how pointer types are recuperated. Pointer types such as `void*` and `int*` are considered distinct. Similar to IFCC, the number of parameters and their types are matched with call-site argument count and types. However, stricter types are taken into consideration. Thus, as seen in Fig. 3 only one target i.e. `CT4` is reachable with the stricter MCFI policy (in addition to `CT1`). Function return types are not considered, similar to IFCC.

④ τ**CFI** [14] considers argument and parameter types along with their counts. The types are contemplated based on the size of the registers $\{0,8,16,32,64\}$ prepared during the indirect call. According to x86-64 calling convention (System V ABI) the first 6 arguments are passed through registers during a function call. τCFI policy allows the call if 1) the number of arguments prepared at the call-site are more or equal to the number of parameters consumed at the call-target, 2) the return type recuperated at the call-site and the call-target is non-void and its size at the call-site is larger than that of the call-target return type; else, if return type recuperated at the call-site is void and then it can also call non-void functions, 3) the size of the argument types at call-site are greater than or equal to their matching arguments at call-targets. Thus, in our example displayed in Fig. 3, `CT3` is the only illegal target that is allowed to be reached from the indirect call-site.

4   Evaluation

4.1   Benchmarks

We evaluate our framework using *sixteen* C and C++ benchmarks from the SPEC 2006[3] integer and floating point suite. We leave out the remaining benchmarks

---

[3] https://www.spec.org/cpu2006/.

either because we didn't find any indirect call-sites in the optimized benchmark version (mcf, libquantum and lbm) or when the benchmarks use Fortran code.

Additionally, we include five popular and large real world applications for this study. Specifically, we performed our evaluation with (a) *Nginx* (v1.22.1 C), an open-source web server software[4], (b) *Node JS*[5] (v10.24.0 C/C++), an open-source, cross-platform JavaScript run-time environment, (c) *Apache Traffic server*[6] (v6.2.3 C/C++), an open-source forward and reverse proxy web server, (d) *postgresql*[7] (v12.0 C), an open-source relational database management framework, and the (e) Tor Browser[8] (v0.4.8.0-alpha-dev C), an open-source web browser focused on privacy and security. We obtained the most primary application binary from these benchmarks for our analysis.

Our benchmarks along with the total number of indirect call-sites and call-targets in each program are listed in Table 1. All the SPECint and SPECfloat benchmarks are presented together in their respective groups in this table (and in all later results).

4.2   Experimental Configuration

We design two benchmark configurations for this study.

I. **Ideal or Baseline Scenario:** For our first configuration, we keep the debugging symbols and compile the binary with optimizations ('-O3'). We refer to this configuration as the *baseline*. This *baseline* configuration can be considered as an idealized representation at the binary level where some source semantics in the form of debug symbols are available to guide the binary analysis frameworks.

II. **Practical Scenario:** For our second configuration, we strip the debugging symbols using 'strip --strip-debug'. This is a practical scenario for most COTS (Commercial off-the-shelf) binaries and presents a more challenging case for the binary analysis algorithms. All benchmarks are still optimized by '-O3'.

All experiments are performed on Fedora 34 operating system with x86-64 Intel Xeon processor. The LLVM/Clang version used is (v.12.0.0) to compile binaries and get the ground truth program information, and 64-bit version of *IDA Pro* (v7.5.2) is used to conduct binary analysis and extract the program information used by the binary-level CFI models.

---

[4] https://nginx.org/en/download.html.
[5] https://nodejs.org/en/download/current.
[6] https://archive.apache.org/dist/trafficserver/.
[7] https://www.postgresql.org/download/.
[8] https://www.torproject.org/download/.

Table 1. Inverse of Benchmark Properties

Benchmark	SPECint	SPECfp	nginx	postgresql	trafficserver	tor	node
call-targets	15594	2341	1237	11089	6886	5761	133496
call-sites	20304	1179	448	9367	8311	273	8239

4.3   Evaluation Metric

To compare and evaluate the *precision* of binary-level CFI policies with their source aware counterparts in terms of the *correct* reachable call-targets at each call-site, we introduce new metrics that calculate not only the number of targets reached (fewer the better), but also employ the known ground-truth targets information to check if there are any false positives or false negatives generated by the CFI policy under evaluation. Such a detailed evaluation of CFI policies is crucial, as mere call-target reduction results, as measured by most earlier CFI metrics, can not characterize the number of:

- true positives – illegal (unreachable) targets that are correctly marked by the CFI policy under evaluation,
- false positives – legal (reachable) targets in the ground truth, but are marked as illegal by the CFI policy under evaluation,
- true negatives – legal targets in the ground truth that are correctly marked by the CFI policy under evaluation, and
- false negatives – targets illegal in the ground truth that are incorrectly marked as legal by the CFI policy.

Thus, it is very important to know the exact targets reached, i.e. we not only need to check how many functions are reached using *Binary-CFI*, but also how many of these functions match the functions detected using our ground truth. We introduce new metrics named $RelativeCTR$ ($RelativeCTR_T$ and $RelativeCTR_F$) to check whether the actual targets reached when Binary-CFI policies are applied are in fact equivalent to the actual targets reached when Source-level CFI policies are applied. $RelativeCTR_T$ (higher the better) represents the number of call-targets that are accurately reached at a particular call-site using binary-CFI policy, compared to source-level CFI policy, and $RelativeCTR_F$ (lower the better) presents the call-targets that are incorrectly reached at a particular call-site using binary-level policy, compared to its source aware CFI policy counterpart.

Suppose that P is a program with total indirect call-sites IC and total reachable call-targets CT. Let IC_i be an indirect call-site in program P with number of reachable call-targets CT_i after applying the CFI constraints for source aware policy P_c and CT_i' be number of reachable call-targets after applying source independent policy P_c' at the same call-site. Then, $RelativeCTR_T$ and $RelativeCTR_F$ are defined as follows.

Definition 1. *$RelativeCTR_T$ is the ratio of the intersection of targets in Source-CFI (CT_i) and in Binary-CFI (CT_i') to the total number of actual targets in Source-CFI (CT_i) at an indirect call-site ICi.*

$$RelativeCTR_T \quad (R_T) = \sum_{i=1}^{n} (CT_i \cap CT_i')/CT_i$$

Definition 2. *RelativeCTR$_F$ is the ratio of the total number of call-targets in (CT$_i'$) reachable with Binary-CFI but not reachable with Source-CFI (CT$_i$) to the total number of targets in Binary-CFI (CT$_i'$) at an indirect call-site ICi.*

$$RelativeCTR_F \quad (R_F) = \sum_{i=1}^{n} (CT_i' \setminus CT_i)/CT_i'$$

We illustrate our new metrics using the hypothetical example from Fig. 1. This program has eight different functions 'A', 'B', 'C', 'D', 'E', 'F', 'G', and 'H'. For some indirect call-site IC_1 in the program, the set of reachable targets as identified by the source-level CFI policy (our ground truth) are 'A', 'C', 'D', 'F' and 'H' (CT_1, CT_3, CT_4, CT_6 and CT_8). However, the binary-level CFI policy under evaluation determines the reachable set of targets from the same call-site to be 'A', 'B' and 'D' (CT_1', CT_2' and CT_4'). Thus, with reference to the ground truth, 'B' is an unintended target, and 'C', 'F' and 'H' are correct targets that are missed. Therefore, the $RelativeCTR_T$ for this call-site is 2/5, which indicates the correctly detected, or true negative targets (and, correspondingly, also the false positive targets). $RelativeCTR_F$ is 1/3, which indicates the incorrectly detected or the false negative call-targets. Thus, a high $RelativeCTR_T$ indicates a high true negative (and low false positive) rate for the CFI technique, i.e., a low likelihood of throwing a fault when there is none. A high $RelativeCTR_F$ indicates a more relaxed CFI policy and a higher likelihood for the CFI technique to allow unsupported control flow paths that can lead to attacks.

In addition, since we target the same weakness in all previous CFI metrics, we use only one, the popular CTR metric [15], as representative of the category of metrics that only use the measure of reduction in the number of call-targets from each call-site to rate different CFI policies. The CTR metric depicts the absolute values of the number of call-targets accessible from a call-site after hardening with a particular CFI policy. The CTR metric is defined as follows.

$$CTR = \sum_{i=1}^{n} ct_i$$

where ct_i is number of call-targets reachable from an indirect call-site ic_i. A lower value of CTR implies a better CFI policy, as it ostensibly reduces the number of *extraneous* targets allowed from a call-site. In this paper, we highlight some important shortcomings of the CTR (and similar) metrics for our work. Specifically, such metrics do not fairly and accurately assess the precision of CFI policies compared to some known *ground truth*.

4.4   CFI Policy Comparison

We present and discuss our results in this section. We use our framework and models to collect the *RelativeCTR* and *CTR* numbers for all our benchmark programs. We use *Dwarf* symbols at every call-site to match the call-sites detected

Table 2. Mean *RelativeCTR* comparison results of our 4 CFI policies (*TypeArmor, IFCC, MCFI* and τcfi)

Benchmark	TypeArmor R_T (I)	R_F (I)	R_T (II)	R_F (II)	IFCC R_T (I)	R_F (I)	R_T (II)	R_F (II)	MCFI R_T (I)	R_F (I)	R_T (II)	R_F (II)	τCFI R_T (I)	R_F (I)	R_T (II)	R_F (II)
SPECint	0.93	0.24	0.92	0.25	0.26	0.45	0.22	0.48	0.14	0.65	0.13	0.66	0.74	0.27	0.75	0.27
SPECfp	0.91	0.13	0.87	0.28	0.49	0.44	0.29	0.53	0.40	0.51	0.19	0.67	0.89	0.16	0.71	0.28
nginx	0.92	0.03	0.91	0.19	0.68	0.30	0.35	0.37	0.47	0.43	0.24	0.72	0.89	0.03	0.67	0.12
postgresql	0.80	0.02	0.75	0.12	0.45	0.53	0.25	0.52	0.28	0.66	0.23	0.76	0.74	0.11	0.42	0.32
trafficserver	0.93	0.22	0.93	0.22	0.31	0.39	0.29	0.40	0.10	0.51	0.11	0.52	0.48	0.22	0.48	0.22
tor	0.96	0.12	0.64	0.29	0.70	0.26	0.18	0.51	0.49	0.32	0.14	0.76	0.75	0.10	0.31	0.22
node	0.99	0.05	0.95	0.24	0.74	0.17	0.31	0.38	0.64	0.22	0.28	0.51	0.92	0.16	0.69	0.38

Table 3. Mean *CTR* comparison results of our 4 CFI policies (*TypeArmor, IFCC, MCFI* and τcfi)

Benchmark	TypeArmor Source	Bin-I	Bin-II	IFCC Source	Bin-I	Bin-II	MCFI Source	Bin-I	Bin-II	τCFI Source	Bin-I	Bin-II
SPECint	3327.33	3966.70	3967.50	1608.22	606.83	591.66	1296.44	356.30	370.67	2105.19	2092.90	2088.97
SPECfp	308.05	307.51	333.59	101.71	78.05	52.72	86.55	48.11	28.00	167.72	155.00	120.70
nginx	506.06	487.85	570.47	277.97	201.50	153.71	130.45	69.33	142.92	366.34	357.17	366.55
postgresql	6637.11	5337.80	5515.54	1825.17	1233.95	1009.84	997.45	720.76	932.53	2415.92	2372.24	1585.11
trafficserver	3049.97	3882.86	3905.23	1866.46	809.56	754.68	1699.28	229.41	250.19	1622.12	990.37	991.23
tor	2896.82	3123.42	2578.18	923.81	730.51	365.42	470.58	385.08	330.14	1610.27	1231.44	786.90
node	70251.10	73847.82	89280.00	25418.30	23934.50	10240.00	17394.30	16165.50	8000.88	37759.30	37679.10	40666.90

during the source-level LLVM pass with the call-sites in the binary executable. We leverage the *llvm-symbolizer* tool to match *Dwarf* symbols with the address of the respective call-site in the binary. Note that the binary address to *Dwarf* mapping is one-to-many and thus we consider all the call-sites that appear in the binary for each source-level call-site.

We leverage our new *RelativeCTR* metrics to show correctly and incorrectly reachable call-targets at each call-site. Table 2 shows the *RelativeCTR* metrics with "Mean" values for our benchmarks in both our binary configurations **I** and **II**. The results in Table 2 allow us to make some important observations that would be missed by earlier CFI comparison metrics that use a reduction in the number of reachable targets from each call-site as the only measure to evaluate the effectiveness of CFI techniques [2,6,7,15,20,25].

Table 3 presents the results using the CTR metric for 4 CFI policies - ① TypeArmor, ② IFCC, ③ MCFI and ④ τCFI, and for our benchmark set when using the analysis information from LLVM (*Source-CFI*), and our two binary configurations, *Binary-CFI* (**I**) and *Binary-CFI* (**II**), respectively. The CTR metrics in Table 3 present the absolute values of reachable targets.

We employ the *RelativeCTR* and *CTR* results, presented in Tables 2 and 3, respectively to make several observations. Of the four CFI policies modelled in this work, TypeArmor is the most *permissive*, since it only considers argument counts and discards argument type information. By contrast, MCFI is most *strict* as it considers both basic types and mature pointer types. Accordingly, we can see higher CTR numbers across the board for TypeArmor and relatively lower CTR numbers for MCFI, which confirms this property about the CFI policies.

For this work though, it is more pertinent to compare the binary-level CFI CTR numbers with the corresponding Source-CFI numbers to assess the accuracy of CFI methods at the binary-level (with Source-CFI acting as ground truth for each policy). When using the CTR metric, the difference between the binary and source-level numbers indicates the potential error in the binary-level CFI models. We find that, **the binary-level CTR numbers differ significantly from the source-level CTR metrics for all our CFI models. Besides, this difference is greater for the more restrictive CFI policies.** Thus, CFI policies, such as MCFI and IFCC, that rely on more precise program data type information appear to be more erroneous as compared to the simpler CFI models, like TypeArmor and τCFI. This is an intuitive result as it indicates that errors in correctly reconstructing the type information at the binary level negatively impacts the algorithms employing such data during their computations.

While this observation derived with the CTR metric appears to be correct, a deeper analysis reveals critical issues and misleading outcomes. For instance, the results in Table 3 also show that the Binary-CFI CTR ratios are often tighter (which is better, according to the CTR metric) than the Source-CFI numbers. We find that in 3 of the 7 benchmark categories with TypeArmor, and in all of the 7 benchmark categories with IFCC, MCFI, and τCFI, the number of *mean* reachable targets from each call-site is smaller with Binary-CFI (**I**) compared with the Source-CFI numbers. This result with the CTR metric is confusing since it suggests that the binary-level techniques achieve better effectiveness with fewer extraneous call-targets compared to the source-level techniques. Likewise, in many cases, especially for the stricter CFI policies, we can observe that the CTR numbers are tighter with the *stripped* benchmarks in the Binary-CFI (**II**) configuration, compared with the Binary-CFI (**I**) configuration, which is again a confusing and likely misleading outcome.

Results with our new *RelativeCTR* metric in Table 2 can help resolve this confusion caused when looking solely at the CTR numbers in Table 3. Thus, we find that the tighter CTR numbers with the binary-level CFI models are not a result of only eliminating the extraneous or false negative call-target edges for each call-site. Rather, the lack of precise program analysis information at the binary-level causes the CFI models to produce significant numbers of *false positive* (indicated by $RelativeCTR_T$) and *false negative* (indicated by $RelativeCTR_F$) edges. Thus, we conclude that **all CFI models for the binary configurations display high error rates that is not captured by the existing metrics used to measure the performance of CFI policies, like CTR.**

We also observe that the *Mean RelativeCTR_T* values are significantly lower for all benchmark categories with the stricter MCFI and IFCC CFI policies compared to TypeArmor and τCFI. Likewise, the *Mean RelativeCTR_F* values are much higher for MCFI and IFCC compared to TypeArmor and τCFI. While this is not a particularly surprising result in hindsight, the extent of the observed error is quite staggering. Thus, we find that the *mean* number of *correct* or *true negative* ($RelativeCTR_T$) edges recovered by the MCFI policy even in the Binary config. **I** (with debug symbols available) drops to as low as 0.10 and 0.14 for the `trafficserver` and SPECint benchmark categories, respectively, and with less than 50% of the *true negative* edges recovered for all but one benchmark suite. Likewise, the number of *incorrect* or *false negative* ($RelativeCTR_F$) edges recovered is as high as 0.66 and 0.65 with the MCFI policy in the Binary config. **I** for benchmark suites `postgresql` and SPECint, respectively. It is also interesting to note that binary-level SRE tools struggle to recover precise program analysis information even for binaries with debug symbol information available, resulting in poor performance by CFI models employing such information. This level of imprecision by binary-level CFI techniques is not something that has been observed or reported by earlier works that used simple metrics like the CTR. Thus, we conclude that, **binary-level CFI models, like MCFI and IFCC, that rely on more precise program analysis information are significantly more erroneous, compared to the simpler CFI models, like TypeArmor and τCFI.**

From Fig. 2 we can also observe that in almost every case, the $RelativeCTR_T$ values are lower, while the $RelativeCTR_F$ values are higher for benchmarks that have been stripped of debug symbols (binary config. **II**) compared to programs with debug information intact (config. **I**). Thus, it is clear that the greater imprecision in static analysis information that is recovered by SRE tools for stripped binaries results in degrading the performance for security and optimization algorithms that rely on such data. While this is also an expected and intuitive result, there has never previously been an attempt or a mechanism to observe, measure, and report the amount of error in CFI policies. If anything, it is interesting to note that the magnitude of error displayed by binary-level CFI policies in config. **II** programs, with symbols stripped, is not very large in several cases, compared to the inherent error already present in CFI models in config. **I**. We even find that in a few cases, like the *mean* $RelativeCTR_T$ for `trafficserver` with the MCFI policy, and the *mean* $RelativeCTR_F$ for `postgresql` with the IFCC policy, stripped benchmarks produce marginally better performance compared with unstripped benchmarks. Overall, we can conclude that **binary-level CFI policies produce significantly more erroneous results for benchmarks that are *stripped* of debugging symbols, compared to binaries that retain their debug symbols information.**

4.5 On the Accuracy of Program Analysis Information

Our results demonstrate that all the binary-level CFI policies modelled in this work show high levels of inaccuracy. This inaccuracy may be manifested by the CFI policies allowing incorrect control flow transfers while tagging correct control flow transfers as erroneous at run-time. The limitations in binary-level CFI models are caused by the imprecision in the extracted program analysis information from binaries by the SRE tools. Therefore, we further investigated the causes of inaccuracies of the relevant program analysis information collected by advanced SRE tools (IDA Pro, in this case). We present some interesting observations from this analysis in this section.

We observe that state-of-the-art SRE tools can accurately detect *the number of* call-site (89% in **I** and 88% in **II**) and function argument counts (95% in **I** and 85% in **II**) in most cases. Interesting is the observation that the lack of symbol information (in **II**) does not significantly affect the accuracy of argument count detection. This high accuracy is reflected in the relatively high $RelativeCTR_T$ and low $RelativeCTR_F$ numbers for most benchmark suites in Table 2.

We discover that the accuracy of preliminary type detection at call-sites and functions is 62% and 89% respectively in setting **I**. But the accuracy decreases significantly (44% and 45% respectively) in **II**. Likewise, the detection accuracy of base pointer types is around 35% and 84% at call-site and call-targets respectively in setting **I**, but the decreases to about 9% and 5% in setting **II**. With some manual analysis with the Nginx benchmark, we found that the mischaracterization of the struct* type as int64 by the binary analysis tool is one important reason for the high error rate. The poor preliminary and pointer type detection by the SRE tools, especially with config. **II**, likely results in the high error rates witnessed in the MCFI and IFCC CFI policies at the binary level.

5   Future Work and Conclusion

Our goal in this work was to explore and quantify the precision of binary-level CFI techniques, and study how that precision is impacted by the inaccuracies in the program analysis information recovered by modern SRE tools. We developed a comprehensive infrastructure, a thorough mechanism, and new metrics to achieve this goal. Our modular framework can model and evaluate different binary-level type-based CFI policies by comparing their outcomes with their source-based counterparts. We demonstrated our framework and reported results for four binary-level CFI policies. The results with our novel mechanism and metrics highlight the unresolved challenges for modern SRE tools in correctly extracting the relevant program information, and their potentially staggering impact on the precision of binary-level CFI techniques that use such data.

There are several avenues for future work. We only study type-based CFI policies in this work. In the future we will augment our current target set analysis by using advanced type propagation and pointer analysis to extend this work to other CFI mechanisms. Likewise, the *false positive* and *false negative* numbers for the evaluated binary-level CFI policies in this work report the *incorrect* call-target edges according to the CFI algorithm. In the future we will develop experiments and metrics to understand how these false edges actually cause a legal program execution to fail or increase program vulnerability at run-time.

References

1. Abadi, M., Budiu, M., Erlingsson, U., Ligatti, J.: Control-flow integrity. In: Proceedings of the 12th ACM Conference on Computer and Communications Security (CCS 2005). Association for Computing Machinery, New York (2005)
2. Burow, N., et al.: Control-flow integrity: precision, security, and performance. ACM Comput. Surv. **50**(1), 1–33 (2017)
3. Checkoway, S., Davi, L., Dmitrienko, A., Sadeghi, A.R., Shacham, H., Winandy, M.: Return-oriented programming without returns. In: Proceedings of the 17th ACM Conference on Computer and Communications Security (CCS 2010), pp. 559-572. Association for Computing Machinery, New York (2010)
4. Designer, S.: Getting around non-executable stack (and fix) (1997). http://ouah.bsdjeunz.org/solarretlibc.html
5. Farkhani, R.M., Jafari, S., Arshad, S., Robertson, W., Kirda, E., Okhravi, H.: On the effectiveness of type-based control flow integrity. In: Proceedings of the 34th Annual Computer Security Applications Conference (ACSAC 2018), pp. 28–39. Association for Computing Machinery, New York (2018)
6. Frassetto, T., Jauernig, P., Koisser, D., Sadeghi, A.R.: Cfinsight: a comprehensive metric for CFI policies. In: 29th Annual Network and Distributed System Security Symposium (NDSS) (2022)
7. Ge, X., Talele, N., Payer, M., Jaeger, T.: Fine-grained control-flow integrity for kernel software. In: 2016 IEEE European Symposium on Security and Privacy (EuroS&P), pp. 179–194 (2016)
8. hexrays. Interactive Disassembler (IDA) (2022). https://hex-rays.com/ida-pro/
9. Lan, B., Li, Y., Sun, H., Su, C., Liu, Y., Zeng, Q.: Loop-oriented programming: a new code reuse attack to bypass modern defenses. In: 2015 IEEE Trustcom/BigDataSE/ISPA, vol. 1, pp. 190–197 (2015)
10. Lettner, J., et al.: Subversive-C: abusing and protecting dynamic message dispatch. In: 2016 USENIX Annual Technical Conference (USENIX ATC 16), pp. 209–221. USENIX Association, Denver (2016)
11. Li, Y., Wang, M., Zhang, C., Chen, X., Yang, S., Liu, Y.: Finding cracks in shields: on the security of control flow integrity mechanisms. In: Proceedings of the 2020 ACM SIGSAC Conference on Computer and Communications Security (CCS 2020). Association for Computing Machinery, New York (2020)
12. LLVM. Clang (2022). https://clang.llvm.org/docs/controlflowintegrity.html
13. LLVM. The LLVM Compiler Infrastructure (2023). https://llvm.org
14. Muntean, P., Fischer, M., Tan, G., Lin, Z., Grossklags, J., Eckert, C.: τ-CFI: type-assisted control flow integrity for x86-64 binaries. In: Bailey, M., Holz, T., Stamatogiannakis, M., Ioannidis, S. (eds.) Research in Attacks, Intrusions, and Defenses, pp. 423–444. Springer, Cham (2018). https://doi.org/10.1007/978-3-030-00470-5_20
15. Muntean, P., Neumayer, M., Lin, Z., Tan, G., Grossklags, J., Eckert, C.: Analyzing control flow integrity with LLVM-CFI. In: Proceedings of the 35th Annual Computer Security Applications Conference (ACSAC 2019), pp. 584–597. Association for Computing Machinery, New York (2019)
16. Niu, B., Tan, G.: Modular control-flow integrity. In: PLDI 2014. Association for Computing Machinery, New York (2014)
17. Schuster, F., Tendyck, T., Liebchen, C., Davi, L., Sadeghi, A.R., Holz, T.: Counterfeit object-oriented programming: on the difficulty of preventing code reuse attacks in c++ applications. In: 2015 IEEE Symposium on Security and Privacy, pp. 745–762 (2015)

18. Shacham, H.: The geometry of innocent flesh on the bone: return-into-LIBC without function calls (on the x86). In: Proceedings of the 14th ACM Conference on Computer and Communications Security (CCS 2007), pp. 552–561 (2007)
19. Team, P.: Rap: rip rop. In: Hackers 2 Hackers Conference (H2HC) (2015)
20. Tice, C., et al.: Enforcing forward-edge control-flow integrity in GCC & LLVM. In: Proceedings of the 23rd USENIX Conference on Security Symposium (SEC 2014), pp. 941–955. USENIX Association, USA (2014)
21. van der Veen, V., et al.: A tough call: mitigating advanced code-reuse attacks at the binary level. In: 2016 IEEE Symposium on Security and Privacy (SP), pp. 934–953 (2016)
22. Wang, M., Yin, H., Bhaskar, A.V., Su, P., Feng, D.: Binary code continent: finer-grained control flow integrity for stripped binaries. In: Proceedings of the 31st Annual Computer Security Applications Conference (ACSAC 2015), pp. 331–340. Association for Computing Machinery, New York (2015)
23. Xu, X., Ghaffarinia, M., Wang, W., Hamlen, K.W., Lin, Z.: Confirm: evaluating compatibility and relevance of control-flow integrity protections for modern software. In: Proceedings of the 28th USENIX Conference on Security Symposium (SEC 2019), pp. 1805–1821. USENIX Association, USA (2019)
24. Zhang, C., et al.: Practical control flow integrity and randomization for binary executables. In: 2013 IEEE Symposium on Security and Privacy, pp. 559–573 (2013)
25. Zhang, M., Sekar, R.: Control flow integrity for cots binaries. In: Proceedings of the 22nd USENIX Conference on Security (SEC 2013). USENIX Association, USA (2013)

A Small World–Privacy Preserving IoT Device-Type Fingerprinting with Small Datasets

Maxwel Bar-on[1], Bruhadeshwar Bezawada[2]([✉]), Indrakshi Ray[1], and Indrajit Ray[1]

[1] Computer Science and Engineering Department, Colorado State University, Fort Collins, CO 80526, USA
{Maxwel.Bar-on,Indrakshi.Ray,Indrajit.Ray}@colostate.edu
[2] Mathematics and Computer Science Department, Southern Arkansas University, Magnolia, AR 71753, USA
bbezawada@saumag.edu

Abstract. Internet-of-Things (IoT) device-type fingerprinting is the process of identification of the specific type of an IoT device based on its characteristics, such as network behavior. Such fingerprinting can be used to detect anomalous behavior of the device, or even predict its behavior should it get compromised. The typical approach to *fingerprint* an IoT device-type is by collecting a significant number of short network trace samples from these devices when it performs various activities and use machine learning on these samples to construct the fingerprint. There are several challenges to this approach. The first challenge is identifying the exact set of packets that correspond to the observed device-type behavior when it is performing some activity. The second challenge is that a single organization may not have enough data corresponding to all possible activities of the IoT device. We propose techniques to overcome the above mentioned challenges. First, to enhance device-type fingerprinting from small data sets, we designed a sliding-window based packet analysis behavioral model that provides improved data coverage associated with the activities of the tasks. Second, to get a model of the network behavior for the different activities of IoT devices deployed at various organizations, we use distributed deep-learning model so as to protect the privacy and confidentiality of the data. Finally, we alleviate the issue of data shortage by supplementing the training data with synthetic data generated using an Adversarial Autoencoder (AAE) neural network. We evaluated our approach using three different sets of experiments using a small set of representative devices. We estimate the best sliding window size for modeling device behavior by comparing the distributed learning performance over a range of window sizes. For our distributed approach, we achieve fingerprinting accuracy in the range of 94–99%, which is an improvement over the centralized approach for the same data sets and experiments. We demonstrate accuracy of 97%, on-par with state-of-the-art fingerprinting approaches, when using synthetic training data generated by our AAE. We note that, this is the first such method of fingerprinting device-types in a collaborative privacy preserving manner while alleviating small data sets.

© The Author(s), under exclusive license to Springer Nature Switzerland AG 2024
M. Mosbah et al. (Eds.): FPS 2023, LNCS 14551, pp. 104–122, 2024.
https://doi.org/10.1007/978-3-031-57537-2_7

Keywords: Device-type Fingerprinting · Internet-of-Things · Privacy Preserving · Machine Learning · Collaborative Learning

1 Introduction

1.1 Motivation

Internet-of-Things (IoT) now has a default presence in home and organizational networks where they provide a wide range of services. A majority of IoT devices are plug-and-play, and any user can connect an IoT device to an existing network. However, an insecure or incorrectly configured IoT device is a significant security risk as these devices have proven [1] to be easy targets for attackers. Therefore, a network administrator needs to correctly identify the IoT device-types and enforce the necessary security controls to prevent and detect attacks.

The traditional device-type identification approach is to create a digital *fingerprint* from the network data generated by an IoT device and applying machine or deep learning techniques. Therein lies the major shortcoming of this approach, for a given timing window of packet capture, some devices generate a small amount of data while others generate larger volume of data making generalized analysis difficult. Therefore, a critical challenge in IoT device-type fingerprinting is to generate an accurate fingerprint even with a limited amount of data.

1.2 System Model and Assumptions

Our system model consists of a network of IoT devices whose network traffic can be captured by a network analyst. We assume the capability of capturing all kinds of traffic such as device-to-device, device to the Internet and from the Internet to a device. We do not make any assumptions on nature of the payload, which may be encrypted, compressed, binary or plain-text.

1.3 Problem Statement

The problem of device-type fingerprinting is to identify the device-type of an unknown IoT device based on the network traffic observed from the device. Let, $T = \{t_1, t_2, \cdots, t_n\}$ be the set of traffic traces collected from a known device-type D where each trace is a group of one or more network packets of fixed size and indicative of different behavioral features of the device. The goal is to build a machine learning model $M(T)$ that will output $True$ when tested on a sample trace T of the same device-type D, and output $False$ when tested on a sample trace of some other device-type. Ideally, the selected traffic-traces should encompass all possible behaviors of the device to enable a machine learning model to accurately identify the device regardless of the sample of traffic-trace being tested. However, it may not be possible or practical for one single observer to collect all possible network traces of a given device-type. Therefore, we assume that several entities are independently collecting sufficient number of traces from the device-type.

Now, the problem statement is as follows: to build a machine-learning model for fingerprinting IoT device-types using traces collected by diverse entities. Let $(D, P, T) = \{(P_1, T_1), (P_2, T_2), \cdots, (P_n, T_n)\}$ denote the collection of traces $T = \{T_1, T_2, \cdots, T_n\}$ of device-type D by a collection of parties $P = \{P_1, P_2, \cdots, P_n\}$ where P_i collects the packets in T_i and does not share with any other party. From these traces, the parties collaborate to build a single machine learning model $M(T)$ for accurate IoT device-type fingerprinting.

1.4   Limitations of Prior Art

Prior solutions [2–14] have one or both of the following limitations:

- *Identifying IoT Device-type Behavior.* For a network analyst, it is difficult to accurately identify the boundaries of the behavior of the IoT device-type as this requires a significant amount of data that encompasses the entire set of behaviors of the device. In prior art, analysts spent considerable time with the set of devices at their disposal to extract such behaviors, but it may not be practically possible for an independent analyst to cover all behaviors of the device.
- *Unknown Devices and Privacy of Data.* In prior art, if a new device is introduced into the network, the machine learning models need to be trained again, which is a significant effort and overhead. To avoid this, one may try to obtain data of unknown devices from other networks, but due to the privacy concerns this is difficult in practice.

In our work, we attempt to address the identified shortcomings of prior art and provide an accurate device-type fingerprinting model.

1.5   Overview of Proposed Approach

First, to solve the problem of small data sets, we make the best possible use of the collected device data with help of a sliding window packet analysis method. Further, we employ AAEs to generate synthetic data to improve the fingerprinting performance. We chose the AAE for our purpose, as opposed to a Generative Adversarial Networks (GANs), due to the limited volume of available data and the nature of our dataset. AAEs are better at handling heterogeneous data and require less training samples to produce high-quality synthetic data. In our experiments with synthetic data, 10% of samples in the training sets were generated by our AAE.

Second, to learn about unknown behaviors of devices and also, possibly unknown devices, we use a collaborative machine learning model where multiple parties train their local learning models using privately collected data and share the trained parameters using an aggregation algorithm. The end result is that the local machine learning models of individual parties are trained on the combined data of all the parties without any exchange of the actual data. The major advantage of the distributed deep learning model is that an individual party will be able to fingerprint unknown device-types without having trained on that device-type data.

Finally, we performed three major sets of experiments to validate our approach. In the first set of experiments, we compared the performance of the distributed learning model over a range of window sizes to estimate the window size which is optimal for modeling device behavior. We found that a window size of 10 packets gives the best performance with an average accuracy of 97%. In the second set of experiments, we tested the sliding window protocol using centralized and distributed learning models. Our results show that the distributed learning model performs on par and better when compared with the centralized learning models with an accuracy range of 94–99% in testing. In the third set of experiments, we tested the distributed learning model using real and mixed data sets where the mixed data sets contain 10% of synthetic data from the AAE. We found that the synthetic data did not degrade the model performance and achieved a similar range of 94–99% accuracy.

1.6   Key Contributions

First contribution is that, we describe an approach to generate machine learning models in a *privacy preserving* manner from small data sets. Second contribution, is the proof-of-concept usage of synthetic data for generating fingerprints of IoT devices, which are of similar quality to the fingerprints generated from real data. Third contribution is a comprehensive experimental validation of our fingerprinting approach. Here we show that our approach achieves a minimum-maximum true-positive rate (TPR) for fingerprinting IoT devices of 92%–99%, respectively, with a mean TPR of 95%, which is the performance of state-of-the-art centralized solutions.

Organization. In Sect. 2, we give an overview of related literature on IoT device-type identification and fingerprinting work. In Sect. 3, we give the detailed outline of our IoT device-type behavioral model using the sliding window approach, the feature engineering for accurate device-type fingerprinting and the privacy preserving deep learning model for collaborative fingerprinting. In Sect. 4, we describe the adversarial auto-encoder design for generating synthetic data. In Sect. 5, we describe our experimental evaluation and show the results of our fingerprinting approach. We summarize our work in Sect. 6 and outline important future challenges.

2   Related Work

2.1   IoT Device-Type Fingerprinting

Device-type fingerprinting has received considerable attention from the research community. General device fingerprinting [15–17] explore several techniques ranging from packet header features to physical features such as clock-skews. Wireless device fingerprinting techniques have been discussed in [10–14]. These works explore device-type identification by exploiting the implementation differences of a common protocol such session initiation protocol (SIP), across similar devices. Physical layer based device fingerprinting has received considerable attention [18–22] where the focus is on analyzing the physical aspects of devices to fingerprint them. All these prior works focus on general wireless devices and their applicability to IoT devices is an open question.

Vladimir et al. [18] developed a radiometric approach based on imperfections in analog components for fingerprinting network interface cards (NICs). Such variations result in imperfect emissions when compared with the theoretical emissions and manifest in the modulation of the transmitted signals of the device. However, this work relies on the availability of link-layer frames from the given device, which may not be possible for IoT devices as they are spread over an area and are interconnected via different switches and routers.

François et al. [12,23] describe a protocol grammar based approach for fingerprinting. They characterize a device based on the set of messages transmitted. A message is represented using the protocol grammar syntax. To classify a given device, the messages emitted by the device are compared with syntactic trees of the stored fingerprints and depending on a similarity metric, the device label is assigned. However, this approach is again specific to protocols that are well known and whose grammar rules are available.

Gao et al. [24] develop a wavelet analysis technique to fingerprint wireless access points based on frame inter-arrival time deltas. The approach does not apply to IoT devices as these devices are usually end-points and do not forward data to other devices.

Radhakrishnan et al. [20] described a technique for device-type identification on general purpose devices like smartphones, laptops and tablet PCs using the inter-arrival times of different packets to extract features specific to a particular application, such as Skype. However, most IoT devices do not generate much traffic and obtaining such statistics will involve considerable time and effort.

Franklin et al. [10] describe a passive fingerprinting method for identifying the different types of 802.11 wireless device driver implementations on clients. The authors explore the statistical relationship of the active channel scanning strategy in a particular device driver implementation. This technique is useful for identifying the type of device driver implementation but not for the type of device.

In the IoT fingerprinting problem space, IoTSentinel by Miettinen et al. [25] and IoTScanner by Siby et al. [26] are the currently known solution frameworks. Miettinen et al. [25] describes IoTSentinel, a framework for device fingerprinting and securing IoT networks. It focuses on device-type identification at the time of device registration into a network. This approach uses packet header based features to identify a particular device-type and applies machine learning models to perform the fingerprinting. One shortcoming of this work is that it is susceptible to packet header spoofing. Our approach provides better accuracy and stronger security. IoTSentinel reports a mean identification rate of 50–100%, whereas our approach reports a mean identification rate of 93–99%.

Siby et al. describe IoTScanner [26], an architecture that passively observes network traffic at the link layer, and analyzes this traffic using frame header information during specific observation time windows. This work is more concerned with discerning the distinct devices and their presence based on the traffic patterns observed during the traffic capture time window. A shortcoming of this approach is that two identical device-types could be classified as two different device-types due to the variations in traffic generated during the traffic capture time window. This approach is useful for network mapping at a high level, but performing this analysis periodically can be cumbersome. In [27], Bezawada *et al.* presented a centralized machine learning based model for fingerprinting IoT devices. They experimented with 23 different device-types and showed that the fingerprinting model was 99% accurate for identifying a majority of the device-types. We select this model for this work as it has a small number of features.

2.2 Privacy Preserving Deep Learning For Fingerprinting

The collaborative privacy preserving deep learning approach was described by Shokri *et al.* [28] and explored in depth by others [29–36]. The process considers a group of N-participants in the training process and a global server that maintains the final machine learning model and serves as a point of dissemination for the necessary information. During local training, each participant trains the neural network on its own private data using an optimization algorithm, such as Stochastic Gradient Descent (SGD). Once the training of the model begins, each client maintains a list of local parameters, *i.e.*, weight-gradients and bias-gradients. At the end of each training epoch, each participant selects exactly Θ_u most significant values from each layer, which contribute more towards the gradient descent, and shares them with the global parameter server.

To date, there is one recently published paper that focuses on federated learning for IoT (Fl4IoT) [37]. The work focuses on identifying unknown devices in the network. The first step of their approach is to use a clustering method to generate vector fingerprints, *i.e.*, short representation of a device, using an unsupervised clustering approach. Then, using supervised learning, they use these fingerprints to identify the presence of unauthorized devices in the network. Their work has similarities and dissimilarities with our work. The similarity is that both works attempt to fingerprint devices for the purposes of security. The dissimilarity is that their work focuses on identifying unauthorized devices based on a set of fingerprints identified in the given network whereas our work focuses on generalizing the fingerprint representation and can be used in unknown networks where we have not collected any data from the IoT devices. Importantly, our work focuses on using small data sets and a small number of features, making it simple to implement and deploy.

3 Device-Type Behavioral Model

In this section, we describe our behavioral model for fingerprinting IoT devices and the pertinent features.

3.1   Sliding Window Analysis for Behavior Coverage

We focus on designing the fingerprint of an IoT device-type based on the set of observable network behaviors of the device as we intend that the fingerprints are used by the network administrator for enforcing the necessary security policies. IoT devices typically provide specific services such as video camera monitoring the premises and sending the data feed to a network operator. A specific feature and/or service of an IoT device-type is obtained by sending a network command to the device. Therefore, a specific network behavior, b_i of an IoT device may be quantified by capturing the network packet trace t_i generated during such an interaction with the IoT device and extracting useful features. However, the network analyst performing the fingerprinting might not be able to identify the exact boundaries, starting and ending, of the packet trace t_i that corresponds to the specific behavior, b_i. One plausible reason is that there may be other control traffic from the IoT device that is being regularly transmitted regardless of the service specific related traffic of the IoT device.

To address this issue, we use a *sliding window* mechanism to extract the features of the network behavior where the term *window* refers to a fixed length sequence of captured packets. The intuition is that as we slide the window over a sequence of the captured network packets, at some point, the exact set of packets that correspond to the behavior will be *covered*. Note that there will still be other unrelated packets within the correct behavioral window, but that is unavoidable in practice.

We illustrate this in Fig. 1, where we consider a network trace of n packets $Pi, \cdots, P_{n+i}$ as the first *window* of behavior under the assumption that a device behavior can be accurately modeled within n packets. The choice of n is subject to practical considerations and complexity of the device. The next window is given by the set of packets $P_{i+1}, \cdots, P_{i+n+1}$, *i.e.*, the next set of n packets starting from the 2nd packet of the first window. Therefore, we do not miss any sequence of n packets, one of which is the most probable candidate covering the specific device-type behavior. Now, the challenge is to define the exact value of n. In our work, we have used the existing experimental data of the IoT device-types to estimate this number and set it to 10. This may not be true for all devices; however, because of the tight coupling of windows, this is a reasonably good estimate of n. Finally, it is important to note that the size of the window,

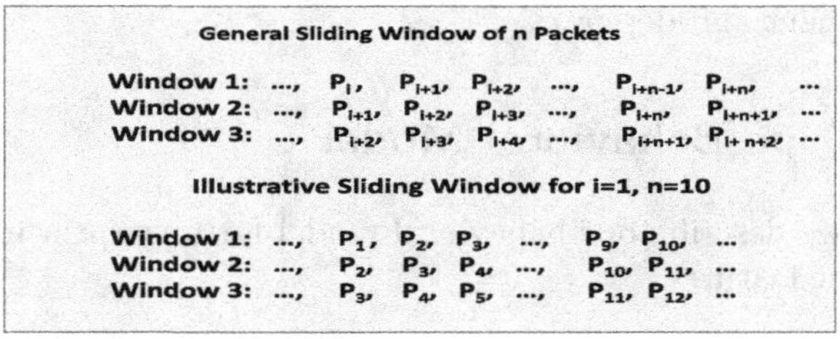

General Sliding Window of n Packets

Window 1: ..., P_i, P_{i+1}, P_{i+2}, ..., P_{i+n-1}, P_{i+n}, ...
Window 2: ..., P_{i+1}, P_{i+2}, P_{i+3}, ..., P_{i+n}, P_{i+n+1}, ...
Window 3: ..., P_{i+2}, P_{i+3}, P_{i+4}, ..., P_{i+n+1}, P_{i+n+2}, ...

Illustrative Sliding Window for i=1, n=10

Window 1: ..., P_1, P_2, P_3, ..., P_9, P_{10}, ...
Window 2: ..., P_2, P_3, P_4, ..., P_{10}, P_{11}, ...
Window 3: ..., P_3, P_4, P_5, ..., P_{11}, P_{12}, ...

Fig. 1. Sliding window coverage of a specific device-type behavior

n, represents the minimum number of packets that need to be observed from an IoT device-type to verify its registered fingerprint.

3.2 Network Traffic Features of Interest

Now, given a window of packets, the next important step is to extract the network traffic features of interest. Prior research work [4–9,27] has identified various features of interest to fingerprint IoT device-types. We categorize such features into two specific types: protocol and behavioral.

Protocol specific features are used to identify the presence of a particular protocol in a given packet header. These features may only be partially specific to a particular device-type. Sample protocol specific features are: presence of TCP, UDP, HTTPS, HTTP, IPv6, ICMP, and DHCP. These are all binary features, *i.e.*, if the protocol appears in the packet header, the feature is set to 1 otherwise it is set to 0.

Behavior specific features are used to quantify the nature of data or connections within a given window of packets. For instance, the payload lengths of small IoT device-types like smart lights could be considerably different from the payload lengths of a large IoT device-types such as video cameras. Furthermore, some device-types make many connections to neighboring devices while some device-types maintain silence and only communicate when requested. These are behavior specific trends of an IoT device-type and are valuable for generating the fingerprint for the IoT device-type. A few illustrative behavior specific features for a given window of packets are: `payload length, payload entropy, packet header length, the number of unique IP addresses observed, the number of distinct sub-net IP addresses, number of distinct external destination IP addresses, IP address variance, length of the longest IP flow, number of packets with same source port` and `number of packets with same destination port`. Some of these features are extracted per packet and stored while the other features are extracted from the entire window of packets. As shown in Table 1, these features are numeric features. The intuition

Table 1. Packet Features

Feature	Value
Payload Length	Length in bytes (float)
Payload Entropy	Byte entropy of payload (float)
Header Length	Length of packet header in bytes
Common Source Port	1 if src.port $\leq$ 1023, else 0
Common Destination Port	1 if src.port $\leq$ 1023, else 0
IP Flows	Count of packets with largest number of same source and destination IP
Unique IP Addresses	Number of unique IP addresses in a packet window
IP Addresses in Subnet	Number of IP addresses that belong to the same subnet in a packet window
External IP Addresses	Number of IP addresses that do not belong to the same subnet
IP Variance	Variance in IP addresses
TCP/UDP/HTTP/HTTPS	1 if packet has a protocol field, else 0

for using these features in device-type fingerprinting is that they are likely to have different distributions across different device-types.

3.3 Privacy Preserving Deep Learning Model for Fingerprinting

Now, based on the features identified, we proceed to build a privacy preserving deep learning model for fingerprinting IoT device-types. Unlike the approach in [28], which described the first practical distributed deep learning model, we engineer a neural network design that suits the current problem.

The process considers a group of N-participants in the training process and a global server that maintains an aggregated deep learning model. Each participant maintains a local parameter vector that it updates using its own private training data and from the updates received from the global server. A parameter vector consists of the weights and biases of a respective neural network. The server periodically aggregates the parameter vector updates received from the users and disseminates the information to the participants. The participants then swap out their local parameters for the aggregated parameters that they received from the server and begin the next round of training. After each round of aggregation, all participants and the server will have equivalent parameter vectors. The number of updates and aggregation steps that occur during the process is determined by the number of training samples and two predefined hyper-parameters: $batch\_size$ and $epochs$. Each participant has the same number of training samples, N, and the swaps occur after each batch so the total number of swaps is: $\frac{N}{batch\_size} *$ $epochs$. Therefore, the parameter aggregation method is a critical factor in the distributed learning process.

Decentralized Optimization. In our distributed learning model, parameter aggregation is done through selective parameter swapping. Participants send the parameters of their local model to the server and the server selects a portion of the parameters in its model to swap out for the ones it received. The selective parameter swapping operation is shown below.

- Server maintains an aggregated parameter vector, w_a
- Server receives parameter vector, w_i, from participant, P_i
- Server computes $index = indices\ of\ sort(|w_i - w_a|)$
- Sets $w_a[index[0:\Theta]] = w_i[index[0:\Theta]]$ where Θ is a hyper-parameter that determines how many parameters are swapped out; the server selects the parameters with the greatest absolute difference between the received and aggregated parameter vectors.

We found that the best value for Θ is the length of the parameter vector divided by the number of participants. We call this method "Decentralized Optimization" because, instead of performing parameter optimization on the server, the participants optimize their parameters locally then send their optimized parameters to the server during each round of aggregation. The participants optimize the parameters of their local model using Adam optimization, an extension of Stochastic Gradient Descent, described by [38].

4 Data Synthesis

To address the problem of small data sets, we used an AAE [39] to generate synthetic data for the IoT devices. We define and use the following terminology for describing our AAE.

- *Network fingerprint*: a feature vector extracted from the network traffic of a device.
- *Latent vector*: the compact and hidden representation of the input data, the output of the bottleneck layer of the autoencoder.
- *Prior distribution*: the target distribution of the latent space produced by the encoder given the training data. We used a Gaussian distribution with a mean of 0.5 and standard deviation of 1.0.
- *Reconstruction loss*: the loss function minimized by the autoencoder, we used mean squared error (MSE).

4.1 AAE Architecture

Our AAE consists of the following key components: encoder, decoder, reconstruction discriminator and latent discriminator as shown in Fig. 2. The encoder is a neural network with three hidden layers, which takes the network fingerprint as the input and outputs a 20-by-1 latent vector. The decoder is a neural network with three hidden layers, which takes a 20-by-1 vector as input and outputs either a synthetic or a reconstructed fingerprint (depending on the source of the input vector). The latent discriminator is a neural network classifier with two hidden layers, that takes a 20-by-1 input vector and classifies it into one of two classes: synthetic latent vector (output of encoder), or vector from prior distribution. X represents original network fingerprint samples and is the input to the encoder. The output of the encoder, Z, is a latent vector and has the same dimensions as prior. The latent discriminator takes samples from prior and Z as inputs.

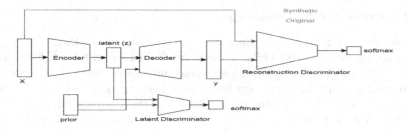

Fig. 2. Adversarial Auto-Encoder

AAE Training. In the first step, of autoencoder update, the encoder and decoder are updated on a mini-batch of samples from the original data. The reconstruction loss from the decoder is back propagated through the decoder and encoder to calculate the gradient. The encoder and decoder weights are updated using the gradient. In the second step, of adversarial update, the mini-batch of samples is fed forward through the encoder to produce the generated latent batch (Z). The latent discriminator gradient is calculated using the latent vector (Z) and a batch from the prior distribution and its weights are updated using the gradient. The batch is fed forward through the encoder and the discriminator to calculate the adversarial error by taking the classification error with the class label inverted. The error is back propagated through the discriminator and the encoder to calculate the gradient. The encoder's weights are updated with the gradient while the discriminator's gradient is discarded.

Adversarial Decoder Training. The decoder training is quite similar as that of the encoder training. In this round, the decoder is fine-tuned to generate believable samples. This round also uses mini-batches from the original data; however, the mini-batches are used as positive samples to train the discriminator. The decoder's weights are updated with the calculated gradient and the discriminator's gradient is discarded.

Synthetic Data Generation. Compared to training the AAE, generating synthetic data samples is straightforward. After the model is trained, the encoder, latent discriminator, and reconstruction discriminator neural networks can all be discarded. The only component that is used to generate data is the decoder. To generate data, the decoder is given a random vector from the prior distribution and it outputs a synthetic vector that is similar to the training data. Given a random vector with shape (num_samples, latent shape), the decoder will produce an output with shape (num_samples, num_features).

5   Performance Evaluation

5.1   Experimental Methodology

We implemented our approach using the numpy library in Python 3.11.4 on a laptop running Windows 11 OS with Intel core® i9-13900H CPU© 2600 MHz processor with 32 GB RAM. We implemented our models using numpy expressions instead of a machine learning framework because this gave us more control. We used a multi-layer perceptron (MLP) as the common neural network architecture for every participant. For training, we used a one-vs-all model of classification where a separate neural network binary classifier was trained for each device-type. Each neural network has a different target vector where the specific device-type was given the positive label while the rest of the device-types were given the negative labels.

All versions of the experiment used a MLP with two hidden layers, sizes 60 and 40. The rectified linear activation function (ReLU) has been used on the hidden layers and softmax on the network outputs. In all the experiments, the batch size is 256 and learning rate is 0.001 with the Binary Cross Entropy (BCE) as the loss function and Adam optimization with 0.9 beta1 and 0.999 beta2 as the parameters. The weights are initialized randomly but any initialization scheme can be used by participants. During the local training, the participants communicate asynchronously with the global parameter server. Once the participant's local model is updated with new weights downloaded from the server, the next training epoch starts. In all the experiments, the value of θ is set to the value (1.0/number of participants).

During classification, we denote a correctly classified positive sample by true positive (TP), an incorrectly classified positive sample as false negatives (FN), a correctly classified negative sample as true negative (TN), and an incorrectly classified negative sample as false positive (FP). We report standard classification metrics as shown in Table 2.

Table 2. Machine Learning Metrics

Metric Name	Definition
Recall (True Positive Rate)	$\frac{TP}{TP+FP}$
Accuracy	$\frac{TP+TN}{TP+FP+FN+TN}$
F1 (F-Score)	$\frac{2TP}{2TP+FP+FN}$
False Positive Rate	$\frac{FP}{FP+TN}$

Communication Model. All of the distributed learning experiments use a single network model. We use a client-server architecture with four clients where the parameter training is done by the clients and the aggregation is done by the server. In our experiments, we simulate dispersed datasets by artificially partitioning the data into five, non-overlapping, subsets of equal size. This partitioning is done by the server using 5-fold cross validation and the server maintains a cumulative sum of confusion matrices of each iteration. We use this confusion matrix to calculate the metrics, which we use to evaluate the model's performance. At the beginning of each iteration, the server partitions the data into four training sets and one test set and sends each client a different training set. Next, the clients send the means and standard deviations for each feature in their training data to the server. Then, the server calculates the combined means and standard deviations for each feature and sends them back to the clients. The clients use the combined means and standard deviations to standardize their training data, which they use to train their local models. At the end of the iteration, the server computes a confusion matrix by testing its aggregated classifier with the data from the test set after standardizing it using the combined means and standard deviations. Training is synchronized so each client sends an update after every batch then waits for the server to send aggregated parameters back before resuming the training. Also, the server does not send the aggregated parameters to the clients until each client has sent its parameters.

5.2   Data Sets

We collected data sets from a sample set of IoT devices such as Amazon Echo, Philips Smart Light etc., as shown in Table 3. We also used some data collected by one of our team members from WiFi access points (with prior permission), standard access points and taxi-cab hot-spots (data available on request). The access points in cabs are specifically meant for providing communication services like WiFi, GPS and radio. We considered these aspects and treated them as IoT devices. Also, since these devices are slightly more generic than a regular IoT device, they pose some technical challenges in fingerprinting due to the noise in their traffic. In our experiments with data synthesized by the AAE, the training sets included 10% synthetic data while the testing sets only included original data samples.

Table 3. Device Network Data

Device Type	Packets
Amazon Echo	18670
Philips Smart Light	49910
Taxi Cab WiFi APs	49910
Standard WiFi APs	11770
Omna	3110
Somfy	49910

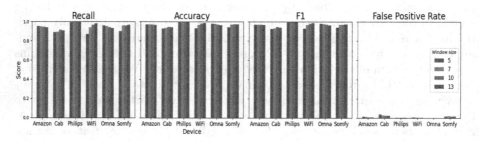

Fig. 3. Packet Window Size Estimation

5.3 Window Size Estimation

One of the difficult choices is the window size of the packets that should be observed to fingerprint a device. Towards this, we measured the performance of our distributed learning model with window sizes 5, 7, 10 and 13. From this experiment, we found that the best value for window size is 10 packets. However, as shown in Fig. 3, the response in the model's performance on individual devices to different window sizes varied. We chose 10 as our estimated window size because it had the best overall performance. The average Recall score with window size 10 was 95.4% which is 2.7% higher than the worst performing window size, 5, and 0.1% higher than the next best window size, 13. We note that identifying the best window size is a difficult task as the device needs to exhibit significant device specific behavior in that window.

5.4 Centralized Learning Performance

To measure the baseline performance, we first performed experiments on the centralized learning mode, *i.e.*, a single party training the machine learning model using all the data.

We compare the performance of the sliding window approach on real and synthetic data. As shown in Fig. 4, our sliding window approach performs well, achieving recall in the range of 83% to 99% across all devices with an average of 92%. The accuracy was in the range of 89% to 99% with an average of 95%. One interesting note is that fingerprinting performance is greater when using synthetic data. This is an encouraging aspect because it shows that the AAE is able to generalize important features in the dataset. If good quality synthetic data is available then it would help other researchers in the community to utilize our method to enhance their experiments as well.

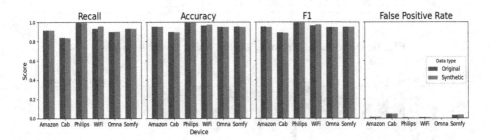

Fig. 4. Baseline Centralized Training Performance On Real and Synthetic Data

5.5 Distributed Learning Performance

The distributed learning method performs well for both real training data and synthetic training data. We tested the distributed learning by training on the

actual data samples and synthetic data samples while the testing was performed
real data samples. From Fig. 5, we note that the recall was in the range of 92%
to 99% while the accuracy ranged from 95% to 99%. In Fig. 6, we show that our
model performs better with four (4) clients than with two (2) clients. Finally,
in Fig. 7 we present a comparison of the best results across all the experiments,
i.e., the best of centralized against the best of distributed learning model. The
distributed model in this case uses four clients and a window size of 10. The
distributed model performs better than the centralized model in all metrics.
The average recall score for the distributed model is 95.4% which is 3.4% higher

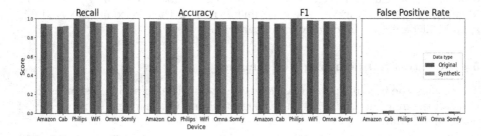

Fig. 5. Distributed Training Model On Real and Synthetic Data

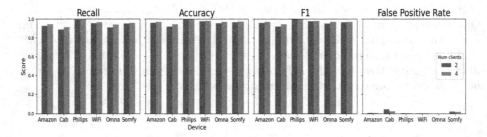

Fig. 6. Distributed Training Model Using 2 and 4 clients

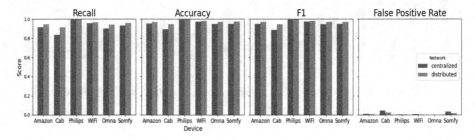

Fig. 7. The Comparison of Best of Distributed and Centralized Fingerprinting Models

than the average recall of the best performing centralized model. One possible reason for this surprising result is that the noise in local data sets seems to be reduced considerably before updating the global neural network model. However, we intend to explore this aspect more rigorously to verify if the same results are achievable for a larger device collection.

6   Conclusion and Future Work

We addressed the problem of fingerprinting IoT devices when sufficient data is not available to the analyst. Our sliding window approach attempts to maximize the chances of covering behavior of device-type and also, increases the packet traffic utilization for machine learning. Our approach generates the fingerprinting model by sharing individual learning model parameters from collaborating parties. We also described an adversarial auto-encoder mechanism to generate synthetic samples that are useful in training the fingerprinting model. Our results show that our approaches perform as good as the centralized learning models with a TPR ranging from 92% to 99% and accuracy ranging from 95% to 99%.

There are several key challenges and future directions for our work. First, the window size of packets is a difficult parameter to estimate as various devices exhibit variable behavior in different packet windows. Second, the IoT devices perform periodic upgrades to their firmware, which might make these devices behave differently at times. Adapting to such changes and evolution in IoT devices is a challenging task as the fingerprinting model might have to learn "on-the-fly". Third, the quality of synthetic data can dramatically change the landscape of IoT fingerprinting. Better synthetic data can resolve the challenges in data collection and analysis and could help the community immensely. Finally, the future scope of our work is to explore the induction of new features into the deep learning model as time evolves and to be able to handle adversarial or noisy data samples from misbehaving participants.

Acknowledgement. This work has been partially supported by funding from the NIST under award number 60NANB18D204, from NSF under award numbers DMS 2123761, CNS 2027750, CNS 1822118 and from the member partner of the NSF IUCRC Center for Cybersecurity Analytics and Automation – Statnett, Cyber Risk Research, AMI, NewPush, and ARL.

References

1. Krebs, B.: Mirai IoT botnet co-authors plead guilty? Krebs on security, November 2017
2. Acar, A., et al.: Peek-a-boo: i see your smart home activities, even encrypted! In: Proceedings of the 13th ACM Conference on Security and Privacy in Wireless and Mobile Networks, pp. 207–218 (2020)

3. OConnor, T.J., Mohamed, R., Miettinen, M., Enck, W., Reaves, B., Sadeghi, A.-R.: HomeSnitch: behavior transparency and control for smart home IoT devices. In: Proceedings of the 12th Conference on Security and Privacy in Wireless and Mobile Networks, pp. 128–138 (2019)

4. Bai, L., Yao, L., Kanhere, S.S., Wang, X., Yang, Z.: Automatic device classification from network traffic streams of Internet of Things. In: 2018 IEEE 43rd Conference on Local Computer Networks (LCN), pp. 1–9. IEEE (2018)

5. Sivanathan, A., et al.: Classifying IoT devices in smart environments using network traffic characteristics. IEEE Trans. Mob. Comput. **18**(8), 1745–1759 (2018)

6. Dong, S., Li, Z., Tang, D., Chen, J., Sun, M., Zhang, K.: Your smart home can't keep a secret: towards automated fingerprinting of IoT traffic. In: Proceedings of the 15th ACM Asia Conference on Computer and Communications Security, pp. 47–59 (2020)

7. Perdisci, R., Papastergiou, T., Alrawi, O., Antonakakis, M.: IoTFinder: efficient large-scale identification of IoT devices via passive DNS traffic analysis. In: 2020 IEEE European Symposium on Security and Privacy (EuroS&P), pp. 474–489. IEEE (2020)

8. Ahmed, D., Das, A., Zaffar, F.: Analyzing the feasibility and generalizability of fingerprinting Internet of Things devices. Proc. Priv. Enhancing Technol. **2**, 2022 (2022)

9. Sharma, R.A., Soltanaghaei, E., Rowe, A., Sekar, V.: Lumos: identifying and localizing diverse hidden {IoT} devices in an unfamiliar environment. In: 31st USENIX Security Symposium (USENIX Security 2022), pp. 1095–1112 (2022)

10. Franklin, J., McCoy, D.: Passive data link layer 802.11 wireless device driver fingerprinting. In: Proceedings of the 15th USENIX Security Symposium, Vancouver, BC, Canada, 31 July–4 August 2006

11. Pang, J., Greenstein, B., Gummadi, R., Seshan, S., Wetherall, D.: 802.11 user fingerprinting. In: Proceedings of the 13th ACM MOBICOM, pp. 99–110. ACM (2007)

12. François, J., Abdelnur, H.J., State, R., Festor, O.: Automated behavioral fingerprinting. In: Proceedings of the 12th RAID Symposium, pp. 182–201 (2009)

13. Arackaparambil, C., Bratus, S., Shubina, A., Kotz, D.: On the reliability of wireless fingerprinting using clock skews. In: Proceedings of the Third ACM WiSec, pp. 169–174, New York, NY, USA. ACM (2010)

14. Kurtz, A., Gascon, H., Becker, T., Rieck, K., Freiling, F.: Fingerprinting mobile devices using personalized configurations. Proc. Priv. Enhancing Technol. **1**, 4–19 (2016)

15. Martin, A., Doddington, G., Kamm, T., Ordowski, M., Przybocki, M.: The DET curve in assessment of detection task performance. Technical report, National Institute of Standards and Technology Gaithersburg MD (1997)

16. Lippmann, R., Fried, D., Piwowarski, K., Streilein, W.: Passive operating system identification from TCP/IP packet headers. In: Workshop on Data Mining for Computer Security, p. 40 (2003)

17. Kohno, T., Broido, A., Claffy, K.C.: Remote physical device fingerprinting. IEEE Trans. Dependable Secure Comput. **2**(2), 93–108 (2005)

18. Brik, V., Banerjee, S., Gruteser, M., Oh, S.: Wireless device identification with radiometric signatures. In: Proceedings of the 14th ACM MOBICOM, pp. 116–127. ACM (2008)

19. Jana, S., Kasera, S.K.: On fast and accurate detection of unauthorized wireless access points using clock skews. IEEE Trans. Mobile Comput. **9**(3), 449–462 (2010)

20. Radhakrishnan, S.V., Uluagac, A.S., Beyah, R.A.: GTID: a technique for physical device and device type fingerprinting. IEEE Trans. Dependable Secure Comput. **12**(5), 519–532 (2015)
21. Formby, D., Srinivasan, P., Leonard, A., Rogers, J., Beyah, R.A.: Who's in control of your control system? Device fingerprinting for cyber-physical systems. In: 23rd Annual ISOC NDSS (2016)
22. Van Goethem, T., Scheepers, W., Preuveneers, D., Joosen, W.: Accelerometer-based device fingerprinting for multi-factor mobile authentication. In: Caballero, J., Bodden, E., Athanasopoulos, E. (eds.) ESSoS 2016. LNCS, vol. 9639, pp. 106–121. Springer, Cham (2016). https://doi.org/10.1007/978-3-319-30806-7_7
23. François, J., Abdelnur, H.J., State, R., Festor, O.: Machine learning techniques for passive network inventory. IEEE Trans. Netw. Serv. Manage. **7**(4), 244–257 (2010)
24. Gao, K., Corbett, C., Beyah, R.: A passive approach to wireless device fingerprinting. In: Proceedings of IEEE/IFIP DSN, pp. 383–392. IEEE (2010)
25. Miettinen, M., Marchal, S., Hafeez, I., Asokan, N., Sadeghi, A.-R., Tarkoma, S.: IoT SENTINEL: automated device-type identification for security enforcement in IoT. In: Proceedings of 37th IEEE ICDCS, pp. 2177–2184 (2017)
26. Siby, S., Maiti, R.R., Tippenhauer, N.: IoTScanner: detecting and classifying privacy threats in IoT neighborhoods. arXiv preprint arXiv:1701.05007 (2017)
27. Bezawada, B., Bachani, M., Peterson, J., Shirazi, H., Ray, I., Ray, I.: Behavioral fingerprinting of IoT devices. In: Proceedings of the 2018 Workshop on Attacks and Solutions in Hardware Security, ASHES CCS 2018, Toronto, ON, Canada, 19 October 2018, pp. 41–50. ACM (2018)
28. Shokri, R., Shmatikov, V.: Privacy-preserving deep learning. In: 2015 53rd Annual Allerton Conference on Communication, Control, and Computing (Allerton), pp. 909–910 (2015)
29. McMahan, B., Moore, E., Ramage, D., Hampson, S., y Arcas, B.A.: Communication-efficient learning of deep networks from decentralized data. In: Proceedings of the 20th International Conference on Artificial Intelligence and Statistics, AISTATS 2017, 20–22 April 2017, Fort Lauderdale, FL, USA, vol. 54, pp. 1273–1282. PMLR (2017)
30. Gupta, O., Raskar, R.: Distributed learning of deep neural network over multiple agents. J. Netw. Comput. Appl. **116**, 1–8 (2018)
31. Lévy, D., Jain, A.: Breast mass classification from mammograms using deep convolutional neural networks. CoRR, abs/1612.00542 (2016)
32. Vepakomma, P., Gupta, O., Swedish, T., Raskar, R.: Split learning for health: distributed deep learning without sharing raw patient data. CoRR, abs/1812.00564 (2018)
33. Vepakomma, P., Raskar, R.: Split learning: a resource efficient model and data parallel approach for distributed deep learning. In: Ludwig, H., Baracaldo, N. (eds.) Federated Learning - A Comprehensive Overview of Methods and Applications, pp. 439–451. Springer, Cham (2022)
34. Niyaz, Q., Sun, W., Javaid, A.Y.: A deep learning based DDoS detection system in software-defined networking (SDN). EAI Endorsed Trans. Secur. Saf. **4**(12), 12 (2017)
35. Deval, S.K., Tripathi, M., Bezawada, B., Ray, I.: "X-Phish: Days of Future Past": adaptive & privacy preserving phishing detection. In: 2021 IEEE Conference on Communications and Network Security (CNS), pp. 227–235 (2021)
36. Phong, L.T., Phuong, T.T.: Privacy-preserving deep learning via weight transmission. IEEE Trans. Inf. Forensics Secur. **14**(11), 3003–3015 (2019)

37. Wang, H., Eklund, D., Oprea, A., Raza, S.: FL4IoT: IoT device fingerprinting and identification using federated learning. ACM Trans. Internet Things **4**, 1–24 (2023)
38. Kingma, D.P., Ba, J.: Adam: a method for stochastic optimization. In: 3rd International Conference on Learning Representations, ICLR 2015, San Diego, CA, USA, 7–9 May 2015, Conference Track Proceedings (2015)
39. Makhzani, A., Shlens, J., Jaitly, N., Goodfellow, I., Frey, B.: Adversarial autoencoders. arXiv preprint arXiv:1511.05644 (2015)

URSID: Automatically Refining a Single Attack Scenario into Multiple Cyber Range Architectures

Pierre-Victor Besson[1,3]([✉]), Valérie Viet Triem Tong[1,2], Gilles Guette[1,3], Guillaume Piolle[4], and Erwan Abgrall[2]

[1] Inria, Rennes, France
pierre-victor.besson@inria.fr
[2] CentraleSupelec, Rennes, France
[3] University of Rennes, Rennes, France
[4] Thales, Rennes, France

Abstract. Contrary to intuition, insecure computer network architectures are valuable assets in IT security. Indeed, such architectures (referred to as cyber-ranges) are commonly used to train red teams and test security solutions, in particular ones related to supervision security. Unfortunately, the design and deployment of these cyber-ranges is costly, as they require designing an attack scenario from scratch and then implementing it in an architecture on a case-by-case basis, through manual choices of machines/users, OS versions, available services and configuration choices. This article presents URSID, a framework for automatic deployment of cyber-ranges based on the formal description of attack scenarios. The scenario is described at the technical attack level according to the MITRE nomenclature, refined into several variations (instances) at the procedural level and then deployed in virtual multiple architectures. URSID thus automates costly manual tasks and allows to have several instances of the same scenario on architectures with different OS, software or account configurations. URSID has been successfully tested in an academic cyber attack and defense training exercise.

Keywords: Network security · Computer security · Attack scenario · Cyber Range · Cyber Security Education

1 Introduction

The numbers of cybersecurity incidents keeps increasing every year and cybercrime is nowadays a threat to any organization. In 2021 the FBI reported a 64% increase in losses related to cybercrime compared to 2020, and more than 4 times what it was in 2017 [6].In particular, the rise of Advanced Persistent Threats (APT) has proven problematic for companies and governments alike, leading

P.-V. Besson is funded by the Direction Générale de l'Armement (CREACH LABS).

M. Mosbah et al. (Eds.): FPS 2023, LNCS 14551, pp. 123–138, 2024.
https://doi.org/10.1007/978-3-031-57537-2_8

to massive data breaches, spying and ransomware-based extortion campaigns. Advanced Persistent Threats are well organized stealthy threat actors, who gain unauthorized access to an information system and for extended periods of time in order to avoid detection and better reach their goals. In order to deal with this increasing threat, cyber defenders have an array of tools at their disposal, one of them being cyber-ranges.

Cyber-Ranges are defined by the National Institute of Standards and Technology (NIST) [15] as "interactive, simulated representations of an organization's local network, system, tools, and applications that are connected to a simulated Internet level environment". They are a complete information system similar to those used in production, on which a previously specified attack scenario can be run. A cyber-range can be used to improve the technical level of the security teams. A so-called red team attacks the cyber-range. Their goal is to reach the target as soon as possible while remaining undetected. Such a training allows the red team to acquire the reflexes and working methods of the attackers and an efficient threat hunting during a real incident response. In order to guarantee an entry point and make the exercise valuable, cyber-ranges may be populated with flawed configurations and exploits on purpose [5,18,21,22]. A so-called blue team defends the cyber-range. Its objective is to track down the attacker in the cyber-range, to prevent his progression, to explain the meaning of the security alerts and thus ultimately to improve the supervision tools.

The deployment of a cyber range first requires the definition of an attack scenario and an architecture in which this scenario can effectively be played. The scenario definition includes the initial compromise of the system by the attacker, an exit point that represents the goal of the attacker (this can range from user accounts to be compromised, database to be exfiltrated, services to be rendered inaccessible, *etc.*), possibly one or more milestones. The architecture must contain at least the machines, user accounts, services, files and configurations to play the scenario. This architecture must also be populated with credible data, system and network activities similar to what would exist on a real architecture in use. A cyber-range tends to be specific to a unique chain of exploits, and its implementation requires very specific combinations of machines, accounts, software , operating system or configuration files. Once such a cyber-range has been used by teams or tools, it is rendered of little value because both the attacker and the defender know the scenario. Another one must then be created, which comes with additional design and deployment costs.

In this article, we present URSID an automated cyber-range deployment pipeline. URSID automatically deploys several architectures where multiple variations of a same attack scenario can be run and aims to address the challenges raised by cyber-range reusability and description genericity. Our contribution can be summarized as in the following perspectives:

- **High level attack scenario definition using a graph-based model** (Sect. 3). We propose a model to describe both an attack scenario and the attacker's required skills to achieve this scenario. The description first occurs at the technical level according to the MITRE nomenclature. Similarly to a

kill chain model, it gives a first general overview of the different movements of the attacker in the targeted architecture.
- **Instantiation**
  through multiple low-level attack scenarios(Section 4.1). We provide a methodology to refine an high level scenario towards more precise descriptions. This refinement process provides variations at the procedural level of the initial scenario in a way that guarantees the consistency of the resulting architecture, by associating attack procedures with architecture constraints.
- **Available implementation**. We provide a git repository of URSID [2] showcasing the entire generation process, alongside an attack scenario which was used as part of a live experiment and instructions on how to refine and deploy it.

2 Background

The generation of a cyber-range first requires choosing an attack scenario and then instantiating it on an actual architecture. In our opinion, this need lies at the junction of two types of work in the literature. On the one hand, models that represent architectures that have been or are likely to be attacked. On the other hand, the models that represent the attacker's skills.

Attack Graphs. Attack graphs are formal structures aiming to represent one or more possible attacks on an architecture using nodes and transitions between those nodes. They differ in the literature by how they decide to represent the architecture (which depends on their use case). In particular, host-based models (such as in [1] are attack graph models in which nodes represent an architecture device and edges the access available between these devices. This type of model seemed the most relevant for our purposes, as information about devices can be more easily converted into virtual machine configurations than system states or a list of exploits. Mensah [12] proposes an attack graph model with a novel approach on host-based graphs. Nodes hold information about not only the device the attacker is currently logged on, but also their level of privilege on this connection. A node may also indicate whether it contains interesting data for the attacker, such as a password or a secret file. An attacker may move in this model by taking a transition between 2 nodes, which may have preconditions or consequences on the state of the devices and the attacker. Some transitions have triggers, which indicate that a transition can only be taken if an other specific node has been visited by the attacker beforehand. The formalization used by URSID shares similarities with this work such as the choice of representing nodes as devices and users but differs significantly as a consequence of different use cases. Indeed, Mensah's proposed formalization was ultimately designed for modeling existing architectures, a goal opposite to our own goal of creating architectures from scratch. In summary, their work thus contains a level of exhaustivity in particular in how modeling a transition requires specifying all consequences and conditions of that transition which would make it difficult to

a) write scenarios manually and b) deploy different scenarios based on a single description. Furthermore the set of actions available to the attacker used in [12] to label their transition is not clearly defined, putting actions such as "CVE-2009–1918" or "CONNECT" on the same level. A clear set of attacker actions is required for our purposes in order to properly convert scenario descriptions into architectures.

Attacker Representation. The modeling of attacker actions depends on the scientific objective. Based on observations of actual attacks, the MITRE corporation proposes the ATT&CK Matrix [13], a cyber-adversary behavior knowledge base aiming to describe the different steps of a given attack scenario. In this article, we rely on this nomenclature to describe attacker actions, which are defined on 3 levels of abstraction known as Tactics, Techniques and Procedures, or TTPs. Tactics represent the main goal of an action performed by an attacker an attacker may try to gain higher-level permissions on a system or network (TA004: *Privilege Escalation*). Techniques represent the means used by an attacker to reach his tactical goals: an attacker may exploit a vulnerability to elevate his privileges on a machine (T1068: *Exploitation for Privilege Escalation*[1]). Finally, procedures describe the specific implementation details of an attack: an attacker may attempt to exploit a flaw in the pkexec process on older Linux versions [16] in order to escalate his privileges on a machine. The ATT&CK matrix is currently comprised of 14 tactics, over 200 techniques and describes a few procedures for each technique. There is however to our knowledge no exhaustive list of procedures for a given technique, although some projects (such as [9]) provide tools to make such a connection. Reusing this nomenclature provides URSID with a standardized way to describe any given step of a scenario, which is needed for its application. The ATT&CK matrix is also used by several other projects in the literature [9] [20] [17] or by attack reports and emulation compendiums [14]. While these projects ultimately have different scopes and goals than URSID, reusing the ATTA&CK matrix makes any potential future combination of these tools easier.

3   Attack Scenario at the Technical Level

3.1   Representation of an Attack Scenario

In this work, we propose to describe an attack scenario through a directed graph of attack positions. We model the attacker through the footholds he acquires by holding attack positions. An attacker may progress from one attack position he holds to another if he is able to execute the attack corresponding to the transition between these two attack positions. An attacker can also remain in the same attack position but increase his knowledge by discovering information hosted on the compromised account/machine. Its progression is made possible by the use of an attack technique, itself implemented by the execution of an attack

---

[1] We are here using the official MITRE numerotation for techniques.

procedure. Depending on the required level of abstraction, a scenario may be described on a technical or on a procedural level. This section describes attack scenarios at the technical level. The proposed formalism is generic. It can be used to describe one or many attack paths allowing to reach a targeted attack position. This formalism does not require the description of all the elements of the architecture but only the useful part of the scenario.

An **attack position** corresponds to a session of an attacker, under the identity of a user on a machine of the compromised network. For a given architecture we define $\mathcal{M}$ as the set of all machines available in the architecture, $\mathcal{U}$ as the set of all users with an account on these machines and $\mathcal{D}$ as the data existing in the architecture. The data can be credentials, passwords, cryptographic keys, addresses, or any other data useful to the attacker to progress through the scenario. We define an attack position by a pair (m, u) where $m \in \mathcal{M}$ is a machine of the compromised network and $u \in \mathcal{U}$ a declared user.

Among these attack positions, a **starting position** is a position controlled by default by the attacker at the beginning of the scenario and from which he will be able to play the scenario. The starting position is usually (*Attacker, SuperUser*), we consider that the attacker has full control over his own machine(s), but could also be a machine from the network, in the case of an insider threat. A **winning position** is a position that is of particular interest to the attacker and which corresponds to one of his ultimate goals in the architecture. For instance this may correspond to an account hosting sensitive data or the admin account of a Windows Active Directory domain controller. In this formalization, we consider that an attacker can hold multiple attack positions at the same time, by compromising multiple accounts on several machines concurrently.

The progression of an attacker in a compromised network is made possible by the use of an attack technique, itself executed through an attack procedure according to the terminology proposed by the MITRE. In our model, this is formalized by edges between the nodes (attack positions) of a scenario graph.

Finally, an attack scenario at the technical level and over an architecture with $\mathcal{M}$ machines and $\mathcal{U}$ declared users is a graph $\mathbf{S}^{\text{tech}} = (\mathbf{P}, \mathbf{A}^{\text{tech}})$ where

- the set of nodes $\mathbf{P} \subseteq \mathcal{M} \times \mathcal{U}$ is a set of attack positions.
- the set of edges $\mathbf{A}^{\text{tech}}$ is $(p_1, p_2, (\tau, \mathbf{pre}, \mathbf{post}))$ where:
  - $p_1, p_2 \in \mathbf{P}$ are attack positions,
  - τ is an attack technique (or an attack procedure depending on the level of abstraction),
  - $\mathbf{pre} \in \mathcal{D}$ are the data required to execute τ
  - $\mathbf{post} \in \mathcal{D}$ are the data granted to the attacker when he successfully completes τ

Note that while URSID shares similarities with the modelization of Mensah [12] - particularly in how nodes are defined -, the use of secret requirements and rewards as well as the ATTK&CK matrix are both unique to this work.

For a given scenario $\mathbf{S}^{\text{tech}} = (\mathbf{P}, \mathbf{A}^{\text{tech}})$, we model the attacker's progression as **an attack state** defined by $\mathcal{A} = (\mathcal{P}, \mathcal{K})$, where $\mathcal{P} \subseteq \mathbf{P}$ is the set of all attack positions he controls, and $\mathcal{K} \subseteq \mathcal{D}$ the data he acquired. In our model, we

consider that an attacker may not lose the control of an attack position after
he acquires it once. Indeed, we suppose that once he manages to open a session
on a given machine by taking a sequence of transitions, the attacker is able to
get back to that attack position by applying the same sequence, or by using
a persistence tactic [13]. While this hypothesis may exclude some destructive
attacks or unstable exploits, these represent a small proportion of attacks in
practice and considering node acquisition to be permanent will make it easier to
traverse the graph in later algorithmic treatments.

The attacker progresses in the scenario by controlling new attack positions
or increasing his knowledge on the architecture. If an attacker controls an attack
position p_1 and if in the attack scenario there exists a position p_2, a technique τ,
two data sets **pre** and **post** such that the attacker already knows **pre** then the
attacker can progress from p_1 to p_2 by applying τ. If the execution of τ succeeds,
the attacker is rewarded with **post**.

An attack path is thus a finite sequence of attack states $\mathcal{A}_0 \xrightarrow{\tau_1} \mathcal{A}_1 \xrightarrow{\tau_2} \ldots \xrightarrow{\tau_n}$
$\mathcal{A}_n$. An attacker can progress from a state $\mathcal{A}_i = (\mathcal{P}_i, \mathcal{K}_i)$ to a state $\mathcal{A}_{i+1} =$
$(\mathcal{P}_{i+1}, \mathcal{K}_{i+1})$ by applying a technique τ in a scenario $\mathbf{S}^{\text{tech}} = (\mathbf{P}, \mathbf{A}^{\text{tech}})$ if the
attacker controls the attack position $p_i \in \mathcal{P}_i$ and there is a transition to move
from p_1 to the position p_2 i.e. $(p_1, p_2, (\tau, \mathbf{pre}, \mathbf{post})) \in \mathbf{A}^{\text{tech}}$ and the attacker
masters the prerequisite to apply the transition $\mathbf{pre} \in \mathcal{K}_i$. Then the attacker can
progress to p_2: $\mathcal{P}_{i+1} = \mathcal{P}_i \cup \{p_2\}$ and its knowledge increases $\mathcal{K}i + 1 = \mathcal{K}_i \cup \mathbf{post}$.
An attack path $\mathcal{A}_0 \xrightarrow{\tau_1} \mathcal{A}_1 \xrightarrow{\tau_2} \ldots \xrightarrow{\tau_n} \mathcal{A}_n$ is said executable if the attacker can
progress from $\mathcal{A}_0$ to $\mathcal{A}_n$.

Among the scenarios which can be described with this formalism, we distinguish the so-called **winnable scenarios** in which there is, at least, one exe-
cutable attack path $\mathcal{A}_0 \xrightarrow{\tau_1} \mathcal{A}_1 \xrightarrow{\tau_2} \ldots \xrightarrow{\tau_n} \mathcal{A}_n$, a starting attack position p_0 such
that $p_0 \in \mathcal{P}_0$ and a winning position p_w such that $p_w \in \mathcal{P}_n$.

3.2 Smash and Grab Attack Case Study

To illustrate this article, we rely on the MITRE Adversary Emulation Plans [14],
which outlines the behavior of persistent threat groups mapped to ATT&CK
techniques. Our first case study scenario is directly inspired from the "smash
and grab attack" of Day 1 of the MITRE APT29 Adversary Emulation Plan
and is referred in the following as "Smash and Grab attack scenario". In this
scenario, the attacker first gets access to a machine and escalates his privileges
on it. He then acquires passwords and files from this position before performing
lateral movement to an other machine, which he will also loot and exfiltrate files
from.

Our own scenario thus follows the same outline, with a few differences. First,
some techniques (such as ones related to tactics like Extraction or Defense Evasion) do not usually lead to a new position or secrets for the attacker, and are
less relevant to our generation purposes. Thus, while it would be possible to
include these techniques anyway using the same formalism, most of them were
left out in order not to clutter the scenario. We also added 2 more machines in

order to give the attacks more options after lateral movement and to diversify his possible attack paths.

The Smash and Grab attack scenario is played out on 4 machines, named *Bear, Raccoon, Badger and Skunk*. Each machine has 2 users, with one of them being a *SuperUser* with elevated privileges. There is also an additional node $(Attacker, SuperUser)^2$ representing the starting position of the attacker. The goal of the attacker is to reach the winning position $(Skunk, root)$.

At a technical level, the Smash and Grab attack scenario can be described by the graph $\mathbf{S}_e^{\text{tech}} = (\mathbf{P}_e, \mathbf{A}_e^{\text{tech}})$ where $\mathbf{P}_e = (p_i)_{i \in [0,8]}$, $\mathbf{A}_e^{\text{tech}} = (\tau_i)_{i \in [0,15]}$, $\mathbf{S}_e = \{p_0\}$ and $\mathbf{W}_e = \{p_8\}$. A graphical representation of this scenario detailing the values of $(p_i)_{i \in [0,8]}$ and $(\tau_i)_{i \in [0,15]}$ is available in Fig. 1 where the notation Txxxx refers to the official MITRE numerotation for techniques. The attacker has 2 main paths from the starting position to the winning one: one which requires him to access machine *Raccoon* to acquire credentials in order to perform T1078 on machine *Skunk*, and one which performs T1053 instead. It has to be noted that machine *Badger* is unnecessary for both of these winning attack paths here, acting as a dead end to diversify the paths an attacker may explore.

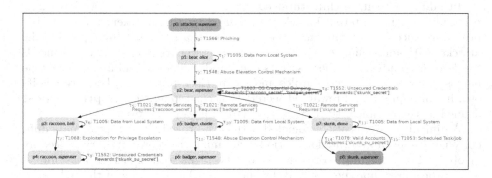

Fig. 1. Scenario "Smash and Grab attack" at a technical level

4 Scenario Instances at the Procedural Level

4.1 From Attack Techniques to Attack Procedures

The high-level description of a technical-level attack scenario is by design not sufficient to grasp the implementation details necessary to actually deploy the cyber-range. The cyber-range architecture is defined by its machines (including the version of the operating system, the version of the installed services, the files and their contents) and the declared users (names, passwords and privileges) on

---

[2] We throughout this work will refer to the attacker's machine as Attacker and consider they have complete control of it.

these machines. To reach this level of detail we propose to refine the description of an attack scenario at the level of attack procedures.

For each technique τ allowing to move from an attack position (u_1, m_1) to a position (u_2, m_2), the choice of an attack procedure π instantiating τ induces architectural constraints on machines m_1 and m_2. We consider here that an attack procedure **instantiates** an attack technique when it is a possible practical implementation of this technique.

The choice of one procedure to instantiate a technique implies constraints on the machines of the architecture on which the scenario will be played. A **constraint** $\mathcal{C}$ is related to a specific machine m and is denoted by $\mathcal{C}(m)$. A single constraint $\mathcal{C}$ includes Operating System constraints, Account constraints, Software constraints and File constraints. Formally, we define $\mathcal{C}(m) = \{OS, Account, Software, Files\}$, with $OS = \{type, version\}$, $Account$ a list of $\{name, group, privilege, services, credentials\}$, $Software$ a list of $\{software, version, port\}$ and $Files$ a list of $\{path, permissions, content\}$. Note that some procedures (such as ones related to techniques corresponding to the Extraction tactic) do not induce any architectural constraint: the attacker is free to use their own tools and means to execute them, regardless of what is available on the machine.

In addition to its architectural constraints, a π procedure may have π_{pre} preconditions, i.e. external knowledge required by the attacker to execute the procedure successfully. Similarly, the execution of a procedure may provide the attacker with additional knowledge we refer to as scenario secrets, which he needs to discover to advance. These secrets can be identifiers, IP addresses, machine names, the contents of certain files and so on. Each procedure therefore has its own list of required and rewarded secrets that corresponds to the **pre** and **post** defined at the technical level. $\pi_{secrets} = \{\textbf{pre} : [type_1, \ldots]; \textbf{post} : [type_1, \ldots]\}$

A difficulty score is also associated with each procedure to approximate difficulty level to each generated scenario by summing the scores of every procedure involved. This difficulty score, chosen by the scenario designer as they implement procedures, may be tweaked depending on the skill level of the red teams which will attack the scenario. This may provide additional data to the defenders, for instance by studying the correlation between an instance's difficulty and the speed at which it gets compromised, or to provide attackers with a greater variety of challenges in case their skills are heterogeneous.

4.2   Inferring Cyber-Range Configurations

A procedural level scenario follows the same formalism as a technical level scenario, except that the edge sets are labeled by attack procedures rather than by techniques. The constraints generated by the choice of procedures make it possible to specify the architecture when these constraints are not inconsistent between them. We propose a **backtracking refinement algorithm** (Algorithm 1) to generate an architecture that can play a scenario described at the procedure level. This algorithm walks through the scenario graph and try to replace each attack technique labeling an edge in the scenario by an attack procedure instantiating the technique as long as the constraints on the architecture stay coherent. The rules for adding constraints are given in Fig. 2 . Intuitively, two constraints on the same machine add up if they have different software, users, credentials or if one of the two constraints is more restrictive than the other in terms of OS and software versions. Otherwise, they are considered to be inconsistent.

To this aim, we need to determine whether individual subconstraints (OS, Accounts, Software and Files) on comparable parameters are compatible, and if so, the result of their combination. We therefore introduce the $\bowtie$ operator, applicable to the various types of subconstraints already defined. Given two subconstraints Sc_1 and Sc_2, $Sc_1 \bowtie Sc_2$ returns a new subconstraint Sc_3, which can be either $\perp$, which is the unsatisfiable subconstraint and a conclusion of incompatibility, or a valid combination of Sc_1 and Sc_2. Of course, the details of this combination depend on the nature of the operands. Formally, there is a different $\bowtie$ operator for each type of subconstraint. For the sake of clarity, we choose to use the same symbol, while always making sure that both operands are of the same type. Let us take OS constraints as an example. An OS constraint is a tuple of a type subconstraint and a version subconstraint. Quite intuitively, the $\bowtie$ operator applied to "type = Linux" and "type = Debian" would return "type = Debian", while on "type = Linux" and "type = Windows" it would return $\perp$. This version of the operator cannot be defined in a very formal way. When it comes to version numbers, however, it behaves much like a linear constraint solver, under the hypothesis that version numbers can always be compared in a safe manner. In a comparable fashion, we define the semantics of the $\bowtie$ operator on other types of subconstraints. Based on this combination operator, we are then able to define a fusion operator $\sqcup$ over constraint sets, and to determine whether the result remains satisfiable or not. Given two constraints C_1 and C_2, $C_1 \sqcup C_2$ returns a new constraint C_3, which can be either the unsatisfiable constraint $\perp$ or a valid combination of C_1 and C_2.

Finally, the set of all constraints over the resulting architecture is represented as a dictionary of constraints C containing entries for every machine m. This dictionary will be filled and edited throughout the course of our backtracking algorithm, and is considered to be unsatisfiable ($C = \perp$) if any of its entries are unsatisfiable. It is to be noted that any refined scenario (described on a procedural level) will be executable/winnable as long as the scenario described on a technical level was itself executable/winnable. Indeed any winning attack path available to the attacker on a technical level can also be followed on a procedural level by chaining the procedures corresponding to the techniques executed in this attack path.

The virtual machine configuration file resulting from all the procedure choices and their associated constraints is a list of machines and their configuration. For each machine m, the corresponding entry in the configuration file $Conf[m]$ is initialized with generic values and constantly updated as constraints are added through Algorithm 1. Note that these initial constraints are customizable: for

Subconstraint type	Sc_i^{type}	$Sc_1^{type} \sqcup Sc_2^{type}$
OS	$type_i, version_i$	$((type_1 \bowtie type_2), (version_1 \bowtie version_2))$
Account	$name_i, group_i, priv_i, serv_i, cred_i$	$(name_1, group_1, priv_1, serv_1 cred_1) \sqcup (name_2, group_2, priv_2, serv_2, cred_2)$ if $name_1 \neq name_2$ $(name_1, (group_1 \bowtie group_2), (priv_1 \bowtie priv_2), (serv_1 \bowtie serv_2), (cred_1 \bowtie cred_2))$ if $name_1 = name_2$
Software	$type_i, version_i, port_i$	$(type_1, version_1, port_1) \sqcup (type_2, version_2, port_2)$ if $(type_1 \neq type_2 \wedge port_1 \neq port_2)$ $(type_1, (version_1 \bowtie version_2), (port_1 \bowtie port_2))$ if $type_1 = type_2$
Files	$path_i, perm_i, content_i$	$(path_1, (perm_1 \bowtie perm_2), (content_1 \bowtie content_2))$ if $path_1 \neq path_2$ $(path_1, perm_1, content_1) \sqcup (path_2, perm_2, content_2)$ if $path_1 = path_2$

Fig. 2. Constraint combination rules for 2 procedures

instance one may wish to restrict machines to a specific set of OS, or to install logging software by default. This configuration file contains enough information about the machines comprising the network - which users to add, which software and OS to install, which files to add and create - to be used for virtual machine deployment, a process we will describe in Sect. 5. We also make sure that the set of transitions $\mathbf{A}^{tech}$ is sorted to put transitions requiring or reward secrets first, in order to optimize computation times. This is done because secret types are one of the more common causes of architecture incompatibilities. Secrets throughout the scenario refinement process are generated on a first come first served basis. Each time a procedure is picked that requires or rewards secrets, a value for this secret will be generated according to its type (such as ssh key or plaintext password) if it has not been generated already. After the refinement process, some values (such as account credentials or privilege) may have no constraints attached to them, in which case they are set to default values.

We implemented at least 2 procedures for each technique involved in scenario 1, some of which are detailed with their constraints in Fig. 3. We then ran the backtracking refinement algorithm on the scenario. This process goes through every transition (starting with the ones requiring or rewarding secrets), picks one of the available procedures for that transition at random and checks for architectural constraints incompatibility. This experiment resulted in a variety of different architectures, all corresponding to the same scenario that was described on a technical level, but having a variety of operating systems, file corpuses, software, services and randomized passwords. Some remarks on the process are as follows:

- The choice of procedure for technique T1552: *Unsecured Credentials* has consequences on the techniques available for T1021: *Remote Services* between (*Bear, SuperUser*) and (*Skunk, Diana*). Indeed if T1552 rewards a SSH key to the attacker, this instance of T1021 cannot pick a procedure requiring a password (for instance a RDP connection).
- The procedure chosen for technique T1021: *Remote Services* between (*Bear, SuperUser*) and (*Racoon, Bob*) can only be a procedure fit to require a secret, and thus cannot be "Weak SSH Password".

Algorithm 1. Backtracking refinement algorithm for a scenario $\mathbf{S}^{\text{tech}} = (\mathbf{P}, \mathbf{A}^{\text{tech}})$ [7]

Require: $\mathbf{S}^{\text{tech}} = (\mathbf{P}, \mathbf{A}^{\text{tech}})$ a scenario described at the technical level ($\mathbf{A}^{\text{tech}}$ are attack techniques)

Require: $\mathbf{C}$ a set of architectural constraints.

Require: $\{\pi_{\tau_i}\}_i$ a list of procedures instantiating each τ_i
    $\mathbf{S}^{\text{proc}} := (\mathbf{P}, \emptyset)$
    $L_t := \mathbf{A}^{\text{tech}}$ the list of all transitions to refine, sorted to prioritize transitions requiring or rewarding secrets.

Ensure: $\mathbf{S}^{\text{proc}} = (\mathbf{P}, \mathbf{A}^{\text{proc}})$ a scenario described at the procedural level ($\mathbf{A}^{\text{proc}}$ are attack procedures) and $\mathbf{S}^{\text{proc}} \triangleright \mathbf{S}^{\text{tech}}$
    function BACKTRACK($\mathbf{S}^{\text{tech}}, \mathbf{S}^{\text{proc}}, L_t, \{\pi_{\tau_i}\}_i, \mathbf{C}$)
        if $L_t = \emptyset$ **then return** True, $\mathbf{C}$
        else
            Sort L_t, putting transitions requiring or rewarding secrets first.
            $t = L_t[0] = ((u1, m1),(u2, m2),(\tau, \mathbf{pre}, \mathbf{post}))$
            if $\{\pi_\tau\} = \emptyset$ **then return** False, $\emptyset$
            end if
            Get the set of all compatible procedures $\{Comp(t)\}_i$
            for all $\{\pi \in Comp(t)\}$ **do**
                $\mathbf{C}_{new} = \mathbf{C}$
                $\mathbf{C}_{new}[m1] = \mathbf{C}_{new}[m1] \sqcup \pi[m1]$
                $\mathbf{C}_{new}[m2] = \mathbf{C}_{new}[m2] \sqcup \pi[m2]$
                if $\mathbf{C}_{new} \dashv \perp$ **then**
                    $\mathbf{S}^{\text{proc}}_{new} = (P, \mathbf{A}^{\text{proc}} + \pi)$
                    $L_{tnew} = L_t - \{t\}$
                    isValid, $\mathbf{C}_{final} = $ backtrack($\mathbf{S}^{\text{tech}}, \mathbf{S}^{\text{proc}}, L_{tnew}, \{\pi_{t_i}\}_i, \mathbf{C}_{new}$)
                    if isValid **then return** True, $\mathbf{C}_{final}$
                end if
            end if
            end for
            return False, $\mathbf{C}$ $\triangleright$ No valid procedure was found
        end if
    end function

Technique	Possible procedures	Constraints and secrets summary for each procedure
$\tau_{4,8} =$ T1552	π_9: Password in bash history	Linux, append a secret to the bash history file, rewards a plaintext password
	π_{10}: Private keys in .ssh	Requires Linux, creates files using a secret, rewards SSH keys
	π_{11}: Passwords in text file	Creates a file using a secret, rewards a plaintext password
$\tau_{5,9,12}=$ T1021	π_{12}: Weak SSH password	Linux, ssh service on port 22, sshd_config allowing password authentication
	π_{13}: SSH access from key	Linux, a ssh service on port 22, authorized_keys to be edited using a secret
	π_{14}: SSH access from password	Linux, a ssh service on port 22, ssh_config to allow password connections
	π_{15}: RDP from Password	Windows, a RDP service on port 3389, Windows registry + user password edits.
$\tau_7 =$ T1068	π_{16}: Dirty COW	Specific Linux version
	π_{17}: Vulnerable sudo version	Requires Linux, specific sudo package, edit sudoers
$\tau_{14} =$ T1078	π_{20}: Password from secret	Requires the user password to match a secret
	π_{21}: Weak Password	Requires the user password to be easy to brute-force.

Fig. 3. Excerpt of available procedures for each technique in the "Smash and Grab attack" scenario.

- Since T1078: *Valid Accounts* procedures only accept passwords, T1552: *Unsecured Credentials* between *(Raccoon, SuperUser)* and itself may not give a SSH key as a reward.
- The output architectures have varying numbers of Windows and Linux on them. Machine *Raccoon* must be on a Linux (because of our available procedures for T1068), but *Skunk*, *Badger* and *Bear* can be either.
- The number of possible resulting architectures exponentially grows as we increase the number of machines deployed, procedures implemented or amount of OS we are able to deploy. This does not however lead to computation complexity issues (running this experiment took a few seconds at most), as resolving the refinement backtracking algorithm only picks out one of these results.

5   Cyber-Range Experiment Using URSID

In the previous section we discussed the procedural refinement process, which lets us refine a single scenario described on a technical level into several possible scenarios described on a procedural level. This refined description states architecture constraints, such as the required operating systems, software, files that need to be created or edited and credential values. This description (in json format) contains all the information needed to deploy the corresponding architecture, using Vagrant [7] and Ansible [11] to instantiate and populate the virtual machines, and VirtualBox [4] to deploy them. Note that generated file contents may be used to append or edit a file naturally present on the virtual machine (for instance */etc/sudoers*), or be copied as a whole. The deployment part of URSID takes such a configuration file as an input, and converts it into a Vagrantfile and several Ansible playbooks (one for each machine). This Vagrantfile is responsible for initializing VM images and network status, and each playbook describes which operations (installing software, copying files, launching services...) have to be ran on each VM. An additional layer of work is thus needed to convert this description into formats acceptable by these tools. For instance, operating system names need to be translated into virtual machine box names and services need to be installed and launched. Installing old version of packages (such as `sudo` or `python3`) may also require a dedicated script to do so, as these versions are not available on main package repositories anymore. While adding new procedures may unfortunately require additional engineering cost (especially if legacy packages are involved, or more OS versions are made available), adding procedures only requiring simple operations - such as installing a package available through traditional repositories, editing files or tweaking the version of a package- is fairly straightforward.

As a proof of concept for the uses of URSID as an educational tool, a real life experiment (denoted as CERBERE in the following) was ran at a local university by a group of 13 voluntary Master students (familiar with cybersecurity), aiming to develop cyber attack-defense skills. This paper will focus on URSID's technical involvement in the red-team aspect of this project: a separate publication [3] details CERBERE as a whole. The scenario deployed for this occasion is shown on a technical level in Fig. 4. It consists of 3 machines sharing a local network, 6 attack positions and 7 transitions showcasing 4 different techniques. The scenario requires the students to complete 7 transitions (i.e. apply 7 attack procedures) in order to access the winning attack position. The attack procedure were distributed over 3 levels of difficulty. In total, 20 variations of this scenario were generated, even though only 13 were really used. The instances differed by which procedures were picked during the refinement process, which in turn influenced the files, OS, software and account installed on the machines. For instance, the privilege escalation on machine Zagreus achieved either exploiting a vulnerability of the sudo package [8] or of the pkexec process [16]. All passwords and keys were also unique to each instance, making it impossible to copy other answers directly. In total, 14 procedures were implemented and out of these 10 made it into one of the instances (the others being incompatible with this specific scenario). A list of all the implemented procedures is available in the repository [2]. Each machine was also setup with logging software (in this case audited). This was done by adding default constraints - one software to install the package and one file to tweak the configuration - for each machine during the refinement process.

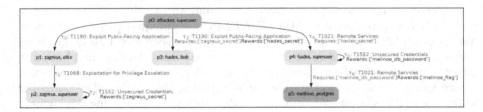

Fig. 4. Scenario "CERBERE educational CTF" at the technical level

All generated virtual machines were hosted on a single host, sporting 80 GB of RAM on 36 cores, with each machine in a given instance existing in their own virtual network. In order to give each attacker their own separate instance accessible remotely (and avoid having outside attacks/bots pollute the experiment), a double proxy was set-up. Students could only access the machine through a specific unique URL which was given to them at the beginning of the experiment.

The CERBERE scenario is simpler than the Smash and Grab scenario, as it is an exercise for students. The time allowed for this exercise was 1 h 30 min. In the end, this was very little time for a single student who couldn't benefit from the help of others who had another scenario, to complete the whole exercise. For students at this level, we felt it was counter-productive to present a scenario that was too long and contained too many unnecessary machines/accounts. Nonetheless, 4 of the 13 students managed to finish the whole scenario with hints, and 1 without hints. Additionally, 7 managed to beat the first out of all 3 machines. This analysis was done after the experiment by recovering and analyzing the audited log files for every machine. Since we also had access to the procedural-level description of each scenario, the log analysis process was partly automatized by writing customized SIGMA [10] rules for each procedure. This let us know for each instance which transitions were successfully attacked and when.

The publicly accessible version of the CERBERE instances has since been shut down. However, the URSID repository contains instructions to deploy an instance locally, alongside directions on how to attack it. Note that the networking setup in this local deployment will differ from the one that was used during the experiment, as machines will be deployed on a local virtual network as opposed to a public one.

6   Related Works

Cyber-range and cyber-training generation tools have varying scopes in the literature, ranging from being used as a learning tool for academic students, to being a training platform for AI-based attackers. In particular, recent researches did tackle the issue of cyber-range re-usability and deployment based on a scenario description. VulnerVAN [21] is a tool aiming to generate vulnerable architectures ready to be deployed for red team training, based on a user provided description. The user describes the network architecture and an attack sequence, which is represented as a sequence of MITRE ATT&CK techniques [13]. The work of Yamin et al. [22] and Costa et al. [5] also converts scenarios into cyber-range architectures using formal description languages (such as Datalog) and both also incorporate a notion of constraints between exploits which needs to be checked before validating a scenario. While not advertising itself as a cyber-range per se, SecGen [19] is a publicly available vulnerable virtual machine deployment tool made for educational purposes, with the goal of being a Capture-The-Flag and student lab deployment platform. It relies on low-level XML description of architectures (and which specific exploits to implement) to be deployed. While all of these tools are of immense use to researchers, it is to be noted that they tend to rely on low-level description of attack scenarios, all requiring specific information about which exploits to implement and software to install before being able to deploy a scenario. VulnerVAN and the work of Yamin et al. [22] come close, but do not go as far as deploying several scenarios corresponding to a single high-level description. We believe URSID's formalization main perk to be its genericity, and URSID's deployment main interest to be the refinement process. The ability to deploy architectures with only a high-level description (once the preliminary work of writing out procedure constraints is achieved) seems fairly unique in the literature so far, and an interesting field of research to expand in the future.

7   Conclusion and Future Works

In this work we presented URSID, an automatic cyber-range generating tool with a new approach toward attack scenario and insecure architecture deployment.

Starting from a formal representation at the technical level, URSID refines a single scenario into several low level description (at the procedural level), which represent the same overall attacker scenario but all differ procedure wise. All these low level descriptions may then be deployed in virtual machine networks and attacked following the same path as described in the high level description, but with varying exploits. While there is an unavoidable engineering cost in the implementation of procedures and the translation of low level descriptions into virtual machine architectures, given a rich enough database of procedures, enhancing, tweaking, or re-deploying a given scenario has a very low cost. URSID was tested as part of a public training Capture-The-Flag experiment in a university, where its refinement abilities meant students were all following the same overall attack path while all having a unique experience. As future works, we first aim to automatize the process of populating a network with additional machines even more, by making it possible to add prefab machines instead of having to write every single attack position manually. Scenarios would thus be a combination of a written-by-hand attack path and automatically generated machine clusters to populate the network. We are also working on combining URSID with pattern matching for system logging tools, such as SIGMA [10] rules. Indeed, associating pattern matching with procedures could let the user automatically track in real time the path of an attacker through the scenario, by checking for known exploit patterns which were specifically implemented in this instance. Finally more practical experiments involving URSID are on their way, first an improvement upon the CERBERE experiment, then tests of URSID's abilities as a honeynet generation platform.

References

1. Ammann, P., Wijesekera, D., Kaushik, S.: Scalable, graph-based network vulnerability analysis. In: Proceedings of the 9th ACM Conference on Computer and Communications Security, pp. 217-224. CCS '02, Association for Computing Machinery, New York, NY, USA (2002). https://doi.org/10.1145/586110.586140, https://doi.org/10.1145/586110.586140

2. BESSON, P.V.: Ursid repository (2023). https://gitlab.inria.fr/pibesson/ursid-final

3. Besson, P.V., et al.: CERBERE: cybersecurity exercise for red and blue team entertainment, reproducibility. In: CyberHunt 2023 - 6th Annual Workshop on Cyber Threat Intelligence and Hunting. IEEE Computer Society, Sorrento, Italy (Dec 2023). https://centralesupelec.hal.science/hal-04285565

4. Corporation, O.: Virtualbox (2005). https://www.virtualbox.org/

5. Costa, G., Russo, E., Armando, A.: Automating the generation of cyber range virtual scenarios with VSDL. J. Wirel. Mobile Netw., Ubiquit. Comput., Dependable Appl. **13**(4), 61–80 (dec 2022). https://doi.org/10.58346/jowua.2022.i4.004, https://doi.org/10.58346

6. FBI: Internet crime report 2021 (2021). https://www.ic3.gov/Media/PDF/AnnualReport/2021_IC3Report.pdf

7. HashiCorp: Vagrant (2010). https://www.vagrantup.com/

8. Hat, R.: Cve-2019-14287 (2019). https://access.redhat.com/security/cve/cve-2019-14287
9. Hemberg, E., et al.: Linking threat tactics, techniques, and patterns with defensive weaknesses, vulnerabilities and affected platform configurations for cyber hunting (2021)
10. HQ, S.: Generic signature format for siem systems (2017). https://github.com/SigmaHQ/sigma
11. Inc, A.: Ansible (2012). https://www.ansible.com/
12. Mensah, P.: Generation and Dynamic Update of Attack Graphs in Cloud Providers Infrastructures. Ph.D. thesis, CentraleSupélec, Châtenay-Malabry, France (2019). https://tel.archives-ouvertes.fr/tel-02416305
13. MITRE: The mitre att&ck matrix for enterprise (2018). https://attack.mitre.org/matrices/enterprise//
14. MITRE: Apt29 adversary emulation (2021). https://github.com/center-for-threat-informed-defense/adversary_emulation_library/tree/master/apt29
15. NIST: Cyber ranges (2018). https://www.nist.gov/system/files/documents/2018/02/13/cyber_ranges.pdf
16. NIST: Cve-2021-4034 detail (2021). https://nvd.nist.gov/vuln/detail/cve-2021-4034
17. Outkin, A.V., Schulz, P.V., Schulz, T., Tarman, T.D., Pinar, A.: Defender policy evaluation and resource allocation using mitre attck evaluations data (2021)
18. Russo, E., Costa, G., Armando, A.: Scenario design and validation for next generation cyber ranges. In: 2018 IEEE 17th International Symposium on Network Computing and Applications (NCA), pp. 1–4 (2018). https://doi.org/10.1109/NCA.2018.8548324
19. Schreuders, C.: Security scenario generator (secgen). https://github.com/cliffe/secgen (2017), https://github.com/cliffe/SecGen
20. Sharma, Y., Birnbach, S., Martinovic, I.: Radar: A ttp-based extensible, explainable, and effective system for network traffic analysis and malware detection (2023)
21. Venkatesan, S., et al.: Vulnervan: A vulnerable network generation tool. In: MILCOM 2019 - 2019 IEEE Military Communications Conference (MILCOM), pp. 1–6 (2019). https://doi.org/10.1109/MILCOM47813.2019.9021013
22. Yamin, M.M., Katt, B.: Modeling and executing cyber security exercise scenarios in cyber ranges. Comput. Secur. **116**, 102635 (2022). https://doi.org/10.1016/j.cose.2022.102635, https://www.sciencedirect.com/science/article/pii/S0167404822000347

Phishing and Social Network

Does the Anchoring Effect Influence Individuals' Anti-phishing Behavior Intentions?

Yukiko Sawaya[1]([✉])[iD], Ayane Sano[1,2][iD], Takamasa Isohara[1][iD],
Akira Yamada[3][iD], and Ayako Komatsu[4][iD]

[1] KDDI Research Inc., 2-1-15 Ohara, Fujimino, Saitama 356-8502, Japan
{yu-sawaya,ay-sano,ta-isohara}@kddi-research.jp
[2] Shizuoka University, 3-5-1 Johoku, Naka-ku, Hamamatsu,
Shizuoka 432-8011, Japan
[3] Kobe University, 1-1, Rokkodai-cho, Nada-ku, Kobe 657-8501, Japan
akirayamada@people.kobe-u.ac.jp
[4] Notre Dame Seishin University, 2-16-9 Ifuku-cho, Kita-ku,
Okayama 700-8516, Japan
aya@m.ndsu.ac.jp

Abstract. Phishing is one of the most common types of attacks that internet users face. To combat them, it is necessary to consider the human aspect and increase users' awareness since users are forced to decide in the moment whether information they see is legitimate or an attack. In privacy and security research, the anchoring effect, one of the nudging approaches using cognitive biases, is expected to change people's attitudes and/or behaviors, but its effectiveness has not been deeply explored. In this paper, we develop nudging messages against phishing attacks, using the anchoring effect. We conducted two online surveys and analyzed a total of 5000 participant responses. We observed the anchoring effect in the participants' perception of people's probability of being victims. Then, we used questions about this probability as anchoring messages and found that the anchoring techniques increased secure behavior intentions against phishing attacks. In addition, nudging messages that combine the anchoring effect and availability heuristics improved intentions more. Our findings suggest the use of effective nudging messages to increase people's awareness of attacks.

Keywords: Anchoring effect · Nudge · Protection motivation theory · Phishing attacks

1 Introduction

One of the most common types of attacks encountered by internet users is phishing. According to reference [24], phishing attacks may occur in email messages, SMSs, or other communication and deceive people into installing malicious software or visiting malicious web sites to steal their personal information.

© The Author(s), under exclusive license to Springer Nature Switzerland AG 2024
M. Mosbah et al. (Eds.): FPS 2023, LNCS 14551, pp. 141–156, 2024.
https://doi.org/10.1007/978-3-031-57537-2_9

To combat phishing attacks, a system for detecting and deleting phishing messages or phishing sites is needed. Furthermore, support is needed to increase users' awareness of these attacks since users are forced to decide in the moment whether messages are legitimate or attacks. Nudge techniques are effective in supporting users' decisions without economic incentives [35]. These techniques are appropriate for increasing awareness of attacks by changing the premise of users' behaviors and/or users' behaviors against attacks. Nudging approaches that use cognitive biases for security and privacy have been widely studied. One of the nudging approaches, the anchoring effect is expected to change people's behavioral premises and/or behaviors toward privacy and security [1], but its effectiveness has not been deeply explored. In this paper, we focus on applying the anchoring effect into nudging messages against phishing attacks from the background mentioned above. To generate an anchoring effect, numerical and semantic priming stimuli should be presented to users based on the literature [23]. To satisfy this requirement, we focus on protection motivation theory (PMT), which promotes the formation of people's protective motivation against risks by presenting risks as fear appeals [25,26]. Perceived threat vulnerability, one of the major elements of PMT [3], is related to people's perception of the likelihood of victimization as a semantic priming stimulus and can be expressed by the percentage likelihood of being victimized as a numerical stimulus. Based on these expectations, we develop messages that aim to produce the anchoring effect of the probability of people being victims and evaluate whether the messages improve people's secure behavior intentions against phishing attacks through online surveys. We first evaluate whether the anchoring effect is observed in people's perceived probability of victimization by phishing attacks. Then, we evaluate whether the messages that produce higher-value estimation in the first evaluation can lead to secure premises and/or behavior against phishing attacks. In addition, we evaluate the effectiveness of the combination of the anchoring effect and other cognitive bias techniques for further improving people's premises of behavior and/or secure behavior. We observe anchoring effects in the value estimation of the probability of being victimized by phishing attacks. Additionally, we find that anchoring techniques enhance secure behavior against phishing attacks. Finally, our results show that nudging messages that combine the anchoring effect and availability heuristics can improve people's secure behavior intentions. Section 2 of this paper describes the related work, Sect. 3 provides a detailed discussion of the approaches. Then, results are reviewed in Sect. 4 and discussed in Sect. 5. Finally, Sect. 6 concludes the paper.

2   Related Work

2.1   Nudge Techniques with Cognitive Biases

Nudging approaches are widely studied and summarized in the literature. For instance, Caraban et al. presented a systematic review of the use of nudging in human-computer interaction research with the goal of describing the design space of technology-mediated nudging. They identified 23 distinct nudging mechanisms grouped into 6 categories that leverage 15 different cognitive biases [5].

Nudging approaches are also studied in the areas of security and privacy. Sharma et al. focused on two types of digital nudging, framing and priming, and examined their impact on users' behavior in a cybersecurity setting. They found that priming users to information security risks reduced their risk-taking behavior, whereas positive and negative framing of information security messages regarding the potential consequences of available choices did not change users' behavior [29]. Acquisti et al. performed a multidisciplinary assessment of the literature pertaining to privacy and security decision-making. They explored research on soft paternalistic interventions in individuals' privacy and security choices that nudge users toward beneficial choices, discussed the potential benefits and shortcomings of these interventions and identified key ethical, design, and research challenges [1]. Masaki et al. conducted an online survey to compare how different nudge designs influenced decisions in 9 scenarios featuring various privacy and safety threats to adolescent SNS users. They found that adolescents were more likely to avoid potentially risky choices when presented with negative frames than when presented with affirmative frames. They also found that social nudges that displayed statistics on how likely other people were to make potentially risky decisions could have a negative effect compared to nudges with only general privacy and safety suggestions [18]. Zang et al. proposed the frequency nudge, which indicates how frequently user information is used, and the social nudge, which indicates the percentage of other users who give certain data permissions. The results of their online survey showed that privacy nudges were effective in altering privacy attitudes but that the direction of effects depended on the framing valence of the nudges, and the feeling of creepiness mediated the relationship between nudging and privacy attitudes [37]. Kankane et al. conducted an online survey in which participants experienced different types of nudges before indicating their comfort levels with an autogenerated password and their intention to create a new password. They found that the nudges reduced people's comfort level when maintaining the autogenerated password [16]. There are two types of nudges based on dual process theory: type 1 nudges and type 2 nudges. According to the literature [12], "Both types of nudges aim at influencing automatic modes of thinking. But while type 2 nudges are aimed at influencing the attention and premises of - and hence the behaviour anchored in - reflective thinking (i.e. choices), via influencing the automatic system, type 1 nudges are aimed at influencing the behaviour maintained by automatic thinking, or consequences thereof without involving reflective thinking." We call type 1 and 2 nudges behavior-change nudges and premise-change nudges, respectively.

2.2   Protection Motivation Theory

Protection motivation theory (PMT) was proposed and developed by Rogers et al. [25, 26] and has been the subject of many studies. Based on the literature [26], PMT postulates that the three crucial components of a fear appeal are the magnitude of noxiousness of a depicted event, the probability of that event's occurrence, and the efficacy of a protective response. In recent years, it has been said that the premises of protection motivation are composed of five main factors: perceived threat severity, threat vulnerability, response costs, response efficacy, and self-efficacy. These factors affect protection motivation, behavioral intention, and actual behavior [3]. PMT is frequently applied in the area of privacy and security. Story et al. proposed nudging interventions based on PMT and implementation intentions (II) to encourage participants to use secure mobile payments. Both PMT-only and PMT with II interventions made participants more likely to make mobile payments relative to the control group [31]. Story et al. also tested an informational nudge based on PMT designed to raise awareness of the Tor browser and found that the nudge helped participants form accurate perceptions of the browser [32].

2.3 Anchoring Effect

The anchoring effect is one of the cognitive biases proposed and developed by Kahneman et al. [10] whereby an individual's decisions are influenced by particular reference values. There are two types of anchoring in estimating uncertain quantities: self-generated and experimenter-provided [7–9]. In experimenter-provided anchoring, people are shown numeric values and consider the estimation based on the values. An example question [9] is "Is the population of Chicago more or less than 200,000?" In self-generated anchoring, people make decisions based on values in their knowledge or experience. An example of this anchoring [7] is "What is the highest recorded body temperature in a human being?" In the studies of anchoring effects, participants are asked the estimated values after showing the questions and evaluates whether the values are skewed to the anchor values. Many studies aim to reveal the mechanism of the anchoring effect in the estimation of numeric values. Onuki et al. revealed that both numerical and semantic priming stimuli must be presented for anchoring effects to occur [23]. Sudgen et al. found anchoring effects only when the anchor value was framed as plausible in decision-making [33]. Acquisti et al. noted that the anchoring effect may significantly affect privacy decision-making [1]. However, detailed analyses of the anchoring effect on security and privacy have not yet been conducted.

3   Method

3.1   Overview

Our goal is to develop nudging messages that can change people's behavior to counter threats using the anchoring effect. An anchoring effect occurs when numerical and semantic priming stimuli are presented [23], and it is expected to change people's premises of behavior and/or their behavior itself [1]. The effectiveness of the anchoring effect as a nudge has not been studied in depth in the area of privacy and security, although some possibilities have been discussed.

In this paper, we describe how the anchoring effect affects people's premises of behavior and/or behavior intentions toward security threats with a focus on phishing attacks. Based on reference [23], the numerical and semantic priming stimuli of phishing attacks should be presented to generate anchoring effects. Here, we focus on PMT, which promotes the formation of people's protective motivation against risks by presenting risks as fear appeals. The major elements of PMT are perceived threat severity, threat vulnerability, response costs, response efficacy, self-efficacy, and protection motivation [3]. These elements are considered the premises of behavioral intentions and actual behaviors. Among them, perceived threat vulnerability is related to an individual's probability of being a victim as a numeric value. For this reason, we construct messages that aim to produce the anchoring effect in the probability of victimization and evaluate whether the messages produce the anchoring effect. To our knowledge, similar studies have not been conducted. If the anchoring effect is produced, then we expect that a higher probability of being victimized leads to the premise of behavior and/or behavior intention changes among people [1]. In addition, if the anchoring effect is used with other techniques that produce cognitive biases, we expect to create more effective messages for nudges that change premises of behaviors and behavioral intentions. Therefore, our hypotheses are as follows:

H1 The anchoring effect is observed in the perceived probability of people being victims of phishing attacks.
H2 Messages that produce a higher perceived probability are behavior-changing and/or attitude-changing nudges against phishing attacks.
H3 If the anchoring effect is combined with other cognitive bias techniques, the effect of the nudges increases.

As the first step, we evaluated H1. We conducted an online survey that asked participants for their perception of the probability that people would be victimized after showing different numeric values of the percentage to different groups and evaluated whether the distribution of perceived probability showed differences among participants. If the distributions differed according to the numeric values, we regarded H1 as supported. If H1 was supported, we evaluated H2 and H3 as the second step. We assessed whether the anchoring messages that were used in the first step changed the participants' premise of behaviors and/or behavioral intentions. In addition, we created messages that aimed to produce both anchoring effects and other cognitive bias techniques and evaluated their effectiveness. We selected availability heuristics [36], a famous cognitive bias. We summarize the PMT components and evaluation steps described above in Fig. 1. Grey part shows the PMT model. Severity (SV), vulnerability (VN), response efficacy (RE), cost (CS), self-efficacy (SE), and motivation (MV) indicate perceived threat severity, threat vulnerability, response efficacy, response cost, self-efficacy, and protection motivation in PMT, respectively, as premises for threats. Behavior intention (noAccess) denotes the intention to engage in secure behavior and, in this paper, the intention to not access the phishing link. Blue and red part of the figure summarizes the steps of our analyses.

3.2   Ethical Considerations

We used the services of Cross Marketing, Inc. [6] to collect the survey responses. Cross Marketing, Inc. is a Japanese company that offers online research ser-

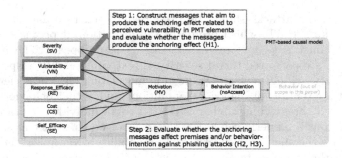

Fig. 1. PMT components and overview of our evaluation.

vices with a pool of 4 million participants within Japan and is widely used in both marketing research and academic research [27,28,34]. The surveys were conducted in Japanese. No personal data were collected, and the responses of the participants were anonymized. A consent form including this description was shown to the candidates for participation, and they were asked whether they were willing to participate. If they were not willing to continue answering the questionnaire, they had the right to stop answering the questions, and records of their answers were not saved. These protocols followed the principles of the Japan Marketing Research Association [15], which are based on the ICC/ESOMAR International Code [14]. We do not know the precise amount of the incentives that were offered to the participants as compensation (although it was ~1USD) because we recruited the participants through the marketing survey company. However, the compensation was well considered and the participants agreed to it. The protocol was approved by the ethics review committee of our office.

4   Experimental Results

4.1   Step 1

Study Design and Participants. First, we evaluated H1. We verified that different values shown to the user could result in different user responses. More precisely, we asked the participants their perceived probability of being victims of phishing attacks after showing the different numeric values of the percentage to different groups. We then evaluated whether the distribution of perceived probability showed differences among the participants. We designed the messages to allow the participants to imagine the approximate values. Participants in Group 1 were shown a message that asked their perceived probability of people being victims without the numeric value as self-generated anchoring, as shown in Table 1. Participants in Groups 2, 3, 4 and 5 were shown messages that asked about the perceived probability of people being victims with numeric values of

1, 10, 50, and 90, respectively. These messages aimed to produce experimenter-provided anchoring. After the participants were shown the messages, they were asked to answer the values they imagined.

Table 1. Questions for each group

Group	Description
1	What percentage of internet users do you think become victims of phishing attacks in their lifetime?
2	Do you think the percentage of internet users who become victims of phishing attacks in their lifetimes is higher or lower than 1%?
3	Do you think the percentage of internet users who become victims of phishing attacks in their lifetimes is higher or lower than 10%?
4	Do you think the percentage of internet users who become victims of phishing attacks in their lifetimes is higher or lower than 50%?
5	Do you think the percentage of internet users who become victims of phishing attacks in their lifetimes is higher or lower than 90%?

Participants were recruited from February 4th to 6th, 2022. To reduce possible influences of the participants' traits related to gender and age, 50 participants of each age decade (20 s, 30 s, 40 s, 50 s, and 60 s) for each gender were recruited and 500 participants were recruited per group. As five groups were assumed for this survey, we collected totally 2500 participants responses.

Analysis and Results. To evaluate the distribution differences of the answers among groups, we used the Kruskal-Wallis test, which is a nonparametric method for testing whether samples originate from the same distribution, because we did not observe normality by conducting the Kolmogorov-Smirnov test ($D = 0.952$, $p < 0.001$). We used the Steel-Dwass test, which is also a nonparametric method for evaluating whether each pair has significant differences.

Figure 2 shows the distribution of the answers of each group's participants. The Kruskal-Wallis test ($p < 0.001$, $H = 635.3$) and the Steel-Dwass test (all pairs' p-values were < 0.01) showed significant differences among the values. The results indicate an anchoring effect in the perceived probability of people being victims; in other words, H1 was supported. The value of the answers increases according to the anchor values, and median values are saturated when the anchor value is 50. The variance of the answers is greater in Group 4 than in Group 5. Focusing on the distribution of Group 1, the median is higher than that of Group 3 and lower than that of Group 4.

4.2 Step 2

Study Design and Participants. As H1 was supported, we then evaluated H2 and H3. We verified whether anchoring messages that generated higher probabilities in people's being victims could result in the greater changes of users'

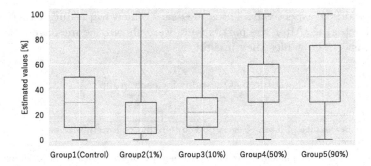

Fig. 2. Boxplot of the answer distribution in each group

Table 2. Messages patterns and the correspondences of groups

Message	Description	Group				
		1	2	3	4	5
NoAnchorA	What percentage of internet users do you think become victims of phishing attacks in their lifetime?	✓				
AnchorA	Do you think the percentage of internet users who become victims of phishing attacks in their lifetimes is higher or lower than 50%?		✓			
NoAnchorB	What percentage of you do you think become a victim of phishing attacks within a year?			✓		
AnchorB	Do you think the percentage of you becoming victims of phishing attacks within a year is higher or lower than 50%?				✓	

premise of behaviors and/or behavior intentions. We also verified the effectiveness of the combination of anchoring effect and availability heuristics. In step 1, in Groups 2, 3, 4, and 5 (experimenter-provided anchoring), the message shown to Group 4 resulted in the highest median values and lower variance than Group 5, which produced the same median values as Group 4 in the participants' perception of the probability of victimization. We selected the message shown to the participants in Group 1 to determine whether the message aimed to produce self-generated anchoring worked to produce anti-phishing behavioral intention. These messages are denoted in Table 2 as noAnchorA and AnchorA. To test H3, we created messages that added the essence of availability heuristics into noAnchorA and AnchorA. The messages noAnchorB and AnchorB in Table 2 showed more familiar examples of victims for the participants and aimed to recall the participants' probability of being victims in a year rather than in their lifetimes. Four messages, noAnchorA, AnchorA, noAnchorB, and AnchorB, were shown to the different participants. The participants in each group were provided with different information about the phishing attacks and the messages that aimed to produce the anchoring effect shown in Table 2.

```
Notification from <mobile carriers>  This message is brought to you by <mobile carriers> of
customers. You can check the communication fee for this month by clicking the following link:
 https://<domain>.<hostname>.<TLD>/
```

Fig. 3. Description of the phishing message

After showing the nudging messages, we showed a phishing message that mimicked the mobile phone carrier that the participant used, as shown in Fig. 3, and asked whether the participant would access the link. The names of the carriers that the participants used were placed in the <carrier> section. The fields <domain> and <hostname> were the actual domain name and hostname in the carriers' URLs, and the string that did not exist in the top-level domain defined by ICANN was placed in the <TLD> section, which means that the URLs did not actually exist. After showing the phishing messages, we asked them the following questions to understand their behavioral intentions regarding the links and their behavioral premise toward phishing attacks.

- Intention to access the link to determine whether behavioral intention differs due to the nudging messages
- Major elements of PMT defined in [3] to identify the premises of behaviors differs due to nudging messages

In addition to the above questions, participants were asked to answer the estimated values for each anchoring messages same as step 1, as a postquestion.

We recruited 2500 participants who used the three largest mobile carriers in Japan, which account for 84.3% of all mobile phone users [22], from July 22nd to 29th, 2022. A total of 250 participants of each age decade (20s, 30s, 40s, 50s, and 60s) for each gender were recruited for the survey. We created five groups, from Group 1 to Group 5, with identical composition, as in the survey in Sect. 4.1. The participants in each group were provided different information about the nudging messages. The information shown for each group is described in Table 2. The participants in Group 5 were the control group and were not shown any of the messages.

Analysis and Result. We used structural equation modeling (SEM) to analyze which information affected the premise of behaviors and behavioral intention because our hypotheses consisted of multiple factors that correlated with one another. We used semopy [19], which calculates covariance-based SEM, and Wishart log-likelihood estimation. Our model for validating H2 and H3 is shown in Fig. 4. In this model, nudging messages affect both premises (i.e., PMT's major elements) and behaviors intention (i.e., the intention to access the link). Each of PMT's elements also affect behavioral intentions in our model. We evaluated the model and removed the non-significant paths between nudging messages and components of PMT (red arrows in Fig. 4) based on the literature [11,17,20] with a p-value above 0.1 [4,30]. In this process, we did not remove the paths of

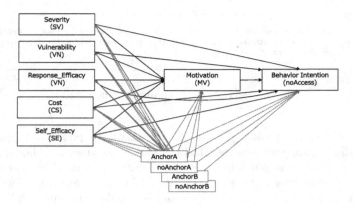

Fig. 4. Model for evaluating H2 and H3. (Color figure online)

PMT (black arrows) since these paths were based on the existing theory. NoAccess refers to the behavioral intention where the participant's answer was "I don't click the link." It is expressed as binary. Each nudging message, AnchorA, noAnchorA, AnchorB, and noAnchorB, is also expressed as binary independent variables according to whether it was shown to each participant. We treated each major elements of PMT as the latent variables, since Cronbach's alpha values of answers to questions for each element were high (SV: 0.878, VN: 0.905, RE: 0.916, CS: 0.918, SE: 0.915, and MV: 0.917). Details of the questions about behavioral intention and premises are shown in Table 3. After a iteration of removing the paths of with a p-value higher than 0.1 as mentioned the above, we obtained the model shown in Fig. 5. We validated the model by the goodness-of-fit indicators, CFI, GFI, TLI, and RMSEA. Our model resulted in CFI, GFI, TLI, and RMSEA values of 0.994, 0.989, 0.992, and 0.023, respectively. The model is good at sufficiently explaining the dataset when CFI, GFI, and TLI are greater than 0.9 and RMSEA is below 0.06 [13,21]. From the results, the model in Fig. 5 can reasonably explain the relationships among the factors and behavioral intention.

The path weights in Fig. 5 were normalized from 0 to 1 to compare the degree of the relationships among the components. As shown in the figure, we found that the intention to click on the phishing link was reduced with significant p-values by the messages we provided. The effect was not strong but had a significant level, while the premise of behavior, which was composed of major PMT elements, was not affected. These results show that messages that include the anchoring effect are likely to be nudges that change behavioral intention more than they change premises. None of PMT elements did not affect the intention to access the link with the significant level but motivation affected the intention to access the link the most. This means that people who naturally have motivation are aware of phishing links. Comparing the path weights between AnchorA and AnchorB concerning the intention to access the link, the weight was higher for AnchorB. Similarly, noAnchorB reduced the intention to access the link more than noAnchorA. The results show that messages that include both the anchor-

Table 3. Questions after showing the information

Question	Description	μ
noAccess	Do you access the link?	0.82
SV1	I think I could be seriously harmed if I am involved in a phishing attack	3.77
SV2	I think I could experience serious monetary loss if I am involved in a phishing attack	3.81
SV3	I think I could be seriously harmed if I am involved in a phishing attack and have my password stolen	4.00
VN1	I think I could be seriously harmed by a phishing attack in the near future	3.40
VN2	I think I could become a victim of a phishing attack and experience financial harm in the near future	3.37
VN3	I think I could get hit by a phishing attack and have my ID or password stolen in the near future	3.41
RE1	Checking whether messages or websites are fake is a good way to prevent serious harm from phishing attacks	3.82
RE2	Checking whether messages or websites are fake is a good way to prevent monetary loss from phishing attacks	3.81
RE3	Checking whether messages or websites are fake is a good way to prevent password theft from phishing attacks	3.79
CS1	Preventing serious harm from a phishing attack is a burden for me	3.28
CS2	Preventing monetary loss from a phishing attack is a burden for me	3.26
CS3	Preventing password theft from a phishing attack is difficult for me	3.28
SE1	Preventing serious harm from a phishing attack is difficult for me in terms of skills and knowledge*	2.64
SE2	Preventing monetary loss from a phishing attack is difficult for me in terms of skills and knowledge*	2.65
SE3	Preventing password theft from a phishing attack is difficult for me in terms of skills and knowledge*	2.65
MV1	I would like to take measures to prevent serious harm from phishing attacks	3.89
MV2	I would like to take measures to prevent financial harm from phishing attacks	3.91
MV3	I would like to take measures to prevent ID/password theft from phishing attacks	3.93

For the behavior intention, we set the values 0 for the answer 'yes' and 1 for the answer 'no.' For the attitude question, we set the values as follows; I don't think so: 1, I rathe don't think so: 2, neutral: 3, I rather think so:4, I think so: 5, and * denotes reversed questions.

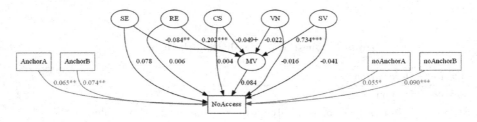

Fig. 5. Results of the causal model. (***: p < 0.001, **: p < 0.01, *: p < 0.05, +: p < 0.1)

ing effect and availability heuristics are more likely to reduce the intention to access the link; in other words, they produce "stronger" behavioral intention changing nudges. These results support our Hypothesis H2 for behavioral intention changes but do not support the premise of behavioral change. In addition, H3 is supported.

5   Discussion

5.1   Effectiveness of Nudging Messages

Our nudging messages aimed to recall the users' perceptions of threat vulnerability and worked as behavior-changing nudges. These messages did not affect perceived threat vulnerability, and perceived threat vulnerability itself did not affect behavioral intention, indicating that the messages did not work as premise-changing nudges. People did not explicitly recognize the threat vulnerability, but they did recognize it implicitly, and their intention to access the link decreased. Our nudging messages were effective in encouraging people to be secure because they changed behavioral intentions without changing the premises of the behavior. The combination of the anchoring effect and availability heuristics showed a better effect from the results comparing AnchorA with AnchorB, and noAnchorA with noAnchorB. We conclude that anchoring techniques combined with other cognitive biases, such as availability heuristics, are more effective in changing people's behavioral intention.

The comparison of the paths from AnchorA to NoAccess and from noAnchorA to NoAccess supports our expectation: messages that produce a higher estimation of being a victim lead users to have more secure behavioral intentions, as described in step 2. However, the comparison of the paths from AnchorB to NoAccess and from noAnchorB to NoAccess showed that the behavioral intention of accessing the link was reduced when the anchor value was not included. Here, we evaluated the estimated values of participants. Figure 6 shows the estimated values of the participants in the postquestion in step 2. Note that there are no significant differences in value estimation between Group 1 in step 1 and Group 1 in step 2 ($U = 121648.5$, $p = 0.460$) and between Group 4 in step 1 and Group 2 in step 2 ($U = 132609.5$, $p = 0.094$), respectively, using the Mann-Whitney U test. This means that the value estimates for the messages were consistent across

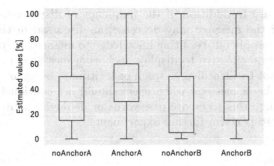

Fig. 6. Value estimation in the step 2

different participants. We observed a similar tendency in the pairs of AnchorA and noAnchorA, and AnchorB and noAnchorB: there were significant differences between AnchorB and noAnchorB in the estimated values from the result of the Mann-Whitney U test (U $= 91918.5$, p < 0.001), but we observed the opposite effect in AnchorB and noAnchorB compared to AnchorA and noAnchorA. This result may be due to the different mechanisms of the anchoring effect in the estimation of numeric values and decision-making by numeric values described in Sect. 2.3. In the anchoring effect for value estimation, the answers for estimated values are considered from numerical and semantic priming, whereas for decision-making, anchoring becomes effective when the values provided are plausible. The value of 50 may have been implausible for the probability of the participants being victims in a year, and it may have been too high to increase people's motivation to protect against phishing attacks. We expect that we can produce more effective nudging messages that include the anchoring effect by prioritizing consideration of the anchor's plausibility. Further experiments will be performed in the future.

5.2 Limitations

Our procedures in step 2 explored whether behavioral intentions rather than actual behaviors change according to the anchoring effect through an online survey. We used this procedure because we sought to understand the participants' behavior from a macro perspective. In future work, we will perform appropriate tests to determine whether actual behaviors change as a result of our proposed messages in a natural way.

5.3 Application of Our Findings

Despite the limitations mentioned above, we consider our findings applicable to some scenarios. For instance, regarding the timing of when people click links in email messages, we anticipate that the anchoring effect will last until just after the messages are displayed to users because this is a nudge technique that uses cognitive biases. In addition, if the frequency of displaying the message is high, the effect of the message may decrease, as discussed in the literature on habituation [2]. To apply our resulting knowledge to messaging applications such as mailers, it may be effective to display anchoring messages when an email is received that cannot be identified as spam or legitimate by spam filters. Another scenario is to display a message when users should act cautiously and securely, such as encouraging users to create passwords or deploying multifactor authentication. We plan to perform further experiments.

6   Conclusion

In this paper, we developed nudging messages against phishing attacks using the anchoring effect and evaluated their effectiveness. We observed anchoring effects in the value estimation of the probability of people being victims of phishing attacks and found that the anchoring techniques enhanced secure behavior against phishing attacks. We also found that nudging messages that combined the anchoring effect and availability heuristics could improve people's secure behaviors. We plan to conduct further experiments mentioned in this paper as future work.

References

1. Acquisti, A., et al.: Nudges for privacy and security: understanding and assisting users' choices online. ACM Comput. Surv. **50**(3), 1–41 (2017)
2. Amran, A., Zaaba, Z.F., Singh, M.K.M.: Habituation effects in computer security warning. Inf. Secur. J. Global Perspect. **27**(4), 192–204 (2018)
3. Boss, S.R., Galletta, D.F., Lowry, P.B., Moody, G.D., Polak, P.: What do systems users have to fear? Using fear appeals to engender threats and fear that motivate protective security behaviors. MIS Q. **39**(4), 837–864 (2015)
4. Botetzagias, I., Dima, A.-F., Malesios, C.: Extending the theory of planned behavior in the context of recycling: the role of moral norms and of demographic predictors. Resour. Conserv. Recycl. **95**, 58–67 (2015)
5. Caraban, A., Karapanos, E., Gonçalves, D., Campos, P.: 23 ways to nudge: a review of technology-mediated nudging in human-computer interaction. In: Proceedings of the 2019 CHI Conference on Human Factors in Computing Systems, CHI 2019, pp. 1–15, New York, NY, USA. Association for Computing Machinery (2019)
6. Cross Marketing Inc. Cross marketing, Inc. (2022). https://www.cross-m.co.jp/en/. Accessed 29 May 2023
7. Epley, N., Gilovich, T.: Putting adjustment back in the anchoring and adjustment heuristic: differential processing of self-generated and experimenter-provided anchors. Psychol. Sci. **12**, 391–396 (2001)
8. Epley, N., Gilovich, T.: When effortful thinking influences judgmental anchoring: differential effects of forewarning and incentives on self-generated and externally provided anchors. J. Behav. Decis. Making **18**, 199–212 (2005)
9. Epley, N., Gilovich, T.: The anchoring-and-adjustment heuristic: why the adjustments are insufficient. Psychol. Sci. **17**(4), 311–318 (2006). PMID: 16623688

10. Frederick, S., Kahneman, D., Mochon, D.: Elaborating a simpler theory of anchoring. J. Consum. Psychol. **20**, 17–19 (2010)
11. Hanley, A.W., Garland, E.L.: Clarity of mind: structural equation modeling of associations between dispositional mindfulness, self-concept clarity and psychological well-being. Personality Individ. Differ. **106**, 334–339 (2017)
12. Hansen, P., Jespersen, A.: Nudge and the manipulation of choice. Eur. J. Risk Regul. **1**, 3–28 (2013)
13. Litze, H., Bentler, P.M.: Cutoff criteria for fit indexes in covariance structure analysis: conventional criteria versus new alternatives. Struct. Equ. Model. **6**(1), 1–55 (1999)
14. ICC/ESOMAR. ICC/ESOMAR international code on market, opinion and social research and data analytics (2016). https://esomar.org/uploads/attachments/ckqtawvjq00uukdtrhst5sk9u-iccesomar-international-code-english.pdf. Accessed 29 May 2023
15. Japan Marketing Research Association. Japan marketing research association (JMRA) (2022). https://www.jmra-net.or.jp/Portals/0/aboutus/en/index.html. Accessed 29 May 2023
16. Kankane, S., DiRusso, C., Buckley, C.: Can we nudge users toward better password management? An initial study. In: Extended Abstracts of the 2018 CHI Conference on Human Factors in Computing Systems, CHI EA 2018, pp. 1–6, New York, NY, USA. Association for Computing Machinery (2018)
17. Liu, K.T., Kueh, Y.C., Arifin, W.N., Kim, Y., Kuan, G.: Application of transtheoretical model on behavioral changes, and amount of physical activity among university's students. Front. Psychol. **9**, 1–8 (2018)
18. Masaki, H., Shibata, K., Hoshino, S., Ishihama, T., Saito, N., Yatani, K.: Exploring nudge designs to help adolescent SNS users avoid privacy and safety threats. In: Proceedings of the 2020 CHI Conference on Human Factors in Computing Systems, CHI 2020, pp. 1–11, New York, NY, USA. Association for Computing Machinery (2020)
19. Meshcheryakov, G., Igolkina, A.A., Samsonova, M.G.: semopy 2: a structural equation modeling package with random effects in Python. arXiv, abs/2106.01140 (2021)
20. Mirhashem, R., Allen, H.C., Adams, Z.W., van Stolk-Cooke, K., Legrand, A., Price, M.: The intervening role of urgency on the association between childhood maltreatment, PTSD, and substance-related problems. Addict. Behav. **69**, 98–103 (2017)
21. Netemeyer, R.G., Bearden, W.O., Sharma, S.: Scaling Procedures: Issues and Applications. Sage Publications, London (2003)
22. The Ministry of Internal Affairs and Japan Communications (MIC). Announcement of quarterly data on the number of telecommunications service contracts and market share (FY2022 Q2 (End of September)) (2022). https://www.soumu.go.jp/main_sosiki/joho_tsusin/eng/pressrelease/2022/12/16_03.html. Accessed 2 May 2023
23. Onuki, Y., Honda, H., Ueda, K.: What stimuli are necessary for anchoring effects to occur? Front. Psychol. **12**, 1–10 (2021)
24. Osterman Research. How to reduce the risk of phishing and ransomware (2021). https://resources.trendmicro.com/rs/945-CXD-062/images/Reduce-Phishing-Ransomware_Trend-Micro.pdf. Accessed 23 May 2023
25. Rogers, R., Prentice-Dunn, S.: Protection motivation theory. Phys. Rev. Lett. **1** (1997)
26. Rogers, R.W.: A protection motivation theory of fear appeals and attitude change1. J. Psychol. **91**(1), 93–114 (1975). PMID: 28136248

27. Sakakibara, H., Uramoto, S.: Empirical analysis of the reference point effect in residential choices under the risk of slope disasters. In: 2016 IEEE International Conference on Systems, Man, and Cybernetics (SMC), pp. 004112–004117 (2016)
28. Sawaya, Y., Sharif, M., Christin, N., Kubota, A., Nakarai, A., Yamada, A.: Self-confidence trumps knowledge: a cross-cultural study of security behavior. In: Proceedings of the 2017 CHI Conference on Human Factors in Computing Systems, CHI 2017, pp. 2202–2214, New York, NY, USA. Association for Computing Machinery (2017)
29. Sharma, K., Zhan, X., Nah, F.F.-H., Siau, K., Cheng, M.X.: Impact of digital nudging on information security behavior: an experimental study on framing and priming in cybersecurity. Organ. Cybersecur. J. Pract. Process People 1(1), 69–91 (2021). Research Unit(s) information for this publication is provided by the author(s) concerned
30. Stockley, R., et al.: Phase II study of a neutrophil elastase inhibitor (AZD9668) in patients with bronchiectasis. Respir. Med. 107(4), 524–533 (2013)
31. Story, P., Smullen, D., Acquisti, A., Cranor, L.F., Sadeh, N., Schaub, F.: From intent to action: nudging users towards secure mobile payments. In: Sixteenth Symposium on Usable Privacy and Security (SOUPS 2020), pp. 379–415. USENIX Association, August 2020
32. Story, P., et al.: Increasing adoption of tor browser using informational and planning nudges. Proc. Priv. Enhancing Technol. 2022(04), 152–183 (2022)
33. Sugden, R., Zheng, J., Zizzo, D.J.: Not all anchors are created equal. J. Econ. Psychol. 39, 21–31 (2013)
34. Tanaka, Y., Inuzuka, M., Arai, H., Takahashi, Y., Kukita, M., Inui, K.: Who does not benefit from fact-checking websites? A psychological characteristic predicts the selective avoidance of clicking uncongenial facts. In: Proceedings of the 2023 CHI Conference on Human Factors in Computing Systems, CHI 2023, New York, NY, USA. Association for Computing Machinery (2023)
35. Thaler, R.H., Sunstein, C.R.: Nudge. Yale University Press, New Haven, CT and London (2008)
36. Tversky, A., Kahneman, D.: Availability: a heuristic for judging frequency and probability. Cogn. Psychol. 5(2), 207–232 (1973)
37. Zhang, B., Xu, H.: Privacy nudges for mobile applications: effects on the creepiness emotion and privacy attitudes. In: Proceedings of the 19th ACM Conference on Computer-Supported Cooperative Work & Social Computing, CSCW 2016, pp. 1676–1690, New York, NY, USA. Association for Computing Machinery (2016)

IntelliTweet: A Multifaceted Feature Approach to Detect Malicious Tweets

Eric Edem Dzeha[✉] and Guy-Vincent Jourdan

Faculty of Computer Science, University of Ottawa, Ottawa, Canada
{edzeh094,gjourdan}@uOttawa.ca

Abstract. Twitter faces an ongoing issue with malicious tweets from deceptive accounts engaged in phishing, scams, and spam, negatively impacting the overall Twitter user experience. In response to growing security concerns, various machine learning-based methods have been deployed to detect and analyze these malicious activities. However, the evolving nature of the threats and tactics used by malicious actors cast doubts on the effectiveness of previously employed techniques. These methods often encounter challenges in addressing URL obfuscation techniques and managing false positive predictions. In this paper, we present "IntelliTweet", an innovative solution designed to comprehend tweet content and accurately identify malicious tweets. This is achieved by incorporating a combination of contextual and content-based features, surpassing the use of conventional features alone. IntelliTweet takes a holistic approach that includes URL analysis, sentiment analysis, Twitter user analysis, and TFIDF-based content analysis, all working in tandem to enhance malicious tweet detection. For this system, our evaluation strategy places emphasis on reducing false positives while maintaining high precision. Through comparative experiments, we have demonstrated that IntelliTweet effectively counters URL obfuscation techniques, is robust, and minimizes the false positive rate. The system achieved a 98.38% precision, a 97.54% f-measure, and yielded a false positive rate of 0.14.

Keywords: Twitter · Malicious tweets · Machine learning · Phishing · Scam · Spam · Features · Text classification · Sentiment analysis · Obfuscation techniques · Social media · Cybercrime

1 Introduction

Twitter, as a social media platform, is prone to malicious activities such as phishing, scams, and spamming targeted at its users [15]. Malicious actors take advantage of the platform's features to deceive users [7,40]. With over 200 million active users generating 400 million daily tweets [2], Twitter serves as a hub for real-time conversations, news dissemination, and event discussions. However, this widespread usage also exposes users to various vulnerabilities through the spread of malicious content [32]. Addressing and mitigating these risks is crucial to harness Twitter's potential for positive interactions.

© The Author(s), under exclusive license to Springer Nature Switzerland AG 2024
M. Mosbah et al. (Eds.): FPS 2023, LNCS 14551, pp. 157–173, 2024.
https://doi.org/10.1007/978-3-031-57537-2_10

Until October 2018, Twitter had a 140-character limit for tweets, which was then increased to 280 characters [22]. To include URLs within this limit, users commonly use shortening services like bit.ly [10]. Malicious actors exploit these shortened URLs for redirection [5, 24, 26, 34], leading users to intermediary servers set up by attackers and potentially exposing them to harmful web pages [8]. In 2022, phishing attacks reached a record high of over 4.7 million reported cases, a 150% increase since 2019, according to the Anti-Phishing Working Group.

Twitter has taken steps to address malicious URLs [37]. They automatically scan URLs to flag potential threats and offer users a reporting system for suspicious URLs [25]. Although these efforts are being pursued, these malicious activities remain a persistent setback to the users of Twitter. This results from the fact that scammers and phishers are constantly evolving their tactics to avoid detection [24]. As a result, detecting and preventing such malicious activities remains a critical challenge for both platform owners and users.

Some researchers [28, 33, 36] investigate phishing and other malicious activity reports shared on Twitter. They identify and analyze phishing attacks and raise more awareness through these reports, which have low interaction from other users on Twitter, especially from the targeted domains and organizations. Other researchers propose using more advanced machine learning techniques, such as deep learning or neural networks, to better distinguish between legitimate and malicious tweets.

In this study, we suggest that relying solely on malicious URLs in a tweet may not be sufficient for accurate classification. The presence of these URLs does not always mean that the tweet is part of a phishing or scam campaign. It could be shared by a legitimate user trying to raise awareness or by someone unaware of the URL's association with a phishing or scam campaign. Our paper introduces "IntelliTweet", a machine learning-based system designed for a precise identification of malicious tweets. IntelliTweet takes a multifaceted approach, combining URL features, user profile attributes, sentiment analysis, and TFIDF-based content analysis. Our research's main contribution lies in considering both the content and context of tweets, as well as the behavior of the accounts sharing them to effectively distinguishes between malicious and legitimate tweets, including user reports. We achieve this by:

1. **Data Collection:** Gathering live tweets to build a comprehensive dataset, encompassing malicious, legitimate tweets, and user reports.
2. **Feature Enhancement:** Introduction of more features to create a holistic approach that accounts for the nuances of tweet context and content.
3. **Model Selection:** Conducting experiments with seven different models to identify the best fit for our dataset, ensuring optimal performance.
4. **Feature Fusion:** Combining text classification, Twitter user features, and tweet text features for robust model training.
5. **Text Analysis Evaluation:** Looking at the value added by the fusion of contextual feature (sentimental analysis and Term Frequencies) with conventional features.

Our code and datasets have been made publicly accessible and can be found within our GitHub repository [13]. The paper is structured as follows: In Sect. 2, we review pertinent literature discussing methods and approaches for detecting malicious activities on Twitter. Section 3 details our methodology, explaining our approach, the collection of malicious, reported, and legitimate tweets, and the analysis of relevant features; Sect. 4.1 presents the key experiments and discusses the results; and in Sect. 5, we summarize our findings, draw conclusions, highlight limitations, and offer recommendations.

2   Review of Literature in Related Approaches

This section gives an overview of current literature on detecting malicious tweets. It starts by exploring traditional methods for identifying misinformation, scams, phishing, and spam, followed by insights into recent advancements, their strengths and weaknesses, and potential areas for improvement and research gaps.

2.1   Traditional Approaches to Detecting Phishing, Spam, and Scams

List-Based Techniques: Traditionally, list-based methods have been commonly used to combat phishing, spam, and scams [16]. Organizations like the Anti-Phishing Working Group (APWG) have played a pivotal role in this battle [41]. They collect, analyze and maintain lists of known phishing URLs, which serve as references for authentication [41]. Services like PhishTank, Google Safe Browsing, and OpenPhish adopt similar techniques, identifying phishing attempts or providing access to databases for quick lookups. These databases contain blocklists with suspicious URLs and IP addresses [30] for authenticity verification and allowlists for presumed safe websites, effectively treating all others as blocklisted [3]. List-based methods are favored for their cost-effectiveness and speed but encounter challenges in maintaining global blocklists due to the constant emergence of new phishing sites, often lagging in updates and missing new attacks [6]. Maintaining a comprehensive global allowlist is equally challenging and may need automatic updates [3] due to the vast number of legitimate websites and the potential for minor URL changes that can disrupt matching within these lists.

Rule-Based Methods: Rule-based approaches offer an alternative strategy for identifying phishing, spam, and scams. These systems use predefined rules or patterns to flag potentially malicious content [19,23]. The CANTINA study by Zhang et al. [42], introduced a content-based approach for malicious webpage detection. Utilizing Term Frequency-Inverse Document Frequency (TF-IDF) and Google search queries, they created a unique lexical signature with top TF-IDF weighted words and integrated the webpage's domain name. Querying Google search results for domain verification effectively reduced false positives and enhanced accuracy. The basic TF-IDF variant achieved a 94% true positive rate with a 30% false positive rate. Incorporating domain names significantly mitigated false positives to 10%, albeit with a trade-off, lowering accuracy to 67%. Introducing the "zero results mean phishing" heuristic dramatically improved accuracy to 97%, maintaining low false positives.

Rule-based methods, while heuristic-driven and very valuable, are not immune to false positives and may require fine-tuning. They have limitations in adapting to the dynamic nature of Twitter-based phishing attacks.

Machine Learning-Based Methods: In response to these challenges, researchers have turned to machine learning-based methods emerging as powerful tools in the fight against phishing.

Korkmaz et al.'s research [24] demonstrated the promise of machine learning algorithms in creating robust phishing detection systems. Their methodology hinged on the utilization of eight distinct machine learning algorithms in conjunction with three diverse datasets. The outcomes underscored the remarkable efficiency of machine learning in enhancing phishing detection, yielding commendable levels of accuracy.

Similarly, Jain and Gupta [21] introduced a client-side anti-phishing method using machine learning. Identifying nineteen critical website characteristics from source code and URLs, their approach achieved a 99.39% true positive rate and an overall detection accuracy of 99.09%. Despite their promise, machine learning-based methods face limitations, such as the need for continuous model updates and representative datasets.

2.2   Uncovering Malicious Tweets on Twitter

Aggarwal et al.'s PhishAri [1] emphasizes Twitter's historically high spam URL clickthrough rate, surpassing email spam rates. To tackle real-time Twitter phishing, PhishAri integrates URL features with Twitter-specific attributes, achieving a 92.52% accuracy in detecting phishing tweets. Twitter-specific features, such as tweet length, hashtags, mentions, content, and user characteristics (account age, tweet count, follower-to-followee ratio), complement URL-based ones when combined with machine learning classification techniques.

Djaballah et al. [12] in 2015 introduced a 3-step approach to detect phishing attacks on Twitter. Their pipeline began with a Twitter-focused pre-processing step: scanning shared URLs against blocklists like PhishTank. Surviving URLs underwent rigorous ML-based scrutiny using URL shortener usage, page content, and account features to classify their legitimacy. This multi-pronged approach achieved 95% accuracy, surpassing previous benchmarks. Critically, it accounted for Twitter-specific risks like shortened links obfuscating phishing sites.

Inuwa-Dutse et al. [18] present a technique for spam-posting account detection on Twitter. Their approach distinguishes between spam and non-spam social media posts, emphasizing features independent of historical tweets. These features encompass user-related attributes, account characteristics, and engagement patterns. The method demonstrates efficacy, robustness, and real-time deployment potential, enhancing the validity of research data.

Some researchers, like Federico Concone et al. [11], use URL inspection and tweet clustering to identify common behaviors among spammers and legitimate users. Their clustering technique achieves approximately 80% accuracy in labeling accounts.

Additionally, some research efforts [20] focus on educating users about identifying and avoiding phishing scams on Twitter by sharing reports and raising awareness. These multifaceted approaches aim to enhance Twitter's security and user protection.

2.3   Malicious Tweet Reports on Twitter

Phishing detection on Twitter is not limited to URL-based methods. In the dynamic Twitter landscape, the public reporting of phishing attacks has garnered attention. In 2021, Sayak Roy et al. [33] conducted the first study on identifying phishing attacks through reports shared by vigilant Twitter users. Their research revealed that these reports contained legitimate phishing URLs and provided extensive information about malicious websites, aiding in threat detection and mitigation. URLs in Twitter reports remained active for extended periods and had limited overlap with PhishTank and OpenPhish listings, underscoring the reports' significance as an open-source knowledge base for swiftly identifying and raising awareness about new phishing websites.

Tang et al. [36] introduced SpamHunter, a novel method for collecting recent SMS spam data from Twitter using user-reported spam messages. Their automated pipeline identified tweets reporting SMS spam, extracted message content from attached screenshots, and over four years, amassed a dataset of 21,918 SMS spam messages in 75 languages. This collection stands as one of the largest publicly accessible datasets, supporting ongoing efforts to reduce SMS spam through continuous monitoring of new spam messages.

Nakano et al. [28] proposed CrowdCanary, a system capable of structurally and accurately extracting phishing information (e.g., URLs and domains) from tweets about phishing by users who have actually discovered or encountered it. They identified 35,432 phishing URLs and out of 38,935 phishing reports, 31,960 (90.2%) of the phishing URLs were later detected by anti-virus engines.

While these studies emphasize the potential of machine learning in countering Twitter phishing, it's essential to acknowledge their limitations. Machine learning approaches are not immune to adversarial attacks and may generate false positives. Also, obtaining the substantial high-quality data required for model training and testing can pose practical challenges. The lack of comprehensive evaluations, primarily due to the scarcity of large ground truth datasets, hinders the assessment of algorithm performance in real-time Twitter spam detection [9].

To address these limitations, Chen et al. [9] collected a large dataset of over 600 million public tweets, labeled around 6.5 million spam tweets, and extracted 12 lightweight features, which can be used for online detection. In addition, they experiment on six machine learning algorithms under various conditions to better understand their effectiveness and weakness for timely Twitter spam detection.

Despite extensive literature on malicious tweets, the issue persists due to evolving phishing attacks, raising questions about the relevance and effectiveness of previous features. Comprehensive studies are necessary to identify pertinent features. Some prior research, e.g., [1], reported low metric scores, and Sharma et al. [35], records that systems like "PhishAri" are obsolete due to Twitter's authentication requirements. Other works focused primarily on machine learning techniques analyzing only URLs [11] or user account information [18], potentially limiting overall detection system effectiveness. Notable approaches, like [12,14] combine URLs, tweet content, and blocklists. However, in [12], reliance on datasets from the University of California, Irvine (UCI) [27] raises concerns about real-world applicability.

In this paper, we overcome these challenges by combining context and content-based features to improve malicious tweet detection and mitigation. The UCI Machine Learning phishing dataset [27] is incompatible with our approach due to its lack of live tweet access, essential for our text analysis features. Additionally, existing works in this field [11,18,33] do not provide access to their datasets for further evaluation. Our solution involves collecting real-time Twitter data from the Twitter stream, including crucial meta features for effective performance.

We recognize the need for a more comprehensive system that can effectively address the evolving nature of malicious activities on social media platforms.

3   Methodology of the IntelliTweet

This section outlines our system's methodology, covering data collection, feature selection, and modeling techniques.

3.1   Approach

Our approach to Twitter malicious content detection considers various factors like URLs, sentiment, term frequencies, and user profiles, aiming for a holistic understanding. We prioritize minimizing false positives, measured by the false positive rate and global precision, as our system identifies malicious users and aims for accurate information provision to Twitter.

Data Collection and Characterisation

Crawling Tweets: For this research, we built our dataset by collecting live tweets. We made use of the Twitter Public Streaming API [38] which offers samples of public data flowing through Twitter around the world in real-time. We collected over 20k samples of Tweets across a period of 3 months from September 2022 to November 2022. We performed cleaning procedures, including removing stopwords, punctuations, emojis, and stemming, for each batch of 1k tweets obtained.

In previous research such as [11,12], we observe that while it is possible to use Twitter to send spam and other messages without using URLs, majority of spam and other malicious messages on the platform contain URLs. We also found that among thousands of spam tweets we manually inspected, very few lacked URLs. Spammers commonly use embedded URLs to direct victims to external sites for phishing, scams, and malware [24]. Therefore, our focus was on tweets with URLs, although we also tested tweets without URLs.

Ground Truth Formalization: Extracted tweets from the Twitter API include a wealth of information such as user details, tweet content, creation time, language, engagement metrics, geolocation, and more. Relevant data were used to create features for efficient Twitter data classification, as discussed in Subsect. 3.1.

To establish ground truth, we considered tweet text and user accounts. Malicious Twitter users often employ URL shortening services to hide harmful links within tweet text [1]. Investigations into such links involved searches using "bit.ly," tracing URL redirections to retrieve complete URLs, and utilizing VirusTotal [39] for scanning with 80 anti-phishing engines. If flagged as malicious, the tweet was labeled as such. Additionally, if the user account was suspended, it was also labeled as malicious. Reported tweets often contain hashtags like #phishing, #spam, and #scam, aimed at raising awareness of malicious content. Some users may defang URLs to prevent accidental clicks, such as by replacing "http"/"https" with "hxxp"/"hxxps" [33]. We collected and labeled reports by searching for tweets using keywords like phishing, scam, spam, and hxxp. After initial processing, we used VirusTotal to check for malicious URLs in the tweets. If no flags were detected, we manually inspected the tweets for report-like characteristics. Additionally, we collected tweets with media attachments, including images and screenshots, and extracted their content using an OCR engine, which was then integrated with the main tweet text before labeling. Legitimate tweets were randomly sampled and involved no reported malicious activity, no VirusTotal flags, and no suspended user accounts.

Note that data collection based on specific keywords may lead to skewed data representation and potentially overlook various malicious tweet patterns not associated with those keywords.

Feature Selection and Analysis

Text Classification Features: These features include textual content and sentiment analysis of tweets. We use BertTweet [29] to gauge tweet sentiment, considering language usage and emotional intensity. Sentiment analysis is crucial in our approach, as tweets with negative sentiment or strong emotional language may indicate phishing or scam content [31]. We derive two sentiment measures from tweets: subjectivity (0-1), which gauges personal opinions, and polarity (-1 to 1), where 1 represents a positive statement and -1 a negative one. Additionally, we utilize TF-IDF (Term Frequency-Inverse Document Frequency) analysis to assess term significance within tweets.

Twitter User Features: Analyzing the user behind a tweet can also help identify malicious content. For example, a user with a history of posting spam or phishing content is more likely to continue doing so. Additionally, reporters frequently report URLs and actively work to raise awareness. Our user feature analysis involves analyzing the number of Twitter users who follows the user (Follower count), the number of Twitter users who are followed by the user (Following count), the number of days since the creation of the account (Age of account), and the number of lists that the user was subscribed to (Lists count).

Tweet Text Features: Malicious tweets seek maximum visibility on Twitter, using tactics like hashtags, mentions, and trending topics to attract attention and enhance discoverability. They often mention users randomly to increase noticeability. Reported tweets often utilize regular expressions and hashtags and may also include images of phishing websites. To leverage this information, we extracted tweet text features from metadata, including message length, retweet count, URL count, hashtag count, digit count, mention count, and favorite count (Table 1).

Table 1. Twitter Related Features

User Features	Tweet Features	Text Analysis Features
Follower count	Message length	TFIDF
Following count	Retweet count	Subjectivity measure
Age of account	Favourites count	Polarity measure
Favourites count	URL count	Sentiment
Lists count	Hashtag count	
	Mention count	
	digit count	

URL Features: URLs in tweets are significant indicators of malicious intent [4,17], and their features provide insights into tweet categorization (malicious, reported, or legitimate). We analyzed URL features related to the address bar, HTML content, JavaScript, whois lookups, domain-specific attributes and assessed URL redirections to account for defanging and obfuscation techniques commonly used by malicious users. Our URL feature selection were inspired by the UCI Machine Learning phishing dataset [27] (Table 2).

3.2   System Flow of IntelliTweet

The general internal system flow of our solution is illustrated in Fig. 1. In the utilization of IntelliTweet, collected Tweets from the stream undergo filtering through the filter function, which operates based on provided arguments. For testing purposes, arguments like "phishing" or "scam" can be applied to retrieve specific reports. Additionally, using "bit.ly" as a keyword helps retrieve tweets

Table 2. URL Features

Having IP Address	Website Traffic	HTTPS in URL
Having "@" Symbol	Domain Registration Length	Website Forwarding
Prefix/Suffix in Domain	Non-Standard Port	PageRank
Request URL	Disabling Right Click	Google Index
Multi Sub Domains	URL of Anchor	Pop-up Window
IFrame Redirection	Age of Domain	DNS Record
Links in <Meta>, <Script> and <Link> tags,		

containing blocklisted URLs, as certain malicious users resort to URL shortening services. Following this, the tweets undergo a cleaning process, eliminating stop-words, punctuations, emojis and stemming the content. The feature extractor then separates the URLs from the main tweet text for feature extraction. The system visits each URL to collect the raw data associated with it, which includes the webpage's HTML content and JavaScript, whois lookups, and domain-specific information. It then encodes and converts these raw features into a usable format.

URL Encoding: Fifteen of these URL features are assessed based on their presence or absence in a URL. These features return values of 1, −1, or 0, reflecting their detection status as shown in the function Eq. 1. For example, the "Having_IP_Address" feature checks for the presence of an IP address in the URL and returns 1 if found, −1 if absent, and 0 if the URL cannot be fetched. Similarly, the "Having_@_Symbol" feature identifies the "@" symbol in the URL, assigning 1 for presence, −1 for absence, and 0 if the URL cannot be fetched.

$$F(feature) = \begin{cases} 1, & \text{if the feature is present in the URL} \\ -1, & \text{if the feature is absent in the URL} \\ 0, & \text{if the URL cannot be fetched} \end{cases} \qquad (1)$$

Encoding URLs with Count Property: It's important to note that four of the URL features incorporate counting mechanisms in their encoding process. The "Having_Sub_Domain" feature counts the number of subdomains within a URL, assigning -1 when none are found, 0 for a single subdomain, and 1 for multiple subdomains. The "Redirect" feature counts the redirections a URL experiences classifying them as -1 for none, 0 for one or two, and 1 for more than two. The "URL_of_Anchor" feature evaluates the ratio of external to total links on a webpage, returning values of -1 for a ratio < 0.31, 0 for 0.31 <= ratio >= 0.67, and 1 for a ratio higher than 0.67. The "Request_URL" feature calculates the count of external domains in loaded resources, returning -1, if the threshold is < 0.22, 0 if 0.22 <= threshold >= 0.61 and 1 for a threshold higher than 0.61. These features offer a nuanced analysis of URLs by incorporating quantitative assessments.

After URL encoding, the feature extractor extracts tweet metadata, including user account features (following count, follower count, age of the account, user favorites count, list count) and full-text features (message length, retweet count, favorites count, URL count, hashtag count, mention count). The processed tweet text is fed into the text analyzer, trained to discern various aspects of the tweet, including its sentiment, subjectivity, polarity, and TF-IDF score. This information is stored as additional features, and all features are combined into one set of feature vectors for classification.

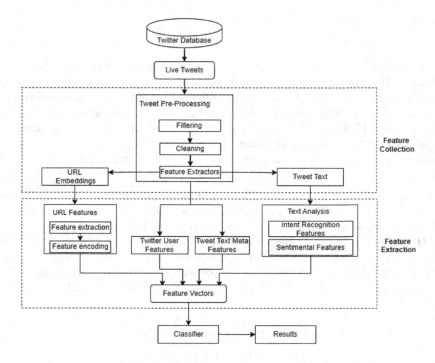

Fig. 1. IntelliTweet System Flow

4   Experiments and Results

We present, in this section, the results obtained for the different criteria explained in our methodology.

4.1   Model Selection and Evaluation

To select the optimal model for our malicious tweet classification system, we conducted an experiment evaluating several models on a dataset of 6,000 tweets. This dataset contained an even distribution of 2,000 malicious tweets, 2,000 legitimate tweets, and 2,000 tweets reporting malicious content that we categorized as legitimate data. By establishing a legitimate-to-malicious ratio of 2:1, we could assess each model's ability to handle class imbalance, a key challenge in malicious tweet detection. Our strategy emphasizes comprehensive evaluation based on minimizing false positives and optimizing global weighted average precision, not merely maximizing accuracy. By prioritizing the reduction of false positives, we account for the real-world implications of misclassifying benign users.

To ensure a robust evaluation, we employed a stratified 5-fold cross-validation methodology, repeating it five times across the dataset. This approach provided a thorough and reliable assessment of the models. Table 3 shows the results obtained for the performance of the evaluated models.

Table 3. Average Metrics for Models after 5 Repetitions of Stratified 5-fold CV

Classifier	Class	Precision (%)	Recall (%)	F1(%)	FPR
Random Forest	Malicious	96.559	**99.850**	98.161	**0.150**
	Legitimate	**99.689**	92.750	96.011	
Decision Tree (DT)	Malicious	88.800	98.475	93.153	1.525
	Legitimate	95.969	72.950	80.630	
Bagging DT	Malicious	92.217	99.090	95.454	0.910
	Legitimate	97.910	82.620	89.095	
Gradient Boosting	Malicious	97.944	98.915	98.423	1.085
	Legitimate	97.799	95.820	96.781	
Support Vector	Malicious	**98.570**	98.490	**98.529**	1.510
	Legitimate	96.989	**97.140**	**97.062**	
Logistic Regression	Malicious	97.691	95.730	96.700	4.270
	Legitimate	91.797	95.470	93.593	

Among the models tested, our selection criteria led us to choose the Random Forest Classifier. We then fine-tuned it with optimal specific parameters. This system achieved a global weighted average precision of 98.38% (standard deviation 0.004), recall of 96.86% (standard deviation 0.009), F1-measure of 97.54% (standard deviation 0.007), accuracy of 97.86% (standard deviation 0.006), and a false positive rate of 0.14.

Intellitweet and TextAnalyst Evaluation: IntelliTweet incorporates the TextAnalyst parameter, which enhances model training. When TextAnalyst is activated, it utilizes Bertweet for sentiment analysis and employs TF-IDF to capture intricate text patterns. Disabling it reverts to standard features. After model selection, we used stratified repeated cross-validation to assess the effectiveness of text analysis features. We conducted an experiment comparing three approaches: TextAnalyst with parameters enabled, TextAnalyst with parameters disabled, and a baseline method used in Kamel's [12] on our dataset. We adopted Kamel's solution as our baseline since it was among the papers utilizing a pipeline of Twitter related features and techniques for detecting malicious tweets. This implementation served as our baseline when applied to our dataset.

The results, shown in Fig. 2, reveal: When IntelliTweet's TextAnalyst parameter is enabled, there is reduced variability in the results, as indicated by smaller box sizes. Conversely, when TextAnalyst is disabled variability slightly increases, with more outliers in the baseline. Nevertheless, both states of IntelliTweet exhibit stability, with minimal differences in the median lines. More importantly, the improved system consistently outperforms the baseline, as evidenced by the higher median values across all metrics (Tables 4 and table:TextspsParameterPerformance2).

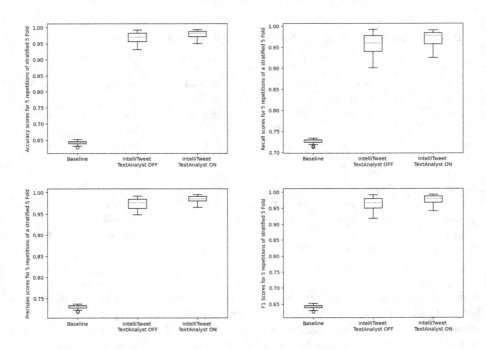

Fig. 2. Box Plot for performance evaluation

Table 4. Mean of confusion matrices (IntelliTweet TextAnalyst parameter ON)

		Predicted	
		Malicious	Non-Mal
Actual	Malicious	1877.0	123.0
	Non-Mal	5.6	3994.4

Table 5. Mean of confusion matrices (IntelliTweet TextAnalyst parameter OFF)

		Predicted	
		Malicious	Non-Mal
Actual	Malicious	1839.4	160.6
	Non-Mal	27.8	3972.2

It is worth noting that the approach in [12] does not account for reports within their dataset. Instead, their approach primarily focuses on detecting the presence of malicious URLs and blocklists to predict phishing tweets. Their user account analysis was only an extra verification step. Consequently, when we tested the approach in the work of Kamel [12], as a baseline on our dataset, the system's performance was relatively poor. The confusion matrix shown in Table 6 highlights a significant number of false positives. This outcome can be attributed to the fact that Kamel's approach, when applied to our dataset, is unable to differentiate reports from other types of tweets. Table 7 offers a potential explanation for this observation, proposing that Kamel's system labels reports as malicious when blocklisted URLs are present.

Table 6. Mean of confusion matrices of Kamel's approach

		Predicted	
		Malicious	Non-Mal
Actual	Malicious	1962.2	37.8
	Non-Mal	2111.6	1888.4

Table 7. Mean of confusion matrices with emphasis on Non-Malicious Predictions

		Predicted	
		Malicious	Non-Mal
Actual	Legitimate	168.0	1832.0
	Report	1943.6	56.4

We conducted runtime analysis comparing the system with and without the "text_features" component, along with the baseline system. Including text features enhances malicious tweet detection but increases runtime to 2753 milliseconds, compared to 2327 milliseconds without this feature. The baseline system achieved a runtime of 1902, which is efficient but yielded poorer metric results with a precision of 73.12%. TextAnalyst's advantage lies in the improved false positive rate, allowing users to customize IntelliTweet by activating or deactivating the feature according to their needs.

Mutual Information scores in Fig. 3 reveals a nuanced interplay of all other features, with TF-IDF standing out as the most influential. This underscores the pivotal role of textual content in distinguishing tweet categories, particularly in malicious tweet detection. The findings highlight the multifaceted nature of our model, demonstrating how the integration of features like account age, follower count, number of tweets, web traffic, page rank, subjectivity, and others alongside TF-IDF contributes to effective tweet categorization.

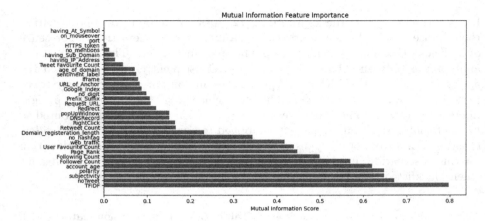

Fig. 3. Feature Importance by Mutual Information

5 Conclusion and Future Work

"IntelliTweet" introduces an innovative system that advances malicious tweet detection by combining contextual and content-based features. The comprehensive approach incorporates TF-IDF, sentiment analysis, user profiles, and URL features, resulting in a multifaceted tweet representation for robust classification.

Comparative experiments highlight IntelliTweet's capabilities in countering URL obfuscation, significantly reducing false positives. The system demonstrates strong, consistent performance across key metrics like 98.38% precision, 97.54% F1-measure and 0.14 false positive rate based on real-world Twitter data. The consideration of user reports further empowers IntelliTweet to avoid mislabeling of legitimate awareness-raising content.

While acknowledging constraints like dataset scope and potential biases, this research significantly advances malicious tweet detection through a holistic feature fusion. Recognizing limitations in data collection, it underscores the imperative to diversify assessments on a large scale to effectively address evolving real-world threats. Future endeavors will address these concerns and be benchmarked against recent advancements in the field. Overall, IntelliTweet represents a vital step toward enhanced Twitter security and positive user experiences, providing valuable insights for mitigating emerging threats on the platform.

References

1. Aggarwal, A., Rajadesingan, A., Kumaraguru, P.: Phishari: automatic realtime phishing detection on twitter. In: 2012 eCrime Researchers Summit, pp. 1–12 (2012). https://doi.org/10.1109/eCrime.2012.6489521

2. Alom, Z., Carminati, B., Ferrari, E.: A deep learning model for twitter spam detection. Online Soc. Netw. Media **18**, 100079 (2020). https://doi.org/10.1016/j.osnem.2020.100079

3. Azeez, N.A., Misra, S., Margaret, I.A., Fernandez-Sanz, L., et al.: Adopting automated whitelist approach for detecting phishing attacks. Comput. Sec. **108**, 102328 (2021)

4. Bell, S., Paterson, K., Cavallaro, L.: Catch me (on time) if you can: understanding the effectiveness of twitter url blacklists. arXiv preprint arXiv:1912.02520 (2019)

5. Bouijij, H., Berqia, A.: Machine learning algorithms evaluation for phishing urls classification. In: 2021 4th International Symposium on Advanced Electrical and Communication Technologies (ISAECT), pp. 01–05 (2021). https://doi.org/10.1109/ISAECT53699.2021.9668489

6. Cao, J., Li, Q., Ji, Y., He, Y., Guo, D.: Detection of forwarding-based malicious urls in online social networks. Int. J. Parallel Prog. **44**, 163–180 (2016)

7. Casanove, O.d., Sèdes, F.: Malicious human behaviour in information system security: contribution to a threat model for event detection algorithms. In: Foundations and Practice of Security, pp. 208–220. Springer Nature Switzerland, Cham (2023)

8. Chen, C., et al.: Investigating the deceptive information in twitter spam. Futur. Gener. Comput. Syst. **72**, 319–326 (2017). https://doi.org/10.1016/j.future.2016.05.036

9. Chen, C., Zhang, J., Chen, X., Xiang, Y., Zhou, W.: 6 million spam tweets: a large ground truth for timely twitter spam detection. In: 2015 IEEE International Conference on Communications (ICC), pp. 7065–7070 (2015). https://doi.org/10.1109/ICC.2015.7249453

10. Choi, D., Han, J., Chun, S., Rappos, E., Robert, S., Kwon, T.T.: Bit.ly/practice: uncovering content publishing and sharing through url shortening services. Telematics and Informatics **35**(5), 1310–1323 (2018). https://doi.org/10.1016/j.tele.2018.03.003

11. Concone, F., Re, G.L., Morana, M., Ruocco, C.: Assisted labeling for spam account detection on twitter. In: 2019 IEEE International Conference on Smart Computing (SMARTCOMP), pp. 359–366. IEEE (2019)

12. Djaballah, K.A., Boukhalfa, K., Ghalem, Z., Boukerma, O.: A new approach for the detection and analysis of phishing in social networks: the case of twitter. In: 2020 Seventh International Conference on Social Networks Analysis, Management and Security (SNAMS), pp. 1–8 (2020). https://doi.org/10.1109/SNAMS52053.2020.9336572

13. Dzeha, Eric Edem, J., Guy-Vincent: eric-edem/The_intellitweet: A Multifaceted Feature Approach to Detect Malicious Tweets. https://github.com/eric-edem/The_IntelliTweet

14. Gangwar, S.S., Rathore, S.S., Chouhan, S.S., Soni, S.: Predictive modeling for suspicious content identification on twitter. Soc. Netw. Anal. Min. **12**(1), 149 (2022)

15. Gheewala, S., Patel, R.: Machine learning based twitter spam account detection: a review. In: 2018 Second International Conference on Computing Methodologies and Communication (ICCMC), pp. 79–84 (Feb 2018). https://doi.org/10.1109/ICCMC.2018.8487992

16. Hong, J., Kim, T., Liu, J., Park, N., Kim, S.W.: Phishing url detection with lexical features and blacklisted domains. Adaptive Autonom. Sec. Cyber Syst. 253–267 (2020)
17. Horawalavithana, S., De Silva, R., Nabeel, M., Elvitigala, C., Wijesekara, P., Iamnitchi, A.: Malicious and Low Credibility URLs on Twitter during the AstraZeneca COVID-19 Vaccine Development, arXiv:2102.12223 (Feb 2021), [cs] version: 1
18. Inuwa-Dutse, I., Liptrott, M., Korkontzelos, I.: Detection of spam-posting accounts on twitter. Neurocomputing **315**, 496–511 (2018)
19. Jabardi, M., Hadi, A.S.: Twitter fake account detection and classification using ontological engineering and semantic web rule language. Karbala Inter. J. Mod. Sci. **6**(4), 8 (2020)
20. Jain, A.K., Gupta, B.: A survey of phishing attack techniques, defence mechanisms and open research challenges. Enterprise Inform. Syst. **16**(4), 527–565 (2022)
21. Jain, A.K., Gupta, B.B.: Towards detection of phishing websites on client-side using machine learning based approach. Telecommun. Syst. **68**, 687–700 (2018)
22. Karami, A., Lundy, M., Webb, F., Dwivedi, Y.K.: Twitter and research: a systematic literature review through text mining. IEEE Access **8**, 67698–67717 (2020). https://doi.org/10.1109/ACCESS.2020.2983656
23. Khonji, M., Iraqi, Y., Jones, A.: Phishing detection: a literature survey. IEEE Commun. Surv. Tutorials **15**(4), 2091–2121 (2013). https://doi.org/10.1109/SURV.2013.032213.00009
24. Korkmaz, M., Sahingoz, O.K., Diri, B.: Detection of phishing websites by using machine learning-based url analysis. In: 2020 11th International Conference on Computing, Communication and Networking Technologies (ICCCNT), pp. 1–7 (2020). https://doi.org/10.1109/ICCCNT49239.2020.9225561
25. Madisetty, S., Desarkar, M.S.: A neural network-based ensemble approach for spam detection in twitter. IEEE Trans. Comput. Soc. Syst. **5**(4), 973–984 (2018). https://doi.org/10.1109/TCSS.2018.2878852
26. Marchal, S., Saari, K., Singh, N., Asokan, N.: Know your phish: novel techniques for detecting phishing sites and their targets. In: 2016 IEEE 36th International Conference on Distributed Computing Systems (ICDCS), pp. 323–333 (2016). https://doi.org/10.1109/ICDCS.2016.10
27. Mohammad, R., McCluskey, L.: Uci machine learning repository. https://archive.ics.uci.edu/dataset/327/phishing+websites
28. Nakano, H., et al.: Canary in twitter mine: collecting phishing reports from experts and non-experts. arXiv preprint arXiv:2303.15847 (2023)
29. Nguyen, D.Q., Vu, T., Nguyen, A.T.: Bertweet: a pre-trained language model for english tweets. arXiv preprint arXiv:2005.10200 (2020)
30. Rao, R.S., Vaishnavi, T., Pais, A.R.: Catchphish: detection of phishing websites by inspecting urls. J. Ambient. Intell. Humaniz. Comput. **11**, 813–825 (2020)
31. Rodrigues, A.P., Fernandes, R., Shetty, A., Lakshmanna, K., Shafi, R.M., et al.: Real-time twitter spam detection and sentiment analysis using machine learning and deep learning techniques. Comput. Intell. Neurosci. (2022)
32. Rout, R.R., Lingam, G., Somayajulu, D.V.L.N.: Detection of malicious social bots using learning automata with url features in twitter network. IEEE Trans. Comput. Soc. Syst. **7**(4), 1004–1018 (2020). https://doi.org/10.1109/TCSS.2020.2992223
33. Roy, S.S., Karanjit, U., Nilizadeh, S.: Evaluating the effectiveness of phishing reports on twitter. In: 2021 APWG Symposium on Electronic Crime Research (eCrime), pp. 1–13 (2021). https://doi.org/10.1109/eCrime54498.2021.9738786

34. Sameen, M., Han, K., Hwang, S.O.: Phishhaven-an efficient real-time ai phishing urls detection system. IEEE Access **8**, 83425–83443 (2020). https://doi.org/10.1109/ACCESS.2020.2991403
35. Sharma, N., Sharma, N., Tiwari, V., Chahar, S., Maheshwari, S., et al.: Real-time detection of phishing tweets. In: Fourth International Conference on Computer Science Engineering Application, pp. 215–27 (2014)
36. Tang, S., Mi, X., Li, Y., Wang, X., Chen, K.: Clues in tweets: twitter-guided discovery and analysis of sms spam. In: Proceedings of the 2022 ACM SIGSAC Conference on Computer and Communications Security, pp. 2751–2764 (2022)
37. Twitter: About unsafe links. https://help.twitter.com/en/safety-and-security/phishing-spam-and-malware-links
38. Twitter: Twitter API Documentation. https://developer.twitter.com/en/docs/twitter-api
39. VirusTotal: Home. https://www.virustotal.com/gui/home/upload
40. Wani, K., Patil, A., Mukherjee, S., Sarkar, S.: Malicious twitter bot detector. In: 2021 4th Biennial International Conference on Nascent Technologies in Engineering (ICNTE), pp. 1–6 (2021). https://doi.org/10.1109/ICNTE51185.2021.9487674
41. Wikipedia: https://en.wikipedia.org/wiki/Anti-Phishing_Working_Group
42. Zhang, Y., Hong, J.I., Cranor, L.F.: Cantina: a content-based approach to detecting phishing web sites. In: Proceedings of the 16th International Conference on World Wide Web, pp. 639–648 (2007)

Web Scams Detection System

Emad Badawi[1,2]($\boxtimes$), Guy-Vincent Jourdan[1,2], and Iosif-Viorel Onut[1,2]

[1] University of Ottawa, Ottawa, ON, Canada
{ebada090,gjourdan}@uottawa.ca
[2] IBM Centre for Advanced Studies, Ottawa, ON, Canada
vioonut@ca.ibm.com

Abstract. Web-based scams rely on scam websites to provide fraudulent business or fake services to steal money and sensitive information from unsuspecting victims. Despite many researchers' efforts to develop anti-scam detection techniques, their main focus has been on understanding, detecting, and analyzing scam sites. State-of-the-art anti-scam research still faces several challenges, such as acquiring a properly labeled scam dataset, especially when there is no blacklist, central repository, or previous large-scale analysis. The researchers have created labeled datasets in different ways, such as manually collecting and labeling the dataset or using a semi-automatic crawler followed by manual inspection. However, this process requires previous knowledge and understanding of the scam and much manual work.

In this paper, we propose a data-driven model to create a labeled training dataset for web-based scams that have a web presence. Given a small scam sample, our model formulates scam-related search queries and uses them on multiple search engines to search for, and collect, potential scam pages. After collecting a sufficiently large corpus of web pages, our model semi-automatically clusters the search results and creates a labeled training dataset with minimal human interaction. We have validated our model using two different scam types that we have studied in our previous work. We tested our classifiers against the databases of web pages we collected during our previous analysis of the scams and successfully detected more than 87% of the scam pages while maintaining a false positive value as low as 0.23%.

Keywords: Training dataset · Scam analysis · Fraud detection · Cyberattack · Web mining

1 Introduction

The Internet has caused a shift in people's lifestyles by providing companies and people with a new way of connecting which created a more connected world. For example, online games have begun to match, or even replace, traditional games. This has also caused companies to focus on creating new Internet services and products with which to dominate the market. However, this shift has also made it possible for criminals to launch new types of crime using computers

© The Author(s), under exclusive license to Springer Nature Switzerland AG 2024
M. Mosbah et al. (Eds.): FPS 2023, LNCS 14551, pp. 174–188, 2024.
https://doi.org/10.1007/978-3-031-57537-2_11

and networks. These kinds of action are known as cybercrime. These cybercrime attacks include, but are not limited to, game-related scams [7,8], cryptocurrency scams [6,26,61], survey scams [21,37], and technical support scams [30,41,56].

Scam attacks are a type of cybercrime by which attackers trick unsuspecting victims into willingly revealing sensitive information, dispensing cash, or even doing harmful actions for the scammer's benefit. The attackers use social engineering to misrepresent themselves by impersonating familiar contacts of the victims, or someone with authority or skill, such as a company representative, police officer, lawyer, or internal revenue officer. Despite the efforts of industry and academia in recent years, anti-scam research still faces several challenges, especially when collecting a reliable dataset to train a classification model that can detect scam pages with a low false-positive rate.

Cybercriminals' activities have caused enormous losses over the years. According to Scam Watch[1], the value of stolen money and scam cases has been increasing over the years. As shown in Fig. 1, the losses in value in 2020, 2021, 2022, and the first 8 months of 2023 are 175,694,583 USD, 325,287,041 USD, 568,640,274 USD, and 328,645,604 USD respectively. The amount of stolen money in 2022 is approximately more than double the total loss of 2020, and the amount of stolen money in the first 8 months of 2023 exceeded the total loss of 2021.

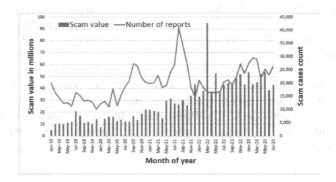

Fig. 1. Scam statistics (reproduced from scamwatch)

Collecting a scam dataset is an essential part of every scam study and investigation. This dataset can be used to analyze the scam and train a classifier to detect more scam instances. However, collecting a reliable source of labeled data is quite challenging. It requires considerable work, especially when there is no blacklist, central repository, or previous large-scale analysis in the studied area [37]. Researchers have used different methods to collect their datasets, such as conducting interviews, publishing questionnaires, collecting data manually, and employing a semi-automatic data collection procedure. We have also used a

---

[1] https://www.scamwatch.gov.au/scam-statistics.

combination of automated crawling and manual inspection to collect datasets to study two types of web-based scams, the "Game Hack" Scam (GHS) [7] and the "Bitcoin Generator" Scam (BGS) [6]. In BGS, attackers attempt to convince the victims that they can "hack the blockchain" and provide them free cryptocurrency for a small mining fee. In GHS, scammers promise to provide the victims with free, unlimited "resources" or other advantages for their favorite game in exchange for completing one or more tasks. These approaches effectively collected a training dataset, but they required previous knowledge and an understanding of how the scam functioned, and both required much manual work.

This paper details how we leveraged the expertise and insights gained from studying the BGS and GHS scams to automate the training dataset collection and significantly reduce the manual efforts required to set up such a study. We propose a data-driven approach to prepare a training dataset for detecting web-based scams. Given a small set of scam pages as initial input, our model generates scam-related search queries and uses them as a seed to search for more scam pages. We cluster the collected pages and automatically select clusters with a high probability of containing scam pages. We then use our model to create a dataset of benign pages to form a training dataset. To validate our model, we have successfully generated training datasets for both BGS and GHS scam sites. This took less effort and time than it did during our initial studies. We used the datasets to train classification models and used them to detect new scam instances. Our classifiers detected the BGS and GHS scam instances with good accuracy. We detected the scam instances with a true positive rate of more than 87% and a false positive rate of 0.23%.

The remainder of this paper is structured in the following manner. After this introduction, we detail our methodology in Sect. 2. In Sect. 3, we compare the manual and semi-automated approaches and discuss the model persistence over time. In Sect. 4, we provide a literature review. In Sect. 5 discusses some of the most important limitations in our model and our future enhancements. Finally, we conclude our paper in Sect. 6[2].

2   Methodology

Our analysis of the BGS and GHS scams have shown that when scammers target a specific online service, the scam instances share common criteria that we can use to group them and create a training dataset. Some of the criteria are:

- The presence of specific keywords. Attackers create a website with content, words, and language related to the original service or product to lure victims to the scam website. As a result, the scam websites have very similar content to that of the targeted service [41,56]. For example, Miramirkhani *et al.* [41],

---

[2] We describe applying the model to create and validate the training datasets for identifying BGS and GHS scams in a separate report hosted with our dataset https://bit.ly/DatasetPaper.

have shown that technical support scammers (TSS) use the words "call", "technicians" and "virus", in the content of a scam web page to convince the victims that their devices are infected with a virus. In the TSS, scammers combine online scams and telephone fraud activities to convince their prey that their machines are infected with malware, and offer a fake technical support service. The same applies to BGS [6] and GHS [7]; for example, the words "hack", "tool", and "online" were widely used in GHS sites, and the words "bitcoin", "btc", and "mining" were widely used in BGS sites.

– Attackers use pre-built templates to create their attacks. Our analysis of GHS sites [7] has shown the existence of online tutorials on how to copy, customize, and deploy existing templates to target online games. These templates are so easy to use that a scammer without any technical skills can customize and publish them without any great effort. Furthermore, the majority of the scam instances we have found have similar templates. We have also found that many BGS instances use similar templates.

– The presence of the scam payload: In some cases, the attackers provide unique identifiers that link the scammer to the scam pages. These identifiers are used for different purposes, such as collecting the victim's information, receiving payments, or communicating phone numbers or emails. For example, in the TSS [56], the scam site contains a phone number that can be used to contact the scammer. In the BGS, the scam page contains a cryptocurrency address to receive the victim's payment.

Our system includes three modules:

1. **Search query generator.** This module generates keywords that are likely to be used in the scam pages.
2. **Web crawler.** This module uses the previous queries to search for scam pages using search engines, such as *Google.com*, and customized historical search engines such as cutestat.com. We crawled through the resulting pages and collected the HTML content of the pages, URL redirections, as well as screen-shots.
3. **Clustering and dataset creation.** This module uses the previously collected web pages to create our labeled training dataset.

2.1 Search Query Generator

Finding good search queries that are very likely to lead to scam pages is a critical task. In this section, we discuss the three techniques that we used to generate our search queries:

1. **Using the context-specific corpus** to generate search phrases that are very likely to lead to the scam. As discussed in Sect. 2, scam instances share many similar contents that are usually related to the product or service targeted by the scam. We can use the high correlation between instances of scam content to generate search queries that are likely to lead to new pages similar to those previously identified, i.e., the initial scam instances used as a seed. Generating relevant search queries from a context-specific corpus has been

used effectively in the past for TSS detection and analysis [56]. We have taken a similar approach to create GHS search queries [7].

2. **The "Keywords" meta tag:** represents a comma-separated list of keywords that are relevant to the web page, and are used to inform search engines of its content [5] . The contents of the "Keywords" meta tag can be extracted from the scam dataset to generate more representative search queries. We have used this approach to create BGS search queries [6].

3. **Google Trends service:** A Google Trends' analysis reflects the popularity of search queries as used by normal web users. We can use the prepared queries created in step 1 and step 2 to crawl the Google Trends API[3] and generate more queries related to a particular scam. For example, Kharraz *et al.* [37] used it to generate a list of 10,000 search queries related to survey scams. We have also used the Google Trends service to generate 1,604 unique queries related to GHS in [7].

2.2   Web Crawler

The primary purpose of the work described in this module was to browse the web and collect web pages to use in our clustering process. We used the previously identified search queries as a seed to search for and collect new scam pages. We used two ways to search for and collect our pages. These are:

– Using **search engines** such as *Google.com*, *Bing.com*, and *search.yahoo.com*. For each query, the crawler visited a predefined number of the pages returned by each engine. For example, we evaluated those links contained in the first two pages (that is, 20 search results).
– Using the **customized historical search engines** to collect domains and URLs with any content related to the search. For example, **urlscan.io**[4] custom search reports previously scanned domains and URLs with DOM structure similar to the performed search. Other websites that can be used are **website.informer.com**[5] and **cutestat.com**[6], which are websites that gather detailed information about other websites. These websites have custom search services that report domains and URLs with text content similar to the search already performed. This search attempts to collect many scam instances with contents similar to those obtained in the initial scam samples. If the domain is no longer available, we use the **Internet Archive**[7] and **urlscan.io** to collect up to five previous snapshots of the domain. The **Internet Archive** is an online digital library that provides a mostly free collection of readily available digitized materials, including music, public-domain books, Internet sites, and games.

---

[3] https://trends.google.com/trends/?geo=US.
[4] https://urlscan.io/.
[5] https://website.informer.com/.
[6] https://www.cutestat.com/.
[7] https://web.archive.org/.

After collecting the URLs, we filtered out the URLs hosted on the Alexa top one thousand domains[8]. Our analysis of the BGS and GHS websites has shown that the URLs hosted on these domains do not contain scam instances. Additionally, scam detection and analysis done by other, prior studies [16,37,56] identified the Alexa Top Domains list as a good source from which to collect benign samples with which to create a training dataset.

The crawler can be built and customized using different technologies and libraries. We chose to build our crawler based on ChromeDriver[9] and Python Selenium[10]. We then used the Python Beautiful Soup library[11] and the CSS selectors to collect and crawl the URLs we gathered from the search results. We used a lightweight scripted headless browser, that was built using Python, by integrating Selenium, ChromeDriver, and BeautifulSoup to implement our crawler.

2.3 Clustering and Dataset Creation

The goal of the clustering step is to group scam pages, based on some common features, into the same cluster. We then label the true positive clusters semi-automatically and select the pages within the clusters as our scam website dataset. To carry out this step, we use a two-step clustering process. An initial clustering is done on a small collection of web pages. We manually inspect a small set of clusters that have a high probability of containing mostly scam pages and label the true positive clusters. We then use the true positive clusters to automatically label a larger dataset. To select the benign samples, we randomly select pages from the clusters that we do not label as true positive clusters.

In carrying out this step, we use the common, shared criteria between the scam pages that we noted earlier to group them in the same cluster.

3 A Comparison Between the Manual and Semi-automated Approach

In this section, we compare the time and effort required to create the training dataset in manual and automated approaches. We also discuss our model persistence and validity over time[12].

3.1 A Comparison Between the Manual and Automated Approaches

To prepare the GHS training dataset, we manually searched the web for approximately a week to collect our initial scam samples. On average, we spent 4 h per

---

[8] https://www.alexa.com/.

[9] http://chromedriver.chromium.org/.

[10] https://selenium-python.readthedocs.io.

[11] https://pypi.org/project/beautifulsoup4/.

[12] We attached the dataset creation and validation process on a separate report hosted with our dataset https://bit.ly/DatasetPaperReport.

day searching for and understanding the scam, which constitutes a total of 28 h of work. We then used the collected samples to create search queries to use with our crawler. After one month of crawling, we manually inspected approximately 600 pages to create the benign dataset. On average, we spent 10 s visually inspecting each page for a total time expenditure of 1.5 h. We have spent approximately 31 h on manual search and inspection.

We used a similar process to prepare our BGS training dataset. On average, we spent 4 h per day searching and collecting scam samples, constituting a total of 28 h. We also manually inspected approximately 1,500 snapshots that belong to 307 possible scam domains[13] that we collected from the Internet Archive. Finally, we manually inspected 400 randomly selected pages collected during the first week of crawling to create our benign dataset. On average, we have spent 10 s visually inspecting each page, constituting 5 h. In total we spent approximately 33 h doing manual search and inspection.

While using our automated process, our manual efforts were reduced as much as possible. In our initial clustering, we automatically selected a maximum of 70 clusters and only inspected 2 to 3 pages from each cluster for visual analysis. On average, we spent 10 s visually inspecting each page, constituting half an hour on manual inspection.

Finally, although the automated approach results are not as good as the results from our manual work in [6,7], our most important gain was achieved in significantly reducing the amount of manual effort while maintaining good accuracy. Ultimately, we saved more than 98% of the effort we spent to create the datasets manually[14].

3.2 Model Persistence

Search engines have become a fundamental part of our daily lives and one of the most powerful tools on the Internet. This is evidenced by the fact that 68% of all website traffic comes from search engines[15]. Our work and model uses the popularity and widespread use of search engines to search for and detect scam pages. In our searches, we depend on common features that are shared between the scam instances to identify and detect them. However, scammers may change their tactics to evade our model. Moreover, technology may change with time, and attackers will likely use other tools to create more sophisticated attacks. For example, attackers may use an AI to customize their attacks and obfuscate the attack traces. Using social engineering attacks, attackers can also evade search engines and target a specific audience.

Note, however, that scammers do not have unlimited freedom with regard to the techniques that they choose to use. Evading our model will make it harder

---

[13] We collected the domains by crawling cutestat.com search engine and a blacklist maintained by Bitcoin.fr.
[14] In our analysis, for both the manual and automated approaches, we did not include any automated process, such as crawling time. We only included the time we spent manually searching, inspecting, and labeling the pages.
[15] https://websitesetup.org/news/internet-facts-stats/,accessedin2022.

for scammers to spread their scams widely, thus reducing the amount of profit that they may gain. Scammers will also need to spend more effort and time creating customized attacks and targeting their victims. Similar to previous observations [32], our analysis of the GHS and BGS sites showed that scammers use automation to manage their campaigns and use toolkits to create attack pages. Therefore, while an attacker could evade our model, this would have a price: creating successful scams that escape detection is harder, more costly, and presents a narrower set of targets, thus making the endeavour less profitable while simultaneously reducing the number of victims.

4   Related Work

Although recent research has provided important insights into different scams, the main focus has been on understanding the scam strategy, analysis, and detection. The researchers used different methods to collect the datasets that were used to investigate the scams or train a classifier to collect and identify scam instances. These different methods have two factors in common: the need for previous knowledge and an understanding of the scams and the human factors throughout the process of dataset creation and validation. To the best of our knowledge, none of these studies have focused on automatically creating the dataset with no previous knowledge about the scam, minimal human interaction, and a small initial sample.

Some researchers collected the training data by using a semi-automated crawling process followed by manual data collection [61,64,69]. Other researchers followed a completely manual process, such as interviewing the victims [15,55, 66], distributing questionnairs [42,73], or by searching online forums such as bitcointalk.org [11]. Our analysis shows that different methods were used to prepare the training dataset:

- Using online blogs and forums, such as Reddit and bitcointalk.org where the scammers advertise their schemes [2,11,22,24,40,43,54,61–64,68–70,74]. For example, Vasek and Moore [68] collected the data from a thread on bitcointalk.org that aggregates a blacklist of suspected fraudulent services being maintained. They then manually inspected the services and identified 192 scam samples that they used in their investigation. In [22], the authors indicate that they searched ransomware removal guides (such as BleepingComputer.com and MalwareTips.com) and online ransomware knowledge (such as ESET, Kaspersky Lab, and Symantec) to collect the scam samples.
- Conducting interviews and distributing questionnaires [15,25,42,47,55,66,67, 72,73]. For example, Buchanan and Whitty [42] created and published a questionnaire for 5 months in 2011. Throughout that period, the questionnaire was accessed 1,096 times and was fully completed by 853 individuals.
- Using a previously prepared dataset from third parties, such as previous studies, online services, public blacklists, and police departments [2–4,10,12,13,17–19,21,27–29,31,33,35,39,45,48–50,52,53,58,60]. For example,

Shaari *et al.* [53], and [12] acquired their datasets from police departments. In [21], MyPageKeeper Facebook, an application which receives a feed of scam pages published on Facebook was used. They then manually inspected and verified the data related to the scam. Chen *et al.* [18], used a leaked transaction history of a Bitcoin exchange in their analysis. Jung *et al.* [33] and Chen *et al.* [19] used a previously disclosed tranche of data in a dataset from Bartoletti *et al.* [9] in their study.

– Collecting data from online exchanges, free online sources, social-media groups, and public service source code. These sources require deep knowledge about the targeted scam and a need for manual analysis to prepare the data [1,9,20,34,36,46,57,71,72]. For example, Hagemann [71] collected the chat histories from Telegram P&D groups (fraudulent ads), the price and volume of cryptocurrencies from Binance exchange, and general data about currency capitalization from *coinmarketcap.com.*

– Preparing search queries that are very likely to lead to the scam and then using them to crawl the web and search for a training dataset. This type of research requires prior knowledge of the scam and an initial dataset from which to extract the search queries from [6–8,37,38,41,56,59,65]. For example, Miramirkhani *et al.* [41] prepared a search query set and used it to crawl the web for several days. The authors then analyzed a scam sample and extracted heuristic features to filter out the scam pages. Subsequently, they manually inspected 17,000 pages to validate their results.

Unlike these approaches, we do not rely on previous knowledge to create the dataset. Our system uses a scam sample as small as five pages to create a complete training dataset that contains both scam and benign pages. Furthermore, the manual intervention is kept to a minimum level where we inspect a minimal number of pages to validate our dataset.

Other researchers [14,16,32,44] have proposed a similar approach to improve the effectiveness of training dataset collection by starting from a seed of known, malicious instances and exploiting the similarities between these instances. They then use search engines to search for more scam pages. Invernizzi and Comparetti [16] have proposed EVILSEED, which is a search process that increases the efficiency of searching for malicious web pages that are similar to previously identified malicious pages. Starting from 604 seeds of known malicious pages, EVILSEED automatically generated search queries to search for and collect other scam pages. The authors generated the search queries using, 1) random alphabetic phrases, 2) random phrases with words taken from an English dictionary, 3) manually-generated Google dorks, taken from an online repository, and 4) trending topics taken from Twitter and Google Hot Trends. The model then uses Google's Safe Browsing, Wepawet [23] which is a client honeypot that uses anomaly-based techniques to detect drive-by download attacks, and a custom-built tool that detects pages that host fake anti-virus software to filter out the malicious web pages.

Canali *et al.* [16] proposed Prophiler, a filter to reduce the number of web pages to be inspected to identify malicious web pages. Prophiler automatically discards benign web pages and only forwards the pages that are likely to contain malicious code to the costly analytic tools. The model uses static analysis techniques based on features extracted from the HTML contents, JavaScript, and the page URL. The authors have used Twitter, Google, and Wikipedia trends as search terms to create their search queries to identify more malicious pages using search engines. To detect the malicious pages, the authors have trained a classifier, using 787 pages that are known to be triggering drive-by-download attacks, extracted from Wepawet's database, and 51,171 benign web pages crawled from the first two levels of the top 100 Alexa websites.

Bouma-Sims and Reaves [14] constructed a set of 74 search queries likely to lead to YouTube scam videos based on their previous experience with YouTube scams. The authors then used the YouTube Data API to collect the first 50 search results of each query, accumulating 3,700 videos. Manual analysis was then used to categorize the collected videos and remove false positive results.

Compared to the previous discussed methods, our approach is more generic and is more automated. Only five malicious pages were used as a seed to train our model, which is less than 1% of what was used by any of these other approaches. Furthermore, our approach is directed toward the most troublesome portion of any scam analysis study, which is automating the collection of the training dataset. Our work can be considered a starting point to collect the required seeds to start a scam analysis study (such as the previously mentioned two approaches), training a classifier to detect more scam instances, and for other purposes. In [16,32] the authors used blacklists or previously collected datasets as a seed for their work, and in [14], the authors depended on their familiarity of the scam and previous experience. However, this approach is not viable for new scam types that have not been studied before, or when there are no available blacklists.

5 Limitations and Future Work

One of the greatest limitations of our study is that we validated our methodology using only two types of web-based scams. Furthermore, we did not run complete experiments to collect our testing corpus of pages. Instead we used the corpus of pages we had collected in our previous work as our testing dataset. In our future work, we will further validate our methodology by studying other web-based scams where we depend entirely on the automated process to collect the scam dataset.

Another limitation is that our result is biased by the five initial pages we used as a starting point in our experiments. There is no guarantee that we could achieve the same results if we started with different scam samples. However, we believe that the overall results will not vary significantly when changing the initial scam samples because we followed a completely random selection process to pick our initial five pages.

Attackers can use cloaking to hide their traces and evade automated solutions such as ours. "Clocking" is the attempt to hide malicious content from automated crawlers by serving benign pages and showing the harmful content only to normal web clients/users [51]. The attackers use this technique to lengthen the life span of their attacks and prevent their websites from being detected and taken down. However, our analysis of the BGS and GHS scams has shown that no active preventive steps have been taken to stop the attack or even blacklist the scam instances. Thus, we believe that the BGS and GHS scammer does not need to take an extra step to protect their scam instances, and cloaking has no significant effect on our approach for the time being.

Finally, in our work, we have validated our approach using a scam category in which the adversary promises the victim some benefit or gains when performing the scam and the scam pages share common information such as similar keywords. However, this approach will be ineffective when the attacker fakes a legitimate website, such as when carrying out phishing attacks, or when the scam pages do not have common keywords. In our future work, we will expand our analysis to include different types of scams and further generalize our approach.

6   Conclusion

In this paper, we have proposed a semi-automatic process to create a labeled training dataset for detecting web-based scams with a web presence. Given a small set of scam samples, our model formulates scam-related search queries and applies them to different sources, such as search engines and customized historical search engines, to search for and collect potential scam pages. After collecting a sufficient corpus of web pages, our model semi-automatically clusters the search results and creates a labeled training dataset with minimal human interaction.

We have used our model to create training datasets for the BGS and GHS scams by using an initial scam sample of only five web pages. Our analysis showed that we can create a good labeled training dataset that can detect the scam pages with good accuracy while significantly reducing the manual effort required. The classifiers successfully detected more than 87% of the scam pages while classifying less than 0.24% of the benign pages incorrectly.

References

1. Abhishta, A., Joosten, R., Dragomiretskiy, S., Nieuwenhuis, L.J.: Impact of successful ddos attacks on a major crypto-currency exchange. In: 2019 27th Euromicro International Conference on Parallel, Distributed and Network-Based Processing (PDP), pp. 379–384. IEEE (2019)
2. Afandi, N.A., Hamid, I.R.A.: Covid-19 phishing detection based on hyperlink using k-nearest neighbor (knn) algorithm. Appli. Inform. Technol. Comput. Sci. 2(2), 287–301 (2021)
3. Alarab, I., Prakoonwit, S., Nacer, M.I.: Comparative analysis using supervised learning methods for anti-money laundering in bitcoin. In: Proceedings of the 2020 5th International Conference on Machine Learning Technologies, pp. 11–17 (2020)

4. Alarab, I., Prakoonwit, S., Nacer, M.I.: Competence of graph convolutional networks for anti-money laundering in bitcoin blockchain. In: Proceedings of the 2020 5th International Conference on Machine Learning Technologies, pp. 23–27 (2020)
5. ARSLAN, A.: On the usefulness of html meta elements for web retrieval. Eskişehir Tech. Univ. . Sci. Technol. A-Appl. Sci. Eng. **21**(1), 182–198 (2020)
6. Badawi, E., Jourdan, G.V., Bochmann, G., Onut, I.V.: An automatic detection and analysis of the bitcoin generator scam. In: 2020 IEEE European Symposium on Security and Privacy Workshops (EuroS&PW), pp. 407–416. IEEE Computer Society, Los Alamitos, CA, USA (sep 2020)
7. Badawi, E., Jourdan, G.V., Bochmann, G., Onut, I.V.: Automatic detection and analysis of the "Game Hack" Scam. J. Web Eng. **18**(8) (2020)
8. Badawi, E., Jourdan, G.-V., Bochmann, G., Onut, I.-V., Flood, J.: The "Game Hack" scam. In: Bakaev, M., Frasincar, F., Ko, I.-Y. (eds.) ICWE 2019. LNCS, vol. 11496, pp. 280–295. Springer, Cham (2019). https://doi.org/10.1007/978-3-030-19274-7_21
9. Bartoletti, M., Carta, S., Cimoli, T., Saia, R.: Dissecting ponzi schemes on ethereum: identification, analysis, and impact. Futur. Gener. Comput. Syst. **102**, 259–277 (2020)
10. Bartoletti, M., Lande, S., Loddo, A., Pompianu, L., Serusi, S.: Cryptocurrency scams: analysis and perspectives. IEEE Access **9**, 148353–148373 (2021)
11. Bartoletti, M., Pes, B., Serusi, S.: Data mining for detecting bitcoin ponzi schemes. In: 2018 Crypto Valley Conference on Blockchain Technology (CVCBT), pp. 75–84. IEEE (2018)
12. Bidgoli, M., Grossklags, J.: "hello. this is the irs calling.": a case study on scams, extortion, impersonation, and phone spoofing. In: Electronic Crime Research (eCrime), 2017 APWG Symposium on, pp. 57–69. IEEE (2017)
13. Bistarelli, S., Parroccini, M., Santini, F.: Visualizing bitcoin flows of ransomware: Wannacry one week later, In: ITASEC (2018)
14. Bouma-Sims, E., Reaves, B.: A first look at scams on youtube. arXiv preprint arXiv:2104.06515 (2021)
15. Buchanan, T., Whitty, M.T.: The online dating romance scam: causes and consequences of victimhood. Psychol. Crime Law **20**(3), 261–283 (2014)
16. Canali, D., Cova, M., Vigna, G., Kruegel, C.: Prophiler: a fast filter for the large-scale detection of malicious web pages. In: Proceedings of the 20th international conference on World wide web, pp. 197–206 (2011)
17. Charan, A.N.S., Chen, Y.H., Chen, J.L.: Phishing websites detection using machine learning with url analysis. In: 2022 IEEE World Conference on Applied Intelligence and Computing (AIC), pp. 808–812 (2022)
18. Chen, W., Xu, Y., Zheng, Z., Zhou, Y., Yang, J.E., Bian, J.: Detecting" pump & dump schemes" on cryptocurrency market using an improved apriori algorithm. In: 2019 IEEE International Conference on Service-Oriented System Engineering (SOSE), pp. 293–2935. IEEE (2019)
19. Chen, W., Zheng, Z., Cui, J., Ngai, E., Zheng, P., Zhou, Y.: Detecting ponzi schemes on ethereum: towards healthier blockchain technology. In: Proceedings of the 2018 World Wide Web Conference, pp. 1409–1418 (2018)
20. Chen, W., Zheng, Z., Ngai, E.C.H., Zheng, P., Zhou, Y.: Exploiting blockchain data to detect smart ponzi schemes on ethereum. IEEE Access **7**, 37575–37586 (2019)
21. Clark, J.W., McCoy, D.: There are no free ipads: an analysis of survey scams as a business. In: Presented as part of the 6th USENIX Workshop on Large-Scale Exploits and Emergent Threats. USENIX, Washington, D.C. (2013)

22. Conti, M., Gangwal, A., Ruj, S.: On the economic significance of ransomware campaigns: a bitcoin transactions perspective. Comput. Sec. **79**, 162–189 (2018)
23. Cova, M., Kruegel, C., Vigna, G.: Detection and analysis of drive-by-download attacks and malicious javascript code. In: Proceedings of the 19th International Conference on World Wide Web, pp. 281–290 (2010)
24. Crawford, J., Guan, Y.: Knowing your bitcoin customer: money laundering in the bitcoin economy. In: 2020 13th International Conference on Systematic Approaches to Digital Forensic Engineering (SADFE), pp. 38–45. IEEE (2020)
25. Custers, B., Oerlemans, J.J., Pool, R.: Laundering the profits of ransomware: money laundering methods for vouchers and cryptocurrencies. Euro. J. Crime Criminal Law Criminal Justice **28**(2), 121–152 (2020)
26. Dashevskyi, S., Zhauniarovich, Y., Gadyatskaya, O., Pilgun, A., Ouhssain, H.: Dissecting android cryptocurrency miners. In: Proceedings of the Tenth ACM Conference on Data and Application Security and Privacy, pp. 191–202 (2020)
27. Farrugia, S., Ellul, J., Azzopardi, G.: Detection of illicit accounts over the ethereum blockchain. Expert Syst. Appl. **150**, 113318 (2020)
28. Gopal, R.D., Hojati, A., Patterson, R.A.: Analysis of third-party request structures to detect fraudulent websites. Decis. Support Syst. **154**, 113698 (2022)
29. Goyal, P.S., Kakkar, A., Vinod, G., Joseph, G.: Crypto-ransomware detection using behavioural analysis. In: Varde, P.V., Prakash, R.V., Vinod, G. (eds.) Reliability, Safety and Hazard Assessment for Risk-Based Technologies. LNME, pp. 239–251. Springer, Singapore (2020). https://doi.org/10.1007/978-981-13-9008-1_20
30. Harley, D., Grooten, M., Burn, S., Johnston, C.: My pc has 32,539 errors: how telephone support scams really work. Virus Bulletin (2012)
31. Hong, G., et al.: Analyzing ground-truth data of mobile gambling scams. In: 2022 IEEE Symposium on Security and Privacy (SP), pp. 2176–2193. IEEE (2022)
32. Invernizzi, L., Comparetti, P.M., Benvenuti, S., Kruegel, C., Cova, M., Vigna, G.: Evilseed: a guided approach to finding malicious web pages. In: 2012 IEEE symposium on Security and Privacy, pp. 428–442. IEEE (2012)
33. Jung, E., Le Tilly, M., Gehani, A., Ge, Y.: Data mining-based ethereum fraud detection. In: 2019 IEEE International Conference on Blockchain (Blockchain), pp. 266–273. IEEE (2019)
34. Kamps, J., Kleinberg, B.: To the moon: defining and detecting cryptocurrency pump-and-dumps. Crime Sci. **7**(1), 18 (2018)
35. Karhade, A., Yogi, A., Gupta, A., Landge, P., Galphade, M.: CNN for detection of COVID-19 using chest x-ray images. In: Verma, P., Charan, C., Fernando, X., Ganesan, S. (eds.) Advances in Data Computing, Communication and Security. LNDECT, vol. 106, pp. 251–259. Springer, Singapore (2022). https://doi.org/10.1007/978-981-16-8403-6_22
36. Kharraz, A., et al.: Outguard: detecting in-browser covert cryptocurrency mining in the wild. In: The World Wide Web Conference, pp. 840–852 (2019)
37. Kharraz, A., Robertson, W., Kirda, E.: Surveylance: automatically detecting online survey scams. In: 2018 IEEE Symposium on Security and Privacy (SP), pp. 70–86. IEEE (2018)
38. Kikerpill, K., Siibak, A.: Mazephishing: the covid-19 pandemic as credible social context for social engineering attacks. Trames: J. Humanities Soc. Sci. **25**(4), 371–393 (2021)
39. Kumar, N., Singh, A., Handa, A., Shukla, S.K.: Detecting malicious accounts on the ethereum blockchain with supervised learning. In: Dolev, S., Kolesnikov, V., Lodha, S., Weiss, G. (eds.) CSCML 2020. LNCS, vol. 12161, pp. 94–109. Springer, Cham (2020). https://doi.org/10.1007/978-3-030-49785-9_7

40. Liao, K., Zhao, Z., Doupé, A., Ahn, G.J.: Behind closed doors: measurement and analysis of cryptolocker ransoms in bitcoin. In: 2016 APWG eCrime, pp. 1–13. IEEE (2016)
41. Miramirkhani, N., Starov, O., Nikiforakis, N.: Dial one for scam: a large-scale analysis of technical support scams. arXiv preprint arXiv:1607.06891 (2016)
42. Modic, D., Anderson, R.: It's all over but the crying: the emotional and financial impact of internet fraud. IEEE Sec. Priv. **13**(5), 99–103 (2015)
43. Mohan, K.J., Poojitha, P.A., Reddy, V.A., Ajay, Y., Vardhan, T.H.: Prediction and analysis of crime rate for tourists by using data mining **13**(2), 1–12 (2022)
44. Moore, T., Clayton, R.: Evil Searching: compromise and recompromise of internet hosts for phishing. In: Dingledine, R., Golle, P. (eds.) FC 2009. LNCS, vol. 5628, pp. 256–272. Springer, Heidelberg (2009). https://doi.org/10.1007/978-3-642-03549-4_16
45. Musch, M., Wressnegger, C., Johns, M., Rieck, K.: Thieves in the browser: web-based cryptojacking in the wild. In: Proceedings of the 14th International Conference on Availability, Reliability and Security, pp. 1–10 (2019)
46. Phillips, R., Wilder, H.: Tracing cryptocurrency scams: clustering replicated advance-fee and phishing websites. arXiv preprint arXiv:2005.14440 (2020)
47. Ravenelle, A.J., Janko, E., Kowalski, K.C.: Good jobs, scam jobs: detecting, normalizing, and internalizing online job scams during the covid-19 pandemic. New Media Soc. **24**(7), 1591–1610 (2022)
48. Razali, M.A., Mohd Shariff, S.: CMBlock: in-browser detection and prevention cryptojacking tool using blacklist and behavior-based detection method. In: Badioze Zaman, H., et al. (eds.) IVIC 2019. LNCS, vol. 11870, pp. 404–414. Springer, Cham (2019). https://doi.org/10.1007/978-3-030-34032-2_36
49. Sadi, S.H., Pk, M.R.H., Zeki, A.M.: Threat detector for social media using text analysis. Inter. J. Perceptive Cognit. Comput. **7**(1), 113–117 (2021)
50. Sahin, M., Relieu, M., Francillon, A.: Using chatbots against voice spam: Analyzing lenny's effectiveness. In: Thirteenth Symposium on Usable Privacy and Security (SOUPS 2017), pp. 319–337. USENIX Association, Santa Clara, CA (2017)
51. Samarasinghe, N., Mannan, M.: On cloaking behaviors of malicious websites. Comput. Sec. **101**, 102114 (2021)
52. SatheeshKumar, M., Srinivasagan, K., UnniKrishnan, G.: A lightweight and proactive rule-based incremental construction approach to detect phishing scam. Inform. Technol. Manag., 1–28 (2022)
53. Shaari, A.H., Kamaluddin, M.R., Paizi, W.F., Mohd, M., et al.: Online-dating romance scam in malaysia: An analysis of online conversations between scammers and victims. GEMA Online® J. Lang. Stud. **19**(1) (2019)
54. Shalke, C.J., Achary, R.: Social engineering attack and scam detection using advanced natural langugae processing algorithm. In: 6th International Conference on Trends in Electronics and Informatics, pp. 1749–1754. IEEE (2022)
55. Sherman, I.N., Bowers, J., McNamara Jr, K., Gilbert, J.E., Ruiz, J., Traynor, P.: Are you going to answer that? measuring user responses to anti-robocall application indicators. In: NDSS (2020)
56. Srinivasan, B., Kountouras, A., Miramirkhani, N., Alam, M., Nikiforakis, N., Antonakakis, M., Ahamad, M.: Exposing search and advertisement abuse tactics and infrastructure of technical support scammers. In: WWW 2018, pp. 319–328 (2018)
57. Starov, O., Zhou, Y., Wang, J.: Detecting malicious campaigns in obfuscated javascript with scalable behavioral analysis. In: 2019 IEEE Security and Privacy Workshops (SPW), pp. 218–223. IEEE (2019)

58. Tanana, D.: Behavior-based detection of cryptojacking malware. In: 2020 Ural Symposium on Biomedical Engineering, Radioelectronics and Information Technology (USBEREIT), pp. 0543–0545. IEEE (2020)
59. Tashtoush, Y., Alrababah, B., Darwish, O., Maabreh, M., Alsaedi, N.: A deep learning framework for detection of covid-19 fake news on social media platforms. Data **7**(5), 65 (2022)
60. Torres, C.F., Baden, M., State, R.: Towards usable protection against honeypots. In: 2020 IEEE International Conference on Blockchain and Cryptocurrency (ICBC), pp. 1–2. IEEE (2020)
61. Toyoda, K., Mathiopoulos, P.T., Ohtsuki, T.: A novel methodology for hyip operators' bitcoin addresses identification. IEEE Access **7**, 74835–74848 (2019)
62. Toyoda, K., Ohtsuki, T., Mathiopoulos, P.: Time series analysis for bitcoin transactions: the case of pirate@ 40's hyip scheme. In: IEEE ICDMW 2018, pp. 151–155. IEEE (2018)
63. Toyoda, K., Ohtsuki, T., Mathiopoulos, P.T.: Identification of high yielding investment programs in bitcoin via transactions pattern analysis. In: GLOBECOM 2017, pp. 1–6. IEEE (2017)
64. Toyoda, K., Ohtsuki, T., Mathiopoulos, P.T.: Multi-class bitcoin-enabled service identification based on transaction history summarization. In: iThings/ GreenCom/ CPSCom/ SmartData/ Blockchain/ CIT/Cybermatics 2018, pp. 1153–1160. IEEE (2018)
65. Tripathi, A., Ghosh, M., Bharti, K.: Analyzing the uncharted territory of monetizing scam videos on youtube. Soc. Netw. Anal. Min. **12**(1), 1–18 (2022)
66. Tu, H., Doupé, A., Zhao, Z., Ahn, G.J.: Users really do answer telephone scams. In: 28th {USENIX} Security Symposium, pp. 1327–1340 (2019)
67. Ueno, D., et al.: Mild cognitive decline is a risk factor for scam vulnerability in older adults. Front. Psychiatry, 2365 (2021)
68. Vasek, M., Moore, T.: There's no free lunch, even using bitcoin: tracking the popularity and profits of virtual currency scams. In: Böhme, R., Okamoto, T. (eds.) FC 2015. LNCS, vol. 8975, pp. 44–61. Springer, Heidelberg (2015). https://doi.org/10.1007/978-3-662-47854-7_4
69. Vasek, M., Moore, T.: Analyzing the bitcoin ponzi scheme ecosystem. In: Zohar, A., Eyal, I., Teague, V., Clark, J., Bracciali, A., Pintore, F., Sala, M. (eds.) FC 2018. LNCS, vol. 10958, pp. 101–112. Springer, Heidelberg (2019). https://doi.org/10.1007/978-3-662-58820-8_8
70. Vasek, M., Thornton, M., Moore, T.: Empirical analysis of denial-of-service attacks in the bitcoin ecosystem. In: Böhme, R., Brenner, M., Moore, T., Smith, M. (eds.) FC 2014. LNCS, vol. 8438, pp. 57–71. Springer, Heidelberg (2014). https://doi.org/10.1007/978-3-662-44774-1_5
71. Victor, F., Hagemann, T.: Cryptocurrency pump and dump schemes: Quantification and detection. In: 2019 International Conference on Data Mining Workshops (ICDMW), pp. 244–251. IEEE (2019)
72. Whitty, M.T.: Anatomy of the online dating romance scam. Secur. J. **28**(4), 443–455 (2015)
73. Whitty, M.T.: Do you love me? psychological characteristics of romance scam victims. Cyberpsychol. Behav. Soc. Netw. **21**(2), 105–109 (2018)
74. Xu, J., Livshits, B.: The anatomy of a cryptocurrency pump-and-dump scheme. In: 28th {USENIX} Security Symposium, pp. 1609–1625 (2019)

Vulnerabilities and Exploits

VulMAE: Graph Masked Autoencoders for Vulnerability Detection from Source and Binary Codes

Mahmoud Zamani⬮, Saquib Irtiza(✉)⬮, Latifur Khan⬮,
and Kevin W. Hamlen⬮

The University of Texas at Dallas, Richardson, TX 75080, USA
{mahmoud.zamani,saquib.irtiza,lkhan,hamlen}@utdallas.edu

Abstract. The first *graph masked auto-encoder* (GraphMAE) model for software vulnerability detection is designed and developed, with a comparative evaluation against other self-supervised learning (SSL) methods. Evaluation of the domain-specific GraphMAE model (VulMAE) for the vulnerability detection task shows exceptional promise, outperforming all other baseline models in the study. The approach is particularly well-suited for cybersecurity applications where gathering substantial real-world labeled samples is difficult, since graph SSL methods (e.g., contrastive and generative models) offer data classification in AI tasks without requiring vast amounts of labeled data for effective training.

The study fills a key gap in the literature on automated and machine-assisted discovery and patching of software security vulnerabilities, which has become increasingly critical with the dramatic increase in modern software complexity, but for which graph neural network (GNN) approaches are understudied relative to traditional processes, such as manual source code auditing and fuzzing. To conduct the study, the evaluation applies models to source and binary software components sourced from the National Vulnerability Database (NVD). A new dataset is curated by extracting vulnerable code fragments from six applications with NVD-documented security flaws and converting them to four graph types using specialized tools based on code property graphs and binary semantics lifting. The data is used to train contrastive and generative learning models for comparison. VulMAE achieves a weighted F1 score of 0.936 and a weighted Recall of 0.938, which is the highest of all tested methods.

Keywords: Contrastive Learning · Generative Model · Vulnerability Detection · Graph Neural Network · Autoencoder

1 Introduction

The exponential increase in software complexity over the past few decades has made it increasingly difficult for human software developers to reliably discover and fix security vulnerabilities in large software systems. This has motivated a

M. Mosbah et al. (Eds.): FPS 2023, LNCS 14551, pp. 191–207, 2024.
https://doi.org/10.1007/978-3-031-57537-2_12

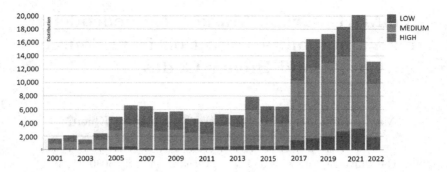

Fig. 1. Common Vulnerability Scoring System (CVSS) severity by year [26]

search for efficient vulnerability detection systems that can distinguish between vulnerable and non-vulnerable programs. Cybersecurity experts have traditionally employed a variety of techniques to address this problem, including elaborate code auditing procedures, voluminous lists of best programming practices, extensive software unit testing such as fuzzing, and vulnerability reporting and patching procedures.

Nevertheless, Fig. 1 illustrates that critical vulnerabilities continue to be discovered and exploited by cyber criminals at an increasing rate despite these precautions. For example, in the first quarter of 2022 critical vulnerabilities were discovered in Sudo (Linux superuser authority delegation command) and OpenSSH (secure network tunneling) whose exploitation gave attackers remote control over affected systems and files [6,25]. Despite large-scale scrutiny of these open-source codes, these vulnerabilities remained exploitable for 6 months and 12 years, respectively, before they were finally discovered and patched.

To overcome this issue, Deep Learning (DL) methods have been used to automatically extract features and investigate whether successes in other problem domains can be translated to vulnerability detection. Prior work has shown that DL models are efficient for detecting many software security issues, achieving high accuracy in many cases [17,19,20]. However, existing DL approaches suffer at least two major drawbacks: First, most are supervised, requiring a large volume of labeled data for adequate training. Vulnerability data collection is notoriously difficult because it requires high expertise and time, and the resulting data is prone to human error due to the diversity and complexity of software products and their vulnerabilities [28]. Second, DL models typically treat codes as natural language inputs, which misses many essential aspects of their structure and semantics, including control-flows, dataflows, and abstract syntax trees.

Self-supervised learning (SSL) [34,40] has helped reduce this dependency on supervision, facilitating training on larger, unlabeled datasets. This is achieved by generalizing learned, transferable knowledge from existing unlabeled data with pretext tasks to downstream tasks. Graph tasks have been solved with SSL-based *contrastive learning* [7,34]. However, this requires high-quality negative samples as a contrast during training, and the training process is complex, resulting in varying degrees of effectiveness from graph to graph [41].

Graph auto-encoders (GAEs) [13,29] aim to resolve these issues through dedicated objective targets in reconstruction of input graph data. In this paper we show that a domain specific version of *graph masked auto-encoders* (GraphMAE), which we call VulMAE, offers exceptional promise for addressing the software vulnerability detection problem at large scales. We evaluate its performance in comparison to contrastive learning methods using a new curated graph dataset. All relevant source code and our dataset are publicly available for download.[1] Our key contributions are as follows:

- We curate a custom dataset for binary classification task using vulnerable code snippets from six applications. They were identified using NVD [1], and then converted to four graph types using Joern [38] and BAP [2].
- We develop VulMAE, a domain specific version of the state-of-the-art Graph-MAE algorithm, by incorporating the most optimal combination of encoder, decoder and loss function.
- We perform comparative analysis between contrastive and generative learning algorithms to identify which one performs best for vulnerability detection. The comparison includes GraphCL [40], InfoGraph [32] and DGI [34].
- Most prior works have either considered source- or binary-level graphs for analysis, but have never compared their efficacy against one another. Our study is the first to perform a comprehensive analysis of source-level graphs such as CFG, AST, and CPG with binary-level CFG, which we call B-CFG.

2 Background

2.1 Self-supervised Graph Learning

Deep learning models are typically trained in either a semi-supervised or supervised manner, relying on labeled data. However, because labeling is expensive, SSL algorithms were developed to train on unlabeled data. Applying SSL to graphs involves pretext training, which captures dependencies in multiple augmentations of the data. These tasks are then used to train *convolutional neural networks* (CNNs) to retain node relationships. Pretext tasks for Graph SSL can be subdivided into two main learning types: contrastive and generative.

2.2 Contrastive Learning

The key idea of contrastive learning is to generate multiple augmentations of graphs that are slightly different from the original and treat them as positive pairs so that their representations are pulled closer together during the training phase. Conversely, negative pairs are formed using augmented graphs that are distinct, and the training process pushes their representations farther apart.

---

[1] https://github.com/Saquibirtiza/VulMAE.git

GraphCL [40] proposes four augmentations for generating views: node dropping, edge perturbation, sub-graph sampling and node attribute masking. However, generalizing these strictly static view generation methods to different kinds of datasets has sometimes proved to be problematic.

Table 1. Summary of existing contrastive learning algorithms considered in this work.

Model	Data Augmentation	Pretext Goal	Objective Function	Use Case
GraphCL	Masking, Edge Perturbation, Random Sampling	Instance Discrimination	Noise-Contrastive Estimation	Graph Classification
DGI	Arbitrary	MI Maximization	JS Estimator	Node/Graph Classification
InfoGraph	None	MI Maximization	SP Estimator	Graph Classification

Table 1 summarizes some of the key properties of relevant contrastive learning algorithms. Deep Graph InfoMax (DGI) [34] is a node classification algorithm that learns patch representations of graphs and tries to maximize the mutual information of these patches with their corresponding high-level graph summaries. The patches can then be used for different downstream tasks. InfoGraph [32] is another unsupervised method motivated by Deep InfoMax (DIM) [9] that learns graph-level representations by maximizing the mutual information between the augmented substructures and the original graph.

2.3   Generative Learning Techniques and Graph Autoencoders

Generative SSL is an alternative technique that treats depth information embedded inside data as a source of self-supervision. In a recent study, GraphMAE revisits the pitfalls of generative learning and proposes a new *masked* Graph Auto-Encoder technique to learn graph representations [44]. An auto-encoder in a self-supervised neural network first compresses input data to an encoded representation to learn how to reconstruct the data to mimic the original input. This is accomplished by introducing masked feature reconstruction and scaled cosine error, which performs better on feature vectors of variable magnitude and handles class imbalances more efficiently. In this work we tailor this method for our domain-specific downstream task and evaluate how well it performs on vulnerability detection on source and binary graphs.

2.4   Encoders and Decoders

Graph representation learning techniques have been less aggressively studied in the domain of software vulnerability detection. To evaluate which encoder and decoder combination offers the most promise for this problem, we considered four of the most popular representation learning algorithms: Graph Attention Network (GAT) [33], Graph Isomorphism Network (GIN) [35], Multi-Layer Perceptron (MLP), and Graph Convolutional Networks (GCN) [14].

GAT is a neural network framework that uses masked self-attention layers to perform convolutions on graph structures. It can accommodate various neighborhood sizes by assigning different weights to the nodes without requiring information about the whole graph. MLP is a decoder-only learning algorithm that uses general feed forward network to decode in a linear fashion. It starts with a Linear layer, followed by a ReLU, Dropout and Linear layer.

GIN is based on the Weisfeiler-Lehman (WL) test [30] to determine whether two graphs are non-isomorphic. In contrast to traditional GNN, GIN uses MLP instead of linear transformation in a multi-layer setting, and then aggregates using sum function instead of mean or max. GCNs are convolutional neural networks for graphs that uses semi-supervised learning while leveraging the spectral structures of the graphs to predict/classify them. The algorithm first performs linear transformation on the node representations. Then it multiplies the newly transformed representations with a normalized affinity matrix. Finally, the results are passed through a non-linear layer to generate the final outputs.

2.5 Loss Functions

We evaluated a variety of loss functions in this work—namely, Mean Squared Error (MSE), Binary Cross Entropy with Logits Loss (BCEWLL), and Scaled Cosine Error (SCE). MSE is mostly used in regression setting where the output is usually a real number within a certain range. It is computed by taking the mean of the squared differences between the predicted and the original outputs. The smaller the MSE, the closer the predicted values are to the original and the better the prediction model is. BCEWLL, also known as log loss, penalizes based on the distances between the predicted values and the expected ones. The penalty is a function of the negative average of the log of the corrected predicted probabilities. GraphMAE introduces a modified loss function more suited to classification tasks involving graphs. This addresses the common class imbalance issue in graphs between easy and difficult samples during the masked feature reconstruction phase. Cosine error is used because it better handles the varying magnitudes of the node attributes in graphs [11].

2.6 Graph Types

This work explores four popular graph types used in vulnerability detection tasks: Source Control Flow Graphs (S-CFGs), Abstract Syntax Trees (ASTs), Code Property Graphs (CPGs) and Binary Control Flow Graphs (B-CFGs). *S-CFGs* [36,42] encode the set of execution paths that a program might traverse during its execution. The nodes represent basic blocks (i.e., lines of code that are always executed consecutively) whereas the edges represent the flow of execution between the blocks. *ASTs* [21,22,24] on the other hand, model the structure of the literal code instructions and expressions that constitute the computer program. Nodes consist of mathematical operators, programming language keywords, assembly language instruction mnemonics, etc., while edges capture nesting relationships, such as arguments to operators and instructions.

CPGs [3,37,43] are an emerging approach for integrating many of the features found in S-CFGs, ASTs, and Program Dependence Graphs (PDGs) into a single database for deeper analysis. The nodes represent high-level constructs, such as methods, variables, and control structures whereas edges are labeled to encode different relationships between program constructs in the same graph. *B-CFGs* represent control-flow paths at the binary level rather than the source level. They are finer grained but also tend to introduce greater flexibility in their control flow, since binary code places fewer semantic constraints on the possible destinations of computed control-flow transfers relative to source code. This flexibility can be attributed to reasons like loss of high level abstractions when transitioning from source to binary code, use of different optimization during compilation, programs that dynamically change its execution during run-time etc. However, real-world attacks frequently exploit this fact to hijack control-flows of victim applications in ways that are not apparent at the source level [10]. B-CFGs are therefore important for effective vulnerability analysis and detection.

2.7 Related Works

General code analysis techniques can be categorized into static, dynamic, and hybrid approaches. The static techniques [23], such as rule-based analysis [5] and code similarity detection [18], mainly rely on the analysis of source code, but often suffer from high false positives [16]. Dynamic analysis includes fuzz testing [27] and taint analysis [31], but often have issues with high false negative rates due to low code coverage.

Devign [43] and Reveal [3] uses new advanced GNN models to identify vulnerabilities in graph-level classification. Devign experiments on different source level graphs including AST, S-CFG, Data Flow Graph (DFG), and Natural Code Sequence (NCS). Reveal combines Devign data with other available real application datasets to facilitate more comprehensive evaluations. The graph datasets in both projects are limited to source-level CPGs which is a research gap we address by experimenting with binary-level graphs also. LineVD [8] detects vulnerabilities at the statement level using GNNs with performance improvement. It uses two popular GNN variants, GCN and GAT, to evaluate the effect of different GNN architectures; and its features are drawn from source-level PDGs and CDGs only. Our research differs from the existing works in its introduction of comparative evaluation of both source and binary level graphs (S-CFG, AST, CPG, B-CFG) and a wide variety of SSL methods (GraphCL, InfoGraph, DGI, and GraphMAE). The format of graph datasets generated for this research are usable by pytorch-geometric libraries for general graph learning purpose and are organized similar to other general graph datasets such as MUTAG [12].

3 Proposed Methodology

Prior work on vulnerability detection has examined the problem at different levels of granularity, such as component-level, file-level, class-level, function-level, and instruction-level. Coarser granularity yields better accuracy because of its higher volume of information but necessitates additional manual exploration that requires human skill and time to make practical use of the results. Finer granularity provides more precise results but can incur higher false negatives. For example, instruction-level granularity can miss vulnerable inter-procedural interactions leading to false negatives, while coarser level might fail to localize the precise bug. This generally inverse relationship between granularity and accuracy raises several challenges for our research:

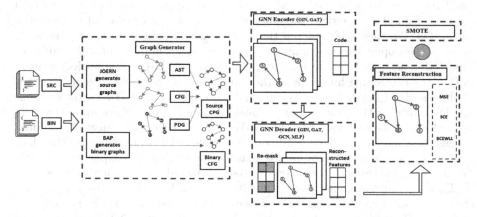

Fig. 2. High-level architecture of VulMAE to detect software vulnerabilities in binary and source graphs

- **Better Localization:** Useful detection systems must enable end users to quickly locate vulnerabilities. This requires finer granularity.
- **Data Imbalance:** The scarcity of reported vulnerabilities relative to the vast volumes of overall code makes realistic datasets highly imbalanced. As a result, subtle vulnerabilities are difficult to find, and tend to be eclipsed by reports of easily spotted, lower severity vulnerabilities.
- **Data Reliability:** Some vulnerabilities remain undetected by defenders for months or years. For instance, the Shellshock vulnerability evaded detection for 25 years in open-source software before it was patched. These hidden vulnerabilities make the non-vulnerable class of the dataset highly unreliable.

Our work provides the following solutions to the identified challenges. For better localization, VulMAE is executed at the function level. We collect source-level function features using Joern [37]. Joern provides a combination of detailed graph representations of source code, namely S-CFG, Data Dependency Graph (DDG), and AST. This results in a composite CPG. However, our approach goes beyond coarse function-level granularity to collect finer-grained features down to the binary instruction level. We parse the binary data using the widely popular

BAP [2] to collect the binary features. BAP was our platform of choice because of its open-source nature as opposed to platforms such as IDA Pro that are commercial. Also, to account for imbalance in the dataset, we use VulMAE that has components capable of performing well even if the dataset is imbalanced. But to ensure that we do not lose any performance of our model, we also use SMOTE [4] to partially reduce the severity of imbalance in our dataset by over-sampling the minority class slightly. This helps VulMAE to deal with the rest of the imbalance without compromising its optimal performance.

Finally to ensure data reliability, as part of an ongoing effort, we accumulated functions from six real-world open source applications to form our own dataset. Table 2 summarizes the dataset along with the number of instances in each class. We specifically picked these applications because of their popularity amongst the open source community and the large number of vulnerabilities reported against them in NVD. Each application is a large-scale project written in C/C++ containing hundreds or thousands of functions, and tens or hundreds of thousands of lines of code. By manually studying all NVD records for these applications over the past decade, we assembled a dataset where approximately 10% of the instances are vulnerable. We improved the reliability of our data by ensuring multiple experts agree on the labels of the data. Because this data collection process is resource intensive and requires multiple experts to commit for many hours, we had to restrict our dataset to only six applications for now.

Figure 2 illustrates our system architecture for VulMAE, consisting of four steps: (1) Our Graph Generator first uses Joern to prepare graphs from source code, and BAP for binary-level graph collection. (2) The GNN Encoder masks extracted node features with a mask token. These altered graphs are encoded using a GNN (*viz.*, GIN and GAT). (3) GNN Decoder next employs four types of GNNs (*viz.*, GAT, GIN, GCN and MLP) to re-mask the code from the previous step with other tokens. (4) The output of the decoder block is then leveraged to reconstruct input node features of masked nodes using multiple loss functions (*viz.*, SCE, MSE, and BCEWLL).

4   Evaluation

GraphMAE has been shown to outperform all existing algorithms when tested against seven benchmark datasets: MUTAG, IMDB-B, IMDB-M, PROTEINS, COLLAB, REDDITB, and NCI1 [39]. However, none of these datasets contain graphs that have the complex relationships characteristic of dependencies found within large real-world software applications. We therefore formulate a new version, VulMAE, that is better suited for detecting vulnerabilities from our challenging real world dataset. Our new method outperforms other state-of-the-art contrastive learning methods for downstream vulnerability detection tasks, as demonstrated by the experimental outcomes reported in this section. Our experiments address the following research questions (RQs):

- **RQ1:** Do the VulMAE encoders and decoders generalize well for the vulnerability detection task? If they do, which encoder-decoder combination proves to be the most suitable for addressing this problem?
- **RQ2:** Does SCE loss function [39] yield high F1 and recall scores? If not, can we find a better alternative for this imbalanced dataset?
- **RQ3:** Prior works evaluate with graphs from either source or binary but not both. If multiple types are considered, which one yields the best results?
- **RQ4:** Do generative learning algorithms such as VulMAE outperform existing contrastive learning algorithms in detecting software vulnerabilities?

Table 2. Dataset description. Vul and Non-Vul represents the number of vulnerabilities and non-vulnerabilities respectively.

App Name	Graph Types	Edges	Nodes	Graphs	Vul	Non-Vul
LibPNG	CPG	1845382	82413	324	25	299
	S-CFG	3104607	12487			
	B-CFG	7861098	28248			
	AST	2628710	81777			
LibTIFF	CPG	5125862	79009	438	33	405
	S-CFG	4498837	13142			
	B-CFG	9156127	47104			
	AST	3679494	78132			
TCPDump	CPG	2074116	33461	100	15	85
	S-CFG	328240	6018	100	15	85
	B-CFG	607635	13679	100	15	85
	AST	6092203	57465	200	20	174
Sudo	CPG	5636108	41858	187	9	178
	S-CFG	740870	6213			
	B-CFG	2664002	25731			
	AST	4384746	41506			
TinTin	CPG	8764300	44903	270	4	266
	S-CFG	1006857	6636			
	B-CFG	3747693	24376			
	AST	586926	44363			
OpenSSH	CPG	5750707	70560	100	21	79
	S-CFG	732305	1003			
	B-CFG	1965966	36199			
	AST	4186296	70352			

4.1   Evaluation Metrics

In our experiments, we present both F1 and Recall scores. Recall plays a crucial role in evaluating the number of potential true positives that might be overlooked by the method. This metric is particularly valuable for cyber defenders, as it aids in quantifying the reliability of the classification process during security-critical code reviews. Also F1 score helps in determining the accuracy of the model by using both precision and recall during its calculation. We specifically report the weighted recall and F1 because it is the best metric for representing the performance on imbalanced datasets. These metrics consider the number of instances in each class when computing the score.

4.2   Compute Resources and Experimental Details

All our experiments were run on an internal cluster containing a single Nvidia Quadro RTX 4000 GPU with 8 GB of GPU memory. Each experiment was run for 20 epochs and repeated five times with random seed values. The results from each of the five runs were then averaged to obtain the scores that are reported in the tables. We take 60% of the dataset as training data, 20% for testing data and the rest for validation. We used a learning rate of 0.001 and a batch size of 6 for all the experiments.

Table 3. Comparative analysis of VulMAE using different encoders, decoders and loss functions and how they perform against different graphs

			B-CFG	CPG	S-CFG	AST
Encoders	**GIN**	Weighted-F1	0.748	0.756	0.770	0.776
		Weighted-Recall	0.813	0.820	0.826	0.842
	GAT	Weighted-F1	**0.822**	**0.855**	**0.898**	**0.936**
		Weighted-Recall	**0.858**	**0.870**	**0.900**	**0.938**
Decoders	**GIN**	Weighted-F1	0.762	0.772	0.813	0.838
		Weighted-Recall	0.820	0.832	0.848	0.865
	MLP	Weighted-F1	0.768	0.798	0.800	0.895
		Weighted-Recall	0.822	0.838	0.833	0.903
	GCN	Weighted-F1	0.818	0.828	0.868	0.893
		Weighted-Recall	0.855	0.852	0.883	0.902
	GAT	Weighted-F1	**0.822**	**0.855**	**0.898**	**0.936**
		Weighted-Recall	**0.858**	**0.870**	**0.900**	**0.938**
Loss Function	**MSE**	Weighted-F1	0.670	0.678	0.678	0.678
		Weighted-Recall	0.770	0.773	0.773	0.773
	BCEWLL	Weighted-F1	0.702	0.730	0.73	0.73
		Weighted-Recall	0.783	0.810	0.810	0.810
	SCE	Weighted-F1	**0.822**	**0.855**	**0.898**	**0.936**
		Weighted-Recall	**0.858**	**0.870**	**0.900**	**0.938**

4.3   RQ1: Encoder and Decoder Analysis

We run two sets of experiments, one for encoders and one for decoders. For each encoder and decoder, we run VulMAE on all four graph types for the six applications. We then generate the final results for each *encoder-graph type* and *decoder-graph type* combination by averaging the F1 and Recall scores over all the applications. While running the experiments, we ensure that the other parameters remain unchanged across all graph types for fair comparison. We consider a total of four different GNNs as decoders (*viz.*, GIN, GAT, GCN and MLP), and two as encoders (*viz.*, GIN and GAT), since these are the most popular choices in this domain.

Table 3 shows the result, where the best encoders and decoders for each graph type are highlighted. Each score in the table is the average of five different runs using random seed values to show that our results are consistent. Results show that GAT is the best choice for both decoders and encoders. This is because GAT uses multi-head attention that focuses on the important nodes in its neighborhood instead of treating all neighboring nodes equally. This makes sense in the context of codes, because not all lines surrounding a particular point of interest should be relevant when detecting vulnerabilities. Rather those lines that have higher chance of contributing to the vulnerability should be given more priority.

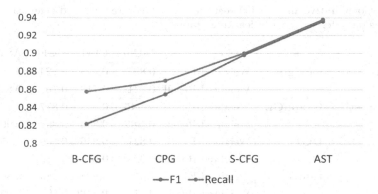

Fig. 3. Weighted F1 and Recall scores given by VulMAE for all four graph types. Control parameters are fixed.

Table 4. Effect of graph types on VulMAE. Best parameters from previous RQs used. All scores are averaged over five runs with random seeds for 20 epochs.

	B-CFG	CPG	S-CFG	AST
Weighted-F1	0.822	0.855	0.898	**0.936**
Weighted-Recall	0.858	0.870	0.900	**0.938**

4.4   RQ2: Loss Function Analysis

The goal of RQ2 is to identify whether changing the loss function affects the performance of the model and whether existing loss functions perform better than the one used in GraphMAE. We also wanted to see whether the loss function proposed in GraphMAE was a good fit for our domain-specific downstream task. The experiments include widely used loss functions, such as MSE and BCEWLL, as well as loss functions modified for GraphMAE, called SCE. We run experiments for each *loss function-graph type* combination for each of the six applications and compute the average of the F1 and Recall scores. Similar to RQ1, we repeat the experiments with five random seeds and reported the average results for all graph types.

Table 3 shows the results of this experiment. The superior performance of SCE compared to the other two loss functions is evident from the results. The advantage in performance of SCE is due to its ability to account for imbalances in the dataset. Also, SCE is better suited to handle differences in magnitudes of feature vectors, which are common in graph node attributes. This means that the effectiveness of this loss function is generalizable to this domain, and can be used to detect vulnerabilities with good accuracy.

Table 5. Comparative analysis between supervised, contrastive, and generative graph algorithms on different types of learning graphs

			B-CFG	CPG	S-CFG	AST
Sup.	**Devign**	Weighted-F1	0.832	0.828	0.824	0.909
		Weighted-Recall	0.741	0.713	0.707	0.865
Contrastive	**GraphCL**	Weighted-F1	**0.845**	0.843	0.877	0.876
		Weighted-Recall	**0.882**	0.883	0.897	0.905
	DGI	Weighted-F1	0.821	0.846	0.880	0.855
		Weighted-Recall	0.830	0.883	0.882	0.900
	InfoGraph	Weighted-F1	0.842	0.848	0.880	0.865
		Weighted-Recall	0.878	**0.893**	0.897	0.903
Gen.	**VulMAE**	Weighted-F1	0.822	**0.855**	**0.898**	**0.936**
		Weighted-Recall	0.858	0.870	**0.900**	**0.938**

4.5   RQ3: Graph Type Analysis

Now that we know which encoder, decoder and loss function yields the best score for VulMAE, we next confirm which graph type gives us the best result. We run experiments with GAT as encoder and decoder and SCE as the loss function, since these were the ones that gave us the best scores in the previous RQs.

Table 4 shows the average of the resulting scores across all applications for each graph type. Each experiment is run with five different random seed values and the scores averaged. The results show that AST is the best performing graph type, whereas B-CFG is the worst. The lower performance observed in B-CFG can be attributed to the loss of high level abstractions when the source code is converted to binary code. The compiler translates high-level constructs into a more direct representation of machine code which provides limited features to train an efficient model. This contributes to the observed performance disparity.

Graph size and adjustable model parameters (e.g., mask ratio) also affect results. The optimal ratio varies across graphs and must be tuned. The graphs in our dataset are larger than those in other available datasets, which can result in information redundancy due to high node degree or homogeneity. Additionally, we observed that the source codes can provide enough syntactic and semantic information, which makes it easier to know how the data and inputs drive the paths of execution [15]. That is the reason why semantic based graphs such as AST perform better than other graph types in this case.

4.6 RQ4: Comparing Contrastive and Generative Algorithms

Table 5 compares VulMAE with other baselines, which includes graph contrastive learning algorithms (GraphCL, DGI, and InfoGraph) and a popular graph based vulnerability detection baseline called Devign [43]. Best F1 and Recall scores, averaged over the six applications in the dataset, are highlighted. Although the architectures and the model parameters are different, they were kept fairly similar for unbiased comparison. Figure 4 visualizes the performance of the models.

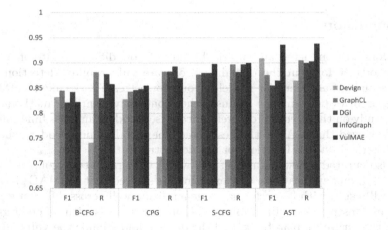

Fig. 4. VulMAE versus other baseline SSL and vulnerability detection methods.

Results show that VulMAE is the best in majority of the cases except for B-CFG where GraphCL performs the best. This is because binary graphs represent machine code that is difficult to generate when masked by our model, due to the loss of high level abstraction from source code. Also, in case of AST, VulMAE outperforms the other methods by a fair margin. Among the source-level graphs, only InfoGraph exhibits a higher recall than VulMAE for CPG, but this advantage is offset by its lower F1 score when compared to VulMAE. Devign on the other hand has fairly competitive F1 scores compared to the SSL methods but its sub-optimal recall scores makes it a poor choice for the downstream task. This trend in performance could be attributed to the fact that generative algorithms accommodate a wider variety of downstream tasks that retrieve the distribution of original data. This gives them flexibility for more tasks, such as classification and generation. Contrastive learning algorithms rely on data augmentation that can be ambiguous and unsuited to graphs with discrete and abstract data. They also require negative samples that are difficult to collect and oftentimes biased. This makes VulMAE better suited for vulnerability detection.

Furthermore, we ran experiments to see whether the severity of the data imbalance had any effect on the performance of our model, even though VulMAE was designed to handle imbalanced data. We used SMOTE to slightly oversample the minority class which makes up 10% of the whole dataset by 30% so that the imbalance in the dataset could be partially alleviated making it easier for the model to handle the rest of the imbalance. The results showed that the overall F1 and Recall scores across all graph types improved by an average of 1% over five runs with random seed values. This establishes that even though our model can handle imbalanced data, the severity of the imbalance determines whether the optimal performance of the model is achieved.

5   Conclusion

In this work we conducted an empirical study of how different state-of-the-art SSL methods perform in the domain of software vulnerability detection. We tailored a masked autoencoder model for our downstream task called VulMAE, and compared its performance against other contrastive learning methods. An ablation study on the effects of different encoders, decoders and loss functions on VulMAE showed that GAT is the best choice for encoder and decoder, whereas SCE loss is the best loss function for the downstream task.

We also curated a new dataset of real-world vulnerable code collected from six C/C++ Linux applications. Our experiments showed that VulMAE gives the best overall result, with its performance generalizing well across different graphs types. This constitutes the first comparison of these models with different graph types. In the future we plan to expand the dataset and include the vulnerability types, so that it can be used for multiclass classification. Also, our current dataset contains labels for each graph instead of individual nodes, which restricts its use for finding line-level vulnerabilities. We plan to address this in future work.

Acknowledgments. This research was supported in part by DARPA Award N66001-21-C-4024, ONR Award N00014-21-1-2654, and ARO Award W911NF-21-1-0032. All recommendations, opinions, and conclusions are those of the authors and not necessarily of the above supporters.

References

1. Booth, H., Rike, D., Witte, G.A.: The national vulnerability database (NVD): Overview. ITL Bulletin, National Institute of Standards and Technology (2013)
2. Brumley, D., Jager, I., Avgerinos, T., Schwartz, E.J.: BAP: a binary analysis platform. In: Proceedings of International Conference on Computer Aided Verification, pp. 463–469 (2011)
3. Chakraborty, S., Krishna, R., Ding, Y., Ray, B.: Deep learning based vulnerability detection: are we there yet. IEEE Trans. Softw. Eng. **48**, 3280–3296 (2022)
4. Chawla, N.V., Bowyer, K.W., Hall, L.O., Kegelmeyer, W.P.: SMOTE: synthetic minority over-sampling technique. J. Artifi. Intell. Res. **16**(1), 321–357 (2002)
5. Croft, R., Newlands, D., Chen, Z., Babar, M.A.: An empirical study of rule-based and learning-based approaches for static application security testing. In: Proceedings of ACM/IEEE International Symposium Empirical Software Engineering and Measurement (2021)
6. DevNest: How to bypass sudo – exploit CVE-2023-22809 vulnerability. Medium (2023). https://medium.com/@dev.nest/how-to-bypass-sudo-exploit-cve-2023-22809-vulnerability-296ef10a1466
7. Hassani, K., Khasahmadi, A.H.: Contrastive multi-view representation learning on graphs. In: Proceedings of International Conference on Machine Learning, pp. 4116–4126 (2020)
8. Hin, D., Kan, A., Chen, H., Babar, M.A.: LineVD: statement-level vulnerability detection using graph neural networks. In: Proceedings of International Conference on Mining Software Repositories, pp. 596–607 (2022)
9. Hjelm, R.D., et al.: Learning deep representations by mutual information estimation and maximization. In: Proceedings of International Conference on Learning Representation (2019)
10. Hohnka, M.J., Miller, J.A., Dacumos, K.M., Fritton, T.J., Erdley, J.D., Long, L.N.: Evaluation of compiler-induced vulnerabilities. J. Aerospace Inform. Syst. **16**(10), 409–426 (2019)
11. Hou, Z., Liu, X., Cen, Y., Dong, Y., Yang, H., Wang, C., Tang, J.: GraphMAE: self-supervised masked graph autoencoders. In: Proceedings of ACM Conference on Knowledge Discovery and Data Mining, pp. 594–604 (2022)
12. Kazius, J., McGuire, R., Bursi, R.: Derivation and validation of toxicophores for mutagenicity prediction. J. Med. Chem. **48**(1), 312–320 (2005)
13. Kipf, T.N., Welling, M.: Variational graph auto-encoders. arXiv:1611.07308 (2016)
14. Kipf, T.N., Welling, M.: Semi-supervised classification with graph convolutional networks. In: Proceedings of International Conferen on Learning Representation (Poster) (2017)
15. Le, T., et al.: Maximal divergence sequential autoencoder for binary software vulnerability detection. In: Proceedings of International Conference on Learning Representation (2019)
16. Li, X., Feng, B., Li, G., Li, T., He, M.: A vulnerability detection system based on fusion of assembly code and source code. Sec. Commun. Netw. **2021** (2021)

17. Li, Z., Zou, D., Xu, S., Chen, Z., Zhu, Y., Jin, H.: VulDeeLocator: a deep learning-based fine-grained vulnerability detector. IEEE Trans. Dependable Sec. Comput. **19**(4), 2821–2837 (2021)
18. Li, Z., Zou, D., Xu, S., Jin, H., Qi, H., Hu, J.: Vulpecker: an automated vulnerability detection system based on code similarity analysis. In: Proceedings of Annual Computer Security Applications Conference, pp. 201–213 (2016)
19. Li, Z., Zou, D., Xu, S., Jin, H., Zhu, Y., Chen, Z.: SySeVR: a framework for using deep learning to detect software vulnerabilities. IEEE Trans. Dependable Sec. Comput. **19**(4), 2244–2258 (2021)
20. Li, Z., et al.: Vuldeepecker: a deep learning-based system for vulnerability detection. In: Proceedings of Annual Network & Distributed System Security Symposium (2018)
21. Lin, G., Zhang, J., Luo, W., Pan, L., Xiang, Y.: POSTER: vulnerability discovery with function representation learning from unlabeled projects. In: Proceedings of ACM Conference on Computer and Communications Security, pp. 2539–2541 (2017)
22. Lin, G.: Cross-project transfer representation learning for vulnerable function discovery. IEEE Trans. Indus. Inform. **14**(7), 3289–3297 (2018)
23. Lipp, S., Banescu, S., Pretschner, A.: An empirical study on the effectiveness of static C code analyzers for vulnerability detection. In: Proceedings of ACM International Symposium on Software Testing and Analysis, pp. 544–555 (2022)
24. Ma, R., Jian, Z., Chen, G., Ma, K., Chen, Y.: ReJection: a AST-based reentrancy vulnerability detection method. In: Proceedings of Chinese Conference on Trusted Computing and Information Security, pp. 58–71 (2020)
25. Mizrahi, Y.: OpenSSH pre-auth double free CVE-2023-25136 – writeup and proof-of-concept. JFrog (2023). https://jfrog.com/blog/openssh-pre-auth-double-free-cve-2023-25136-writeup-and-proof-of-concept
26. NIST: CVSS severity distribution over time. https://nvd.nist.gov/general/visualizations/vulnerability-visualizations/cvss-severity-distribution-over-time#CVSSSeverityOverTime, (Accessed 12 Sep 2023)
27. Pinconschi, E., Abreu, R., Adão, P.: A comparative study of automatic program repair techniques for security vulnerabilities. In: Proceedings of IEEE International Symposium on Software Reliability Engineering, pp. 196–207 (2021)
28. Russell, R., et al.: klM.: Automated vulnerability detection in source code using deep representation learning. In: Proceedings of IEEE International Conference on Machine Learning and Applications, pp. 757–762 (2018)
29. Schlichtkrull, M., Kipf, T.N., Bloem, P., van den Berg, R., Titov, I., Welling, M.: Modeling relational data with graph convolutional networks. In: Proceedings of European Semantic Web Conference, pp. 593–607 (2018)
30. Shervashidze, N., Schweitzer, P., Leeuwen, E.J.V., Mehlhorn, K., Borgwardt, K.M.: Weisfeiler-Lehman graph kernels. J. Mach. Learn. Res. **12**(9) (2011)
31. Shimchik, N., Ignatyev, V., Belevantsev, A.: Improving accuracy and completeness of source code static taint analysis. In: Ivannikov Ispras Open Conference, pp. 61–68 (2021)
32. Sun, F.Y., Hoffmann, J., Verma, V., Tang, J.: Infograph: unsupervised and semi-supervised graph-level representation learning via mutual information maximization. In: Proceedings of International Conference on Learning Representations (2020)
33. Veličković, P., Cucurull, G., Casanova, A., Romero, A., Liò, P., Bengio, Y.: Graph attention networks. In: Proceedings of International Conference on Learning Representation (2017)

34. Veličković, P., Fedus, W., Hamilton, W.L., Liò, P., Bengio, Y., Hjelm, R.D.: Deep graph infomax. In: Proceedings of International Conference on Learning Representation (2019)
35. Xu, K., Hu, W., Leskovec, J., Jegelka, S.: How powerful are graph neural networks? In: Proceedings of International Conference on Learning Representation (2019)
36. Xu, L., Sun, F., Su, Z.: Constructing precise control flow graphs from binaries. The University of California, Davis, Tech. rep. (2009)
37. Yamaguchi, F., Golde, N., Arp, D., Rieck, K.: Modeling and discovering vulnerabilities with code property graphs. In: Proceedings IEEE Symposium on Security & Privacy, pp. 590–604 (2014)
38. Yamaguchi, F., Lindner, F.F., Rieck, K.: Vulnerability extrapolation: assisted discovery of vulnerabilities using machine learning. In: Proceedings of USENIX Workshop Offensive Technologies, pp. 118–127 (2011)
39. Yanardag, P., Vishwanathan, S.: Deep graph kernels. In: Proceedings of ACM International Conference on Knowledge Discovery and Data Mining, pp. 1365–1374 (2015)
40. You, Y., Chen, T., Sui, Y., Chen, T., Wang, Z., Shen, Y.: Graph contrastive learning with augmentations. In: Proceedings of Conference on Neural Information Processing Systems, pp. 5812–5823 (2020)
41. Zhang, H., Wu, Q., Yan, J., Wipf, D., Yu, P.S.: From canonical correlation analysis to self-supervised graph neural networks. In: Proceedings of Conference on Neural Information Processing Systems, pp. 76–89 (2021)
42. Zhou, M., et al.: A method for software vulnerability detection based on improved control flow graph. Wuhan University J. Nat. Sci. **24**(2), 149–160 (2019)
43. Zhou, Y., Liu, S., Siow, J., Du, X., Liu, Y.: Devign: effective vulnerability identification by learning comprehensive program semantics via graph neural networks. In: Proceedings of Conference on Neural Information Processing Systems, pp. 10197–10207 (2019)
44. Zhu, Q., Du, B., Yan, P.: Self-supervised training of graph convolutional networks. In: Proceedings of International Conference on Machine Learning, Online (2020)

Analysis of Cryptographic CVEs: Lessons Learned and Perspectives

Raphaël Khoury[(✉)], Jérémy Bolduc, Jason Lafrenière-Nickopoulos, and Abdel-Gany Odedele

Université du Québec en Outaouais, Gatineau, QC, Canada
{raphael.khoury,bolj10,lafj53,odea04}@uqo.ca

Abstract. Cryptographic vulnerabilities can have a particularly far-reaching impact due to the ubiquity of cryptographic software. In this paper, we describe 30 cryptographic vulnerabilities, classify them according to a taxonomy published in previous work, and compile useful information about this class of vulnerabilities. After discovering that many cryptographic vulnerabilities are caused by the use of functions that are known to be insecure, we investigate the efficacy of a straightforward lexical checker to warn programmers of the most typical errors.

Keywords: Vulnerabilities · CVE · cryptographic vulnerabilities

1 Introduction

Cryptographic vulnerabilities can have particularly far-reaching impacts due to the ubiquity of cryptographic software in the Internet infrastructure. The problem is compounded by the relative lack of diversity of the ecosystem: a relatively small number of cryptographic libraries are widely relied upon by thousands of different systems. An exploitable vulnerability in one of these libraries may thus endanger thousands of software products from many different vendors.

In this paper, we examine 30 cryptographic vulnerabilities, collected from the NVD database and provide a detailed analysis of various aspects of these vulnerabilities. We limit our analysis to cryptographic vulnerabilities, and to vulnerabilities for which source code is available. We examine and categorize these vulnerabilities and draw lessons, observations, and perspectives for future research.

Additionally, after determining that most vulnerabilities can be uncovered by a simple lexical checker, we extend the VCG tool so that it is able to detect a wide variety of cryptographic vulnerabilities.

This paper makes the following contributions:

- We create a dataset of 30 cryptographic vulnerabilities for which the vulnerable source code as well as the mitigation is available. We compile useful data related to these vulnerabilities, and make this dataset available to other researchers.

M. Mosbah et al. (Eds.): FPS 2023, LNCS 14551, pp. 208–218, 2024.
https://doi.org/10.1007/978-3-031-57537-2_13

- We create extensions of VCG's configuration files for 6 widely used languages: C\C++, Java, C#\VB and Php. For each language, we include all instances of potential misuse from commonly used libraries that can be detected lexically.

The remainder of this paper is organized as follows. Section 2 describes our dataset. Section 3 presents our analysis of the vulnerabilities it contains. Section 4 discusses the use of Visual Code Grepper as mitigation tool. Concluding remarks are given in Sect. 5.

2 Description of the Dataset

We crawled the NVD database for vulnerabilities labelled with one of 30 CWEs that are indicative of a cryptographic vulnerability. We further limited our analysis to vulnerabilities for which the source code is open and freely available, and to vulnerabilities that postdate 2010. The list of CWEs judged to be of interest, including the vulnerable and patched source code, is reproduced in the author's Github repository[1].

In total, we obtained 31 CVE reports, describing 30 distinct vulnerabilities. In order to verify that every vulnerability is cryptography related, we manually analyzed the code of each vulnerability, and classified it in a taxonomy of cryptographic vulnerabilities developed by Blochberger et al. [4]. This taxonomy classifies cryptographic vulnerabilities according to the programming mistake at its source. Of particular interest to this paper are the following classes:

Initialization: a vulnerability is present because a user-provided value that the library relies upon (such as a nonce or a seed) is chosen incorrectly or reused.

Insecure Defaults: a vulnerability is present because the programmer uses default values as function parameters, while proper usage requires that the value be explicitly set. A typical example is an implementation of AES that defaults to ECB mode.

Weak Algorithms: a vulnerability results from the use of a weak or deprecated algorithm, such as MD5.

Validation: a vulnerability occurs at the transport layer of a protocol, such as failure to validate a certificate.

Usage complexity: a vulnerability exists because proper use of an encryption library requires complex manipulations that are beyond the capabilities of the average programmer.

Vulnerabilities marked as 'other' capture a number of different issues, such as memory corruption issues that can lead to a buffer that should contain a random seed being filled with zeros (CVE-2013-2548) or a miscalculation of cryptographic-values caused by an integer overflow (CVE-2014-3570).

---

[1] https://github.com/RaphaelKhoury/CryptographicVulnerabilities.

Table 1 contains a list of the 30 vulnerabilities that are the focus of this study. The table also indicates the type of vulnerability, the programming language of the code, and the usage complexity and impact level of the vulnerability, as recorded in the NVD database. We used CVSS v.3 whenever available, and CVSS v.2 otherwise. The final column indicates if the vulnerability is present in a library that implements cryptographic services (C), in software that implements cryptographic protocols (P) or in more general software that use cryptographic services (G).

3   Analysis and Lessons Learned

We start off by describing the key insight of a manual study of the security vulnerabilities and fixes in our dataset.

Most Cryptographic Vulnerabilities Are Usage Errors, Rather Than Errors in the Cryptographic Algorithms Themselves. This confirms previous results, notably in [3]. Nearly all of the 30 vulnerabilities are usage errors, rather than errors in the implementation of cryptographic algorithms. Even most vulnerabilities in cryptographic software fall in the former category. The only outliers are the vulnerabilities listed in Table 1 as being Validation errors, as well as CVE-2014-8275 which deals with incorrect certificate validation.

This result lends further support in favour of attempts to design cryptographic libraries in such a way as to minimize the burden on the programmer required to write secure code, such as the Tafelsalz cryptographic library [4]. The presence of insecure default values, which accounts for 2 of the vulnerabilities in our dataset, is particularly egregious since it was observed as early as 1975 that secure systems should not allow such values [15].

In fact, only 7 of the vulnerabilities in our dataset are vulnerabilities in cryptographic libraries (an additional 7 are vulnerabilities in the implementation of cryptographic protocols, such as SSL). The remainder are vulnerabilities in more general software that uses cryptography.

Preliminary Analysis Shows that the Vulnerabilities do not Appear to be Highly Exploitable. Only a small number (2) of these vulnerabilities exhibit the particular combination of high impact and low complexity. This is somewhat fortunate since prior research [10] has shown that vulnerabilities that exhibit this particular combination of attributes are more likely to be exploited by malicious adversaries. However, this is just one element in the exploitability equation. In particular, cryptographic libraries tend to be widely reused in multiple different software systems, making them particularly tempting targets for malicious adversaries.

Table 2 shows the average complexity and impact for each class of vulnerability. A scale derived from the CVSS documentation was used to convert the categorical complexity rating to a scalar value in order to compute an average[2].

---

[2] Low=.35, med=.61. high=.71.

Table 1. Description of the dataset.

CVE id	Vulnerability type	Programming Language(s)	Complexity	Impact	Crypto
CVE-2011-0766	Initialization	Erlang, C	Low	6.9	C
CVE-2012-2417	Initialization	Python	Medium	2.9	C
CVE-2013-1445	Initialization	Python	Medium	2.9	C
CVE-2014-5386	Initialization	C++	Low	2.9	G
CVE-2015-8867	Initialization	C	Low	3.6	P
CVE-2018-12520	Initialization	C++	High	5.9	G
CVE-2019-11808	Initialization	Java	High	1.4	G
CVE-2020-12735	Initialization	Php	Low	5.9	G
CVE-2020-28924	Initialization	Go	Low	3.6	G
CVE-2021-3538	Initialization	Go	Low	5.9	G
CVE-2021-41117	Initialization	JavaScript	Low	5.2	C
CVE-2022-36045	Initialization	JavaScript	Low	5.9	G
CVE-2019-15075	Initialization	PHP	Low	3.6	G
CVE-2022-1434	Initialization	C	High	3.6	P
CVE-2019-10908	Initialization	Java	Low	5.9	G
CVE-2022-1235	Initialization	PHP	Low	4.2	G
CVE-2012-3458	Insecure Defaults	Python	Medium	2.9	G
CVE-2016-1000352 & CVE-2016-1000344[a]	Insecure Defaults	Java	High	5.2	C
CVE-2017-7526	Usage complexity	C	High	4.0	C
CVE-2018-16870	Usage complexity	C	High	3.6	P
CVE-2018-19653	Usage complexity	Go	High	3.6	G
CVE-2019-9155	Usage complexity	JavaScript	High	3.6	C
CVE-2020-26263	Usage complexity	Python	Low	3.6	P
CVE-2016-2053	Validation	C	High	3.6	G
CVE-2019-11578	Validation	C	High	3.6	P
CVE-2021-32738	Validation	TypeScript (JavaScript)	Low	3.6	G
CVE-2013-2548	Other	C	Low	2.9	C
CVE-2014-3570	Other	C	NA	2.9	P
CVE-2014-8275	Other	C	Low	2.9	P
CVE-2016-10530	Other	JavaScript	High	3.6	G

[a] These two CVEs were combine since they seem to refer to the same vulnerability, and were fixed by the same patch.

As can be seen in the table, Initialization errors, aside from being the most common type of errors, also have both the highest average impact and the second lowest attack complexity.

Table 2. Average impact and complexity for each category of vulnerabilities.

Type	Average Impact	Average Complexity
Initialization	4.39	0.45
Insecure default	4.05	0.66
Usage complexity	4.4	0.64
Validation	3.6	0.44
Other	3.07	0.47
All	4.11	0.51

Further analysis shows that none of these vulnerabilities appear in the CISA list of actively exploited vulnerabilities[3]. A single vulnerability, CVE-2018-12520, appears in the exploit-db database of known exploit code[4] while a PoC exploit for a different vulnerability, CVE-2021-41117, is available on github. Both CVEs are related to weak number generators. At the time of writing, data gathered by Greynoise[5] recorded activity on a single vulnerability from this sample, CVE-2022-1434.

Since prior research has found that about 5% of vulnerabilities are exploited [9], it would appear that the sample under consideration in this study is representative of the broader trend, though the small size of the sample makes a definitive determination difficult.

The EPSS scores of these vulnerabilities confirm this intuition. EPSS is a metric that can be used to predict the probability that a vulnerability will be actively exploited [9]. It is commonly used to prioritize vulnerability patching. Computing the EPSS score of the vulnerabilities in our dataset reveals that all but three of the vulnerabilities have an EPSS score below 1%, indicating a very low probability of exploitation. Indeed, CVE-2014-3570 refers to a miscalculation in an implementation of RSA, caused by a carry when computing a borderline value. The conditions that allow exploitation occur with probability $1\backslash 2^6 4$ on 32 bit systems or $1\backslash 2^1 28$ on 64 bit systems.

The three outliers are CVE-2018-12520 (25.8%), CVE-2019-9155 (1.28%) and CVE-2014-8275 (1.06%). CVE-2018-12520 refers to an unseeded PRNG in a network monitoring software. The latter two vulnerabilities are both caused by missing checks during cryptographic protocols.

---

[3] https://www.cisa.gov/known-exploited-vulnerabilities-catalog.

[4] https://www.exploit-db.com/.

[5] https://viz.greynoise.io/.

There is Insufficient Data to conclude if Some Usage Errors are More Common in Some Languages than in Others. Some programming languages "protect the programmer" against particular categories of vulnerabilities, for example, Java was designed in such a way as to prevent memory corruption errors. In the same vein, it would be interesting to determine if specific classes of cryptographic vulnerabilities are more common in some programming languages. If this were to be the case, further investigation could identify the features that underpin the development of secure cryptographic libraries.

In this optic, Table 3 provides a breakdown of the vulnerabilities by programming language. We once again use Blochberger et al.'s taxonomy as the basis of the analysis. Unfortunately, the small size of our dataset does not allow us to draw definitive conclusions. Nonetheless, it is interesting to observe that over half of the vulnerabilities in our dataset are initialization vulnerabilities, a finding that points to a particular difficulty in the proper usage of cartographic libraries. This is the only category of vulnerability that spans every programming language.

Mitigation often Necessitates only Minimal Code Changes. We examined the mitigation for each of the vulnerabilities in our dataset. In most cases, the corrective was simple, often less than five lines of code in a single file. This was specially the case for vulnerabilities of type 'Initialization', 'Insecure Defaults' and 'Weak Values'. In these cases, the mitigation often simply consists in replacing a method call with a call to a different method. For instance, the case of CVE-2014-5386, in which the mitigation simply consists in replacing a call to rand() with a call to f_rand() is representative.

Vulnerabilities in cryptographic libraries are naturally outliers in this regard, and all but one necessitate elaborate code modifications, often affecting several files. In a single case, CVE-2018-19653, the mitigation does not require the application of a patch, though one is available. In this case, the vendor provides a reconfiguration that adequately addresses the vulnerability without requiring a software upgrade.

We also examined each code patch to determine if the security justification for the code changes was adequately explained in the accompanying comments. In the absence of comments, there is always the possibility that later code changes will undo a security fix and reintroduce the vulnerability. This situation famously occurred in an implementation of the DUAL EC PRNG in Juniper routers [5].

We found that while most security patches did not include descriptive comments, such comments were included in cases where the patch involved what could be considered elaborate code modification. A representative example of this case is CVE-2013-1445. The program properly seeds a PRNG, and subsequently forks a process. In this context, the two processes share the same PRNG, leading to a vulnerability. The patch clearly documents the reason for the more elaborate structure of the code. This was one of the vulnerabilities whose patch required the most elaborate code modification in our dataset.

Code Review Tools are Ineffective. For the next stage of our study, we used code analysis tools to try to detect the vulnerabilities in the code. We employed 4 different code analysis tools: Bandit [2], for python programs, Visual Code Grepper (VCG) [12], for C, C++, Java and PHP programs, DeepScan [1] for Javascript and TypeScript programs and StaticCheck [8] for Go programs.

The results were disappointing. In only one case, CVE-2022-1235, a code analysis tool, VCG, was able to detect the vulnerability. This case concerns the use of an insecure PRNG, mt_rand.

Interestingly, VCG flagged the use of another potentially unsafe function, the hash function MD5 in the source code of CVE-2020-12735, even though the vulnerability itself is unrelated to the use of this hash function. The tool also flagged the use of a number of other potentially dangerous memory manipulation functions in the code of other CVEs. Further analysis is required to determine if these warnings are indicative of real security vulnerabilities, or are merely false positives.

Insecure Defaults Seem to be Related to Insufficient Documentation. As mentioned above, the dataset contained 2 vulnerabilities of type 'Insecure default', namely CVE-2012-3458 and CVE-2016-100352. In both cases, the vulnerability is present because encryption is performed using the AES algorithm, and the encrypting function uses ECB mode by default while other more secure modes must be requested explicitly.

Table 3. Distribution of programming languages by vulnerability type.

	C	JavaScript	Python	PHP	Go	Java	C++	Erlang
Initialization	3 (30%)	2 (40%)	2 (50%)	3 (100%)	2 (67%)	2 (67%)	2 (100%)	1 (100%)
Insecure Defaults			1 (25%)			1 (33%)		
Usage	Complexity 2 (20 %)	1 (20%)	1 (25%)		1 (33%)			
Validation	2 (20%)	1 (20%)						
Other	3 (20%)	1 (20%)						

Vulnerabilities of this type can often be partly blamed on the difficulty of finding documentation about a library's proper usage. To determine if this is the case for the vulnerabilities under consideration, we manually examined the documentation of the cryptographic libraries used in each case to determine if security critical information is easy to come across, from the perspective of a novice programmer.

CVE-2016-100352 is a vulnerability in a Java program that employs the Bouncy Castle cryptography APIs, while CVE-2012-3458 refers to a python program that relies upon the cryptographic library pycryptopp. In both cases, we found it difficult to find information about the default mode of AES encryption, or about the risks inherent to ECB mode in the software's official documentation. In fact, the section of the documentation of Bouncy Castle that lists the possible encryption modes for AES does not even mention that ECB is default.

A related question is the security level of code fragments that programmers can obtain on question-answer websites such as stackoverflow. Fischer et al. [7], found that programmers routinely reuse code verbatim from stackoverflow, and that the code found on this resource is often vulnerable. In the case of the libraries under consideration here, we found that usage examples of pycryptopp were generally correct, at least with respect to the encryption mode, but that most Bouncy Castle code fragments used ECB (by default). Interestingly, one of the first threads we found on stackoverflow related to Bouncy Castle was a discussion of the default mode, which correctly identified it as being ECB. Further research is needed to determine if this situation represents a common lacuna in the documentation of cryptographic libraries.

Most Initialization Errors are related to the Use of Pseudorandom Number Generation Functions That are Commonly Known to be Weak. 11 of the 16 (69%) initialization errors are related to pseudorandom number generation. In most cases, the vulnerability is caused by the use of a seeding function that is well known to be inadequate for security-sensitive contexts. For example, CVE-2019-10908 is related to the use of `RandomStringUtils` (which uses java.util.Random internally) to generate passwords. Other vulnerabilities are related to the use of `rand()` or `Math.random()`. Since it is common knowledge that these functions should not be used in a security-relevant context, a simple lexical tool, such as VCG, could be able to detect a potential vulnerability and inform the programmer of the cautions he\she should take.

Other causes of initialization errors include hard-coded values (CVE-2019-15075) as well as a case where AAD data was mistakenly used in lieu of a key (CVE-2022-1434).

Programming Errors Often Cause Cryptographic Failures. Our analysis of the source code revealed that programming mistakes account for 12.9% (4) of the cryptographic vulnerabilities in our dataset. In addition to the integer overflow mentioned above, we also note the case of CVE-2021-4117 in which the programmer mistakenly called the fromCharCode function twice on the same input data, resulting in a buffer containing mostly zeros being used as seed for a PRNG. Another instructive example is CVE-2013-2548. A stack buffer, whose content is controlled by the user, is filled using memcpy. If the destination buffer is larger than the amount of data to be written, memcpy transfers arbitrary bytes from memory. The issue is solved by using strncpy. This vulnerability is reminiscent of the widely know heartbleed vulnerability [6], and serves as an illustration of the fact that the same type of vulnerabilities seem to recur over time.

4   Visual Code Grepper

One of the most interesting observations of this analysis is that a large portion of cryptographic errors are related to either the use of functions that are known to be insecure (e.g. Math.random), or to specific misuse of cryptographic functions (e.g. insecure default values). Indeed, we found that as many as 22 of the 30 cryptographic vulnerabilities in our dataset fall in this category. A comparatively simple lexical checker could in theory detect most of these vulnerabilities (or at least the potential for a vulnerability), simply by checking for the presence of a specific method call and alerting the programmer of the security considerations related to usage of this function. For example, if the checker encounters the token "Math.Random" in a java program, it can advise the programmer that this function does not generate cryptographically secure random numbers. If the checker encounters a call to the "AESEngine()" method (from the Bouncy Castle library), it can inform the programmer that this method uses ECB mode by default, and advise him to change the encryption mode if necessary.

Lexical checkers are limited, since they do not perform syntactic or data flow analysis. Nonetheless, the use of such a tool does offer several advantages. A simpler tool can be used by even novice programmers, and unlike more complex model checkers, does not require advance training to be used effectively. Furthermore, false positives, while inevitable for any bug detection tool, can be dealt with quickly when they originate with a simple lexical checker. Lexical checkers can be used earlier in the software development process, which simplifies mitigation.

Indeed, a number of tools specially dedicated to the detection of cryptographic vulnerabilities have been presented in the literature. Amongst them we note static analyzers such as CrySL [11] or Cryptoguard [14]; and dynamic analyzers such as Crylogger [13] or RVSec [16]. While some of these methods may exhibit greater precision or scope, they often require an expertise in order to be used effectively. For instance, CrySL rules are written in a custom specification language, and its creators "designed CrySL specifically with crypto experts in mind" [11]. VCG, on the other hand, can be used with minimal training, and allows for substantial left-shifting of the process.

We decided to investigate the potential of lexical checkers to address this specific category of vulnerabilities. We chose VirtualCodeGrepper (VCG), a free open source lexical checker for 8 different languages. A particular feature of VCG is that it relies upon a language-specific configuration file that lists dangerous functions, alongside with an associated error message that is to be communicated to the programmer if this function is encountered. This file can be edited, expanding the range of errors detected by the tool.

We found that 17 of the 30 vulnerabilities in our dataset are coded in languages that are supported by VCG. Of these, 9 (52%) could likely be uncovered by a lexical checker that scans the code for specific dangerous functions, and informs the programmer of the risks associated with their use.

We extended 4 of VCG's configuration files, for C\C++, Java, C# and PHP, so that they include each of the risky functions encountered in our dataset, alongside a number of other vulnerable or deprecated cryptographic functions present in commonly used cryptographic APIs. In aggregate, we added 90 new checks to VCG's config files. These represent over 65 deprecated or vulnerable method names, from 33 commonly used libraries, as well as checks for the names of commonly used cryptographic functions that are known to be cryptographically insecure, such as MD5 and SHA1. For each, the config files includes a severity rating derived from the CVSS impact score of similar vulnerabilities in the NVD database, as well as an informative error message. Table 4 details the number of vulnerable libraries, functions and keywords detected for each language.

The error messages were specifically designed to be as informative as possible, and to assist the developer in rapidly ruling out potential false positives. For example, a typical error message is: "FunctionCryptReleaseContext from Library libtomcrypt is deprecated". We endeavoured to insure that the messages are sufficiently clear as to be comprehensible to a programmer with only limited knowledge in cryptography.

Whenever possible, the error message also includes a link to a page in the library's documentation that reports on the vulnerability. We also included a replacement function whenever such a replacement was suggested by the authors of the original library, and a link to further information, for example:

"Class HybridDecryptConfig was deprecated in the Google tink library, use Config and HybridConfig instead. For more info: https://google.github.io/tink/javadoc/tink/1.0.0/deprecated-list.html".

In other cases, the error message provides a cogent explanation of a particular precaution that the programmer must take when using a specific library. For example, if VCG detects the token "Cipher.getInstance(AES)" (from library Javax.crypto.Cipher), the programmer will be informed that this method uses ECB by default.

Table 4. Number of vulnerable libraries, functions and keywords for each language.

Language	Libraries	Functions	Keywords
C\C++	7	34	43
C#	3	2	9
Java	16	18	26
PHP	7	11	12

The config files are available on the author's github repository[6].

An initial test confirmed that by using the updated config files, VCG is able to detect 9 of the 30 vulnerabilities in our dataset.

5   Conclusion and Perspective

In this paper, we examined a dataset of cryptographic vulnerabilities, and drew insights into the causes of these flaws. Finding that in many cases, a simple lexical checker is sufficient to detect many such vulnerabilities, we extended the VCG tool with configuration files designed for this purpose. Excluding CVEs for which the corresponding source code is unavailable somewhat limits the scope of this

---

[6] https://github.com/RaphaelKhoury/VCG-config-files.

study, however, the availability of source code is necessary for a thorough analysis of the vulnerability. Further research is needed to determine if our observations hold in a more general context.

References

1. How to ensure javascript code quality. deepscan. https://deepscan.io/
2. Welcome to bandit - bandit documentation. https://bandit.readthedocs.io/en/latest/
3. Blessing, J., Specter, M.A., Weitzner, D.J.: You really shouldn't roll your own crypto: An empirical study of vulnerabilities in cryptographic libraries. arXiv preprint arXiv:2107.04940 (2021)
4. Blochberger, M., Petersen, T., Federrath, H.: Mitigating cryptographic mistakes by design. Mensch und Computer 2019-Workshopband (2019)
5. Checkoway, S., Maskiewicz, J., Garman, C., Fried, J., Cohney, S., Green, M., Heninger, N., Weinmann, R.P., Rescorla, E., Shacham, H.: A systematic analysis of the juniper dual ec incident. In: Proceedings of the 2016 ACM SIGSAC Conference on Computer and Communications Security, CCS 2016, pp. 468-479. Association for Computing Machinery, New York(2016). https://doi.org/10.1145/2976749.2978395, https://doi.org/10.1145/2976749.2978395
6. Durumeric, Z., et al.: The matter of heartbleed. In: Proceedings of the 2014 Conference on Internet Measurement Conference, pp. 475–488 (2014)
7. Fischer, F., et al.: Stack overflow considered harmful? the impact of copy&paste on android application security. In: 2017 IEEE Symposium on Security and Privacy (SP), pp. 121–136 (2017). https://doi.org/10.1109/SP.2017.31
8. Honnef, D.: staticcheck-action: Staticcheck's official github. https://github.com/dominikh/staticcheck-action
9. Jacobs, J., Romanosky, S., Adjerid, I., Baker, W.: Improving vulnerability remediation through better exploit prediction. J. Cybersec. 6(1) (2020). https://doi.org/10.1093/cybsec/tyaa015
10.) Khoury, R., Vignau, B., Hallé, S., Hamou-Lhadj, A., Razgallah, A.: An analysis of the use of CVEs by IoT malware. In: 13th International Symposium -Foundations and Practice of Security, FPS 2020, Montreal, Canada, 1-3 Dec, pp. 47–62 (2020). https://doi.org/10.1007/978-3-030-70881-8_4
11. Krüger, S., Späth, J., Ali, K., Bodden, E., Mezini, M.: Crysl: an extensible approach to validating the correct usage of cryptographic APIs. IEEE Trans. Software Eng. 47(11), 2382–2400 (2021). https://doi.org/10.1109/TSE.2019.2948910
12. Nccgroup: Nccgroup/vcg: Visualcodegrepper - code security scanning tool. https://github.com/nccgroup/VCG
13. Piccolboni, L., Guglielmo, G.D., Carloni, L.P., Sethumadhavan, S.: Crylogger: detecting crypto misuses dynamically. In: 2021 IEEE Symposium on Security and Privacy (SP), pp. 1972–1989 (2021). https://doi.org/10.1109/SP40001.2021.00010
14. Rahaman, S., et al.: Cryptoguard: high precision detection of cryptographic vulnerabilities in massive-sized java projects. In: Proceedings of the 2019 ACM SIGSAC Conference on Computer and Communications Security, CCS 2019, pp. 2455-2472. Association for Computing Machinery, New York (2019). https://doi.org/10.1145/3319535.3345659, https://doi.org/10.1145/3319535.3345659
15. Saltzer, J.H., Schroeder, M.D.: The protection of information in computer systems. Proc. IEEE 63(9), 1278–1308 (1975)
16. Torres, A., et al.: Runtime verification of crypto apis: an empirical study. IEEE Trans. Softw. Eng. 1–16 (2023). https://doi.org/10.1109/TSE.2023.3301660

A BERT-Based Framework for Automated Extraction of Behavioral Indicators of Compromise from Security Incident Reports

Mohamed El Amine Bekhouche$^{(\boxtimes)}$ (ID) and Kamel Adi (ID)

Department of Computer Science and Engineering, University of Quebec in
Outaouais (UQO), Quebec, Canada
{bekm04,kamel.adi}@uqo.ca

Abstract. The exponential growth of cyberattacks in recent years has highlighted the inadequacy of existing detection mechanisms and therefore the need to develop more relevant predictive models and methods in the field of Cyber Threat Intelligence (CTI). Many cybersecurity systems use behavioral indicators of compromise (IoCs), such as tactics, techniques, and procedures (TTPs), to design their defense strategies and detect future attacks attempts in an early stage. Typically, behavioral IoCs are gathered from unstructured incident reports, often written in natural language, and are typically extracted with manual analysis by cybersecurity experts. However, due to the huge number of reports daily released, this task has become more difficult and time-consuming to make it effective. In this paper, we propose a framework based on Bidirectional Encoder Representations from Transformers (BERT) to identify and recognize behavioral IoCs in incident reports. The results of our contribution showed a significant improvement of the F1-score compared to the state-of-the-art works.

Keywords: Cyber Threat Intelligence · Indicators of compromise · Named Entity Recognition · TTPs · BERT

1 Introduction

Nowadays, cybercriminals pose significant challenges for organizations that must defend their data and systems against cyberattacks. They employ a variety of methods to carry out cyberattacks, serving multiple purposes ranging from simple identity theft to sophisticated attacks on critical infrastructure. However, while various cyberattacks may seem to use different infection methods, they essentially have a somewhat similar lifecycle, starting from victims machine reconnaissance to the execution of a malicious code [10]. Moreover, the rising number and diversity of cyberattacks have made cybersecurity analysis more complex, exposing the limitations of traditional semi-manual approaches for incident detection and response. To address this challenge, there is an urgent need

© The Author(s), under exclusive license to Springer Nature Switzerland AG 2024
M. Mosbah et al. (Eds.): FPS 2023, LNCS 14551, pp. 219–232, 2024.
https://doi.org/10.1007/978-3-031-57537-2_14

to develop a new Cyber Threat Intelligence (CTI) approach to fully automate this process. Typically, CTI has been a manual process aiding cybersecurity professionals in identifying Indicators of Compromise (IoCs) and gathering attack details [3]. CTI analysis generates strategic insights into cyber threats, extracted from incident reports, and manually analyzed by cybersecurity experts. This information is often represented as a set of behavioral IoCs such as tactics, techniques, and procedures (TTPs) used by cyber attackers [18].

Unlike atomic IoCs (IP addresses, URLs, md5, etc.), which have a relatively short lifetime [2], behavioral IoCs have a longer lifetime, making it more difficult for an attacker to modify them [17]. In addition, behavioral information can be merged and used to develop comprehensive attacker profiles that can help cyberanalysts draw conclusions to better predict future attacks and, hence, support the resilience of threat detection. Specifically, the structure of TTPs allows analysts to understand which actions performed by the adversary belong to specific procedures related to specific techniques and tactics [18]. This enables analysts to grasp what an adversary is trying to achieve and how to better defend against it.

Behavioral IoCs come often from incident reports, and are extracted by text manual analysis. Unfortunately, due to the number of reports released daily, this task has become more difficult and time consuming for humans. In this regard, several research works have been proposed to automate this task using Natural Language Processing (NLP) techniques. Among them, numerous architectures of neural networks using Convolutional Neural Networks (CNN), Unidirectional/Bidirectional Long short-term memory (LSTM/Bi-LSTM), etc. or a combination of them in order extract features from text, extract entities and capture the dependencies between them, and then, classify incident reports. However, these types of model are not efficient in capturing text semantics and offer a poor generalization to efficiently deal with specific domains such as cybersecurity documents.

The appearance of transformers in 2017 has revolutionized the field of natural language processing (NLP), providing powerful language representations, which are crucial for various NLP tasks [19]. Moreover, pretrained transformers such as Bidirectional Encoder Representations from Transformers (BERT), are trained on massive amounts of text data, which can be fine-tuned on specific tasks with smaller dataset such as sentiment analysis, Named Entity Recognition (NER), text generation, etc. leading to better performance and faster convergence. These strengths can be adopted to address the problems of NLP in the field of cybersecurity, such as the insufficiency of annotated data and the particular format of incident reports. In this context, the present work proposes a BERT-Based framework for automated named entity recognition to identify and recognize behavioral IoCs in incident reports. These reports are written in natural language, in unstructured format and are obtained from several sources such as MITRE ATT&CK, FireEye, Crowdstrike and others security blogs (this work focuses on English reports). Moreover, the framework employs a hybrid approach that combines BERT word embedding for general terms with another word embedding model for CTI-specific terms. This technique can be a powerful way to manage domain-specific words while taking advantage of the contextual comprehension of BERT. For training and testing phase, the framework takes an unstructured document as input, passing it through a rigorous pipeline, and then outputs a structured information that can be exploited by analysts. The pipeline includes four units: data aggregation, data cleaning, data preprocessing, and Entities Classification, which we describe in detail below.

To summarise, the main contributions of the proposed work are as follows:

- NER-IoCs: a fine-tuned framework based on a combination of BERT embedding and domain-specific embedding for NER tasks in Cyber Threat Intelligence (CTI).
- An effective data pipeline to prepare security incident reports for NLP tasks.
- A comparison of the proposed framework with state-of-the-art architectures such as CNN and LSTM/Bi-LSTM, to demonstrate the empirical strength of our work.

The remainder of this paper is organized as follows. Section 2 reviews related work. The framework architecture is explained in Sect. 3. The end-to-end data pipeline is described in Sect. 4, followed by experimental results in Sect. 5. The conclusion is drawn in Sect. 6.

2   Related Works

The studies on Named Entity Recognition for Cyber Threat Intelligence (CTI) can be classified into three categories: rules-based approaches, machine learning-based approaches, and deep learning-based approaches.

The rules-based approach is the most widely used method for NER tasks in CTI. In [7,12,16], the authors use a template of regular expression rules to map different entities within text, such as IPV4, CVE, SHA256, etc. These methods are effective in extracting atomic IoCs due to their well-defined patterns, but they prove less effective when confronted with behavioral IoCs characterized by their elusive patterns. Furthermore, the rule-based approach has obvious limitations, requiring the laborious manual creation of rule templates and a significant depth of domain knowledge, especially in cybersecurity.

Methods based on supervised machine learning rely on feature engineering techniques to build statistical models by exploiting training corpora. In [8], the conditional random field (CRF) algorithm is used to extract concepts and entities related to cybersecurity through a data set that has been manually annotated. [1] treated the NER task as a multiclass classification problem. They employed the term frequency-inverse document frequency (TF-IDF) as the feature extraction algorithm and subsequently trained a support vector machine (SVM) model to classify different tokens within the text. These methods are relatively efficient, but may also have limitations, particularly in terms of generalization on new data.

Among deep learning methods, many authors make use of known architectures based on CNN, LSTM/bi-LSTM, or a combination of them to perform

NER tasks. Therefore, the research work [11] proposes a Bi-LSTM/CFR model, in [9] the authors adopt CNN as a feature extractor network, a Bi-LSTM to capture relationships between entities, and then classify tokens into different classes. These models are effective in local/global features extraction from text and capture the dependencies between entities within sequence of text. However, these models are inefficient in capturing textual semantics and are unsuitable due to their inscalability when confronted with lengthy sequences, such as those found in cybersecurity documents.

3   Framework Architecture

In this section, the framework architecture is explained in detail. This architecture defines four layers (input, embedding, Bi-LSTM, and entity classification) to achieve a named entity recognition as indicators of compromise (NER-IoCs). The architecture of this BERT-Based framework is shown in Fig. 1.

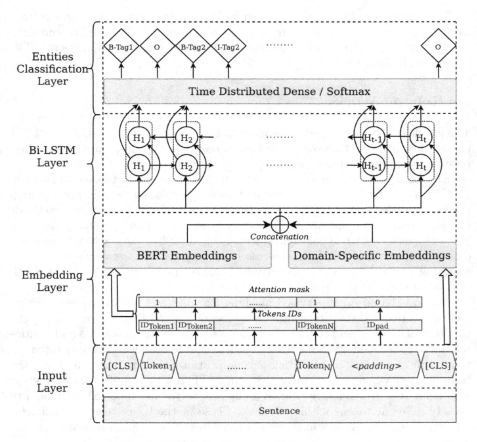

Fig. 1. NER-IoCs: Framework Architecture

3.1   Input Layer

The Input layer serves as the entry point of our framework. It takes pre-processed sentences extracted from incident reports. These sentences are then tokenized into labeled sequences. The sequences are then delimitted by "[CLS]" and "[SEP]" tokens to comply with the format expected by the Embedding BERT model. To ensure that all input sequences have the same length (size of the longest sentence), we pad shorter sequences with a special "[PAD]" token.

3.2   Embedding Layer

In the embedding layer, we adopt an hybrid method that includes BERT word embedding for general terms, and another word embedding model for CTI terms. This approach, can be a powerful way to handle domain-specific terms while benefiting from the contextual understanding of BERT.

BERT Embedding. BERT is a pre-trained representation that uses a bidirectional Transformers model and multi-head attention mechanism [5]. The way in which BERT was trained is composed of two distinct unsupervised tasks. First, it tackles Masked LM (MLM), a process where it randomly masks some input tokens and then predicts these masked tokens enabling it to understand word semantics and relationships. Second, it delves into Next Sentence Prediction (NSP), where the model learns to predict whether two sentences are consecutive in a given text, which helps to capture sentence-level relationships. By performing these two tasks, BERT is able to encompass the strengths of models such as GPT and ELMO [13,14] in language comprehension.

For the fine-tuning phase of pre-trained BERT, a specific format of input is required. First, we map each token in the tokenized sentence with a unique ID according to the BERT vocabulary. These token IDs are used to index into the BERT model. Second, an attention mask is created to indicate which tokens are actual words and which tokens are padding tokens. The attention mask contains binary value, 1 for real tokens and 0 for padding tokens.

Domain-Specific Embedding. We use a domain-specific word embedding technique for the cybersecurity domain proposed by [15]. The work introduces the embedding model which is trained with 596,414 unique words related to the cybersecurity area. This technique also serves as a domain-specific term representation, such as acronyms or abbreviations, that may not be well represented by the BERT model. Moreover, we have optimized this model to output the same vector dimension as with the BERT model, which serves as an essential step for the combination.

Model Combination. This operation serves to combine the general term representation and the domain-specific term representation. The resulting vector contains the average of domain-specific embedding with BERT embedding for

CTI terms. Conversely, we keep the same resulting vector obtained by BERT for terms that are not linked to the CTI area. Consequently, we preserve BERT capabilities in contextual understanding and give the ability to handle domain-specific terms, resulting in a more robust and domain-adaptive NER-IoCs framework.

3.3   Bi-LSTM Layer

A Bi-LSTM layer is connected to the combined embedding vector, which has two main components: a forward LSTM and a backward LSTM. Each LSTM processes the input sequence in one direction, hence, capturing dependencies in both directions. The output of the Bi-LSTM layer at each time step (token) is a vector that encodes contextual information for that token. The output of the Bi-LSTM layer for each token is used as input features to make classification of entities.

3.4   Entities Classification Layer

To obtain the desired output of our proposed architecture, we follow the Bi-LSTM layer by a time-distributed dense layer, which applies a specified classification operation to each time step independently, treating them as individual tokens in the sequence. It assigns a label to each token based on the information extracted by the Bi-LSTM, and then applies a softmax activation function to compute the probability distribution over the entity classes (Tags) for each token.

4   Data Pipeline

In this section, we present the data pipeline designed to prepare security incident reports for the training and testing phases. The proposed pipeline is shown in Fig. 2.

4.1   Data Aggregation

The initial phase of our pipeline focuses on data aggregation, comprising two main steps: identification of CTI sources and collection of CTI reports. These steps lay the groundwork for assembling a diverse and representative corpus of security incident reports, a fundamental aspect of our framework's success. Hence, the process begins with the identification of CTI sources. Prominent CTI sources in the cybersecurity domain have been incorporated into our pipeline: MITRE ATT&CK [18], FireEye [6], CrowdStrike [4] and other several sources that have a minor usage. These sources are chosen based on their credibility, the breadth of their coverage, and the diversity of threat intelligence, which implies a better generalization of the AI model during the production phase. We then collected security incident reports from these sources. This process is done by

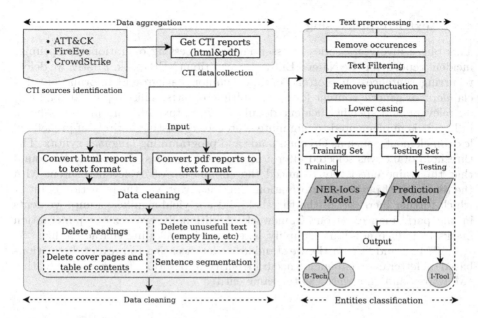

Fig. 2. End-to-End Data Pipeline

querying an API, which provides access to the repositories of security reports maintained by these sources. In total, 1776 reports were collected in two formats (HTML and PDF).

4.2   Data Cleaning

In the second phase, our main focus is preparing and refining collected incident reports from phase 1. We apply processing steps to transform the raw reports into a suitable format for subsequent analysis, annotation, and feature extraction. Initially, we convert the reports, which come in HTML and PDF formats, into standardized plain text. This is crucial because these formats may contain complex structural elements and non-textual content that hinder processing. By homogenizing the data through plain text conversion, we ensure consistent handling. Additionally, we remove unnecessary elements like cover pages, tables of contents, headers, and introductory sections, which do not contribute to the substantive content of security incident reports. This streamlines the processing pipeline, reducing noise and improving efficiency. Furthermore, we address extraneous lines within the text, including empty lines and single-word lines, which can distract during analysis. This refinement enhances the clarity and coherence of the reports, focusing on substantive descriptions of security incidents. Lastly, we segment the text into individual sentences to prepare for Natural Language Processing (NLP) tasks, facilitating subsequent phases while accommodating the necessary granularity for accurate NER.

4.3 Text Pre-processing

This phase involves a series of essential pre-processing operations to optimize incident reports for the Named Entity Recognition (NER) task. Firstly, we delete recurring sentences that often contain common background information, disclaimers, or generic content found in multiple reports. This step ensures a focus on relevant and specific incident details. Next, a text filtering process (shown in Fig. 3) is implemented to eliminate sentences consisting entirely of predefined lexicon elements, such as OS commands and programming language syntax. The threshold of 0.5 was selected after a preliminary analysis of our data. We found that this value effectively balanced the elimination of irrelevant content with the retention of pertinent information. Specifically, it was the inflection point at which further increases in the threshold did not yield significant improvements in the performances of our framework. Additionally, we remove punctuation marks to reduce noise and simplify text analysis, including characters like ".", ",", ";", "?", and "!". Lastly, we standardize letter casing to prevent distinctions based on letter case, enhancing accurate entity recognition, for example, treating "Malware" and "malware" as the same entity.

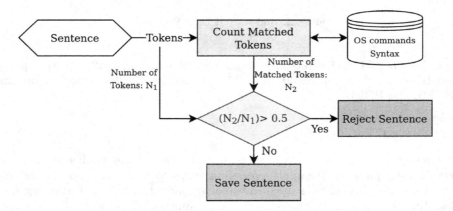

Fig. 3. Sentences filter

4.4 Entities Classification

The pre-processed data from the previous phase is partitioned into training and testing dataset. Subsequently, the proposed framework in Sect. 3, is then trained with the annotated training data to predict relevant tags for each token. These tags correspond to different categories of behavioral IoCs.

5 Experimental Results

5.1 Dataset

Table 1 illustrates the number of reports obtained from each source, as eluci-
dated in Sect. 4. After the execution of various phases of the pipeline on these
documents, the resulting pre-processed data are transformed into a DataFrame
to attain a file in a standardized input format for the NER task. The dataset
is partitioned into two subsets: 85% for training (including validation) and 15%
for testing. Table 2 presents the statistics for the experimental data.

Table 1. Number of incident reports obtained from each identified source

Source	PDF	HTML	Total
MITRE ATT&CK	55	373	428
FireEye	35	324	359
Crowdstrike	27	206	233
Others	110	646	756

Table 2. Dataset statistics

Dataset	Sentence	Token	Entity
Train set	12059	585811	19124
Test set	2128	103379	3375
Total	14187	689190	22499

5.2 Data Annotation

Sequence annotation for NER tasks involves labeling specific entities with their
corresponding classes. For our experiment, we define five behavioral IoCs, including tactic, technique, sub-technique, tool, and adversary group entities, which are
labeled on two steps. The first part of our data was labeled using a dictionary-
based method. This dictionary is constructed by leveraging reports previously
annotated by cybersecurity experts, particularly those aligned with the MITRE
ATT&CK framework. Second, a manual annotation was used for the second part
of data due to the dictionary-based method's limitations in recognizing new entities. Our team examined each sentence to tag entities not in the dictionary. The
distribution of different entities in the dataset is illustrated in Table 3. Additionally, following the universal NER annotation method, the initial word of an
entity is marked as 'B-TagName,' the words within the entity are marked as
'I-TagName,' and any words outside of entities are labeled as 'O' for 'Outside'.
An example of an annotated sentence is shown in Fig. 4.

Table 3. Entities distribution in the dataset

Dataset	Entities				
	Tactic	Technique	Sub-Technique	Tool	Adversary Group
Train set	4103	561	355	10458	3648
Test set	725	99	63	1845	644
Total	4828	660	418	12303	4292

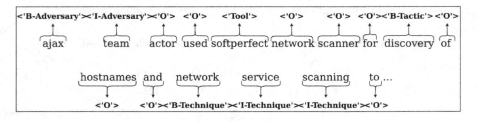

Fig. 4. Example of labeled sentence

5.3   Experimental Settings

In our experimental setup, we use a NVIDIA GeForce RTX GPU with 8 GB of memory. We have used PyTorch to implement different phases of the framework. For training, all models have trained with 25 epochs, with the following hyperparameters: Optimizer = Adam, batch size = 32, learning rate = 0.001. The loss function adopted for training was categorical cross-entropy.

5.4   Results Analysis

Our NER-IoCs framework was trained and tested with the CTI Dataset consisting of five distinct classes (explained in Sect. 5.1). The analysis encompasses the impact of different embedding models: we fix the Domain-Specific embedding (denoted D-S) as a baseline, and we explore different models including BERT base, BERT large embedding (denoted BERT-B and BERT-L), as well as state-of-the-art architecture including CNN, Bi-LSTM, and a combined CNN with Bi-LSTM model.

Evaluation Metrics. NER-IoCs and baseline architectures have been evaluated using Precision, Recall, and F1-score metrics.

– **Precision:** precision in NER tasks measures the accuracy of correctly identified entities among all entities predicted by the model.

$$Precision = \frac{True\ Positives}{True\ Positives + False\ Positives}$$

- **Recall:** recall assesses the ability of a model to identify all relevant entities within the text.

$$\text{Recall} = \frac{\text{True Positives}}{\text{True Positives} + \text{False Negatives}}$$

- **F1-score:** the F1-score is the harmonic mean of precision and recall, providing a balanced measure of the model's performance in both precision and recall.

$$\text{F1} - \text{score} = \frac{2 \cdot \text{Precision} \cdot \text{Recall}}{\text{Precision} + \text{Recall}}$$

Training Results. Figure 5 illustrates the loss and F1-score of training/validation of our framework over epochs, by deploying BERT-L embedding combined (denoted $\oplus$) with D-S embedding. In particular, our framework exhibits a distinct convergence pattern, with discernible improvement in F1-score performance after epoch 15.

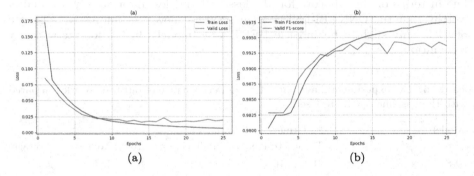

Fig. 5. (a) Training and Validation Loss, (b) Training and Validation F1-score

For entity level performance, Table 4 provides a detailed breakdown of the BERT-L $\oplus$ D-S metrics across five distinct entity classes on the test set. The results are striking: the model achieves an impressive average precision of 92.84%, signifying its precision in entity predictions, while the average recall, standing

Table 4. The performances of the proposed framework using BERT-L $\oplus$ D-S on the test set

Metric	BERT-L $\oplus$ D-S Embedding					
	Tactic	Technique	Sub-Technique	Tool	Adversary	Average
Precision %	91.3	90.5	97.1	94.6	90.7	92.84
Recall %	89.7	89.1	93.4	91.9	88	90.42
F1-score %	91.5	89.8	95.2	93.2	89.3	91.8

at 90.42%, demonstrates its effectiveness in identifying a substantial portion of actual entities. Furthermore, the model achieves a commendable average F1-score of 91.8%, confirming its overall robustness in recognizing a diverse array of entity types.

Comparison with State-of-the-Art Works. In this part, we provide a detailed comparison of our proposed BERT-based framework with existing state-of-the-art models. To facilitate this comparison, our team has implemented three widely recognized architectures for NER tasks in the general domain, namely using CNNs, Bi-LSTMs, and a combination of both. Additionally, the Domain-Specific embedding model is employed alongside these state-of-the-art architectures. It is important to note that both the training and testing of these state-of-the-art models were conducted using the same dataset as our BERT-Based framework. In result, the Table 5 illustrates the average F1-score performance of the proposed framework versus the state-of-the-art models across the five entity classes in the test set. The results clearly demonstrate the superiority of our framework when using BERT-L ⊕ D-S embedding, which outperforms the baseline in terms of the F1-score for all classes of entities. Interestingly, it is noteworthy that the CNN+Bi-LSTM architecture achieves an impressive F1-score of 94%, only slightly behind the BERT large model's 91.5% for tactic entity recognition.

Table 5. The experimental average F1-score performance of our framework compared with the baseline on the test set

Model	Performance F1-score (%)					
	Tactic	Technique	Sub-Technique	Tool	Adversary	Average
D-S+CNN	61	16	15	88	48.5	45.7
D-S+Bi-LSTM	16	3	2	27.5	20.2	13.74
D-S+CNN+Bi-LSTM	**94**	22	20	91.5	60	57.5
BERT-B ⊕ D-S+Bi-LSTM	87	85	77	93.1	83	85.02
BERT-L ⊕ D-S+Bi-LSTM	91.5	**89.8**	**95.2**	**93.2**	**89.3**	**91.8**

6   Conclusion and Future Work

In this paper, we presented NER-IoCs: a BERT-based framework for named entity recognition task in the Cyber Threat Intelligence (CTI) domain. The framework contributes significantly to the automation and acceleration of the CTI analysis process. The experimentation results underscore the effectiveness of combining BERT embedding with domain-specific embedding, with an average F1-score of 91.8%. Furthermore, our framework is trained and tested on diverse incident reports sources, which give it more capabilities and robustness in terms of generalization.

In future research, we aim to explore the transformation of the extracted IoCs from our framework into a standardized format, such as STIX (Structured Threat Information eXpression), making them compatible with a wide range of cybersecurity tools, and ultimately fortifying the collective defense against dynamic cyber threats.

Acknowledgments. I am grateful to Prof. Kamel ADI for his mentorship and guidance throughout this paper. I also extend my thanks to the members of the Computer Security Research Laboratory (LRSI) at the University of Quebec in Outaouais for their collaborative support and insightful discussions that greatly enhanced this work.

References

1. Alves, F., Ferreira, P.M., Bessani, A.: Design of a classification model for a Twitter-based streaming threat monitor. In: 2019 49th annual IEEE/IFIP International Conference on Dependable Systems and Networks Workshops (DSN-W), pp. 9–14. IEEE (2019)
2. Asiri, M., Saxena, N., Gjomemo, R., Burnap, P.: Understanding indicators of compromise against cyber-attacks in industrial control systems: a security perspective. ACM Trans. Cyber-phys. Syst. **7**(2), 1–33 (2023)
3. Brown, S., Gommers, J., Serrano, O.: From cyber security information sharing to threat management. In: Proceedings of the 2nd ACM Workshop on Information Sharing and Collaborative Security, pp. 43–49 (2015)
4. CrowdStrike, Inc. https://www.crowdstrike.com/
5. Devlin, J., Chang, M.W., Lee, K., Toutanova, K.: BERT: pre-training of deep bidirectional transformers for language understanding. arXiv preprint arXiv:1810.04805 (2018)
6. FireEye, Inc. https://www.fireeye.com/
7. Fujii, S., Kawaguchi, N., Shigemoto, T., Yamauchi, T.: CyNER: information extraction from unstructured text of CTI sources with noncontextual IOCs. In: Cheng, CM., Akiyama, M. (eds.) Advances in Information and Computer Security, IWSEC 2022. LNCS, vol. 13504, pp. 85–104. Springer, Cham (2022). https://doi.org/10.1007/978-3-031-15255-9_5
8. Ghazi, Y., Anwar, Z., Mumtaz, R., Saleem, S., Tahir, A.: A supervised machine learning based approach for automatically extracting high-level threat intelligence from unstructured sources. In: 2018 International Conference on Frontiers of Information Technology (FIT), pp. 129–134. IEEE (2018)
9. Jang, B., Kim, M., Harerimana, G., Kang, S., Kim, J.W.: Bi-LSTM model to increase accuracy in text classification: combining Word2vec CNN and attention mechanism. Appl. Sci. **10**(17), 5841 (2020)
10. Lehto, M.: Apt cyber-attack modelling: building a general model. In: International Conference on Cyber Warfare and Security, vol. 17, pp. 121–129. Academic Conferences International Limited (2022)
11. Ma, P., Jiang, B., Lu, Z., Li, N., Jiang, Z.: Cybersecurity named entity recognition using bidirectional long short-term memory with conditional random fields. Tsinghua Sci. Technol. **26**(3), 259–265 (2020)

12. Mohammad, R.M., Thabtah, F., McCluskey, L.: Intelligent rule-based phishing websites classification. IET Inf. Secur. **8**(3), 153–160 (2014)
13. Peters, M.E., et al.: Deep contextualized word representations. In: Proceedings of the 2018 Conference of the North American Chapter of the Association for Computational Linguistics: Human Language Technologies (NAACL-HLT), Volume 1 (Long Papers) (2018)
14. Radford, A., Narasimhan, K., Salimans, T., Sutskever, I., et al.: Improving language understanding by generative pre-training (2018)
15. Roy, A., Park, Y., Pan, S.: Learning domain-specific word embeddings from sparse cybersecurity texts. arXiv preprint arXiv:1709.07470 (2017)
16. Sapienza, A., Ernala, S.K., Bessi, A., Lerman, K., Ferrara, E.: DISCOVER: mining online chatter for emerging cyber threats. In: Companion Proceedings of the The Web Conference 2018, pp. 983–990 (2018)
17. Shahi, M.A.H.: Tactics, techniques and procedures (TTPs) to augment cyber threat intelligence (CTI): a comprehensive study (2018)
18. Strom, B.E., Applebaum, A., Miller, D.P., Nickels, K.C., Pennington, A.G., Thomas, C.B.: MITRE ATT&CK: Design and Philosophy. Technical report. The MITRE Corporation (2018)
19. Vaswani, A., et al.: Attention is all you need. In: Advances in Neural Information Processing Systems, vol. 30 (2017)

Enhancing Code Security Through Open-Source Large Language Models: A Comparative Study

Norah Ridley[✉], Enrico Branca, Jadyn Kimber, and Natalia Stakhanova

University of Saskatchewan, Saskatoon, SK, Canada
`norah.ridley@usask.ca`

Abstract. Significant advances in the language processing field are providing new innovations, including the ability to analyze code for weaknesses. Typically, analyzing code security is performed by tools that use known vulnerable patterns, which may not adequately represent the intricacies of vulnerabilities in real-world projects. Such tools can fail to detect non-standard weaknesses in code samples, potentially leading to a loss of personal and financial information for end users of the code. Using language-based models to detect weaknesses that would have otherwise been missed by the currently available analysis tools is a promising new avenue of vulnerability detection. In this research, we employ 25 different models to evaluate the security of code samples. Using an existing dataset of insecure code, we prompt each model to detect weaknesses in the vulnerable code. Our findings indicate that most models are ill-equipped to deal with insecure code. Through our analysis, we identify strategies for improving weakness detection using language models.

Keywords: Large language model · Code weakness · Code security

1 Introduction

The wide application of large language models (LLMs) is changing our perception of technology. Significant advances in the language processing field are providing new innovations, including the ability to write, analyze, and correct code written in different programming languages. The innovations in AI are continuously increasing the capabilities of language models and allowing for a more flexible approach to code generation.

Several studies have examined the code quality produced by LLM tools, assessing correctness, validity, dependability, and maintainability [1,2,6,34,41]. While these considerations are extensively explored, the security aspect often remains overlooked. Recent research studies have explored the presence of vulnerabilities in code generated by GitHub's Copilot [29], the ability of OpenAI's Codex to generate hardware security assertions [20], and the security implications of using AI-generated code [33].

© The Author(s), under exclusive license to Springer Nature Switzerland AG 2024
M. Mosbah et al. (Eds.): FPS 2023, LNCS 14551, pp. 233–249, 2024.
https://doi.org/10.1007/978-3-031-57537-2_15

In this work, we perform a comprehensive comparative analysis of popular LLM tools to explore their ability to recognize the presence of security weaknesses in code. Typically, code security analysis is performed by tools relying on known vulnerable patterns. Generating these patterns is an error-prone and time-consuming process. Using language-based models to detect code weaknesses can significantly expedite this process, potentially offering a promising new avenue of vulnerability detection.

In this study, we employ 25 different LLMs to evaluate the security of code samples. Using a dataset of insecure code, we ask each of our models to detect common weakness enumerations (CWEs) in the code samples. CWEs are a widely used community-developed list of software and hardware weaknesses that provide a baseline for detecting vulnerabilities in code. Through this approach, we explore how LLMs have evolved over time, looking at how models based on GPT-3 were improved to create new LLaMA models. To gain a comprehensive understanding of the current state of language models and code weakness detection, we focus our study on large models. Our smallest model is based on seven billion parameters (7B) and trained using one trillion tokens while our largest model uses 70 billion parameters and are trained using 1.4 trillion tokens.

Our work presents several findings that expand our understanding of LLMs as code analysis tools:

- Overall, our findings show that models are ill-equipped to offer sufficient reasoning for identifying code weaknesses. Models that are trained on general datasets outperform models that are specifically trained on coding data.
- Our analysis highlights that models tended to identify more CWEs that are represented as text rather than CWEs that must be inferred by the LLMs. Hence, LLMs should be trained on both code and code evaluation data to develop sufficient reasoning about code weaknesses.
- We investigate strategies for improving weakness detection. Our results suggest that pairing static analysis tools with LLMs can detect a wider range of CWEs in code.

2   Background and Related Work

Large Language Models Overview. Large language models are transformer-based neural networks that are trained on a large amount of text datasets. The datasets often include code samples written in different programming languages. These models have billions of parameters, which are the adjustable elements that allow the model to learn the relationships and patterns in text data. Input to an LLM is known as a *prompt*, which is a limited length sequence of tokens. Large language models have a wide range of applications, including natural language understanding, text generation, language translation, and code analysis. Building an LLM is a complex and expensive task. Training a model from scratch requires a significant amount of time and resources. However, it is often easier to fine-tune a pre-existing model for a specific task. Fine-tuning through data, in the context of this work, refers to adjusting the weight of input training data to optimize outputs.

Related Work. Code vulnerability analysis has been at the centre of research in computing for over a decade. Longstanding papers in the research area of vulnerability detection have often focused on identifying code weaknesses to prevent code vulnerabilities from occurring. The application of machine learning as a means of detecting code vulnerabilities has been the focus of Yamaguchi et al. [40] and Bilgin et al. [5]; both of which outline specific techniques for detecting vulnerabilities using AI-based language processing. While these works are important, our paper maintains a particular focus on using LLMs for detecting code weaknesses.

A few works have focused on the role of LLMs in creating and editing code. Taecharungroj et al. [38] explored a wider view of an LLM's ability to write code. Surameery et al. [37] used LLM models to detect bugs in code. These works explore the capabilities of LLMs, but they do not delve deeply into the weakness detection capabilities of LLMs.

Some works have explored LLMs as code vulnerability detection tools such as Khoury et al. [21], which explored the performance of GPT-3.5 in detecting vulnerabilities. Our work differs from this approach in two ways. First, we focus on code weaknesses rather than vulnerabilities. Second, we employ a more comprehensive approach by analyzing and comparing the performance of a large cross-section of LLMs. Siddiq et al. [35] provided the framework for the security evaluation of generated code. Lastly, Pearce et al. [30] recently published a work detailing a large-scale comparison of LLM-generated code. However, their study focuses on repairing vulnerabilities rather than detecting weaknesses. As such, there has never been a large-scale comparison of LLMs in the context of detecting weaknesses. Thus, we address this gap in the existing literature by evaluating the abilities of 25 popular LLMs in assessing vulnerable code.

3 Methodology

In our study, we evaluate a set of 25 widely-used LLMs. To establish a reliable baseline for our subsequent evaluation, we used an existing dataset that contained vulnerable and generally weak code, which served as a reference point for comparing the models' evaluations of code vulnerabilities. Additionally, we enhanced this evaluation by incorporating CodeQL [22], a static analysis tool.

3.1 Large Language Models

Our work focused on 25 popular open-source LLMs employed by both industry and academia. We selected LLMs with over 500 downloads in the past month[1] from the Hugging Face platform [13], an open-source AI community. The exceptions were the two Samantha models, which we included due to their specialized training datasets.

The initial version of GPT-3 that was released by OpenAI displayed three key abilities: language generation, in-context learning, and world knowledge [14].

---

[1] At the time of writing.

Since the GPT model is proprietary, we focused our efforts on evaluating approximate open source alternatives; one such alternative to GPT-3 is LLaMA, an open-source LLM released by Meta.

Our models include the original *Guanaco 7B* [23] model, which is a fine-tuned variant of the original LLaMA model with four-bit QLoRA tuning. We included one other model based on the original LLaMA model in the form of Vicuna, a LLaMA model that is fine-tuned with user conversations from ShareGPT [19]. Additionally, we used the *Samantha 33B* model, which is based on Vicuna. This model was trained on a curated dataset of 6,000 conversations in ShareGPT [15].

We also leveraged models trained against LLaMA models such as *Wizard Vicuna 7B Uncensored* and *Wizard Vicuna 30B Uncensored*, which removes alignment and moralizing data from the original Wizard Vicuna model [16].

LLaMA 2 models are the next generation of LLaMA [26] that improve on the original LLaMA model by training on 40% more tokens, having a longer context length, and using grouped-query attention. We included the LLaMA 2 models with seven billion and 13 billion parameters in our analysis, referring to these models as *LLaMA 2 7B* and *LLaMA 2 13B*, respectively.

The *Luna AI LLaMA Uncensored model* fine-tunes the LLaMA 2 model using 40,000 long-form chat discussions from real users [39]. In addition, we included the seven billion parameter, 13 billion parameter, and 70 billion parameter versions of the StableBeluga2 [25] model in our analysis, consequently referred to as *StableBeluga2 7B*, *StableBeluga2 13B*, and *StableBeluga2 70B*. StableBeluga2 models are trained on an Orca style dataset [27] and fine-tuned on LLaMA2. Our evaluation also includes the *LLaMA 2 Coder 7B* model, which was based on the LLaMA2 model and trained on the CodeAlpaca 20K dataset (based on Stanford Alpaca) [32].

Additionally, we included the LLaMA 2 version of Guanaco, called LLaMA 2 Guanaco QLoRA. We analyzed the seven billion parameter, 13 billion parameter, and 70 billion parameter versions of this model (*LLaMA 2 7B Guanaco QLoRA*, *LLaMA 2 13B Guanaco QLoRA*, and *LLaMA 2 70B Guanaco QLoRA*).

Another model in the GPT-3 series was the initial Codex, which has the ability to understand and generate code. One approximate open-source alternative is the Salesforce GodeGen models. Thus, we included the *CodeGen2.5 7B Mono* model [12] in our evaluation.

Models in the GPT-3.5 series not only have the ability to understand and generate code, they also exhibit a capability for complex reasoning and possibly long-term dependency. The StarCoder model is an approximate open source alternative. We included the *StarCoder* and *StarCoderPlus* models in our set since both of these models are trained on over 80 programming languages [24].

The *Chronos Hermes 13B* model [4] uses a mixture of the LLaMA derived model, Chronos-13B, and the Nous Hermes model trained on a variety of data including data from technical forums and repositories, as well as coding documentations for various products.

We also evaluated the mixed model *Nous Hermes LLaMA 2 13B*, which was fine tuned on over 300,000 instructions to produce an enhanced LLaMA 2 13B model that aims to rival the performance of the GPT-3.5-turbo model [31].

We included in our analysis several LLaMA-based models that were trained using output based on GPT-4.0. Similar to GPT-3.5, GPT-4.0 was trained on technical forums, code repositories, and coding documentation. We included the *Airoboros 7B GPT4-1.2* and *Airoboros 13B GPT4-1.4* models, which are QLoRA models that were trained on, among other things, programs written in multiple programming languages, and fine-tuned on entirely synthetic data using seven billion and 13 billion parameters, respectively [3].

We evaluated the *OpenOrca Platypus2 13B* model that was trained on the Platypus dataset, which includes Python coding exercises [23]. This model mixes the LLaMA 2-based Platypus2 model with the GPT-4 based OpenOrca model [28].

Our analysis also included the *Falcon 7B Instruct* model, a causal decoder-only model [18] trained on a variety of instruct and chat datasets, and its variant *Samantha Falcon 7B* model, which like Samantha 33B, was trained on ShareGPT data.

3.2 Code Dataset

To assess the models' abilities to recognize insecure code, we employed the SecurityEval dataset produced by Siddiq and Santos [35]. This dataset includes code samples collected from four different sources: CodeQL [22] documentation, the CWE website [7], from SonarSource [36] rules, and the study by Pearce et al. [29]. To supplement their dataset, the authors generated additional code samples. Each sample targets a specific CWE. The collected samples were assessed by their original source and assigned a CWE. The authors of the SecurityEval dataset used these CWE assignments to organize their dataset by CWE. The generated samples were created to address specific CWEs that were not already in the dataset, meaning that the authors intentionally developed insecure code. In the current version of this dataset, there are 121 programs written in Python language targeting 69 CWEs. Table 1 shows the distribution of code samples in the dataset sorted by CWE.

3.3 Baseline Analysis

To determine how efficient the selected models are at detecting code weaknesses, we use CodeQL [22], an open source semantic code analysis engine created by the Github Security Lab. CodeQL leverages a set of predefined or customized queries to analyze code for security issues and code correctness. We scanned all 121 programs from SecurityEval dataset using the CodeQL tool. These results establish our baseline when analyzing the LLMs' assessments of the dataset, allowing us to gain an understanding of the models' performances against a widely used static analysis tool.

Table 1. CodeQL performance on the SecurityEval dataset

Code samples

CWE Number	CWE-020	CWE-022	CWE-078	CWE-079	CWE-080	CWE-089	CWE-090	CWE-094	CWE-095	CWE-099	CWE-113	CWE-116	CWE-117	CWE-1204	CWE-193
SecureEval	6	4	2	3	1	2	2	3	1	1	2	2	3	1	1
CodeQL	0	7	2	8	0	0	4	2	0	0	0	1	1	0	0

CWE Number	CWE-215	CWE-250	CWE-252	CWE-259	CWE-269	CWE-283	CWE-285	CWE-295	CWE-306	CWE-319	CWE-321	CWE-326	CWE-327	CWE-329	CWE-330
SecureEval	1	1	2	2	1	1	1	3	1	4	3	2	4	1	2
CodeQL	1	0	0	0	0	0	0	1	0	0	0	2	6	0	0

CWE Number	CWE-367	CWE-377	CWE-379	CWE-385	CWE-400	CWE-406	CWE-414	CWE-425	CWE-434	CWE-454	CWE-462	CWE-477	CWE-502	CWE-521	CWE-522
SecureEval	2	2	2	1	2	1	2	1	2	1	2	2	4	2	2
CodeQL	0	2	0	0	0	0	0	0	0	0	0	2	0	0	0

CWE Number	CWE-605	CWE-611	CWE-641	CWE-643	CWE-703	CWE-730	CWE-732	CWE-759	CWE-760	CWE-776	CWE-798	CWE-827	CWE-835	CWE-841	CWE-918
SecureEval	1	6	1	2	3	3	1	1	1	1	2	1	1	1	2
CodeQL	0	2	0	1	0	3	1	0	1	1	51	0	0	0	2

CWE Number	CWE-200	CWE-209	CWE-595	CWE-601	CWE-331	CWE-339	CWE-941	CWE-943	CWE-347
SecureEval	1	1	1	5	1	2	1	1	4
CodeQL	0	0	0	4	0	0	0	0	0

3.4   Model Assessment

Similar to the baseline analysis, we prompted each model to evaluate the 121 code samples. Since manually querying each model for each code sample takes a significant amount of time, we automated this process with the Python library, llama2-wrapper [17]. Using a custom Python script, the models evaluated the code samples using the following query: *Does the following code contain a CWE-ID? If so, what is the CWE-ID? [code sample].* By design, each model's responses (and similarly the prompts) are limited by character count and time; once these limits are exceeded, the response is terminated and the model is presented with the next query. We query each model only once regardless of the received response quality.

4   Results

Experimental Setup. We downloaded and ran the models on a Linux Pop OS 22.04 machine with two NVIDIA GeForce RTX 3090 GPUs. Each GPU has 24 GB of memory, 10,496 CUDA cores, and 328 tensor cores, providing us with sufficient power to evaluate the collected models.

CodeQL Assessment. Table 1 presents the results of baseline assessment with CodeQL. Although CodeQL is generally regarded as a state-of-the-art code assessment tool, our analysis shows that its results in most cases do not agree with the dataset labelling. Overall, CodeQL identified CWEs only in 50 samples from the dataset. CodeQL identified fewer CWEs than what was present according to the dataset labelling. For four different CWEs, CWE-079, CWE-90, CWE-327, and particularly with CWE-798 (the use of hard coded credentials), CodeQL detected more instances of these CWEs than were actually present.

Since there is no guarantee that initial dataset labelling is more accurate than the CodeQL assessment, we further provide comparison along both assessment results.

LLM Assessment Compared to the SecurityEval Dataset. Table 2 shows the outcome of each model's attempt to detect CWEs compared to the SecurityEval baseline. For each model, we categorize the models' responses to the 121 Python samples as follows:

Table 2. LLM code assessment compared to the SecurityEval dataset labelling

Model	Provided CWE matched	CWE did not match	No response	No CWE found	Other response
LLaMA 2 13B	6	99	4	11	1
LLaMA 2 7B	3	79	8	22	9
StarCoderPlus	3	17	85	16	0
OpenOrca Platypus2 13B	2	24	3	92	0
Nous Hermes LLaMA 2 13B	1	11	89	20	0
LLaMA 2 13B Guanaco QLoRA	1	28	74	17	1
StarCoder	1	41	74	4	1
Vicuna 33B	0	0	121	0	0
Airoboros 13B GPT4-1.4	0	0	121	0	0
LLaMA 2 7B Guanaco QLoRA	0	24	49	44	4
StableBeluga 7B	0	10	83	28	0
CodeGen2.5 7B Mono	0	1	120	0	0
Airoboros 7B GPT4-1.2	0	0	121	0	0
Guanaco 7B	0	0	121	0	0
Falcon 7B Instruct	0	0	4	117	0
Wizard Vicuna 7B Uncensored	0	0	121	0	0
Samantha 33B	0	0	121	0	0
Luna AI LLaMA Uncensored	0	10	35	76	0
StableBeluga 13B	0	5	58	58	0
Chronos Hermes 13B	0	0	121	0	0
LLaMA 2 Coder 7B	0	0	121	0	0
Samantha Falcon 7B	-	-	-	-	-
Wizard Vicuna 30B Uncensored	-	-	-	-	-
LLaMA2 70B Guanaco QLoRA	-	-	-	-	-
StableBeluga2 70B	-	-	-	-	-

- **Provided CWE matched.** The model identified a CWE in a given code sample that matched the SecurityEval CWE labelling for that sample.
- **CWE did not match.** The model identified a CWE that did not match the CWE indicated in the dataset.
- **No response.** The model did not respond to our query.
- **No CWE found.** The model assessed the code sample and stated that there were no CWEs present in the sample.
- **Other.** Model responded with uncertainty or with a fragmented response.

As our results in Table 2 show, the vast majority of models did not agree on the presence of CWEs according to the SecurityEval labels.

Only seven models responded with at least one identification of a CWE that matched the baseline. Among them, LLaMA 2 13B appears to be the most successful model (detected six CWEs matching the SecurityEval labelling). This means that the model most in line with SecurityEval labelling agreed with it only five per cent of the time. The StarCoderPlus model performed the second best after the LLaMA 2 models. Surprisingly, the most common result from the models was a failure to answer, which mostly consisted of the models returning a timeout error when attempting to provide a response. Of the tested models, eight returned this response for all 121 code samples.

Interestingly, most of the models that were trained or fine-tuned using technical repositories and documentation did not stand out in their performance. For example, the Airoboros 7B GPT4-1.2 model, which was trained on data specifically focused on coding examples that were written in multiple programming languages, failed to identify any CWEs in the code samples. Rather, it did not answer the prompt for any of the samples as shown in Tables 2 and 3. Similarly, the Chronos Hermes 13B and LLaMA 2 Coder 7B models gave no response in all cases.

Similar to incorrect responses, a significant number of responses from models claimed that no CWEs were present in code despite the indication of the baseline. Three models returned this response for over half the submitted code while nine models never returned this response.

Falcon 7B Instruct was an outlier in this case, claiming a lack of weaknesses in code for most (117 out of 121) of the analyzed samples. The Falcon 7B Instruct model's pre-training data consisted of public data from the web. The model was optimized, meaning that only the data with the most positive hits was retained. As a result, it appears that the Falcon 7B Instruct model can not recognize code.

Lastly we received a negligible amount of miscellaneous responses from the models which did not fit into any of the previous categories.

LLM Assessment Compared to the CodeQL Results. Table 3 presents the results of comparing the models' assessments for the 50 code samples that were deemed insecure by the CodeQL scan. The results show the number of times a model's assessment of a specific code sample matched with results of the CodeQL scan for that file.

The LLaMA 2 13B performed the best, identifying four CWEs that agreed with CodeQL's results. Interestingly, this model also performed the best according to the original dataset labelling. However, it also had the highest number of cases (44 out of 50) identifying CWEs that did not correspond with CodeQL's assessment. The StarCoderPlus model, which was intended to help developers with coding tasks, performed the second best.

Nine of the models did not answer the query for all 50 samples of our subset. Among them were the models based on GPT-3.5 and GPT-4: Airoboros and Chronos Hermes. The performance of the OpenOrca Platypus2 model, which was trained on data that included Python code, was not remarkable either.

Over half of the models identified at least one sample in the subset that did not contain a CWE (i.e., the model answered "no" to our query). Given that the Falcon 7B Instruct model found no CWEs in the highest number of files from the full dataset, it is not surprising that it identified 48 (96%) samples with no CWEs in this experiment.

Analysis of Detected CWEs. Table 4 shows the number of unique CWEs and CWE combinations identified by the models during the code assessment of the samples. The LLaMA 2 7B and 13B models suggested the highest number of unique CWEs. Across all of the models, CWE-311, CWE-77, CWE-78, CWE-434 and CWE-319 were the top five most identified CWEs. CWE-311 (Missing Encryption of Sensitive Data), which occurs when data is improperly encrypted, was identified 21 times. CWE-77 and CWE-78 were detected 19 and 18 times, respectively. Both of these CWEs are concerned with variations of command injection, which can give an attacker a privilege or capability that they would not otherwise have.

When comparing the LLM assessments to the SecurityEval dataset, CWE-311, CWE-77, CWE-78, CWE-434, and CWE-319 were the most commonly identified CWEs that did not match the labelling used by SecurityEval. CWE-311 and CWE-77 were mismatched 21 and 19 times respectively, corresponding to the number of times they were identified across all of the models. However, CWE-78 was mismatched only 15 times, meaning that CWE-78 was correctly matched to the SecurityEval dataset three times since it was detected 18 times. Some of the LLMs that we evaluated learned from text to differentiate between secure and insecure code (e.g., code containing CWE-78), making it possible for LLMs to detect this form of weakness.

When comparing the results of the model assessments to the CodeQL scan, CWE-77, CWE-311, CWE-78, CWE-434 and CWE-122 were the most commonly identified CWEs that also did not match the CodeQL result for that corresponding file. CWE-77 was the most commonly mismatched CWE; mismatches occurred 13 times.

In Table 5 we present the agreement between each variety of model and our two baselines. Specifically, we show the percentage of evaluations done by each model type that detected the same CWE in a code sample as either one of our baselines. These percentage rates are counted separately for each baseline. For both comparisons, the baseline LLaMA 2 model performed the best in this metric with a 7.4% overlap with the SecurityEval baseline and a 10% agreement with the CodeQL evaluation. Interestingly, many of the models that were derivatives of LLaMA 2 performed much worse than the base model. We believe that this is due to the fine-tuning toward chat data of these derivative models, which reduces the weight of code analysis data in the training sets. To support this, the other two model types showing any overlap at all with the baselines were the Nous Hermes and the LLaMA 2 Guanaco QloRA models, both of which contain non-chat-based fine-tuning. In addition, with the exception of OpenOrca Platypus, all chat tuned models showed zero overlap. The original Guanaco model was also not chat trained, but it was based on the original LLaMA instead of LLaMA 2, which could account for its variance.

Table 6 shows the distribution of the models' assessments sorted by the 10 pillars of the Research Concepts view (CWE-1000) defined by the CWE community. In the CWE community, views are hierarchical structures used to organize weaknesses, and this view is intended to include every CWE weakness [11].

Pillars exist within this view with the purpose of grouping weaknesses. The models identified numerous CWEs in the code samples, and we sort these CWEs into their top-level pillar entry to present a more cohesive relationship between the models and the CWEs they identified. We observe that LLaMA 2 7B identified 45 CWE-707s, which is 37% of the code samples it assessed. CWE-707 (Improper Neutralization) typically occurs when input (and in some cases, output) is not correctly validated to ensure that it is safe and will behave as expected when used in the code [10]. Additionally, LLaMA 2 13B identified 40 instances of CWE-664 (Improper Control of a Resource Through its Lifetime) and 30 instances of CWE-693 (Protection Mechanism Failure) during its code assessments. Together these two CWEs account for 58% of this model's assessments. Code contains the CWE-664 when it fails to properly create, use and destroy resources according to the resource's instructions [8]. CWE-693 occurs when a protection mechanism is missing, insufficient, or not applied in all relevant situations in the code [9].

CWE-664, CWE-693 and CWE-707 are similar in the sense that they can be represented in text as patterns. LLaMA 2 13B identified a high number of CWE-664 and CWE-693 rather than identifying small numbers of many different CWEs. We also see this trend with the LLaMA 2 7B model where it identified a high number of one CWE (CWE-707). Presumably, since the 13B model is exposed to more patterns than the 7B due to the size of its training data, it detects a wider range of CWEs at a high number compared to the rest of the dataset.

In other words, larger models should identify more variety of CWEs with less specificity (i.e., numbers should be more spread out and not as high). We see this when we examine the CWE breakdown for the LLaMA 2 7B and 13B models. The 7B model peaks higher since it identifies 45 files with the CWE-707 weakness, and the 13B model peaks twice with slightly lower numbers.

Interestingly, the LLaMA 2 13B model flagged three files that matched the SecurityEval labelling, but, due to the limited number of CWE rules defined by CodeQL, these files were not flagged by CodeQL. Two of these files contained CWE-259 (Use of Hard-coded Password) and one file contained CWE-200 (Exposure of Sensitive Information to an Unauthorized Actor). Similarly, the StarCoderPlus model correctly identified (according to the SecurityEval labelling) one file that contained CWE-321 (Use of Hard-coded Cryptographic Key). These three CWEs can be represented as text, and they are not CWEs that are currently detected by CodeQL according to the defined rules in CodeQL's repository on Github. These results suggest that LLMs and CodeQL can pair well together to detect a wider range of weaknesses in code.

5   Discussion

The use of CWEs is an attempt to formalize the effect of weakness in code, and it is a valuable way to standardize weakness across the community. As indicated by the differences in CWE identification between the models' assessments, the CodeQL scan, and the labelling of the SecurityEval dataset, identifying code

Table 3. Models' code assessments compared to the CodeQL scan

Model	Provided CWE matched	CWE did not match	No response	No CWE found	Other response
LLaMA 2 13B	4	44	0	2	0
StarCoderPlus	2	6	38	4	0
LLaMA 2 7B	1	32	3	8	6
LLaMA 2 7B Guanaco QLoRA	1	13	19	13	4
Nous Hermes LLaMA 2 13B	1	3	38	8	0
StarCoder	1	15	29	4	1
Vicuna 33B	0	0	50	0	0
Airoboros 13B GPT4-1.4	0	0	50	0	0
OpenOrca Platypus2 13B	0	11	2	37	0
LLaMA 2 13B Guanaco QLoRA	0	17	24	8	1
StableBeluga 7B	0	5	32	13	0
CodeGen2.5 7B Mono	0	0	50	0	0
Airoboros 7B GPT4-1.2	0	0	50	0	0
Guanaco 7B	0	0	50	0	0
Falcon 7B Instruct	0	0	2	48	0
Wizard Vicuna 7B Uncensored	0	0	50	0	0
Samantha 33B	0	0	50	0	0
Luna AI LLaMA Uncensored	0	3	15	32	0
StableBeluga 13B	0	4	15	31	0
Chronos Hermes 13B	0	0	50	0	0
LLaMA 2 Coder 7B	0	0	50	0	0
Samantha Falcon 7B	-	-	-	-	-
Wizard Vicuna 30B Uncensored	-	-	-	-	-
LLaMA2 70B Guanaco QLoRA	-	-	-	-	-
StableBeluga2 70B	-	-	-	-	-

weaknesses can be challenging. Programming languages are continually evolving; subsequently, code weaknesses also evolve. Using LLMs to detect weaknesses in code allows us to shift away from having to continually redefine version- and code-dependent weaknesses.

Specifically, our findings emphasize several important points:

- **Model size and parameter number.** Our analysis shows that the size of a model and its number of parameters is not a reflection of a model's ability to assess weakness in code. For example, the LLaMA 2 13B model outperformed other larger models.
- **Best performing model.** Out of the evaluated models, LLaMA 2 13B performed the best. Overall, it was robust in response to the provided code samples, and it provided a CWE for 105 code samples. Its assessments were most in line with the SecurityEval dataset's CWE labelling and the CodeQL results. It also provided the highest number of unique CWEs.

244 N. Ridley et al.

Table 4. The number of unique CWEs identified by models during code assessment

Model	Unique CWEs
LLaMA 2 13B	38
LLaMA 2 7B	35
StarCoder	24
LLaMA 2 13B Guanaco QLoRA	19
LLaMA 2 7B Guanaco QLoRA	17
OpenOrca Platypus2 13B	17
StarCoderPlus	12
Luna AI LLaMA Uncensored	10
Nous Hermes LLaMA 2 13B	9
StableBeluga 13B	5
StableBeluga 7B	4
CodeGen2.5 7B Mono	1
Airoboros 13B GPT4-1.4	0
Vicuna 33B	0
Airoboros 7B GPT4-1.2	0
Guanaco 7B	0
Falcon 7B Instruct	0
Wizard Vicuna 7B Uncensored	0
Samantha 33B	0
Chronos Hermes 13B	0
LLaMA 2 Coder 7B	0
Samantha Falcon 7B	-
Wizard Vicuna 30B Uncensored	-
LLaMA2 70B Guanaco QLoRA	-
StableBeluga2 70B	-

- **Model training datasets.** Models that were trained on more generalized data tended to identify a higher number of CWEs that were in line with the SecurityEval dataset categorization and the CodeQL analysis. Models that were specifically trained on code displayed mediocre performances with the exception of the StarCoderPlus model. However, this model was still outperformed by the LLaMA 2 13B model. Hence, it appears that models equipped to solve coding-related questions do not have sufficient reasoning to identify code weaknesses.
- **LLM code evaluation.** Detecting weakness is a form of code evaluation and not a property of code. Developing models that can identify code weaknesses requires a training dataset of both code data as well as non-coding data related to code evaluation (i.e., a mixed model).

Table 5. Detection rate for each model type

Model Type	Parent Model	Rate (SE)	Rate (CodeQL)
LLaMA 2	NA	7.40%	10%
Luna AI LLaMA	LLaMA 2	0.00%	0%
Nous Hermes	LLaMA 2	0.80%	2%
Vicuna	LLaMA	0.00%	0%
Airoboros*	LLaMA	0.00%	0%
OpenOrca Platypus*	LLaMA 2	1.70%	0%
LLaMA 2 Guanaco QloRA	LLaMA 2	0.80%	2%
StableBeluga	LLaMA 2	0.00%	0%
Guanaco	LLaMA	0.00%	0%
Falcon	NA	0.00%	0%
Wizard Vicuna	LLaMA + WizardLM	0.00%	0%
Samantha	GPT-4	0.00%	0%
Chronos Hermes*	LLaMA + LLaMA 2	0.00%	0%
Starcoder*	StarCoderBase	0.80%	2%
StarcoderPlus*	StarCoder	2.50%	4%
LLaMA 2 Coder	LLaMA 2	0.00%	0%
CodeGen2.5*	CodeGen2	0.00%	0%

* Presence of code samples, data from technical forums, or coding documentations in the training or fine-tuning stages

- **CWE representation.** Models often detected the same types of CWEs, which were mainly patterns of CWE concepts represented as text. CWEs that are not represented as text, and therefore must be inferred by the LLM, are not easily detected by LLMs. This finding suggests that LLMs require more knowledge about code evaluation to reason about code weakness.
- **Pairing LLMs with static analysis tools.** As we saw in our analysis, two LLMs detected CWEs that were outside the scope of CodeQL. Tool pairings such as this can potentially detect a wider range of code weaknesses before significant problems arise. Since the process of defining the vulnerable patterns used by static analysis tools is time consuming and prone to errors, using LLMs to complement the existing tools may expedite the process of identifying weaknesses in code.

5.1 Limitations

Although CodeQL offers vulnerability detection at an industry standard, it does have some limitations. CodeQL is composed of queries defined only for a small range of CWEs for Python code, and it does not support detection for other CWEs that can affect Python code. As a result, this limits our ability to fully compare the models' assessments to the full range of CWEs.

Hugging Face provides several popular models for use within the AI community. Despite this accessibility, some models did not successfully load on our system despite our system meeting the model's requirements. It is unclear if there was an internal issue with the model, or another reason entirely. Four of our selected models (three of which had parameters greater than or equal to 30B) did not load and were not evaluated, therefore limiting our ability to evaluate larger models.

Table 6. Breakdown of model responses by CWE pillars

Model	CWE 284	CWE 435	CWE 664	CWE 682	CWE 691	CWE 693	CWE 697	CWE 703	CWE 707	CWE 710	No corresponding CWE pillar	No CWE	Total
CodeQL	1	0	6	0	0	8	0	0	3	8	24	71	121
LLaMA 2 13B	4	0	40	1	1	30	0	0	14	1	14	16	121
LLaMA 2 7B	2	3	17	0	4	1	5	1	45	0	4	39	121
LLaMA 2 7B Guanaco QLoRA	2	0	5	2	0	1	0	0	4	4	6	97	121
LLaMA 2 13B Guanaco QLoRA	2	0	13	0	0	8	1	0	0	1	4	92	121
Luna AI LLaMA Uncensored	1	0	3	0	0	1	0	1	2	0	2	111	121
Nous Hermes LLaMA 2 13B	1	0	3	0	0	6	1	0	1	0	0	109	121
OpenOrca Platypus2 13B	1	0	8	0	2	5	0	0	3	0	7	95	121
Vicuna 33B	0	0	0	0	0	0	0	0	0	0	0	121	121
Airoboros 13B GPT4-1.4	0	0	0	0	0	0	0	0	0	0	0	121	121
CodeGen2.5 7B Mono	0	0	0	0	0	0	0	0	1	0	0	120	121
StableBeluga 7B	0	0	5	0	0	4	0	1	0	0	0	111	121
Airoboros 7B GPT4-1.2	0	0	0	0	0	0	0	0	0	0	0	121	121
Guanaco 7B	0	0	0	0	0	0	0	0	0	0	0	121	121
Falcon 7B Instruct	0	0	0	0	0	0	0	0	0	0	0	121	121
StarCoderPlus	0	0	11	0	0	0	0	0	1	0	8	101	121
Wizard Vicuna 7B Uncensored	0	0	0	0	0	0	0	0	0	0	0	121	121
LLaMA 2 Coder 7B	0	0	0	0	0	0	0	0	0	0	0	121	121
Samantha 33B	0	0	0	0	0	0	0	0	0	0	0	121	121
StarCoder	0	0	10	0	0	1	0	0	0	1	31	78	121
StableBeluga 13B	0	0	2	0	0	2	0	0	1	0	0	116	121
Chronos Hermes 13B	0	0	0	0	0	0	0	0	0	0	0	121	121
Samantha Falcon 7B	-	-	-	-	-	-	-	-	-	-	-	-	-
Wizard Vicuna 30B Uncensored	-	-	-	-	-	-	-	-	-	-	-	-	-
LLaMA 2 70B Guanaco QLoRA	-	-	-	-	-	-	-	-	-	-	-	-	-
StableBeluga2 70B	-	-	-	-	-	-	-	-	-	-	-	-	-

6   Conclusion

In this study, we compared the weakness assessment capabilities of various LLMs. Our analysis sheds light on how different types of models detect code weakness. We asked each model to assess a dataset of Python code and detect any CWEs. The models' assessments were compared to the original CWE labelling assigned to the code samples by the SecurityEval authors. We further explored the models' abilities to identify weaknesses by comparing their assessments to the results of CodeQL, a widely used static analysis tool.

We show that a model's success in detecting CWEs is more influenced by the content of its training dataset rather than its size and parameter number alone. Overall, the LLaMA 2 models, which were trained on general datasets, outperformed models that were specifically trained on code samples. Additionally, some of the models in our dataset did not have sufficient knowledge of code and CWEs, resulting in a high number of false negatives. This result suggests that models require a knowledge of code as well as an understanding of how code is evaluated to reliably detect code weaknesses.

Out of the models in our evaluation, only a small portion of models identified a CWE in at least one code sample. Upon closer examination, certain CWEs were frequently detected; many of which were CWEs that are represented as text and can therefore be detected by the model. CWEs that are not represented as text (i.e., CWEs that are detected through model inference) are not easily detectable.

Our analysis of popular LLMs demonstrates that certain types of models are better suited for use in code weakness detection. Ultimately, the goal with detecting weakness in code is to detect as many weaknesses as possible before such weaknesses cause significant problems for end users. Pairing LLMs with static analysis tools such as CodeQL to detect weaknesses in code is the next step toward comprehensive code analysis.

References

1. Adamson, V., Bägerfeldt, J.: Assessing the effectiveness of ChatGPT in generating Python code (2023)
2. Ahmed, I., Kajol, M., Hasan, U., Datta, P.P., Roy, A., Reza, M.R.: ChatGPT vs. Bard: a comparative study. UMBC Student Collection (2023)
3. Airoboros: Airoboros: using large language models to fine-tune large language models. https://github.com/jondurbin/airoboros
4. Austism: Chronos-hermes-13b. https://huggingface.co/Austism/chronos-hermes-13b
5. Bilgin, Z., Ersoy, M.A., Soykan, E.U., Tomur, E., Çomak, P., Karaçay, L.: Vulnerability prediction from source code using machine learning. IEEE Access **8**, 150672–150684 (2020)
6. Bull, C., Kharrufa, A.: Generative AI assistants in software development education: a vision for integrating generative AI into educational practice, not instinctively defending against it. IEEE Softw. **41**, 52–59 (2023)
7. MITRE Corporation: Common weakness enumeration. https://cwe.mitre.org/
8. CWE: CWE-664: improper control of a resource through its lifetime. https://cwe.mitre.org/data/definitions/664.html
9. CWE: CWE-693: protection mechanism failure. https://cwe.mitre.org/data/definitions/693.html
10. CWE: CWE-707: improper neutralization. https://cwe.mitre.org/data/definitions/707.html
11. CWE: CWE view: research concepts. https://cwe.mitre.org/data/definitions/1000.html
12. Nijkamp, E., Hayashi, H., Zhou, Y., Xiong, C.: CodeGen2.5: small, but mighty. https://blog.salesforceairesearch.com/codegen25/
13. Hugging Face: The AI community building the future. https://huggingface.co/
14. Fu, Y., Peng, H., Khot, T.: How does GPT obtain its ability? Tracing emergent abilities of language models to their sources. Yao Fu's Notion, December 2022. https://yaofu.notion.site/How-does-GPT-Obtain-its-Ability-Tracing-Emergent-Abilities-of-Language-Models-to-their-Sources-b9a57ac0fcf74f30a1ab9e3e36fa1dc1
15. Hartford, E.: Samantha-33b. https://huggingface.co/ehartford/samantha-33b

16. Hartford, E.: Wizard Vicuna 7B Uncensored. https://huggingface.co/ehartford/Wizard-Vicuna-7B-Uncensored
17. Python Package Index: llama2-wrapper 0.1.12. https://pypi.org/project/llama2-wrapper/
18. Technology Innovation Institute: Falcon 7b instruct. https://huggingface.co/tiiuae/falcon-7b-instruct
19. Ji, B.: VicunaNER: zero/few-shot named entity recognition using Vicuna. arXiv preprint arXiv:2305.03253 (2023)
20. Kande, R., et al.: LLM-assisted generation of hardware assertions (2023)
21. Khoury, R., Avila, A.R., Brunelle, J., Camara, B.M.: How secure is code generated by chatgpt? arXiv preprint arXiv:2304.09655 (2023)
22. GS Lab: CodeQL. https://codeql.github.com/
23. Lee, A.N., Hunter, C.J., Ruiz, N.: Platypus: quick, cheap, and powerful refinement of LLMs (2023)
24. Li, R., et al.: StarCoder: may the source be with you! (2023)
25. Mahan, D., Carlow, R., Castricato, L., Cooper, N., Laforte, C.: Stable beluga models. https://huggingface.co/stabilityai/StableBeluga2
26. Meta: Meta and Microsoft introduce the next generation of Llama. https://about.fb.com/news/2023/07/llama-2/
27. Nayak, A., Timmapathini, H.P.: LLM2KB: constructing knowledge bases using instruction tuned context aware large language models. arXiv preprint arXiv:2308.13207 (2023)
28. Open-Orca/OpenOrca-Platypus2-13B. https://huggingface.co/Open-Orca/OpenOrca-Platypus2-13B
29. Pearce, H., Ahmad, B., Tan, B., Dolan-Gavitt, B., Karri, R.: Asleep at the keyboard? Assessing the security of GitHub Copilot's code contributions. In: 2022 IEEE Symposium on Security and Privacy (SP), pp. 754–768 (2022)
30. Pearce, H., Tan, B., Ahmad, B., Karri, R., Dolan-Gavitt, B.: Examining zero-shot vulnerability repair with large language models. In: 2023 IEEE Symposium on Security and Privacy (SP), pp. 2339–2356. IEEE (2023)
31. Nous Research: Nous-Hermes-Llama2-13b. https://huggingface.co/NousResearch/Nous-Hermes-Llama2-13b
32. Romero, M.: Llama-2-Coder-7B (revision d30d193) (2023). https://huggingface.co/mrm8488/llama-2-coder-7b
33. Sandoval, G., Pearce, H., Nys, T., Karri, R., Garg, S., Dolan-Gavitt, B.: Lost at C: a user study on the security implications of large language model code assistants. In: USENIX (2023)
34. Sharma, S., Sodhi, B.: Calculating originality of LLM assisted source code (2023)
35. Siddiq, M.L., Santos, J.C.S.: SecurityEval dataset: mining vulnerability examples to evaluate machine learning-based code generation techniques. In: Proceedings of the 1st International Workshop on Mining Software Repositories Applications for Privacy and Security, MSR4PS 2022 (2022). https://doi.org/10.1145/3549035.3561184
36. SonarSource: Sonarsource static code analysis. https://rules.sonarsource.com/
37. Surameery, N.M.S., Shakor, M.Y.: Use ChatGPT to solve programming bugs. Int. J. Inf. Technol. Comput. Eng. (IJITC) 3(01), 17–22 (2023). ISSN 2455-5290
38. Taecharungroj, V.: "What can ChatGPT do?" Analyzing early reactions to the innovative AI Chatbot on Twitter. Big Data Cogn. Comput. 7(1), 35 (2023)
39. Tap-M: Luna AI Llama uncensored. https://huggingface.co/Tap-M/Luna-AI-Llama2-Uncensored

40. Yamaguchi, F., Rieck, K., et al.: Vulnerability extrapolation: assisted discovery of vulnerabilities using machine learning. In: 5th USENIX Workshop on Offensive Technologies, WOOT 2011 (2011)
41. Yetiştiren, B., Özsoy, I., Ayerdem, M., Tüzün, E.: Evaluating the code quality of AI-assisted code generation tools: an empirical study on GitHub Copilot, Amazon CodeWhisperer, and ChatGPT (2023)

Network and System Threat

Green-Fuzz: Efficient Fuzzing for Network Protocol Implementations

Seyed Behnam Andarzian$^{(\boxtimes)}$, Cristian Daniele, and Erik Poll

Radboud Universiteit, Nijmegen, The Netherlands
seyedbehnam.andarzian@ru.nl

Abstract. Recent techniques have significantly improved fuzzing, discovering many vulnerabilities in various software systems. However, certain types of systems, such as network protocols, are still challenging to fuzz. This article presents two enhancements that allow efficient fuzzing of network protocols. The first is Desock+, which simulates a network socket and supports different POSIX options to make Desock+ suitable for faster network protocol fuzzing. The second is Green-Fuzz, which sends input messages in one go and reduces the system-call overhead while fuzzing network protocols. We applied this modification to AFLNet, but it could be applied to any fuzzer for stateful systems. This is the maximum overhead we can avoid, when doing out-process fuzzing on stateful systems. Our evaluation shows that these enhancements make AFLNet up to four times faster.

Keywords: Testing · Fuzzing · Software Security · Network Protocol Fuzzing

1 Introduction

Fuzzing (a.k.a. fuzz testing) is an effective technique for testing software systems, with popular fuzzers such as AFL++ [22] and LibFuzzer [1] having found thousands of bugs in both open-source and commercial software. For instance, Google has discovered over 25,000 bugs in their own software (e.g. Chrome) and over 36,000 bugs in over 550 open source projects [3].

Unfortunately, not all software can benefit from such fuzzing campaigns. One important class of software is network protocols which are challenging to fuzz [9] [6]. One of the challenges in fuzzing network protocols is performance overheads caused by the network stack, and context switching between the fuzzer and Software Under Test (SUT).

There are two main approaches for testing such software. One approach is in-process fuzzing [1] to exercise different parts or APIs of the SUT. Although this method is fast and can yield positive results, it needs considerable manual effort (including source code modification), and system-level testing still needs to be

E. Poll—This research is funded by NWO as part of the INTERSCT project (NWA.1160.18.301).

performed. Another approach is out-process fuzzing [13], where the fuzzer runs outside of SUT, generates random input messages, and sends them to the SUT. While this approach requires less manual effort and no source code modification, it is very slow and takes a lot of computation power.

We propose two enhancements to have an efficient fuzzer:

- We offer a new method that leverages a simulated socket library named Desock+, a modified version of **preeny**. Unlike **preeny** [2], Desock+ works with a wide range of SUTs, allowing for efficient fuzzing of network protocols.
- We present the Green-Fuzz fuzzer, which sends input message traces in one go to the SUT. Therefore, it can avoid some system-call and context-switching overhead between the fuzzer and SUT.

These enhancements are different: Desock+ is a simulated socket library that can work with any fuzzer, and Green-Fuzz is a network protocol fuzzer that uses a specific version of Desock+ named Fast-desock+.

Our evaluation of the execution speed on ProFuzzBench [12] shows that Green-Fuzz is up to four times faster than AFLNet [13]. We also compared our approach with related work, which shows that our solution has the advantage of supporting more types of SUT for fuzzing, which use complex socket functionalities.

This paper is structured as follows: Sect. 2 presents the background and our motivation for this research. In Sect. 3, we talk about the issue of network communication overhead and how we solve it with Desock+. Section 4 presents our new approach used in Green-Fuzz and its architecture to reduce the overhead in fuzzing. In Sect. 5, we discuss the related work. In Sect. 6, we discuss the limitations and future work, and finally, in Sect. 7, we provide the conclusion of this paper.

2   Background and Motivation

In the realm of software security, one of the major challenges is ensuring the robustness and safety of software against malicious inputs. Fuzzing, a dynamic code testing technique, is a useful way of identifying vulnerabilities in software. There are many factors considered for effective fuzzing of software. The main ones are code-coverage, performance, and applicability. Each of these factors is essential for effectively fuzzing and finding vulnerabilities. Performance, as one of these factors, is critical in fuzzing because more fuzzing speed means we need less computing resources and energy.

For example, Google is spending a lot of computing resources for OSS fuzz [26] to find bugs. By having an efficient fuzzer, these companies can spend less time and resources on fuzzing. Furthermore, time is critical when it comes to integrating fuzzing in the CI/CD[1] pipelines for software. As mentioned in [27], the reasonable amount of time that should be spent on fuzzing in the CI/CD pipeline is around 10 min per day, which is very short.

---

[1] Continuous Integration/Continuous Deployment.

The issues mentioned above get worse when it comes to fuzzing network protocol implementations. When fuzzing regular command line software[2], on average, we are 100 times faster than fuzzing network protocol implementations. This observation led us to do more research and find different hurdles in efficiently fuzzing network protocol implementations. After addressing these hurdles, we believe this is the maximal amount of speed gain we can have when doing out-process fuzzing (see Sect. 4.3).

3   Removing Network Communication Overhead with Desock+

In this section, we discuss our approach to avoid network communication overhead. We provide Desock+ as a simulated socket library that works with any fuzzer to avoid network communication overhead. Existing fuzzers for network protocols, such as AFLNet [13], rely on network communication to send inputs to the SUT. However, this approach has two drawbacks. The fuzzer sends an input message to the SUT and gets a response. Each round of fuzzing[3] is done by sending a sequence of input messages, which we call a trace of input messages. For each trace of input message $T = <m_1, m_2, ..., m_n>$, the fuzzer must create a new connection, which adds overhead. Additionally, sending each input message m_n through the network also incurs overhead due to the time-consuming steps in the network stack, which are unnecessary for the fuzzing.

To reduce this overhead, we propose using a simulated socket instead of sending inputs through the network stack. By taking this approach, we do not have to use emulation or modify the source code of the SUT, and it is faster. We accomplish this by using a modified version of the simulated socket library called **preeny**, which communicates with the SUT via the standard I/O. However, we found that **preeny** does not work out of the box. We addressed this issue by modifying **preeny** and introducing a new simulated socket library named Desock+.

3.1   Network Protocol Fuzzing Using Desock+

Desock+ can be used by the SUT instead of the standard POSIX library to fuzz network protocols more efficiently. The overview of a fuzzer working with Desock+ is shown in Fig. 1. In this case, the fuzzer is the slightly modified AFLNet which sends and receives input messages through standard I/O instead of network sockets. As we can see, the SUT is intact, and the only thing that is changed is the underlying socket library, which the SUT would load instead of the real socket library. Figure 2 shows AFLNet fuzzing using Desock+ as a simulated socket-library.

---

[2] This is just an estimation based on our experience with out-process fuzzing using AFL fuzzer.

[3] One round of fuzzing consists of sending one input to the SUT to test it, and refreshing the SUT for the next input.

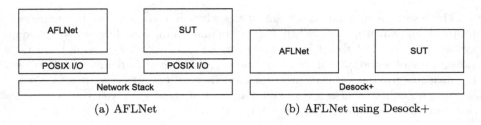

(a) AFLNet   (b) AFLNet using Desock+

Fig. 1. Removing network communication overhead using Desock+.

The difference between **preeny** and Desock+ is that **preeny** can not support specific socket-related system-calls and arguments. However, by modifying **preeny**, we have provided Desock+, which can handle any types of SUT that use POSIX network I/O. The arguments in socket-related system-calls that Desock+ supports are listed in Table 1. The advantage of Desock+ over **preeny** is that it can also support SUTs that:

– Contain socket system-calls using blocking or non-blocking network I/O.
– Receive the input messages as datagram, streams, sequenced, connection-less, and raw.
– Use **connect** and **accept4** system-calls.

The modifications made to **preeny** to make Desock+ are implemented in the **socket** system-call, which is responsible for creating the socket file descriptor. We have added a function named **setup**, which modifies the socket file descriptor by considering different arguments provided to the **socket** system-call. Based on the arguments passed to the **socket** system-call, Desock+ uses **fcntl** and **setsockopt** to set different arguments on the socket file descriptor. This way, other socket-related system-calls can use this socket file descriptor without resulting in an error. In **preeny**, these arguments are ignored while creating the socket file descriptor, resulting in an error when other socket-related system-calls try to use different arguments inside the SUT.

Desock+ is only helpful for fuzzing network protocols, whereas **preeny** is also intended to be used for SUT interaction with other services on the system or using a loopback address[4]. To be able to set different arguments on the socket file descriptor, Desock+ avoids assigning an IP address and port number to the socket file descriptor (setting arguments on a simulated file descriptor with assigned IP and port results in an EINVAL error). However, since **preeny** is meant to be used for many other purposes, this can break its functionality. Therefore, we made Desock+ a separate library for use by fuzzers.

---

[4] A loopback address is a unique IP address, that is used to refer to the localhost.

Table 1. Socket-related POSIX system-calls and their arguments supported by Desock+.

System-Call	Arguments	System-Call	Arguments
socket()	AF_LOCAL		SOCK_NONBLOCK
	AF_INET	connect3()	SOCK_CLOEXEC
	AF_INET6		SOCK_SEQPACKET
	SOCK_STREAM		SOCK_DGRAM
	SOCK_DGRAM		SOCK_STREAM
	SOCK_SEQPACKET		SOCK_NONBLOCK
	SOCK_RAW	dup3()	SOCK_CLOEXEC
	SOCK_RDM	recv()	MSG_CMSG_CLOEXEC
	SOCK_PACKET	recvfrom()	SCM_RIGHTS
accept4()	SOCK_NONBLOCK	recvmsg()	MSG_DONTWAIT
	SOCK_CLOEXEC		MSG_ERRQUEUE
	SOCK_SEQPACKET	send()	SOCK_STREAM
	SOCK_STREAM	sendto()	SOCK_SEQPACKET
bind()	AF_INET	sendmsg()	MSG_CONFIRM
	AF_INET6		MSG_DONTWAIT

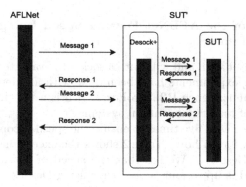

Fig. 2. AFLNet fuzzing using Desock+, which is a simulated socket library.

3.2 Extending Desock+

Although Desock+ supports many SUTs for fuzzing network protocols, there are corner-case SUTs that it does not support, because of system-calls that are not simulated. To address this issue, we must identify which system-calls and their input arguments are causing the errors (EAGAIN, EBADF, etc.) and simulate them correctly. However, manually identifying these error-prone system-calls (for example, epoll or select) and their arguments among thousands of system-calls is not possible.

Table 2. Speed in message per second, of AFLNet with and without Desock+ on ProFuzzBench [12].

SUT	AFLNet	AFLNet with Desock+	Speed up
lightFTP	12	49	+308%
dnsmasq	15	19	+26%
live555	14	29	+107%
dcmqrscp	17	21	+23%
tinydtls	12	19	+58%

To solve this problem, we have developed an automated system-call filtering module. As shown in Fig. 3, when the fuzzer starts fuzzing the SUT, the system-call filtering module begins monitoring the SUT by using the Ptrace to intercept system-calls between the operating system and the SUT. The module then filters the socket-related system-calls and looks for the ones that have returned -1 as an error. Then, it extracts the system-call arguments using GDB debugger. The error-prone system-calls and their arguments are then saved as the output of this module. Therefore, the user of Desock+ can simulate these system-calls into Desock+ to support different SUTs.

3.3 Evaluation of the AFLNet Fuzzing Speed Using Desock+ on ProFuzzBench

We have used AFLNet with and without Desock+ to evaluate the fuzzing speed. Both sets of fuzzing experiments have been done with an identical setup on the five SUTs from ProFuzzBench [12]. ProFuzzBench is a benchmark that is used for the evaluation of fuzzers for stateful systems.

We ran our experiment five times to ensure the speed is consistent. Each time the fuzzing went on for an hour. Table 2 shows the execution speed of AFLNet with and without Desock+. We see that the speed of fuzzing traces of input messages per second is up to four times faster using Desock+.

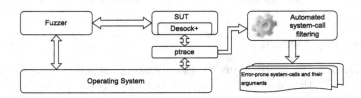

Fig. 3. Extracting the error-prone POSIX system-calls and their arguments.

4   Green-Fuzz Fuzzer

Monitoring the execution of AFLNet reveals that specific system-calls and context-switches between the fuzzer and SUT impose much overhead in the fuzzing process. In this section, we present Green-Fuzz, a new fuzzer to reduce the number of `sendto`, `setsockopt`, `recvfrom` system-calls, and also the context-switches between the fuzzer and SUT in the fuzzing process.

As seen in Sect. 2, current fuzzers for network protocols consider a trace of input messages $T =< m_1, m_2, ..., m_n >$, and send the input message m_n one by one to fuzz the SUT. By using the Green-Fuzz, we do not send input messages one by one but as a trace. We do this because when the fuzzer sends input messages one by one, the fuzzer has to call two (or more) system-calls for each input message and call the same number of system-calls to receive the respective response from the SUT. However, by sending the entire trace of input messages in one go, the number of system-calls is reduced: for a trace of input messages T with n messages, we only have the overhead once, instead of n times. This approach can be applied to any network protocol fuzzer, assuming the fuzzer can decide on the input trace in advance. In our case, we applied it to AFLNet. In Fig. 4, we can see how Green-Fuzz has reduced this overhead compared to AFLNet.

4.1   Design

To apply our approach to AFLNet, we had to make a slight change to it. We call the new fuzzer Green-Fuzz, which sends a trace of the input messages to the SUT in one go. For this purpose, we implemented another simulated socket library named Fast-desock+. Fast-desock+ intercepts and buffers the trace of input messages T sent by Green-Fuzz fuzzer. After that, it takes each message m_n from trace T and sends it to the SUT. Consequently, the SUT finishes processing and sends back a response r_j, which Fast-desock+ intercept and save into a response buffer.

When Fast-desock+ has sent all input messages and saved all the respective responses into the buffer, it sends the responses back to Green-Fuzz in one go. These responses are a list of responses. Because an individual input message m_n can produce several responses or none. We send the list of responses as a list of tuples to the Green-Fuzz. This list of tuples would be in the form of $\{(n, r) | r \in R = \{r_1, ..., r_j\}\}$, where n is the index of the input message and r is the respective response to input message m_n. This way, the Green-Fuzz can relate the input messages and their respective response (or responses).

The difference between Fast-desock+ and Desock+ is that Fast-desock+ also hooks `sendto`, `recvfrom`, and `setsockopt` to intercept and buffer trace of input messages and responses between the fuzzer and SUT.

Figure 5-a shows the AFLNet interaction with the SUT, where the fuzzer sends each input message one by one. Figure 5-b shows the Green-Fuzz interaction with the SUT, which sends a trace of the input messages to the SUT in one go.

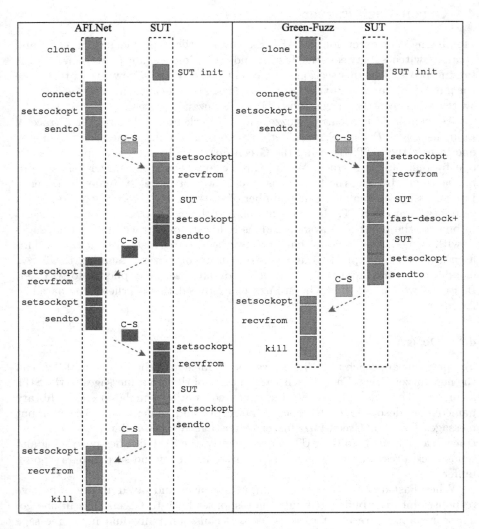

Fig. 4. Comparison of fuzzing overheads in AFLNet (left) and Green-Fuzz (right). Green-Fuzz avoids the overheads colored in red; as shown in Table 3, this can be from 0% to 80%. C-S stands for a context-switch, shown in orange. The time spent by SUT in processing input is shown in green and other system-calls are shown in blue. (Color figure online)

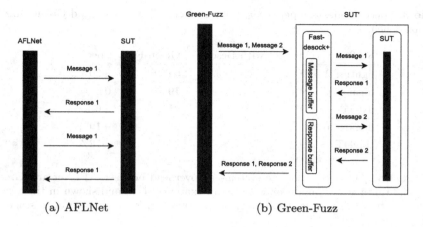

(a) AFLNet　　　　　　　　(b) Green-Fuzz

Fig. 5. Sending a trace of input messages in AFLNet (a) vs Green-Fuzz (b). By sending all messages/entire trace in one go, unlike one by one in AFLNet, we save overhead from context switches and system-calls.(Color figure online)

4.2 Evaluation of Green-Fuzz on ProFuzzBench

To show the benefits of Green-Fuzz, in this section, we evaluate it on Pro-FuzzBench [12]. After that, we compare the absolute fuzzing overhead and its difference between AFLNet using Desock+ and Green-Fuzz.

Table 3 shows the execution speed of Green-Fuzz compared to the AFLNet using Desock+. Five of the ten SUTs included in ProFuzzBench use the socket options our tool supports. We fuzzed the SUTs for an hour and repeated our experiment to ensure the numbers are reliable. The results show that the trace of input messages fuzzed per second is higher when using Green-Fuzz than AFLNet using Desock+, but not that much.

We used ptrace to monitor different system-calls that are a source of the overhead while fuzzing. Table 4 shows the absolute overhead difference, where we can see Green-Fuzz decreases overhead in `recvfrom`, `sendto`, `setsockopt`, and `connect` system-calls. There is no change in overhead regarding the `kill` and `clone` system-calls because both AFLNet and Green-Fuzz are out-process fuzzers and have to use these system-calls for each trace of input messages.

4.3 Comparison with In-Process Fuzzing

Fuzzers are broadly classified into out-process and in-process fuzzers. Like AFLNet [13], out-process fuzzing involves forking, (i.e., duplicating a process by calling `clone` system-call) and killing, (i.e., terminating a process by calling `kill` system-call) the SUT for each input. Although this approach imposes overhead, it does not require patching or modification of the SUT's source code. Moreover, out-process fuzzing can be applied to closed-source programs, which is not feasible using in-process fuzzing.

Table 3. Speed in message per second, of AFLNet with Desock+ and Green-Fuzz on ProFuzzBench.

SUT	AFLNet with Desock+	Green-Fuzz	Speed up
lightFTP	49	64	+30%
dnsmasq	19	19	0%
live555	29	31	+6%
dcmqrscp	21	25	+19%
tinyDTLS	19	34	+78%

Table 4. Comparison of absolute system-call overhead between AFLNet and Green-Fuzz. The times are in milliseconds (from an example SUT) and shown in the format of $n \times m \times time$ where n is the number of traces and m is the number of messages in one trace.

System-call	AFLNet	Green-Fuzz	Overhead Difference
`clone`	$n \times 6.5$	$n \times 6.5$	0%
`kill`	$n \times 8.7$	$n \times 8.7$	0%
`recvfrom`	$n \times m \times 1.2$	$n \times 1.2$	−80%
`sendto`	$n \times m \times 1.3$	$n \times 1.3$	−80%
`setsockopt`	$n \times m \times 0.1$	$n \times 0.1$	−80%
`connect`	$n \times 11$	$n \times 4$	−63%

In contrast, for in-process fuzzing [1,7], we manually modify the SUT so that instead of processing a single input, it can process multiple. To do this, we introduce a loop, where after processing one input message, we jump back to the program point where it begins processing an input message. This method avoids frequent forking, initialization, and killing of the SUT, resulting in a much faster fuzzing speed. In-process fuzzing is also known as in-memory fuzzing in some publications [8,15].

In this section, we compare the speed of sending input message traces per second between Green-Fuzz (out-process fuzzer) and in-process fuzzers [1,7]. For this purpose, we make a hypothetical comparison based on our experiment in Sect. 3.2 and the expected overheads that in-process fuzzing can save. First, we discuss the overhead difference between the two types of fuzzers. After that, we present our comparison based on previous experiments (see Sect. 3.2) and our expectations from the in-process fuzzing overheads. Figure 6 shows the fuzzing overhead occurring while doing out-process and in-process fuzzing for a network protocol.

Table 5 shows the comparison between the Green-Fuzz (out-process fuzzer) and an in-process fuzzer. Since in-process fuzzing only fork and kills the SUT once, it does not have overheads regarding `clone` and `kill` system-calls. Furthermore, the input messages are mutated inside the SUT (in-memory) and

Table 5. comparison of Green-Fuzz and in-process fuzzing based on different overheads for fuzzing n trace of m input messages. The times are in milliseconds (from an example SUT) and shown in the format of $n \times m \times time$.

Source of Overhead	Green-Fuzz	In-process Fuzzer	Overhead Difference
`clone`	$n \times 6.5$	6.5	$\approx -100\%$
`kill`	$n \times 8.7$	8.7	$\approx -100\%$
`recvfrom`	$n \times m \times 1.2$	0	-100%
`sendto`	$n \times m \times 1.3$	0	-100%
`setsockopt`	$n \times m \times 0.2$	0	-100%
`connect`	$n \times 11$	0	-100%
Context-switching	$n \times m \times 0.8$	2×0.8	$\approx -100\%$
SUT initialization	$n \times 5.1$	5.1	$\approx -100\%$

not sent through simulated sockets, so it does not have overhead regarding `recvfrom`, `sendto`, `setsockopt` and `connect` system-calls. There is also the context-switching overhead between the fuzzer and SUT, which the in-process fuzzer saves. Finally, the overhead of SUT initialization differs between the two types of fuzzing. Because in-process fuzzing patches the start of the fuzzing loop right after the initialization of the SUT and right before the processing of a new input. However, the out-process fuzzing has to go through the SUT initialization each time it forks the SUT to send a new input.

Green-Fuzz, as an out-process fuzzer, does not require changing the program's source code and can also be applied to closed-source SUT. Overall, there is a trade-off between the fuzzing speed and modifying the source code of the SUT. For SUTs in which the time of SUT execution (the green part in Fig. 6) is very high, using in-process fuzzing does not save much overhead relatively. Using in-process fuzzing also introduces the risk of missing some parts of the SUT behavior because we have to introduce a loop inside the SUT, where only the code inside that loop would be exercised. Finally, since Green-Fuzz avoids any out-process fuzzing overhead in network protocol fuzzing possible, it is the most efficient out-process fuzzer that we could have for network protocol implementations.

5   Related Work

Using grey-box fuzzing solutions to test network services has become a popular research topic. One example is Peach* [18], which combined code coverage feedback with the original Peach [19] fuzzer to test Industrial Control Systems (ICS) protocols. It collected code coverage information during fuzzing and used Peach's capabilities to generate more effective test cases.

IoTHunter [20] applied grey-box fuzzing for network services in IoT devices. It used code coverage to guide the fuzzing process and implemented a multi-stage testing approach based on protocol state feedback.

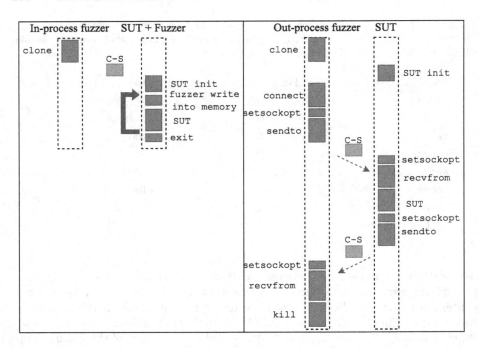

Fig. 6. In-process fuzzer (left) and out-process fuzzer (right) overheads while fuzzing network protocols. The blue colors are system-call overhead, and the green ones are the time spent by the SUT in processing input message. C-S stands for context-switching between the fuzzer and the SUT, shown in orange. (Color figure online)

AFLNet [13] is a grey-box fuzzer for protocol implementations which uses state feedback to guide fuzzing. It acts as a client and replayed different variations of the original message sequence sent to the server. It kept the variations that increased code or state space coverage effectively.

StateAFL [21] is a variation of AFLnet that utilizes a memory state to represent the service state. It instrumented the target server during compilation and determined the current protocol state at runtime. It gradually built a protocol state machine to guide the fuzzing process.

5.1   Related Work with Desock+

Zeng et al. [17] also made a simulated socket library, named Desockmulti, to avoid network communication overhead when fuzzing network protocols. However, compared to Desock+, Desockmulti does not support connect and accept4 system-calls, which limits its applicability.

Maier et al. [11] introduced the Fuzzer in the Middle (FitM) for fuzzing network protocols. Instead of using a simulated socket library, FitM intercepts the emulated system-calls inside the QEMU emulator and sends the input messages to the SUT without the network communication overhead. Because FitM has emulation overhead, it is slower than our approach. Compared to our approach, FitM has the capability to fuzz both the client and server of a network protocol as the SUT.

There are also ad-hoc approaches [4,5,25] where by manually modifying the SUT, the fuzzer would send the input messages to the SUT without network communication. These approaches change the source code of SUT to read the inputs from a file or argument variables to avoid network communication. These approaches require manual effort for each SUT, which is not ideal, but are more stable because of SUT specific fuzzing harnesses that are built per SUT.

5.2   Related Work with Green-Fuzz

Nyx-Net [14] utilizes hypervisor-based snapshot fuzzing incorporated with the emulation of network functionality to handle network traffic. Nyx-Net uses a customized kernel module, a modified version of QEMU and KVM, and a custom VM configuration where the target applications are executed. Nyx-Net also contains a custom networking layer miming certain POSIX network functionalities, which currently needs more support for complicated network targets. In contrast, Green-Fuzz adopts a user-mode approach that avoids complexity. Green-Fuzz is also an orthogonal approach to be added on top of Nyx-Net, to speed up the fuzzing.

In-process (a.k.a in-memory) fuzzing [1,7] is an approach where a fuzzer does not restart or fork the SUT for each trace of input messages, and the fuzzing is done within the same process. The input values are mutated inside the memory. Therefore, it also avoids network communication overhead. However, these methods involve manual work to modify a piece of code as the SUT and specifying the exact position of variables inside the memory. Using a simulated socket library, Green-Fuzz does not require these manual steps. However, in-process fuzzing is faster (around 200 to 300 times in our experiments) than our approach because it has less fuzzing overhead. Another issue of in-process fuzzing is that usually it can not test the whole system, because of the fuzzing loop that is defined for the harness.

6   Limitations and Future Work

Currently, Desock+ only works with the SUTs using system-calls and their arguments shown in Table 1. Some SUTs use other socket options. For example, input arguments for `epoll` system-call must be simulated in Desock+ to work correctly if the SUT is using this system-call. Because part of Green-Fuzz is based on Fast-desock+, these limitations also apply to Green-Fuzz. Since the non-simulated options in Desock+ and Fast-desock+ can be complex. As our future work, we would like to complete these engineering efforts and use Green-Fuzz to fuzz network protocols such as OPC-UA [23] and Modbus [24] protocols. To Fuzz protocols that require a handshake, the Green-Fuzz needs a minor modification to do the handshake before sending the whole trace in one go.

Desock+ and Green-Fuzz are general solutions to fuzzers for stateful systems, so we plan to apply them to other fuzzers for stateful systems. In this paper, we applied our improvements to AFLNet. However, any fuzzer that sends the inputs to a network protocol via network sockets or sends the input messages from a trace of messages can be upgraded by using our solutions, except if it needs feedback after sending each input message, as [10] does. For example, SGPFuzzer [16] and Nyx-net [14] are network protocol fuzzers that can be upgraded by Green-Fuzz, to have an efficient fuzzer. The modification for applying Green-Fuzz to other fuzzers is relatively simple. The user has to modify the harness to send and receive the messages in a trace format to the SUT.

7 Conclusion

Fuzzing is an effective technique for identifying bugs and security vulnerabilities in software systems. However, it's application to network protocols has been challenging because of low fuzzing throughput.

This work proposes a solution to improve the efficiency of network protocol fuzzing by introducing a simulated socket library, Desock+, that enables efficient fuzzing without modifying the source code of the SUT. The study also presents Green-Fuzz, a novel approach that utilizes a trace-based input message-sending method to increase efficiency further. Green-Fuzz can be easily applied to other fuzzers for stateful systems to gain more performance.

Our evaluation shows that the proposed method outperforms AFLNet by being up to four times faster and can be applied to a broader range of SUTs. Green-Fuzz removes as much overhead as possible without resorting to in-process fuzzing, which requires non-trivial manual changes to the SUT and introduces the risk of missing parts of the SUT behavior (as discussed in Sect. 3.3). Therefore, we can achieve this maximum performance gain with a generic solution that works for any network protocol. While it substantially improves out-process fuzzing, we may still want to do the extra work to move to in-process fuzzing.

References

1. Libfuzzer: A library for coverage-guided fuzz testing (2023). https://llvm.org/docs/LibFuzzer.html. Retrieved 2 Feb 2023
2. Zardus: preeny (2023). https://github.com/zardus/preeny. Retrieved 6 Jan 2023
3. Google: ClusterFuzz Trophies (2022). https://google.github.io/clusterfuzz/#trophies. Retrieved 12 Feb 2023
4. Tuveri, N.: Fuzzing open-SSL (2021). https://github.com/openssl/openssl/blob/master/fuzz/README.md. Retrieved 6 Feb 2023
5. Low, W.C.Y.: Dissecting Microsoft IMAP Client Protocol (2022). https://www.fortinet.com/blog/threat-research/analyzing-microsoft-imap-client-protocol. Retrieved 6 Feb 2023
6. Aschermann, C., Schumilo, S., Abbasi, A., Holz, T.: Ijon: exploring deep state spaces via fuzzing. In: 2020 IEEE Symposium on Security and Privacy (SP), pp. 1597–1612. IEEE (2020)

7. Ba, J., Böhme, M., Mirzamomen, Z., Roychoudhury, A.: Stateful greybox fuzzing. In: 31st USENIX Security Symposium (USENIX Security 22), pp. 3255–3272 (2022)

8. Cui, B., Wang, F., Hao, Y., Chen, X.: WhirlingFuzzwork: a taint-analysis-based API in-memory fuzzing framework. Soft. Comput. **21**, 3401–3414 (2017)

9. Daniele, C., Andarzian, S.B., Poll, E.: Fuzzers for stateful systems: survey and research directions (2023). arXiv preprint arXiv:2301.02490

10. Isberner, M., Howar, F., Steffen, B.: The TTT algorithm: a redundancy-free approach to active automata learning. In: Bonakdarpour, B., Smolka, S.A. (eds.) RV 2014. LNCS, vol. 8734, pp. 307–322. Springer, Cham (2014). https://doi.org/10. 1007/978-3-319-11164-3_26

11. Maier, D., Bittner, O., Munier, M., Beier, J.: FitM: binary-only coverage-guided fuzzing for stateful network protocols. In: Workshop on Binary Analysis Research (BAR), vol. 2022 (2022)

12. Natella, R., Pham, V.-T.: Profuzzbench: a benchmark for stateful protocol fuzzing. In: Proceedings of the 30th ACM SIGSOFT international symposium on software testing and analysis, pp. 662–665 (2021)

13. Pham, V.-T., Böhme, M., Roychoudhury, A.: AFLNet: a greybox fuzzer for network protocols. In: 2020 IEEE 13th International Conference on Software Testing, Validation and Verification (ICST), pp. 460–465. IEEE (2020)

14. Schumilo, S., Aschermann, C., Jemmett, A., Abbasi, A., Holz, T.: Nyx-net: network fuzzing with incremental snapshots. In: Proceedings of the Seventeenth European Conference on Computer Systems, pp. 166–180 (2022)

15. Sutton, M., Greene, A., Amini, P.: Fuzzing: Brute Force Vulnerability Discovery. Pearson Education, London (2007)

16. Yu, Y., Chen, Z., Gan, S., Wang, X.: SGPFuzzer: a state-driven smart graybox protocol fuzzer for network protocol implementations. IEEE Access **8**, 198668–198678 (2020)

17. Zeng, Y., et al.: Multifuzz: a coverage-based multiparty-protocol Fuzzer for IoT publish/subscribe protocols. Sensors **20**(18), 5194 (2020)

18. Luo, Z., Zuo, F., Shen, Y., Jiao, X., Chang, W., Jiang, Y.: ICS protocol fuzzing: coverage guided packet crack and generation. In: 2020 57th ACM/IEEE Design Automation Conference (DAC), pp. 1–6. IEEE (2020)

19. Mozilla Security: Peach (2021). https://github.com/MozillaSecurity/peach. Retrieved 2 Feb 2023

20. Yu, B., Wang, P., Yue, T., Tang, Y.: Poster: fuzzing IoT firmware via multi-stage message generation. In: Proceedings of the 2019 ACM SIGSAC Conference on Computer and Communications Security (CCS 2019), pp. 2525–2527 (2019)

21. Natella, R.: StateAFL: Greybox fuzzing for stateful network servers. Empir. Softw. Eng. **27**(7) (2022)

22. Fioraldi, A., Maier, D., Eißfeldt, H., Heuse, M.: AFL++: combining incremental steps of fuzzing research. In: 14th USENIX Workshop on Offensive Technologies (WOOT 20) (2020)

23. The OPC foundation 2023: The OPC Unified Architecture (UA) (2023). https:// opcfoundation.org/about/opc-technologies/opc-ua/. Retrieved 2 Apr 2023

24. Modbus Organization: Modbus data communications protocol (2023). https:// modbus.org/. Retrieved 2 Apr 2023

25. Cheremushkin, T.: OPC UA security analysis 2023. Technical report, Kaspersky (2023). https://ics-cert.kaspersky.com/publications/reports/2018/05/10/opc-ua-security-analysis/. Retrieved 14 Apr 2023

26. Serebryany, K.: OSS-Fuzz-Google's continuous fuzzing service for open source software. In: USENIX 2017 (2017)
27. Klooster, T., Turkmen, F., Broenink, G., Hove, R.T., Böhme, M.: Continuous fuzzing: a study of the effectiveness and scalability of fuzzing in CI/CD pipelines. In: 2023 IEEE/ACM International Workshop on Search-Based and Fuzz Testing (SBFT), pp. 25–32. IEEE (2023)

Unmasking of Maskware: Detection and Prevention of Next-Generation Mobile Crypto-Ransomware

Farnood Faghihi[1]([✉]), Mohammad Zulkernine[2], and Steven Ding[2]

[1] Security Compass, Toronto, Canada
ffaghihi@securitycompass.com
[2] Queen's University, Kingston, Canada

Abstract. Malware is advancing at a rapid pace, and it is becoming more stealthy, resilient, and aware of the existing detection methods. A similar trend in mobile crypto-ransomware can be expected soon. Thus, it is crucial to investigate the problem of new variants of mobile crypto-ransomware that may emerge in the near future. Hence, this work investigates how next-generation advanced mobile crypto-ransomware can evade the existing state-of-the-art detection metrics and how it is possible to neutralize this threat. After reviewing the current data-centric crypto-ransomware detection metrics, we investigate the possibility of evading them. We demonstrate the threat posed by next-generation mobile crypto-ransomware by implementing a crypto-ransomware targeted for the Android operating system called Maskware. Maskware uses partial encryption and mimics the behavior of legitimate applications in terms of data manipulation. We evaluate the effectiveness of common crypto-ransomware detection metrics, including entropy, data transformation, and file structure, in the detection of Maskware. We demonstrate that such metrics are ineffective in detecting Maskware. Hence, this article suggests using more efficient and effective methods to combat such malware and proposes a novel solution. The evaluation results of the proposed solution demonstrate that it can effectively detect Maskware and protect users' data.

Keywords: Crypto-ransomware · Malware detection · User data protection

1 Introduction

The threat posed by mobile ransomware is increasing at a rapid pace. In the last year, more than 4.2 million mobile users have suffered ransomware attacks on their phones in the United States [26]. In just 30 days, more than 900 thousand Android phones were hit by ScarePackage mobile ransomware [24]. US Treasury has reported that it has tied $5.2 billion in cryptocurrency transactions to ransomware payments [10], and the average ransom payment has increased from

---

F. Faghihi—This work was carried out while the first author was a PhD candidate at Queen's University.

M. Mosbah et al. (Eds.): FPS 2023, LNCS 14551, pp. 269–284, 2024.
https://doi.org/10.1007/978-3-031-57537-2_17

around ten thousand dollars in 2018 to more than a hundred thousand dollars in 2020, according to the Canadian Center for Cyber Security [4]. These alarming numbers call for more attention to the critical issue of ransomware and how it can affect mobile devices.

Along with the advancements in malware detection techniques [1,28], crypto-ransomware is also advancing and becoming more stealthy. For instance, recent crypto-ransomware has demonstrated the abuse of cutting-edge obfuscation techniques [27], The Onion Router (TOR) network [12], exploit kits [18], partial encryption [16], and public-key cryptography [15]. Some researchers have proposed data-centric (focusing on user's data) defense techniques to combat crypto-ransomware [5,6,8,9,17,23], and some works have explored various techniques that next-generation crypto-ransomware can use to evade the existing data-centric methods [19]. However, none of the existing works has explored next-generation mobile crypto-ransomware, nor has any work proposed and implemented a solution to detect and neutralize next-generation crypto-ransomware.

To close this gap, in this paper, we first demonstrate the vulnerability of the existing data-centric crypto-ransomware detection metrics. We show that crypto-ransomware can evade data-centric detection metrics by leaving a minimum footprint and imitating the behavior of legitimate applications in terms of data manipulation. Afterwards, we illustrate the vulnerability of the existing techniques by implementing a next-generation mobile crypto-ransomware, called Maskware. We demonstrate that the common data-centric crypto-ransomware detection metrics, including entropy, data transformation, and file structure, can be evaded by Maskware using a custom partial encryption mechanism. Finally, this paper proposes a novel solution based on the entropy of the changes made to user data. We evaluate the proposed solution and show that it can effectively detect Maskware.

In summary, the major contributions of this paper can be highlighted as follows:

- This article investigates the critical threat of advanced next-generation mobile crypto-ransomware, which is aware of the existing data-centric methods and mimics the data manipulation patterns of legitimate applications to prevent detection.
- Through experiments, we demonstrate that it is possible to evade common data-centric metrics such as file entropy, structure, and data transformation using a custom partial encryption technique.
- We are the first to propose and implement a solution for detecting crypto-ransomware that uses partial encryption. We show that the proposed solution can outperform the existing methods in detecting crypto-ransomware.

The rest of this paper is organized as follows. Section 2 reviews some of the most recent and comprehensive related works. We discuss the architecture of Maskware and the attack scenario in Sect. 3. In Sect. 4, we perform some experiments to evaluate the resiliency of Maskware against data-centric crypto-ransomware detection techniques. Section 5 proposes a potential solution for detection and mitigation of Maskware and evaluates its effectiveness. Section 6 concludes this paper and discusses some of its limitations.

2   Related Work

This section reviews the most related and recent works in this area. We start this section by discussing different types of crypto-ransomware detection methods. Afterwards, we continue our discussion by focusing on data-centric crypto-ransomware detection methods and discuss some of the most important works in this domain.

2.1   Categories of Ransomware Detection Methods

From one perspective, ransomware detection methods can be grouped into three categories [9]: programmatic, data-centric, or user-centric. Programmatic approaches usually focus on features of the code using static or dynamic analysis. User-centric approaches rely on user education and training to mitigate crypto-ransomware. Data-centric approaches can better suit the problem of ransomware since they focus on users' data, and they have gained more popularity in the past few years. This is due to the fact that these approaches do not rely on the user's awareness or the application's code. Thus, data-centric approaches are resilient against common static and dynamic analysis evasion approaches. Furthermore, they have been shown to outperform most other approaches in terms of detection rate and file loss [3].

2.2   Data-Centric Crypto-Ransomware Detection Methods

The existing data-centric approaches have employed various features for the detection of crypto-ransomware. Faghihi et al. [9] propose an Android ransomware detection and mitigation method. They monitor the changes made to the user's data and look for anomalies. They consider creating high-entropy files that do not have a known structure (file type) as anomalies. In case an application creates a significant amount of anomalous data, they warn the user about possible ransomware detection. Chen et al. [5] propose a real-time mobile crypto-ransomware detection method based on file entropy and by analyzing the user interface widgets of applications. They monitor entropy changes of user files, and in case the entropy of a file reaches the upper bound (8), they consider it an encrypted file. The application modifying the file is considered to be suspicious. To decrease false positives, they analyze the user interface of suspicious applications and determine if the encryption behaviors are with the user's consent or not.

Scaife et al. [23] propose a ransomware detection method based on three primary metrics. These metrics include file type change, similarity measurement, and Shanon entropy. They monitor changes made to user files, and in case they observe significant changes in the mentioned metrics, they report the detection of crypto-ransomware. Similarly, Davies et al. [8] propose a ransomware detection method calculating the entropy of the first few bytes of the file's header. They show that fully encrypted files can be differentiated from unencrypted files based on the entropy values of file headers. McIntosh et al. [19] suggest that

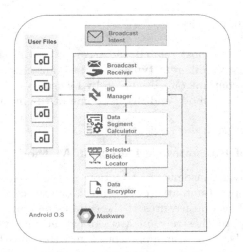

Fig. 1. Architecture of Maskware

crypto-ransomware detection methods can be improved by considering the file's structure. May et al. [17] propose a ransomware detection method based on file life-cycle and complex file events. They monitor file content types using Apache Tika, and in case the type of file is changed during modifications, they flag this change as a crypto-ransomware attack. McIntosh et al. [20] design and implement a situation-aware access control framework to combat crypto-ransomware. They claim that the proposed framework can preserve file content integrity by enforcing that files written to the file system should have consistent internal file structures with the declared file types. They evaluate their proposed framework against some ransomware applications and report that the proposed method can protect users against file corruption and ransomware attacks.

3   Threat Model

To illustrate the threat model, we implement a mobile crypto-ransomware called Maskware. Maskware uses partial encryption and imitates legitimate applications' behavior in terms of data manipulation to evade data-centric crypto-ransomware detection methods. Figure 1 shows an overview of Maskware and its components. The following subsections discuss each component in more detail.

3.1   Broadcast Receiver

Intents serve as messaging objects that facilitate the exchange of information between the OS and applications as well as among applications. Broadcast intents are a special class of intents that are dispatched by the Android OS in response to specific events, such as device boot-up or screen locking, and are sent to all registered applications monitoring these events. Maskware's Broadcast Receiver component listens for the phone unlock event, launching when the user unlocks their device. This design ensures that with each device unlock, Maskware encrypts a single file, mimicking the resource usage of legitimate applications and evading detection methods reliant on resource consumption within short time windows.

3.2   I/O Manager

The I/O manager is responsible for all the interactions between the application and device storage. This component reads the contents of the files and overwrites the original files with (partially) encrypted data. Additionally, it keeps track of the files that have been encrypted previously to prevent files from being encrypted twice.

3.3   Data Segment Calculator

This component receives the contents of the files from the I/O Manager, and determines the data section of the file that can be safely encrypted without damaging the structure of the file. Different types of files have different signatures. These signatures are usually stored as a series of bytes at the beginning of the files. The signatures (also referred to as magic numbers or magic bytes) are particular to each file type, and help programs determine the type of the file and data it contains. The goal of Maskware is to manipulate the file's data but keep its structure (signature) intact. Thus, we keep the signatures of files intact by skipping the magic bytes and only manipulating the data section of user files. After determining the file's data section, this component passes the file's data section to the File Name Hash Calculator.

3.4   Selected Block Locator

This component is responsible for locating the block of data to be encrypted (Selected Block, or SB from here onward) within the file's Data Section (DS). The size of the block is calculated based on the Encryption Threshold. The Encryption Threshold value is a float number in the range 0–1, which specifies what proportion of the data section in the file will be encrypted. The higher the number, the bigger the portion of the file that Maskware will encrypt, and the malware can potentially deal more damage. However, a high number could reduce the stealthiness of Maskware and make it less resilient to detection. Assuming that the Selected Block Size is denoted by SBS, Data Section Size is denoted by DSS, and the Encryption Threshold is denoted by ET, the value of SBS can be calculated as follows:

$$SBS = DSS * ET \qquad (1)$$

After calculating the SBS, we take the following approach to randomize the location of the encryption in files. We calculate the location of the Selected

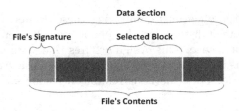

Fig. 2. An overview of the proposed partial encryption mechanism

Block based on the SHA256 hash value of the file's name. Assuming that $SHA(f)$ indicates the SHA256 hash value (number) of the name of the file f, and Start denotes the starting position of the Selected Block (SB) in that file's Data Section (DS), we can calculate the value of Start using the following formula:

$$Start = SHA(f) mod(DSS - SBS) \qquad (2)$$

To better illustrate how the Selected Block is located inside a file, let us consider the example demonstrated in Fig. 2. After reading the file's content's by the I/O Manager, we locate the Data Section of the file by skipping the file's signature using the Data Segment Calculator. Afterward, we locate the Selected Block (green block) within the file's Data Section. The Encryption Threshold determines the size of the Selected Block (SBS), and its location (Start) is determined using the hash value of the file's name as shown in Formula 2. After locating the Selected Block by calculating its start index (Start) and its size (SBS), we pass it to the Data Encryptor component.

3.5 Data Encryptor

The Data Encryptor component is responsible for the encryption of the Selected Block. Essentially, it receives the data to be encrypted (Selected Block) from the previous component and encrypts it using a secure encryption algorithm. To eliminate the need for network communications, we employ an offline (on-device) key generation algorithm. We employ the dynamically generated symmetric key encryption scheme [2].

In this scheme, the ransomware generates a random encryption key offline on the device. This key is used to encrypt user's data using symmetric key encryption algorithms such as the Advanced Encryption Standard (AES). To protect the encryption key from being exposed, the ransomware encrypts it using the public key of the (ransomware) developer and stores the resulting value on the device. In this way, only the attacker can recover the encryption key using the stored value on the device, as well as her/his private key. Assuming that the encryption key used by ransomware to encrypt user's data is denoted by s, malware developer's public key is indicated by P_{pub}, and its private key is denoted by P_{priv}, the encryption and decryption process can be summarized as follows:

Encryption:

$$s = \mathrm{random}()$$

$$\mathrm{data} \xrightarrow{\text{encryption using key } s} \{data\}_s$$

$$s \xrightarrow{\text{encryption using public key } P_{pub}} \{s\}_{P_{\mathrm{pub}}}$$

Decryption:

$$\{s\}_{P_{\mathrm{pub}}} \xrightarrow{\text{decryption using private key } P_{priv}} s$$

$$\{data\}_s \xrightarrow{\text{decryption using key } s} \mathrm{data}$$

After the Selected Block is encrypted using this component, it passes the encrypted data to the IO Manager to write the encrypted data into the file.

4   Resiliency Against Detection

This section evaluates the resiliency of Maskware to being detected. We start this section by discussing the dataset of user files. We proceed by evaluating the resiliency and stealthiness of Maskware against the common data-centric metrics used for the detection of crypto-ransomware.

4.1   User Files

In order to evaluate the performance of Maskware, we create a dataset of user files. The dataset contains various types of files and represents an average user's data on their smartphone. Since there exists no work that has explored the distribution of user's data on smartphones, we follow the distribution of user files on personal computers [11] to create this collection as suggested by Faghihi et al. [9]. Table 1 shows the distribution and types of the files. As shown in Table 1, the generated collection contains different file types. In total, it contains 5,100 files, with the majority of the files being documents (books, text files, spreadsheets, etc.) and media files (images, videos, audio files, etc.).

4.2   Entropy

Entropy can be defined as the average level of information inherent to a variable's outcome. In Information Theory, the entropy of data is usually measured in bits. A single byte of data can have 256 possible combinations of bits (2^8). Thus, by replacing ω with B_i, where B_i indicates a possible byte, the formula for calculating the entropy of information measured in bits can be rewritten as follows:

$$H(X) = -\sum_{i=0}^{255} P(B_i) log_2 P(B_i) \tag{3}$$

Table 1. Distribution of user files and their corresponding types

#	Category	Extensions	Percentage	#	Category	Extensions	Percentage
1	Applications	ini, msi	1.43	10	Internet	html, js	5.90
2	Audio	mp3, wav, wma	1.25	11	Presentation	ppt	1.72
3	CAD	dwf	3.98	12	Project	mpp	0.19
4	Code	f, php	7.47	13	Simulation	mat	1.21
5	Compressed	zip	2.45	14	Spreadsheet	xls	4.25
6	Data	csv, xml	4.5	15	Text	doc, pdf, ps, txt	20.58
7	Database	dbase3, sql, mdb	0.56	16	Unknown	unk	23.88
8	Graphics	pub	0.37	17	Video	avi, mp4	0.17
9	Image	gif, jpg, png, tif	20.03				

Encrypted data usually tend to have high entropy since the chance of the occurrence of different bytes is almost identical. Thus, many crypto-ransomware detection methods [5, 9, 13, 14, 21, 23] rely on this metric to detect crypto-ransomware.

We investigate the impact of the proposed partial encryption scheme on the entropy of user files by using various Encryption Thresholds to encrypt user data, following the approach mentioned in Sect. 3.5. Figure 3a shows the entropy of the original files. It can be observed that different types of files (and different kinds of data) have different characteristics in terms of entropy. For instance, certain types of files such as code (text data), database, and simulation have lower entropy. These types of files usually contain text and only a limited set of characters. Thus, their entropy does not reach the upper bound of 8. However, some other files, such as compressed zip files, images, and videos, contain high-entropy data. This is due to the fact that many of the modern encoding standards use image and video compression to decrease the size of the files [25]. Compression algorithms usually minimize data redundancy by re-encoding the data. Hence, compressed media files and compressed data naturally have higher entropy. Figure 3f shows the results of fully encrypting the files. The entropy of the data reaches its maximum limit for almost all types when files are fully encrypted. Taking a closer look at Fig. 3b to Fig. 3e, it can be observed that by gradually increasing the Encryption Threshold and encrypting bigger proportions of the files, the entropy of the data is increasing. However, since Maskware only encrypts a rather small proportion of the file's contents, the encrypted files cannot be distinguish easily from non-encrypted files. For instance, by setting the Encryption Threshold to 0.1 and encryption 10% of the data in the files, the entropy of many of the files still does not reach 6. Hence, Maskware can successfully evade many of the existing methods [9, 21, 29].

4.3 Similarity Digest Hash

This experiment evaluates the effectiveness of Maskware against crypto-ransomware detection methods that are based on data transformation. These

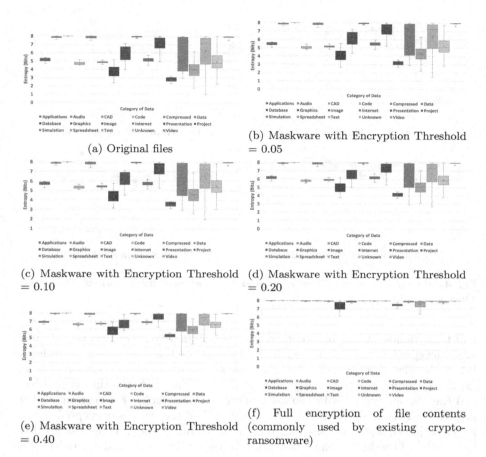

(a) Original files

(b) Maskware with Encryption Threshold = 0.05

(c) Maskware with Encryption Threshold = 0.10

(d) Maskware with Encryption Threshold = 0.20

(e) Maskware with Encryption Threshold = 0.40

(f) Full encryption of file contents (commonly used by existing crypto-ransomware)

Fig. 3. Entropy values of files encrypted by Maskware using various Encryption Thresholds versus full file encryption

methods measure the similarity of the data before and after modification. Normally, after the modifications of files by legitimate applications, the transformation in the data is not significant. For instance, after a user edits a document or an image on their device, only a certain proportion of the data is usually affected (added, deleted, modified). Thus, a significant transformation in the data can indicate crypto-ransomware behavior.

We use the popular sdhash tool [22] which is commonly used for the detection of crypto-ransomware based on data transformation [21,23]. The sdhash tool calculates data similarity scores, ranging from 0–100, indicating how certain it is that the two files have non-trivial amounts of commonality. Figure 4 shows the similarity score of encrypted files using various Encryption Thresholds. Since increasing the Encryption Threshold increases the proportion of the data that is being encrypted, the encrypted files will be less similar to the orig-

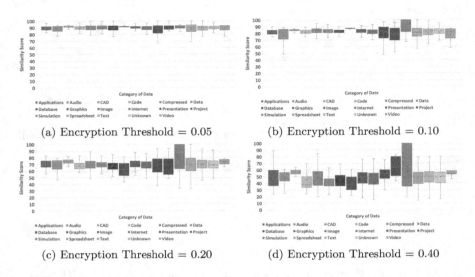

(a) Encryption Threshold = 0.05   (b) Encryption Threshold = 0.10

(c) Encryption Threshold = 0.20   (d) Encryption Threshold = 0.40

Fig. 4. Similarity scores of files encrypted by Maskware using various Encryption Thresholds

inal files. Hence, it can be observed that the similarity score between original and encrypted files decreases with the increase of the Encryption Threshold. While the files encrypted with an Encryption Threshold of 0.4 shown in Fig. 4d exhibit low similarity to the original files, the difference between the original files and the files encrypted with the low Encryption Threshold of 0.05 seems rather negligible. This is due to the fact that only 5% of the data is encrypted in the latter scenario, and thus, the files remain rather untouched. Thus, using a low Encryption Threshold ensures low transformation in the user data and avoids detection by methods that rely on data transformation.

4.4   File Structure

This experiment investigates the impact of the proposed partial encryption method on the structure of user files. We use popular file tool [7] to check the structure of files before and after encryption. Figure 5a shows an example bitmap (BMP) image on the user device. As illustrated by Fig. 5d, the file tool recognizes the image as a BMP file and extracts its features from the image. Figure 5b exhibits the result of the full encryption of the image (similar to how existing crypto-ransomware encrypt the data). Since all the bits are encrypted in this scenario, the file after encryption has no structure anymore. As a result, Fig. 5e, shows that the image is no more recognized by the file tool. Thus, this kind of encryption can be detected using tools that investigate the structure of the data. Figure 5c presents the same image encrypted by Maskware. In this scenario, only parts of the image are encrypted. Thus, the structure of the image is preserved. Figure 5f shows the result of the execution of the file tool on the same image. We

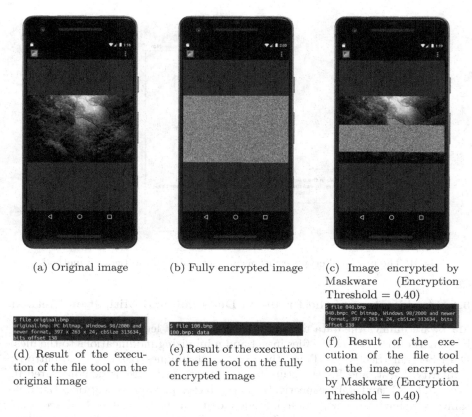

(a) Original image

(b) Fully encrypted image

(c) Image encrypted by Maskware (Encryption Threshold = 0.40)

(d) Result of the execution of the file tool on the original image

(e) Result of the execution of the file tool on the fully encrypted image

(f) Result of the execution of the file tool on the image encrypted by Maskware (Encryption Threshold = 0.40)

Fig. 5. The impact of Maskware's encryption versus full file encryption on the file structure

can observe that the file tool still recognizes the image. Thus, the partial encryption scenario used in Maskware can eliminate this metric and successfully evade the tools that detect crypto-ransomware based on the structure of the data. It is worth noting that the file tool can sometimes provide inaccurate results when detecting the file type. Hence, we advise readers to avoid solely relying on the file tool for encryption detection.

5   Proposed Detection Method

In this section, we design a method that can be used to detect and neutralize Maskware. We also perform experiments to evaluate the efficiency of the proposed defense mechanism and compare its detection performance with the performance of the traditional entropy metric.

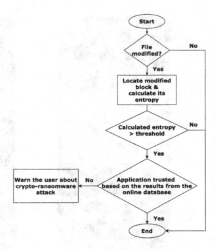

Fig. 6. The proposed crypto-ransomware detection and mitigation method

5.1 Architecture of the Proposed Detection and Mitigation Method

Maskware mimics the data manipulation behavior of legitimate applications by keeping the structure of the files intact and minimizing modifications to the files' Data Section (Sect. 3.4). Thus, the existing techniques based on file entropy, similarity digest, and file structure fail to detect Maskware as demonstrated in Sects. 4.2, 4.3, and 4.4, respectively. These techniques fail to capture the ransomware behavior because these methods focus on the whole files to detect ransomware (instead of focusing exclusively on the changes made by the applications). Since Maskware makes minimal modifications to the files, and the files look very similar before and after encryption (apart from the Selected Block), it can evade the existing detection methods. Hence, if we manage to isolate the changes made to user files and shift our focus on the modifications exclusively (rather than the whole file), we can detect Maskware's ransomware-like behavior.

Let us assume that $file_{old}$ denotes the contents of the old file (before modification), and $file_{new}$ denotes the contents of the new file (after modifications). $SelectedBlock$ denotes the modified file bytes, and Δ denotes the byte-wise operator returning the differences in two data streams. The entropy of the encrypted data can be calculated in the following way:

$$SelectedBlock = file_{new} \Delta file_{old}$$

$$Entropy_{EncryptedData} = Entropy_{SelectedBlock}$$

By solely focusing on the entropy of the modified data, it is possible to capture the partial encryption behavior of the proposed Maskware ransomware and neutralize it.

Figure 6 shows the proposed crypto-ransomware detection and mitigation approach. Every time a file is opened for modifications, a copy is created (before

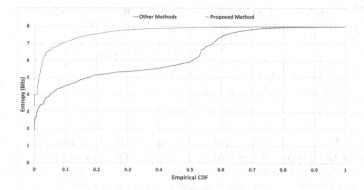

Fig. 7. CDF of entropy values calculated using the proposed method and techniques based on the entropy metric as used by others [5, 9, 21, 23]

the file has been modified). Once the file is closed and after the modifications are saved, the proposed technique compares the file contents with the previous copy and locates the changes made to the file. If the entropy of the modified bytes (after the modifications) exceeds the threshold, this modification is considered a potential ransomware behavior. In case the application making the modifications is not in the whitelist of benign applications, we warn the user and restore the file to its original state.

5.2 Detection Performance

This section evaluates the detection performance of the proposed approach and compares it with the existing metrics. We encrypt the files in the user files dataset using the proposed partial encryption method discussed in Sect. 3 with an Encryption Threshold value of 0.1. While the existing data-centric crypto-ransomware detection metrics [5, 9, 21, 23] employ the (traditional) file entropy metric, in this work, we locate and calculate the entropy of the modified bytes.

Figure 7 shows the empirical Cumulative Distribution Function (CDF) of entropy values calculated using other methods using traditional metrics [5, 9, 21, 23] as well as our proposed technique. The proposed technique is significantly more sensitive to (partial) encryption of data. The higher sensitivity of the proposed method stems from the fact that instead of calculating the entropy of all data in the file, we only calculate the entropy of the modified (encrypted) blocks. Hence, by isolating the encrypted data from non-encrypted bytes, we minimize the impact of non-encrypted bytes in calculating the entropy.

Table 2 shows the results of the encryption detection using the proposed method versus the traditional file entropy metric used in other works [5, 9, 21, 23]. Using an entropy threshold of 6, as suggested by other researchers [21], it can be observed that 97.3% of file encryptions can be detected using the proposed detection method. However, using the traditional file entropy metric used by

Table 2. The results of encryption detection using the proposed approach versus the traditional file entropy metric

Approach	Files Detected (percentage)
Proposed Method	97.3
Traditional File Entropy	49.5

others, only 49.5% of the encryptions are detected. This indicates the higher sensitivity of the proposed method to partial encryption of the files. Hence, it ensures much faster detection of crypto-ransomware and guarantees that fewer data will be lost before the crypto-ransomware is detected.

The proposed ransomware detection technique relies on the entropy of data to detect crypto-ransomware. Hence, if an application modifies large volumes of high-entropy data, it can raise the alarm (a false positive). However, this scenario is not a typical use case for smartphones. Nevertheless, to reduce the potential false positives, we employ a signature-based application analysis module that submits the signatures of suspicious apps to an online database and marks applications that have been analyzed before as benign.

6 Conclusion and Future Extensions

With the growth and advancement of mobile malware and the alarming rise of ransomware attacks, it is critical to study and investigate the possible threats posed by next-generation mobile crypto-ransomware. This work addresses this issue by investigating the vulnerability of the existing data-centric crypto-ransomware metrics to evasion and proposing a solution to combat next-generation mobile crypto-ransomware. We demonstrate the vulnerability of the existing data-centric crypto-ransomware detection methods to mimicry attacks by implementing a proof-of-concept Android application called Maskware. We demonstrate that by leaving a minimal footprint in terms of data manipulation and mimicking the behavior of legitimate applications, Maskware can evade detection.

We evaluate the performance of the common data-centric crypto-ransomware metrics in the detection of Maskware. We demonstrate that the proposed technique can evade the existing entropy, data transformation, and file structure metrics. Furthermore, this article proposes a solution to detect and neutralize Maskware. We demonstrate that the proposed solution effectively detects Maskware and can outperform others by detecting 97.3% of encryption behaviors even when only a small fragment (10%) of a file's data is encrypted. One of the limitations of the present work is that if ransomware writes data to new files (instead of modifying the existing files), it may evade detection. However, this issue can be addressed by complementing the proposed method with taint tracking. In this way, it is possible to follow the flow of information across the files and use the same technique to detect ransomware.

References

1. Abdel-Basset, M., Moustafa, N., Hawash, H., Ding, W.: Deep Learning Techniques for IoT Security and Privacy. Springer, Cham (2022). https://doi.org/10.1007/978-3-030-89025-4
2. Bajpai, P., Enbody, R.: An empirical study of key generation in cryptographic ransomware. In: 2020 International Conference on Cyber Security and Protection of Digital Services (Cyber Security), pp. 1–8. IEEE (2020)
3. Berrueta, E., Morato, D., Magaña, E., Izal, M.: A survey on detection techniques for cryptographic ransomware. IEEE Access **7**, 144925–144944 (2019)
4. Canadian Centre for Cyber Security: National cyber threat assessment (2020). https://cyber.gc.ca/en/guidance/national-cyber-threat-assessment-2020. Accessed Dec 2021
5. Chen, J., Wang, C., Zhao, Z., Chen, K., Du, R., Ahn, G.J.: Uncovering the face of android ransomware: characterization and real-time detection. IEEE Trans. Inf. Forensics Secur. **13**(5), 1286–1300 (2017)
6. Continella, A., et al.: Shieldfs: a self-healing, ransomware-aware filesystem. In: Proceedings of the 32nd Annual Conference on Computer Security Applications, pp. 336–347 (2016)
7. Darwin, I.F.: File - Linux man page (2008). https://linux.die.net/man/1/file. Accessed Dec 2021
8. Davies, S.R., Macfarlane, R., Buchanan, W.J.: Differential area analysis for ransomware attack detection within mixed file datasets. Comput. Secur. **108**, 102377 (2021)
9. Faghihi, F., Zulkernine, M.: Ransomcare: data-centric detection and mitigation against smartphone crypto-ransomware. Comput. Netw. **191**, 108011 (2021)
10. Financial Crimes Enforcement Network, US Treasury: Financial trend analysis (2020). Accessed Dec 2021
11. Hicks, B.J., Dong, A., Palmer, R., Mcalpine, H.C.: Organizing and managing personal electronic files: a mechanical engineer's perspective. ACM Trans. Inf. Syst. **26**(4) (2008)
12. Kaspersky Lab: The onion ransomware (encryption trojan) (2021). https://www.kaspersky.com/resource-center/threats/onion-ransomware-virus-threat. Accessed Dec 2021
13. Kharaz, A., Arshad, S., Mulliner, C., Robertson, W., Kirda, E.: {UNVEIL}: a large-scale, automated approach to detecting ransomware. In: 25th {USENIX} Security Symposium ({USENIX} Security 16), pp. 757–772 (2016)
14. Lee, K., Lee, S.-Y., Yim, K.: Effective ransomware detection using entropy estimation of files for cloud services. In: Esposito, C., Hong, J., Choo, K.-K.R. (eds.) I-SPAN 2019. CCIS, vol. 1080, pp. 133–139. Springer, Cham (2019). https://doi.org/10.1007/978-3-030-30143-9_11
15. Lessing, M.: Case study: archievus ransomware (2020). https://www.sdxcentral.com/security/definitions/case-study-archievus-ransomware/. Accessed Dec 2021
16. Sophos Ltd.: Lockfile ransomware's box of tricks: intermittent encryption and evasion (2021). https://news.sophos.com/en-us/2021/08/27/lockfile-ransomwares-box-of-tricks-intermittent-encryption-and-evasion/. Accessed Dec 2021
17. May, M.J., Laron, E.: Combating ransomware using content analysis and complex file events. In: 2019 10th IFIP International Conference on New Technologies, Mobility and Security (NTMS), pp. 1–5. IEEE (2019)

18. McAfee: An analysis of the wannacry ransomware outbreak (2017). https://www.mcafee.com/blogs/other-blogs/executive-perspectives/analysis-wannacry-ransomware-outbreak/. Accessed Dec 2021
19. McIntosh, T., Jang-Jaccard, J., Watters, P., Susnjak, T.: The inadequacy of entropy-based ransomware detection. In: Gedeon, T., Wong, K.W., Lee, M. (eds.) ICONIP 2019. CCIS, vol. 1143, pp. 181–189. Springer, Cham (2019). https://doi.org/10.1007/978-3-030-36802-9_20
20. McIntosh, T., Watters, P., Kayes, A., Ng, A., Chen, Y.P.P.: Enforcing situation-aware access control to build malware-resilient file systems. Futur. Gener. Comput. Syst. **115**, 568–582 (2021)
21. Mehnaz, S., Mudgerikar, A., Bertino, E.: RWGuard: a real-time detection system against cryptographic ransomware. In: Bailey, M., Holz, T., Stamatogiannakis, M., Ioannidis, S. (eds.) RAID 2018. LNCS, vol. 11050, pp. 114–136. Springer, Cham (2018). https://doi.org/10.1007/978-3-030-00470-5_6
22. Roussev, V.: Data fingerprinting with similarity digests. In: Chow, K.-P., Shenoi, S. (eds.) DigitalForensics 2010. IAICT, vol. 337, pp. 207–226. Springer, Heidelberg (2010). https://doi.org/10.1007/978-3-642-15506-2_15
23. Scaife, N., Carter, H., Traynor, P., Butler, K.R.: Cryptolock (and drop it): stopping ransomware attacks on user data. In: 2016 IEEE 36th International Conference on Distributed Computing Systems (ICDCS), pp. 303–312. IEEE (2016)
24. Sjouwerman, S.: The evolution of mobile ransomware (2020). https://blog.knowbe4.com/evolution-of-mobile-ransomware. Accessed Dec 2021
25. Sullivan, G.J., Wiegand, T.: Video compression-from concepts to the h. 264/avc standard. Proc. IEEE **93**(1), 18–31 (2005)
26. Varonis: Ransomware statistics, data, trends and facts (2020). https://www.varonis.com/blog/ransomware-statistics-2021/. Accessed Dec 2021
27. Varonis: Return of the darkside: analysis of a large-scale data theft campaign (2021). https://www.varonis.com/blog/darkside-ransomware. Accessed Dec 2021
28. Wu, B., et al.: Why an android app is classified as malware: toward malware classification interpretation. ACM Trans. Softw. Eng. Methodol. (TOSEM) **30**(2), 1–29 (2021)
29. Xia, T., Sun, Y., Zhu, S., Rasheed, Z., Shafique, K.: Toward a network-assisted approach for effective ransomware detection. arXiv preprint arXiv:2008.12428 (2020)

Automated Attacker Behaviour Classification Using Threat Intelligence Insights

Pierre Crochelet[1], Christopher Neal[1,2](✉), Nora Boulahia Cuppens[1], Frédéric Cuppens[1], and Alexandre Proulx[1,3]

[1] Polytechnique Montreal, Montreal, Canada
{pierre.crochelet,christopher.neal,nora.boulahia-cuppens
frederic.cuppens,alexandre-2.proulx}@polymtl.ca
[2] IRT SystemX, Palaiseau, France
[3] Thales Research and Technology, Quebec City, Canada

Abstract. As the sophistication and occurrence of cyberattacks continues to rise, it is increasingly crucial for organizations to invest in threat intelligence. In this research, we propose a way to automate some part of the threat intelligence process by leveraging the MITRE ATT&CK knowledge base of attackers to correlate and attribute attackers to a specific threat group. We propose a proof of work algorithm that does not aim to completely replace network administrators, but would rather help them by giving guidance, to expedite the attribution process. We show how this algorithm can be used to give insights on attackers by using it on real-world data gathered from a honeypot made publicly available on the Internet, over a two months period. We demonstrate how we are able to first discover the different techniques used by the attackers. Then, we identify various modi operandi of different threat groups collected from the MITRE ATT&CK framework and leverage that information to expose the behaviour of attackers targeting our Honeypot. By correlating the attackers together, we manage to reconstruct more complex attack vectors and are finally able to find higher similarities between the observed attackers and the knowledge base.

Keywords: Attacker Attribution · Threat Intelligence · Honeypot Data · MITRE ATT&CK

1 Introduction

Threat intelligence and attribution investigate the authors of the attacks to understand their behaviours and motives. It is key to keeping an organisation safe but currently lacks a generic framework and proper automated tools to help organisations. A report by Mandiant in 2023 [16] explains that many organisations do not even consider threat intelligence when making decisions about their

---

This research was supported by Thales Research and Technology (TRT) Canada.

M. Mosbah et al. (Eds.): FPS 2023, LNCS 14551, pp. 285–301, 2024.
https://doi.org/10.1007/978-3-031-57537-2_18

defensive needs. As such, they often craft defensive strategies and make purchasing decisions to defend from actors who actually have no interest in attacking them [16]. To prevent this, organisations should dedicate more time in understanding who are behind the attacks and their goals.

In [1], Bada M. et al. mention that attribution, or cyber-criminal profiling, is quite a recent research objective with a growing interest. However, it crucially lacks a common definition and a systematic approach. In this paper, we use the MITRE ATT&CK [18] knowledge base as the basis of our work. It provides a detailed overview of different tactics and techniques that attackers use, representing respectively the "why" and the "how" an attack occurs. To help with attribution, it also provides intelligence on threat groups and their preferred techniques, representing a kind of modus operandi of those threat groups.

A first attempt in the field by Lim C. et al. [22] introduces a manual threat categorisation algorithm to gain some information on attackers targeting a honeypot in terms of the techniques used from the MITRE ATT&CK framework. Honeypots are decoy servers on a network that aim to lure attackers and record their attacks [19]. Therefore, they have no production functionality and only gather malicious activity. This allows the interesting property to treat the detection and attribution problems separately.

As a basis of our work, we aim to use the algorithm proposed in [22] to manually label traffic from a Cowrie honeypot [21] using the techniques defined in MITRE ATT&CK. This algorithm proposes to sequentially go through all commands observed in a dataset and find a corresponding technique. This allows representing an attacker only by the techniques that they employ. With this representation, we look at two ways of clustering those attackers. First, we cluster them individually using the DBSCAN algorithm [9], suited for our kind of data representation as we explain later. Second, we define our own algorithm to perform correlation on the attackers as during a clustering phase. This correlation is induced from semantic information provided by the MITRE ATT&CK framework.

As such, we propose a novel method to group and correlate the attackers who attacked our honeypot, then link those to a specific threat group defined in the MITRE ATT&CK framework. We devise a clustering algorithm based firstly on the similarity between an attacker or a group of attackers and a threat group, then secondly on a metric measuring the correlation between the grouped attackers. This allows us to use the insights from the MITRE ATT&CK framework as a priori information for the clustering. Using those groups as a priori information allows to us to direct the clustering towards understandable and interpretable results. The contributions of this work are summarised as the following:

- Propose a method to represent attackers as binary vectors in terms of the MITRE ATT&CK techniques they used.
- Propose a clustering of attackers by who used similar techniques.
- Use the MITRE ATT&CK threat groups for interpretation of the clusters.
- Propose an unsupervised algorithm to correlate and cluster attackers. The correlation uses the MITRE ATT&CK threat group as a priori knowledge.
- Provide some understanding of the current threat landscape and the techniques used by the attackers who targeted our honeypot.

The remainder of this work is organised as follows. In Sect. 2, we discuss recent developments in attacker attribution. Section 3 introduces our data collection process and methodology. In Sect. 4, we apply the methodology to our collected data and demonstrate the results. Finally, Sect. 5 discusses the results and the limitations of our approach.

2   Background and Related Work

Attribution aims to discover information about the authors of an attack. Different ways of gathering and analysing such information have been proposed in recent years. Some researchers study the use of attack graphs [10,14] to represent the possible paths the attacker can take in breaching the network. However, when constructing an attack graph, one needs expert knowledge of the system to derive the probabilities that make the different paths, which is challenging to scale. Others use Hidden Markov Models (HMMs) [2,6] which discretize the attack vector in states and model the transition between these states. By definition, the states and transition probabilities in an HMM are strongly dependent on the dataset, which makes these techniques difficult to generalise and scale. Finally, researchers have also tried using different sets of rules, with fuzzy [15] or argumentative [12] logic that aim to give some insight as attacker categories and intelligence about the state of the world respectively. These works usually use their own derivation of rules which can quickly lag behind the rapidly evolving realities present in the real-world. This inevitably makes the attribution task fall behind as well.

These mentioned works propose to tackle the attribution problem in their own way, each giving their own definition for attribution and attacker, as well as the different categories to categorise the attackers. Bada M. et al. [1] identify this problem and suggest adopting common definitions and a common approach when approaching this problem. We follow their guideline by taking advantage of rules and definitions rigorously derived by an organization whose sole goal is providing such a framework to the world to better inform and help with threat hunting task such as attribution.

With the rise of interest in attribution, researchers have realised that the attribution task requires intelligence as a basis of the work, in forms of indicators such as domain names, Internet Protocol (IP) addresses, common Tactics, Techniques, and Procedures (TTPs), and network artefacts, to name a few. However, not all indicators have the same relevance. Warikoo explains in [26], through the use of the pyramid of pain by David J. Bianco [3], that hash values and IP addresses are not good indicators for attribution as attackers can change these very easily. On the other hand, TTPs are a good basis for attribution as "they refer to an attacker's behaviour and tradecraft" which are very difficult to change.

These TTPs are present in the MITRE ATT&CK matrix that researchers have started to use in their attribution processes, and which is a good way of defining the common approach that is needed. Some use it to gain insight into open-source intelligence such as Cyber-Threat Intelligence (CTI) reports [5] or simply crawling all available information on the Internet [23] and calculate similarities between the different threat groups. However, those researches have the same pitfall in that they can hardly be used in real-time as they need information which is generated after an incident has occurred and someone has already investigated it. Other researchers use the MITRE ATT&CK matrix to correlate information collected from Intrusion Detection System (IDS) alerts [24] or the malware themselves [13] to reconstruct the whole incident and attribute it to a specific threat group. Our research follows a similar process, but by working directly on the commands that attackers typed on our honeypot. Thus, the need for third party software, such as an IDS, to analyse malware is alleviated.

In [22], Lim C. et al. propose an algorithm to label attackers' commands gathered on their Cowrie Honeypot [21] and present a small subset of their labelling list. Then, in [7], the same authors use this list and present the big picture of what is happening on their honeypot, presenting the frequency of usage of each technique. However this analysis does not use the information provided by the MITRE ATT&CK concerning the different threat groups. Thus, it does not perform any attribution task. We think this information can greatly help in defining a rigorous framework for attribution, which is the focus of our work.

3   Methodology

3.1   Data Collection

Finding a suitable dataset to study the attribution problem is not a straightforward task. A lack of data was identified as one of the main shortcomings in conducting research in this field [1,8]. Indeed, to the best of our knowledge, there does not exist any open-source dataset with information on the attackers, that would make it suited for attribution or threat intelligence. However, Doynikova E. et al. [8] propose using data collected from honeypots to separate the attribution and detection problems as honeypots have no production functionality. This gives the property that all gathered data is at least suspicious. Also, they mention that gathering data from honeypots is as close to a real-world scenario as one can presently achieve. However, because honeypots are designed to gather information, they are usually less defended than a real company server. Still, this is the approach that we consider in this work due to lack of better options.

We use a Cowrie honeypot made publicly accessible on the Internet. The full implementation details of our honeypots are omitted here to preserve the intellectual property of an industrial partner. We collected data over a 2 month period, starting in December 2021, and ended up having over a million attack log entries. These logs are in "NDJSON" format and contain information as key-value fields, such as attacker's IP addresses, time of attacks, the session cookies, the commands, etc. A simplified example of the kind of logs it generates can be found in Table 1. With the honeypot deployed on public, unused, IP addresses, we collected a vast diversity of attacks: from simple ones where the attackers simply gather some information on the honeypot to more complex ones where botnets download and execute several malwares after an initial phase of information gathering. Out of these logs, all the information needed for this work is the IP address of the attackers, the timestamp, and the commands they typed, i.e. the payload data which we later translate in techniques used.

Table 1. Simplified example of a log

Attribute	Value
Session	233ed93a0c46
Timezone	Central Standard Time
Source IP	157.245.101.31
Command	cat /proc/cpuinfo | grep name | wc -l
Timestamp	2021-12-27T19:26:09.727623Z

On the other hand, we also derive a labelling list to associate a specific command that attackers can use to a MITRE ATT&CK technique. This is done using the algorithm proposed in [22] and the information provided by MITRE ATT&CK. The techniques presented in MITRE ATT&CK provide a mention to the commands that can be used to implement the technique. For example, for the technique "File and Directory Discovery", it is mentioned that commands like "dir", "tree", "ls", "find", and "locate" can be used. This information is added to our labelling list, referencing this technique. With this methodology, we generate a list of about 100 rules, linking commands to MITRE ATT&CK techniques, similar to the one shown by Lim et al. [22]. Looking back at the example in Table 1, the attacker tries to access information about the CPU and this accounts for technique "$T1082$: System Information Discovery".

3.2 Attacker and Technique Representation Process

Using the labelling list defined in the previous step, we derive an attack vector from the commands entered by attackers, representing the techniques those attackers executed. However, taking the logs as individual incidents makes our representation very sparse and the results rather limited. Therefore, we make the assumption that two logs coming from the same IP address in under an hour are considered to be part of the same attack, from the same attacker. This assumption is also used in several other works [2,20] as a method to get a tangible representation of an attack.

In this way, we identify slightly more than 10000 attackers in our collected data. For each attacker, we have a binary vector with a 1 at position i if the technique i was used and a 0 otherwise. These vectors are of length T, with T being the number of techniques of the MITRE ATT&CK matrix. For this work, we consider $T = 26$, as this is the number of techniques observed in our honeypot dataset. At the time of writing, the total number of techniques in the MITRE ATT&CK matrix is 185.

To identify the techniques we first replicate the process from [7] on our dataset, which analyses on a high level, the techniques used on a honeypots.

This process involves identifying all the techniques used and ranking them by their frequencies. The results of this procedure are presented in Sect. 4.1. In [7], the authors explain each technique in greater detail, which we refrain from doing here as the interested reader can find those in their article or in the MITRE ATT&CK website directly.

3.3 Individual Attacker Clustering

A straightforward way to analyse attackers is to use a clustering algorithm to group together attackers who use the same techniques. With our data, one readily sees that the number of possible representations of an attacker is 2^T. As such, the data is sparse and can be very noisy, which would disrupt a prototype-based clustering algorithm like K-means. Luckily, density-based clustering algorithms such as DBSCAN work well in these settings as explained in [9]. This clustering algorithm groups together all data points that are a distance smaller than ϵ from each other. Grouped data points are only considered a cluster if there exists at least a predefined minimum number of points, min_points, in a group. Thus, ϵ and min_points are both parameters of the algorithm and will influence the results and the number of clusters found. We use this algorithm and fix the parameters as explained in [4]. The min_points parameter is then set to $(2 * dim) - 1$ where dim is the dimensionality of the data, represented by T, the number of techniques in our case. The ϵ parameter is evaluated using a K-distance plot, which can be found in Fig. 1. This figure shows that we can form clusters by setting the ϵ parameter, i.e. a distance between clusters, to 0. This means that two attackers will be considered as being in the same cluster, or group, if they use exactly the same techniques.

After identification of the clusters, we interpret them using the information provided in the MITRE ATT&CK threat groups by looking at the similarity between each cluster and each threat group. Interestingly, the algorithm does not try to fit every data point into a cluster and defines a "noisy" cluster for all data points that do not belong to a cluster. The results of this method are presented in Sect. 4.1. With this kind of clustering we are only treating the attackers individually and using the information from MITRE ATT&CK a posteriori for interpretation. However, with the manner we treat the attackers so far, based only on the IP addresses and a time constraint, it is more than likely that there are correlations between them. Indeed, a very easy way to implement a deception technique is to perform an attack using multiple IP addresses [11]. We now propose a clustering algorithm that takes advantage of the information from the MITRE ATT&CK threat group to correlate attackers as the clustering is being done.

3.4 Proposed Attacker Correlation and Clustering Process

In Algorithm 1, we present our proposed procedure that loops through each attacker of a set "S" to find correlations that satisfy a certain confidence thresh-

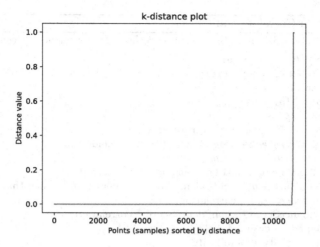

Fig. 1. K-distance plot

old "*ct*" and maximises the similarity score "*ft*" to the considered threat group "*g*". We provide an explanation of this algorithm in the following text.

The confidence threshold is a parameter that controls the amount of attempts the algorithm makes when trying to link attackers to the same attack. When it cannot find any new attacker that satisfies the confidence threshold and improve the similarity, if the similarity is higher than a specified fit threshold, it adds the grouped attackers to the cluster represented by the threat group. The fit threshold is the second parameter of this algorithm and aims at separating real malicious behaviours from more benign ones. Both the confidence threshold and the fit threshold have values falling in the $[0, 1]$ range.

This approach is greedy in that it attempts to maximise the similarity at each iteration. One could instead look at each possible group of attackers that satisfy the confidence threshold but this would make the time complexity explode. The algorithm uses this greedy approach as a trade-off between complexity and completeness and gets the complexity to $\mathbf{O}(n^2)$ on average, with n being the number of attackers (by Gauss [25]). This algorithm can in turn be applied to each threat group under consideration, which will elevate the time complexity to $\mathbf{O}(gn^2)$, with g being the number of threat groups considered. When considering multiple threat groups, it is possible that the same attackers will be associated with different threat groups. In this case, one can either decide to only retain those with greatest similarity or to have a probability of membership dictated by the similarity scores.

We need to define two formulas for this algorithm. First, to express the similarity between a threat group and a group of attackers, we use Eq. 1, where, s stands for "same" and is the number of techniques shared by the threat group and the grouped attackers, o stands for "overhead" and is the number of techniques used by the grouped attackers but not used by the threat group, and N is the

---

Algorithm 1: Correlate and Cluster

---

input: Attackers S, threatGroup g, fitThreshold ft, confidenceThreshold ct

for *each attacker a_i in S* **do**
    // Variable initialization
    confidenceScore $\leftarrow$ 1
    grouped $\leftarrow \{a_i\}$
    lastSimilarity $\leftarrow$ -1
    similarity $\leftarrow$ FindSimilarity(grouped, g)
    // Loop while a better similarity is found
    while *similarity > lastSimilarity* **do**
        // Find next candidate and update variables
        Find attacker a_j in S that maximises similarity to g such that
        confidenceScore * correlation > ct
        confidenceScore $\leftarrow$ confidenceScore * correlation
        grouped $\leftarrow$ grouped $+ \{a_j\}$
        lastSimilarity $\leftarrow$ similarity
        similarity $\leftarrow$ FindSimilarity(grouped, g)
    end
    if *similarity > ft* **then**
        // Assign cluster group g to all attackers in grouped
        S $\leftarrow$ S - grouped
    end
end

---

total number of techniques used by the threat group acting as a normalisation value.

$$similarity = (s - o)/N \tag{1}$$

Then, to define the correlation between attackers, we use Eq. 2, where t represents the amount of days between the attacker's activity (with a minimum of 1) and m represents a match in the IP addresses used as the number of leading similar bits. We also use a factor $\alpha \in [0,1]$ which modulates how much the IP match interferes in the calculation of the correlation. In our experiment, we set α to 0.125 because we want the correlation to be based mainly on the time difference. But in case of sensibly similar time differences, we still want to get a higher correlation for attackers in the same network and this value of α proved efficient. One can easily verify that the correlation values falls in the $[0,1]$ range.

$$correlation = (1/\sqrt{t}) - \alpha\frac{32 - m}{32} \tag{2}$$

On one hand, the algorithm is regulated through these two formulas. On the other hand, it is regulated by the two thresholds that are passed as arguments, which will have a large impact on the results. The fit threshold allows to modulate how the semantic links between attackers and threat groups should be set. If set to 0, it will accept any positive similarity between attackers and threat groups.

In this case, we shall have a lot of false positives as even a legitimate user could be associated to a threat group. If set to 1, it will only find links between attackers and threat groups if there is a perfect match between them. However, this one-to-one similarity is not likely to happen in most cases and thus prevents the algorithm from making most attributions. As such, this value should be set according to a given set needs and the considered threat groups.

The confidence threshold modulates the correlations made by the algorithm. If set to 0, all attackers can be correlated together. This will most likely result in false correlations. However, setting it to 1 is very strict and prevents the algorithm from making most correlations. This confidence threshold also has an impact on the speed of the algorithm as setting it to 1 almost prevents the algorithm from going into the while loop and setting it to 0 forces the algorithm to exhaust every possible correlation in the while loop. Thus, it is necessary to tune this value to achieve the best results.

We apply our algorithm to the data collected from our honeypot in Sect. 4.2. We also present the formulas that we use to calculate the correlation between attackers and the similarities between attackers and threat groups.

4   Evaluation

4.1   Overview of Techniques and Clustering of Individual Attackers

We begin by performing a global analysis of the techniques used by all attackers, similar to what was done by Lim C. et al. [7], by counting frequencies of each technique. The results for the 10 most frequent techniques are shown in Fig. 2. We can see that attackers are usually initially more concerned with understanding the machine itself by trying to get insight into the system, the credentials, or software. Only after having gathered this information do they begin their attacks. Since we do not have the complete labelling list of Lim C. et al., this allows us to validate our list as we end up with similar conclusions.

With our data, 17 clusters were identified and 587 attackers were labelled as "noisy". This means there are 587 attackers who used a different attack vector than the majority of attackers. These should be identified and considered for further manual investigation by an analyst. The results of the clustering are shown in Fig. 3. The different clusters are represented by their most similar threat groups. Here, this similarity is simply defined as the number of techniques they have in common, divided by the total number of techniques of the threat group. This explains why some threat groups, such as "FIN6" are found twice in Fig. 3, as they correspond to different clusters and therefore have different similarities. The similarities of each cluster can be found in Table 2.

Next, we can go one step further and predict the attackers' next moves by finding the techniques of the most similar threat group that were not used yet by the attackers. An example of this, for one of the clusters, can be found in Table 3. This relates to a cluster of 165 attackers where the "Putter Panda" [17] threat group was identified as most similar and we can thus expect the following techniques as being used later on their attack vectors: $T1055$, $T1057$, $T1071$,

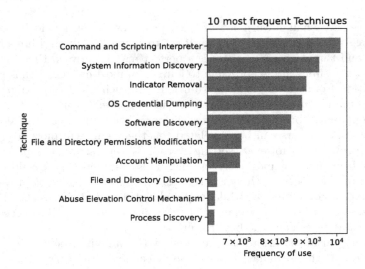

Fig. 2. Frequently used techniques on our Honeypot

$T1083$ and $T1555$, which are all explained in details on the MITRE ATT&CK website. These were the five techniques used by the threat group and not used by our attackers in this cluster. For concision, we only included in Table 3 those techniques that were used by the threat group or our clustered attackers.

As one can see from Table 2, most similarities are subpar. This can be explained by the fact that those attackers are treated individually, based on the IP address. In practice, attackers scarcely use only one IP address when performing their attacks. This drives us to create Algorithm 1 which correlates attackers together when calculating the clusters. This allows us to find multiple attackers, and thus multiple IP addresses as being part of the same attack and alleviates this problem, resulting in improved similarities found, with all of them being higher than 0.6 and some reaching 1.0, i.e. full similarity with a threat group. This analysis is the subject of the next section.

4.2 Results of Correlation and Clustering of Attacker Groups

Clustering the attackers using the DBSCAN algorithm only treats them as individual data points and does not link those data points. We thus apply Algorithm 1 on our data to perform correlation between the attackers at the same time as the clustering gets calculated. In order to use this algorithm we use the two formulas defined earlier for the correlation between attackers and the similarity between a group of attacker and a threat group.

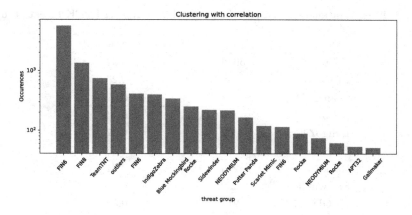

Fig. 3. DBSCAN Clustering

The results of the algorithm are presented in Fig. 4. To get these results, we set the confidence threshold, ct, to 0.8 and the fit threshold, ft, to 0.6. The value of ct is chosen to be somewhat strict on the correlation. Indeed, it forces the algorithm to focus on the attackers that have performed their attack within 1.6 days, when looking for correlations. This value can be found by equating 0.8 to Eq. 2 and setting $m = 32$ (for the best-case). With this, the algorithm groups attackers by 2 or 3 on average, with the largest group made up of 5 attackers. The value of ft has been decided empirically, starting maximum value of 1 and decreasing it until the algorithm finds matches. A more detailed discussion on selecting these values appears in Sect. 5.

It can be seen in Fig. 4 that most attackers are in the *unclustered* group. This represents attackers where the algorithm did not manage to find high enough similarities between them and the threat group, to pass the fit threshold. The algorithm could not find correlations between these attackers that would get their similarities close enough to a threat group, with the chosen parameters ($ct = 0.8$ and $ft = 0.6$). In our case, we are using honeypot data and we know all of them are suspicious since our honeypot has no production functionality. Upon further investigation, we find in the *unclustered* group, the attackers who never really performed an attack. There are indeed many suspicious users who simply opened a connection and sent basic commands such as "this is a test", or just moved in the file system using successions of "cd" and "ls" commands. In a real world scenario, it is legitimate to separate these suspicious behaviours from other malicious behaviours.

It is worth mentioning that we are using the threat groups information from the MITRE ATT&CK framework as intelligence on different ways of breaching into a network. However, we want to stress that those results do not necessarily mean we have discovered those exact threat groups attacking our network, but that we have discovered attackers whose modi operandi are similar to those of the corresponding threat groups.

Table 2. Interpretation of DBSCAN clusters with MITRE ATT&CK threat groups

Cluster	Number of attackers	Similarity
FIN6	5646	0.33
FIN8	1335	0.25
TeamTNT	744	0.50
FIN6	413	0.14
IndigoZebra	402	0.37
Blue Mockingbird	345	0.33
Rocke	253	0.61
Sidewinder	222	0.67
NEODYMIUM	217	0.56
Putter Panda	165	0.45
Scarlet Mimic	119	0.33
FIN6	115	0.40
Rocke	89	0.57
NEODYMIUM	75	0.27
Rocke	62	0.31
APT32	54	0.55
Gallmaker	52	0.58

Table 3. Prediction of attackers' future actions

Technique	Clustered Attackers	"Putter Panda"
$T1027$: Obfuscated Files of Information	X	X
$T1055$: Process Injection		X
$T1057$: Process Discovery		X
$T1059$: Command and Scripting Interpreter	X	X
$T1070$: Indicator Removal	X	X
$T1071$: Application Layer Protocol		X
$T1082$: System Information Discovery	X	X
$T1083$: File and Directory Discovery		X
$T1547$: Boot or Logon Autostart Execution		X
$T1552$: Unsecured Credentials	X	X
$T1562$: Impair Defences	X	X

5   Discussion

As explained in Sect. 3.1 the whole basis of this work is to find a way to represent attackers with the techniques they used. To achieve this, we derive a list of techniques based on the attackers' commands. Obviously, this list influences the

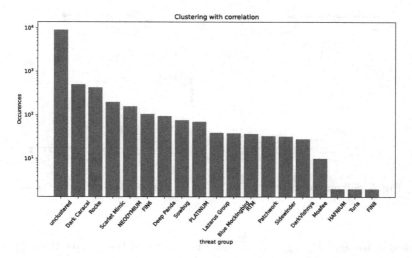

Fig. 4. Clustering with Algorithm 1

results a lot and great care should be taken when making it. We decided to mainly use the information from MITRE ATT&CK's description of the techniques, but other ways of labelling the commands could be considered as well for a more exhaustive list. Since we consider our research as a proof of work, we decide to keep our list somewhat simple. However, even with this simple list, we still manage to correlate attackers and identify different modi operandi.

As shown in Sect. 4, there are different ways of using the information from the MITRE ATT&CK framework. Either, (1) studying only the techniques used by attackers, as done in Sect. 4.1 and more extensively in [7], (2) trying to link individual attackers with different threat groups as done, in Sect. 4.1, or (3) trying to look at the bigger picture and induce correlations between attackers through semantic links derived from the MITRE ATT&CK threat groups, as done in Sect. 4.2. Looking at the techniques can give an idea of what most attackers are concerned with when breaching into a network. It can help give guidance on what to consider with when evaluating systems and making purchasing decisions on defensive needs.

Clustering the attackers individually requires finding an algorithm suited to the particularities of a dataset. With our representation of the attackers, we utilise the DBSCAN algorithm, regulated by two parameters: ϵ, the distance between two points to be in the same cluster, and *min_points*, the minimum number of points that need to be close enough to be considered as a cluster. The number of clusters itself is not a parameter for this algorithm and is instead induced by the two parameters. The *min_points* parameter is induced by the dimensions of the data, as explained in [4]. The ϵ parameter has been derived by the K-distance plot as explained in Sect. 4.1 and shown in Fig. 1. To confirm

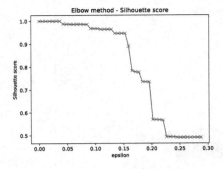
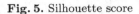
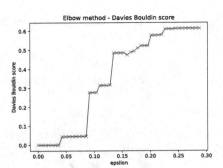

Fig. 5. Silhouette score   **Fig. 6.** Davies Bouldin score

this choice, we also consider the Silhouette score and the Davies Bouldin score with different values of ϵ.

The Silhouette score measures the similarity of objects in the same cluster. Values range within $[-1, 1]$, where 1 indicates that all objects in each given cluster are the same. We demonstrate the Silhouette score in Fig. 5 and see 1 for small values of ϵ. This makes sense since a 0 value for this parameter means all data points in a single cluster are exactly the same. Then, as ϵ increases, with clusters of different data points the Silhouette score decreases.

The Davies Bouldin score measures the separation of the clusters and it can have positive values, with 0 being the best. We see in Fig. 6 that smaller values of ϵ result in better clustering as the Davies Bouldin scores are very close to 0, meaning there is a clear separation between the clusters. Then, as ϵ increases, the clusters overlap more as the Davies Bouldin scores get higher.

We see here that both those metrics indicate that a smaller value of ϵ gives us a better clustering, as suggested by the K-distance plot in Fig. 1. After the clustering, we use the threat groups as labels to perform a very simple attribution task. It might work well in some cases, when an attacker performs his or her whole attack in one go from one IP address. However, in real-world scenarios, this is hardly ever likely to happen. Most attackers use multiple IP addresses and spend some time when making an attack, not everything is instantaneous.

Attacker correlation solves this problem by catching those attackers who use multiple IP addresses. The amount of effort put into making those correlations is regulated through our confidence threshold (ct) parameter. In practice, this threshold as well as the fit threshold should both be chosen diligently, and depending on the aims when using Algorithm 1. The best way of setting these parameters is through supervised learning, by comparing the results of the algorithm with a ground truth. However, to the best of our knowledge, an attribution dataset, providing ground truth on the different attackers behind the attacks, does not exist. For this reason, one can also define a specific range of time when the correlations should be done (a certain number of days) and find the corresponding correlation threshold by plugging this into Eq. 2. Then, the fit threshold will control the number of indications the algorithm gives, as suggested in Sect. 4.2, setting it with a high value at first and then reducing it, analysing the results slowly as they come.

We also want to stress that the algorithm in itself does not totally replace the human factor in the attribution task. Instead, it gives guidance to network analysts, providing some support when performing attribution tasks. It can greatly help in automating the most cumbersome tasks and help analysts focus their attention to spend more time on the most dangerous attackers. This identifies promising leads and finds needles in a haystack, so to speak, but should then be further considered by the analysts, who can also change the parameter variables as their investigation advances and to better orient their focus.

Finally, we decided to use honeypot data for our work as suggested by [8] but it is important to remember that the data gathered is still somewhat different to real-world data as most of the times honeypot are not as protected as company servers. However, this kind of data is hardly accessible for academic purposes. Still, our methodology, being based on the command typed, is not limited to the technology we use to test it, i.e. honeypots but can be utilized with other types of defense mechanism as well such as an IDS.

6 Conclusion

This paper investigates how the MITRE ATT&CK framework can be used to tackle the attribution problem from suspicious log commands. Our approach is validated by using a publicly accessible honeypot to collect samples of nefarious traffic entries. We first characterize individual attackers based on the commands they performed, then we correlate and cluster these attackers with a novel algorithm that groups attackers based on these commands. We demonstrate how the found clusters of attackers can be directly linked to known threat groups published by MITRE. Our approach can be used to guide network administrators and automate some of the most cumbersome parts of attacker attribution tasks.

For future work, we suggest creating a dataset that can be used to validate and compare attribution frameworks. Building such a dataset would go a long way in the attribution process, but is a large undertaking to perform, hence is why most researchers use honeypot data for now. As such, we leave the parameters of our proposed correlation algorithm as variables and propose an empirical way to set them. Once such a dataset is made publicly available, the parameters could be approximated, as is often the case for supervised learning parameters.

References

1. Bada, M., Nurse, J.R.: Profiling the cybercriminal: a systematic review of research. In: 2021 International Conference on Cyber Situational Awareness, Data Analytics and Assessment (CyberSA). pp. 1–8. IEEE (2021)

2. Bar, A., Shapira, B., Rokach, L., Unger, M.: Identifying attack propagation patterns in honeypots using Markov chains modeling and complex networks analysis. In: 2016 IEEE International Conference on Software Science, Technology and Engineering (SWSTE 2016), pp. 28–36 (2016)

3. Bianco, D.J.: Pyramid of pain (2014). http://detect-respond.blogspot.com/2013/03/the-pyramid-of-pain.html

4. Caliński, T., Harabasz, J.: A dendrite method for cluster analysis. Commun. Stat. Theory Methods **3**(1), 1–27 (1974)

5. Charan, P.S., Anand, P.M., Shukla, S.K.: Dmapt: study of data mining and machine learning techniques in advanced persistent threat attribution and detection. In: Data Mining-Concepts and Applications. IntechOpen (2021)

6. Deshmukh, S., Rade, R., Kazi, D., et al.: Attacker behaviour profiling using stochastic ensemble of hidden Markov models. arXiv preprint arXiv:1905.11824 (2019)

7. Djap, R., Lim, C., Silaen, K.E., Yusuf, A.: Xb-pot: revealing honeypot-based attacker's behaviors. In: 2021 9th International Conference on Information and Communication Technology (ICoICT), pp. 550–555. IEEE (2021)

8. Doynikova, E., Novikova, E., Kotenko, I.: Attacker behaviour forecasting using methods of intelligent data analysis: a comparative review and prospects. Information **11**(3) (2020)

9. Ester, M., Kriegel, H.P., Sander, J., Xu, X.: A density-based algorithm for discovering clusters in large spatial databases with noise. In: Proceedings of the Second International Conference on Knowledge Discovery and Data Mining. KDD'96, pp. 226–231. AAAI Press (1996)

10. GhasemiGol, M., Ghaemi-Bafghi, A., Takabi, H.: A comprehensive approach for network attack forecasting. Comput. Secur. **58**, 83–105 (2016)

11. Goutam, R.K.: The problem of attribution in cyber security. Int. J. Comput. Appl. **131**(7), 34–36 (2015)

12. Karafili, E., Wang, L., Lupu, E.C.: An argumentation-based reasoner to assist digital investigation and attribution of cyber-attacks. Forensic Sci. Int. Digit. Invest. **32**(S) (2020)

13. Kim, K., Shin, Y., Lee, J., Lee, K.: Automatically attributing mobile threat actors by vectorized ATT&CK matrix and paired indicator. Sensors **21**(19), 6522 (2021)

14. Kotenko, I., Chechulin, A.: A cyber attack modeling and impact assessment framework. In: 2013 5th International Conference on Cyber Conflict (CYCON 2013), pp. 1–24. IEEE (2013)

15. Mallikarjunan, K.N., Shalinie, S.M., Preetha, G.: Real time attacker behavior pattern discovery and profiling using fuzzy rules. J. Internet Technol. **19**(5), 1567–1575 (2018)

16. Mandiant: The Majority of Business Cyber Security Decisions are Made Without Insight into the Attacker (2023). https://www.mandiant.com/company/press-releases/mandiant-security-perspectives-report

17. MITRE ATT&CK: Putter panda. https://attack.mitre.org/groups/G0024/

18. MITRE ATT&CK, February 2023. https://attack.mitre.org/

19. Mokube, I., Adams, M.: Honeypots: concepts, approaches, and challenges. In: Proceedings of the 45th Annual Southeast Regional Conference, pp. 321–326 (2007)

20. Nawrocki, M., Wählisch, M., Schmidt, T.C., Keil, C., Schönfelder, J.: A survey on honeypot software and data analysis. arXiv preprint arXiv:1608.06249 (2016)
21. Oosterhof, M.: Cowrie (2022). https://www.cowrie.org
22. Ryandy, Lim, C., Silaen, K.E.: Xt-pot: exposing threat category of honeypot-based attacks. In: Proceedings of the 2021 International Conference on Engineering and Information Technology for Sustainable Industry, pp. 1–6 (2020)
23. Shin, Y., Kim, K., Lee, J.J., Lee, K.: Art: automated reclassification for threat actors based on ATT&CK matrix similarity. In: 2021 World Automation Congress (WAC), pp. 15–20. IEEE (2021)
24. Soliman, H.M., Salmon, G., Sovilj, D., Rao, M.: Rank: AI-assisted end-to-end architecture for detecting persistent attacks in enterprise networks. arXiv preprint arXiv:2101.02573 (2021)
25. University of Cambridge: Clever Carl (2012). https://nrich.maths.org/2478
26. Warikoo, A.: The triangle model for cyber threat attribution. J. Cyber Secur. Technol. 5(3–4), 191–208 (2021)

UDP State Manipulation: Description of a Packet Filtering Vulnerability in Stateful Firewalls

Wassim Koribeche[1,2]([✉]), David Espes[1,2], and Cédric Morin[1]

[1] Institute of Research and Technology b<>com, Rennes, France
{wassim.koribeche,david.espes,cedric.morin}@b-com.com
[2] Université de Bretagne Occidentale, Brest, France
{wassim.koribeche,david.espes}@univ-brest.fr

Abstract. Firewalls are essential components for security enforcement in a network, as they are the first layer of protection from unwanted traffic and cyber-attacks. While the requirements for efficiency led to the design of ever more complex systems, evolving from stateless to stateful firewalls, this complexity induced new vulnerabilities. In this paper, we discuss a new vulnerability present in Packet Filtering that we called Vulnerability on Firewall States (Von-FS). It is due to three factors: 1) once a state is up, traffic going through it is not checked anymore, 2) a state timeout is refreshed when a packet matches it, and 3) pushing a blocking/dropping rule in the firewall does not automatically delete obsolete states. This vulnerability can be used by legacy attacks to be more stealthy and more difficult to stop when detected. Our study shows that many commercial and open-source firewalls are subject to this vulnerability. We propose a mitigation solution that consists of deleting all obsolete states whenever a dropping rule is pushed. We evaluated this idea by patching a well-known open-source firewall, FreeBSD. Experiments show that the impact on firewall performance is very low.

Keywords: Stateful firewalls · Packet Filtering · connection-less protocols · state table vulnerability

1 Introduction

Firewalls are essential for network security as they allow to filter out unwanted traffic and stop it from entering/exiting the network. To determine whether a given packet is legitimate or not, the firewall matches it against a set of rules that need to be configured for both entering and exiting traffic. These rules are either written directly by an administrator or pushed automatically. Firewalls are located in the path of user data. As a consequence, they must be carefully designed to be efficient enough to avoid causing bandwidth reduction and added latency to the traffic they monitor.

The most basic firewalls are called stateless firewalls [7]. They apply their rules packet by packet, without having any notion of context. While those firewalls can offer some protection against attacks, they are not sufficient when it

M. Mosbah et al. (Eds.): FPS 2023, LNCS 14551, pp. 302–317, 2024.
https://doi.org/10.1007/978-3-031-57537-2_19

comes to filtering large and complex amounts of traffic requiring a high level of security, such as the traffic flowing through a 5G network. In this case, the firewall must be able to enforce more complex security policies, while avoiding becoming a bottleneck for the traffic. To reach this objective it is possible to use what can be considered as an evolution of stateless firewalls: stateful firewalls. As opposed to their stateless counterparts, stateful firewalls analyze incoming packets taking into account the context. Typically, the stateful firewall can create a *state* to track the evolution of a communication based on a connection protocol. This would allow the firewall, for example, to reject a response if no request has been sent first. Two identical packets can then be treated differently, depending on the context. Furthermore, while the firewall can have a large number of rules, having a smaller number of active states reduces the time required to apply filtering decisions for the packets matching those states.

While stateful firewalls provide better performances for traffic filtering under normal conditions, they also offer new opportunities for attackers. As an example, a relatively small amount of carefully crafted packets can force the firewall to open and maintain a large number of states, depleting its resources. Additionally, sending many packets that do not match any current state also consumes a high amount of CPU resources to fully match those new packets against the rule table, bypassing the state table optimization mechanism.

This paper presents another vulnerability that can be exploited by attackers, referred to as Von-FS. This vulnerability can be summarized as follows. As long as a state for connection-less protocols remains active, packets that match this state can go through the firewall without further inquiry. Knowing this, an attacker may then alter any field except the header required to match the state, and its packets will still be allowed to pass despite carrying a potentially harmful payload [11]. Furthermore, a state remains active as long as either the connection is not closed or its timeout has not expired. The timeout is refreshed each time a packet matches the state, this allows an attacker to keep a state open as long as it wants by regularly sending packets matching the state. This open state allows the attacker to launch different attacks such as amplification or integrity-based ones. Finally, if the attack is detected it cannot be stopped with filtering rules until either the state's timeout expires, which the attacker can easily avoid by sending packets regularly, or when the state is killed directly.

This problem was already known for iptables in Linux systems where the connection track present in a table called "conntrack table" was not deleted after adding a drop rule[1,2]. Although solutions were proposed, like flushing the conntrack table immediately after adding the drop rule or give lesser priority to the rule handling the conntrack than DROP rules, they only work for iptables. As our tests will demonstrate, this vulnerability can also be found in the packet filtering [9] function that is present in most operating systems and a wide range of firewalls, which generally do not delete active states when a contradictory

---

[1] https://access.redhat.com/discussions/5165651.
[2] https://unix.stackexchange.com/questions/527867/force-iptables-to-immediately-put-drop-rule-into-effect.

dropping rule is pushed. Additionally, this vulnerability poses a severe threat to network traffic filtering as it allows attackers to perform stealthy attacks and it lowers dropping rules' effectiveness. To address these problems in packet filtering, a solution is proposed to mitigate the vulnerability's impact on firewalls. Since performance remains a crucial aspect of firewalls, an evaluation is conducted to measure the impact of the solution on the rule reloading time.

We first discuss in Sect. 2 the existing contributions related to the security of stateful firewalls. Section 3 presents a detailed description of the vulnerability itself and a solution to mitigate it is proposed in Sect. 4. An implementation of this solution, along with its evaluation and a study of the spread of the vulnerability among commonly used firewalls, are detailed in Sect. 5, and 6. Finally, Sect. 7 presents our conclusion and prospects for future works while Sect. 8 presents the full disclosure of the vulnerability.

2   Related Work

Connection-less protocols [1,2] are widely used nowadays on the internet. UDP, for example, is omnipresent as it is the most effective for multimedia and streaming purposes, but also for common network configuration protocols like Domain Name System (DNS) and Network Time Protocol (NTP). Over the years, many attacks were developed to benefit from the connection-less aspect and lack of verification of these protocols to harm one or multiple victims. In this section, we focus on the specific case of stateful firewalls handling connection-less protocols and the attacks that can result from this situation.

Attacks on connection-less protocols can be difficult to perform, especially in the presence of a stateful firewall that uses a state table to prevent these attacks. It helps to confirm whether the flow passing through is authorized while preserving the firewall's performance by avoiding the need to check the filtering rules one by one every time a packet arrives.

Stateful firewalls are commonly used in networks to improve traffic filtering performances. As opposed to stateless firewalls, a stateful firewall does not analyze all the packets passing through it and their possible response. It uses a state table where a packet matching the expected information of a state passes through without checking the loaded filtering rules. Once a packet matches a passing rule in the firewall, a state is created using the packet's header. The state typically consists of: Protocol, Source IP, Source Port, Destination IP, Destination Port, a timeout, and a connection state. The timeout can be changed and its default value varies depending on the type of state.

The security concerns related to stateful firewalls, their performance, and state tables are widely addressed in the literature. They treat the limitation of possible states or source nodes to avoid most Flood and Denial of Service (DoS) attacks and propose solutions to optimize rules treatment and make it harder to perform overloading-based attacks. However, none of the contributors address the weaknesses present in one state only and how an attacker can exploit them.

Many attacks focus on using major weaknesses present in stateful firewalls or protocols to succeed. In [8], the authors propose an in-depth analysis of four major non-disruptive attacks based on global states, as well as two other attacks but only effective on NetBSD to subvert stateful firewalls. Articles [4,10] leverage on the lack of security of the connection-less User Datagram Protocol (UDP) to perform a DrDoS attack, overloading the victim and possibly its firewall. Both articles use the NTP protocol to perform the attack. The articles highlight that NTP has the highest bandwidth amplification factor among UDP-based protocols, which makes it particularly suitable to carry out Distributed Reflection Denial of Service (DrDoS) attacks. [4] proposes a solution called IEWA for "increasing expense and weak authentication". They apply their algorithm on the NTP protocol to make it more robust and harder to use for attacks. After the initial connection, two hashes are first computed by the client and the server. These hashes are computed with various variables known by both parties, including the client's IP address and a random number generated by the server, shared with the client, and updated every 12 h. During the initial connection, the server checks if the two hashes are identical. The server will then answer to client's NTP request only if the check is successful. A comparison with the original NTP protocol shows that the modified version is immune to DrDoS attacks. The same result could be achieved with other UDP-based protocols. [10] proposes to protect the routers with Reflexive Access Control Lists (RACL) and Committed Access Rate Limiting (CAR) to deny the possibility of applying the DrDoS attack and reduce drastically the CPU usage and ping time. Although those two solutions have been proven efficient to solve the problem of DrDoS attacks, they do not deal with the state table and thus do not close entirely the possibility of such an attack occurring as they treat the consequences instead of the cause.

3 Vulnerability Description

In this Section, we first detail how a stateful firewall applies states to connection-less protocols, and then explain the vulnerability induced by this technique.

3.1 State Tables with Stateless Protocols

Initially, stateful firewalls were proposed for connection-based protocols such as TCP [3]. They significantly improve the controls that can be performed on these protocols. State tables are used both to check if a given packet received in a given context should be allowed to pass, and to enhance the overall performance of the firewall. While context awareness can only apply to stateful protocols, performance improvement is also desirable for connection-less ones like UDP and Internet Control Message Protocol (ICMP). As opposed to Transmission Control Protocol (TCP), UDP is a stateless protocol. Consequently, the firewall cannot rely on the state of the UDP communication to determine whether or not the communication is finished, or even to determine if two packets are part of the same communication. To solve this problem, the firewall considers fictive UDP connections. For example, two UDP packets between the same sources and destinations, identified by their Internet Protocols (IPs) and ports, are considered

```
root@freebsd:/etc # pfctl -vs state
No ALTQ support in kernel
ALTQ related functions disabled
all tcp 10.51.105.105:22 <- 10.51.104.100:34412        ESTABLISHED:ESTABLISHED
   [23984528 + 2151744512] wscale 6  [592934639 + 3221225728] wscale 7
   age 00:12:25, expires in 24:00:00, 818:759 pkts, 61133:446922 bytes, rule 26
all udp 10.0.2.4:123 -> 151.80.211.8:123        SINGLE:NO_TRAFFIC
   age 00:00:57, expires in 00:00:03, 1:0 pkts, 76:0 bytes, rule 20
all udp 8.8.8.8:53 <- 10.102.11.42:53        SINGLE:MULTIPLE
   age 00:00:02, expires in 00:00:28, 2:1 pkts, 164:76 bytes, anchor 33, rule 1
all udp 10.0.2.4:58680 (10.102.11.42:53) -> 8.8.8.8:53        MULTIPLE:SINGLE
   age 00:00:02, expires in 00:00:28, 2:1 pkts, 164:76 bytes, rule 13
```

Fig. 1. FreeBSD State table

as part of the same UDP connection. Hence, the firewall can create a state for this connection, and corresponding UDP packets can match this state instead of matching the firewall rules. As there is no clear end to this fictive connection, an arbitrary timeout is defined for the state. This timeout is refreshed each time a packet matches the state, and the state is deleted once the timeout reaches zero.

Figure 1 shows how states are depicted in FreeBSD[3]'s packet filtering state table. We can see for example that "udp.single" states have a default timeout of 30 s.

3.2   Von-FS Vulnerability

Several attacks take advantage of the vulnerabilities induced by the handling of connection-less protocols by stateful firewalls. While Von-FS is also based on the fact that stateful firewalls apply state to inherently stateless protocols, it is not an attack in itself, but a vulnerability that can be used to amplify existing attacks.

The Von-FS vulnerability works as follows: connection-less protocol packets that match a state can normally pass through the firewall without being verified again by the filtering table as long as the said state remains active. This means that 1) an attacker can transport through the firewall altered or malicious harmful payloads as long as the header of the packets matches an existing state, and 2) if the attacker manages to create his own state in the firewall targeting one of his malicious destination IPs, redirection attacks will occur more frequently and efficiently as the firewall sees them as legitimate traffic. Furthermore, the attacker can keep a state constantly active by periodically sending a packet with a header matching the state's requirements before the timeout is reached to refresh it. Due to this vulnerability, even a detected attack cannot be stopped with filtering rules alone, unless the state is killed or its timeout expires. The latter can be easily avoided, as explained earlier. Exploiting this vulnerability thus opens various new ways to perform existing attacks and maybe new ones.

Figure 2 represents an exploitation of the vulnerability. Here, a flow is a set of connection-less protocol packets that match the same state in a stateful firewall,

---

[3] https://www.freebsd.org.

typically packets with the same IP and Port for source and destination. The first packet of a given flow matches no state in the firewall's state table and has to match a rule in the rule table. While doing so, the firewall creates the corresponding state, with a timeout. For example, a UDP state has a timeout of 30 s when the state is first created. Subsequent packets of the same flow only match this state, without having to go through the rule table. Each new packet matching the state refreshes the timeout. In the case of UDP, the refreshed timeout is set to 1 min. There are two ways for an attacker to take advantage of this situation.

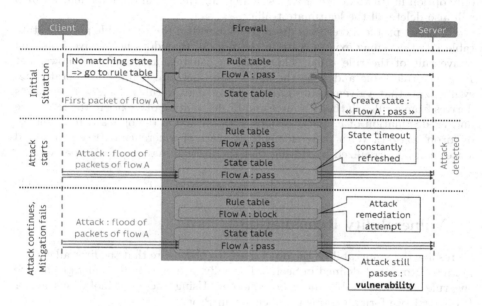

Fig. 2. Vulnerability utilization to pass through a firewall

Firstly, the attacker can either identify a legitimate communication that goes through the firewall (so a legitimate state exists for this communication) and forge its malicious traffic to match this legitimate state or manage to create its own state. Creating its state is relatively easy as most firewalls usually allow all their users to access some services, such as DNS or NTP. If that attacker somehow gains access to a machine within the network it is then simple to create a seemingly legitimate state toward a malicious server using the right protocol. The targeted state can then be maintained open by sending regularly a packet of the flow before the state's timeout expires. The attacker can then use this open state to perform its attack. As long as the attacker remains in the same state the firewall is unlikely to raise any alarm, as the state itself is viewed as legit. Indeed, most state-related detection and protection mechanisms focus on the overall number of states, but not on the behavior and impact on a given state. Thus, an attacker is likely to remain undetected as long as it stays in a single open state.

Secondly, the attacker can take advantage of the autonomy of the state table. Even if the network operator notices the attack and updates the rule table, this will have no effect as long as the state itself is not killed. This problem is caused by the fact that many firewalls do not automatically update the state table when new rules are pushed. In particular, when a "drop" rule is pushed against a given flow, if any state that allows this flow to pass is still active then the flow will still be allowed through the firewall, as represented in Fig. 2. This is because the only option in PF to delete states is by flushing the whole table manually which will also delete all the legitimate traffic.

This last problem creates a discrepancy between the rule table and the state table i.e., there may exist a state in the firewall that does not derive from any active rule of the rule table. This problem can be formalized as follows. Let R be the rule table and S be the state table. Let also define the operator $\ggg$ symbolizing that a given state s is derived from a given rule r if $s \ggg r$. A state s derives from a rule r if the IP source and IP destination of s exist in the IP source and IP destination of r, and r defines a "pass" action (as opposed to a "block" or "drop" action). With these elements, the lack of coherence between rules and states can be formalized by stating that the firewall may satisfy Property 1.

$$\forall\, r \in R,\ \exists\, s \in S\ s.a.\ s\,!\ggg\ r \tag{1}$$

4   Vulnerability Remediation

To resolve the vulnerability, the objective is to make sure that the firewall cannot fall into Property 1 defined in Sect. 3. Formally, it means that at any given time the rule and state table must be coherent. Using the same notations as for Property 1, we formalize this requirement in Property 2.

$$\forall\, s \in S,\ \exists\, r \in R\ \text{such as:}\ s \ggg\ r \tag{2}$$

To reach this objective, any state that does not derive from any existing rule must immediately be discarded. To formalize this condition, we define S_R as the set of states that derive from rules in R. In this case, the condition to achieve non-vulnerability to Von-FS can be formalized by Property 3.

$$\forall r \in R,\ R' = R \setminus r \implies S_{R'} = S_R \setminus \{s \in S_R \mid s \ggg r\} \tag{3}$$

To comply with Property 3, a solution is to kill all states that derive from a given rule when this rule is discarded. This typically occurs when an attack is detected and a "drop" rule is pushed in response to this attack, which effectively cancels out any previously existing "pass" rules. In this case, any state that derived from the canceled rules, and are now in contradiction with the newly pushed "drop" rule, should be deleted. An attack may be using only one state or a restricted number of states. For example, the Data Exfiltration attack typically involves one single victim sending data to one single rogue server and hence uses a single state. In this case, it is possible to identify clearly both source and destination IPs involved in the attack, and shut down specifically the corresponding state(s), instead of fully blocking an otherwise legitimate user.

The following Section details the patch implemented to kill specific active states related to a source and destination IP once a drop/block rule is added.

5 Implementation

In this Section, we first present the security architecture test-bed used to test the vulnerability, presented in Sect. 3. We then demonstrate that many commercial and open-source, widely used firewalls are subject to the vulnerability.

5.1 Architecture

To demonstrate the vulnerability and the proposed solution, a test-bed based on a DNS-spoofing attack was carried out. This attack consists of performing first an Address Resolution Protocol (ARP) spoofing by changing the MAC addresses present in the ARP table for the client and server to dupe them into thinking they are exchanging packets while in reality, they are forwarded first to the attacker. From this point onward, the attacker is able to receive and read the DNS messages and can change the DNS IP to redirect the client to a malicious website [5]. The architecture used to perform the experiments and measures, later described in this section, is represented in Fig. 3. It may be divided into two main parts: the 5G system and the security system that is attached to it. The 5G system is composed of a data plane, that carries the data of the user, and a control plane, which is not represented in the figure. The security system consists of an Autonomous System (AS) that can be described as the implementation of a loop that fully or partially automates the security processes [6]. It can be divided into 4 major parts: 1) the Monitoring Engine (ME), which collects and aggregates data, 2) the Analysis Engine (AE), which analyzes the collected data and raises an alert when an attack is detected, 3) the Decision Engine (DE), which is responsible for designing an action plan in reaction to the alerts received from the AE, and 4) the Actuator that executes DE's action plan.

The main components used to implement the 5G system are:

- **UERANSIM**: a customized version of an open source simulator UERAN-SIM[4] for the User Equipment (UE) and Radio Access Network (RAN) parts of the system. It is used to send user traffic into the network.
- **UPF**: a custom user plane function used to handle user traffic. The UPF is controlled by the 5G Control Plane (CP).
- **5G CP**: a custom 5G control plane (not represented in Fig. 3).

---

[4] https://github.com/aligungr/UERANSIM.

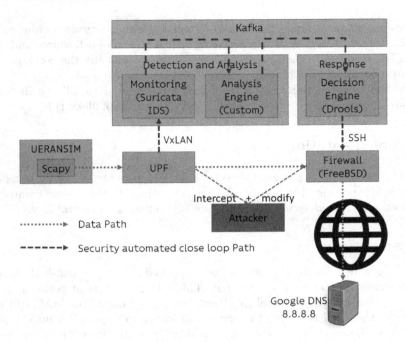

Fig. 3. Proof of concept of the solution

The main components used to implement the security system are:

- **Suricata**[5]: an open source network analysis and threat detection software. Its role is to analyze traffic passing through an interface and raise an alert if it matches a registered rule (Intrusion Detection System (IDS) mode). It is used in the architecture as the ME as it monitors the traffic and raises alerts when suspicious activities are detected.
- **Custom AE**: The custom-made AE analyzes the alerts received from Suricata, confirms if the alert is pertinent, and formalizes an attack detection event.
- **Drools**[6]: a Business Rule Management System (BRMS). Drools works as a DE as it takes AE's alerts as inputs, takes a decision based on them, and produces an action plan as an output. In our architecture, it is also used as the actuator as it is the component that will transmit the actions to the firewall.
- **FreeBSD**[7]: FreeBSD is an operating system with advanced capabilities in network security. In this architecture, it is used for its "Packet Filtering" functionality, which effectively turns it into a firewall. As a firewall, FreeBSD can be installed along the path of user plane traffic and analyzes the packets.

---

[5] https://suricata.io/.

[6] https://www.drools.org/.

[7] https://www.freebsd.org/.

The analysis is made based on the rules loaded in FreeBSD. These rules can take as input IP addresses and ports for both source and destination, as well as the protocols used. Based on this, packets can be allowed to pass through, dropped, or rejected (equivalent to drop, but with a notification sent to the source).

– **Apache Kafka**[8]: This is an open-source software that is used in our architecture to connect the security system's components together. It allows applications to produce messages, called events, that are stored in databases called topics. Those messages can then be consumed by other components. This solution offers good performance, including low latency, and allows to decouple the different components of the architecture.

With this setup in place, we can first assess whether or not this vulnerability is widespread among commercial firewalls.

5.2   Spread of the Vulnerability

In this section, we consider several well-known firewalls, both commercial and open source. We chose those specific firewalls because they are either among the most used BSD-based [9] ones or commercial ones that were available for testing. Two properties are evaluated: 1) whether they can detect if an adversary is using the vulnerability (Detection), and 2) whether they can remediate attacks that take advantage of the vulnerability (Remediation) via their filtering rules. Results are summarized in Table 1.

Table 1. Status of different firewalls regarding the Von-FS vulnerability

Firewall	Detection	Remediation
OpenBSD	✗	✗
FreeBSD	✗	✗
PFsense	✗	✗
Palo Alto	✗	✓
Stormshield	✗	✗
Juniper	✗	(✗)

To establish whether a firewall can detect or remediate the vulnerability we use the following protocol:

1. We set up the test-bed following the architecture presented in Sect. 5.1.
2. In the firewall, DNS packets are whitelisted.
3. In the UE, we use Scapy[9] to constantly forge DNS packets that always have the same header, and which target Google DNS to query IP addresses of different websites.

---

[8] https://kafka.apache.org/.
[9] https://scapy.net.

4. The attacker intercepts the request and changes the requested server's IP address during the reception phase into a malicious one he possesses and transmits it to the UE. Then, the attacker keeps sending the same packet through the firewall to keep the state constantly open.
5. At this point we observe if an alert or action of some sort is performed by the firewall automatically, or if the firewall offers some kind of rule that we can push to trigger such alert or action. If the firewall can detect the vulnerability, an alert or action should be visible. Else, the firewall is considered unable to detect the vulnerability.
6. We then, push a rule that blacklists all DNS packets.
7. At this point, if the DNS requests still pass then the firewall is considered unable to perform a remediation against the vulnerability.

The first thing to note is that no firewall can detect the presence of the vulnerability. Indeed, even next-gen firewalls that integrate an IDS do not track the activity of individual states. Hence suspicious activities linked to the state life cycle, such as artificially maintaining a state open, are not monitored. Consequently, none of the tested firewalls can detect the anomaly as they all consider the different packets received to keep the state active for the attack as one regular session. Figure 4 shows the results of the DNS spoofing from the User's point of view. We can see that he is not receiving the same answer when trying to query the IP address of "google.com" compared to before the attack as he is now, in fact, receiving the IP address to access "Facebook.com".

Before the attack

After the attack

Fig. 4. Effect of DNS spoofing using the vulnerability against a legitimate user

Regarding remediation, the Palo Alto firewall is the only one that passes the test. It displays a "Rematch sessions" feature, activated by default, that applies new rules even to existing sessions (states), killing them if they match a deny rule. The Juniper firewall also possesses this option, which is referred to as "Policy rematch". However, it is not activated by default. To fully pass the test it should have been the default behavior. Juniper's documentation[10] precises that this feature is disabled by default because it induces a risk of mistakes. As an example, it may cause to locking oneself out if SSH-related states are deleted. In this case, however, we expect the security system to trigger this action only if necessary. Considering that soft locks are only a secondary problem compared to malicious attacks using the vulnerability, it should be better to enable the "policy rematch" feature by default.

---

[10] https://www.juniper.net/documentation/us/en/software/junos/security-policies/index.html.

As of the day of our tests, this feature is still not implemented in other firewalls. Only the scheduler option, which allows scheduling filtering rules in an ulterior date and hour, offers a way to kill related states when a drop rule is applied. Note that the Packet filter has a command "-F" to flush the state table, but will result in deleting all states, legitimate ones included.

6   Evaluation

In this part, we detail our proposed implementation to remediate the vulnerability presented in Sect. 4, along with a performance evaluation.

6.1   Remediation

As highlighted in the previous section, no firewall can detect the vulnerability, and few can remediate it. In this contribution, the focus is made on the remediation of the vulnerability, not its detection. As a consequence, the rule written in Suricata to define suspicious activity is quite trivial: an alert is raised if 5 messages with the same IP and port source and destination and same protocol are received within a 60-s sliding time window. This mimics the behavior of an attacker trying to keep a given state open.

Once the alert is raised by Suricata it is transmitted to Drools via the Analysis Engine. This, as well as the next steps of the workflow, is represented in Fig. 5. Considering that the machine behind the source IP is an attacker, Drools automatically pushes an adequate drop rule in the firewall and starts a rule reload. As detailed in the previous section, such action should have no effect, as the open state would still allow the messages to pass through the firewall. To fix this and enable vulnerability remediation in the FreeBSD firewall packet filtering, we developed a dedicated patch. When this patch is applied, if a rule contains the action "drop" the rule reload will trigger the firewall to kill all the states related to the infected victim's IP address. This avoids using the flush option which will delete the whole state table including legitimate traffic.

If the specific destination IP address of the rogue server/attacker is added to the drop rule, the kill state will only target states that contain both destination and source IPs, thus avoiding blocking completely a UE IP address that can be the victim of the actual attacker.

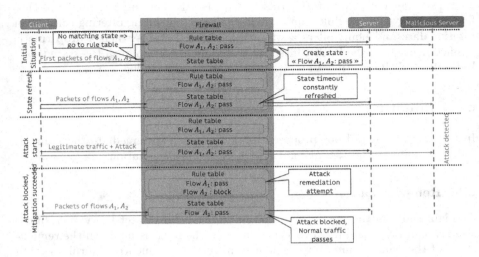

Fig. 5. Vulnerability remediation after application of the patch

Figure 6 shows Packet Capture (PCAP) traces of the same type of traffic before and after the patch. It shows that, after the patch, the traffic is dropped by the firewall since no response is received. It is because no existing state is found matching the received header and an active policy is stating to drop everything coming from that source.

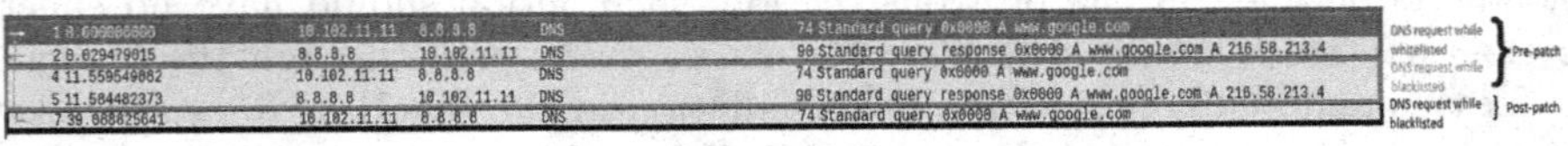

Fig. 6. Traffic filtering before and after patch

6.2 Evaluation

In this part, we evaluate the impact of the proposed patch on the performance of the firewall. To do so, we compare the time necessary to perform a rule reload in the default and the patched versions of the firewall, according to the number of rules added. To perform the experiment, states are first created in the firewalls by generating two thousand requests as traffic. Drop rules targeting some IP sources present in the states are then added, and we measure the time taken by the firewall to apply the new rules (in both default and patched versions) and kill the related states (in the patched version only). For each test, an increasing number of drop rules is pushed.

Results are displayed in Fig. 7. It shows that the performance gap is limited, with the patched version taking on average 9.4% more time to perform the reload. Even when going up to two thousand, the firewall still managed to treat the reload and kill the malicious states without adding too much delay compared to its original configuration as it rose by 9.8% only.

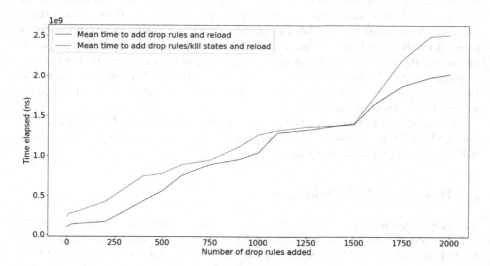

Fig. 7. Time required to reload firewalls' rules, with and without patch

7 Conclusion

Firewalls are essential elements of a network security system, as they enforce the security policies designed to keep malicious traffic at bay. The need for efficiency leads to more and more complex solutions, evolving from stateless firewalls to stateful ones. The latter do not only filter traffic packet by packet but can create states to follow the life cycle of a connection and take decisions based on this context. To this day, performance improvement is still an open research field. But those security tools are themselves subject to weaknesses and vulnerabilities, and with increased complexity come new risks. Today, many contributions are focused on protecting stateful firewalls and developing countermeasures focused on detecting abnormal numbers of states used to conduct attacks. The behavior of a single state, however, is generally ignored.

In this paper, we presented a new vulnerability that we named Von-FS. This vulnerability is based on the facts that 1) once a state is created any packet matching this state is allowed to pass without further inquiry and 2) states timeout are refreshed anytime a packet matches it. Legacy attacks can take advantage of this vulnerability in three ways. Firstly, they can craft their packets in a way to match an existing state and make themselves more difficult to detect. Secondly, once a suitable state is found, the attacker can maintain it open indefinitely by refreshing it. Thirdly, once the attack is detected it is harder to stop if the firewall does not automatically kill exploited states when the block/drop rules are pushed.

To evaluate this vulnerability we first design and implement a security architecture to use as a test-bed. Several open source and commercial firewalls are tested and most of them are found to be subject to the vulnerability, being unable to detect a malicious use of their states, as well as to block an attack using the vulnerability. To solve this problem we implemented a patch on one of those firewalls, FreeBSD. When a blocking/dropping rule is pushed, this patch automatically kills all states that go in contradiction with it, allowing the firewall to block an attack that is using the vulnerability. The evaluation shows that the performance impact of the patch is very low. This patch could be adapted to all vulnerable stateful firewalls.

The proposed patch solves the problem of the remediation of attacks exploiting the Von-FS vulnerability. However, the detection part is still an issue, which will be the subject of future works.

8   Responsible Disclosure

The ANSSI-CERT-FR[11] was notified of the vulnerability as of June 8th, 2023. A full proof of concept for the vulnerability and remediation method was transmitted as well as a CVE deposit request. A response was received stating that the request was under review and that all subsequent procedures like notifying the different vendors will be handled by the organization after the tests have been successfully assessed.

References

1. Gregg, M. (ed.): Hack the Stack, pp. 151–203. Syngress. https://doi.org/10.1016/B978-159749109-9/50009-5, https://www.sciencedirect.com/science/article/pii/B9781597491099500095
2. Garcia, N.M., Gil, F., Matos, B., Yahaya, C., Pombo, N., Goleva, R.I.: Keyed user datagram protocol: concepts and operation of an almost reliable connectionless transport protocol. IEEE Access **7**, 18951–18963 (2018). https://doi.org/10.1109/ACCESS.2018.2886707
3. Gouda, M.G., Liu, A.X.: A model of stateful firewalls and its properties. In: 2005 International Conference on Dependable Systems and Networks (DSN'05), pp. 128–137. IEEE (2005)
4. Huang, H., Hu, L., Chu, J., Cheng, X.: An authentication scheme to defend against UDP DrDoS attacks in 5g networks. IEEE Access **7**, 175970–175979 (2019). https://doi.org/10.1109/ACCESS.2019.2957565
5. Hussain, M.A., Jin, H., Hussien, Z.A., Abduljabbar, Z.A., Abbdal, S.H., Ibrahim, A.: DNS protection against spoofing and poisoning attacks. In: 2016 3rd International Conference on Information Science and Control Engineering (ICISCE), pp. 1308–1312 (2016). https://doi.org/10.1109/ICISCE.2016.279
6. IBM whitepaper: An architectural blueprint for autonomic computing

---

[11] https://cert.ssi.gouv.fr.

7. Kim, H., Pak, W., Ju, H.: Correlation analysis between inference accuracy and inference parameters for stateless firewall policy. In: 2013 15th Asia-Pacific Network Operations and Management Symposium (APNOMS), pp. 1–6 (2013)
8. Klein, A.: Subverting stateful firewalls with protocol states. In: Proceedings 2022 Network and Distributed System Security Symposium. Internet Society. https://doi.org/10.14722/ndss.2022.23037, https://www.ndss-symposium.org/wp-content/uploads/2022-37-paper.pdf
9. McCanne, S., Jacobson, V.: The BSD packet filter: a new architecture for user-level packet capture. In: USENIX Winter, vol. 46 (1993)
10. Sassani, B.A., Abarro, C., Pitton, I., Young, C., Mehdipour, F.: Analysis of NTP DRDoS attacks' performance effects and mitigation techniques. In: 2016 14th Annual Conference on Privacy, Security and Trust (PST), pp. 421–427 (2016). https://doi.org/10.1109/PST.2016.7906966
11. Trabelsi, Z., Zeidan, S.: Resilence of network stateful firewalls against emerging dos attacks: a case study of the blacknurse attack. In: 2019 IEEE/ACS 16th International Conference on Computer Systems and Applications (AICCSA), pp. 1–8 (2019). https://doi.org/10.1109/AICCSA47632.2019.9035323

Malware Analysis

Following the Obfuscation Trail: Identifying and Exploiting Obfuscation Signatures in Malicious Code

Julien Cassagne[1]($\boxtimes$) ⓘ, Ettore Merlo[1], Guy-Vincent Jourdan[2], and Iosif-Viorel Onut[3]

[1] Polytechnique Montreal, Montreal, Canada
{julien.cassagne,ettore.merlo}@polymtl.ca
[2] University of Ottawa, Ottawa, Canada
gjourdan@uottawa.ca
[3] IBM Centre for Advanced Studies, Ottawa, Canada
vioonut@ca.ibm.com

Abstract. In this paper, we delve into the intricate world of dynamic code generation in script languages. One way that malicious code authors can evade detection through static analysis is using obfuscation and relying on dynamic code generation to deobfuscate the code at runtime. These obfuscation techniques can be highly intricate, involving numerous recursive "*eval*" calls to ultimately reveal the payload, or requiring the deobfuscation of separately generated code segments. This complexity presents significant challenges for researchers studying such code and for tools attempting static analysis. However, the very effort invested by attackers in obfuscation and the structures they create and reuse across attacks can also serve as a distinctive signature of the attacker. In this paper, we propose leveraging the structure of these obfuscation mechanisms as a similarity metric for malicious software.

Our proposed method focuses on extracting obfuscation strategies, which we evaluate using two extensive datasets comprising over 30,000 phishing kits. Within these datasets, we identified approximately 18,000 instances of dynamically generated code, resulting in only 569 unique signatures. One notable advantage of our method compared to the state-of-the-art approaches is that it can extract a partial signature even if the deobfuscation process remains incomplete. Other methods heavily rely on the payload, rendering them inconclusive when the payload cannot be extracted.

Keywords: Deobfuscation · Static Analysis · Dataflow

1 Introduction

In this paper, we look into the challenge of analyzing malicious code that employs dynamic code execution as a means to evade detection and analysis. Dynamic code execution refers to a method wherein programs generate and execute code during runtime, often utilizing complex structures to conceal the malicious payload and intent. The process of payload deobfuscation involves recovering the

M. Mosbah et al. (Eds.): FPS 2023, LNCS 14551, pp. 321–338, 2024.
https://doi.org/10.1007/978-3-031-57537-2_20

original code from the obfuscated arguments. This is important because of the prevalence of languages like PHP, JavaScript, and Python that support dynamic code execution, typically through "*eval*" statements. Consequently, static code analysis becomes exceedingly difficult without executing the source code. Malicious code authors leverage this technique to conceal vital information or malicious code from both static analysis tools and human analysts.

Previously, several methods have been proposed to extract the payload from obfuscated source code executed dynamically [2,13]. However, these methods have certain limitations. Firstly, they primarily concentrate on the final deobfuscation of the payload and disregard the underlying structure resulting from the deobfuscation process, referred to as the *signature* in this article. The signature represents the computational approach used to transform an obfuscated argument into a dynamically executable payload. It can involve processes like base64 decoding, AES decryption, or evaluating a string containing escaped characters. We will demonstrate the significance of this structure, as it contains valuable information that should not be overlooked. Secondly, these prior methods often fail to achieve their main objective of extracting the payload from obfuscated arguments, owing to various challenges like encryption, compression, encoding, and other anti-analysis techniques. Since the focus is solely on payload extraction, if this objective is not accomplished, no progress is made.

We believe that signatures play a crucial role in the analysis of malicious code due to several reasons. Firstly, signatures are separate and distinguishable from the source code and payloads. This means that even if payload deobfuscation proves unsuccessful, signatures can still be extracted successfully. Secondly, signatures offer insights into the obfuscation design, shedding light on the level of sophistication and intent employed by the authors of the malicious code. Thirdly, signatures enable the correlation of attack campaigns by identifying shared patterns and variations across multiple instances of malicious code. This aids in recognizing commonalities and distinguishing characteristics among different malicious code samples.

In this article, we analyze the signature of obfuscated code embedded in two large datasets of so-called "Phishing Kits", a collection of tools, resources, and scripts that are designed and assembled for the purpose of conducting phishing attacks.

We present the following contributions:

- Introducing a novel approach to extract, store, and analyze obfuscation strategies (signatures) utilized in malicious code employing dynamic code execution.
- Conducting an evaluation of our method using a publicly available dataset comprising 3,776 phishing kits sourced from GitHub [18]. The results demonstrate the successful extraction of both signatures and payloads. Also confirming that authors of malicious code tend to reuse their obfuscation mechanism.
- Extending the evaluation to a larger private dataset of 28,134 phishing kits, showcasing similar outcomes.

- Performing a statistical analysis of the extracted signatures and payloads, examining the overall similarity among the phishing kits in which they were identified, as well as the variety of payloads associated with them. Furthermore, we compare the signatures and payloads extracted from the two datasets, highlighting both divergences and similarities.
- Releasing our source code [5] and a datasets of 569 unique signatures extracted from 18,056 "*eval*" calls found in 31,910 kits, and the php files in which the "*eval*" calls are found[1].

The remainder of this paper is organized as follows: we first introduce the related work in Sect. 2. We then present our approach in Sect. 3, then our experiments and results in Sect. 4. In Section 5 we discuss some findings in our experiments and some possible future improvements to our work. Finally, future work and conclusions are discussed in the Sect. 6.

2   Related Work

Two papers from 2012 [11,14] explored the use of benign "*eval*" calls in JavaScript applications and provided methods to automatically identify and replace these calls with static code alternatives. Their findings demonstrated that in many cases, "*eval*" calls in JavaScript can be substituted with safer and more efficient alternatives. Of course, this does not apply when the goal of using "*eval*" is obfuscation.

One approach to analyze "*eval*" calls is to examine the string being evaluated. Analyzing strings in a program is a common practice in static analysis, as seen in previous studies [6,8,12,16,21,22]. These approaches enable tracking string values for all variables using data-flow analysis. However, these methods alone do not perform any deobfuscation. In [23], the authors proposed a novel architecture that can detect "*eval*" calls and extract hidden payloads at runtime by utilizing an interpreter add-on for the SpiderMonkey[2] engine. This approach is specific to the JavaScript engine, requires dynamic code execution, and solely focuses on payload extraction without uncovering the obfuscation structure.

Some studies on obfuscated JavaScript, such as [3,10] have demonstrated the use of Abstract Syntax Trees to extract obfuscation patterns in the case of "*eval*" calls. They employed pushdown automaton to characterize these patterns and provided a list of findings. However, their methods do not attempt to resolve dynamically executed code, thus limiting the analysis to the first level of obfuscation and overlooking sub-patterns hidden within the obfuscated code. Consequently, they do not extract payloads or the obfuscation signature.

---

[1] We are publicly releasing [4] the PHP code and signatures coming from public dataset, the signatures from private dataset, while the PHP code from the private dataset will be made available to researchers from academia upon request and after verification.

[2] https://spidermonkey.dev/.

Li et al. [13] proposed an architecture for fully static deobfuscation based on ASTs, specifically focusing on PowerShell malicious scripts. The authors demonstrated that by deobfuscating the payloads within such scripts, the detection rate on scanners like Virus Total[3] can be improved. However, their solution primarily emphasizes payload recovery and does not investigate the obfuscation steps. Furthermore, the implemented dataflow analysis is relatively simple and may face limitations when applied to other programming languages.

The current state-of-the-art approach for analyzing dynamically executed code, including *"eval"*-like statements, is presented in [2]. The authors propose using an intermediate Language (μJS) from which they extract semantic information. This analysis allows over-approximating the possible values of the code to be evaluated and executed. Their approach is fully static, without code execution, and enables the extraction of payloads from obfuscated code utilizing JavaScript *"eval"*-like structures. However, this approach neglects what we refer to as the "signature" - the sequence of operations used for code obfuscation is lost during payload resolution. Additionally, their approach has not been evaluated against real-life code datasets. In this paper, we aim to delve deeper into statements, extract their structures, and compare them using large-scale real-life datasets.

In a recently published review paper by Hajarnis et al. [9], an extensive comparison of existing deobfuscation tools was presented, along with a comprehensive solution for common obfuscation techniques and obfuscation detection. While their work and the surveyed solutions focus on the detection of obfuscated code and deobfuscation, none of them specifically address the study of the obfuscation structure itself.

3   Methodology

In this section, we outline our methodology for identifying and extracting signatures and payloads from obfuscated structures. We begin with a high-level overview of our approach before delving into the specific details of the signature extraction process.

Overview of our Method

Our method consists of the following steps:

1. Pre-processing
   (a) Detection of obfuscated source code.
   (b) Parsing the source code to construct the Abstract Syntax Tree (AST).
   (c) Extraction of Control Flow Graph (CFG) and Data-Flow information for each variable.
2. Utilizing subtree-pattern matching and substitution techniques on the AST.
3. Retrieval of the obtained signature and payloads.

---

[3] https://www.virustotal.com/.

These steps, illustrated in Fig. 1, collectively comprise our approach to identifying and extracting signatures and payloads from obfuscated structures. We released the source code related to this system in a GitHub public repository [5].

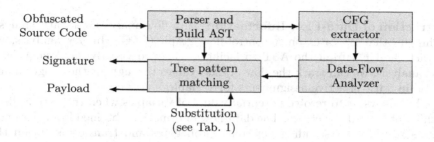

Fig. 1. System diagram

3.1 Step 1: Pre-processing

During the primary stage of our methodology, we implement widely recognized and accepted analysis approaches, which includes a range of techniques like pattern matching, parsing, and the extraction of both control flow and data flow.

Dynamic Code Execution Identification. In this study, our focus is specifically on dynamically executed code facilitated through the PHP function call *"eval"*. However, it is important to note that this approach can be used on other programming languages that support dynamic code execution.

Although PHP provides alternative constructs such as *"preg_replace /e"* or *"assert"*, which also enable the execution of dynamically generated code, our dataset analysis indicates that instances of these cases are relatively rare.

The initial step in our analysis involves identifying all structures associated with dynamically executed code, specifically function calls to *"eval"*, which we find through a simple static analysis of the code. This function call serves as the root of our AST for subsequent analysis. The AST undergoes a series of systematic transformations in the following step using pattern matching techniques.

Parsing and AST Extraction. One of the key challenges in our source code analysis is to comprehend the structure and semantics of the code. To tackle this challenge, we employ abstract syntax trees (ASTs) as the representation of the code. ASTs are tree-based data structures that capture the syntactic elements and their relationships within a program. They offer language independence, making them applicable to programming languages with defined grammars such as PHP, which is the language used in our experiments.

In our analysis, we extract the AST by utilizing a parser [1] generated with JavaCC based on a PHP grammar. The extracted AST undergoes two rounds of analysis. Firstly, it is analyzed to extract the control flow graph (see Sect. 3.1). Secondly, it is further analyzed to examine obfuscation structures (see Sect. 3.1).

Extraction of Data-Flow Information Data-flow analysis is a static analysis technique that operates on a control-flow graph (CFG). In our analysis, we extract the CFG from the AST to facilitate this process. By employing data-flow analysis, we can track the flow of data values throughout the program and maintain a list of active assignments for variables.

This allows us to resolve potential values of variables when they are utilized within obfuscated structures. The data-flow information obtained from this analysis assists in understanding how data propagates and transforms within the program, aiding in the identification and analysis of obfuscated patterns. We limited our data-flow to an intra-procedural analysis and extracted possibles values of variables within functions when possible (complex transformations with loops are not handled here). Additionally, we believe that more signatures could be found using inter-procedural analysis, and by updating data-flow after each deobfuscation step.

3.2 Step 2: Tree Pattern Matching and Substitution

Using the previously extracted information, we then perform tree pattern matching and substitution, a technique utilized for source code analysis enabling the identification and replacement of code fragments based on their structure and semantics. Our algorithms employ this approach by searching for specific patterns (Table 1) within the AST and implementing transformations when a match is found.

During the pattern matching process, additional information from the CFG and Data-Flow analysis is considered when variables are involved. This information is used to generate an equivalent node that replaces a subtree within the AST (Table 1, Dataflow Resolution).

The equivalent node is attached to the original node using a new type of edge, establishing a reference for subsequent iterations of pattern matching. This ensures that the subtree keeps track of all replacements that occur.

We have compiled an exhaustive list of transformations, detailing the specific changes applied during this step. Please refer to Table 1 for more information.

Dynamic Resolution. Given that our analysis is entirely static, all transformations are performed without executing the code. However, in the case of the "dynamic resolution" transformation, we interpret the subtree and generate an equivalent node based on the computed result.

In our first experiment we are describing here, we managed to achieve promising results by using a limited set of PHP functions to dynamically resolve issues related to malicious code.:

– base64_decode – base64_encode – gzinflate – gzcompress – gzuncompress –
str_rot13 – strrev – rawurldecode – urldecode – eval

Table 1. AST Transformation list

Operation	Description	Transformed AST
Dynamic Resolution	Resolve the value of a Function Call and attach the equivalent value to the AST. The equivalent value is computed based on the function name and arguments.	
	Resolve the value of a concatenation of two literal values, and attach the equivalent value to the AST	
Dataflow Resolution	Resolve the value of a variable and attach the last assigned value to the AST.	
Parsing	In the case of a function call that dynamically executes code (e.g "*eval*"), this operation will parse the argument, and attach the resulting AST.	
Error	When one of the operation above failed, a node related to the error is attached to the AST.	
Default	When the encountered structure is not one of the above, a "Failed" node is attached and the analysis will then stop there.	

For each of these functions, we have implemented a procedure that searches for the arguments within the subtree and generates an equivalent node by reversing the transformation done by the function.

Regarding the "*eval*" function, the behavior is a little bit different: the arguments is parsed and the whole resulting subtree is attached.

Additionally, we also found in our dataset few cases of handcrafted functions used to encode data. In this case the dataflow can give us the sequence of transformation and sub-subsequent function called. These transformations, if part of the above list, will be reversed to extract the payload; when not possible, these operations will be part of the extracted obfuscation signature anyway.

3.3   Step 3: Signature and Payload Extraction

After performing all the transformations, we proceed to the final step, which involves extracting the desired information.

Payload. The extraction of payloads is only possible if no errors occurred during the transformations. When extraction is successful, the payload corresponds to the latest parsed and attached subtree (as seen in Sect. 3.2). Extracting the payload can be achieved by simply isolating this subtree.

Signature. In contrast, the extraction of the signature can be performed even if errors occurred. The signature encompasses the transformed AST, excluding any payload-related data. To obtain the signature, we remove the following components from the AST:

- All literal images
- The subtree corresponding to the parsed payload (when no errors occurred)

A visual representation of an example signature is provided in Fig. 3. Excerpt of the corresponding code is given in Fig. 2: in the example, a 86K+ character Base64 encoded string is stored in a variable which is then called after several manipulations inside the eval call. When deobfuscated, the call yields another eval call. Eventually, after full deobfuscation, the code of a password-protected Webshell offering remote code execution to more than 30 predefined functionalities is made available to the attacker.

3.4   Adaptation to Other Languages

One last point we want to discuss before starting the next section is the adaptation of our system to other languages. While the syntax and semantics of different languages vary, the core principle of our method remains consistent across languages. Regardless of the language, our approach involves the transformation of the original code into an AST representation, and the extraction of Dataflow information.

```
[...]
$code="... Large BASE64 String of
         over 86,000 characters ...";
[...]
eval(str_rot13(gzinflate(
  str_rot13(base64_decode($code)))
));
```

Fig. 2. PHP Code corresponding to signature 3 found in the filtered Dataset

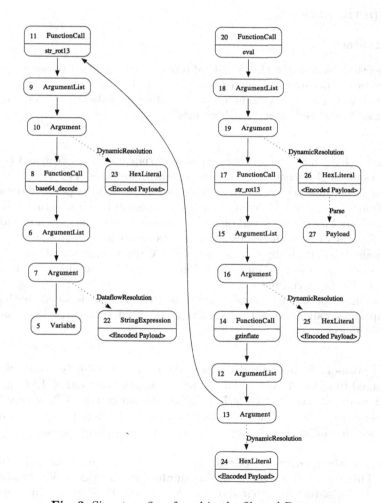

Fig. 3. Signature 3 as found in the filtered Dataset

330 J. Cassagne et al.

The first part that will need adaptation is related to the transformations we called "Dynamic Resolution" (Table 1): a visitor (design pattern on which our implementation is based) will need to be added for each encoding function that needs to be handled. These functions are fairly simple and are often one-line long, they associate to a function name (e.g. *base64_decode*) a decoding mechanism, to return the clear value when called (e.g. base64 decoded string). Most of the time, the pre-defined set of functions we implemented for PHP can be re-used as is, only the function name needs to be updated.

Then the last part will be to properly hook the parser and AST/Dataflow extraction to our system, to allow resolution of recursive structures.

4 Experiments

4.1 Datasets

In this section, we present the details of our experiments and provide a concise summary of the findings obtained from our analysis.
Our experimentation was conducted on two distinct datasets comprising what are commonly referred to as "phishing kits".

A *"Phishing Kit"* refers to a collection of materials and tools designed to facilitate the rapid deployment of convincing phishing websites [17]. These kits offer configurable parameters for the impersonated brand and the point of data exfiltration from the victims, allowing scammers to customize their attacks [7]. Typically, phishing kits are deployed on compromised servers that are not under the control of the scammers themselves. These kits are utilized for large-scale phishing campaigns and typically consist of HTML, CSS, images, and JavaScript files that impersonate various brands. Additionally, PHP files are included to handle the exfiltration of victim data.

While our experiments focused solely on PHP files, it is worth noting that JavaScript files can also contain similar obfuscated structures that could be subject to analysis.

Public Dataset. In our initial dataset, we utilized a publicly accessible database sourced from GitHub [18]. This dataset comprises a total of 4,582 phishing kits that were collected between June 2020 and November 2022. According to the authors of the dataset, they employed a method wherein they searched for archives within malicious websites, utilizing common sources for harvesting these kits.

To ensure the quality and relevance of the dataset, we performed a filtering process. This process involved removing duplicated kits (identified by the same hash) and eliminating kits that did not contain any PHP code. After applying these filters, the resulting dataset consisted of 3,776 unique phishing kits.

Private Dataset. Our second dataset comprises phishing kits that were provided by our industry partner and are not publicly accessible. This dataset consists of 28,134 phishing kits that were collected between March 2018 and August 2022.

To ensure the validity and nature of these kits, each one underwent a dynamic analysis. This analysis involved executing all PHP files within the kits and monitoring for any exfiltration attempts to email addresses or the Telegram API. By comparing the automatically provided input data with the data exfiltrated through email or HTTP API calls, we were able to confirm the authenticity of each kit. All the kits in this dataset successfully passed the confirmed exfiltration test.

Filtered Dataset. In a recent article by Tejaswi et al. [20], they conducted a study on the same public dataset that we utilized in our research. Their findings revealed that some of the phishing kits in this dataset contained hidden code, including vulnerabilities, email addresses, and Telegram tokens. However, they also cautioned that not all files in the dataset may be authentic phishing kits: they performed pre-filtering steps such as removing corrupted archives and archives that do not contain PHP code.

Taking this into consideration, we decided to apply the same dynamic analysis used on the Private Dataset to filter the public dataset. This resulted in a refined selection of kits, which we refer to as the "Filtered Dataset". After applying the filtering process, the number of kits that remained was 1,795, accounting for 48% of the initial set. By applying the same filtering steps to both the filtered dataset and the private dataset, we ensure a fair comparison between the two sets.

Table 2. Datasets Statistics

		Public	Filtered	Private
Kits		3,776	1,795	28,134
Files		7,033,994	472,796	2,982,133
PHP Files		4,963,467	269,671	1,599,859
Evals	Total	9,877	1,454	8,179
	Kits	784	213	2,131
	Signature	353	81	216

4.2 Signature Extraction

We conducted our analysis on the three datasets, utilizing our algorithm to extract signatures and payloads. All signatures and payloads are available in our public source code repository [4].

In the public datasets, we identified 353 different signatures out of 9,877 instances of *"eval"* calls. For the filtered dataset, we discovered 81 different

Table 3. Top 10 largest signatures in each dataset

Dataset

Public				Filtered				Private			
#	$|Nodes|$	$|Kits|$	$|C2|$	#	$|Nodes|$	$|Kits|$	$|C2|$	#	$|Nodes|$	$|Kits|$	$|C2|$
1	337	11	9	1	337	10	8	1	337	24	19
2	336	14	14	2	336	9	9	2	336	407	144
3	137	4	4	3	27	4	4	3	177	6	5
4	33	12	12	4	26	4	3	4	111	13	6
5	32	3	3	5	25	5	5	5	28	10	10
6	28	12	11	6	21	12	10	6	28	6	5
7	28	3	2	7	18	6	3	7	27	11	9
8	28	63	56	8	18	5	5	8	26	60	15
9	28	14	13	9	18	7	5	9	26	12	6
10	27	8	6	10	17	12	8	10	25	7	7

signatures out of 1,454 instances of "*eval*" calls. Finally, in the private dataset, we found 216 different signatures out of 8,179 instances of "*eval*" calls. These figures, along with other pertinent statistics, are summarized in Table 2.

These numbers suggest that creators of phishing kits often reuse obfuscation structures. This phenomenon becomes particularly apparent when examining the most frequently used signatures: across all three datasets, the top 10 signatures account for more than half of the "*eval*" statements.

Furthermore, we compiled a list of signatures that are common to multiple datasets, as presented in Table 4. These findings indicate a significant number of shared signatures among the datasets, implying that these shared signatures could serve as effective fingerprints for obfuscated PHP code.

Table 4. Cross dataset signature analysis: show the percentage of signatures shared between datasets

	Public	Filtered	Private	None
Public		81 (23%)	131 (37%)	217 (61%)
Filtered	81 (100%)		75 (93%)	0 (0%)
Private	131 (60%)	75 (34%)		88 (40%)
	Public	**Filtered**	**Private**	**None**
	Shared with			

We present the most common signatures across phishing kits for each dataset in Table 5. To obtain these results, we determined the number of kits (column $|Kits|$) in which these signatures were found.

While each kit is unique within each dataset (with different hashes), some of these kits are "clones" of each other. Studying the similarity of the overall kits containing common signatures is important to ensure they were used in actual different kits. While testing the hash only would be too sensitive to small changes usually brought to phishing kits. We performed an automated analysis of the source code to examine their similarity. This analysis involved representing the kits as sets of PHP fragments at the function level and creating clusters of kits that consisted of the exact same set of cloned fragments.

In the literature, various types of clones are defined [19]. For our experiments, we focused on type 2 clones, as they are insensitive to changes in:

- Filenames and file paths
- Code fragment permutation
- White space, formatting, and comments
- Identifiers, literals, and constants

Type 2 clones are particularly relevant for phishing kits [15], as they are often modified only in exfiltration parameters. Modifications to extract victim data to a different email address, Telegram chat, etc., result in changes solely in literal and constant values. The number of different type 2 clones in which the signature is present is displayed in the column $|C2|$.

These numbers demonstrate that a significant portion of kits that share an obfuscation signature are, in fact, different. This commonality among these kits would go unnoticed in static analysis, and approaches such as [15] would be unable to link these kits. With our approach, we can identify shared obfuscation structures, suggesting that they may be related or created by the same author. It is important to note that we are not claiming that our obfuscation signatures should replace traditional static code analysis. Instead, we argue that they should complement it, flagging commonalities that might otherwise be overlooked.

Table 5. Top 5 signatures kits statistics and similarity

Dataset

Public			Filtered			Private		
#	$|Kits|$	$|C2|$	#	$|Kits|$	$|C2|$	#	$|Kits|$	$|C2|$
1	239	239	1	30	6	1	407	144
2	223	212	2	19	16	2	271	117
3	174	170	3	15	15	3	180	78
4	161	155	4	12	9	4	152	100
5	142	138	5	12	8	5	151	14

Some of these signatures can be extremely complex, involving recursive code evaluation, variables, and multiple transformations, presumably designed to evade static analysis tools. We consider these complex signatures to be particularly relevant within the scope of this article.

Table 3 presents statistics for the top 10 largest signatures in each dataset. The size of a signature is determined by the number of nodes it contains, which is indicated in the column $|Nodes|$.

These statistics shed light on the intricacy and scale of the obfuscation techniques employed in phishing kits. By quantifying the size of the signatures, we can better understand the level of complexity involved and appreciate the challenges faced by traditional static analysis methods in detecting and analyzing such code structures.

Table 6. Top 10 signatures analysis

Dataset

Public [18]					Filtered					Private				
#	Recur	Calls	Var	Full	#	Recur	Calls	Var	Full	#	Recur	Calls	Var	Full
1	15	48	1	×	1	15	48	1	×	1	15	48	1	×
2	15	48	0	×	2	15	48	0	×	2	15	48	0	×
3	2	12	13		3	0	4	1	×	3	2	9	0	
4	0	4	4		4	0	4	0	×	4	7	10	0	×
5	0	3	2		5	0	2	2		5	0	3	1	
6	0	3	1		6	0	3	0	×	6	0	4	2	×
7	0	1	2		7	0	1	2		7	0	4	1	×
8	0	3	1		8	0	1	2		8	0	4	0	×
9	0	3	1		9	0	3	1		9	0	4	0	×
10	0	4	1	×	10	0	2	1	×	10	0	2	2	

4.3 Signature Analysis

In all three datasets, the top two signature are shared across them, and correspond to a complex chain of fifteen recursive *"eval"* calls and almost fifty encoding functions. We can speculate that they were probably created by a tool dedicated to obfuscate PHP code, such as one of the many PHP Obfuscator tools accessible online. To further characterize how these signatures obfuscate their payloads, we selected the following criteria:

- the number of recursive calls to *"eval"*,
- the number of function called, and
- the number of variable used.

The results of our analysis are presented in Table 6. By sorting, by size we found out that the two largest signatures are the same on all three datasets. After these first two signatures, the complexity of the remaining signatures decreases significantly.

However, it is important to note that some of these signatures are partial, meaning that we were not always able to fully deobfuscate the code using our static analysis approach. The reason for this limitation is that our analyzer may encounter functions that are not yet supported by our reverse-engineering capabilities. For example, functions like "preg_replace" may be present at certain depths in the obfuscated code but are not currently included in our list of reversible functions. As a result, the deobfuscation process may not be able to recover the entire payload.

While full deobfuscation is ideal, our solution demonstrates its strength by being able to work with partially obfuscated signatures. Even in these cases, we can still correlate phishing kits, as mentioned in Table 3, despite not recovering the complete payload. This sets our approach apart from prior methods, which would typically fail in such scenarios.

With this article, we also released a dataset containing all these signatures in a public GitHub repository [4].

4.4 Payloads Comparison

We conducted an analysis of the payloads associated with these signatures to determine whether the obfuscation structures were reused to deliver distinct payloads or if they were simply copy-pasted code resulting in the same payloads. The findings are presented in Table 7, which includes the number of payloads found for each signature (column *Payload*) and the average, minimum, and maximum size of these payloads (measured based on the number of AST nodes). Note that payloads if size "1" correspond to a node containing HTML code. We also included a line labelled "**All**", that shows the total number of payloads we found and information about their sizes.

The results confirmed that the obfuscation structures were indeed reused with different payloads, and rarely did a single obfuscation structure correspond to a unique payload. Manual analysis revealed that smaller payloads often contained exfiltration information, such as the hacker's email address or a Telegram bot token. On the other hand, larger payloads corresponded to complete webshells, which provide attackers with a shell-like interface to the web server. In some cases, this interface can be protected and serve as a backdoor.

These findings highlight the dynamic nature of the payloads associated with obfuscation structures and the various functionalities they can serve, ranging from data exfiltration to providing full control over the compromised web server.

Table 7. Top 3 signatures analysis - Payloads

Dataset

Public					Filtered					Private				
#	|Payl.|	Avg	Min	Max	#	|Payl.|	Avg	Min	Max	#	|Payl.|	Avg	Min	Max
2	16	78	4	170	2	8	64	4	85	2	41	99	1	456
3	1	6	6	6	3	1	1233	1233	1233	3	1	6	6	6
10	1	1233	1233	1233	4	2	71	65	76	4	14	24	24	24
All	1217	202	1	45489	**All**	508	295	2	45489	**All**	2862	545	1	45489

5   Discussion

This section discusses the implications of our findings, the significance of the proposed method, and its potential impact.

Implications of Signature Extraction. Our method leverages dynamic code execution to reveal distinct signatures within obfuscated malicious code. We posit that the effort invested by attackers in creating obfuscation patterns can inadvertently create a distinctive signature, similar to a fingerprint. This fresh perspective complements existing techniques focused on payload extraction.

Comparison with Other Approaches. Unlike state-of-the-art methods that rely on complete payload extraction, our approach can uncover partial signatures even during incomplete deobfuscation, offering valuable insights into obfuscation strategies used by attackers.

Dataset and Significance. We assessed our method with large datasets, each containing over 30,000 phishing kits. This in-depth analysis revealed limited number of unique signatures for each dataset, showcasing our approach's effectiveness. This marks a significant advancement in cybersecurity and forensics, offering a powerful tool for identifying and categorizing malicious code.

6   Conclusion

The primary contribution of this paper is to demonstrate the feasibility and significance of extracting obfuscation structures from dynamically executed code, which are commonly employed by malicious code authors to evade detection and analysis. We have presented a method to identify and extract these obfuscation signatures, highlighting their utility in correlating attacks that share the same obfuscation structure. By leveraging this information, we can infer additional forensic information and insights about the authors and attack campaigns.

Furthermore, we have conducted an evaluation of our approach using two distinct datasets of phishing kits: a publicly available dataset and a private dataset. Our findings provide evidence that obfuscation structures are not exclusive to specific malware families or variants but instead are reused across different campaigns and payloads. This observation emphasizes the prevalence and widespread nature of obfuscation techniques in malicious activities.

In summary, our work contributes to the understanding of obfuscation structures, their extraction through dynamic code execution, and their potential for correlating attacks and gaining insights into the authors and campaigns involved. Our evaluation on diverse datasets strengthens the validity and generalizability of our findings.

References

1. Aho, A.V., Lam, M.S., Sethi, R., Ullman, J.D.: Compilers: Principles, Techniques, and Tools, 2nd edn. Addison-Wesley Longman Publishing Co. Inc. (2006)
2. Arceri, V., Mastroeni, I.: Analyzing dynamic code: a sound abstract interpreter for evil eval. ACM Trans. Priv. Secur. **24**(2), 1–38 (2021). https://doi.org/10.1145/3426470
3. Blanc, G., Miyamoto, D., Akiyama, M., Kadobayashi, Y.: Characterizing obfuscated javascript using abstract syntax trees: experimenting with malicious scripts. In: 2012 26th International Conference on Advanced Information Networking and Applications Workshops, pp. 344–351 (2012). https://doi.org/10.1109/WAINA.2012.140
4. Cassagne, J.: Payloads dataset. https://github.com/weimdall/phishing-evals
5. Cassagne, J.: Source code. https://github.com/weimdall/obfuscation-analyzer
6. Christensen, A.S., Møller, A., Schwartzbach, M.I.: Precise analysis of string expressions. In: Cousot, R. (ed.) Static Analysis, pp. 1–18. Springer, Heidelberg (2003). https://doi.org/10.1007/3-540-44898-5_1
7. Cui, Q., Jourdan, G.-V., Bochmann, G.V., Onut, I.-V.: Proactive detection of phishing kit traffic. In: Sako, K., Tippenhauer, N.O. (eds.) Applied Cryptography and Network Security, ACNS 2021, pp. 257–286. Springer, Cham (2021). https://doi.org/10.1007/978-3-030-78375-4_11
8. Doh, K.G., Kim, H., Schmidt, D.A.: Abstract parsing: static analysis of dynamically generated string output using IR-parsing technology. In: Palsberg, J., Su, Z. (eds.) Static Analysis, pp. 256–272. Springer, Heidelberg (2009). https://doi.org/10.1007/978-3-642-03237-0_18
9. Hajarnis, K., Dalal, J., Bawale, R., Abraham, J., Matange, A.: A comprehensive solution for obfuscation detection and removal based on comparative analysis of deobfuscation tools. In: 2021 International Conference on Smart Generation Computing, Communication and Networking (SMART GENCON), pp. 1–7 (2021). https://doi.org/10.1109/SMARTGENCON51891.2021.9645824
10. Han, K., Hwang, S.O.: Lightweight detection method of obfuscated landing sites based on the AST structure and tokens. Appl. Sci. **10**(17), 6116 (2020). https://doi.org/10.3390/app10176116
11. Jensen, S.H., Jonsson, P.A., Møller, A.: Remedying the eval that men do. In: Proceedings of the 2012 International Symposium on Software Testing and Analysis (ISSTA 2012), pp. 34–44. Association for Computing Machinery, New York (2012). https://doi.org/10.1145/2338965.2336758
12. Kim, H., Doh, K.G., Schmidt, D.A.: Static validation of dynamically generated html documents based on abstract parsing and semantic processing. In: Logozzo, F., Fähndrich, M. (eds.) Static Analysis, pp. 194–214. Springer, Heidelberg (2013). https://doi.org/10.1007/978-3-642-38856-9_12
13. Li, Z., Chen, Q.A., Xiong, C., Chen, Y., Zhu, T., Yang, H.: Effective and lightweight deobfuscation and semantic-aware attack detection for powershell scripts. In: Proceedings of the 2019 ACM SIGSAC Conference on Computer and Communications Security (CCS 2019), pp. 1831–1847. Association for Computing Machinery, New York (2019). https://doi.org/10.1145/3319535.3363187
14. Meawad, F., Richards, G., Morandat, F., Vitek, J.: Eval begone! semi-automated removal of eval from javascript programs. ACM SIGPLAN Notices **47**(10), 607–620 (2012). https://doi.org/10.1145/2398857.2384660

15. Merlo, E., Margier, M., Jourdan, G.V., Onut, I.V.: Phishing kits source code similarity distribution: a case study. In: 2022 IEEE International Conference on Software Analysis, Evolution and Reengineering (SANER), pp. 983–994 (2022). https://doi.org/10.1109/SANER53432.2022.00116

16. Minamide, Y.: Static approximation of dynamically generated web pages. In: Proceedings of the 14th International Conference on World Wide Web (WWW 2005), pp. 432–441. Association for Computing Machinery, New York (2005). https://doi.org/10.1145/1060745.1060809

17. Oest, A., Safei, Y., Doupe, A., Ahn, G.J., Wardman, B., Warner, G.: Inside a phisher's mind: understanding the anti-phishing ecosystem through phishing kit analysis. In: Proceedings of the 2018 APWG Symposium on Electronic Crime Research, eCrime 2018, pp. 1–12. eCrime Researchers Summit, eCrime, IEEE Computer Society (2018). https://doi.org/10.1109/ECRIME.2018.8376206

18. Ramilli, M.: https://github.com/marcoramilli/PhishingKitTracker

19. Roy, C.K., Cordy, J.R., Koschke, R.: Comparison and evaluation of code clone detection techniques and tools: a qualitative approach. Sci. Comput. Prog. **74**(7), 470–495 (2009). https://doi.org/10.1016/j.scico.2009.02.007

20. Tejaswi, B., Samarasinghe, N., Pourali, S., Mannan, M., Youssef, A.: Leaky kits: the increased risk of data exposure from phishing kits. In: 2022 APWG Symposium on Electronic Crime Research (eCrime), pp. 1–13 (2022). https://doi.org/10.1109/eCrime57793.2022.10142092

21. Thiemann, P.: Grammar-based analysis of string expressions. In: Proceedings of the 2005 ACM SIGPLAN International Workshop on Types in Languages Design and Implementation (TLDI 2005), pp. 59–70. Association for Computing Machinery, New York (2005). https://doi.org/10.1145/1040294.1040300

22. Yu, F., Alkhalaf, M., Bultan, T.: Patching vulnerabilities with sanitization synthesis. In: 2011 33rd International Conference on Software Engineering (ICSE), pp. 251–260 (2011). https://doi.org/10.1145/1985793.1985828

23. Yue, C., Wang, H.: A measurement study of insecure javascript practices on the web. ACM Trans. Web **7**(2), 1–39 (2013). https://doi.org/10.1145/2460383.2460386

On Exploiting Symbolic Execution to Improve the Analysis of RAT Samples with angr

Serena Lucca[✉], Christophe Crochet, Charles-Henry Bertrand Van Ouytsel, and Axel Legay

INGI, ICTEAM, Universite Catholique de Louvain, Place Sainte Barbe 2, LG05.02,01, 1348 Louvain-La-Neuve, Belgium
{serena.lucca,christophe.crochet,charles-henry.bertrand, axel.legay}@uclouvain.be

Abstract. This article presents new contributions for Remote Access Trojan (RAT) analysis using symbolic execution techniques. The first part of the article identifies the challenges in the application of such an analysis, as well as the procedures put in place to address these challenges. The second part of the article presents a practical analysis of samples from known RAT families with the help of the SEMA toolchain.

Keywords: Symbolic Execution · Malware Analysis · Reverse Engineering · Remote Access Trojans

1 Introduction

According to Dataprot [16], in 2022, 560 000 new pieces of malware were detected daily. The increasing number of critical infrastructures relying on digital resources exposes society more and more to malware-related threats. It is thus important to develop techniques to detect and classify malware. Scanning a file for specific signatures common to malware provides a means of malware detection. Signatures help identify malware and classify them into malware families.

In the past, signatures have been represented by strings and byte sequences. Initial malware detection only required the *static* identification of these elements directly in the file, which could be completed without executing the malware (see [33]). Malware writers have easily circumvented this static approach by offering obfuscation techniques [27]. Tools like Ghidra [23] allow for an improved understanding of the functioning of a binary by reverse-engineering. However, static analysis is no longer sufficient for malware detection [3]. Contrary to the static approach, *dynamic analysis* consists in executing a binary in a controlled or test environment (e.g., a 'sandbox'). This form of execution makes it possible to reveal and monitor the behavior of the malware without harm to the host system. For example, such an approach can identify the malware signature as a succession of system calls [4,11], monitor the malware's behavior, and detect how the

M. Mosbah et al. (Eds.): FPS 2023, LNCS 14551, pp. 339–354, 2024.
https://doi.org/10.1007/978-3-031-57537-2_21

malware would adversely interact with the host system. Unfortunately, malware can often detect that it is running in test environments. When this happens, the malware hides its behavior so that it is (falsely) considered benign [6]. Dynamic analysis is equally ineffective when analyzing malware designed to interact with the network environment. In this case, malware detection requires either access to the network (which is dangerous) or imitation of the behavior of the network in the protected execution environment [18] (which can be prohibitively resource-intensive). This situation is particularly problematic when analyzing Remote Access Trojan (RAT) malware [35] given most RAT malware is designed to be deployed in a network environment.

Performing analyses manually takes significant time but can offer detailed information about the behavior and impact of the malware. Of course, automated analyses are faster and scale better [36]. Unfortunately, this form of analysis could miss malware information. For example, an automated analysis often focuses on one execution path occurring in a specific environment. Moreover, malware developers are continuously developing new ways to evade detection tools [2].

Symbolic analysis [17,31] solves most of the previously identified issues. Symbolic analysis works with a symbolic mathematical representation of the different values that each variable can take during a piece of malware's execution. This approach permits multiple explorations of various sets of paths at each execution step. Procedures testing the safety properties of very complex systems first promoted symbolic analysis [17]. Along with learning algorithms, malware detection processes now widely use symbolic analysis [22,26,30]. Symbolic analysis allows learning algorithms to create more general signatures thanks to a better exploration of the different behaviors of a piece of malware. Analysts can apply symbolic analysis, often with other tools, to observe, analyze, and understand new malware families [10,25].

In [7], the authors use an extension of *angr* to analyze a RAT of the Enfal family. They demonstrate that it is possible to use symbolic analysis to discover all the commands supported by the RAT and to identify the behavior associated with these commands. The authors point out that obtaining this information is less time-consuming when symbolic analysis is deployed in comparison to a manual static analysis. However, their approach focuses on a single binary. The authors of [7] do not generalize their approach or apply it to different malware from different families. Another issue unaddressed by [7], is the need to automatically generate actionable reports of what is observed during their analysis. Because symbolic analysis can explore all the commands of the RAT, automated reporting would facilitate the quick comparison of different malware. Automated reporting could also aid in more efficiently analyzing the evolution of a malware family over time. In [12], the authors complement their previous work with the reconstruction of a C2 server for a Remote Access Trojan which can then be used to perform in-vivo analysis. Their approach uses symbolic execution on the full software stack to record interesting traces in the command processing loop, considerably increasing execution time. Their approach also requires an analyst.

Our work addresses these issues. This paper presents a generalization of symbolic analysis techniques, accounting for the specific workflow of a RAT. For example, we explore how to manage the command processing loop and competently handle time-consuming functions and external calls. We also propose how to implement our approach in SEMA [8], a toolchain for malware analysis based on *angr*. Our approach includes, among other solutions, creating a database of time-consuming functions, implementing more than 100 SimProcedures to tackle the external system calls, and producing a report that focuses on Indicators of Compromise (IoCs). Our implementations are publicly available [5]. We also present a detailed analysis of a sample from the Warzone family and provide a brief overview of our analysis of a MagicRAT sample. With this last analysis, we show how symbolic analysis can be combined with static analysis.

2   Background

This section reviews concepts used in our work. We start with symbolic execution, which is a technique used to collect behaviors of a program. We then present the tool SEMA (Symbolic Execution for Malware Analysis) to automatize malware analysis. Finally, we discuss Remote Access Trojan (RAT), malware that can be used to gain remote control of a target computer.

Symbolic Execution. allows for the collection of a compact representation of sets of behaviors of a binary without executing it. In contrast, a concrete execution follows only one of many possible paths. While a concrete execution directly updates the variables in memory, symbolic execution replaces variables with symbolic values and saves the logical formulas defining those symbolic values. Symbolic execution abstractly executes a binary, considering multiple inputs concurrently. When the execution flow meets a branch depending on a symbolic value, it forks its current state of execution and continues with two different paths. In many cases, symbolic execution has shown better results than static and dynamic analysis for malware analysis [9,10].

There are many challenges associated with symbolic execution. If the approach aims to explore all the possible execution paths, the situation can degenerate. Symbolic loops can generate an exponential number of paths [24]. This leads to the well-known *path explosion problem*. Another issue is environmental interaction; it is often difficult to symbolically interpret the output of external (and therefore unknown) API calls according to their inputs, which leads to the appearance of over-approximation. This necessitates improving approach efficiency with the design of exploration methods and heuristics [30].

angr [31] is an open-source binary analysis tool that provides a symbolic execution framework. In *angr*, all information related to the current state of execution of a program are stored in a *SimState* and represented by *symbolic bitvectors* (BVS). Relationships between BVS are represented by constraints from which concrete values can be inferred. During the execution, applying instructions generates successor states from a *SimState*. SimProcedures manage external API calls. SimProcedures are function summaries that reflect the effects of the calls on the *SimState*.

SEMA. (Symbolic Execution toolchain for Malware Analysis) [8,9] is a new *angr*-based tool that detects and classifies malware via symbolic execution and machine learning (see Fig. 1). (1) The tool accepts ELF and PE executables. (2) *SEMA* takes binary files as input and performs symbolic execution with *angr*. (3) During the Symbolic Execution process, API calls and their corresponding arguments are collected to create a System Call Dependency Graph (SCDG) [26] that links calls based on their dependencies. The tool implements several Sim-Procedures that are useful for malware analysis. Many of these SimProcedures are not implemented in the standard *angr* framework. Others are also optimized to improve the concretization of symbolic values, mainly of strings. This speeds up the symbolic execution and makes the analysis of the traces more convenient. SCDGs can be seen as an abstraction of malware signatures. (4) Machine learning algorithms can use SCDGs to build models for malware detection and classification [8,9]. The machine learning models rely on graph mining through gSpan [37], graph kernel and support vector machine, or deep learning models. In this paper, we are particularly interested in extending the capabilities of angr in *SEMA*. The tool implements useful heuristics for malware analysis, such as path prioritization strategies to improve code coverage [9], loop handling [30], optimized SMT solver strategies [30],... With these heuristics, we are able to discover new addresses of the malware, avoid infinite symbolic loops, and efficiently explore the program's state space. *SEMA* also offers new *angr* plugins to collect information about malware interactions with the system (e.g., accessed environment variables, windows registries).

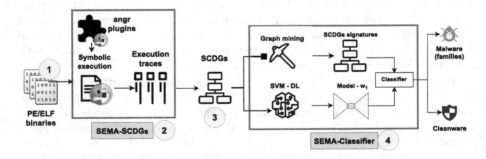

Fig. 1. SEMA

RAT Analysis. RAT malware offers remote access control which allows for multiple transgressions including launching DDoS attacks or stealing sensitive information. Having established persistence on the target computer, a RAT generally sets up a connection to the Command & Control (C2) server to communicate with an attacker. The RAT then enters a command processing loop where it will poll the server for instructions from the attacker. When the RAT receives a command from the attacker, it executes the corresponding function. The set of possible commands depends on the family and version of the RAT. Commands can comprise keylogging, screen capture, execution of payloads, file ex-filtration, etc. RATs are out of the scope of most automatic techniques in malware analysis because they require network interaction to expose their malicious behavior.

3 Contributions to Symbolic Analysis of RATs

This section introduces improvements in symbolic execution to accelerate RAT analysis. Figure 2 shows a RAT generic workflow to present improvements.

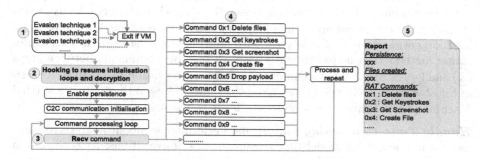

Fig. 2. Workflow of the RAT with our improvements

First, the RAT usually tries to detect if it is running in a monitored environment (e.g., a 'sandbox'). If the RAT determines this to be the case, then it may deploy evasion techniques. Each technique deployed will lead to the creation of a new symbolic path ①. Depending on the environment's reaction, the RAT may terminate its execution, generate a benign behavior, or continue its malicious execution. If the RAT continues malicious execution, it executes several procedures related to the initialization of the memory and some integrity checks ②. These procedures include, for example, the initialization of the allocated virtual memory to zero with a loop, or a CRC32 computation on the whole binary. These procedures are generally present in all variants of the same RAT family [14] and will not contain malicious actions useful in the identification or analysis of new RATs. They can also hinder execution efficiency. As a result, these procedures should be circumvented before the application of symbolic analysis to new candidates. The RAT will then establish persistence by modifying specific Windows configuration files. For example, many RATs add a path to the registry key HKCU\Software\Microsoft\Windows\CurrentVersion\Run. After this, the RAT will initialize a connection with its C2 server and wait for commands ③. Managing the interaction with the C2 server is challenging. Ideally, all the commands need to be explored by the symbolic exploration engine to discover all the capabilities of the RAT. In addition, it is useful to understand the logic behind the different commands (i.e., which command triggers which behavior) when analyzing the recorded network traffic. The SimProcedures of the external calls present in the Commands ④ should be provided to the symbolic analyzer.

General Methodology. Our approach includes manually analyzing a RAT sample and identifying the challenges for its family. We then tackle challenges with subsequently mentioned techniques that, once successful, are generic enough to be generalized across samples.

Explore of the Binary. Several strategies exist to explore symbolic execution paths efficiently. This includes breadth-first search and depth-first search. In [9], the authors proposed a depth-first search procedure (CDFS) that explores paths containing new instruction addresses. This algorithm is very effective when exploring the command processing loop ③. Each new command of the processing loop corresponds to a new path with addresses not yet visited. This exploration method thus helps efficiently visit all possible commands between steps ③ and ④ of Fig. 2. This technique also helps with evasion techniques. As seen in Fig. 2, evasion techniques often reuse the same address if they detect a Virtual Machine ①. A focus on new addresses leads to the malicious behavior.

Handle Time-Consuming Functions. Performing symbolic analysis requires using a mathematical model that represents sets of executions. At each step, a given instruction is applied to symbolic values represented by sets of constraints. This computation takes more time than the dynamic execution, which applies the instruction directly on concrete values [15,38]. In some situations, such as loops, the repetition of identical instructions severely impacts the computation time. Our approach should manage such situations. As an example, consider a function whose objective is to copy part of the memory from one location to another. The code extracted from the binary by Ghidra is given in Listing 1.1. We note that the more the size of the area under replication increases, the more repetitively the code of the loop is executed. Avoiding this repetitive process in the symbolic analysis is preferable to reduce time consumption.

```
 1  int copy_mem(int dest_addr,undefined *src_addr,int length){
 2    int offset;
 3    if (length != 0) {
 4      offset = dest_addr - (int)src_addr;
 5      do {
 6        src_addr[offset] = *src_addr;
 7        src_addr = src_addr + 1;
 8        length = length - 1;
 9      } while (length != 0);
10    }
11    return dest_addr;
12  }
```

Listing 1.1. Exemple of function managing memory

```
1  def copy_data(state):
2      return_addr = state.stack_pop()
3      length = state.stack_pop()
4      src_addr = state.stack_pop()
5      dest_addr = state.stack_pop()
6      data = state.memory.load(src_addr, length)
7      state.memory.store(dest_addr, data)
8      state.stack_push(dest_addr)
9      state.stack_push(src_addr)
10     state.stack_push(length)
11     state.stack_push(return_address)
12     return
```

Listing 1.2. Hook that replaces the time-consuming function

To address this problem, we manually identify the time-consuming functions in one sample from a family. To do this, we monitor the symbolic execution and identify the addresses where the execution stalls. We then manually extract the behavior of each of these functions (e.g., with Ghidra) and create an equivalent Python function. For example, the Python code in Listing 1.2 is equivalent to the function in Listing 1.1. We verify that these models behave similarly to the actual functions by testing them on different inputs and comparing the outputs. Creating these Python models manually is tedious and only applicable to small and unobfuscated functions; it should be automated and generalized to all types of time-consuming functions in future work. When analyzing a new sample from a previously evaluated family, our approach deploys a pattern-matching algorithm to identify problematic functions found with manual identification in other samples from the family, performing a replacement to avoid running a symbolic execution on these functions.

Handle External Calls and Simulate Interaction. Thanks to SimProcedures (see Sect. 2), our approach manages external calls to reflect their environmental modifications ④. SimProcedures provide more visibility and control over the inputs and outputs of the API calls [21]. For example, if a system call receives a pointer to a buffer as an argument, its content is automatically retrieved from memory and saved for future analysis. SimProcedures also support the restriction of return values, helping to prioritize interesting paths and discard unwanted paths (e.g., paths related to successful evasion techniques ① are automatically avoided because they return values not related to any sandbox). Finally, SimProcedures permit us to simulate network interactions. In Windows binaries, network interactions and message communication happen through system calls such as `recv` or `InternetReadFile`. Contrary to dynamic execution, our approach does not require crafting concrete messages to trigger malware behaviors. Instead, our approach returns a symbolic message from the SimProcedures related to those system calls, permitting the automatic discovery of any behavior that depends on the message.

Produce Reports. Initially, SEMA stores all system calls and their arguments found in the various execution traces in a json file. As already highlighted in previous research [7], execution traces from symbolic execution are difficult for analysts to interpret. That is why our improvements include the production of a report that gathers structured information about the behavior of the analyzed malware. More precisely, the report focuses on Indicators of Compromise (IoCs) such as modifications in registry keys, creation of new files/processes, connection to specific IP addresses, etc. Analysts share these IoCs with the infosec community to improve knowledge of malware behavior, incident response, and remediation strategies [34]. In our tool, this information is automatically extracted from the aforementioned json file, selected based on a list of relevant system calls [19]. Since the focus of this paper is RAT malware, a report on the different commands available in the RAT is created as well (5). By recording which received message (3) corresponds to which execution path (4), it is possible to understand the relationship between the message and the associated behavior (i.e., all system calls that occurred during the execution trace between the receipt of two messages). For instance, if command `0x1` triggers the calls `CreateFileA` and `WriteFile`, we can infer that command `0x1` corresponds to the creation of a file on the host.

4   Experiments

In this section, we show how to use techniques introduced in Sect. 3 to obtain a detailed analysis of different RATs families. We propose a detailed analysis of the Warzone RAT and briefly discuss another family of interest. Before diving into the analyses, we quickly show how our work improves on [7]. The experiments presented in this section are performed on a computer with a 12th Gen Intel Core i7-1255U × 12 and 16GB RAM running Ubuntu 20.04.5.

4.1   The Enfal Family from [7]

In [7], the authors present a manual analysis of a sample from the Enfal RAT malware family via symbolic execution. The sample can be found on Malware-Bazaar [1] with the md5 7296d00d1ecfd150b7811bdb010f3e58. The approach used in that paper relies on the capacity of an analyst to identify the portion of code that requires analysis. In practice, the analysis focuses on the extraction of the communication protocol used by the malware. This analysis produces a report that lists the different execution traces and the resulting API calls. From this report, the authors extract the different commands that the RAT features. In their work, the authors mention that their approach does not provide a clear summary of the execution. The authors also claim that a generalization of their approach may be hindered if each sample needs a different setup. Discovering the right setup for each sample requires the intervention of an analyst, which takes time. In this context, the authors raise the question of how one can minimize the manual intervention required to analyze a malware sample. In our approach, we propose to mitigate the problems exposed in [7]. Our tool automatically parses the execution traces to find predefined IoCs related to the malware's behavior (e.g., registry modification, file creation, network communication, etc.). We also devise a number of automatic optimizations to improve the symbolic execution and minimize manual interventions. We develop techniques that, once applied to specific malware, can be automatically applied to similar samples from the same family.

4.2 Warzone RAT

The Warzone malware is written in C++ and targets Windows users. The format of the file is a 32-bit portable executable (PE). For simplicity, we focus on the analysis of a sample that can be found on MalwareBazaar [1] with the MD5 93c5434350e0f5dc53a88202ee48e531. We successfully analyzed 35 samples of this family due to improvements made for the first sample.

General Workflow. At the beginning of the execution, Warzone goes through several time-consuming functions. Because these functions can considerably slow down symbolic execution, they must be identified. Once the initialization is complete, Warzone tries to become persistent by copying itself to the folder C:\Users\User\AppData\Roaming. This path is then added to the registry key HKCU\Software\Microsoft\Windows\CurrentVersion\Run. The execution continues with the privilege escalation. This process is performed differently depending on the host's Windows version. The malware next ensures that it will escape antivirus detection. Warzone achieves this by adding its name to the exclusion list of Windows Defender. The malware then connects with its C2 server and enters the command processing loop where it receives and executes the commands sent by the attacker. There are more than 20 different commands ranging from keylogging to shell execution. The communication between the victim and the C2 server is encrypted with RC4 and the password "warzone160\x00".

Improved Exploration. Our first contribution is to compare the effect of different symbolic exploration strategies. We observe that the CDFS strategy from [9] greatly improves code coverage compared to classical DFS/BFS strategies. This technique enables us to visit all the possible commands that the RAT features. In comparison, we observe that with a DFS strategy, the execution will always go depth-first and therefore get stuck in the infinite loop ④. When using the BFS method, the execution is slower because it explores many redundant paths. For example, the exploration will create two branches to execute the privilege escalation depending on the OS version of the host. After escalating privileges, the rest of the execution of each branch will use the same instructions at the same addresses. In practice, the situation repeats itself and creates an exponential blow-up which impacts the execution time and the instructions that are visited. The CDFS strategy [9] detects this situation and limits its exploration to a single branch. Table 1 shows a comparison. In terms of analysis quality, the technique from [9] identifies all the different commands and finds more system calls than BFS or DFS within the same time limit.

Table 1. Code coverage for three different exploration method

Method	# of instructions visited	# of blocks visited
CDFS	10264	2145
BFS	4141	1001
DFS	2828	644

User Defined Hooks. Several hooks have been implemented to avoid the symbolic exploration of time-consuming functions. Functions for Warzone that require management include data processing functions (as seen in Listing 1.1), cryptographic routines (MurmurHash), and other time-consuming functions. These functions are generic and are reused in other samples from the family. Hence, our pattern-matching algorithm automatically finds the problematic functions in other samples from the family and replaces them with previously created hooks. Figure 3 represents the time (in logarithmic scale) spent in different parts of the execution. The experiment was performed on three equivalent runs of 600 s. In the first run, which does not apply hooks, most of the execution time is spent in cryptographic functions. In the second run, we see that the execution gets trapped in the data processing functions if corresponding hooks are not implemented. Finally, when all hooks are implemented, we see that the time-consuming functions no longer have an impact on the execution.

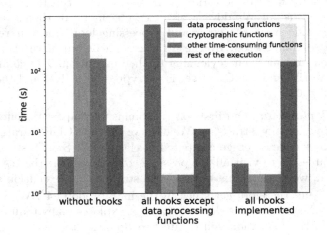

Fig. 3. Execution time with and without hooks

Interaction and SimProcedures. We have implemented all the SimProcedures that correspond to the system calls made by the RAT during its execution. This represents a substantial effort since more than 100 SimProcedures have been considered. As an example, the code provided in Listing 1.3 shows the SimProcedure for the function `GetVersionExA`. This function is used to determine the OS version, which is important in the selection of the privilege escalation technique. The implementation is based on the information found in the Win32 API documentation. For instance, the variable `MajorVersion` can take different values between 5 and 10 depending on the OS. In the SimProcedure, this is represented by creating a symbolic variable and applying constraints. Our strategy in implementing SimProcedures is to limit the symbolic inputs and outputs to what is specified in the Win32 API. We discard only the paths that would lead to an error in real execution. In this way, we mitigate the path explosion problem while preserving all paths that would be dynamically feasible.

```
1  class GetVersionExA(angr.SimProcedure):
2    def run(self, addr):
3      MajorVersion = claripy.BVS("MajorVersion",32)
4      self.state.solver.add(MajorVersion >= 5)
5      self.state.solver.add(MajorVersion <= 10)
6      self.state.memory.store(addr+0x4, MajorVersion)
7      MinorVersion = claripy.BVS("MinorVersion",32)
8      self.state.solver.add(MinorVersion >= 0)
9      self.state.solver.add(MinorVersion <= 3)
10     self.state.memory.store(addr+0x8, MinorVersion)
11     BuildNumber = claripy.BVS("BuildNumber",32)
12     self.state.memory.store(addr+0xc, BuildNumber)
13     PlatformId = claripy.BVV(2,32)
14     self.state.memory.store(addr+0x10, PlatformId)
15     return 0x1
```

Listing 1.3. SimProcedure of `GetVersionExA`

The `recv` SimProcedure plays an important role in the execution of all the RAT malware that communicates through this function. During analysis, a symbolic buffer is created to represent the buffer returned by the `recv` function. This is done in a way that permits the retrieval of the constraints that were applied to the buffer. This helps deduce the concrete value of the buffer for each execution trace and create a report on the commands that the RAT can receive.

Report Extracted. Each execution automatically produces two reports, one for the commands and one for the IoCs. For each execution trace, the commands report produces the command message that triggered this trace and the following system calls. As an example, the first part of Listing 1.4 shows a piece of the report that represents an execution trace. It corresponds to the command that uninstalls the malware. This report supports the comparison of different samples from the same family. If we analyze samples spread over a large time period, we might see a growth in the number of commands in recent versus older malware. The IoC report is divided into several categories. Each category represents a potentially incriminating behavior. Listing 1.4 provides an excerpt of the IoC report from the Warzone analysis. In Category "Network activity", we observe that the address of the C2 server is "`rtyui.nerdpol.ovh`". This category also shows all the system calls that are used to communicate on the network. The next category lists all the activities related to the registers. This is strategic information, as the registers are often used by malware to create persistence. The "Files" category lists all the system calls that concern files and directories. In this example, we see that Warzone asks for a special folder to which it will copy itself later. The categories "Processes" and "Command Line" retrieve information on the processes created by the malware. Here we see that Warzone creates the processes sdclt.exe and cmd.exe, used to escalate privileges in Windows.

```
 1 RAT Commands:
 2 * 0x9123b422d33a244e6018673
 3 - RegDeleteKeyW
 4 - GetModuleFileNameA
 5 - CreateProcessA
 6 - CloseHandle
 7 - ExitProcess
 8 [...]
 9 Network activity:
10 - inet_addr(rtyui.nerdpol.ovh)
11 - ...
12 Registers:
13 - RegOpenKeyExW(Software\Microsoft\Windows\CurrentVersion\
       Explorer\ZU6FTFTS7G)
14 - RegCreateKeyExA(Software\Classes\Folder\shell\open\command)
15 - ...
16 Files:
17 - SHGetSpecialFolderPathW(C:\Users\USERNAME\AppData\Roaming)
18 - ...
19 Processes:
20 - CreateProcessW(C:\Windows\System32\cmd.exe)
21 - ...
22 Command line:
23 - ShellExecuteW(open, C:\Windows\System32\sdclt.exe)
24 - ...
```

Listing 1.4. Report on discovered commands and IoCs

4.3 MagicRAT

We analyzed a sample of the *MagicRAT* family, a malware attributed to the North Korean Lazarus group. The sample can be found on MalwareBazaar with the MD5: b4c9b903dfd18bd67a3824b0109f955b. Cisco Talos [32] recently discovered it. MagicRAT (written in C++, compiled as a 64-bit PE file) uses the widespread and trusted QT graphical framework. This significantly increases the size and complexity of the binary. Since the binary of the RAT is complex and large, we performed the analysis with a combination of Ghidra and SEMA.

General Workflow. With symbolic analysis, we found that the malware starts with an initialization phase of its parameters. Then it creates and hides its configuration inside a file called \ProgramData \WindowsSoftwareToolkit\visual. 1991-06.com.microsoft_sd .kit from the legit QSettings class. The configuration is composed of three strings that start with the common prefix "LR02DPt22R". During the execution, this prefix is removed from each string.

The remaining part of the string is then decoded to obtain the C2 URLs ("LRO2DPt22R<url_i_encoded_in_base64>"). By inspecting the result of the symbolic execution, we were able to retrieve the IP from the string. This allows for threat hunting and forensic analysis of these sources. We then used Ghidra to identify places where suspicious strings (e.g., "cmd.exe /c bcdedit") are exploited. This speeds up workflow deduction. With our analysis, we observe that MagicRAT uses the task scheduler to execute itself at 10:30 a.m. each day. It also hides in a fake "Onedrive" shortcut in the startup folder of the victim. Its command processing loop is simple; it mainly manipulates victims' files (rename, delete, and move). MagicRAT can also execute terminal commands on the victim to collect information which is sent to the attacker in a file named "zero_dump.mix". Finally, the sample has a self-deletion procedure contained in a ".bat". We now show the implementation contributions that allow us to achieve this result.

User Defined Hooks. The QT framework requires specific CPU features for the execution which can be checked with the assembly instruction "cpuid". *angr* does not handle this instruction. Thus, we implement a special hook called "CPUIDHook". This is an advantage when compared to dynamic analysis because our approach works independently of the real CPU used.

Improved Exploration. The QT framework contains code that is not relevant for symbolic analysis but can hinder effectiveness. The logging process of QT induces an exploration of benign behavior associated with different environmental variables. Using Ghidra, we identify 17 QT environment variables associated with such optional behavior. By setting values for these variables, we avoid examining these behaviors and improve the efficiency of the analysis that would otherwise time out before discovery of the malicious behavior.

Interaction and SimProcedures. All API calls present in the command loop are implemented in SEMA. This includes Windows structures containing file information such as _BY_HANDLE_FILE_ INFORMATION, which contains file metadata, or VS_VERSIONINFO, which gives the version of the file. We have also implemented file mapping. This typically starts with a call to CreateFileMappingW to create a handle for the mapping of an input file. MapViewOfFile then maps the content of the file to the memory region.

5   Conclusion and Future Work

We have demonstrated how symbolic analysis can help understand the workflow of RATs by proposing new heuristics implemented in SEMA and by using a combination of manual and automatic actions. While our work significantly improves the analysis of challenging malware such as RATs, more remains to be done. Our approach reduces the cost of symbolic execution by identifying and replacing bottleneck functions. Our pattern-matching approach, while efficient, is prone to syntactic obfuscation. This process could improve with more reliance on obfuscation-resilient semantic functionality identification as in [28]. The bottleneck functions could also be automatically identified with the use of machine learning as in [20]. Monitoring specific symbolic values (e.g., values related to interaction with the network) could also enhance exploration techniques [13,29]. Finally, we will integrate our contributions into the machine learning malware detection process introduced in [26] and implemented in SEMA. In particular, we intend to improve detection and classification of RAT malware families on a larger scale.

Acknowledgments. This research is supported by the Walloon region's CyberExcellence program (Grant #2110186).

References

1. Abuse.ch: Malwarebazaar (2023). https://bazaar.abuse.ch/
2. Afianian, A., Niksefat, S., Sadeghiyan, B., Baptiste, D.: Malware dynamic analysis evasion techniques: a survey. ACM Comput. Surv. **52**(6), 1–28 (2019)
3. Aghakhani, H., et al.: When malware is packin' heat; limits of machine learning classifiers based on static analysis features. In: Network and Distributed Systems Security (NDSS) Symposium 2020 (2020)
4. Amer, E., Zelinka, I.: A dynamic windows malware detection and prediction method based on contextual understanding of API call sequence. Comput. Secur. **92**, 101760 (2020)
5. Bertrand Van Ouytsel, C.-H., Crochet, C., Legay, A., Lucca, S.: SEMA-ToolChain. GitHub. GitHub repository. https://github.com/csvl/SEMA-ToolChain
6. Avllazagaj, E., Zhu, Z., Bilge, L., Balzarotti, D., Dumitras, T.: When malware changed its mind: an empirical study of variable program behaviors in the real world. In: USENIX Security Symposium, pp. 3487–3504 (2021)
7. Baldoni, R., Coppa, E., D'Elia, D.C., Demetrescu, C.: Assisting malware analysis with symbolic execution: a case study. In: Dolev, S., Lodha, S. (eds.) Cyber Security Cryptography and Machine Learning. CSCML 2017. LNCS, vol. 10332, pp. 171–188. Springer, Cham (2017). https://doi.org/10.1007/978-3-319-60080-2_12
8. Bertrand Van Ouytsel, C.-H., Crochet, C., Dam, K.H.T., Legay, A.: Tool paper - SEMA: symbolic execution toolchain for malware analysis. In: Kallel, S., Jmaiel, M., Zulkernine, M., Hadj Kacem, A., Cuppens, F., Cuppens, N. (eds.) Risks and Security of Internet and Systems, CRiSIS 2022, pp. 62–68. Springer, Cham (2023). https://doi.org/10.1007/978-3-031-31108-6_5
9. Bertrand Van Ouytsel, C., Legay, A.: Malware analysis with symbolic execution and graph kernel. In: Reiser, H.P., Kyas, M. (eds.) Secure IT Systems - 27th Nordic Conference, NordSec 2022. LNCS, vol. 13700, pp. 292–310. Springer, Cham (2022). https://doi.org/10.1007/978-3-031-22295-5_16
10. Biondi, F., Given-Wilson, T., Legay, A., Puodzius, C., Quilbeuf, J.: Tutorial: an overview of malware detection and evasion techniques. In: Margaria, T., Steffen, B. (eds.) Leveraging Applications of Formal Methods, Verification and Validation. Modeling - 8th International Symposium, ISoLA 2018. LNCS, vol. 11244, pp. 565–586. Springer, Cham (2018). https://doi.org/10.1007/978-3-030-03418-4_34
11. Blokhin, K., Saxe, J., Mentis, D.: Malware similarity identification using call graph based system call subsequence features. In: 2013 IEEE 33rd International Conference on Distributed Computing Systems Workshops, pp. 6–10. IEEE (2013)

12. Borzacchiello, L., Coppa, E., D'Elia, D.C., Demetrescu, C.: Reconstructing C2 servers for remote access Trojans with symbolic execution. In: Dolev, S., Hendler, D., Lodha, S., Yung, M. (eds.) Cyber Security Cryptography and Machine Learning. CSCML 2019. LNCS, vol. 11527, pp. 121–140. Springer, Cham (2019). https://doi.org/10.1007/978-3-030-20951-3_12
13. Brumley, D., Hartwig, C., Liang, Z., Newsome, J., Song, D., Yin, H.: Automatically identifying trigger-based behavior in malware. In: Lee, W., Wang, C., Dagon, D. (eds.) Botnet Detection, pp. 65–88. Springer, Boston (2008). https://doi.org/10.1007/978-0-387-68768-1_4
14. Calleja, A., Tapiador, J., Caballero, J.: The malsource dataset: quantifying complexity and code reuse in malware development. IEEE Trans. Inf. Forens. Secur. **14**(12), 3175–3190 (2018)
15. Chen, J., et al.: {SYMSAN}: time and space efficient concolic execution via dynamic data-flow analysis. In: 31st USENIX Security Symposium (USENIX Security 22), pp. 2531–2548 (2022)
16. Dataprot: A Not-So-Common Cold: Malware Statistics in 2022 (2023). https://dataprot.net/statistics/malware-statistics/
17. Godefroid, P.: Test generation using symbolic execution. In: D'Souza, D., Kavitha, T., Radhakrishnan, J. (eds.) IARCS Annual Conference on Foundations of Software Technology and Theoretical Computer Science, FSTTCS 2012. LIPIcs, vol. 18, pp. 24–33. Schloss Dagstuhl - Leibniz-Zentrum für Informatik (2012)
18. Gorecki, C., Freiling, F.C., Kührer, M., Holz, T.: TrumanBox: improving dynamic malware analysis by emulating the internet. In: Défago, X., Petit, F., Villain, V. (eds.) Stabilization, Safety, and Security of Distributed Systems, pp. 208–222. Springer, Heidelberg (2011). https://doi.org/10.1007/978-3-642-24550-3_17
19. HackTricks. Common API used in malware (2023). https://book.hacktricks.xyz/reversing-and-exploiting/common-api-used-in-malware
20. Massarelli, L., Di Luna, G.A., Petroni, F., Querzoni, L., Baldoni, R.: Function representations for binary similarity. IEEE Trans. Depend. Secure Comput. **19**(4), 2259–2273 (2021)
21. Microsoft: Programming reference for the win32 API (2023). https://learn.microsoft.com/en-us/windows/win32/api/
22. Namani, N., Khan, A.: Symbolic execution based feature extraction for detection of malware. In: 2020 5th International Conference on Computing, Communication and Security (ICCCS), pp. 1–6. IEEE (2020)
23. NSA. Ghidra (2023). https://ghidra-sre.org/
24. Obdržálek, J., Trtík, M.: Efficient loop navigation for symbolic execution. In: Bultan, T., Hsiung, PA. (eds.) Automated Technology for Verification and Analysis. ATVA 2011. LNCS, vol. 6996, pp. 453–462. Springer, Heidelberg (2011). https://doi.org/10.1007/978-3-642-24372-1_34
25. Park, K., et al.: Identifying behavior dispatchers for malware analysis. In: Proceedings of the 2021 ACM Asia Conference on Computer and Communications Security, pp. 759–773 (2021)
26. Said, N.B., et al.: Detection of Mirai by syntactic and behavioral analysis. In: Ghosh, S., Natella, R., Cukic, B., Poston, R.S., Laranjeiro, N. (eds.) 29th IEEE International Symposium on Software Reliability Engineering, ISSRE 2018, Memphis, 15–18 October 2018, pp. 224–235. IEEE Computer Society (2018)
27. Schrittwieser, S., Katzenbeisser, S.: Code obfuscation against static and dynamic reverse engineering. In: Filler, T., Pevný, T., Craver, S., Ker, A. (eds.) Information Hiding, pp. 270–284. Springer, Heidelberg (2011). https://doi.org/10.1007/978-3-642-24178-9_19

28. Schrittwieser, S., Kochberger, P., Pucher, M., Lawitschka, C., König, P., Weippl, E.R.: Obfuscation-resilient semantic functionality identification through program simulation. In: Reiser, H.P., Kyas, M. (eds) Secure IT Systems. NordSec 2022. LNCS, vol. 13700, pp. 273–291. Springer, Cham (2023). https://doi.org/10.1007/978-3-031-22295-5_15

29. Schwartz, E.J., Avgerinos, T., Brumley, D.: All you ever wanted to know about dynamic taint analysis and forward symbolic execution (but might have been afraid to ask). In: 2010 IEEE Symposium on Security and Privacy, pp. 317–331. IEEE (2010)

30. Sebastio, S., et al.: Optimizing symbolic execution for malware behavior classification. Comput. Secur. **93**, 101775 (2020)

31. Shoshitaishvili, Y., et al.: Sok:(state of) the art of war: offensive techniques in binary analysis. In: 2016 IEEE Symposium on Security and Privacy (SP), pp. 138–157. IEEE (2016)

32. Talos, C.: Magicrat: Lazarus' Latest Gateway into Victim Networks (2022). https://blog.talosintelligence.com/lazarus-magicrat/

33. Team, Y.: Yararules (2023). https://github.com/Yara-Rules/rules

34. TrendMicro: Indicators of Compromise (2023). https://www.trendmicro.com/vinfo/us/security/definition/indicators-of-compromise

35. Valeros, V., Garcia, S.: Growth and commoditization of remote access trojans. In: 2020 IEEE European Symposium on Security and Privacy Workshops (EuroS&PW), pp. 454–462. IEEE (2020)

36. Vasilescu, M., Gheorghe, L., Tapus, N.: Practical malware analysis based on sandboxing. In: 2014 RoEduNet Conference 13th Edition: Networking in Education and Research Joint Event RENAM 8th Conference, pp. 1–6. IEEE (2014)

37. Yan, X., Han, J.: gspan: Graph-based substructure pattern mining. In: 2002 IEEE International Conference on Data Mining, 2002, pp. 721–724. IEEE (2002)

38. Yun, I., Lee, S., Xu, M., Jang, Y., Kim, T.: {QSYM}: a practical concolic execution engine tailored for hybrid fuzzing. In: 27th {USENIX} Security Symposium ({USENIX} Security 18), pp. 745–761 (2018)

Original Entry Point Detection Based on Graph Similarity

Thanh-Hung Pham$^{(\boxtimes)}$ and Mizuhito Ogawa$^{(\boxtimes)}$

Japan Advanced Institute of Science and Technology, Nomi, Japan
hung.pthanh@gmail.com, mizuhito@jaist.ac.jp

Abstract. This paper proposes a method for packer identification and OEP (Original Entry Point) detection based on the graph similarity on control flow graphs of packed codes. Packed code consists of an unpacking stub and a packed payload, which is recovered to the original after the unpacking stub executes. In this paper, the CFGs of packed code are generated by a DSE (Dynamic Symbolic Execution) tool BE-PUM on x86-32/Windows. We define the *template* of the unpacking stub as the pair of the average of Weisfeiler-Lehman histogram vectors and the tail jump sequence. Next, each template is computed packer-wise (i.e., processing packed codes by the same packer) for the ease of covering a new packer. We use the total of 71 samples packed by 12 packers. For unknown packed code, we will find the templates in its CFG generated by BE-PUM.

Among them, the CFG fragment with the highest cosine similarity is regarded as the unpacking stub, which also detects the used packer and the OEP as the jump destination from the exit.

Our first experiment is performed on 700 non-malware samples (of which the original payload is also known) packed by 12 packers above. The used packer is correctly identified for 689 and the OEP is correctly detected for 688. Further, we apply the method to 1239 malware samples. Among them, 1089 samples are detected packed by *unknown packer* and among them 150 samples are detected as packed by the 11 packers (except for TELOCK) and their OEPs are detected. We conclude that our method is highly effective as long as we have access to an executable of a target packer to compute its templates.

Keywords: Original Entry point detection · Packer Identification · Graph similarity

1 Introduction

Malware threat increases every year. Not only new techniques are introduced, but also a systematic development becomes popular, such as the use of a packer. It is said that more than 80% of recent malware is obfuscated by packers to bypass anti-virus software. For x86, more than 50 popular packers are available on the net, and they often encrypt the payload which is decrypted at runtime by

M. Mosbah et al. (Eds.): FPS 2023, LNCS 14551, pp. 355–371, 2024.
https://doi.org/10.1007/978-3-031-57537-2_22

unpacking stubs (Fig. 1). Hence, the detection of the used packer and the OEP (Original Entry Point) is important to understand the hidden actions of the payload of malware. Control obfuscations, such as indirect jumps, code flattening, opaque predicates (mixing dead code), and self-modification, are mostly in the unpacking stub. It is believed that DSE (Dynamic Symbolic Execution) [1,2] is the most powerful de-obfuscation, which exhaustively traces feasible control paths only. We adopt a DSE tool BE-PUM [3] on x86-32/Windows to obtain precise control flow graphs of packed code.

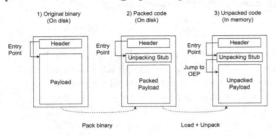

Fig. 1. Packing and Unpacking Process

This paper proposes a method for the packer identification and the OEP (Original Entry Point) detection based on the graph similarity of CFGs (Control Flow Graphs) of packed codes. Packed code consists of an unpacking stub and a packed payload, which is recovered to the original after the unpacking stub executes. We start with the hypothesis that the CFG of the unpacking stub characterizes a packer. Note that when the original payloads and used packers are known (e.g., pack the payload by ourselves) we can identify the unpacking stub. Figure 4 (Sect. 4) shows preliminary observation on UPX, FSG, and Mew, respectively. A packer may have different patterns of CFGs of the unpacking stubs (e.g., WIN-UPACK has 2), but the pattern of the unpacking stubs converges regardless of the payloads. Our tool for the graph similarity is a *Weisfeiler-Lehman histogram vector* (Sect. 3) of a CFG, which is computed iteratively by relabeling each node with the collection of neighbor's labels [4].

First, to confirm the hypothesis, we classify 771 samples packed by 12 packers (UPX v3.95, ASPACK v2.12, FSG v1.0, YODA v1.3, MEW SE v1.2, PACKMAN v1.0, PECOMPACT v2.xx, PETITE v2.1, WINUPACK v0.39 Final, JDPACK v1.01, MPRESS v2.xx, and TELOCK v0.98) by a clustering algorithm DBSCAN wrt the graph similarity, (which is the cosine similarity [5] on Weisfeiler-Lehman histogram vectors). We observe that when the allowance *eps* of DBSCAN is small enough (e.g., $eps = 0.02$), (1) each class does not cross different packers, and (2) the tail jump sequence (the prefix of the exit of an unpacking stub) is the same in each class. Hence, we define the *template* of the class as the pair of the average of Weisfeiler-Lehman histogram vectors (of CFGs of the unpacking stubs) and the tail jump sequence. The length of the vector rapidly increases with respect to the number k of the diameter, and we set $k = 2$.

Next, we prepare the templates of 12 packers, using 71 packed samples. For the ease of introducing a new packer, we compute them packer-wise (i.e., clustering code packed by the same packer). Finally, for an unknown code, BE-PUM incrementally generates the CFG. When the tail jump sequence matches with the tail of a CFG fragment, we check the similarity between its Weisfeiler-Lehman histogram vector and that in prepared templates. Among them, the CFG fragment with the highest cosine similarity is regarded as the unpacking stub, which also detects the used packer and the OEP as the jump destination from the exit.

We perform experiments on 700 non-malware samples (which are packed by 12 packers mentioned above). Our method correctly detects the packer for 689, and the OEP for 688. For the packer identification, `VirusTotal` (a database collected from various resources) identifies 699 beyond our result, but the OEP detection result is distinguished from others, e.g., `GUnpacker` and `QuickUnpack` find 525 and 283, respectively. Further, 1239 malware samples are examined. Among them, 1089 are detected packed by *unknown packer* and 150 are packed by the 11 packers (except for TELOCK). Our main contributions are,

1. Apart from dynamic analysis based on dirty page tracing, we observe the control flow generated by DSE tool BE-PUM [3] (when we have access to an executable of a target packer).
2. We combine statistical similarity (Weisfeiler-Lehman kernel) with the symbolic evidence (the tail jump sequence of the unpacking stub) to characterize the unpacking stub. This pair is called the *template* of a packer.

The paper is constructed as follows. Section 2 introduces basic terminologies and BE-PUM. Section 3 describes Weisfeiler-Lehman Kernel. In Sect. 4, we discuss our hypothesis about CFGs of unpacking stubs. Section 5 describes our method for the packer identification and the OEP detection. Then, our experimental results are shown in Sect. 6. Finally, Sect. 7 concludes the paper.

Related Works. Most of the OEP detection is based on a dynamic analysis. If a packed code is fully executed, the original payload must be somewhere in the memory. `Polyunpack` [6] first applies the static disassembly and then runs dynamic analysis. If an executed instruction is different from disassembly, it is regarded as unpacked. `Omniunpack` [7] observes some sensitive system calls. When such a call is detected, it scans the memory page to find unpacked code. Since the original payload is often unpacked in a newly allocated memory, most of OEP detection tools monitor and/or hook the access to a dirty page (i.e., `write` occurs on a write-protected page) by setting a write protection on a newly allocated area. OllyBonE[1] is a plugin of *Ollydbg*, and tries to stop when the control jumps to a newly allocated region. It prepares a Windows kernel driver for the page protection of a specified region and sets a target memory area and an exception *break-on-execute*. When the control flow moves to the address inside the protected area, it is regarded as the OEP. However, it fails when packers use anti-debugging with the API `IsDebuggerPresent@kernel32.dll`.

The candidates of the OEP are explored either on-the-fly or ahead-of-time. Renovo [8] is built on the top of an emulation environment, TEMU[2] It stores a shadow copy of the memory space of the target file and monitors runtime

---

[1] http://www.joestewart.org/ollybone.
[2] http://bitblaze.cs.berkeley.edu/temu.html.

updates. Alternatively, the entry of recently generated code and data is regarded as the OEP. `QuickUnpack`[3] set the OEP breakpoints, following a common strategy, e.g., pushing breakpoints at `jump` instruction and inspecting near `popa`. `QuickUnpack` chooses the last trigger to OEP breakpoints as the OEP.

The ahead-of-time search of the candidates for the OEP first prepares the candidate list and check it. In [9], OEP candidates are collected at the page faults. They are checked by the entropy (since an encrypted code has larger entropy, i.e., more random) and the number of API calls placed in the memory. `PinDemonium` [10] detects OEP candidates whether the memory dump (using Scylla [11]) can reconstruct the library function table. `Junstin` [12] is often used to collect the OEP candidates. It monitors the control flow and selects an OEP candidate when jumps to a dirty page. It reduces the candidates by heuristics, e.g., *Unpacker Memory Avoidance* (avoid unlikely pages containing unpacked code), *Stack Pointer Check* (check the stack pointer whether the same as the start of the execution), and *Command-line Argument Access* (check whether the command-line argument is put to the stack at the dirty page access). [13] tried to reduce the OEP candidates by identifying decryption routines (by watching writing instructions and written areas) and sorts the candidates. [14] follows [13], and further watching branching instructions to identify decryption routines and tracking system parameters related to the main function. Then, the nearest to the structured exception handler installation (which is located at the last `write` on `fs:[0]` during the system startup) is regarded as the OEP. Apart from the dirty page tracing, [15] combines statistical and symbolic signs which is the pair of the entropy and the single instruction (either `JMP`, `JCC`, `CALL`, or `RET`).

The graph similarity is applied for malware detection and analyses [16,17]. After obtaining CFGs of packed codes by the symbolic execution `Angr`[4], the former uses CNN on CFGs and the latter uses the (1-dimensional) Weisfeiler-Lehman kernel on a call graph. However, they do not care to distinguish the unpacking stubs and the payloads. Apart from them, we apply the symbolic execution `BEPUM` [3] and the graph similarity to classify the targets, instead of their machine learning techniques.

2   Preliminaries

2.1   Terminologies on Graph

We denote the concatenation of two strings s_1 and s_2 by $s_1.s_2$. For a directed graph $G = (V, E)$ with $E \subseteq V \times V$ and $v \in V$, let

$$ancestors(v) = \{u \mid (u, v) \in E\} \qquad successors(v) = \{u \mid (v, u) \in E\}.$$
$$N(v) = (ancestors(v) \cup successors(v)) \setminus \{v\}$$

The *indegree* $\deg^-(v)$ and *outdegree* $\deg^+(v)$ of $v \in V$ is $|ancestors(v)|$ and $|successors(v)|$, respectively. $v \in V$ is a *source node* (resp. *sink node*) if

---

[3] https://www.aldeid.com/wiki/QuickUnpack.
[4] https://angr.io/.

$\deg^-(v) = 0$ (resp. $\deg^+(v) = 0$). We also sometimes denote $u \to v$ if $(u,v) \in E$. A directed graph G is *acyclic* if there are no $v \in V$ with a cycle $v \to^+ v$.

Assuming a DFS on G, we have the order among children nodes. We say,

- Forward edge: from an ancestor to a direct descendant.
- Cross edge: from a righter node to a lefter node.
- Retreating edge: from a descendant to an ancestor.
- Back edge: Retreating edges (u,v) such that v dominates u, i.e., every path from the roof of the DFS tree to u traverses v.

Definition 1. *Let $G = (V,E)$ be a directed acyclic graph. For $u \in V$, the* predecessor graph *from u is a graph $Pre_u^G = (V_u, E_u)$ with*

$$V_u = \{v \in V \mid v \xrightarrow{*} u\} \qquad E_u = E \cap (V_u \times V_u) \tag{1}$$

If G is clear from the context, we may omit it as Pre_u.

The label of $G = (V,E)$ is a labelling function $l_G : V \to \Sigma$. When $l_G(u) = \sigma$, $\sigma \in \Sigma$ is the label of $u \in V$.

2.2 De-obfuscation for CFG Generation

Obfuscation Techniques. The difficulty of analyzing packed malware comes from the use of obfuscation techniques introduced by a packer. When a program is obfuscated (e.g., encryption), it may not be interpreted statically. Hence, these packed codes can evade firewall and antivirus scanners. Typical obfuscation techniques are classified into 14 [18], which are further classified into 6 groups [19].

1. **Entry/code placing obfuscation** (Code layout): overlapping functions, overlapping blocks, and code chunking.
2. **Self-modification code** (Dynamic code): overwriting and packing/unpacking.
3. **Instruction obfuscation**: Indirect jump.
4. **Anti-tracing**: SEH (structural exception handler) and 2API (the use of special APIs, LoadLibrary and GetProcAddress in kernel32.dll).
5. **Arithmetic operation**: Obfuscated constants and checksumming.
6. **Anti-tampering**: Timing check, anti-debugging, anti-rewriting, and hardware breakpoints. Anti-rewriting consists of stolen bytes and checksumming.

Among them, Anti-tampering contains VM-awareness and trigger-based behavior, which often affects on dynamic analysis and monitoring.

- Anti-Debugging: It detects the presence of a debug mode by specific API calls, e.g., *CALL kernel32.IsDebuggerPresent*
- Stolen bytes: This calls *VirtualAlloc* to allocate a buffer, and the unpacked code is written on this area.
- Timing Check: This checks timing anomaly compared to the native Windows environment.
- Hardware breakpoint: Jump destination is stored in debug registers, such as DR0, DR1, DR2, and DR3.

BE-PUM for CFG Generation. DSE is considered to be the most powerful tool for de-obfuscation [2,19]. For instance, DSE overcomes anti-tampering techniques since it can generate satisfiable test instances as long as it is on an executable path. Alternatively, DSE will not explore dead code (e.g., *opaque predicate*) since the constraint for it is detected unsatisfiable.

BE-PUM (Binary Emulation for PUshdown Model)[5] [3] is a DSE tool for binary code on Intel x86/Win32 architecture, which generates the precise CFG of a binary code (including malware). Overall, the architecture of BE-PUM can be illustrated by three main components, which are a CFG storage, a binary emulator, and a symbolic execution (Fig. 2). BE-PUM also adopts JackStab 0.8.3 [20] for one-step disassembly (i.e., interpret one instruction from a given address), Z3 4.3 [21] for a constraint solver (with the *bitvector* backend theory).

Architecture.png

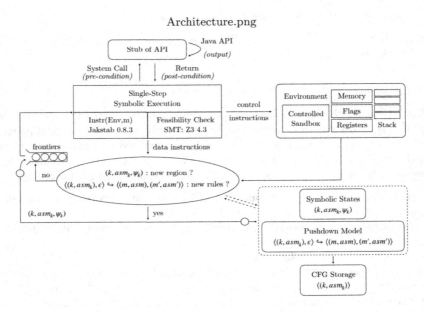

Fig. 2. The architecture of BE-PUM [19]

The frontiers in the left-hand side of Fig. 2 store symbolic states (described by the path constraints on symbolic values) at the leaves of currently explored traces. BE-PUM selects one from it and tries to apply the one-step symbolic execution. If it is an indirect jump, one-step testing by a satisfiable instance decides the next destination before the application of symbolic execution. It extends one step of the possible traces, and the path constraint is expanded. This procedure terminates when either the exploration has converged or comes to

---

[5] https://github.com/NMHai/BE-PUM.

unknown instructions, unknown system calls, or unknown addresses. Currently, BE-PUM supports about 400×86 instructions and >1000 Win32 APIs.

3   Weisfeiler-Lehman Kernel

In order to deal with the graph isomorphism, the 1-*dimensional Weisfeiler-Lehman test* has been introduced [4]. It performs with multiple iterations to relabel nodes by compressing the current node labels with the concatenation of the sorted string of node labels of neighboring nodes.

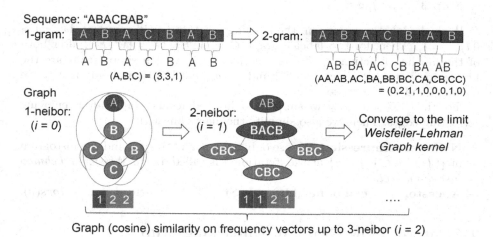

Fig. 3. Weisfeiler-Lehman algorithm

Let $G = (V, E, \ell)$ be a labelled graph with the labelling function $\ell : V \to \Sigma$. We assume that Σ is a totally ordered set. Let $l_0 = \ell$ and $i > 0$. $l_i : V \to \Sigma^*$ is the labeling function after the i-th iteration, which is computed by the following steps. Let $v \in V$ and we assume a total order on Σ.

- **Step 1**: $M_i : V \to \mathcal{M}(\Sigma^*)$ is a multiset-labeling function such that $M_i(v) = \{l_{i-1}(u) \mid u \in N(v)\}$.
- **Step 2**: $s_i : V \to \Sigma^*$ is defined by
  1. $M_i(v)$ is sorted in the ascending order (wrt the lexicographic extension) as $M_i(v) = (l_{i-1}(u_1), l_{i-1}(u_2), \cdots, l_{i-k}(u_k))$.
  2. $s_i(v) = l_{i-1}(v).l_{i-1}(u_1).l_{i-1}(u_2).\cdots.l_{i-k}(u_k)$.
- **Step 3**: $l_i := s_i$.

Figure 3 shows an analogy of the computation of the Weisfeiler-Lehman Kernel of a graph with the n-gram of a word. n-gram collects the labels of the sequence of the length n. At the i-step, the Weisfeiler-Lehman histogram vector inductively computes the collection of labels in the diameter i of each node.

The Weisfeiler-Lehman Kernel continues to compute until the label converges, whereas we use an approximation up to $i = 2$.

For the graph isomorphism, [4] further performs the *label compression* by defining a partial function $f_i : \Sigma^* \to \Sigma$. Adding to the steps above, f_i is incrementally defined starting from $f_0(\sigma) = \sigma$ for $\sigma \in \Sigma$.

- **Step 2':** For $w = s_i(v)$,

$$f_i(w) = \begin{cases} f_{i-1}(w) & \text{if } w \in Dom(f_{i-1}) \\ v' & \text{otherwise, } v' \text{ is a fresh label added to } \Sigma \end{cases}$$

- **Step 3':** $l_i := f_i \circ s_i$.

With the label compression, the labeling function l_1 will converge, i.e., $\exists j > 0.l_{j+1} = l_j$. Then, for two labeled graph $G = (V, E)$, $G' = (V', E')$, after both of the labeling functions l_i, l'_i converge at $i = j$, we can simply compare the histogram vectors of $\{l_j(v) \mid v \in V\}$ and $\{l'_j(v) \mid v \in V'\}$. If and only if they are equal, G and G' are isomorphic.

For the CFG similarity, we simplify to directed acyclic graphs after removing retreating edges. Then, we also simplify the algorithm with

- **No label compression:** We use only **Step 1** and **Step 2** and the histogram of $\{l_i(v) \mid v \in V, i \leq j\}$ at the iteration j is called a j-th *Weisfeiler-Lehman histogram vector*.
- **Ancestors instead of neighbors:** In **Step 1**, $N(v)$ instead of $ancestors(v)$.

4   Control Flow Graph of Unpacking Stub

4.1   The CFG of the Unpacking Stub Characterizes a Packer

We start with our observation that a packed code has a similar unpacking stub regardless of the original payload. Besides, it is necessary to remark that the labels on our graphs only contain the opcode of instructions. Originally, each CFG node is labelled with an instruction and its address. However, the value of address and operands can vary between different packed codes by the same packer. Therefore, we decide to remove this information from the labels in our graph for the ease of graph similarity. The left hand side of Fig. 4 shows the comparison of two CFGs of the packed code by UPX. From this observation, we further set the hypothesis that a similar class of CFGs of unpacking stubs does not cross different packers. If it works, we can identify the used packer and the unpacking stub by the graph matching. (We confirm it by our preliminary experiments in Sect. 6.) Note that the graph matching will be not exact, since even if the CFGs are in the same class, they may have different offsets, which make binary codes different. To remedy this, we apply the graph similarity, i.e., the cosine similarity [5] on Weisfeiler-Lehman histogram vectors, after annealing the labels by stripping arguments from the instructions.

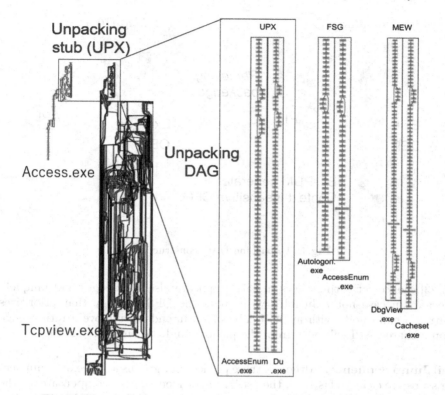

Fig. 4. The similarly among predecessor graphs in the same packer

When we know both the unpacking stub and the original payload, we can identify the body of the unpacking stub as the difference between the memory image after the execution of the packed code and the original payload. Hence, in theory, the CFG of unpacking stubs will be the predecessor graph at the exit of the unpacking stub. However, we sometimes observe a path from the unpacked payload to the unpacking stub. This looks strange since the original payload does not know the unpacking stub in advance. We observe that this happens when the unpacking stub and the unpacked payload call the same API (Fig. 5), and this is because the CFG generated by BE-PUM is context-insensitive, i.e., there are no criteria to distinguish different call-sites.

To remedy the situation, we simply strip the retreating edges in the CFG, and then taking the preceding graph at the exit of the unpacking stub. We call it the *unpacking DAG*. Note that the unpacking DAG avoids a loop in the unpacking stub (e.g., a decrypting loop), which may reduce the size of the unpacking DAG much smaller than the original CFG. The right-hand side of Fig. 4 shows the unpacking DAG examples of UPX, FSG, and Mew. They look similar.

As the last remark, a retreating edge in a directed graph depends on the order of nodes travelled in the DFS. However, CFGs of most programs are reducible

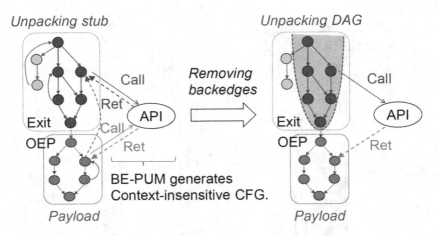

Fig. 5. Unpacking DAG construction

[22,23], hence retreating edges in this graph are also back-edges and uniquely selected. In case not reducible, we prepare the DFS strategy that prioritizes visiting a child node with an API call, which intends to remove a return edge from a shared API call both from the payload and the unpacking stub.

Tail Jump Sequence. Although these predecessor graphs at the exit of unpacking stubs are clearly classified, they still are not identical. To compensate for the approximation, we observe that the tail jump sequence of these graphs in the same class is consistent. Here, the tail jump sequence is the opcode sequence of the last m instructions in these graphs. Currently, we set $m = 5$. The table below shows several tail jump sequences (proceeding left-to-right) for UPX, FSG, and MEW.

Packer	the tail jump sequence of unpacking stub
UPX	`pushl, cmpl, jne, subl, jmp`
FSG	`je, decb, jne, decb, je`
MEW	`GETPROCADDRESS-KERNEL32-DLL, stosl, testl, jne, ret`

The tail jump sequence of unpacking stubs has an important role in our method because Weisfeiler-Lehman kernel is a statistical method and it just approximates a graph into a vector. However, a tail jump sequence is a symbolic property. Therefore, it can reduce the number of unpacking stub candidates and confirm again whether a node in a graph is the exit of an unpacking stub.

4.2 Confirming Hypothesis by Clustering Packed Codes

After intuitive observation, we confirm our hypothesis by clustering 771 samples packed by 12 packers (UPX v3.95, ASPACK v2.12, FSG v1.0, YODA v1.3, MEW

SE v1.2, PACKMAN v1.0, PECOMPACT v2.xx, PETITE v2.1, WINUPACK v0.39 Final, JDPACK v1.01, MPRESS v2.xx, and TELOCK v0.98). After taking Weisfeiler-Lehman histogram vectors of the CFGs of unpacking stubs (since we know both the original payload and the used packer), the clustering algorithm DBSCAN with the cosine similarity is applied. The table shows the results of DBSCAN with fixed parameters $min\_sample = 2$ and $metric = cosine$. We observe the change wrt eps from 0.1 to 0.02.

eps	0.1	0.09	0.08	0.07	0.06	0.05	0.04	0.03	0.02
number of class	11	11	12	14	16	16	18	18	21
Hypothesis (1)	False	False	False	False	False	False	True	True	True
Hypothesis (2)	False	False	False	False	False	False	False	False	True

We observe that when the allowance eps of DBSCAN is small enough,

(1) each class does not cross different packers, and
(2) the end instruction sequence (the prefix of the exit of an unpacking stub of the length 5) is the same in each class.

More precisely, $eps = 0.04$ is enough for (1), and $eps = 0.02$ satisfies both.

5 Packer Identification End OEP Detection Using Template Matching

In Sect. 4, we observe that Weisfeiler-Lehman histogram vectors and the tail jump sequence characterize each class of unpacking stubs. We define a *template* of a packer by the pair of the average of Weisfeiler-Lehman histogram vectors and the tail jump sequence. Note that some packers may have several templates.

5.1 Template Setup for Each Packer

Clustering Procedure. The process of template setup for a fixed packer includes 5 steps. We use the CFG of a packed code generated by BE-PUM.

- **Step 1**: Generate the unpacking DAGs of the unpacking stub.
- **Step 2**: Compute their Weisfeiler-Lehman histogram vector.
- **Step 3**: Apply the 0-aligning, i.e., fulfilling 0 to make the dimensions of vectors the same.
- **Step 4**: Apply the clustering algorithm DBSCAN with the cosine similarity.
- **Step 5**: Pair the average of Weisfeiler-Lehman histogram vectors in each cluster and the tail jump sequence (if it is consistent).

At **Step 4**, we apply DBSCAN with $eps = 0.05$. However, some clusters have inconsistent tail jump sequences. In such a case, we decrease the eps value by the step 0.01 and perform again the clustering until stabilized.

5.2 Template Matching for Packer Identification and OEP Detection

When we face an unknown packed code, the template-matching process consists of 4 steps. We use the CFG of a packed code generated by BE-PUM.

- **Step 1**: During incremental DFS trace of the CFG, remove a retreating edge and generate the predecessor graph at each node.
- **Step 2**: Compute its Weisfeiler-Lehman histogram vector.
- **Step 3**: If the tail jump sequence of the predecessor graph matches that in a template, check the similarity between the Weisfeiler-Lehman histogram vectors.
- **Step 4**: Choose the template of the maximum similarity.

The node at **Step 4** (the sink node of the predecessor graph) is recognized as the exit of the unpacking stub, and the OEP is detected as the jump destination from it. The packer is identified simultaneously. Figure 6 shows an example of steps 3 and 4, in which the node 7 is the exit of the unpacking stub, the node 8 is the OEP, and P is the used packer.

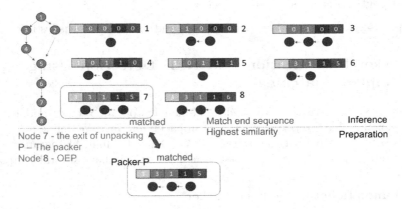

Fig. 6. Template matching for Packer Identification and OEP detection

6 Experiment

A packed code with the used packer name and the original payload is taken from Git Hub pages[6],[7] (the latter for TELOCK). We prepare CFGs of packed code by BE-PUM with a time limit of 1 hour, which results in 771 samples. We also prepared 1259 samples of malware from VXHeaven. Windows environment of BE-PUM is set to Windows 7-32 bit except for TELOCK. Telock requires

---

[6] https://github.com/chesvectain/PackingData.
[7] https://github.com/packing-box/dataset-packed-pe.

sysenter, which currently works in BE-PUM only with Windows XP 32-bit. The experimental environments are built on VMware Workstation Pro 17 with Host OS Ubuntu 20.04 and Processor 13th Gen Intel(R) Core(TM) i9-13900K 3.00 GHz. Details of experiments are shown at the GitHub Link[8].

6.1   Testing on Non-malware Samples

In this experiment, we used 71 samples for obtaining templates, and 700 samples for testing. Our proposed method is compared with

- **Packer identification:** VirusTotal (1), PyPackerDetect[9](2), BE-PUM [19] (which finds the used packer by the frequency of obfuscation techniques).
- **OEP detection:** Gunpacker v0.5[10](3), QuickUnpack v2.2[11](4).

Among OEP detection tools mentioned in **Related Work**, we could not find access to most of them [7–9,13–15], except for Polyunpack [6] source[12]

Roughly speaking, the execution time depends on the number of nodes in the CFG. Our method takes mostly around 6 s for 550 nodes, and 260 s for 3500 nodes, respectively, whereas GunUnpacker and QuickUnpack take 1–2 s.

Packer	Samples	Packer Identification				OEP detection		
		(1)	(2)	BE-PUM	Ours	(3)	(4)	Ours
UPX v3.95	85	85	30	84	85	78	85	85
ASPACK v2.12	68	68	68	68	68	56	68	68
FSG v1.0	75	75	75	75	75	70	75	75
PECOMPACT v2.xx	27	27	27	27	27	0	8	27
MEW SE v1.2	75	75	75	75	75	74	8	75
YODA's Cryptor v1.3	74	74	74	62	74	73	8	74
PETITE v2.1	34	34	34	34	34	0	8	34
WINUPACK v.039 final	26	26	26	26	15	26	4	15
MPRESS v2.xx	78	78	0	78	78	0	8	78
PACKMAN v1.0	79	79	79	0	79	79	8	78
JDPACK v1.01	52	51	0	0	52	45	2	52
TELOCK v0.98	27	27	27	27	27	24	1	27
Total	700	699	515	556	689	525	283	688

6.2   Observation on the Result of Experiments

For the packer identification, our method correctly detects the packer for 689, next to VirusTotal (a database collected from various resources) for 699.

---

[8] https://github.com/hungpthanh/oep-detection-based-on-graph-similarity.
[9] https://github.com/cylance/PyPackerDetect.
[10] https://webscene.ir/tools/show/GUnPacker-v0.5.
[11] https://www.aldeid.com/wiki/QuickUnpack.
[12] https://github.com/PlatonovIvan/PolyUnpack.

- The failure of `PyPackerDetect` and BE-PUM would come from the obsolete setups, i.e., the supported versions of packers seem too old. The packer identification of BE-PUM is in built-in service [19], which compares the frequency of the occurrences of obfuscation techniques, called *metadata signature*. BE-PUM also detects whether packed by the presence of overwrite the code (e.g., self-modification, encryption). However, the metadata signatures are not updated (which causes failures for UPX and YODA), and BE-PUM does not support PACKMAN and JDPACK. Similarly, `PyPackerDetect` fails on MPRESS and JDPACK.
- Our method for the packer identification fails on 11 samples by WINUPACK, which report *"unknown packer"*. The reason is, although WINUPACK has at least 2 templates (Fig. 7), our method found only the left one due to a small number of samples (the total 71 for 12 packers) for the template setup.

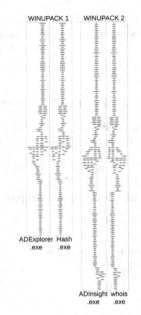

Fig. 7. WINUPACK templates

For the OEP detection, our method correctly detects the OEP for 688, whereas `GunUnpacker` and `QuickUnpack` find 525 and 283, respectively.

- Our method fails 11 samples in WINUPACK (of which the packer identification already fails) and 1 sample in PACKMAN. This shows that once the used packer is correctly identified, our OEP detection is mostly correct. Figure 8 shows the irregular behavior of the failed sample of PACKMAN. We observed that there is an instruction `jmp start`, which strangely repeats the unpacking process one more time before jumping to the OEP.
- The table below shows the metadata signature of BE-PUM [19], in which the number in the top column indicates the categories of obfuscation techniques [18], e.g., (3)

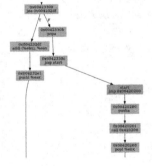

Fig. 8. PACKMAN failure

overwriting and (4) Packing-unpacking. `Gunpacker` fails on PECOMPACT, PETITE, and MPRESS, which seem to have significantly more (3) overwriting and (4) Packing-unpacking obfuscations.

Packer	Average frequency of obfuscation techniques													
	0	1	2	3	4	5	6	7	8	9	10	11	12	13
UPX	0	2.27	0.53	0.1	16.14	17.41	0.41	11	5.57	0.28	0.16	0.03	0.13	0.13
ASPACK	2	0	0	0.5	76.73	8.97	0	1.5	12.92	0	0	0	2	0
FSG	0	0.09	1.54	0.13	14.27	27.34	0.28	16.05	3.74	0	0.16	0.03	0.14	0.1
PECOMPACT	0.53	0.61	0.7	**1.12**	**106.56**	18.8	1.06	6.89	20.63	0	0.04	0	3.03	1.01
MEW	0.3	0	2.65	0.03	55.84	27.66	0.29	14.38	16.67	0.01	0.13	0.02	0.15	0.1
YODA	0	1.77	5.08	0.14	17.15	25.12	1.11	16.75	13.84	1.01	0.17	0.89	0.14	0.96
PETITE	0	0.03	1.65	**3.46**	**180.79**	9.31	2.4	1.81	26.44	0.05	0.11	0	0.25	0.12
WINUPACK	0.47	0.47	0.1	0.09	21.12	22.91	0.07	2.24	4.67	0.76	0.04	0	0.01	0.03
MPRESS	0	0	1.94	**1.88**	**93.81**	0.94	0	0.94	9.82	0	0	0	0	0
PACKMAN	0.48	0	0	0.02	6.87	4.8	0	0.94	0.97	0	0	0	0.99	0
JDPACK	3.09	5.59	0.33	0.07	19.32	27.16	0.16	16.62	2.81	0	0.23	0.01	1.07	0.05
TELOCK	0	2.94	3.96	0	37.42	7.56	9.81	0.21	11.33	0	0.02	0	0	1.98

6.3   Experiment on Real Malware

We also tried 5190 malware samples taken from VXHeaven. Among them, BE-PUM generates CFGs for 1239 within a 1-hour timeout.

From them, our method detects 1089 packed by *unknown packers* (i.e., beyond the prepared templates of 11 packers) and 150 are identified the used packer names (among 11 packers except for Telock). For them, the OEPs are also reported. The table shows the identified packers.

Packer	UPX	ASPACK	FSG	PECOMPACT	YODA	WINUPACK	MPRESS
Sample	80	26	1	9	13	20	1

When a packer is identified, our method also detects the OEP, though currently, we cannot verify its correctness. However, the tail jump sequence of the unpacking stub would rarely match by luck, and their similarity to our template is higher than 0.51, among them, 133 samples have a similarity of more than 0.7.

7   Conclusion

This paper proposed a method for the packer identification and the OEP (Original Entry Point) detection based on the graph similarity of CFGs (Control Flow Graphs) of packed codes. The CFG generation of packed code owes fully on a DSE tool BE-PUM [3] on x86-32/Windows. Our tool for the graph similarity is a *Weisfeiler-Lehman histogram vector* (Sect. 3) of a CFG, which is computed iteratively by relabeling each node with the collection of neibor's labels [4].

First, we confirmed the hypothesis that the CFG of the unpacking stub characterizes a packer by the clustering of 771 samples packed by 12 packers (UPX, ASPACK, FSG, Yoda, Mew, Packman, PECOMPACT, Petite, WINUPACK, JDPACK, MPRESS, and TELOCK). Second, we set the template, which is the pair of the average of *Weisfeiler-Lehman histogram vectors* and the tail jump sequence. Experiments showed the effectiveness of our method, especially on the OEP (Original Entry Point) detection. For 700 non-malware samples (which are packed by 12 packers above), our method correctly detected the packer for 689, and the OEP for 688. For 1239 malware samples, 1089 were detected packed by *unknown packer* and 150 were packed by the 11 packers (except for TELOCK). Throughout the experiments, when the packer identification succeeds, the OEP seems to be correctly detected (except for 1 case packed by PACKMAN). The impact on the OEP detection is much more substantial than on packer identification, since analyzing the original payload would give new sights on malware.

Future Work. In the future, we would like to extend our methods to many other packers. Particularly, we also extend our methods to packers using vm-protect techniques (i.e., themida). In addition, the limitation of our current work is that we need to access the packer's executable to generate the templates. We hope to tackle custom packers, of which executables are not accessible.

Acknowledgement. This research is partially supported by JSPS KAKENHI 20K20625 (Grant-in-Aid for Challenging Research).

References

1. King, J.C.: Symbolic execution and program testing. CACM **19**, 385–394 (1976)
2. Salwan, J., Bardin, S., Potet, M.-L.: Symbolic deobfuscation: from virtualized code back to the original. DIMVA, LNCS **10885**, 372–392 (2018)
3. Hai, N.M., Ogawa, M., Tho, Q.T.: Obfuscation code localization based on CFG generation of malware. FPS, LNCS **9482**, 229–247 (2015)
4. Shervashidze, N., Schweitzer, P., van Leeuwen, E.J., Mehlhorn, K., Borgwardt, K.M.: "Weisfeiler-Lehman Graph Kernels". J. Mach. Learn. Res. **12**, 2539–2561 (2011)
5. Wikipedia. "Cosine similarity." https://en.wikipedia.org/wiki/Cosine_similarity
6. Royal, P., Halpin, M., Dagon, D., Edmonds, R., Lee, W.: PolyUnpack: automating the hidden-code extraction of upack-executing malware. In: ACSAC, pp. 289–300 (2006)
7. Martignoni, L., Christodorescu, M., Jha, S.: OmniUnpack: fast, generic, and safe unpacking of malware. In: ACSAC, pp. 431–441 (2007)
8. Kang, M., Poosankam, P., Yin, H.: Renovo: a hidden code extractor for packed executables. In: WORM 2007, pp. 46–53 (2007)
9. Isawa, R., Kamizono, M., Inoue, D.: Generic unpacking method based on detecting original entry point. NIP, LNCS **8226**, 593–600 (2013)
10. D'Alessio, S., Mariani, S.: PinDemonium: a DBI-based generic unpacker for windows executables. In: BlackHat, pp. 1–56 (2016)
11. NtQuery. Scylla - x64/x86 imports reconstruction. https://github.com/NtQuery/Scylla
12. Guo, F., Ferrie, P., Chiueh, T.C.: A study of the packer problem and its solutions. RAID, LNCS **5230**, 98–115 (2008)
13. Isawa, R., Inous, D., Nakao, K.: An original entry point detection method with candidate-sorting for more effective generic unpacking. IEICE Trans. **E98-D**(4), 883–893 (2015)

14. Kim, G.M., Park, J., Jang, Y.H., Park, Y.: Efficient automatic original entry point detection. J. Inf. Sci. Eng. **35**, 887–901 (2019)
15. Jeong, G., Choo, E., Lee, J., Bat-Erdene, M., Lee, H.: Generic unpacking using entropy analysis. In: MALWARE, pp. 98–105 (2010)
16. Phan, A.V., Nguyen, L.M., Nguyen, H.Y.L., Bui, L.T.: DGCNN: a convolutional neural network over large-scale labeled graphs. Neural Netw. **108**, 533–543 (2018)
17. Van Ouytsel, C.-H.B., Legay, A.: Malware analysis with symbolic execution and graph Kernel. NordSec, LNCS **13700**, 292–310 (2022)
18. Roundy, K.A., Miller, B.P.: Binary-code obfuscations in prevalent packer tools. ACM Comput. Surv. **46**, 4:1–4:32 (2013)
19. Nguyen, M.H., Ogawa, M., Tho, Q.T.: Packer identification based on metadata signature. In: SSPREW-7, pp. 1–11 (2017)
20. Kinder, J., Zuleger, F., Veith, H.: An abstract interpretation-based framework for control flow reconstruction from binaries. VMCAI, LNCS **5403**, 214–228 (2009)
21. Moura, L., Bjørner, N.: Z3: An efficient SMT solver. TACAS, LNCS **4963**, 337–340 (2008)
22. Knuth, D.E.: An empirical study of FORTRAN programs. Softw. Pract. Exp. **1**(2), 105–134 (1971)
23. Hecht, M.S., Ullman, J.D.: Flow graph reducibility. In: ACM STOC, pp. 238–250 (1972)

Attacking and Securing the Clock Randomization and Duplication Side-Channel Attack Countermeasure

Martin Brisfors, Michail Moraitis$^{(\boxtimes)}$, Gabriel Klasson Landin,
and Truls Jilborg

Royal Institute of Technology (KTH), Electrum 229, 196 40 Stockholm, Sweden
{brisfors,micmor,gablan,trulsj}@kth.se

Abstract. The emergence of deep learning has revolutionized side-channel attacks, making them a serious threat to cryptographic systems. Clock randomization is a well-established mitigation technique against side-channel attacks that, when combined with duplication, has been shown to effectively protect FPGA implementations of block ciphers and post-quantum KEMs. In this paper, we present two deep-learning-based side-channel attacks on an FPGA implementation of AES protected with the clock randomization and duplication countermeasure. The attacks are based on identifying sporadic synchronicity in the execution of the encryption rounds of the two AES cores. We remedy this vulnerability by presenting three modular additions to the original design of the countermeasure that restores its security and increases its robustness.

Keywords: Side-channel attack · Random Execution Time · Countermeasure · Deep Learning · FPGA

1 Introduction

Field Programmable Gate Arrays (FPGAs) have become an integral component of technological systems used in a wide range of industries including telecommunications, automotive, aerospace, defense, healthcare, and data centers. Their popularity is due to their flexibility (reconfigurability), high performance, and power efficiency. These attributes make them very attractive for security-demanding applications and cryptographic systems. Encryption algorithms typically involve heavy computations and can therefore greatly benefit from the FPGAs' high performance and power efficiency. Additionally, the reconfigurable nature of FPGAs allows them to adapt to changes in encryption algorithms or cryptographic system requirements.

M. Brisfors and M. Moraitis—Both authors contributed equally to this manuscript. This work was supported in part by the Swedish Civil Contingencies Agency (Grant No. 2020-11632) and the Sweden's Innovation Agency Vinnova (Grant No. 2023-00221).

M. Mosbah et al. (Eds.): FPS 2023, LNCS 14551, pp. 372–387, 2024.
https://doi.org/10.1007/978-3-031-57537-2_23

A critical threat to such cryptographic systems is the side-channel attack (SCA). An SCA gathers and analyses information that is unintentionally emitted from the physical implementations of algorithms such as power consumption, electromagnetic (EM), and thermal emissions. By analyzing this information, cryptographically secure algorithms can be broken and their secret key recovered [1].

An effective countermeasure against such attacks is to create an unpredictable pattern in the execution time of the operations of the cryptographic algorithm [1,2]. In hardware, this is commonly achieved through random delay insertions [3,4] or clock randomization [5–14]. However, clock randomization techniques have been shown to be overcome with a high degree of oversampling [14]. This happens because when the side-channel measurements are taken with a sampling frequency that is significantly higher than the operational frequency of the algorithm under attack, the measurements can be synchronized. To counteract this, a countermeasure that combines clock randomization with encryption core duplication (CRCD)[1] has been proposed in [15]. Adaptations of this countermeasure have been shown to effectively protect FPGA implementations of block ciphers such as the advanced encryption standard (AES) [15] and key encapsulation mechanisms (KEMs) such as CRYSTALS-Kyber [16]. In [17] an analysis of the frequencies used in the clock randomization unit of [15] showed that there is a possible vulnerability in the countermeasure related to concurrent power-consumption peaks. A concurrent peak appears when both encryption cores perform a round of computations almost concurrently, resulting in a unified peak in the power traces.

Our Contributions

- We leverage the existence of concurrent peaks to perform two attacks on the CRCD countermeasure [15]. The first attack is based on attacking the concurrent peaks themselves while the second attack is based on merging two consecutive non-concurrent peaks.
- We present three modular improvements to the original design of CRCD. The first two, make CRCD secure against the concurrent and merged peak attacks. The third one eliminates the encryption errors that CRCD was reported to introduce.
- We experimentally evaluate the proposed attacks as well as the proposed improvements to CRCD on a protected FPGA implementation of AES.

The remainder of the paper is organized as follows. Section 2 reviews the previous work on randomized clock countermeasures. Section 3 briefly presents the AES implementation protected with CRCD introduced in [15] and highlights the vulnerability of concurrent peaks that appears in its power traces. Section 4 describes the modular additions we propose towards making CRCD secure against attacks based on concurrent peaks. Section 5 presents our attack

---

[1] This acronym is not used in the original paper that describes the countermeasure. We decided to introduce it here since we make many references to it throughout the paper.

methodology. Section 6 presents our experimental results from attacking the original CRCD implementation as well as the proposed improved CRCD. Finally, Sect. 7 concludes our paper.

2   Previous Work

In this Section, we present FPGA-based clock randomization techniques that can be found in the literature.

In the earliest works we could find [5,6], the randomized clock is generated by a key scheduler that uses a True Random Number Generator (TRNG) to randomly selects between the outputs of positive-edge and negative-edge flip-flops.

In later works [7–10], Digital Clock Managers (DCMs) [18], are deployed to generate phase-shifted instances $f_{p1}, \ldots, f_{pn}$ of a base frequency f. The phase-shifted frequencies are connected to a multiplexer controlled by a random number generator. The output of the multiplexer is given as a clock to the encryption core. During the execution of the algorithm, the selected clock changes multiple times resulting in a randomized clock. In [11], the candidate frequencies are multiples of a base frequency instead of phase-shifted versions of it.

In [12], a clock randomization technique called runtime frequency tuning countermeasure (RFTC) is presented. There, the generation of the candidate frequencies is performed through Mixed-Mode Clock Managers (MMCMs) [19]. MMCMs are a more advanced version of DCMs that is available in the modern Xilinx FPGAs (7 series and Ultrascale). They allow the generation of up to seven different output frequencies that are defined by applying user-defined scaling factors on an input frequency. In RTFC, $m = 1024$ different configurations (sets of scaling factors) of an MMCM with $n = 3$ output frequencies are stored in FGPA block RAMs (BRAMs). Through dynamic reconfiguration, the MMCM scaling factors and thus their output frequencies are updated over time. The authors test the effectiveness of the countermeasure against a correlation power analysis (CPA) on an FPGA implementation of AES that encrypts in $r = 10$ clock cycles. The application of RFTC generates $_{r+n-1}C_r \times m = {}_{10+3-1}C_{10} \times 1024 = 66 \times 1024 = 67,584$ different cumulative times to completion on the last round of the encryption (which is the preferable attack point for a CPA). The presented experimental results showed that the implementation is secure against attacks with at least 5M power traces.

In RFTC, an MMCM has a static input frequency and a dynamically changing set of scaling factors. In [13] an approach is presented where the input frequency is dynamic (given from a software-based clock randomizer) while the MMCM's scaling factors remain constant. The authors evaluated their countermeasure on an FPGA AES implementation that encrypts in $r = 13$ clock cycles using $n = 4$ and $n = 8$ MMCM-generated output frequencies. This resulted in $_{13+4-1}C_{13} \times 257 = 143,920$ for $n = 4$ and $_{13+8-1}C_{13} \times 257 = 19,922,640$ for $n = 8$ different times to completion on the last round. They found the implementation secure against FFT-CPA, FFT-MLP, and CNN attacks with at least 1M power traces.

In [14], another approach for choosing between frequencies is presented. In this method, both the input frequency and the MMCM scaling factors are constant. The four output frequencies of the MMCM are fed into a LUT-based multiplexer (MUX) that is controlled by the output of an RNG clocked with the same frequency that is given to the MMCM. This results in randomized clock pulses in the output of the MUX with varying frequency and duty cycle. The authors simulated the behavior of this configuration and reported at least $n = 403$ different frequencies. They evaluated the randomized clock on an AES implementation that encrypts in $r = 10$ clock cycles which results in $_{10+403-1}C_{10} \approx 3.478 \times 10^{19}$ different times to completion in the last round. However, due to the asynchronous selection, 3% of the ciphertexts were not calculated correctly. The authors captured power traces with a 40× oversampling rate (sampling frequency 80 times higher than AES operation frequency) and synchronised the power traces. They performed a deep-learning-based attack on the first round of the AES encryption, overcoming the randomness accumulation that occurs in the last round. They showed a model that trained on 10M traces was able to perform a successful attack with 319 power traces. These results suggested that with sufficient oversampling and synchronization, clock randomization can be significantly weakened.

In [15] CRCD, a countermeasure that combines clock randomization with cryptographic hardware duplication is presented. The authors use the randomized clock generator of [14] to create two different randomized encryption clocks that feed two AES cores, a primary, and a dummy. The presented configuration has the following features:

- The parts of power/EM traces generated from the dummy core have a similar shape to the ones generated from the primary core since they are copies of each other.
- The primary and the dummy AES cores operate with a different secret key. In this way, no additional leakage related to the primary secret key is generated.
- Both AES cores are given the same plaintext input. In this way, identification of the segments of the traces that are generated by the dummy core (e.g. by leveraging correlation to the plaintext) is not possible.
- The secret keys of the primary and dummy core are updated concurrently. By using primary and dummy secret keys connected in pairs and giving both AES cores the same input, the noise generated by the dummy core is algorithmic rather than random making the implementation secure against repetition attacks.

The application of this countermeasure results in misaligned power traces that are difficult to synchronize since for every given trace it is not evident which parts are generated from the primary and which from the dummy core. Moreover, a brute force attack to partition the peaks into groups would require 2^m enumerations where m is the number of traces used for a successful attack. In state-of-the-art attacks against FPGA implementations of AES, m is in the order of 10^2 making such an attack infeasible. The attack was reported to be secure for at least 10M encryptions against a deep-learning-based side-channel attack. In [16] the same configuration was used to protect a CRYSTALS-Kyber implementation, however, this time the randomized clock generator was selecting between candidate frequencies synchronously through clock multiplexers (BUFCTRL). The reason for that change was that the CRYSTALS-Kyber implementation required three orders of magnitude more clock cycles to encrypt compared to AES. Therefore using asynchronous switching would result in an unacceptably high error rate. In the presented experimental results, the randomized clock for each core was generated by randomly selecting between only two frequencies. However, it was reported to be sufficient in protecting the implementation against deep-learning-based attacks of at least 10M traces.

In [17] the effect of the MMCM scaling factor selection in the randomized clock generator of [14,15] was investigated since the relative frequencies of the MMCM outputs have an impact on the distribution of the frequency spectrum. The analysis revealed that in the setup of [15] the two AES cores were sporadically calculating an encryption round concurrently, generating a single, high-amplitude peak in the captured power traces. They found that this phenomenon occurred in 11% of the captured power traces on the first round of encryption. This would suggest a possible vulnerability if such traces were isolated and used for an attack.

In this paper, we present a side-channel attack on an FPGA implementation of AES protected with CRCD [15]. The attack leverages the existence of the concurrent peaks in the first round of encryption to perform a deep-learning-based power analysis that can recover the key with 78645 traces on average. Furthermore, we propose an improved version of the countermeasure that 1) mitigates concurrent and merged peak attacks and 2) produces no faulty encryptions. With no faulty encryptions, our version of a randomized clock generator with asynchronous switching becomes suitable for use in more complex algorithms like CRYSTALS-Kyber improving the security of [16].

3   The Concurrent Peak Vulnerability

In this Section, we describe the architecture of CRCD [15] and the concurrent peak vulnerability that it exhibits.

3.1   The Architecture of CRCD [15]

In Fig. 2, the architecture proposed in [15] is shown on white background (the components that are enclosed in colorful background are our additions to the countermeasure design and are discussed in Sect. 4). There, a base frequency f_{base} is given to an MMCM to produce four *candidate frequencies* f_1, f_2, f_3, f_4 and a selector frequency f_5. The candidate frequencies are connected to two 4-to-1 MUXes. Each MUX is controlled by a random number generator (RNG) output that is registered with a different frequency; f_{base} for the top MUX and f_5 for the bottom. In this configuration, each MUX randomly selects one of the four candidate frequencies. The selection happens on the rising edge of the selector signal of each MUX (f_{base}, or f_5), disregarding the state of the candidate frequencies. This results in two different clock signals in the output of the MUXes that have pulses of random frequency and duty cycle. The authors reported that pulses of at least 403 distinct frequencies occur in each individual randomized clock output. Finally, the two (different) randomized clocks are fed to the primary and dummy AES cores, which share the same input but hold a different key as described in Sect. 2.

3.2 Power Trace Analysis

Split Peaks A peak in a power trace (Fig. 1) represents a spike in voltage caused by a round of computations of the underlying hardware. In our case study, the peaks are correlated to the encryption/decryption rounds of the AES cores. When the operations of the two cores do not overlap then we observe two distinct peaks where each of them is associated with the power consumption of one of the two cores. However, connecting a peak in the power trace to the encryption core that generated it is not feasible since the cores operate using different randomized clocks. In this work, we refer to such peaks as *split peaks*.

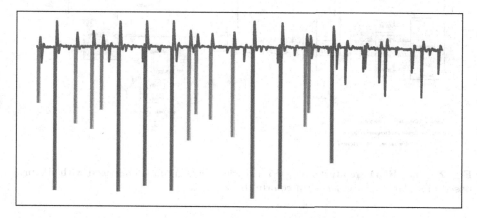

Fig. 1. Sample power trace with concurrent peaks highlighted in red and split peaks in green. (Color figure online)

The attack in [15] was considering split peaks and selecting the first peak every time. If there is no bias this would result in around half of the selected peaks containing the desired information. If there is bias, systematically selecting the same peak is still more likely to succeed than a random guess.

Concurrent Peaks. A concurrent peak occurs when the two encryption cores perform a round of calculations virtually at the same time, resulting in a single peak in the power trace that has a considerably higher amplitude than split peaks. In the power trace sample of Fig. 1 concurrent peaks are highlighted in red while split peaks in green. In [17] it was found that 11% of power traces generated by the countermeasure of [15] have a concurrent peak in the first round of the AES encryption.

Merging Peaks. Considering a first-round attack, in the case of split peaks, a merging of the first two peaks can be attempted to approximate an equivalent concurrent peak. However, since the two clocks are random, there is a chance that the first two peaks are two consecutive rounds of the same core.

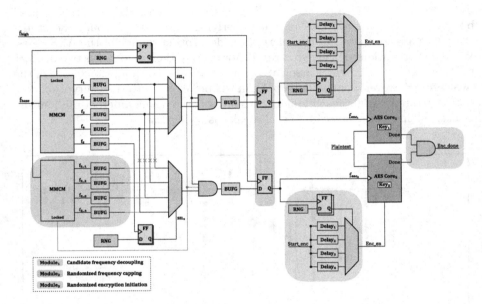

Fig. 2. The CRCD architecture of [15] (in white background) enhanced with the proposed modular improvements (in colorful backgrounds)

4   Improved CRCD

In this Section, we present an improved version of CRCD shown in Fig. 2. The improvements come from three modular additions. Two of them (modules 1 and 3) aim at making the architecture resistant to concurrent and merged peak attacks while a third one (module 2) aims at making the design more robust, by eliminating the 3% error rate that was reported in [15].

4.1   Module 1

The first module we add consists of a second MMCM that takes the same input as the first MMCM and generates four new candidate frequencies. The candidate frequencies of the first MMCM are connected to the MUX that generates the clock for AES $core_1$ while the candidate frequencies of the second MMCM are connected to the MUX that generates the clock for AES $core_2$. By decoupling the candidate frequencies of the two cores we achieve an order of magnitude reduction in the appearance of concurrent peaks.

4.2   Module 2

The second module consists of a register connected to the output of each MUX. The register is clocked with a high frequency, f_{high}. This results in a randomized clock in the output of the register that cannot have pulses of a frequency that surpasses f_{high}. The f_{high} used in our experiments is two orders of magnitude higher than the candidate frequencies. This module combined with asynchronous switching between candidate frequencies can also be a modular addition to RFTC [12] and [13] that can drastically increase the randomness of the clock.

4.3   Module 3

The third module consists of three submodules. The first two submodules consist of four delays connected to a MUX that is controlled by an RNG. These submodules take as input the external signal that requests the start of an encryption/decryption (Start_enc) and delay it by randomly selecting between the four predefined delays. In our implementation, we connected the Start_enc signal to a shift register and connected different stages of it to a MUX to generate the candidate delays. Each of these submodules controls the corresponding Enc_en signal of the two AES cores as shown in Fig. 2. Finally, the third submodule has an AND gate connecting the *Done* signals of the two cores in order to thwart a possible timing attack. The effect of this module is to further decrease the occurrence of concurrent peaks but also to allow the generation of concurrent peaks that do not contain information about the same round of AES (e.g. a concurrent peak where $core_1$ calculates the first round and $core_2$ the third). In the experiments presented in this paper, the delays used range from 1 to 9 clock cycles. To an AES implementation that takes 10 rounds to complete an encryption, this imposes a considerable timing overhead (90% in the worst case). However, in encryption algorithms such as CRYSTALS-Kyber (which was also shown to be protected by CRCD in [16]) the overhead is minimal. For example, the very lightweight implementation of CRYSTALS-Kyber presented in [20] takes 14000 clock cycles to complete the decapsulation procedure. This translates to a miniscule 0, 06% timing overhead in the worst case when adding the proposed module with a maximum delay of 8 clock cycles.

5 Side-Channel Attack Methodology

In this section, we describe the attack methodology we followed to perform the concurrent peak and merged peak attacks. The methodology for both attacks involves three steps, oversampling, pre-processing, and deep-learning-based analysis.

5.1 Oversampling

Oversampling is the practice of sampling a signal with a frequency higher than the Nyquist rate. The Nyquist rate dictates a sampling frequency that is twice as fast as the frequency of the sampled signal. In [14] it was shown that a 40× oversampling rate (i.e. 80 samples per clock cycle) is sufficient to recover the key from a non-duplicated AES core protected with a randomized clock. Therefore, we use the same degree of oversampling for our experiments to not overestimate its security.

5.2 Pre-processing

We define three pre-processing steps; $<1>$ Concurrent peak identification, $<2>$ synchronization and $<3>$ merging. To perform a concurrent peak attack only the first two steps are required, while for the merged peak attack all three steps are required.

Concurrent Peak Identification. We modified the threshold criterion of [14] to distinguish between concurrent and split peaks. Our peak detection function is defined as:

$$Peaks(T) = \{Peak(t)|t \in T\}$$
$$Peak : \mathbb{R}^n \mapsto \{0,1,2\}^n : \tag{1}$$

$$Peak(t) = \begin{cases} 2 \; Concurrent & \text{if } t_i \geq 3\sigma_T \\ 1 \; Split & \text{if } 3\sigma_T > t_i \geq 1.5\sigma_T \\ 0 \; NoPeak & \text{if } 1.5\sigma_T > t_i \end{cases}$$

where T is the set of all traces, t is a single power trace, t_i is the i-th sample point of the selected trace, and σ_T is the standard deviation of the set T. This generates a list of identifiers for all indexes of every trace. By discarding all *NoPeak* indices we are left with a list of where peaks exist in the traces.

Synchronization. To synchronize the traces, an interval is selected around a peak as determined by the *Peak* function. Since the power traces are oversampled there is often more than a single index that corresponds to each peak. In [14] the first point that crosses the threshold is used. This implies that the synchronization is done around the lowest of any clustered set of indices if counting from the beginning, or the highest of the cluster if counting from the end of the trace. In this work, we identify the full cluster of indices and select the median. This makes the method invariant to the direction of counting and possibly less sensitive to mistimed measurements that occur due to insufficient oversampling with regard to randomized clocks. The clusters of indices are created by grouping indices with a difference of less than three into ordered sets. In this way, a single sampling error cannot cause the false identification of a single peak as two separate ones.

Once the concurrent peaks are identified (step 1) and synchronized (step 2), a deep-learning-based concurrent peak attack can be performed.

Merging. To perform a merged peak attack the split peaks identified in step 1 have to be merged to emulate a concurrent peak. We perform the merging through an index-wise addition:

$$Merge(a, b) = a + b : a, b \in \mathbb{R}^n \tag{2}$$

where n is the size of the interval chosen around the peak. It should be noted that in [15], it is mentioned that an attack merging the first two peaks fails. However, no distinction between concurrent and split peaks was performed. This would result in merging concurrent peaks with split peaks resulting in an unintentionally poisoned dataset.

5.3   Deep Learning-Based Analysis

Table 1. MLP Architecture.

Layer (type)	Output Shape	Param #
batch_normalization_1	(None, 50)	200
dense_1 (Dense)	(None, 1024)	52224
batch_normalization_2	(None, 1024)	4096
relu_1 (ReLU)	(None, 1024)	0
dense_2 (Dense)	(None, 512)	524800
batch_normalization_3	(None, 512)	2048
relu_2 (ReLU)	(None, 512)	0
dense_3 (Dense)	(None, 256)	131328
batch_normalization_4	(None, 256)	1024
relu_3 (ReLU)	(None, 256)	0
dense_4 (Dense)	(None, 256)	65792
softmax_1 (Softmax)	(None, 256)	0
Total params:	781,512	
Trainable params:	777,828	
Non-trainable params:	3,684	

Deep Learning-Based Side-Channel Analysis (DLSCA) has been proven to be effective at achieving attacks comparable to or better than alternate methods [21]. Early results indicated that Convolutional Neural Networks (CNNs) can overcome desynchronization [22] and jitter [23] while later results have found that Multilayer Perceptrons (MLP) have comparable performance if synchronization can first be achieved [14].

To train our model, M_0, we use labels l_t corresponding to the basis vectors $e_{b_t+1} \in \mathbb{R}^{256}$ where $b_t \in [0..255]$ is the first round $Sbox$ output value [14] of byte 0 for every trace $t \in T$ where T is the set of all traces.

We captured T using random plaintext values and subjected it to preprocessing, splitting it into T_c (concurrent) and T_s (split). Half of the set is used for training and half for validation. The model is trained for 6 epochs using the *Nadam* optimization algorithm with a learning rate of 0.004, an epsilon value of $1e-8$, and 1024 batch size. We use the same model structure as the one presented in [14] as shown in Table 1.

To evaluate the security we calculate the average rank, rather than accuracy [24], of the correct subkey in the joint probabilities using a given number of traces. Since the predicted value is the $Sbox$ output value rather than the subkey value we first remap all $Sbox$ probabilities p into subkey probabilities $\tilde{p}$:

$$\tilde{p}_t = \{p_{t_j} | j \in \left(Sbox(b \oplus d_t) | b \in [0..255] \right) \} \tag{3}$$

where d_t is the corresponding plaintext byte used for trace $t \in T_t$ where T_t is the set of all testing traces. Then we calculate the joint probability that the subkey is equal to a specific value b as:

$$log(p(k = b|T_t)) = log(\tilde{p}_{0_b}) + log(\tilde{p}_{1_b}) + \ldots + log(\tilde{p}_{t_b}) \tag{4}$$

By sorting the joint probability of each subkey value from most to least probable we can determine at what index the correct subkey value is found. This is called its *rank*. A rank of 0 indicates that the model is predicting the correct subkey as being the most probable. To reduce the variance of the test results we run multiple iterations of this test on different ordered subsets of the test set $\tilde{T}_t \subseteq T_t$. The arithmetic mean is calculated index-wise between each series of test results.

6   Experimental Results

This section presents the results of our experiments.

6.1   Equipment

The power traces used in our experiments are captured with ChipWhisperer [25], an open-source toolkit that facilitates side-channel attacks. We used a CW1173 ChipWhisperer-Lite (for capturing the power traces), coupled with a CW305 Artix 7 FPGA target board (for hosting our design and generating the power traces).

6.2   Test Vector Leakage Assessment (TVLA)

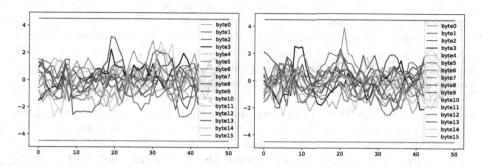

Fig. 3. Comparison of TVLA between Concurrent CRCD (left) and Concurrent Improved CRCD (right). The red lines indicate a 4.5 TVLA threshold. (Color figure online)

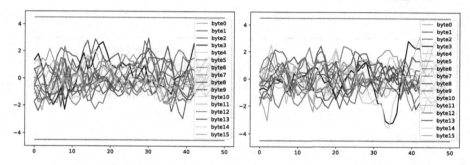

Fig. 4. Comparison of TVLA between Merged CRCD (left) and Merged Improved CRCD (right). The red lines indicate a 4.5 TVLA threshold. (Color figure online)

In SCA, the most popular method to identify potential leakage is TVLA [26].

The general idea behind TVLA is to split a set of side-channel measurements into two subsets and then try to find if there is a significant difference between them. In our case, we partition the set based on the Hamming Weight(HW)[2] of the output bytes from the first round's SubBytes step of AES.

The TVLA method is typically performed using Welch's t-test. The formula used to calculate this t-test score is:

$$t = \frac{\mu_1 - \mu_2}{\sqrt{(\frac{\sigma_1^2}{n_1} + \frac{\sigma_2^2}{n_2})}} \tag{5}$$

---

[2] Hamming Weight is defined as the number of logical 1 s in the binary representation of the value.

where μ is the sample mean, σ^2 is the sample variance, n is the sample size, and the subscript refers to which of the two sets was used as the sample.

The margins that are used most commonly to determine the statistical significance of the test score are 4.5 and −4.5.

In our experiments, we performed a Welch's t-test [27] on randomly selected subsets from our 4 test cases. The size of all subsets used for the t-test was 100k traces. The results of the concurrent peak t-test are shown in Fig. 3, while the results of the merged peak t-test are shown in Fig. 4.

Both figures show that TVLA did not detect any leakage in either the original or the enhanced CRCD countermeasure for both the merged and concurrent peak attacks. However, the experimental results presented in the following subsection show that the original CRCD is susceptible to concurrent peak attacks and somewhat resistant to merged peak attacks. This observation confirms the results presented in [28] where it is argued that TVLA is not a reliable method for evaluating the security of an implementation against SCA.

6.3   Security Analysis

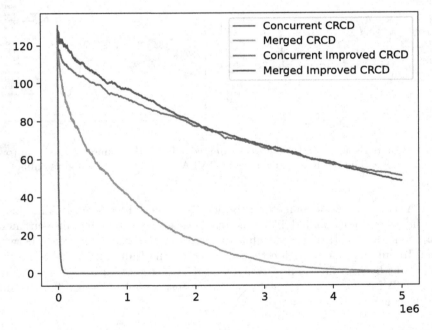

Fig. 5. Average rank of correct subkey byte for the original and improved CRCD.

We evaluated the security of both the original CRCD and the CRCD enhanced with our three modules (improved CRCD) against the concurrent and merged peak attacks.

We captured a set of $10M$ traces of which half is used for training and half is used for validation. For testing, we use the same half of traces that were used for validation. The test was iterated $5k$ times. To present our experimental results, we calculated the average rank of the correct subkey shown in Fig. 5. For traces captured from the original CRCD, 18% of traces have concurrent peaks in the first round and 82% have split peaks (used for merged peak attack). In the traces from the improved CRCD, only 1.6% of traces have concurrent peaks. Therefore to make a fair comparison, the x-axis in Fig. 5 has been adjusted to reflect the number of traces captured rather than the number given to the model.

According to Fig. 5, a concurrent peak attack against CRCD can recover the subkey using 78645 traces on average, revealing a severe vulnerability. The merged peak attack on the same implementation succeeds with 4.7M traces on average. With our proposed improvements implemented, the average rank doesn't fall below 50 for the concurrent peak attack and 48 for the merged peak attack when using 5M traces. This shows that the improved CRCD is secure against attacks with up to at least 5M traces with a large security margin.

It is interesting how our attack results against Concurrent CRCD are so successful and yet the TVLA score for the same traces did not pass the 4.5 threshold which is often used for leakage identification. Perhaps this implies that the leakage after synchronization is distributed across multiple points in some unintuitive fashion; something which Welch's t-test may not find but an MLP model could learn. From this we draw the conclusions that more research into explainable Deep Learning is warranted in this case, and we also reiterate the findings in [28] that Welch's t-test cannot be used as a pass-fail by itself.

7   Conclusion

In this paper, we used a deep learning-based side-channel attack to exploit the sporadic synchronicity in the execution of encryption rounds of the two AES cores in CRCD [15]. We presented an attack based on concurrent peaks that can recover a subkey byte in less than 80K traces on average and an attack based on merged peaks that can do the same with an average of 4.7M traces. We proposed three architectural additions to CRCD that restore the countermeasure's security and make it more robust. Our experimental results show that the improved CRCD is secure for at least 5M traces and with a large security margin (the lowest average rank observed is 48). The improved CRCD no longer generates wrong encryptions, making its application to more complex algorithms possible. We intend to make our source-code available after the review process.

References

1. Kocher, P., Jaffe, J., Jun, B.: Differential power analysis. In: Wiener, M. (ed.) CRYPTO 1999. LNCS, vol. 1666, pp. 388–397. Springer, Heidelberg (1999). https://doi.org/10.1007/3-540-48405-1_25

2. Kocher, P.C., Jaffe, J.M., Jun, B.C.: Using unpredictable information to minimize leakage from smartcards and other cryptosystems. US Patent 6,327,661 (2001)
3. Bucci, M., Luzzi, R., Guglielmo, M., Trifiletti, A.: A countermeasure against differential power analysis based on random delay insertion. In: IEEE International Symposium on Circuits and Systems (ISCAS), vol. 4, pp. 3547–3550 (2005)
4. Lu, Y., O'Neill, M.P., McCanny, J.V.: FPGA implementation and analysis of random delay insertion countermeasure against DPA. In: 2008 International Conference on Field-Programmable Technology, pp. 201–208 (2008)
5. Boey, K.H., Hodgers, P., Lu, Y., O'Neill, M., Woods, R.: 'Security of AES Sbox designs to power analysis. In: 2010 17th IEEE International Conference on Electronics, Circuits and Systems, pp. 1232–1235 (2010)
6. Boey, K.H., Lu, Y., O'Neill, M., Woods, R.: Random clock against differential power analysis. In: 2010 IEEE Asia Pacific Conference on Circuits and Systems, pp. 756–759 (2010)
7. Zafar, Y., Har, D.: A novel countermeasure enhancing side channel immunity in FPGAs. In: 2008 International Conference on Advances in Electronics and Microelectronics, pp. 132–137 (2008)
8. Zafar, Y., Park, J., Har, D.: Random clocking induced DPA attack immunity in FPGAs. In: 2010 IEEE International Conference on Industrial Technology, pp. 1068–1070 (2010)
9. Güneysu, T., Moradi, A.: Generic side-channel countermeasures for reconfigurable devices. In: Preneel, B., Takagi, T. (eds.) CHES 2011. LNCS, vol. 6917, pp. 33–48. Springer, Heidelberg (2011). https://doi.org/10.1007/978-3-642-23951-9_3
10. Ravi, P., Bhasin, S., Breier, J., Chattopadhyay, A.: PPAP and iPPAP: PLL-based protection against physical attacks. In: 2018 IEEE Computer Society Annual Symposium on VLSI (ISVLSI), pp. 620–625. IEEE (2018)
11. Fritzke, A.W.: Obfuscating against side-channel power analysis using hiding techniques for AES (2012)
12. Jayasinghe, D., Ignjatovic, A., Parameswaran, S.: RFTC: runtime frequency tuning countermeasure using FPGA dynamic reconfiguration to mitigate power analysis attacks. In: 2019 56th ACM/IEEE Design Automation Conference (DAC), pp. 1–6. IEEE (2019)
13. Hettwer, B., Das, K., Leger, S., Gehrer, S., Güneysu, T.: Lightweight side-channel protection using dynamic clock randomization. In: 2020 30th International Conference on Field-Programmable Logic and Applications (FPL), pp. 200–207 (2020)
14. Brisfors, M., Moraitis, M., Dubrova, E.: Do not rely on clock randomization: A side-channel attack on a protected hardware implementation of AES. In: Jourdan, G.V., Mounier, L., Adams, C., Sedes, F., Garcia-Alfaro, J. (eds.) FPS 2022. LNCS, vol. 13877, pp. 38–53. Springer, Heidelberg (2022). https://doi.org/10.1007/978-3-031-30122-3_3
15. Moraitis, M., Brisfors, M., Dubrova, E., Lindskog, N., Englund, H.: A side-channel resistant implementation of AES combining clock randomization with duplication. In: 2023 IEEE International Symposium on Circuits and Systems (ISCAS), pp. 1–5 (2023)
16. Moraitis, M., Ji, Y., Brisfors, M., Dubrova, E., Lindskog, N.: Securing CRYSTALS-kyber in FPGA using duplication and clock randomization. IEEE Des. Test (2023)
17. Landin, G.K., Jilborg, T.: Determining the optimal frequencies for a duplicated randomized clock sca countermeasure. arXiv preprint arXiv:2307.13834 (2023)
18. Xilinx. Using Digital Clock Managers (DCMs) in Spartan-3 FPGAs application note (XAPP462) (2006)

19. Xilinx. 7 Series FPGAs Clocking Resources User Guide (UG472) (2018)

20. Xing, Y., Li, S.: A compact hardware implementation of CCA-secure key exchange mechanism CRYSTALS-KYBER on FPGA. IACR Trans. Cryptogr. Hardw. Embed. Syst. 328–356 (2021)

21. Maghrebi, H., Portigliatti, T., Prouff, E.: Breaking cryptographic implementations using deep learning techniques. In: Carlet, C., Hasan, M.A., Saraswat, V. (eds.) SPACE 2016. LNCS, vol. 10076, pp. 3–26. Springer, Cham (2016). https://doi.org/10.1007/978-3-319-49445-6_1

22. Benadjila, R., Prouff, E., Strullu, R., Cagli, E., Dumas, C.: Study of deep learning techniques for side-channel analysis and introduction to ASCAD database. Cryptology ePrint Archive, Paper 2018/053 (2018). https://eprint.iacr.org/2018/053

23. Masure, L., et al.: Deep Learning Side-Channel Analysis on Large-Scale Traces - A Case Study on a Polymorphic AES. Cryptology ePrint Archive, Paper 2020/881 (2020). https://eprint.iacr.org/2020/881

24. Masure, L., Dumas, C., Prouff, E.: A comprehensive study of deep learning for side-channel analysis. IACR Trans. Cryptogr. Hardw. Embed. Syst. 348–375 (2020)

25. NewAE Technology Inc. Chipwhisperer. https://newae.com/tools/chipwhisperer

26. Gilbert Goodwill, B.J., Jaffe, J., Rohatgi, P., et al.: A testing methodology for side-channel resistance validation. In: NIST Non-invasive Attack Testing Workshop, vol. 7, pp. 115–136 (2011)

27. Welch, B.L.: The generalization of 'student's' problem when several different population varlances are involved. Biometrika **34**(1–2), 28–35 (1947)

28. Standaert, F.-X.: How (not) to use Welch's T-test in side-channel security evaluations. In: Bilgin, B., Fischer, J.-B. (eds.) CARDIS 2018. LNCS, vol. 11389, pp. 65–79. Springer, Cham (2019). https://doi.org/10.1007/978-3-030-15462-2_5

Security Design

Hardening Systems Against Data Corruption Attacks at Design Time

John Breton[1]([✉])[iD], Jason Jaskolka[1][iD], and George O. M. Yee[1,2][iD]

[1] Systems and Computer Engineering, Carleton University, Ottawa, ON, Canada
{john.breton,jason.jaskolka}@carleton.ca
[2] Aptusinnova Inc., Ottawa, ON, Canada
g.m.yee@ieee.org

Abstract. Despite advancements in security research, systems continue to be susceptible to all kinds of threats. To better support designers, we present a method and tool called Dubhe that can be employed during the design phase of development to harden systems against data corruption attacks. We highlight the benefits of this approach by applying it to an online seller of merchandise system to analyze various "what-if" scenarios with different defence objectives. Using our approach, Dubhe (1) analyzes the XML form of UML activity diagrams created to define the behavioural view of the system, (2) determines optimal locations for data sanitization using novel protection techniques and activity centrality concepts, and (3) communicates the results to the designers so that they can incorporate the suggestions back into their system designs. This example application of Dubhe shows that our approach can provide valuable security advice to designers to ensure that their systems are designed with protection against data corruption attacks, using only artifacts that designers would normally create during the design phase.

Keywords: Design Security · Model Analysis · Corruption Propagation · UML Activity Diagrams · Security Posture · System Hardening

1 Introduction

As software systems continue to evolve in scope, system designers face an increased challenge when it comes to incorporating security into their designs. Recent examples include Microsoft Outlook's zero-day elevation of privilege vulnerability and data corruption vulnerabilities enabling remote code execution in certain Apple operating systems and Google's Chrome web browser [1,6,15]. These examples underscore the continual introduction of software vulnerabilities during the design phase.

Although tools have been developed to support designers during different points in the software development life cycle (SDLC), tools that consider security in different system views at design time, such as the structural or behavioural view are not as prominent [10]. The structural view of a system delineates its

M. Mosbah et al. (Eds.): FPS 2023, LNCS 14551, pp. 391–407, 2024.
https://doi.org/10.1007/978-3-031-57537-2_24

components and their interrelationships, while the behavioural view details the execution flow between these components and highlights the intended processes the system will execute. Techniques that focus on the structural view of systems have recently been developed, along with the notion of a security posture specific to this structural representation [21]. Using security posture as a basis, we aim to begin defining the behavioural security posture of systems by introducing a system hardening technique applied to UML activity diagrams at design time.

In this work, we focus on hardening systems against data corruption attacks, which leads to our main contributions:

- A methodology to maximize the effectiveness of data sanitization that can be employed during the design phase of the software development life cycle.
- An automated tool called Dubhe[1] and accompanying use case walkthrough to support developers in hardening their systems against data corruption attacks across multiple "what-if" scenarios.

Using an Online Seller of Merchandise (OSM) system to demonstrate the real-world implications and applications of our contributions, we will illustrate three scenarios where Dubhe can be employed by designers to harden their systems against data corruption attacks. Although the OSM system is simplistic, it suffices to highlight how Dubhe works so that designers can have confidence in the results when it is applied to larger and more complex systems.

The rest of this paper is organized as follows. Section 2 discusses existing research for the application of security to software models. Section 3 describes data corruption attacks and the XML Data Interchange. Section 4 highlights our methodology. Section 5 presents the OSM system model case study. Section 6 applies our methodology under different scenarios. Section 7 discusses limitations and avenues for future work. Lastly, Sect. 8 concludes the paper.

2   Related Work

Samuel et al. [21] developed methods and accompanying tools to determine the security posture of early system designs by analyzing UML class diagrams. Also in the vein of UML model analysis, Jürjens [8] created UMLSec, a UML profile that enables designers to incorporate security objectives into their system designs. Lodderstedt et al. [13] presented SecureUML, a modelling language that allowed for the generation of role-based access control architectures. Sindre [22] introduced the concept of mal-activity diagrams to aid in the elicitation of security requirements. Similarly, Rodriguez et al. [20] illustrated a profile for UML activity diagrams that can be used to obtain security requirements. On the side of data corruption attacks, Nie et al. [17] analyzed abstract syntax trees for systems written in C/C++ to protect them against data corruption attacks. Chen et al. [2] showed a new form of memory corruption attack alongside a technique

---

[1] Dubhe is a star in the Ursa Major constellation. It is commonly referred to as a "pointer star" as it helps find Polaris, also known as the North Star.

to detect and combat these attacks by analyzing pointer taintedness at the CPU level. Kontouras et al. [11] used set theory and monitored system network metrics to detect data corruption attacks in operating cyber-physical systems.

While the works discussed above perform security analysis or allow for the addition of security measures for early system designs and models, they do not focus on protecting systems against data corruption attacks by analyzing their behavioural views, such as their activity views. In our work, we leverage a system's behavioural view by analyzing UML activity diagrams to harden software systems against data corruption attacks. We automate this analysis utilizing Dubhe, a tool we developed that implements our approach and eliminates the need for designers to learn new formalisms to perform security analysis.

3   Preliminaries

In this section, we provide an overview of two concepts, data corruption attacks and the XML Data Interchange (XMI) format, which are central to this work.

3.1   Data Corruption Attacks

Data corruption attacks manipulate legitimate data within a system to propagate corruption for malicious purposes. While the goal of corruption attacks can be to render a system inoperable by corrupting the code of the system, other attacks are focused on memory tampering to be able to execute malicious code and steal sensitive information. The potential for harm makes data corruption attacks a topic of interest in research, with numerous works exploring such attacks and their potential countermeasures [3,23,25]. For this reason, we choose to focus on this type of attack in this paper.

The methods in which data corruption attacks are exploited can vary dramatically and fall outside of the scope of this work. While existing literature on data corruption attacks is vast, it is important to note that research thus far has been focused on the analysis of these attacks using completed systems. This allows for the analysis of source code and executable models that are created as development shifts toward the implementation of the functional view of systems.

We were motivated by the previously defined Coupling Corruption Propagation metric presented in [4]. In our work, we view corruption as being possible in any element in a UML activity diagram, and we track the propagation of this corruption throughout the subsequent elements to determine potential locations for data sanitizer objects. For our purposes, a data sanitizer is a component responsible for checking the integrity of data, whether by sanitizing the input in the case of data injection attacks, comparing the data against a set of expected data that should flow between elements, or some other form of detection [5]. The exact nature of the data sanitizer object is outside of the scope of the analysis and will depend on the needs of the current system.

3.2   XML Data Interchange

The XML Data Interchange (XMI) is a format created by the Object Management Group (OMG). OMG is also responsible for the official UML specification [18]. Alongside the UML specification, OMG includes rules to be able to represent any UML-compliant model within the XMI format. While XMI is typically utilized for data exchange between different modelling tools, it is possible to parse the data for non-modelling purposes.

Although XMI is an established format with clear specifications, the goal of easy model exchange between modelling tools has not come to fruition. A survey by Ozkaya [19] concluded that of 58 UML tools tested, only 17 supported XMI exports. The remaining 41 tools did not offer XMI export options, effectively preventing the transfer of models to other UML tools. This lack of support makes the development of a widely applicable tool based on XMI analysis difficult, and we discuss this further in Sect. 7.1.

XMI has been used for model security analysis in the past; however, tools that support this type of analysis were created for a now outdated version of UML (UML 1.5) [9]. Further, the analysis of XMI from UML activity diagrams to harden systems against data corruption attacks, to the best of our knowledge, has not been explored. Our approach supports UML 2.X/XMI 2.X, and we aim to update support if new versions of the UML specification are published.

4   Methodology

Figure 1 presents an overview of our approach while explaining the designers' and Dubhe's responsibilities. Activities coloured green fall outside of the normal Secure SDLC. The Secure SDLC (SSDLC) is an approach to integrating security best practices and standards into the traditional SDLC. The SSDLC aims to ensure that security is considered throughout the lifecycle of a project [7]. Activities coloured in gray fall within the expected activities of the SSDLC and are outside the scope of this work. On top of the activities normally found within the SSDLC, we ask designers to incorporate two additional activities as follows:

Export UML Activity Diagrams to XMI: We ask developers to export their UML activity diagrams to XMI. As previously discussed, support for the XMI specification is not widespread. For our purposes, we created Dubhe to comply with the most recent XMI 2.X specification, which is supported by popular modelling tools such as StarUML and Papyrus [16,24]. With Papyrus, the ability to export to XMI is included with the application, while StarUML allows for XMI export via an officially supported extension [12]. Given the ease of exporting existing diagrams to this file format, designers should not be too inconvenienced to incorporate this activity into their existing development activities.

Analyze Results and Modify Models with Selected Suggestions: The output of Dubhe is a set of recommendations that are meant to assist designers in hardening their systems against data corruption attacks given different security goals. The method by which these recommendations are generated will be

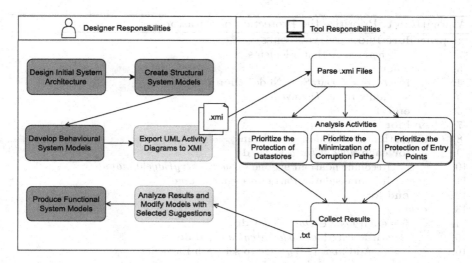

Fig. 1. Overview outlining the responsibilities of designers and of Dubhe

described later in this section. This activity requires designers to select the recommendations they feel best align with their individual needs and apply these modifications to their existing system models. Although Dubhe does not modify the models directly, we provide clear text-based suggestions that designers can add to their system models, leaving the agency to implement these decisions as their prerogative.

Next, we highlight the core responsibilities of Dubhe, which consist of analyzing UML activity diagrams to harden systems against data corruption attacks. Dubhe is available online at: https://gitlab.com/CyberSEA-Public/dubhe.

Parse .xmi Files: Using Python, Dubhe parses a target .xmi file that complies with the XMI 2.X specification that a designer wishes to have analyzed. To do this, we leverage the `lxml` Python library and extract XML attribute data from the XMI tags present within the .xmi file [14]. This data allows for the creation of ActivityElement objects, a custom datatype that encompasses an XMI ID, XMI element type, the labelled name for the element (if it exists), the name of the parent element (if it exists), and two lists of XMI IDs corresponding to the elements connected by incoming edges and the elements connected by outgoing edges. This data is stored as strings.

Analysis Activities: Analysis occurs concurrently in three sub-activities that utilize thread-safe read operations on a fixed set of initial data to avoid potential conflicts. Each activity prioritizes the protection of a system under a different context, which we describe in more detail below. In this context, prioritization refers to focusing on a specific goal for each analysis activity and by considering multiple analysis activities, several goals can be achieved simultaneously. We leave the decision to implement any recommendations generated by Dubhe to the designer.

Algorithm 1. Prioritize the Protection of Datastores

1: **procedure** PROTECTDATASTORES
2:     $E \leftarrow$ Generated ActivityElements
3:     **for each** $e \in E$ **do**
4:         **if** $e.type ==$ "DataStoreNode" **then**
5:             Add e to set *DataNodes*
6:         **end if**
7:     **end for**
8:     **if** length of *DataNodes* $== 1$ **then**
9:         **for each** *node* $\in$ *DataNodes* **do**
10:             RecommendationPartOne $\leftarrow$ *node.entryEdge*[0].*name*
11:             RecommendationPartTwo $\leftarrow$ *node.name*
12:         **end for**
13:     **else**
14:         **for each** *node* $\in$ *DataNodes* **do**
15:             **while** length of *node.entryEdge* ¿ 0 **do**
16:                 Add *node.entryEdge* to set Path Elements
17:                 *node* $\leftarrow$ *node.entryEdge*
18:             **end while**
19:         **end for**
20:         *result* $\leftarrow$ node with max centrality, closest to datastores in Path Elements
21:         RecommendationPartOne $\leftarrow$ *result.entryEdge*[0].*name*
22:         RecommendationPartTwo $\leftarrow$ *result.name*
23:     **end if**
24: **end procedure**

Prioritize the Protection of Datastores: The first sub-activity prioritizes the protection of datastores. As seen in Algorithm 1, each element e in the set of ActivityElements E is checked to see if it is of type DataStoreNode, which is the standard for such elements per the XMI 2.X standard [18]. If no DataStoreNode is present in the XMI, this analysis activity does not generate any suggestions. If exactly one DataStoreNode is detected, the analysis activity will recommend that a data sanitizer object be placed immediately before the datastore element and the element that has an edge entering the datastore. If multiple DataStoreNode elements are detected, Dubhe works backward from each DataStoreNode element to determine the path of elements that lead into it. Once all of the paths have been gathered, Dubhe will find which element is the most common or central across all paths and in the event of a tie, will determine which element among those with the highest occurrences is closest to the datastores. For our purposes, we rank the centrality of an ActivityElement higher the more paths it appears in. In either case, this analysis activity generates a suggestion for the location of a data sanitizer that will protect the most datastores possible by ensuring that data enters the data sanitizer before it reaches a datastore. This will harden a system against data corruption attacks that target datastores with the goal of either gaining access to or corrupting the information contained within.

Algorithm 2. Prioritize the Minimization of Corruption Path Lengths

```
1: procedure MINIMIZECORRUPTION
2:     E ← Generated ActivityElements
3:     for each e ∈ E do
4:         if length of e.entryEdge == 0 then
5:             Add e to set StartNodes
6:         end if
7:     end for
8:     for each node ∈ StartNodes do
9:         currPath ← node
10:        if length of node.exitEdge > 0 then
11:            currPath = currPath + node.exitEdge
12:            node ← node.exitEdge
13:        else
14:            Add currPath to set AllPaths
15:        end if
16:    end for
17:    midPoint ← Middle element of longest path in AllPaths
18:    RecommendationPartOne ← midPoint.entryEdge[0].name
19:    RecommendationPartTwo ← midPoint.name
20: end procedure
```

Prioritize the Minimization of Corruption Paths: The second sub-activity makes the minimization of corruption propagation its goal. As illustrated in Algorithm 2, analysis begins by iterating through the set of all generated ActivityElements E. For each element e in E, Dubhe checks to see if it has no incoming edges, indicating that the element appears at the start of a path. These elements are then collected and iterated through. For each of these elements, Dubhe will determine their total path length. Once every path length has been determined, Dubhe will calculate which path is the longest and attempt to place a data sanitizer object in the middle of the path. In this sense, the largest corruptible path that previously existed in the system will be eliminated in favour of two shorter paths. This accomplishes the goal of minimizing the worst-case corruption propagation scenario for systems, making full system takeovers by data corruption attacks more difficult to accomplish.

Prioritize the Protection of Entry Points: The third sub-activity prioritizes the protection of expected system entry points. As shown in Algorithm 3, Dubhe iterates through the set of ActivityElements E to determine which ActivityElement e has a value of InitialNode, which is the standard for such elements per the XMI 2.X standard [18]. Once this is identified, Dubhe prepares the recommended location for a data sanitizer object to be placed between the identified InitialNode element and the element connected to the InitialNode element by an outgoing edge. Application of this suggestion would result in the sanitization of data entering the system through the expected system entry point, effectively hardening the system against data corruption attacks that use defined entry points as their initial attack vector.

Algorithm 3. Prioritize the Protection of Expected Entry Points

```
1: procedure PROTECTENTRY
2:     E ← Generated ActivityElements
3:     for each e ∈ E do
4:         if e.type == "InitialNode" then
5:             RecommendationPartOne ← e.name
6:             RecommendationPartTwo ← e.exitEdge[0].name
7:         end if
8:     end for
9: end procedure
```

Collect Results: The final step is to collect the analysis results and concatenate them into a single textual representation that can be read by the system designer. Dubhe outputs each recommendation from the three analysis activities described above at once. The results are meant to assist designers in hardening their systems against data corruption attacks and are tailored to three distinct "what-if" security scenarios. We walkthrough these scenarios in Sect. 6. If Dubhe detects that a data sanitizer is already present in a system model, no recommendations are generated to avoid superseding a designer's discretion. Instead, the designer is informed that it appears an attempt at hardening their system against data corruption attacks has already been made.

5   Case Study - Online Seller of Merchandise

To demonstrate our methodology, we adapt an existing Online Seller of Merchandise (OSM) system architecture originally defined in [26]. For our purposes, we only use five components of those defined in the UML class diagram of the OSM system, which are the components coloured in white in Fig. 2.

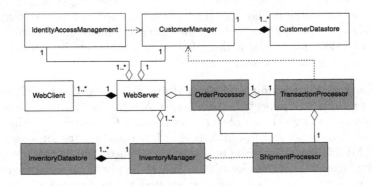

Fig. 2. A UML class diagram of the OSM system

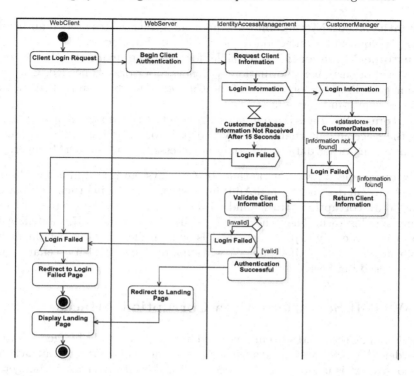

Fig. 3. A UML activity diagram for the Login Flow of the OSM system

UML class diagrams are a type of artifact that designers create during the early phases of the SSDLC, and it maps back to the **Create Structural System Models** activity present in Fig. 1. After structural models are created, behavioural system models such as UML activity diagrams are developed during the **Develop Behavioural System Models** activity present in Fig. 1. This activity then leads directly into our focused methodology activity flow. Using the UML Class Diagram of the OSM system as a basis, we derived a UML activity diagram that captures the login flow for the OSM system. As seen in Fig. 3, the WebClient, WebServer, IdentityAccessManagement, CustomerManager, and CustomerDatabase system components are involved in the login request flow for the OSM system. Of these, the first four are each shown as a swimlane whereas the CustomerDatabase is shown as an embedded datastore object under the CustomerManager swimlane:

- **WebClient** acts as the expected interface for users who interact with the OSM system. The system can be accessed via web browsers, and WebClient is responsible for handling user input and rendering the system to users.
- **WebServer** is responsible for mediating between WebClient and the rest of the OSM system. It handles input from multiple local WebClient components and routes requests to core components of the OSM.

- **IdentityAccessManagement** component authenticates users if authentication is required for an action requested by the WebServer.
- **CustomerManager** is responsible for handling requests related to the retrieval of customer information. Whenever user data is needed, CustomerManager will query for the data from CustomerDatabase and return the data to the requesting component.
- **CustomerDatabase** is a datastore that contains customer information, such as their account usernames, encrypted passwords, and stored cart information, among other data. It can only be accessed via CustomerManager.

For our purposes, we assume that the OSM system is still in active development. A system designer named Ali is interested in hardening their OSM system against data corruption attacks and wishes to make use of our created tool to accomplish this task. They check and confirm that their UML modelling tool allows them to easily export their models as .xmi files that are compliant with the official XMI 2.X specification. We will explore three "what-if" scenarios using this case study in Sect. 6.

6   What-If Scenarios - Data Corruption Attacks

Ali is designing the OSM system presented in Sect. 5 on a tight budget. Ali wishes to harden the OSM system against the threat of data corruption attacks but, as a non-expert is unsure of how to accomplish this effectively. Ali's budget and personal goal to minimize coupling between components afford them the ability to incorporate a single data sanitizer object in their OSM system, but they do not know where to place the data sanitizer object. In this section, we explore three scenarios focusing on: protecting the OSM system's datastores, securing its entry points, and limiting corruption propagation within the system.

6.1   Scenario 1: Protecting Datastores

In this scenario, Ali's goal is to protect datastore objects from data corruption attacks. We assume that an attacker launching such an attack seeks to extract information from the system's datastores. This could involve directly targeting the datastore object or exploiting activities that interact with it. Successful exploitation might enable the attacker to execute arbitrary code or SQL statements, thereby achieving their malicious objectives.

Ali exports the UML activity diagram for their OSM Login Flow as described in Fig. 3 to XMI. They submit this XMI as input to Dubhe and receive output relevant to their security goal, shown in Fig. 4. The recommendations provided by Dubhe were generated following the logic in Algorithm 1.

Using the suggestion provided by Dubhe, Ali modifies their UML activity diagram by adding a data sanitizer object between the accept signal element **Login Information** and the datastore element **CustomerDatabase**. A possible modification following the suggested recommendation can be seen in Fig. 5.

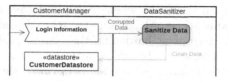

Fig. 4. Output snippet to protect the CustomerDatabase in the OSM system

CustomerManager	DataSanitizer
Login Information	Corrupted Data → Sanitize Data
«datastore» CustomerDatastore	Clean Data

Fig. 5. Modified activity flow to protect the CustomerDatabase in the OSM system

The modification in Fig. 5 demonstrates that corrupted data exiting from the accept signal element **Login Information** can now be checked for corruption before its use by the datastore element **CustomerDatabase**. The corrupted data in this scenario can take many forms, such as malformed SQL statements to dump information from the datastore or garbage data that is meant to stall or overflow system resources. We assume that the activity **Sanitize Data** considers these possibilities and modifies any corrupted data where possible to harden the system against data corruption attacks.

Although an example with one datastore is simplistic, the situation becomes more interesting when multiple datastores are involved. Consider a revised scenario where the OSM system instead queries two different datastores concurrently during the login flow, one for login information and another for client profile information, demonstrated in Fig. 6.

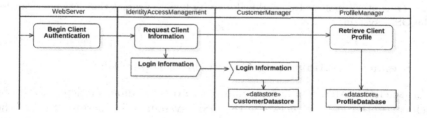

Fig. 6. A revised multi-datastore OSM activity flow

In this scenario, Ali's goal remains unchanged. Following the same steps as before, Dubhe once again applies the logic present in Algorithm 1 and now suggests a revised location for the data sanitizer object to be placed between the activity element **Begin Client Authentication** and the activity element

Request Client Information. The implementation of this recommendation is shown in Fig. 7. Note that while it would be possible to achieve the same effect by placing two references to a data sanitizer object after the activity element **Request Client Information**, this would add an additional call in the activity flow compared to the current recommendation, which may not be desirable in a situation such as Ali's where they wish to minimize coupling between system components. This increase in coupling is avoided with a single activity reference to the data sanitizer object, which is why Dubhe will prioritize this recommendation to designers when multiple datastores need protection. After making the modifications, Ali submits the revised model to Dubhe and the results show that an attempt at hardening the system against data corruption attacks has been detected, shown in Fig. 8. Note that in this case, Dubhe informs users that if they wish to have an analysis performed, they must first remove references to data sanitizer objects within their systems. Further capabilities are planned for future work to check the suitability of existing data sanitizer objects.

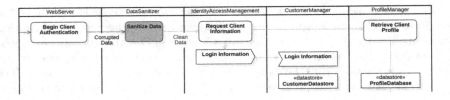

Fig. 7. Modified activity flow to protect multiple datastores in the OSM System

```
----Detected Data Sanitizer----
It appears your submitted XMI already contains a reference to a 'DataSanitizer'. It may be
placed in an optimal location accordingto your specific security goals. If you wish to have
analysis performed, please remove any references to 'DataSanitizer' elementsand resubmit
your modified XMI to Dubhe.
```

Fig. 8. Output snippet for the modified activity flow to protect the CustomerDatabase in the OSM system

6.2   Scenario 2: Minimizing Corruption Propagation

In this scenario, Ali's goal is to minimize the total number of elements through which corruption can propagate in the OSM system. Ali generates XMI of their UML activity diagram for the OSM system. Dubhe applies the logic described in Algorithm 2 and displays the output to the console, shown in Fig. 9.

Ali applies the recommendation to the OSM system, which can be seen in Fig. 10. While this modification is placed one element off of the recommendation outlined in Sect. 6.1, the benefits vary. In this case, the longest activity element path that existed in the OSM system is eliminated. While the data sanitizer object will not catch every instance of corrupted data, placing it in the middle

```
----Minimizing Corruption Propagation----
It is recommended to place a Data Sanitizer object between the following elements:
    - DataStoreNode: CustomerDatabase (parented by CustomerManager)
    - DecisionNode: DecisionNode1 (parented by CustomerManager)
This recommendation should be applied if you have the goal of minimizing the longest path
of corruption within your system, making system wide data corruption attacks more difficult.
```

Fig. 9. Output snippet to minimize corruption propagation in the OSM system

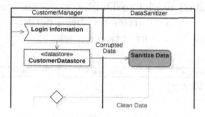

Fig. 10. Modified activity flow to minimize corruption propagation in the OSM system

of the longest activity element path does add a barrier that must be overcome to achieve a total system takeover, either by defeating the data sanitizer or by launching multiple data corruption attacks from different initial attack vectors. While a similar effect is achieved by implementing the recommendation from Sect. 6.1, that recommendation leaves a larger portion of the OSM system as a whole susceptible to a data corruption attack, even if by only one extra element. Ali's goal this time was to minimize the potential for corruption propagation in their system, and this midpoint data sanitizer placement accomplished this. As in Scenario 1, when Ali submits the modified model to Dubhe, they find that their attempt at hardening their system has been detected.

6.3   Scenario 3: Protecting Expected Entry Points

Ali's goal is to protect the entry points of the OSM system. Ali exports their UML activity diagram to XMI and provides this file to Dubhe. Dubhe generates suggestions following the logic presented in Algorithm 3, and these suggestions are then displayed to the console as seen in Fig. 11.

```
----Protecting Expected Entry Points----
It is recommended to place a Data Sanitizer object between the following elements:
    - InitialNode (parented by WebClient)
    - OpaqueAction: Client Login Request (parented by WebClient)
This recommendation is useful if the threat of insider attacks is sufficiently small compared to
the threat of external attacks. Examples of such external attacks include attempting to harm
your system by threatening its availability, or attempting a forceful takeover using arbitrary
code execution via corrupted data.
```

Fig. 11. Output snippet to protect the expected entry points of the OSM system

Ali decides to implement this recommendation and makes a small modification to their UML activity diagram, which is shown in Fig. 12. This modification is not too dissimilar to the modifications suggested in Sect. 6.1 and Sect. 6.3; however, the data sanitizer is placed earlier in the system. Although this may afford insiders more opportunities to intercept and corrupt data in subsequent activities, this modification immediately addresses the security goal in this scenario to protect the expected entry points of the OSM system. Once again, when Ali submits their modified model to Dubhe, they are shown output that indicates their addition of a data sanitizer has been detected as an effort to harden the OSM system against data corruption attacks.

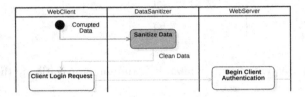

Fig. 12. Modified activity flow to protect the expected entry points of the OSM system

7   Limitations and Future Work

In this section, limitations with the approach of hardening systems against data corruption at design time are discussed, along with avenues for future work.

7.1   Limitations

To the best of our knowledge, our approach is the first attempt at hardening systems against data corruption attacks at design time, but this inherently comes with some limitations.

It remains the designer's decision as to which recommendations they choose to implement or ignore, and Dubhe does not attempt to rank the recommendations against one another. With unlimited resources, it may be the decision of a designer to implement every recommendation, but as previously discussed, this incurs an increase in coupling and a decrease in overall system cohesion. This reliance on a designer's ability to consider which security goals to select could serve as a barrier if they lack security expertise.

Likewise, in its current state, Dubhe is tailored towards the hardening of systems against data corruption attacks. If designers are not concerned about such attacks, they may not see the point of modifying their development cycles to support the use of Dubhe. We hope that as further research into data corruption attacks is published, designers will seek out solutions and in turn find tools such as the one we have developed for this work as beneficial to integrate into their system design process. We understand that designers may wish to know the impact Dubhe has in terms of development time and general effectiveness, but this requires deeper investigation that is planned in future work.

7.2   Future Work

We are exploring multiple avenues to improve Dubhe with the goal of providing designers additional recommendations to harden their systems against threats at design time. Our primary objective is to add more analysis capabilities to Dubhe with the ultimate outcome of presenting the behavioural security posture of a system as was done for the structural view of systems in previous work [21]. Additionally, we aim to improve the features offered by Dubhe. The first of these would be providing a graphical interface rather than the command-line interface currently supported. In a similar vein, we hope to further aid designers by automatically modifying the XMI to incorporate the suggestions presented by Dubhe subject to the designer's approval of the suggestions. This would further reduce the manual tasks of designers and make the incorporation of Dubhe into existing secure software development lifecycles more enticing. We are also exploring the possibility of letting designers specify the number of data santizer objects to optimally place within a UML activity diagram, rather than placing a single data sanitizer as is currently done. Lastly, we have yet to perform any usability analysis or effectiveness measuring on Dubhe. In the future, we hope to rectify this once Dubhe has been further developed. The insights gained from a usability analysis will be used to improve Dubhe while informing the direction for future features.

8   Concluding Remarks

In summary, we described a novel method to harden systems against data corruption attacks during the design phase. We implemented this methodology in Dubhe, a tool that can be used to determine the effective locations of data sanitization objects within systems to satisfy varying "what-if" security scenarios. These "what-if" scenarios were applied to a simple OSM system that highlighted the differences between the three analysis profiles that Dubhe performs and how each hardens the system against data corruption attacks in a unique way. Although the results of the analysis and subsequent recommendations for the OSM system may seem obvious for designers with minimal security expertise, this may not be the case for more complex systems. We hope that by applying Dubhe to the simple OSM system, the method in which Dubhe determines its recommendations could be fully understood to lend confidence to designers who wish to apply Dubhe to their own system models. Finally, we hope that the release of Dubhe along with the files needed to perform the use cases outlined in this work will motivate developers to incorporate Dubhe into their SSDLC going forward.

Acknowledgements. This research is supported by the Natural Sciences and Engineering Research Council of Canada (NSERC) grant RGPIN-2019-06306.

References

1. Apple: CVE-2023-32435. Available from MITRE, CVE-2023-32435 (2023). https://cve.mitre.org/cgi-bin/cvename.cgi?name=CVE-2023-32435
2. Chen, S., Xu, J., Nakka, N., Kalbarczyk, Z., Iyer, R.K.: Defeating memory corruption attacks via pointer taintedness detection. In: 2005 International Conference on Dependable Systems and Networks, pp. 378–387. DSN 2005 (2005)
3. Cheng, L., et al.: Exploitation techniques and defenses for data-oriented attacks. In: 2019 IEEE Cybersecurity Development (SecDev), pp. 114–128. IEEE (2019)
4. Chowdhury, I., Chan, B., Zulkernine, M.: Security metrics for source code structures. In: 4th International Workshop on Software Engineering for Secure Systems, pp. 57–64. SESS 2008, ACM (2008)
5. Fiala, D., Mueller, F., Engelmann, C., Riesen, R., Ferreira, K., Brightwell, R.: Detection and correction of silent data corruption for large-scale high-performance computing. In: 2012 International Conference on High Performance Computing, Networking, Storage and Analysis, pp. 1–12 (2012)
6. Google: CVE-2023-3079. Available from MITRE, CVE-2023-3079 (2023). https://cve.mitre.org/cgi-bin/cvename.cgi?name=CVE-2023-3079
7. Howard, M., Lipner, S.: The Security Development Lifecycle, vol. 8. Microsoft Press, Redmond (2006)
8. Jürjens, J.: UMLsec: extending UML for secure systems development. In: Jézéquel, J.-M., Hussmann, H., Cook, S. (eds.) UML 2002. LNCS, vol. 2460, pp. 412–425. Springer, Heidelberg (2002). https://doi.org/10.1007/3-540-45800-X_32
9. Jürjens, J., Shabalin, P.: Tools for secure systems development with uml: security analysis with ATPs. In: Cerioli, M. (ed.) FASE 2005. LNCS, vol. 3442, pp. 305–309. Springer, Heidelberg (2005). https://doi.org/10.1007/978-3-540-31984-9_23
10. Kang, S., Kim, S.: CIA-level driven secure SDLC framework for integrating security into SDLC process. J. Ambient. Intell. Humaniz. Comput. 13(10), 4601–4624 (2022)
11. Kontouras, E., Tzes, A., Dritsas, L.: Set-theoretic detection of data corruption attacks on cyber physical power systems. J. Mod. Power Syst. Clean Energy 6, 872–886 (2018)
12. Lee, M., Davis, C.: XMI extension for StarUML (2018). https://github.com/staruml/staruml-xmi
13. Lodderstedt, T., Basin, D., Doser, J.: SecureUML: a UML-based modeling language for model-driven security. In: Jézéquel, J.-M., Hussmann, H., Cook, S. (eds.) UML 2002. LNCS, vol. 2460, pp. 426–441. Springer, Heidelberg (2002). https://doi.org/10.1007/3-540-45800-X_33
14. lxml Development Team: lxml: XML and HTML with python (2023). https://lxml.de/. version 4.9.3 [Software library]
15. Microsoft: Microsoft outlook elevation of privilege vulnerability (2023). https://msrc.microsoft.com/update-guide/en-US/vulnerability/CVE-2023-23397
16. MKLabs Co.,Ltd.: StarUML (2023). https://staruml.io. version 6.0 [Software]
17. Nie, X., Chen, L., Wei, H., Zhang, Y., Cui, N., Shi, G.: KPDFI: efficient data flow integrity based on key property against data corruption attack. In: Computers & Security, pp. 103–183 (2023)
18. Object Management Group: Unified Modeling Language (2017). https://www.omg.org/spec/UML/2.5.1/PDF. version 2.5.1
19. Ozkaya, M.: Are the UML modelling tools powerful enough for practitioners? a literature review. IET Softw. 13(5), 338–354 (2019)

20. Rodríguez, A., Fernández-Medina, E., Piattini, M.: Capturing security requirements in business processes through a UML 2.0 activity diagrams profile. In: Roddick, J.F., et al. (eds.) ER 2006. LNCS, vol. 4231, pp. 32–42. Springer, Heidelberg (2006). https://doi.org/10.1007/11908883_6
21. Samuel, J., Jaskolka, J., Yee, G.O.M.: Analyzing structural security posture to evaluate system design decisions. In: 21st IEEE International Conference on Software Quality, Reliability, and Security, QRS 2021, pp. 8–17 (2021)
22. Sindre, G.: Mal-activity diagrams for capturing attacks on business processes. In: Sawyer, P., Paech, B., Heymans, P. (eds.) REFSQ 2007. LNCS, vol. 4542, pp. 355–366. Springer, Heidelberg (2007). https://doi.org/10.1007/978-3-540-73031-6_27
23. Szekeres, L., Payer, M., Wei, T., Song, D.: Sok: eternal war in memory. In: 2013 IEEE Symposium on Security and Privacy, pp. 48–62. IEEE (2013)
24. The Eclipse Foundation: Eclipse Papyrus (2023). https://www.eclipse.org/papyrus/. version 6.5.0 [Software]
25. van der Veen, V., dutt-Sharma, N., Cavallaro, L., Bos, H.: Memory errors: the past, the present, and the future. In: Balzarotti, D., Stolfo, S.J., Cova, M. (eds.) RAID 2012. LNCS, vol. 7462, pp. 86–106. Springer, Heidelberg (2012). https://doi.org/10.1007/978-3-642-33338-5_5
26. Yee, G.O.M.: Reducing the attack surface for private data. In: 13th International Conference on Emerging Security Information, Systems and Technologies, SECURWARE 2019, pp. 28–34 (2019)

Design of an Efficient Distributed Delivery Service for Group Key Agreement Protocols

Ludovic Paillat[1]([✉])(iD), Claudia-Lavinia Ignat[2](iD), Davide Frey[3](iD),
Mathieu Turuani[2], and Amine Ismail[1]

[1] Hive Computing Services, Cannes, France
{ludovic.paillat,amine.ismail}@hivenet.com
[2] Université de Lorraine, CNRS, Inria, LORIA, Nancy, France
{claudia.ignat,mathieu.turuani}@inria.fr
[3] Inria, IRISA, CNRS, Université de Rennes, Rennes, France
davide.frey@inria.fr

Abstract. End-to-end encrypted messaging applications such as Signal became widely popular thanks to their capability to ensure the confidentiality and integrity of online communication. While the highest security guarantees were long reserved to two-party communication, solutions for n-party communication remained either inefficient or less secure until the standardization of the MLS Protocol (Messaging Layer Security). This new protocol offers an efficient way to provide end-to-end secure communication with the same guarantees originally offered by the Signal Protocol for two-party communication. However, both solutions still rely on a centralized component for message delivery, called the Delivery Service in the MLS Protocol. The centralization of the Delivery Service makes it an ideal target for attackers and threatens the availability of any protocol relying on MLS. In order to overcome this issue, we propose the design of a fully distributed Delivery Service that allows clients to exchange protocol messages efficiently and without any intermediary. It uses a Probabilistic Reliable-Broadcast mechanism to efficiently deliver messages and the Cascade Consensus Protocol to handle messages requiring an agreement. Our solution strengthens the availability of the MLS Protocol without compromising its security.

Keywords: Distributed systems · Group key agreement · Consensus protocols · Reliable broadcast

1 Introduction

To protect the privacy of their users, a number of Internet-based services have started to develop solutions based on *end-to-end encryption (E2EE)* that prevent third parties from accessing user data transferred from one endpoint to another.

Secure messaging applications such as Signal and WhatsApp are well-known to advertise their use of *E2EE*. Indeed, the Signal Protocol was the first to propose *E2EE* for two-party conversations using the Double Ratchet algorithm [18].

M. Mosbah et al. (Eds.): FPS 2023, LNCS 14551, pp. 408–423, 2024.
https://doi.org/10.1007/978-3-031-57537-2_25

However, the solutions proposed by these same messaging applications for n-party secure communication were either inefficient by requiring the establishment of encrypted communication between all pairs of group members, or less secure when using a common encryption key (e.g. Sender Keys Protocol [5]) which may not be refreshed as the group dynamically changes.

To address the topic of secure group communication, industrial and academic organizations such as Cisco, Mozilla, Facebook and Inria proposed the Messaging Layer Security Protocol (MLS) standardized as RFC 9420 [6]. This protocol relies on a Group Key Agreement Protocol called TreeKEM [9] allowing members of a group to derive a common secret called *group key* which serves as a basis to secure group communications. It is scalable in terms of the number of operations modifying the group and it supports periodic group-key renewals preventing compromised communication.

The MLS Protocol offers an efficient solution to guarantee the *confidentiality* and *integrity* of communication. However, the *availability* of the protocol depends on the *Delivery-Service* component, which remains centralized most of the time. The centralization of this component makes it an ideal target for attackers who wish to disrupt communication. Notably, with the help of a compromised Delivery Service, an attacker can prevent group members from refreshing their keys and resolving the compromise.

In order to overcome these limitations we propose a fully distributed Delivery Service. It combines two distributed communication mechanisms adapted to the need of the messages exchanged by the protocol. We use a Probabilistic Reliable Broadcast mechanism [13] to reliably deliver messages allowing users to propose changes to the group (i.e. *Proposal* messages) and the Cascade Consensus Protocol [1] to deliver the messages that actually modify the group (i.e. *Commit* messages) and thus require an agreement between members.

Our contribution is two-fold:

- the formalization of the MLS protocol's Delivery Service, detailing the necessary properties of this component;
- a novel algorithm describing a fully distributed Delivery Service.

We start by reviewing the state of the art of distributed communication mechanisms in Sect. 2. We then present the TreeKEM Protocol and formalize the Delivery Service in Sect. 3. Section 4 presents the details of our solution and discusses how it increases the security of the protocol with respect to a centralized approach. Finally, Sect. 5 concludes the paper and presents some future work directions.

2   Related Work

Secure communication requires securely sharing encryption keys thus preventing attackers from gaining access to them. Additionally, as communications can remain established for a long time, protocols must provide a way to mitigate the eventual compromise of some keys. The following security properties need to be ensured:

- *Backward secrecy*: the knowledge of previous keys does not affect the security of the current key and future ones.
- *Forward secrecy*: the knowledge of a key does not affect the security of previous keys.
- *Post-Compromise security*: if a member is compromised, an UPDATE operation from this member will resolve the compromise and restore the security of the group in subsequent states.

The Signal protocol based on the Double Ratchet Algorithm [18] provides strong security guarantees for two-party communication. The Double Ratchet algorithm provides *Forward secrecy* by generating a new encryption key for each message while periodical Diffie-Hellman key exchanges provide fresh security material ensuring *Post-Compromise security*. However, this approach cannot be applied to group (i.e. n-party) communication and the use of pairwise communication channels (i.e. a group member sends a message to the group by using $n-1$ secure communication channels established with the other members) does not scale well.

An alternative, *Sender Keys* [5], allows one member to use pairwise communication channels to share a common encryption key that can be used to encrypt messages. While this key can be used to deterministically generate individual *message keys* to provide *Forward Secrecy*, *Post-Compromise security* is not ensured as the common key is only renewed in rare occasions such as member removal. Thus, the compromise of one member makes it possible to spy on future messages for a long time.

Secure group-communication protocols address these drawbacks. In the following, we first present the main existing protocols for secure group communication and we highlight the advantages of TreeKEM [9]. We then describe the distributed communication mechanisms we selected to make it distributed.

2.1 Secure Group Communication

First attempts to secure group communication were Conference Key Distribution Systems in which a member generates a conference key and distributes it to all group members. Different topologies for Distribution Systems [11] were proposed. However the *Star-Based* topology is inefficient as it requires $\mathcal{O}(n)$ key exchanges, while other topologies such as a *Tree* or a *Cyclic System* cannot tolerate the fault of even one participant.

Group Key Agreement protocols were introduced as a way to establish and manage dynamic groups whose members can derive a common encryption key called *group key*. These protocols mainly provide three operations: the ADD and REMOVE operations to manage the group and the UPDATE operation to allow group members to refresh their secret keys. Each operation leads to a new group key, thereby ADD and REMOVE operations guarantee *backward* and *forward secrecy* for the group key while periodical UPDATEs ensure *post-compromise security*. Thus, if a member does not renew its secret key, this member should be removed from the group as a compromise of this member threatens the security of the group.

Collaborative Group Key Agreement protocols were the first to establish a *group key* built on the principle of the Diffie-Hellman key exchange. The GDH protocols [4,20] allow members to collaboratively build the group key presented in Equation 1. However, the computation of this key requires $\mathcal{O}(n)$ communication rounds. The TGDH (Tree-based Group Key Agreement) protocol [14] establishes a group key more efficiently in $\mathcal{O}(\log n)$ rounds. The underlying binary-tree structure contains the member keys in the leafs, intermediate keys exchanged between sub-groups (i.e. members sharing one node in their path to the root of the tree) and the root representing the group key. The resulting group key for a 5-member group is presented in Equation 2. Additionally, operations on the group only require the modification of $\mathcal{O}(\log n)$ intermediate keys.

$$K = \alpha^{r_1 \times r_2 \times \cdots \times r_n} \qquad (1) \qquad K = \alpha^{\left(\alpha^{\left(\alpha^{(r_1 \times r_2)} \times \alpha^{(r_3 \times r_4)}\right)}\right) \times r_5} \qquad (2)$$

Nevertheless, the TGDH protocol cannot tolerate the fault or disconnection of any member, as each member can only modify their path to the root of the tree. Thus, the removal of one member from the tree requires the participation of the closest neighbor to this member in the tree. The ART (Asynchronous Ratcheting Trees) protocol [12] enhances TGDH with the capability of creating a group in which all members but the group creator are not required to be online. In this protocol, the group creator can create the initial tree by using the X3DH key exchange algorithm [16] with ephemeral keys stored by each group member in a Public Key Infrastructure. This key exchange guarantees that each group member will be able to derive only the keys they should know with the exception of the group creator who initially knows the entire tree.

The more recent TreeKEM protocol [9] allows clients to issue asynchronous group operations. By replacing the tree structure based on Diffie-Hellman with a tree structure based on the principle of *Key Derivation*, the TreeKEM protocol allows any member to carry out operations on the tree without requiring the help of any particular group member. The TreeKEM protocol achieves good performance and was backed by multiple security analyses (i.e. [3,10], ...). It is part of a complete solution for Secure Group Communication, the MLS Protocol [6] standardized in RFC 9420. For all these reasons we rely on TreeKEM as a basis for our proposed distributed Group Key Agreement mechanism.

2.2 Distributed Communication Mechanisms

We extend TreeKEM by focusing on two distributed communication mechanisms adapted for the delivery of Proposal and Commit messages as described in Sect. 3.1.

In the case of Proposal messages, which are sent by members only to propose modifications to the group, and thus do not require agreement, we use a Reliable Broadcast protocol. This protocol only focuses on the correct delivery of a message from a specific sender to all group members.

Specifically we adopt a gossip-based Scalable Reliable Broadcast protocol [13] with a $\mathcal{O}(\log(n))$ per-process communication and computation complexity where n is the number of processes. More precisely, we adopt MURMUR [13], a gossip-based dissemination protocol which only guarantees the delivery of messages without the ability to provide an order of messages for a given member. This protocol perfectly fits the requirements for Proposal messages as these messages do not need to be ordered in any way.

For dealing with Commit messages, which need to be totally ordered and thus require agreement between group members, we use the Cascade Consensus Protocol [1]. Below, we first provide a description of the Context-Adaptative Cooperation abstraction which is an important part of Cascade Consensus and then we detail the Cascade Consensus protocol.

Context-Adaptative Cooperation. Context-Adaptative Cooperation (CAC) is a new broadcast abstraction that sits between reliable broadcast and consensus [1]. It allows multiple senders to send concurrent messages and focuses on the ability to detect when some messages are indeed sent concurrently and conflict with each other.

In CAC, contrary to classical reliable broadcast protocols, the protocol will not only deliver a message but also a *conflict-set* indicating other messages that might conflict with the delivered one. Therefore, CAC can act as a reliable broadcast when there is not any conflict during a broadcast instance. Otherwise, in the case of a conflict between multiple senders, this conflict will be detected and CAC can trigger a classical consensus protocol to handle the conflict.

The protocol works by collecting signatures from other processes about the different broadcast messages. When a process broadcasts a protocol message to others, this process includes the signed messages received from other processes. The use of signatures prevents a malicious process from presenting different views to other processes as processes share their own views by means of these signed messages. Then, after reaching a sufficient count of signatures, the protocol can move forward with the associated messages. The CAC protocol is organized in two phases (Witness and Ready) detailed below.

In the *Witness* phase, each process broadcasts a WITNESS message targeting the first broadcast message that this process received. After receiving WITNESS signatures from a quorum of q_W processes, the current process can move on to the next phase for this given message. However, in the event of multiple broadcast messages, it is possible that none reaches the quorum of q_W processes. Thus, an *unlocking mechanism* is triggered when a process knows that it received a response from at least $n - t$ processes, n being the total number of processes with at most t Byzantine processes. In that case this process will also send a WITNESS message for all witnessed messages that satisfy a lower threshold. These messages are likely to conflict and appear in the *conflict-set* that will later be computed. The size of the quorum $q_W = 2t + k$ is based on a parameter k that tunes the sensitivity of the protocol to conflicting messages: a small k can lead to multiple conflicts whereas with a larger k fewer messages will likely reach the quorum.

The *Ready* phase is reached for a given message when this message reaches the quorum of q_W distinct WITNESS signatures. Then, the process can broadcast a READY message and wait for q_R distinct READY signatures for the same message. The purpose of this phase is to ensure *totality* meaning that if the current process delivers the message then all the other correct processes also deliver it. Finally, as mentioned earlier, CAC associates the delivered messages with a *conflict-set*. This *conflict-set* contains messages that received enough WITNESS signatures to be considered in conflict.

Cascade Consensus Protocol. The CAC abstraction enables the construction of a consensus protocol named *Cascade Consensus*. In this protocol, a process starts by using CAC to broadcast a message. Then, if there are no conflicts, meaning that CAC delivers a single message with a *conflict-set* of size 1, the protocol can directly finish and deliver this message. Otherwise in case of a conflict, with a *conflict-set* containing two messages or more, the protocol triggers a *Restrained Consensus* between the senders associated with the messages in the *conflict-set*. This *Restrained Consensus* involves only the senders in conflict and thus is less costly than regular consensus provided that none of its participants is Byzantine and no period of asynchrony occurs during its execution. Thus, either one of the participants is chosen by *Restrained Consensus* and its message can be delivered, or in the event of a timeout, a classical Consensus algorithm is used to settle the *Cascade Consensus* protocol and reach a final decision.

We choose this protocol as the graceful conditions allowing the early termination of Cascade Consensus match the expected behavior of TreeKEM. Indeed, depending on the size and the dynamics of a group, conflicts may not occur very often, in which cases the consensus ends after a CAC broadcast. Additionally, these conflicts may usually be restricted to a few members of the group, reducing the complexity of consensus by triggering Restrained Consensus.

3   The TreeKEM Protocol and Its Delivery Service

The TreeKEM protocol underlying Messaging Layer Security (MLS) [6] provides a standard and well-secured solution for end-to-end secure group communication such as group messaging and video conferencing. We first present the Propose and Commit approach used by TreeKEM to handle concurrent operations in the group. Next, we introduce the core structure of TreeKEM based on the ratcheting tree. We then describe the Delivery Service component of TreeKEM which is in charge of handling protocol communication and resolving conflicts between members. We present our formalization of the role and the properties of this Delivery Service component. Finally, we describe the centralized solution of the Delivery Service adopted by TreeKEM and its follow-up protocols.

3.1 Propose and Commit

The 8th draft of the MLS Protocol, introduces the principle of *Propose and Commit* in the TreeKEM Protocol which describes the current way of organizing the operations in the protocol. This allows group members to perform concurrent operations in the form of *Proposals*. Then, these proposals can be merged into a *Commit* which materializes these changes into the group and leads to a new *epoch* for the group. In TreeKEM, it is up to the application using the protocol to decide which client commits the *Proposals*.

In the case of conflicting *Proposals* (e.g. multiple add/remove/update *Proposals* for the same member), the *commiter* must choose between those proposals to solve the conflicts. Additionally, if one *Commit* contains *Proposals* to add one or multiple members, the protocol generates a *Welcome* message that allows them to effectively join the group.

Therefore, based on the MLS RFC [6] we propose the following formalization of the TreeKEM protocol:

- $s \leftarrow \text{INIT}(ID)$: initiates the group state s for the user associated with the identity ID.
- $p \leftarrow \text{PROPOSEADD}(s, ID')$: creates a proposal to add the user corresponding to ID' to the group with the current state s. The operation outputs a proposal p.
- $p \leftarrow \text{PROPOSEREMOVE}(s, ID')$: creates a proposal to remove the user corresponding to ID' from the group with current state s. The operation outputs a proposal p.
- $p \leftarrow \text{PROPOSEUPDATE}(s, k)$: creates a proposal to update the current user's key in current state s with k. The operation outputs a proposal p.
- $(C, W) \leftarrow \text{COMMIT}(s, P)$: commits a set P of valid and non conflicting proposals (i.e. according to Sect. 12.2 of the RFC [6]) to make the current group state s progress. The operation outputs a commit message C to make current members transition to the new group state and possibly a welcome message W to allow proposed new users to join the group.
- $(s', K) \leftarrow \text{PROCESS}(s, M)$: processes a commit or welcome message M to transition from the old group state s to the new group state s'. The transition additionally generates a new *group key K*.

3.2 Ratcheting Tree

One way to implement the protocol would be for a member to generate a new group key and encrypt this key with the public keys of each user. However this kind of approach would scale poorly in the case of large groups. Thus, TreeKEM uses the concept of the ratcheting tree in order to improve scalability.

The ratcheting tree is organized as a balanced binary tree of public-private key-pairs whose leaves represent members of the group. Group members do not share the same view of the tree as each member only knows a subset of the private keys: the keys on the path from the leaf associated with this member to the root of the tree. Therefore the only private key known by all members is the root of the tree which gets to be used as the group key. Figure 1 presents the example of a ratcheting tree in the case of a 4-member group. In the tree, members 1 and 2 share the secret associated with A, 3 and 4 share the secret associated with B and C's secret is shared among all members and considered the group key.

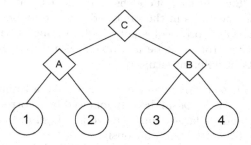

Fig. 1. Example of a TreeKEM ratcheting tree in the case of a 4-user group.

When a member creates a Commit message to advance the group state, this member modifies one or more leaves in the tree to apply the operations described by the associated proposals. Then, this member updates their path to the root in order to ensure the renewal of the group key. This can be done in two steps:

- First, a key derivation mechanism, similar to a hash function, makes it possible to generate the new keys. For example, member 1 would generate a new leaf key $k_{1'}$, and iterate a key derivation mechanism to generate the following keys: $k_{1'} \rightarrow k_{A'} \rightarrow k_{C'}$.
- Then, the tree structure can be used to limit the number of encryptions: $k_{A'}$ can be encrypted to member 2, and $k_{C'}$ can be encrypted to the remaining sub-group using the public key of B.

As members can complete the chain of keys using the key-derivation mechanism, the number of keys and needed encryptions to generate a Commit message is limited to $log(n)$ in a group of size n, which offers good scalability. However, the protocol does not provide a way to merge the modifications conveyed by multiple commits. Thus, in the event of concurrent commits, only one commit must be chosen to be applied by all group members. The task of resolving these conflicts falls under the responsibility of the *Delivery Service* that will be described in the following subsection.

3.3   The TreeKEM's Delivery Service

The MLS Architecture draft [8] describes the typical architecture in which clients implementing the MLS Protocol [6] interact with each other. In this architecture, clients communicate with each other using a *Delivery Service* whose detailed description falls out of the scope of the MLS Protocol.

Thus, the role of the *Delivery Service* is essentially to ensure the delivery of the different types of messages: Application messages exchanged between users, *Proposal* messages and *Commit* messages. The only constraint for Application and *Proposals* messages is that they must eventually reach their recipients.

However, *Commit* messages present different challenges. In fact, the MLS Protocol imposes a linear history of epochs. This means that the members should process the *Commit* messages in the same order and only one *Commit* message can exist per epoch, as the protocol is not capable of merging multiple *Commits*. Ensuring this linear history can be a problem as the members may generate concurrent commits in different situations:

- On the one hand, some members might not take advantage of concurrent operations (i.e. send a *Proposal* directly followed by a corresponding *Commit*) and in dynamic and/or large groups, there is a high probability of members issuing multiple *Commits* simultaneously.
- On the other hand, even when members first send *Proposals* to allow operations to be executed concurrently, there is still the need for one of those members to *commit* the operations. This member can be determined deterministically to limit the cost, for example based on the set of received proposals. But, in a distributed system the presence of failures and asynchronous periods may prevent all members from deciding on the same *commiter*. Thus, even if the probability of conflicts is lowered, it is still possible for concurrent *commits* to be issued. Addressing this situation requires solving consensus.

Therefore, in case of conflicts, the *Delivery Service* must act as a reference, capable of deciding on one *Commit* that all members will consider as the right one for a given *epoch*.

Formalization. Based on the specifications provided in the MLS Protocol [6] and the MLS Architecture draft [8], we now present our formalization of the role and the properties of the TreeKEM Delivery Service.

The Delivery Service is a group communication mechanism that provides two operations and two callbacks:

- `ds_proposal_broadcast`(pm): a process p_i can invoke this operation to submit a proposal message pm.
- `ds_proposal_deliver`(p_i, pm): callback triggered to deliver a proposal message pm broadcast by process p_i.
- `ds_commit_propose`(ep, cm): a process p_i can invoke this operation to submit a commit message cm for the current epoch ep.
- `ds_commit_deliver`(ep, p_i, cm): callback triggered to deliver the commit message cm for the epoch ep and broadcast by process p_i, which allows members to progress to the next epoch and state.

The Delivery Service satisfies the following properties:

- **Proposal Validity.** If a correct process p_i ds-proposal-delivers a pair (p_j, pm), then pm is a valid proposal message, p_j is a correct process and p_j has previously ds-proposal-broadcast pm.
- **Proposal Totality.** If a correct process p_i ds-proposal-broadcasts a proposal message pm, then all correct processes eventually ds-proposal-deliver the pair (p_i, pm).
- **Epoch Validity.** If a correct process p_i ds-commit-delivers a tuple (ep, p_j, cm), then ep is the current epoch, cm is a valid commit message in the current epoch, p_j is a correct process and p_j has previously ds-commit-proposed cm.
- **Epoch Agreement.** If any two correct processes ds-commit-deliver respective tuples $(ep, -, cm)$ and $(ep', -, cm')$, and if $ep = ep'$ then we have $cm = cm'$.
- **Epoch Termination.** If a correct process p_i ds-commit-proposes a commit message cm for the epoch ep, then all correct processes eventually ds-commit-deliver a pair $(ep, -, -)$.
- **Epoch-Content Consistency** If a correct process ds-commit-delivers a tuple $(-, -, cm)$, then for all proposal messages pm referenced by cm all correct processes have previously ds-proposal-delivered a tuple $(-, pm)$.

3.4 Centralized Delivery Service

The approach adopted by TreeKEM and other protocols it inspired (e.g. [2, 15]) is to rely on a central authority to implement the Delivery Service. In this case, the Delivery Service would be operated by a central server. To keep confidentiality this central server is assumed to be *untrusted*. This means that, as the messages are end-to-end encrypted, the server cannot read or modify the messages exchanged between members, but has access to a limited set of metadata necessary to fulfill its task (i.e. group id and epoch).

Due to its limited view on the content of messages, an *untrusted* centralized Delivery Service can only accomplish the role of an ordering server, providing the different messages in the same order for all clients. Then, in case of conflicts, the members can choose the first valid commit message and coherently resolve the conflict.

However, this central server can easily become a target of attacks such as Denial of Service which can impact its availability. In more complex settings, a compromised Delivery Service can be used to mount attacks against specific groups. By blocking the operations of given members, one can prevent these members from refreshing their keys and thus eventually lead to the failure of the Post-Compromise Security property.

4   A Distributed Delivery Service

In this section, we describe our solution for a fully distributed Delivery Service. Instead of relying on a third-party untrusted server, the participants in the key agreement protocols, or a subset of them, directly run the delivery service. We illustrate our solution as a flowchart in Fig. 2 and formally in Algorithm 1. The flowchart in Fig. 2 describes the verification process and the delays that messages can encounter between their receipt from the communication component and their delivery. The Algorithm 1 details how the execution unfolds.

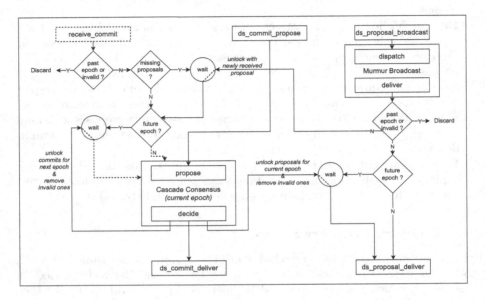

Fig. 2. Diagram detailing our solution for a Distributed Delivery Service

Our solution relies on two basic communication mechanisms adapted to the different messages of the TreeKEM protocol: a Probabilistic Reliable Broadcast (i.e. the MURMUR protocol from [13]) for Proposal messages and the Cascade Consensus Protocol [1] for Commit messages. We introduce a slight modification to the Cascade Consensus Protocol and to the CAC broadcast mechanism on which it is based (see Sect. 2). Specifically, we delay the acknowledgement of a commit (i.e. the emission of a WITNESS message upon receipt of a first WITNESS message) until the client considers this commit as valid. We materialize this validation by a call to ccb.receiveCommit (l. 17). This ensures that the commit message can be introduced as a candidate in the consensus protocol only when all members agree that this commit is valid.

Algorithm 1. Formalization of our solution for a Distributed Delivery Service based on the Cascade Consensus Protocol and the Murmur broadcast protocol.

Implements:
1: DistributedDeliveryService, **instance** dds
Uses:
2: MurmurBroadcast, **instance** mb
3: CascadeConsensusBroadcast, **instance** ccb
4: TreeKEMProtocol, **instance** tkem
5:
6: **upon event** < Init > **do**
7:     $proposals = \emptyset$; $incomplete\_commits = \emptyset$; $future\_commits = \emptyset$;
8:     $future\_proposals = \emptyset$
9:
10: **upon event** < dds.BroadcastProposal | [**Proposal**, $proposal$] > **do**
11:     **trigger** < mb.Dispatch | [**Proposal**, $proposal$] >
12:
13: **procedure** $handleCommit(commit)$ ▷ handle commits that are or became complete
14:     **if** $commit$.epoch > $tkem$.currentEpoch **then**
15:         $future\_commits \leftarrow future\_commits \cup commit$
16:     **else**
17:         ccb.receiveCommit($commit$)
18:     **end if**
19:
20: **upon event** < mb.Deliver | [**Proposal**, $proposal$] > **do**   ▷ ignore past and invalid proposals
21:     $proposals \leftarrow proposals \cup proposal$
22:     **for** $commit \in incomplete\_commits$ **do**
23:         **if** $commit$.proposals $\subseteq proposals$ **then**
24:             $handleCommit(commit)$
25:             $incomplete\_commits \leftarrow incomplete\_commits \setminus commit$
26:         **end if**
27:     **end for**
28:     **if** $proposal$.epoch $= tkem$.currentEpoch **then**
29:         **trigger** < dds.DeliverProposal | [**Proposal**, $proposal$] >
30:     **else**
31:         $future\_proposals \leftarrow future\_proposals \cup proposal$
32:     **end if**
33:
34: **upon event** < dds.ProposeCommit | [**Commit**, $commit$] > **do**
35:     **trigger** < ccb.Propose | $tkem$.currentEpoch,[**Commit**, $commit$] >

```
36: upon event < ccb.ReceiveCommit | [Commit, commit] > do        ▷ ignore past and
        invalid commits
37:     if commit.proposals ⊈ proposals then
38:         incomplete_commits ← incomplete_commits ∪ commit
39:     else
40:         handleCommit(commit)
41:     end if
42:
43: upon event < ccb.Deliver | [Commit, commit] > do
44:     tkem.apply(commit)
45:     for proposal ∈ future_proposals do
46:         if tkem.currentEpoch = proposal.epoch and tkem.isValid(proposal) then
47:             trigger < dds.DeliverProposal | [Proposal, proposal] >
48:             future_proposals ← future_proposals \ proposal
49:         end if
50:     end for
51:     for commit ∈ future_commits do
52:         if tkem.currentEpoch = commit.epoch and tkem.isValid(commit) then
53:             ccb.receiveCommit(commit)
54:             future_commits ← future_commits \ commit
55:         end if
56:     end for
57:     trigger < dds.DeliverCommit | [Commit, commit] >
```

Delaying commits allows our solution to control the flow of epochs, making sure that it only delivers messages belonging to the current epoch, and that all members have moved to the current epoch before deciding on the next one. This prevents an attacker from executing a *Denial of Service attack* by submitting a large number of commits in a short time. To implement this delay, Algorithm 1 employs two waiting queues (*incomplete_commits, future_commits*) initialized on line 7. Together, these queues allow our solution to wait until all the proposals referenced by a commit are received before starting an agreement (i.e. a consensus) on this commit. This leads to the satisfaction of the *Epoch-Content-Consistency* property.

In a similar manner, we also introduce a delay on proposal messages (by means of the *future_proposals* waiting queue initialized on line 8 of Algorithm 1). This makes it possible to delay proposals whose messages belong to a future epoch—that a member suffering from network delays cannot immediately verify—or that were created by an attacker in an attempt to block the progress of the group.

We handle proposal messages using the MURMUR [13] protocol (l. 20), which guarantees *Proposal Totality*. When a member receives a proposal message, two cases can arise. If the proposal belongs to the current epoch, and thus satisfies *Proposal Validity*, we can directly deliver the message (l. 29). Otherwise, we wait for this message to become valid by inserting this message in the list of future proposals (l. 31). Additionally, we check if this proposal is referenced by any commit previously received (l. 22). This check may unblock a commit whose acknowledgment was delayed to ensure *Epoch-Content Consistency*.

To handle commit messages, on the other hand, we employ the modified cascade-consensus mechanism (l. 36). Commits whose proposals are missing are delayed (l. 38), either if some of their proposals are missing to guarantee *Epoch-Content Consistency* or to guarantee *Commit Validity* if the commit belongs to a future epoch (l. 15) that cannot yet be verified. Then, valid commits are transmitted as candidates for the next epoch to the Cascade Consensus Protocol. This protocol ensures the *Epoch Agreement* and *Epoch Termination*.

Finally, when members all agree on the same commit, this commit is delivered by the consensus protocol (l. 43). This commit can be transmitted to the TreeKEM protocol to take effect. Additionally, the change of epoch can unblock proposals (l. 47) and commits (l. 53) that were previously delayed if the client received messages out of order.

5 Conclusion

In this paper we presented a completely distributed solution for the design of the Delivery-Service component of TreeKEM by combining a Probabilistic Broadcast [13] method with the Cascade Consensus Protocol [1]. We formalized the role and the necessary properties of this Delivery-Service component and we proposed a novel algorithm supporting its distributed counterpart. This design allows users to run the TreeKEM protocol or any similar Group Key Agreement protocol without requiring their communication to go through a central server. Our approach increases the security and the availability of group communication making it harder for an attacker to compromise the Delivery Service. Mounting attacks against the group requires compromising one third of the clients [1] instead of only one server in the standard centralized solution.

We plan to implement our Distributed Delivery Service solution and to conduct a performance evaluation in the context of peer-to-peer networks. Additionally, we plan to conduct a formal security analysis of our protocol. We will further extend our solution in order to explicitly support offline group members. Currently, the TreeKEM protocol supports offline members using a central server that stores messages for these users. We plan to design completely distributed alternative solutions for offline communication by relying on State-Machine-Replication [7] mechanisms such as State Transfer. This should allow previously offline members to get up to date with the group by directly synchronizing with some other members. In order to support a completely distributed group-key-management component for our real-time peer-to-peer collaborative editor MUTE [17], we plan to integrate the TreeKEM protocol and our distributed Delivery Service. We further plan to combine this distributed group-key-management mechanism with a distributed access control mechanism such as ACCURE [19].

Acknowledgments. This work is supported by the "Alvearium" Inria and hive partnership.

References

1. Albouy, T., Frey, D., Gestin, M., Raynal, M., Taïani, F.: Context adaptive cooperation (2023). https://arxiv.org/abs/2311.08776
2. Alwen, J., Auerbach, B., Noval, M.C., Klein, K., Pascual-Perez, G., Pietrzak, K., Walter, M.: Cocoa: concurrent continuous group key agreement. In: Advances in Cryptology - EUROCRYPT 2022: 41st Annual International Conference on the Theory and Applications of Cryptographic Techniques, Trondheim, Norway, 30 May–3 June 2022, Proceedings, Part II, p. 815-844. Springer, Heidelberg (2022). https://doi.org/10.1007/978-3-031-07085-3_28
3. Alwen, J., Coretti, S., Dodis, Y., Tselekounis, Y.: Modular design of secure group messaging protocols and the security of mls. In: Proceedings of the 2021 ACM SIGSAC Conference on Computer and Communications Security, CCS 2021, pp. 1463-1483. Association for Computing Machinery, New York (2021). https://doi.org/10.1145/3460120.3484820
4. Ateniese, G., Steiner, M., Tsudik, G.: Authenticated group key agreement and friends. In: Proceedings of the 5th ACM Conference on Computer and Communications Security, CCS 1998, pp. 17–26 (1998). https://doi.org/10.1145/288090.288097
5. Balbás, D., Collins, D., Gajland, P.: Analysis and improvements of the sender keys protocol for group messaging. XVII Reunión española sobre criptología y seguridad de la información. RECSI 2022 **265**, 25 (2022). https://arxiv.org/abs/2301.07045
6. Barnes, R., Beurdouche, B., Robert, R., Millican, J., Omara, E., Cohn-Gordon, K.: The Messaging Layer Security (MLS) Protocol. RFC 9420 (2023). https://doi.org/10.17487/RFC9420, https://www.rfc-editor.org/info/rfc9420
7. Bessani, A., Sousa, J., Alchieri, E.E.: State machine replication for the masses with bft-smart. In: 2014 44th Annual IEEE/IFIP International Conference on Dependable Systems and Networks, pp. 355–362 (2014). https://doi.org/10.1109/DSN.2014.43
8. Beurdouche, B., Rescorla, E., Omara, E., Inguva, S., Duric, A.: The Messaging Layer Security (MLS) Architecture. Internet-Draft draft-ietf-mls-architecture-10, Internet Engineering Task Force (2022). https://datatracker.ietf.org/doc/draft-ietf-mls-architecture/10/
9. Bhargavan, K., Barnes, R., Rescorla, E.: TreeKEM: asynchronous decentralized key management for large dynamic groups a protocol proposal for messaging layer security (MLS). Research report, Inria Paris (2018). https://hal.inria.fr/hal-02425247
10. Brzuska, C., Cornelissen, E., Kohbrok, K.: Security analysis of the mls key derivation. In: 2022 IEEE Symposium on Security and Privacy (SP), pp. 2535–2553 (2022). https://doi.org/10.1109/SP46214.2022.9833678
11. Burmester, M., Desmedt, Y.: A secure and efficient conference key distribution system. In: De Santis, A. (ed.) Advances in Cryptology—EUROCRYPT 1994, vol. 950, pp. 275–286 (1995). https://doi.org/10.1007/BFb0053443. https://www.cs.fsu.edu/~langley/Eurocrypt/euro-pre.pdf
12. Cohn-Gordon, K., Cremers, C., Garratt, L., Millican, J., Milner, K.: On ends-to-ends encryption: asynchronous group messaging with strong security guarantees. In: Proceedings of the 2018 ACM SIGSAC Conference on Computer and Communications Security, CCS 2018, pp. 1802-1819. Association for Computing Machinery, New York (2018). https://doi.org/10.1145/3243734.3243747
13. Guerraoui, R., Kuznetsov, P., Monti, M., Pavlovic, M., Seredinschi, D.A.: Scalable byzantine reliable broadcast (Extended Version). In: 33rd International Symposium on Distributed Computing (DISC 2019) (2019). https://arxiv.org/abs/1908.01738

Efficient Distributed Delivery Service for Group Key Agreement   423

14. Kim, Y., Perrig, A., Tsudik, G.: Simple and fault-tolerant key agreement for dynamic collaborative groups. In: Proceedings of the 7th ACM Conference on Computer and Communications Security, CCS 2000, pp. 235–244. (2000). https://doi.org/10.1145/352600.352638
15. Klein, K., et al.: Keep the dirt: tainted treekem, adaptively and actively secure continuous group key agreement. In: 2021 IEEE Symposium on Security and Privacy (SP), pp. 268–284 (2021). https://doi.org/10.1109/SP40001.2021.00035
16. Moxie, M., Trevor, P.: Signal - specifications - the x3dh key agreement protocol (2016). https://signal.org/docs/specifications/x3dh/
17. Nicolas, M., Elvinger, V., Oster, G., Ignat, C.L., Charoy, F.: MUTE: a peer-to-peer web-based real-time collaborative editor. In: ECSCW 2017 - 15th European Conference on Computer-Supported Cooperative Work. Proceedings of 15th European Conference on Computer-Supported Cooperative Work - Panels, Posters and Demos, vol. 1, pp. 1–4. EUSSET, Sheffield (2017). https://doi.org/10.18420/ecscw2017_p5
18. Perrin, T., Marlinspike, M.: The double ratchet algorithm. Signal - Specifications (2016). https://signal.org/docs/specifications/doubleratchet/
19. Rault, P.A., Ignat, C.L., Perrin, O.: Access control based on CRDTs for collaborative distributed applications. In: The International Symposium on Intelligent and Trustworthy Computing, Communications, and Networking (ITCCN-2023), Proceedings of the 22nd IEEE International Conference on Trust, Security and Privacy in Computing and Communications (TrustCom-2023). Exeter, UK (2023). https://inria.hal.science/hal-04224855
20. Steiner, M., Tsudik, G., Waidner, M.: Key agreement in dynamic peer groups. IEEE Trans. Parallel Distrib. Syst. 11(8), 769–780 (2000). https://doi.org/10.1109/71.877936

A Shared Key Recovery Attack on a Masked Implementation of CRYSTALS-Kyber's Encapsulation Algorithm

Ruize Wang[✉] and Elena Dubrova

KTH Royal Institute of Technology, Stockholm, Sweden
{ruize,dubrova}@kth.se

Abstract. In July 2022, NIST selected CRYSTALS-Kyber as a new post-quantum secure public key encryption and key encapsulation mechanism to be standardized. To safeguard its shared and secret keys from side-channel attacks (SCA), countermeasures such as masking and shuffling are applied. However, the existing SCA-protected implementations of CRYSTALS-Kyber protect the decapsulation algorithm only. The encapsulation algorithm is not covered because single-trace shared key recovery attacks on encapsulation are not considered feasible. Since the same shared key is never encapsulated more than once, the attacker gets only a single trace per shared key from the execution of the encapsulation algorithm. In this paper, we demonstrate a practical single-trace shared key recovery attack on a first-order masked implementation of the encapsulation algorithm of Kyber-768 in ARM Cortex-M4 based on deep learning-assisted power analysis. Our main contribution is a new aggregation method for ensemble learning that enables enumeration during shared key recovery. Our experimental results show that a full shared key can be recovered with a 91% probability on average from a single trace captured from a different from profiling device.

Keywords: Public-key cryptography · Post-quantum cryptography · Kyber · LWE/LWR-based KEM · Side-channel attack

1 Introduction

The majority of side-channel attacks (SCA) on implementations of post-quantum (PQ) key encapsulation mechanisms assume that the attack is preformed during the execution of the decapsulation algorithm by the device under attack (DUA). Decapsulation algorithm is an attractive target as it involves the secret key. SCAs such as [3, 8, 19, 24] can recover the secret key from messages encrypted in chosen ciphertexts which are constructed using various methods. For instance, the horizontal attack method presented in [24] requires three chosen chipertexts to recover the secret key from an unprotected ARM Cortex-M4 implementation of Kyber-768. However, future PQ-secure protocols may shift all secret

© The Author(s), under exclusive license to Springer Nature Switzerland AG 2024
M. Mosbah et al. (Eds.): FPS 2023, LNCS 14551, pp. 424–439, 2024.
https://doi.org/10.1007/978-3-031-57537-2_26

key-related operations from not-well-protected low-end devices to a well-protected server in order to reduce the attack surface for physical attacks. In this case, the shared key generated during the execution of the encapsulation algorithm may become a primary target of physical attacks on low-end devices.

Some of the previous SCAs on PQ cryptographic (PQC) algorithms can recover the shared key during the execution of the decapsulation algorithm [6,19,22,25]. However, the same methods may not be applicable to shared key recovery during encapsulation because it has two specific features:

1. Only a single trace is available for the attack.
2. The DUA cannot be used for profiling.

We are aware of only one single-trace shared key recovery SCA targeting the encapsulation algorithm presented by Sim et al. in [20]. It is a non-profiled machine learning-assisted attack which uses k-means clustering for recovering the encapsulated message based on the leakage of the message encoding operation. The message encoding is performed during the encryption step of the encapsulation algoithm. The attack is demonstrated on an unprotected software reference implementation of CRYSTALS-Kyber by Bos et al. [4] in ARM Cortex-M4. According to the experiments of [20], it achieves 100% success rate of shared key recovery.

Our Contributions: In this paper, we demonstrate a single-trace profiled shared key recovery attack on a first-order masked software implementations of the encapsulation algorithm of CRYSTALS-Kyber in ARM Cortex-M4. The masking approach of Heinz et al. [9] is used to protect the encapsulation algorithm. The deep learning-assisted power-based method of Ngo et al. [12] is applied to extracts messages directly, without extracting each share explicitly. As in the attack of [20], the leakage of the message encoding operation is exploited. The traces for profiling are captured from five devices different from the DUA. The ensemble learning is used to increase neural network's prediction accuracy, with each model being re-trained iteratively on fresh sets of traces to improve its generalization ability.

A main contribution of the paper is a new aggregation method for ensemble learning that enables enumeration during shared key recovery. Instead of using the traditional majority voting or cumulative probability, the presented aggregator decides on a class only if the difference between the number of 0 and 1 classes predicted by the models in an ensemble is larger than a certain threshold Δ. This can be viewed as a type of threshold voting extended to detect the gray zone when the models are "in doubt". In this case, the aggregator outputs "?". Such an aggregation approach allows us to increase the success rate of shared key recovery from 41% (single model) to 91% with at most 2^{32} enumerations (i.e. no more than 32 message bits are marked by "?").

The rest of the paper is organized as follows. Section 2 reviews previous work on side-channel analysis of CRYSTALS-Kyber implementations. Section 3 gives a background on CRYSTALS-Kyber algorithm and shared key establishment protocol. Section 4 discusses main differences in attacking encapsulation and decapsulation and describes the attack scenario on the encapsulation algorithm. Section 5 presents the equipment used in the experiments. Sections 6 and 7 describe our profiling and attack stages, respectively. Section 8 summarizes experimental results. Section 9 suggests countermeasures against the presented attack. Section 10 concludes the paper.

2 Previous Work

In this section, we describe previous shared key/message recovery side-channel attacks related to the presented work.

Pessl and Primas [16] presented an interesting single-trace side-channel attack on an unprotected forward number theoretic transform (NTT) of error polynomial in a lattice-based encryption algorithm. The belief propagation method introduced in [18] is further optimized so that only 213 templates are required to recover the full message. In the experimental setup, both profiling traces and attack traces are acquired from the same device. The templates are constructed using 1900 traces. A success rate of message recovery is 0.95 (for 100 tests).

Another influential work which inspired many follow-up contributions is a single-trace side-channel attack on an unprotected reference implementation of NewHope by Amiet et al. in [1]. It is based on a simple power analysis of the message encoding operation of the encryption algorithm. A success rate of message recovery of over 99% is demonstrated. The authors identified an intermediate variable which evaluates to 0×0000 if the processed message bit is 0, and to 0xFFFF otherwise. Since the Hamming distance between the two values of this variable is large (16 for 16-bit integers), the message bits are easy to distinguish. Later, the name *determiner-leakage* was given to such type of vulnerabilities [20].

In [20], a non-profiled single-trace shared key recovery attack targeting the message encoding operation of the encapsulation algorithm of an unprotected CRYSTALS-Kyber implementation is described. The k-means clustering algorithm is applied to recover the shared key from a power trace. A 100% success rate for 500 tests is reported.

In [25], an near field electromagneic (EM)-based side-channel attack on an unprotected software implementation of CRYSTALS-Kyber is demonstrated. One-versus-the-rest classifier and templates, constructed at the profiling stage for the message encoding operation of the re-encryption step of the decapsulation algorithm, are used for message bit prediction. 120 traces are required to achieve a 100% success rate of shared key recovery.

In [22], a power-based side-channel attack on the first-order masked implementation of CRYSTALS-Kyber [9] targeting the message encoding operation of the re-encryption of the decapsulation algorithm is presented. Neural network trained using message byte values as labels recover the shared key with a close to 100% probability. The traces for profiling stage and attack stages are captured from the same device.

In [6], a message recovery attack on the higher-order masked implementation of CRYSTALS-Kyber, built on the top of the implementation of Heinz et al. in [9], is presented. It targets the message encoding operation of the re-encryption step of the decapsulation algorithm. The average single-trace message bit recovery probability for the first-order masked implementation is 0.9743.

```
KYBER.CPAPKE.KeyGen()                          KYBER.CCAKEM.KeyGen()
 1: (ρ,σ) ← U({0,1}^256)                         1: z ← U({0,1}^256)
 2: A ← U(R_q^{k×k};ρ) ; s,e ← B_η1(R_q^{k×1};σ)  2: (pk,s) = KYBER.CPAPKE.KeyGen()
 3: t = Encode_12(As + e); s = Encode_12(s)      3: sk = (s,pk,H(pk),z)
 4: return (pk = (t,ρ), sk = s)                  4: return (pk, sk)

KYBER.CPAPKE.Enc(pk = (t,ρ), m, r)              KYBER.CCAKEM.Encaps(pk)
 1: t = Decode_12(t)                             1: m ← U({0,1}^256)
 2: A ← U(R_q^{k×k};ρ); r ← B_η1(R_q^{k×1};r)    2: m = H(m)
 3: e_1 ← B_η2(R_q^{k×1};r); e_2 ← B_η2(R_q^{1×1};r)  3: (K̂,r) = G(m,H(pk))
 4: u = A^T r + e_1                              4: c = KYBER.CPAPKE.Enc(pk,m,r)
 5: v = t^T r + e_2 + Decompress_q(Decode_1(m),1) 5: K = KDF(K̂,H(c))
 6: c_1 = Encode_{d_u}(Compress_q(u,d_u))        6: return (c, K)
 7: c_2 = Encode_{d_v}(Compress_q(v,d_v))
 8: return c = (c_1,c_2)                         KYBER.CCAKEM.Decaps(sk,c)
                                                 1: m' = KYBER.CPAPKE.Dec(s,c)
KYBER.CPAPKE.Dec(s,c)                            2: (K̂',r') = G(m',H(pk))
 1: u = Decompress_q(Decode_{d_u}(c_1),d_u)      3: c' = KYBER.CPAPKE.Enc(pk,m',r')
 2: v = Decompress_q(Decode_{d_v}(c_2),d_v)      4: if c = c' then
 3: s = Decode_12(s)                             5:    return K = KDF(K̂',H(c))
 4: m = Encode_1(Compress_q(v − s·u,1))          6: else
 5: return m                                     7:    return K = KDF(z,H(c))
                                                 8: end if
```

Fig. 1. Kyber algorithms from [2] (simplified).

In [23], a power-based side-channel attack on a bitsliced higher-order masked CRYSTALS-Kyber implementation [5] is presented. It targets the masked Boolean to arithmetic conversion procedure which is carried out during the re-encryption step of the decapsulation algorithm. For the first-order masked implementation, the average single-trace shared key recovery probability is 0.83. For the second- and third-order masked implementations, the shared key can be recovered from 16 traces with the average probability of 0.98.

3 Background

In this section, we describe notation used in the paper, the CRYSTALS-Kyber algorithm [2], and the shared key establishment protocol.

3.1 Notation

Let $\mathbb{Z}_q$ be the ring of integers modulo a prime q and R_q be the quotient ring $\mathbb{Z}_q[X]/(X^n + 1)$. We use regular font letters to denote elements in R_q, bold lower-case letters to represent vectors with coefficients in R_q, and bold upper-case letters to represent matrices. The transpose of a vector v (or matrix A) is denoted by v^T (or A^T). The ith entry of a vector v is represented by $v[i]$. The polynomial multiplication is denoted by "·" and the Boolean XOR "⊕". The term $\lceil x \rfloor$ means rounding of x to the closest integer with ties being rounded up.

The term $x ← \mathcal{D}(S;r)$ stands for sampling x from a probability distribution $\mathcal{D}$ over a set S using a seed r. The uniform distribution is denoted by $\mathcal{U}$. The centered binomial distribution with a parameter μ is denoted by B_μ.

3.2 Kyber Algorithm

Kyber [2] consists of a chosen-plaintext attack (CPA)-secure PKE scheme, KYBER.CPAPKE, and a chosen ciphertext attack (CCA)-secure KEM scheme, KYBER.CCAKEM, which is built on the top of KYBER.CPAPKE using a tweaked version of the Fujisaki-Okamoto (FO) transform [7]. These schemes are described in Fig. 1.

Inputs and outputs to all API functions of Kyber are byte arrays. Kyber works with vectors of ring elements in R_q^k, where k is the rank of the module defining the security level. There are three versions of Kyber: Kyber-512, Kyber-768 and Kyber-1024, for $k = 2, 3$ and 4, respectively, see [2] for details. In this paper, we focus on Kyber-768.

The Decode_l function decodes an array of $32l$ bytes into a polynomial with n coefficients in the range $\{0, 1, \cdots, 2^l - 1\}$. The Encode_l function is the inverse of Decode_l. It first encodes each polynomial coefficient individually and then concatenates the output byte arrays.

The $\mathsf{Compress}_q(x, d)$ and $\mathsf{Decompress}_q(x, d)$ functions, for $x \in \mathbb{Z}_q$ and $d < \lceil \log_2(q) \rceil$, are defined by:

$$\mathsf{Compress}_q(x, d) = \lceil (2^d/q) \cdot x \rfloor \bmod^+ 2^d,$$
$$\mathsf{Decompress}_q(x, d) = \lceil (q/2^d) \cdot x \rfloor.$$

The functions $\mathcal{G}$ and $\mathcal{H}$ represent the SHA3-512 and SHA3-256 hash functions, respectively. The KDF is a key derivation function realized by SHAKE-256.

3.3 Shared Key Establishment Protocol

Figure 2 describes a post-quantum secure shared key establishment protocol using Kyber KEM which we assume in this work.

The server initiates the shared key establishment process by generating a key pair (pk, sk) using the key generation algorithm KYBER.CCAKEM.KeyGen() and sends the pk to the client.

The client runs the encapsulation algorithm KYBER.CCAKEM.Encaps() to compute the ciphertext c encrypting a message m and a random seed r which are needed to derive the shared key K. The resulting c is sent to the server.

Finally, the server re-computes K from c using the decapsulation algorithm KYBER.CCAKEM.Decaps().

4 Attack Scenario

In this section, we first highlight the core differences between profiled side-channel attacks on encapsulation and decapsulation algorithms and then describe our attack scenario.

Table 1 summarizes the former. First, in a profiled attack on encapsulation, the DUA cannot be used for collecting profiling traces because an attacker cannot

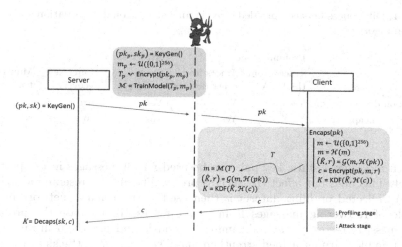

Fig. 2. The attack scenario.

control the random message generation procedure of the encapsulation algorithm of the DUA (see lines 1-2 of KYBER.CCAKEM.Encaps() in Fig. 1) and thus does not have labels for the traces. In contrast, in an attack on decapsulation, an attacker can collect profiling traces from the DUA by first encrypting known messages using the public key of the DUA and then decapsulating the resulting ciphertexts using the DUA. Since the messages encrypted in the ciphrtexts are known, labels for the profiling traces are available. Typically, message bit or byte values, or the Hamming weight of the bytes, are used as labels in side-channel attacks on software implementations, depending on the leakage type.

At the attack stage, messages can be recovered from traces captured during the execution of either encapsulation or decapsulation algorithm because there are message-related operations in both (see line 4 of KYBER.CCAKEM.Encaps() and lines 1 and 3 of KYBER.CCAKEM.Decaps() in Fig. 1). However, the secret key is involved only in decapsulation, thus it can only be recovered from traces captured during the execution of the decapsulation algorithm by the DUA.

Finally, a DUA can typically be used to decapsulate the same ciphertext multiple times, therefore multiple traces corresponding to a given message can be captured for the attack. Contrary, only a single trace corresponding to a given message can be acquired from the DUA during the execution of the encapsulation algorithm, since the same message is never encapsulated more than once.

In our attack scenario on the encapsulation algorithm, shown in Fig. 2, at the profiling stage the attacker first generates a key pair (pk_p, sk_p) using KYBER.CCAKEM.KeyGen(). Then he/she selects uniformly at random a message $m_p \in \{0,1\}^{256}$ and runs KYBER.CPAPKE.Enc() on a profiling device to encrypt m_p with the public key pk_p. The corresponding power trace T_p is recorded. These steps are repeated multiple times until a labeled set of traces of the desired is gathered. Note that it is not necessary to re-generate a fresh key pair (pk_p, sk_p)

Table 1. Differences between profiled side-channel attacks on decapsulation and encapsulation algorithms.

	Profiling stage		Attack stage		
	Traces from the DUA	Traces from other devices	Shared key recovery	Secret key recovery	Multiple traces
Attack on decapsulation	Yes	Yes	Yes	Yes	Yes
Attack on encapsulation	No	Yes	Yes	No	No

for each message; a static key pair can be used for all messages in the profiling dataset. This does not affect the success probability of the presented attack.

The collected profiling dataset is then used to train neural network models capable of recovering messages from power traces. To increase the probability of message recovery, we train multiple models and use them in an ensemble. Ensemble learning helped strenthen many side-channel attacks in the past, e.g. [15,21,26] Our novel contribution is a new aggregation method for ensemble learning that enables enumeration during message recovery. Section 6.1 describes our training strategy in more details.

At the attack stage, the attacker measures the total power consumption of the DUA during the execution of the encapsulation algorithm with an output ciphertext c. The segment of the resulting power trace T representing the points of interest is extracted (Sect. 7 gives details). This segment is given as input to the models trained at the profiling stage to recover the message m encapsulated in c. The shared key K is then computed as $K = \mathsf{KDF}(\hat{K}, \mathcal{H}(c))$, where the pre-key $\hat{K}$ is derived as $(\hat{K}, r) = \mathcal{G}(m, \mathcal{H}(pk))$.

5 Experimental Setup

This section describes the equipment used in our experiments and the target masked implementation of the encapsulation algorithm of CRYSTALS-Kyber.

5.1 Equipment

The equipment used in our experiments is shown in Fig. 3. It consists of a ChipWhisperer-Pro, a CW308 UFO main board and six CW308T-STM32F4 target boards. Each target board contains a STM32F415-RGT6 chip based on ARM Cortex-M4 32-bit RISC core operating at a frequency of 24Mhz. Our lab computer has Intel(R) Core(TM) i7-10750H CPU with a 2.60GHz processor and a 16GB RAM. The traces are acquired with the sampling rate of 96MS/s, i.e. four data points per clock cycle are recorded.

5.2 Target Implementation of Protected Encapsulation Algorithm

To the best of our knowledge, there are no publicly available CRYSTALS-Kyber implementations that protect the encapsulation part. However, the

Fig. 3. Equipment used in the experiments.

```
void masked_poly_frommsg(masked_poly *r, masked_u8_msgbytes *msg)
int i,j;
uint16_t mask;
 1: for (i = 0; i < 32; i++) do
 2:    for (j = 0; j < 8; j++) do
 3:        mask = -((msg->share[0].u8[i] >> j) & 1);
 4:        r->poly[0].coeffs[8*i+j] += (mask & ((KYBER_Q + 1)/2));
 5:    end for
 6: end for
 7: for (i = 0; i < 32; i++) do
 8:    for (j = 0; j < 8; j++) do
 9:        mask = -((msg->share[1].u8[i] >> j) & 1);
10:        r->poly[1].coeffs[8*i+j] += (mask & ((KYBER_Q + 1)/2));
11:    end for
12: end for
13: ...Further processing ...
```

Fig. 4. The C code of masked message encoding procedure of the implementation [9].

re-encryption step of a protected implementation of the decapsulation algorithm of CRYSTALS-Kyber, which runs KYBER.CPAPKE.Enc(), can be adopted.

In our experiments, we use the first-order masked CRYSTALS-Kyber implementation by Heinz et al. [9]. The presented attack exploits a vulnerability located in the masked message encoding operation which is carried out during encryption (see lines marked in red in the C code in Fig. 4).

In the procedure in Fig. 4, the message msg is splitted into two shares, share[0] and share[1], and then the intermediate value mask is computed for each share based on the share's bit value. The value of mask can be either 0 (whose Hamming weight is 0) or -1 (whose Hamming weight 16 since its two's complement is 0xFFFF). Since the difference in Hamming weights is large, it is easy to distinguish between the two cases.

The C code is complied using arm-none-eabi-gcc with the highest optimization level -O3 (recommended default).

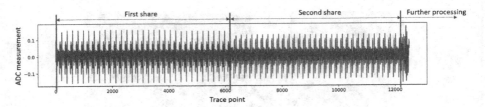

Fig. 5. An average power trace representing the processing of two Boolean shares of the message in the message encoding operation of the encryption algorithm.

6   Profiling Stage

This section describes our training strategy and network parameters.

6.1   Iterative Training Strategy

Using the equipment described in Sect. 5.1, we capture from each profiling device D_i, for $i \in \{1, \ldots, 5\}$, 20K traces during encryption of different messages selected at random. The secret and public key pair for each device is selected at random as well.

Figure 5 shows a trace segment representing the message encoding part of the encryption. The first 32 repeating patterns correspond to the processing of 32 bytes of the first Boolean share of the message. The second 32 patterns correspond to the second share.

Since the patterns representing each byte in both shares are identical, we can apply the byte-wise cut-and-join technique [12] to the training set to expand it to $32 \times 5 \times 20K = 3.2M$. After cut-and-joining, each trace segment is a concatenation of two intervals representing the execution of a given byte in both shares. Thus, we only need to train eight models $\mathcal{M} = \{\mathcal{M}_0, \ldots, \mathcal{M}_7\}$, one per bit, to recover the whole message. A message bit $m[j]$ is recovered using the model $\mathcal{M}_{j \bmod 8}$, for $j \in \{0, 1, \ldots, 255\}$.

It is well-known that more training data is typically useful in deep learning. However, due to its memory limitation, our lab computer can process only at most 3.2M traces at a time. To overcome this limitation, we use iterative re-training. First, the initial eight models $\mathcal{M}_0 = \{\mathcal{M}_{0,0}, \ldots, \mathcal{M}_{0,7}\}$ are trained on 3.2M traces. These models are saved and, at the next iteration r, the next eight models $\mathcal{M}_r$ are trained on a fresh set of 3.2M traces using $\mathcal{M}_{r-1}$ as a starting point, for $r \in \{1, 2, \ldots, R\}$. The re-training is repeated as long as the validation accuracy grows.

We also apply standardization to traces. Given a set of traces $\boldsymbol{T}$ with elements $T = (t_1, \ldots, t_{|T|})$, each $T \in \boldsymbol{T}$ is standardized to $T' = (t'_1, \ldots, t'_{|T|})$ such as:

$$t'_i = \frac{t_i - \mu_i}{\sigma_i},$$

```
TrainModels(N, R) /* N is the number of traces captured from each profiling device and R is
the number of iteration re-training is repeated. */
 1: r = 0
 2: while r ≤ R do
 3:    {T, m} = GetTrainingData(N)
 4:    {T', L} = FindPoI(T, m)
 5:    T' = Standardization(T')
 6:    for each bit ∈ {0, . . . , 7} do
 7:        if r == 0 then
 8:            Train M_{0,j} on {T', L[:, bit]}
 9:        else
10:            Train M_{r,j} on {M_{r-1,j}, T', L[:, bit]}
11:        end if
12:    end for
13:    r = r + 1
14: end while
15: return M_R = {M_{R,0}, . . . , M_{R,7}}

GetTrainingData(N)
 1: T = ∅, m = ∅
 2: for each D_i ∈ {D_1, . . . , D_5} do
 3:    (pk, sk) = KYBER.CCAKEM.KeyGen()
 4:    for each j ∈ {1, . . . , N} do
 5:        m = m ∪ {m_j ∈ {0, 1}^{256} | m_j is generated at random}
 6:        T = T ∪ {T_j ∈ ℝ^{|T|} | T_j ⇐ D_i[KYBER.CPAPKE.Enc(pk, m_j)]}
 7:    end for
 8: end for
 9: return {T, m}

FindPoI(T, m)
 1: T' = ∅, L = ∅
 2: for each byte ∈ {0, 1, . . . , 31} do
 3:    Find points of interest PoI_{byte} containing both shares of byte
 4:    T' = T' ∪ T[:, PoI_{byte}]
 5:    L = L ∪ m[:, 8 * byte : 8 * (byte + 1)]
 6: end for
 7: return {T', L}
```

Fig. 6. A pseudocode of `TrainModels()` algorithm.

where and μ_i and σ_i are the mean and the standard deviation of the elements of T at the ith data point, $i \in \{1, . . . , |T|\}$.

Figure 6 summarizes our training strategy in a pseudocode.

6.2   Network and Training Parameters

The neural networks with the architecture listed in Table 2 are trained with a batch size of 1024 for a maximum of 100 epochs using early stopping with patience 10. We use Nadam optimizer with a learning rate of 0.01 and a numerical stability constant $epsilon = $ 1e-08. Categorical cross-entropy is used as a loss function to evaluate the network classification error. 70% of the training set is used for training and 30% is left for validation. Only the model with the highest validation accuracy is saved.

7 Attack Stage

Table 2. MLP architecture.

Layer type	Output shape
Batch Normalization 1	440
Dense 1	512
Batch Normalization 2	512
ReLU	512
Dense 2	256
Batch Normalization 3	256
ReLU	256
Dense 3	128
Batch Normalization 4	128
ReLU	128
Dense 4	2
Softmax	2

```
RecoverMessage(𝓜_R^1, ..., 𝓜_R^K) /* K models in ensemble. */
1:  T ⇐ DUA[KYBER.CPAPKE.Enc(pk, m)]
2:  for each k ∈ {1, ..., K} do
3:      for each byte ∈ {0, 1, ..., 31} do
4:          for each bit ∈ {0, ..., 7} do
5:              m^k[8 * byte + bit] = 𝓜_{R,bit}^k(T[PoI_byte])
6:          end for
7:      end for
8:  end for
9:  return  m = Aggrerate(m^1, ..., m^K)
```

Fig. 7. A pseudocode of RecoverMessage() algorithm.

As mentioned in Sect. 4, only a single trace is available to an attacker for message recovery during encapsulation. Thus repeated measurements can not be applied to increase the message recovery probability. Instead, we use the ensemble learning [17] with an enhanced aggregation method.

A message is recovered bit by bit. For each bit, the aggregator decides on a class only if the difference between the number of 0s and 1s predicted by the models is above a certain threshold $\Delta \in \{1, 2, ..., K\}$, where K is the number of models in the ensemble. Otherwise, the bit is marked by "?" and we enumerate all "?"s at the end. In other words, the message bit $m[j]$, for $j \in \{0, 1, ..., 255\}$, is determined by:

$$m[j] = \begin{cases} 1, & \text{if } \#1s - \#0s \geq \Delta \\ 0, & \text{if } \#0s - \#1s \geq \Delta \\ ?, & \text{otherwise.} \end{cases} \tag{1}$$

For an odd K and $\Delta = 1$, the Eq. (1) reduces to the traditional *majority voting* [13]. It can be viewed as an extension of the *threshold voting* extended to

Table 3. Empirical probability of recovering a message bit from a single trace using a single model trained with a different number of iterative re-trainings R.

	bit 0	bit 1	bit 2	bit 3	bit 4	bit 5	bit 6	bit 7	Avg
Initial	0.9993	0.9993	0.9993	0.9992	0.9991	0.9992	0.9647	0.9850	0.9931
$R = 1$	0.9993	0.9993	0.9993	0.9993	0.9991	0.9993	0.9716	0.9879	0.9944
$R = 2$	0.9993	0.9994	0.9993	0.9993	0.9991	0.9993	0.9744	0.9891	0.9949
$R = 3$	0.9993	0.9994	0.9993	0.9993	0.9992	0.9993	0.9760	0.9900	0.9952
$R = 4$	0.9993	0.9993	0.9993	0.9993	0.9992	0.9993	0.9801	0.9906	0.9958
$R = 5$	0.9993	0.9994	0.9993	0.9993	0.9992	0.9992	0.9788	0.9898	0.9955
$R = 6$	0.9993	0.9994	0.9993	0.9993	0.9992	0.9993	0.9768	0.9902	0.9954

detect the gray zone when the models cannot come to an agreement. The threshold voting is used in fault-tolerant design [11] and safety monitoring [14]. We dids not find any previous work applying Eq. (1) to ensemble learning in general, or to ensemble learning in side-channel analysis in particular.

Figure 7 summarizes our attack strategy in a pseudocode.

8 Experimental Results

To evaluate the presented attack method, we captured from the DUA 10K test traces representing the execution of the encryption algorithm by the target first-order masked implementation of CRYSTALS-Kyber for 10K different messages selected at random.

Table 3 lists empirical probabilities of recovering ith message bit of a byte from a single trace, for all $i \in \{0, 1, \ldots, 7\}$, using a single neural network model trained with a different number of iterative re-trainings R. All 32 message bytes were used for computing the probabilities in Table 3, i.e. each entry is a mean over $32 \times 10K$ tests.

We can see that, for the initial models $\mathcal{M}_0$, the average probability for all bits is 0.9931. It grows to 0.9958 when R increases to four. After that, the probability drops. Thus, $R = 4$ seems to be the best choice.

Then, we trained 19 neural network models with the architecture listed in Table 2 using $R = 4$. Table 4 lists empirical probabilities (mean over 10K tests) of recovering a full message from a single trace using an ensemble size of up to $K = 19$. Note that the maximum threshold Δ is limited by K, therefore Table 4 is empty for $\Delta > K$.

From Table 4 we can make the following observations:

1. The case of an odd K and $\Delta = 1$ determines the *lower bound* of the message recovery probability. In this case, the decision is made if the size of one group is larger than the size of another and no further enumeration is allowed.

Table 4. Empirical probability of recovering a full message from a single trace with $\leq 2^{32}$ enumerations using a K-model ensemble.

# models K	1	2	3	4	5	6	7	8	9	10	11	12	13	14	15	16	17	18	19
$\Delta = 1$	.4070	.6196	.4687	.5872	.4928	.5647	.4995	.5591	.5117	.5562	.5112	.5473	.5135	.5408	.5134	.5386	.5133	.5392	.5176
$\Delta = 2$		.6196	.7213	.5872	.6532	.5647	.6203	.5591	.6042	.5562	.5930	.5473	.5767	.5408	.5666	.5386	.5634	.5392	.5590
$\Delta = 3$			.7213	.7733	.6532	.6947	.6203	.6601	.6042	.6392	.5930	.6181	.5767	.6027	.5666	.5886	.5634	.5842	.5590
$\Delta = 4$				.7733	.8045	.6947	.7279	.6601	.6916	.6392	.6650	.6181	.6439	.6027	.6246	.5886	.6116	.5842	.6054
$\Delta = 5$					.8045	.8258	.7279	.7560	.6916	.7182	.6650	.6857	.6439	.6614	.6246	.6438	.6116	.6305	.6054
$\Delta = 6$						.8258	.8409	.7560	.7775	.7182	.7384	.6857	.7057	.6614	.6798	.6438	.6631	.6305	.6495
$\Delta = 7$							.8409	.8568	.7775	.7927	.7384	.7507	.7057	.7210	.6798	.6962	.6631	.6782	.6495
$\Delta = 8$								.8568	.8668	.7927	.8059	.7507	.7655	.7210	.7342	.6962	.7118	.6782	.6909
$\Delta = 9$									.8668	.8731	.8059	.8139	.7655	.7732	.7342	.7449	.7118	.7248	.6909
$\Delta = 10$										.8731	.8805	.8139	.8232	.7732	.7829	.7449	.7561	.7248	.7343
$\Delta = 11$											.8805	.8854	.8232	.8312	.7829	.7911	.7561	.7639	.7343
$\Delta = 12$												.8854	.8905	.8312	.8377	.7911	.7988	.7639	.7727
$\Delta = 13$													.8905	.8905	.8377	.8428	.7988	.8070	.7727
$\Delta = 14$														.8939	.8939	.8428	.8479	.8070	.8138
$\Delta = 15$															.8939	.8975	.8479	.8530	.8138
$\Delta = 16$																.8975	.9019	.8530	.8565
$\Delta = 17$																	.9019	.9058	.8565
$\Delta = 18$																		.9058	.9083
$\Delta = 19$																			.9105

2. The case of $K = \Delta$ determines the *upper bound* of the message recovery probability. In this case, the decision is made only if all models predict the same class.
3. If K is even, then the probability for $\Delta = 2i - 1$ is always equal to the probability for $\Delta = 2i$, for all $i \in \{1, 2, \ldots, \frac{K}{2}\}$.
4. If K is odd and $K > 1$, then the probability for $\Delta = 2i$ is always equal to the probability for $\Delta = 2i + 1$, for all $i \in \{1, 2, \ldots, \frac{K-1}{2}\}$.

The reason why we observe (3) and (4) is that the only possible absolute differences between the number of predicted 0s and 1s are $d_{even} = \{0, 2, \ldots, K - 2, K\}$ for an even K and $d_{odd} = \{1, 3, \ldots, K - 2, K\}$ for an odd K. According to eq. (1), the aggregator makes a decision on the class only if the abolute difference between the number of predicted 0s and 1s $d \geq \Delta$. Since the difference in values of all neighbouring elements of d_{even} is two, the probabilities for $\Delta = 2i - 1$ and $\Delta = 2i$ are equal for all $i \in \{1, 2, \ldots, \frac{K}{2}\}$. Similarly, since the difference in values of all neighbouring elements of d_{odd} is two, the probabilities for $\Delta = 2i$ and $\Delta = 2i + 1$ are equal for all $i \in \{1, 2, \ldots, \frac{K-1}{2}\}$.

One can see that the new aggregation method allows us to increase the full message recovery probability from 0.41 (for a single model) to 0.91 (for $K = 19$ and $\Delta = K - 1$) with at most 2^{32} enumerations.

9   Countermeasures

The presented shared key recovery attack would not be possible if the encapsulation algorithm were protected using shuffling. In this case, the attacker would manage to recover the shuffled message bit values, but their correct order would remain unknown. So, only the Hamming weight of the shared key would be revealed by the attack.

Note that the side-channel attack on a masked and shuffled implementation of CRYSTALS-Kyber by Backlund et al. [3] can recover shuffling indexes. However, at most two shuffling indexes can be recovered from a single trace, therefore the attack [3] would not break a shuffled encapsulation algorithm. Another possibility is to use a fault attack to disable shuffling. We are currently investigating if it is possible to do within a single run of encapsulation.

The presented shared key recovery attack would be more difficult if a constant-weight coding of a message were performed, e.g., by using the method of [10]. Since coding-based countermeasures may leave exploitable correlations (unless the balancing is perfect), verifying their effectiveness in protecting implementations of PQC algorithms from single-trace attacks remains a future work.

10   Conclusion

We presented the first shared key recovery attack on a masked implementation of CRYSTALS-Kyber's encapsulation algorithm. The success of the attack is due to a combination of multi-device profiling, a very large profiling set collected by iterative re-training, and a new aggregation method for ensemble learning.

The presented attack method is not specific for CRYSTALS-Kyber. It may help reduce the number of traces required for deep learning-assisted attacks on other cryptographic algorithms. It may also result in more efficient attacks on the decapsulation algorithm of CRYSTALS-Kyber. For example, in the attack on a fifth-order masked implementation of CRYSTALS-Kyber presented in [6], cyclic rotations may become unnecessary for obtaining high bit prediction accuracy, leading to a four-fold reduction in the number of traces required for the attack.

Future work includes developing stronger countermeasures against side-channel and fault attacks on implementations of PQC algorithms.

Acknowledgments. This work was supported in part by the Swedish Civil Contingencies Agency (Grant No. 2020-11632) and the Sweden's Innovation Agency Vinnova (Grant No. 2023-00221).

References

1. Amiet, D., Curiger, A., Leuenberger, L., Zbinden, P.: Defeating NEWHOPE with a single trace. In: Ding, J., Tillich, J.-P. (eds.) PQCrypto 2020. LNCS, vol. 12100, pp. 189–205. Springer, Cham (2020). https://doi.org/10.1007/978-3-030-44223-1_11
2. Avanzi, R., et al.: CRYSTALS-Kyber algorithm specifications and supporting documentation (2021). https://pq-crystals.org/kyber/data/kyber-specification-round3-20210131.pdf
3. Backlund, L., Ngo, K., Gartner, J., Dubrova, E.: Secret key recovery attacks on masked and shuffled implementations of CRYSTALS-Kyber and Saber. Cryptology ePrint Archive, Paper 2022/1692 (2022). https://eprint.iacr.org/2022/1692
4. Bos, J., et al.: CRYSTALS-Kyber: a CCA-secure module-lattice-based KEM. In: 2018 IEEE European Symposium on Security and Privacy (EuroS&P), pp. 353–367. IEEE (2018)
5. Bronchain, O., Cassiers, G.: Bitslicing arithmetic/Boolean masking conversions for fun and profit: with application to lattice-based KEMs. IACR Trans. Crypto. Hardware Embedded Syst. 553–588 (2022)
6. Dubrova, E., Ngo, K., Gärtner, J., Wang, R.: Breaking a fifth-order masked implementation of CRYSTALS-Kyber by copy-paste. In: Proceedings of the 10th ACM Asia Public-Key Cryptography Workshop, pp. 10–20 (2023)
7. Fujisaki, E., Okamoto, T.: Secure integration of asymmetric and symmetric encryption schemes. In: Wiener, M. (ed.) CRYPTO 1999. LNCS, vol. 1666, pp. 537–554. Springer, Heidelberg (1999). https://doi.org/10.1007/3-540-48405-1_34
8. Hamburg, M., et al.: Chosen ciphertext k-trace attacks on masked CCA2 secure Kyber. IACR Trans. Crypto. Hardware Embedded Systems, 88–113 (2021)
9. Heinz, D., Kannwischer, M.J., Land, G., Pöppelmann, T., Schwabe, P., Sprenkels, D.: First-order masked Kyber on ARM Cortex-M4. Cryptology ePrint Archive, Paper 2022/058 (2022). https://eprint.iacr.org/2022/058
10. Maghrebi, H., Servant, V., Bringer, J.: There is wisdom in harnessing the strengths of your enemy: Customized encoding to thwart side-channel attacks. In: Fast Software Encryption, pp. 223–243 (2016)

11. von Neumann, J.: Probabilistic logics and the synthesis of reliable organisms from unreliable components. Automata Studies, pp. 43–98 (1956)
12. Ngo, K., Dubrova, E., Guo, Q., Johansson, T.: A side-channel attack on a masked IND-CCA secure Saber KEM implementation. IACR Trans. Crypto. Hardware Embedded Syst. 676–707 (2021)
13. Pacuit, E.: Voting methods. Stanford Encyclopedia of Philosophy (2019)
14. PARHAMI, B.: Threshold voting is fundamentally simpler than plurality voting. Inter. J. Reliab. Quality Saf. Eng. $\mathbf{1}$(01), 95–102 (1994)
15. Perin, G., Chmielewski, Ł., Picek, S.: Strength in numbers: improving generalization with ensembles in machine learning-based profiled side-channel analysis. IACR Trans. Crypt. Hardware Embedded Syst., 337–364 (2020)
16. Pessl, P., Primas, R.: More practical single-trace attacks on the number theoretic transform. In: Schwabe, P., Thériault, N. (eds.) Progress in Cryptology - LATINCRYPT 2019, pp. 130–149. Springer International Publishing, Cham (2019). https://doi.org/10.1007/978-3-030-30530-7_7
17. Polikar, R.: Ensemble learning. Ensemble machine learning: methods and applications, pp. 1–34 (2012)
18. Primas, R., Pessl, P., Mangard, S.: Single-trace side-channel attacks on masked lattice-based encryption. In: Fischer, W., Homma, N. (eds.) CHES 2017. LNCS, vol. 10529, pp. 513–533. Springer, Cham (2017). https://doi.org/10.1007/978-3-319-66787-4_25
19. Ravi, P., Bhasin, S., Roy, S.S., Chattopadhyay, A.: On exploiting message leakage in (few) NIST PQC candidates for practical message recovery attacks. IEEE Trans. Inform. Forensics Sec. (2021)
20. Sim, B.Y., et al.: Single-trace attacks on message encoding in lattice-based KEMs. IEEE Access $\mathbf{8}$, 183175–183191 (2020)
21. Wang, H., Dubrova, E.: Tandem deep learning side-channel attack against FPGA implementation of AES. In: 2020 IEEE International Symposium on Smart Electronic Systems (iSES) (Formerly iNiS), pp. 147–150 (2020). https://doi.org/10.1109/iSES50453.2020.00041
22. Wang, J., Cao, W., Chen, H., Li, H.: Practical side-channel attack on message encoding in masked Kyber. In: 2022 IEEE International Conference on Trust, Security and Privacy in Computing and Communications, pp. 882–889. IEEE (2022)
23. Wang, R., Brisfors, M., Dubrova, E.: A side-channel attack on a bitsliced higher-order masked CRYSTALS-Kyber implementation. Cryptology ePrint Archive (2023)
24. Wang, R., Dubrova, E.: A side-channel secret key recovery attack on CRYSTALS-Kyber using k chosen ciphertexts. In: International Conference on Codes, Cryptology, and Information Security, pp. 109–128. Springer (2023)
25. Xu, Z., Pemberton, O.M., Roy, S.S., Oswald, D., Yao, W., Zheng, Z.: Magnifying side-channel leakage of lattice-based cryptosystems with chosen ciphertexts: The case study of Kyber. IEEE Transactions on Computers (2021)
26. Zaid, G., Bossuet, L., Habrard, A., Venelli, A.: Efficiency through diversity in ensemble models applied to side-channel attacks:–a case study on public-key algorithms–. IACR Trans. Cryptographic Hardware Embedded Syst., 60–96 (2021)

Tight Differential Privacy Guarantees for the Shuffle Model with k-Randomized Response

Sayan Biswas[1,2,3], Kangsoo Jung[1(✉)], and Catuscia Palamidessi[1,2]

[1] Inria, Palaiseau, France
gangsoo.zeong@inria.fr
[2] École Polytechnique, Palaiseau, France
[3] EPFL, Lausanne, Switzerland

Abstract. Most differentially private algorithms assume a central model in which a reliable third party inserts noise to queries made on datasets, or a local model where the data owners directly perturb their data. However, the central model is vulnerable via a single point of failure, and the local model has the disadvantage that the utility of the data deteriorates significantly. The recently proposed shuffle model is an intermediate framework between the central and local paradigms. In the shuffle model, data owners send their locally privatized data to a server where messages are shuffled randomly, making it impossible to trace the link between a privatized message and the corresponding sender. In this paper, we theoretically derive the tightest known differential privacy guarantee for the shuffle models with k-Randomized Response (k-RR) local randomizers, under histogram queries, and we denoise the histogram produced by the shuffle model using the matrix inversion method to evaluate the utility of the privacy mechanism. We perform experiments on both synthetic and real data to compare the privacy-utility trade-off of the shuffle model with that of the central one privatized by adding the state-of-the-art Gaussian noise to each bin. We see that the difference in statistical utilities between the central and the shuffle models shows that they are almost comparable under the same level of differential privacy protection.

Keywords: Differential privacy · Shuffle model · Privacy-utility optimization

1 Introduction

As machine learning and data analysis using sensitive personal data are becoming more and more popular, concerns about privacy violations are also increasing manifold. The most successful approach to address this issue is differential privacy (DP). Most research performed in this area probes two main directions. One is the so-called central model, in which a trusted third party (the curator) collects

M. Mosbah et al. (Eds.): FPS 2023, LNCS 14551, pp. 440–458, 2024.
https://doi.org/10.1007/978-3-031-57537-2_27

the user's personal data and obfuscates them with a differentially private mechanism. The other is the local model, where the data owners apply the mechanism themselves on their data and send the perturbed data to the collector. A major drawback of the central model is that there is the risk that the curator may be corrupted. On the other hand, in the local model, there is no need to rely on a trusted curator. However, since each record is obfuscated individually, the utility of the data is substantially deteriorated compared to the central model.

In order to address the problem of the loss of utility in the local model, an intermediate paradigm between the central and the local models, known as the *shuffle model (SM)* of differential privacy, was recently proposed [5]. As an initial step, the shuffle model uses a local mechanism to perturb the data individually like the local model. The difference is that, after this first step of sanitization, a shuffler uniformly permutes the noisy data to dissolve their link with the corresponding data providers. Since a potential attacker is oblivious to the shuffling process, the data providers obtain two layers of privacy protection: injection of random noise by the local randomizer and anonymity by data shuffling. This allows the shuffle model to achieve a certain level of privacy protection using less noise than the local model.

The privacy guarantees provided by the shuffle model have been rigorously analyzed in several studies. More specifically, given a local mechanism with a level of privacy parameterised by ϵ_0 (pure local DP) or (ϵ_0, δ_0) (approximate local DP), the aim is to derive a (ϵ, δ) bound on the level of differential privacy guaranteed by applying shuffling on top of the local mechanism. In this paper, we derive the tight (ϵ, δ)-DP guarantee for the shuffle model with the k-RR local mechanism by using the concept of (ϵ, δ)-adaptive differential privacy (ADP) proposed by Sommer et al. in [15]. Next, we consider the question of how convenient the shuffle model is for publishing histograms in terms of the privacy-utility trade-off as opposed to the central model.

We perform various experiments on both synthetic and real data (the Gowalla dataset) and compare the utilities of the two models calibrated with the same privacy parameters. As expected, the utility of the central model is better than that of the shuffle model, consistent with what was observed in the literature [6]. However, in our case, the gap is very small – namely the histograms resulting from the shuffle model, once de-noised, are almost as close to the original ones as those of the central model. The contributions of this paper are as follows.

1. we derive an analytical form of the tight differential privacy guarantee for the shuffle model with k-RR local randomizer under histogram queries, and therefore, show that the shuffle model, essentially, provided a higher level of DP guarantee than what is known by the community, for the same level of locally injected noise to the data.
2. using the tight bound of the (ϵ, δ)-DP provided by the shuffle model, as derived, we compare the privacy-utility trade-off of the shuffle model and the optimized Gaussian mechanism for the histogram queries and show that their performances are comparable.

2   Related Work

Recently, intensive research on shuffle models of differential privacy has been done in various directions. One of the major research directions in this area is the study of privacy amplification by shuffling [3,10]. Erlingsson et al. [10] analysed the privacy amplification of the local randomizer's privacy protection by shuffling. Balle et al. [3] introduced the idea of privacy guarantee in shuffle models and quantitatively analyzed the relationship between the privacy parameter ϵ and the number of participants in the shuffle protocol. Feldman et al. [11] improved Balle et al.'s results and suggested an asymptotically optimal dependence of the privacy amplification on the privacy parameter of the local randomizer. However, neither [3] nor [11] explicitly theorize any guarantee for the tightness of the bounds for the privacy guarantee of shuffle models. Koskela et al. [14] proposed computational methods to estimate tight bounds based on weak adversaries – however, they are not expressed by an analytical formula, they can only be computed via an algorithm. Sommer et al. introduced the notion of adapted differential privacy (ADP) in [15] and laid down specific conditions to achieve the tight (ϵ, δ)-ADP for any abstract and high-level probabilistic mechanism. To derive the tight DP guarantees for SMs, we adapt Sommer et al.'s result and obtain necessary and sufficient conditions for achieving δ that warrants the best (ϵ, δ)- DP guarantee in SMs with a k-RR local randomizer.

3   Preliminaries

Definition 1 (Differential privacy [9]). *For a certain query, a randomizing mechanism $\mathcal{K}$ is (ϵ, δ)-differentially private (DP) if for all adjacent datasets, D_1 and D_2, and all $S \subseteq Range(\mathcal{K})$, we have:*

$$\mathbb{P}[\mathcal{K}(D_1) \in S] \le e^\epsilon \, \mathbb{P}[\mathcal{K}(D_2) \in S] + \delta$$

Definition 2 (Adaptive differential privacy [15]). *For $x_0, x_1 \in \mathcal{X}$, where $\mathcal{X}$ is the space of the original data, and for a member u in the dataset, a randomizing mechanism $\mathcal{K}$ is (ϵ, δ)-adaptive differentially private (ADP) for x_0 and x_1 if for all datasets, $D(x_0)$ and $D(x_1)$, and all $S \subseteq Range(\mathcal{K})$, we have:*

$$\mathbb{P}[\mathcal{K}(D(x_0)) \in S] \le e^\epsilon \, \mathbb{P}[\mathcal{K}(D(x_1) \in S] + \delta$$

where $D(x_0)$ and $D(x_1)$ are datasets differing only in the entry of the fixed member u: $D(x)$ means that u reports x for every $x \in \mathcal{X}$, keeping the entries of all the other users the same.

Remark 1. $\mathcal{K}$ is (ϵ, δ)-DP implies that $\mathcal{K}$ is (ϵ, δ)-ADP for every $x_0, x_1 \in \mathcal{X}$.

Definition 3 (Tight DP (or ADP) [15]). *Let $\mathcal{K}$ be (ϵ, δ)-DP (or ADP for $x_0, x_1 \in \mathcal{X}$). We say that δ is tight for $\mathcal{K}$ (w.r.t. ϵ and x_0, x_1 in case of ADP) if there is no $\delta' < \delta$ such that $\mathcal{K}$ is (ϵ, δ')-DP (or ADP for x_0, x_1).*

Definition 4 (Local differential privacy [8]). *Let $\mathcal{X}$ denote a possible alphabet for the original data and let $\mathcal{Y}$ be the alphabet of noisy data. A randomizing mechanism $\mathcal{R}$ provides ϵ-local differential privacy (LDP) if for all $x_1, x_2 \in \mathcal{X}$, and all $y \in \mathcal{Y}$, we have*

$$\mathbb{P}[\mathcal{R}(x_1) = y] \le e^\epsilon \, \mathbb{P}\,(\mathcal{R}(x_2) = y)$$

Definition 5 (k-Randomized Response [13]). *Let $\mathcal{X}$ be a discrete alphabet of size k. Then* k-randomized response *(k-RR) mechanism, $\mathcal{R}_{kRR}$, is a locally differentially private mechanism that stochastically maps $\mathcal{X}$ onto itself (i.e., $\mathcal{Y} = \mathcal{X}$), given by*

$$\mathcal{R}_{kRR}(y|x) = \begin{cases} c\, e^\epsilon & , \text{ if } x = y \\ c, & , \text{ otherwise} \end{cases}$$

for any $x, y \in \mathcal{X}$, where $c = \frac{1}{e^\epsilon + k - 1}$.

Definition 6 (Shuffle model [10]). *Let $\mathcal{X}$ and $\mathcal{Y}$ be discrete alphabets for the original and the noisy data respectively. For any dataset of size $n \in \mathbb{N}$, the shuffle model (SM) is defined as $\mathcal{M} : \mathcal{X}^n \mapsto \mathcal{Y}^n$, $\mathcal{M} = \mathcal{S} \circ \mathcal{R}^n$, where*

- *$\mathcal{R} : \mathcal{X} \mapsto \mathcal{Y}$ is a local randomizer, stochastically mapping each element of the input dataset, sampled from $\mathcal{X}$, onto an element in $\mathcal{X}$, providing ϵ_0-local differential privacy.*
- *$\mathcal{S} : \mathcal{Y}^n \mapsto \mathcal{Y}^n$ is a shuffler that uniformly permutes the finite set of messages of size $n \in \mathbb{N}$, that it takes as an input.*

A SM can be perceived as having a sequence of messages going through the mechanism $\mathcal{M}$ and then coming out as the frequencies of each of the noisy messages, as the idea of the layer of "shuffling" is to randomize the noisy messages w.r.t. their corresponding senders by a random permutation. Let us call this particular brand of query on SM as the *histogram query*.

Definition 7 (Histogram query [2]). *Let $\mathcal{X}$ and $\mathcal{Y}$ be discrete alphabets for the original and the noisy data respectively. For any dataset of size $n \in \mathbb{N}$, the histogram query on SM, $\mathcal{M} : \mathcal{X}^n \mapsto \mathbb{R}^{+n}$, is defined as $\mathcal{M} = \mathcal{T} \circ \mathcal{R}^n$, where*

- *$\mathcal{R} : \mathcal{X} \mapsto \mathcal{Y}$ is a local randomizer providing ϵ_0-local differential privacy, as in Definition 6.*
- *$\mathcal{T} : \mathcal{Y}^n \mapsto \mathbb{R}^n$ is a function that gives the frequency of each message in finite set of messages of size $n \in \mathbb{N}$, that it takes as an input.*

In other words, if we have a dataset $D_\mathcal{X} = (x_1, \dots, x_n) \in \mathcal{X}^n$, then $D_\mathcal{Y} = \mathcal{M}(D_\mathcal{X}) = \mathcal{T}((\mathcal{R}(x_1), \dots, \mathcal{R}(x_n)) = (s_1, \dots, s_n)$, where $s_i = n_i/n$ with n_i denoting the number of times $\mathcal{R}(x_i)$ occurs in $D_\mathcal{Y}$.

Definition 8 (Privacy loss random variable [15]). *For a probabilistic mechanism mapping messages from the alphabet of original messages to the alphabet for noisy messages, $M : \mathcal{X} \mapsto \mathcal{Y}$, let us fix $x_0, x_1 \in \mathcal{X}$ and a potential output*

$y \in \mathcal{Y}$. *The* privacy loss random variable *of* y *for* x_0 *over* x_1 *is defined as: where* $M(x_i)$ *is the probability distribution of the noisy output for the original input* x_i *for* $i \in \{0,1\}$.

$$\mathcal{L}_{M(x_0)/M(x_1)}(y) = \begin{cases} +\infty & \begin{cases} \mathbb{P}(M(x_0) = y) \neq 0, \\ \mathbb{P}(M(x_1) = y) = 0 \end{cases} \\ \ln \frac{\mathbb{P}(M(x_0)=y)}{\mathbb{P}(M(x_1)=y)} & \begin{cases} \mathbb{P}(M(x_0) = y) \neq 0, \\ \mathbb{P}(M(x_1) = y) \neq 0 \end{cases} \\ -\infty & o.w. \end{cases} \quad (1)$$

Definition 9 (Privacy loss distribution [15]). *Let* P_1 *and* P_2 *be two probability distributions on* $\mathcal{Y}$ *(the finite alphabet for noisy messages). The* privacy loss distribution, ω, *for* A *over* B *is defined as:*

$$\omega(u) = \sum_{y:\mathcal{L}_{A/B}(y)=u} \mathbb{P}(A = y) \text{ for all } u \in \mathcal{U} \text{ , where } \mathcal{U} = \bigcup_{y \in \mathcal{Y}} \{\mathcal{L}_{A/B}(y)\} \subset \mathbb{R} \text{ .}$$

4   Tight Privacy Guarantee for SM

4.1   Overview

Sommer et al. in [15] proposed a notion of adaptive differential privacy and derived a very important sufficient and necessary result for any probabilistic mechanism to have the best formal privacy guarantee. Adaptive differential privacy essentially translates the idea of a differential privacy guarantee with respect to a chosen pair of elements in the dataset. Exploiting this result (Result 1), we derived the necessary and sufficient condition needed to warrant the best DP guarantee for SM with the most popularized LDP satisfying local randomizer, the k-RR mechanism. This essentially draws the tight DP guarantee that an SM can induce being locally randomized with a k-RR mechanism. At the crux of this paper, the importance of deriving the tight DP guarantee by SM under the k-RR local randomizer implies that we show that the SM provides a higher level of privacy than what is known by the existing work in the literature that focuses on improving the privacy bound for the SM.

Table 1. Value of δ derived from the existing work and our proposed result

	[10]	[3]	[11]	[14]	Proposed tight δ
$\epsilon = 0.1$	0.97	0.229	0.066	9.01E-4	2.38E-28
$\epsilon = 0.2$	0.89	0.002	1.91E-5	1.89E-6	1.61E-42
$\epsilon = 0.3$	0.77	1.77E-6	2.43E-11	2.19E-10	5.22E-57
$\epsilon = 0.4$	0.64	5.95E-11	1.35E-19	3.14E-16	5.14E-72

Table 1 presents the values of δ obtained from the results in [3,10,11,14] and the proposed derivation in (6) of this paper, by varying ϵ from 0.1 to 0.4, fixing $n = 100$ and $\epsilon_0 = 0.5$. We observe that, indeed, the value of δ computed from (6) in Definition 11 is significantly less compared to the other existing improvements proposed, highlighting that our proposed result engenders the best possible DP guarantee for SMs under the k-RR local randomizer.

4.2 Framework

Let $\mathcal{X} = (x_0,\ldots,x_{k-1})$ be the alphabet of messages of size $k \in \mathbb{N}$, $k > 1$ and $\mathfrak{U}$ be the set of all users involved in the environment. For simplicity, we assume the alphabets of the original and noisy messages to be the same, both being $\mathcal{X}$. Therefore, the local randomizer of our shuffle mechanisms locally sanitizes the dataset by mapping original messages sampled from $\mathcal{X}$ to elements of $\mathcal{X}$.

Let ϵ_0 be the privacy parameter of $\mathcal{R}_{\text{kRR}}$, which is used as the local randomizer for the shuffle mechanisms discussed in this paper. Furthermore, letting $D_{\mathcal{X}}$ be the dataset of the original messages of n users, each of which is sampled from (and obfuscated to) $\mathcal{X}$, we denote $D_{\mathcal{X}\,z}$ as the original message of $z \in \mathfrak{U}$ in $D_{\mathcal{X}}$ for any $z \in \mathfrak{U}$. Let $D_{\mathcal{Y}} = \mathcal{R}_{\text{kRR}}^n(D_{\mathcal{X}}) = \{\mathcal{R}_{\text{kRR}}(D_{\mathcal{X}\,z}) : z \in \mathfrak{U}\}$ be the noisy dataset going through $\mathcal{R}_{\text{kRR}}$.

For the purpose of analysing the adaptive differential privacy, let us fix a certain user, $u \in \mathfrak{U}$, whose data is in $D_{\mathcal{X}}$. Since the only major distinction that k-RR mechanism makes in the process of mapping a datum from its original value to the obfuscated value is whether the original value and the obfuscated value are the same or not (i.e., the probability that the x is being reported as x' is the same for every $x' \in \mathcal{X}$ when $x \neq x'$), it is reasonable for us to study the adaptive differential privacy guarantee with respect to a couple of potential original messages of u, say x_0, $x_1 \in \mathcal{X}$, $x_0 \neq x_1$ in the environment where the shuffle model uses a k-RR local randomizer.

The idea behind adaptive differential privacy w.r.t. x_0, x_1 is to make it significantly difficult to predict whether u's original message is x_0 or x_1. In the context of this work, since we will be focusing on the case of having the local randomizer as the k-RR mechanism, the only gravity x_1 holds as far as the shuffle model is concerned is the fact that it is different from x_0. Thus x_1 could represent any $x \in \mathcal{X}$ such that $x \neq x_0$. Therefore, we shall be analysing the privacy of u's original message being x_0 and compare its privacy level of being identifiable with a different potential original message, which we fix as x_1 w.l.o.g. Let's call x_0 as the *primary input* for u and x_1 be the *secondary input*. For a fixed set of values reported by every user in $\mathfrak{U} \setminus \{u\}$, let $D(x_0)$ represent the edition of the dataset where u reports x_0, and let $D(x_1)$ represent the one where u reports x_1.

The most important result from literature - Lemma 5 in [15] - that is heavily exploited in this paper is as follows:

Result 1: (Lemma 5 [15]) For every probabilistic mechanism $M : \mathcal{X} \mapsto \mathcal{Y}$, for any x_0, $x_1 \in \mathcal{X}$ and any ϵ, $\delta(\epsilon) > 0$, M is tightly (ϵ, δ)-ADP for x_0, x_1 iff

$$\delta(\epsilon) = \omega(\infty) + \sum_{\substack{u \in \mathcal{U} \setminus \{\infty, -\infty\} \\ u > \epsilon}} (1 - e^{\epsilon - u})\omega(u) \tag{2}$$

4.3 Theorems and Results

As we are interested in finding $\epsilon > 0$ and, correspondingly, $\delta > 0$ that provide a tight ADP guarantee for $\mathcal{M}$ for x_0, x_1, we define the constants $\kappa_1, \kappa_2, \kappa_3$ to simplify the mathematical results derived in the subsequent sections as follows:

$$\kappa_1 := \frac{e^{\epsilon_0}(e^{\epsilon_0} + k - 2)}{k - 1} \tag{3}$$

$$\kappa_2 := \frac{k - 1}{e^{\epsilon_0} + k - 2} \tag{4}$$

$$\kappa_3 := \frac{(k - 1)^{n_{x_0}}(e^{\epsilon_0} + k - 2)^{n - n_{x_0} - s}}{(e^{\epsilon_0} + k - 1)^n} \tag{5}$$

Remark 2. Note that $\kappa_1, \kappa_2, \kappa_3 > 0$ for any $\epsilon_0 > 0$, $n \in \mathbb{N}$, $k \in \mathbb{N}_{\geq 2}$, $s \in \mathbb{N}$.

From now on we shall focus on the histogram query of the shuffle model. For the same ϵ_0-LDP mechanism $\mathcal{R}_{kRR}$ to be used as the local randomizer for histogram query, let $\mathcal{M} = \mathcal{T} \circ \mathcal{R}_{kRR}$ denote the shuffle model that takes in a sequence of original messages, obfuscates them locally using $\mathcal{R}_{kRR}$, and broadcasts the frequency of each message in the noisy dataset. In other words, having u having x_i as her original message for $i \in \{0, 1\}$, $\mathcal{M}(D(x_i)) = (\mathcal{M}_{x_0}(x_i), \dots, \mathcal{M}_{x_{k-1}}(x_i))$ where $\mathcal{M}_{x_j}(x_i)$ is a random variable giving the frequency of $x_j \in \mathcal{X}$ in the noisy dataset, $D_\mathcal{Y}$, obfuscated by $\mathcal{R}_{kRR}$. Assuming that u's original data is x_0 (w.l.o.g.), let n_{x_0} denote the number of times x_0 has appeared in $D_\mathcal{X}$ for the original entries from all users in $\mathfrak{U} \setminus u$.

Definition 10. *By Definition 8, the* privacy loss random variable *for the histogram query for shuffle model of x_0 over x_1 with respect to a certain output $s \in \mathbb{N}$, in $\mathcal{M}$ is $v_s(x_0, x_1) = \ln \frac{\mathbb{P}(\mathcal{M}_{x_0}(x_0) = s)}{\mathbb{P}(\mathcal{M}_{x_0}(x_1) = s)}$.*

Definition 11. *For $s \in \{0, \dots, n\}$, $r \in \{0, \dots, s\}$, let $\mu(s, r) = \binom{n_{x_0}}{r}\binom{n - n_{x_0}}{s - r}\kappa_1^r$ and $\tau_r = \kappa_2(n - n_{x_0}) + (e^{\epsilon_0} - \kappa_2)(s - r)$. For any $\epsilon > 0$, let us define*

$$\hat{\delta}(\epsilon) := \sum_{s=0}^{n} \mathbb{1}_{\{v_s(x_0, x_1) > \epsilon\}}(1 - e^{\epsilon - v_s(x_0, x_1)})\frac{\kappa_3}{n - n_{x_0}}\sum_{r=0}^{s}\mu(s, r)\tau_r \tag{6}$$

where $\mathbb{1}_E$ is the indicator function for any event E.

Theorem 1. *For any $\epsilon > 0$, we get the tight (ϵ, δ)-ADP guarantee for $\mathcal{M}$ with respect to x_0, x_1 iff $\delta = \hat{\delta}(\epsilon)$ as in as in (6) of Definition 11 where*

$$v_s(x_0, x_1) = \ln\left(\kappa_2 + \frac{\frac{(e^{\epsilon_0}-\kappa_2)}{n-n_{x_0}}\left(\sum_{r=0}^{s}(s-r)\binom{n_{x_0}}{r}\binom{n-1-n_{x_0}}{s-1-r}\kappa_1^r\right)}{\sum_{r=0}^{s}\binom{n_{x_0}}{r}\binom{n-n_{x_0}}{s-r}\kappa_1^r}\right).$$

Corollary 1. *For any $\epsilon > 0$, we get the tight (ϵ, δ)-DP guarantee for $\mathcal{M}$ iff:*

$$\delta(\epsilon) := \sum_{s=0}^{n}\mathbb{1}_{\{v_s>\epsilon\}}(1-e^{\epsilon-v_s})\frac{\kappa_3}{n-n_{x_0}}\sum_{r=0}^{s}\mu(s,r)\tau_r \qquad (7)$$

where $v_s = \max_{x_0,x_1 \in \mathcal{X}} v_s(x_0, x_1)$ and $v_s(x_0, x_1)$ is as derived in Theorem 1.

5   Evaluating the Utility of the Shuffle Model

It is crucial to have the tight bound in the privacy guarantee for shuffle models to be able to conduct a fair comparison of utilities of shuffle models with other forms of differential privacy under a certain level of privacy protection.

Suppose with ϵ, δ, we get a tight (ϵ, δ)-ADP guarantee for $\mathcal{M}$ w.r.t. x_0 as the primary input. We wish to compare how the utility of $\mathcal{M}$ would perform against that of a central model of differential privacy for histogram query implemented on $D_{\mathcal{X}}$ with the same privacy parameters ϵ and δ. For this, we will be sticking to the most optimal framework, known until now [4], of one of the most popular mechanisms for the central model for (ϵ, δ)-DP: the *Gaussian mechanism*. The details of the theoretical build-up are provided in Appendix B.

In [7], Cheu et al. give theoretical evidence that the accuracy of the SM lies in between the central and local models of DP. However, no experimental analysis had been performed to dissect how low the accuracy of SMs lies when compared to the central model when both provide the same level of privacy protection. Thus, the main goal of our experiments was to empirically show the scale of difference in accuracy between SM and the central model by comparing their statistical utilities under the tight and equal DP guarantee. To do this end, we compared the statistical approximation of the true distribution from the SM with k-RR local randomizer to that of the central model by applying the Gaussian mechanism [4], using the value of δ derived from (6), ensuring the tight (ϵ, δ)-DP guarantee.

5.1   Experimental Results on Synthetic Data

In this section, we carry out an experimental analysis to illustrate the comparison of utilities for histogram query of the shuffle model using k-RR local randomizer and the optimal Gaussian mechanism using synthetically generated data sampled from $\mathcal{N}(0, 2)$. We experimented and demonstrated our results in the two categories: (i) trend analysis of δ providing the tight ADP guarantee for $\mathcal{M}$ and (ii) utility comparison between $\mathfrak{N}$ and $\mathcal{M}$ under the same level of differential privacy.

To analyze the values of δ providing a tight ADP guarantee for $\mathcal{M}$, we change the values of ϵ, ϵ_0, n, n_0, and k that enable us to see the change in the trend of δ. For comparing the utilities of the central model and the shuffle model, we considered $\hat{\delta}$ as in (15), providing the worst possible tight ADP over every $x_0, x_1 \in \mathcal{X}$, and therefore, by Remark 1, a DP guarantee. Table 2 shows the default values of the parameters used for the experiment.

Table 2. Experimental parameters used for synthetic data

Parameter name	Values
ϵ	0.1 to 3
ϵ_0	0.1 to 3
n	50, 100, 150, 1000, 100000
x_0	1 to 15
k	5, 10, 15

Tight δ for Histogram Queries. We show the experimental results for deriving δ providing (ϵ, δ)-ADP guarantee, as given by Theorem 1, by changing the values for ϵ, ϵ_0, n and k. We use the *total variation distance*, $d_{TV}(.)$, to evaluate $\mathcal{W}(\mathcal{M})$ and $\mathcal{W}(\mathfrak{N})$ – the "distances" of the estimated original distribution obtained from shuffle model with k-RR local randomizer, using matrix inversion, (shuffle+INV), and the distribution sanitized with Gaussian mechanism from the original distribution itself. Table 3 shows δ when we vary ϵ, for three categories:

(a) We change ϵ_0, fixing $n_{x_0} = 80$, $n = 100$, and $k = 10$. We observe that δ decreases as ϵ increases for the same ϵ_0, and δ increases as ϵ_0 increases under a fixed value of ϵ. When it does not satisfy the $v_s > \epsilon$ condition of equation (57), δ becomes 0. For a fixed ϵ and ϵ_0, a high value of δ decreases the level of privacy protection. Thus, experimentally, we can validate that for a constant ϵ, δ increases as ϵ_0 used for k-RR increases, ensuring that the privacy protection of the shuffle model decreases with a decrease in the privacy level of its local randomizer.

(b) We vary n fixing $k = 10$, $\epsilon_0 = 2$, and $n_{x_0} = 80$. For the same ϵ, δ becomes smaller as the value of n increases. A lower δ means higher privacy protection, reassuring that the shuffle model provides higher privacy protection as the number of users (samples) increases.

(c) We alter k fixing $n = 100$, $\epsilon_0 = 2$, and $n_{x_0} = 80$. As the value of k increases, δ decreases. This is also due to the characteristic of the k-RR mechanism, which is used as the local randomizer for $\mathcal{M}$. The inference probability for a potential adversary decreases as the size of the domain for the data increases.

Table 3. Tight δ for different ϵ

Varying ϵ_0	$\epsilon = 0.1$	$\epsilon = 0.5$	$\epsilon = 1.0$	$\epsilon = 1.5$	$\epsilon = 2.0$	$\epsilon = 2.5$	$\epsilon = 3.0$
$\epsilon_0 = 1$	2.08E-20	3.42E-43	0	0	0	0	0
$\epsilon_0 = 2$	2.49E-15	3.25E-22	2.20E-30	1.57E-40	0	0	0
$\epsilon_0 = 3$	8.79E-11	5.73E-13	3.52E-16	4.49E-20	1.09E-25	4.52E-33	0
Varying n							
$n = 50$	1.91E-08	5.02E-12	2.40E-15	4.49E-21	0	0	0
$n = 100$	2.49E-15	3.25E-22	2.20E-30	1.57E-40	0	0	0
$n = 150$	6.58E-22	7.83E-32	2.75E-44	6.99E-59	0	0	0
Varying k							
$k = 5$	1.96E-10	2.51E-14	1.08E-19	2.02E-27	0	0	0
$k = 10$	2.49E-15	3.25E-22	2.20E-30	1.57E-40	0	0	0
$k = 15$	1.66E-18	7.13E-28	1.49E-38	7.35E-50	0	0	0

Comparing the Utility of the Shuffle and the Central Models. In this section, we compare the utilities of the central model and the shuffle models, providing the same level of privacy protection. For neutral comparison, we perform the experiments into two cases: individual specific utility and community level utility, as described in Appendix B. We use the *total variation distance* to estimate the difference between original distribution and estimated distributions.

Table 4. Individual specific utility comparison of central and shuffle models for synthetic data ($\epsilon = 4$)

x_0	$n = 1,000$		$n = 100,000$	
	Gaussian	shuffle+INV	Gaussian	shuffle+INV
1	3E-3	1E-3	6E-6	3E-3
3	6E-4	2E-4	1E-5	5E-4
5	12E-4	11E-4	1E-5	5E-4
7	1E-4	4E-3	8E-6	3E-5

Table 4 shows the results from the experimental analysis of comparing the individual specific utilities of $\mathcal{M}$ and $\mathfrak{N}$ as the primary input, x_0, is changed. We performed the experiments for the case of $n = 1,000$ and $n = 100,000$, setting $\epsilon_0 = 4$, $\epsilon = 4$, and $k = 15$, calculating δ for each x_0. When $n = 1,000$, shuffle+INV is comparable with the Gaussian mechanism, depending on the value of x_0. However, when n is $100,000$, the Gaussian mechanism shows better results regardless of x_0. This is explained through our choice of δ (given by Theorem 1), which depends on n_{x_0}, which, in turn, varies with x_0 and that

Gaussian mechanism inserts fixed noise regardless of n. However, even for a large value of n, the utility of shuffle+INV, although slightly worse than the Gaussian mechanism, is quite good as $\overline{\mathcal{W}}(\mathcal{M}, x_0)$ remains very low across different x_0.

For the community level utility, we apply the worst case (highest value) of δ computed over all the primary inputs for all the users in $\mathfrak{U}$, given as $\hat{\delta}$ in (15), to sanitize all input messages of the dataset – thus establishing the worst tight ADP guarantee possible on the shuffle model. This is used to determine the community level utility of the corresponding shuffle model with the estimated differential privacy guarantee. Similar to the case of individual specific utility, experiments were performed for the case of $n = 1,000$ and $n = 100,000$, and the other parameters used for the experiment being the same. The experiments results are similar to what we showed for individual specific utility. When n is small, the utility of shuffle model is almost as much as that of the central model. As n increases, the utility of the Gaussian mechanism, $\mathfrak{N}$, improves slightly over that of the shuffle model under the same level of differential privacy, however they still are fairly close (Fig. 1).

5.2   Experimental Results on Real Data

Now we focus on the experimental results obtained using real location data from the Gowalla dataset [12]. Figure 2 illustrate the estimations of the original distributions of location data from San Francisco and Paris, respectively. We sanitize the original distribution using the shuffle model giving a tight differential privacy guarantee with parameters ϵ and $\hat{\delta}$, as in (15). We use the same ϵ and $\hat{\delta}$ to privatize the original data using the Gaussian mechanism as same in the previous experiment, thus getting a $(\epsilon, \hat{\delta})$-DP guarantee for both cases.

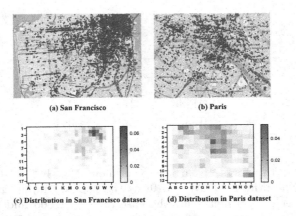

(a) San Francisco   (b) Paris

(c) Distribution in San Francisco dataset   (d) Distribution in Paris dataset

Fig. 1. (a) and (b): Location data from Gowalla check-ins from a northern part of San Francisco and a part of Paris. (c) and (d) give the heatmap of the locations in the areas of San Francisco and Paris as an alternative visualization.

To compare the utility of the two mechanisms under the same privacy level, we estimate the original distributions using shuffle+INV for the shuffle model and the Gaussian mechanism itself for the central model, as described in (13) and (14) and evaluate how far the corresponding estimations lie from the original distributions. We observe that the Gaussian mechanism approximates the original distributions slightly better than the shuffle+INV, but they are comparable.

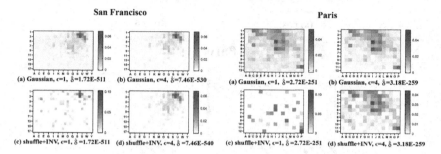

Fig. 2. Estimation of the original distribution from the noisy data obfuscated with the Gaussian mechanism and the SM in San Francisco and Paris dataset

As we observe in the previous experiment results, the number of samples, ϵ affects the utility. In Fig. 3, we show how the number of samples and the differential privacy parameters affect the utilities in more detail. In summary, we observe a consistency with the existing work in the trend of the Gaussian mechanism having a better utility than the shuffle model across all settings. However, when the number of samples is small and the privacy level is low, the utilities of the shuffle model and the central model are comparable.

Figure 3 (a) and (b) illustrate the evaluation of the TV distance between the original and the estimated distributions for San Francisco dataset. n ranges from 10,000 to 100,000, which is used to sample locations from the aforementioned San Francisco region. We set $\epsilon = 4$ and $\epsilon = 6$ to capture the change of distance between the original and the estimated distributions by varying n. We use $\hat{\delta}$, as in (15), to calculate community-level utility and we run the mechanism 10 times to obtain the boxplots. The results exhibit that shuffle model, $\mathcal{M}$, gives worse utility than the central model $\mathfrak{N}_{\epsilon,\hat{\delta}}$, and shuffle+INV shows better utility than shuffle. This trend is harmonious across the different settings for ϵ. It is reassuring to observe that the shuffle+INV is slightly closer or comparable with the Gaussian mechanism especially when the value of n is small ($n = 10,000$) and the privacy level is low ($\epsilon = 6$). Figure 3 (c) and (d) shows the TV distance between the estimated and the original distributions and the utility difference for locations in Paris dataset with n ranging from 1,000 to 10,000 and the other parameters being the same as the experiments for the San Francisco dataset.

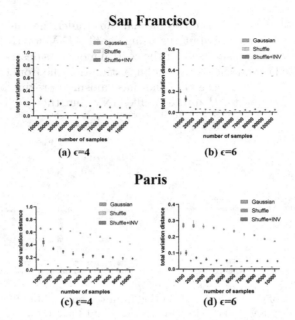

Fig. 3. Illustrating the comparison of community level utilities between Gaussian, shuffle and shuffle+INV for varying n and ϵ in San Francisco and Paris dataset

The overall trend of TV distance for the dataset of Paris is the same as that of San Francisco. Again, we observe that the utility of the shuffle+INV is better than that of just shuffle with k-RR, and the utilities of the shuffle+INV and the optimal Gaussian mechanism are almost indistinguishable when the number of samples and the privacy level are low. As we see from the heatmaps in Fig. 2, when the value of ϵ is 4, both the Gaussian mechanism and shuffle+INV generate results very close to the original distribution. Individual-specific utilities for the Paris and San Francisco datasets are described in Table 5.

Table 5. Individual specific utility comparison of central and shuffle models for Gowalla data ($\epsilon = 4$, $\epsilon_0 = 4$)

x_0	San Francisco		x_0	Paris	
	Gaussian	shuffle+INV		Gaussian	shuffle+INV
40	4E-6	1E-3	20	2E-6	3E-4
80	3E-5	5E-4	40	3E-5	2E-3
120	9E-6	1E-3	60	4E-5	2E-3
160	4E-5	2E-4	80	5E-5	4E-4
200	2E-5	2E-4	100	7E-5	1E-4

6   Conclusion

In this paper, we have compared the privacy-utility trade-off of two different models of differential privacy for histogram queries: the classic central model with the optimal Gaussian mechanism and the shuffle model with k-RR mechanism as the local randomizer, enhanced with post-processing to de-noise the resulting histogram. In order to do this comparison, we needed to derive the tight bounds for the level of privacy provided by the shuffle model, so that we could tune the parameters of the Gaussian mechanism to provide the same privacy.

First, we have used a result on the condition for tightness of ADP given by Sommer et al. in [15] and translated it in the context of shuffle models, giving rise to a closed form expression of the least δ for any ϵ and, thus, we obtained a necessary and sufficient condition to have the tight DP guarantee for the shuffle models. This result shows that the differential privacy ensured by the shuffle models under a certain level of local noise is much higher than what has been known by the community so far. Then, we performed experiments on synthetic and real location data from San Francisco and Paris, and we compared the statistical utilities of the shuffle and the central models. We observed that, although the central model still performs better than the shuffle model, only ever so slightly – the gap between their statistical utilities is very small and tends to vanish as the number of samples is small.

Acknowledgment. The work is supported by the European Research Council (ERC) project HYPATIA under the European Unions Horizon 2020 research and innovation programme. Grant agreement no. 835294 and ELSA - European Lighthouse on Secure and Safe AI funded by the European Union under grant agreement No. 101070617.

A   Proof of Theorem Theorem 1

Setting $p = \mathbb{P}[x_0|x_0]$, $\overline{p} = \mathbb{P}[x_0|y \neq x_0]$ in $\mathcal{R}_{k\mathrm{RR}}$, $\forall s \in [n]$, $\mathbb{P}[\mathcal{M}_{x_0}(x_0) = s]$

$$
= p \sum_{r=0}^{s-1} \left[\binom{n_{x_0}}{r} p^r (1-p)^{n_{x_0}-r} \binom{n-1-n_{x_0}}{s-1-r} \overline{p}^{\,s-1-r} (1-\overline{p})^{n-n_{x_0}-s+r} \right]
$$

$$
+ (1-p) \sum_{r=0}^{s} \left[\binom{n_{x_0}}{r} p^r (1-p)^{n_{x_0}-r} \binom{n-1-n_{x_0}}{s-r} \overline{p}^{\,s-r} (1-\overline{p})^{n-n_{x_0}-1-s+r} \right]
$$

$$
= \frac{e^{\epsilon_0}}{e^{\epsilon_0}+k-1} \sum_{r=0}^{s-1} \left[\binom{n_{x_0}}{r} \frac{e^{r\epsilon_0}(k-1)^{n_{x_0}-r}}{(e^{\epsilon_0}+k-1)^{n_{x_0}}} \binom{n-1-n_{x_0}}{s-1-r} \frac{(e^{\epsilon_0}+k-2)^{n-n_{x_0}-s+r}}{(e^{\epsilon_0}+k-1)^{n-1-n_{x_0}}} \right]
$$

$$
+ \frac{k-1}{e^{\epsilon_0}+k-1} \sum_{r=0}^{s} \left[\binom{n_{x_0}}{r} \frac{e^{r\epsilon_0}(k-1)^{n_{x_0}-r}}{(e^{\epsilon_0}+k-1)^{n_{x_0}}} \binom{n-1-n_{x_0}}{s-r} \frac{(e^{\epsilon_0}+k-2)^{n-n_{x_0}-1-s+r}}{(e^{\epsilon_0}+k-1)^{n-1-n_{x_0}}} \right]
$$

$$
= \frac{e^{\epsilon_0}(k-1)^{n_{x_0}}(e^{\epsilon_0}+k-2)^{n-n_{x_0}-s}}{(e^{\epsilon_0}+k-1)^n} \sum_{r=0}^{s-1} \binom{n_{x_0}}{r} \binom{n-1-n_{x_0}}{s-1-r} \kappa_1^r
$$

$$+ \frac{(k-1)^{n_{x_0}+1}(e^{\epsilon_0}+k-2)^{n-n_{x_0}-1-s}}{(e^{\epsilon_0}+k-1)^n} \sum_{r=0}^{s} \binom{n_{x_0}}{r}\binom{n-1-n_{x_0}}{s-r}\kappa_1^r$$

$$= \kappa_3 \left[e^{\epsilon_0} \sum_{r=0}^{s-1}\binom{n_{x_0}}{r}\binom{n-1-n_{x_0}}{s-1-r}\kappa_1^r + \kappa_2\sum_{r=0}^{s}\binom{n_{x_0}}{r}\binom{n-1-n_{x_0}}{s-r}\kappa_1^r \right]$$

Using elementary combinatorial identities, we reduce to:

$$\kappa_3 \left[\kappa_2 \sum_{r=0}^{s}\binom{n_{x_0}}{r}\kappa_1^r \left(\binom{n-1-n_{x_0}}{s-1-r} + \binom{n-1-n_{x_0}}{s-r} \right) \right.$$

$$\left. + (e^{\epsilon_0}-\kappa_2)\left(e^{\epsilon_0}\sum_{r=0}^{s-1}\binom{n_{x_0}}{r}\binom{n-1-n_{x_0}}{s-1-r}\kappa_1^r \right) \right]$$

$$= \kappa_3 \left[\kappa_2 \sum_{r=0}^{s}\binom{n_{x_0}}{r}\binom{n-n_{x_0}}{s-r}\kappa_1^r + (e^{\epsilon_0}-\kappa_2)\left(\sum_{r=0}^{s}\binom{n_{x_0}}{r}\binom{n-1-n_{x_0}}{s-1-r}\kappa_1^r \right) \right]$$

$$= \kappa_3 \left[\kappa_2 \sum_{r=0}^{s}\binom{n_{x_0}}{r}\binom{n-n_{x_0}}{s-r}\kappa_1^r + \frac{(e^{\epsilon_0}-\kappa_2)(s-r)}{n-n_{x_0}} \sum_{r=0}^{s}\binom{n_{x_0}}{r}\binom{n-n_{x_0}}{s-r}\kappa_1^r \right]$$

$$= \frac{\kappa_3}{n-n_{x_0}} \sum_{r=0}^{s}\mu(s,r)\tau_r \quad [\mu \text{ and } \tau \text{ are as in Definition 11}] \tag{8}$$

By similar arguments as above, for any $s \in \{0,\ldots,n\}$, $\mathbb{P}[\mathcal{M}_{x_0}(x_1) = s]$

$$= \frac{1}{e^{\epsilon_0}+k-1} \sum_{r=0}^{s-1} \left[\binom{n_{x_0}}{r} \frac{e^{r\epsilon_0}(k-1)^{n_{x_0}-r}}{(e^{\epsilon_0}+k-1)^{n_{x_0}}} \binom{n-1-n_{x_0}}{s-r} \frac{(e^{\epsilon_0}+k-2)^{n-n_{x_0}-s+r}}{(e^{\epsilon_0}+k-1)^{n-1-n_{x_0}}} \right]$$

$$+ \frac{e^{\epsilon_0}+k-2}{e^{\epsilon_0}+k-1} \sum_{r=0}^{s} \left[\binom{n_{x_0}}{r} \frac{e^{r\epsilon_0}(k-1)^{n_{x_0}-r}}{(e^{\epsilon_0}+k-1)^{n_{x_0}}} \binom{n-1-n_{x_0}}{s-1-r} \frac{(e^{\epsilon_0}+k-2)^{n-n_{x_0}-1-s+r}}{(e^{\epsilon_0}+k-1)^{n-1-n_{x_0}}} \right]$$

$$= \kappa_3 \left(\sum_{r=0}^{s}\binom{n_{x_0}}{r}\binom{n-1-n_{x_0}}{s-1-r}\kappa_1^r + \sum_{r=0}^{s}\binom{n_{x_0}}{r}\binom{n-1-n_{x_0}}{s-r}\kappa_1^r \right)$$

$$= \kappa_3 \sum_{r=0}^{s}\binom{n_{x_0}}{r}\binom{n-n_{x_0}}{s-r}\kappa_1^r \tag{9}$$

Using Result 1, for every $k > 2$ and $s \in \{0,1,\ldots,n\}$, we can say that $\mathcal{M}$ induces a tight (ϵ, δ)-ADP guarantee with respect to $x_0, x_1 \in \mathcal{X}$ for any $\epsilon > 0$ and δ iff δ is defined as:

$$\delta(\epsilon) = \sum_{v:v>\epsilon} (1 - e^{\epsilon-v}) \sum_{\substack{s=0 \\ v=\ln\frac{\mathbb{P}[\mathcal{M}_{x_0}(x_0)=s]}{\mathbb{P}[\mathcal{M}_{x_0}(x_1)=s]}}}^{n} \mathbb{P}[\mathcal{M}_{x_0}(x_0) = s] \tag{10}$$

Using the expressions derived for $\mathbb{P}[\mathcal{M}_{x_0}(x_0) = s]$ and $\mathbb{P}[\mathcal{M}_{x_0}(x_1) = s]$ in (8) and (9), respectively, to get v_s:

$$= \ln \frac{\mathbb{P}[\mathcal{M}_{x_0}(x_0) = s]}{\mathbb{P}[\mathcal{M}_{x_0}(x_1) = s]} = \ln \frac{e^{\epsilon_0} \sum_{r=0}^{s-1} \binom{n_{x_0}}{r}\binom{n-1-n_{x_0}}{s-1-r}\kappa_1^r + \kappa_2 \sum_{r=0}^{s} \binom{n_{x_0}}{r}\binom{n-1-n_{x_0}}{s-r}\kappa_1^r}{\sum_{r=0}^{s-1} \binom{n_{x_0}}{r}\binom{n-1-n_{x_0}}{s-1-r}\kappa_1^r + \sum_{r=0}^{s} \binom{n_{x_0}}{r}\binom{n-1-n_{x_0}}{s-r}\kappa_1^r}$$

$$= \ln \left(\kappa_2 + \frac{(e^{\epsilon_0} - \kappa_2)\left(\sum_{r=0}^{s-1} \binom{n_{x_0}}{r}\binom{n-1-n_{x_0}}{s-1-r}\kappa_1^r \right)}{\sum_{r=0}^{s} \binom{n_{x_0}}{r}\binom{n-n_{x_0}}{s-r}\kappa_1^r} \right)$$

$$= \ln \left(\kappa_2 + \frac{\frac{(e^{\epsilon_0} - \kappa_2)}{n - n_{x_0}}\left(\sum_{r=0}^{s} (s - r)\binom{n_{x_0}}{r}\binom{n-1-n_{x_0}}{s-1-r}\kappa_1^r \right)}{\sum_{r=0}^{s} \binom{n_{x_0}}{r}\binom{n-n_{x_0}}{s-r}\kappa_1^r} \right) \qquad (11)$$

Combining (10) and (11), $\displaystyle \delta(\epsilon) = \sum_{\substack{u:u>\epsilon; s=0 \\ v=\ln \frac{\mathbb{P}[\mathcal{M}_{x_0}(x_0)=s]}{\mathbb{P}[\mathcal{M}_{x_0}(x_1)=s]}}}^{n} (1 - e^{\epsilon-v})\mathbb{P}[\mathcal{M}_{x_0}(x_0) = s]$

$$= \sum_{s=0}^{n} \mathbb{1}_{\{v_s > \epsilon\}}(1 - e^{\epsilon - v_s})\mathbb{P}[\mathcal{M}_{x_0}(x_0) = s]$$

$$= \sum_{s=0}^{n} \mathbb{1}_{\{v_s > \epsilon\}}(1 - e^{\epsilon - v_s})\frac{\kappa_3}{n - n_{x_0}}\sum_{r=0}^{s} \mu(s,r)\tau_r = \hat{\delta}(\epsilon)$$

[Substituting $\mathbb{P}[\mathcal{M}_{x_0}(x_0) = s]$ from (8)].

B   Theoretical outline

In $\mathcal{M}$, we extend the idea of ADP to a non-adapted, general DP by using the highest value of δ across the primary inputs of every member in $\mathfrak{U}$, for a fixed ϵ. This essentially ensures the worst possible tight differential privacy guarantee for the shuffle model. After that, we focus on estimating the original distribution of the primary initial dataset.

Let $\mathcal{R}_{\text{kRR}}^{-1}$ denote the inverse[1] of the probabilistic mechanism $\mathcal{R}_{\text{kRR}}$, which is used as the local randomizer for $\mathcal{M}$. Note that $\mathcal{R}_{\text{kRR}}^{-1}$ and $\mathcal{R}_{\text{kRR}}$ are both $k \times k$ stochastic channels as $|\mathcal{X}| = k$. Staying consistent with our previously developed notations, let us, additionally, introduce $H_{\mathfrak{N}}$ broadcasting the frequencies of the elements in $\mathcal{X}$ after they have been sanitized with $\mathfrak{N}$. In other words, $H_{\mathfrak{N}} = \mathfrak{N}_{\epsilon,\delta}(D_{\mathcal{X}}) = (H_{x_0}, \ldots, H_{x_{k-1}})$, where H_{x_i} is the random variable giving the frequency of x_i after $D_{\mathcal{X}}$ has been obfuscated with $\mathfrak{N}_{\epsilon,\delta}$.

Since both $\mathcal{M}$ and $\mathfrak{N}$ are probabilistic mechanisms, to estimate their utilities we study how accurately we can estimate the true distribution from which $D_{\mathcal{X}}$ is sampled, after observing the response of the histogram queries in both the scenarios.

---

[1] the inverse of a k-RR mechanism always exists [1,13].

Let $\pi = (\pi_{x_0}, \ldots, \pi_{x_{k-1}})$ be the distribution of the original messages in $D(x_0)$. Our best guess of the original distribution by observing the noisy histogram going through the Gaussian mechanism is the noisy histogram itself, as $\mathbb{E}(H_{x_i}) = n\pi_{x_i}$ for every $i \in \{0, \ldots, k-1\}$.

However, in the case where $D(x_0)$ is locally obfuscated using $\mathcal{R}_{kRR}$ and the frequency of each element is broadcast by the shuffle model $\mathcal{M}$, we can use the matrix inversion method [1,13] to estimate the distribution of the original messages in $D(x_0)$. So $\mathcal{M}(D(x_0))\mathcal{R}_{kRR}^{-1}$ (referred as *shuffle+INV* in the experiments) should be giving us $\hat{\pi} = (\hat{\pi}_{x_0}, \ldots, \hat{\pi}_{x_{k-1}})$ – the most likely estimate of the distribution of each user's message in $D(x_0)$ sampled from $\mathcal{X}$ – where $\hat{\pi}_{x_i}$ denotes the random variable estimating the normalised frequency of x_i in $D(x_0)$.

$$\mathbb{E}(\hat{\pi}) = \mathbb{E}(\mathcal{M}(D(x_0))\mathcal{R}_{kRR}^{-1}) = \pi\mathcal{R}_{kRR}\mathcal{R}_{kRR}^{-1} = \pi \qquad (12)$$

We recall that $\mathcal{M}$ provides tight (ϵ, δ)-ADP for x_0, x_1, where δ is a function of ϵ_0, ϵ, and x_0 – essentially $\mathcal{M}$ privatizes the true query response for x_0 to be identified as that for any $x_1 \neq x_0$. On the other hand, $\mathfrak{N}_{\epsilon,\delta}$ ensures (ϵ, δ)-DP, which essentially means it guarantees (ϵ, δ)-ADP for every $x_i \in \mathcal{X}$. Therefore, in order to facilitate a fair comparison of utility between the central and shuffle models of differential privacy under the same privacy level for the histogram query, we introduce the following concepts:

i) Individual specific utility: Suppose the primary input of u is x_0. *Individual specific utility* refers to measuring the utility for the specific message x_0 in the dataset $D(x_0)$ in a certain privacy mechanism. In particular, the individual specific utility of x_0 in $D(x_0)$ for $\mathcal{M}$ is

$$\overline{\mathcal{W}}(\mathcal{M}, x_0) = |n\hat{\pi}_{x_0} - n\pi_{x_0}|,$$

and that for $\mathfrak{N}_{\epsilon,\delta}$ is

$$\overline{\mathcal{W}}(\mathfrak{N}_{\epsilon,\delta}, x_0) = |n\pi_{x_0} - H_{x_0}|$$

ii) Community level utility: Here we consider the utility privacy mechanisms over the entire community, i.e., all the values of the original dataset, by measuring the distance between the estimated original distribution obtained from the observed noisy histogram and the original distribution of the source messages itself.

In particular, fixing any $\epsilon_0 > 0$ and $\epsilon > 0$, the *community level utility* for $\mathcal{M}$ is

$$\mathcal{W}(\mathcal{M}) = d(n\hat{\pi}, n\pi), \qquad (13)$$

and that for $\mathfrak{N}_{\epsilon,\delta}{}^2$ is

$$\mathcal{W}(\mathfrak{N}_{\epsilon,\delta}) = d(H_{\mathfrak{N}_{\epsilon,\delta}}, n\pi), \qquad (14)$$

where $d(.)$ is any standard metric[3] to measure probability distributions over a finite space.

---

[2] where δ is correspondingly obtained using Result 1.

[3] we consider Total Variation Distance for our experiments.

For an equitable comparison between $\mathcal{M}$ and $\mathfrak{N}$, we take the worst tight ADP guarantee over every user's primary input and call this the *community level tight DP guarantee for* $\mathcal{M}$. That is, for a fixed ϵ_0, $\epsilon > 0$, we have $\mathcal{M}$ satisfying $(\epsilon, \hat{\delta})$-DP as the community level tight DP guarantee if

$$\hat{\delta} = \max_{x \in \mathcal{X}}\{\delta : \mathcal{M} \text{ is tightly } (\epsilon, \delta(x))\text{-ADP for } x \in D_{\mathcal{X}}\} \tag{15}$$

Therefore, we impose the worst tight ADP guarantee on $\mathcal{M}$ over all the original messages with ϵ and $\hat{\delta}$, implying that $\mathcal{M}$ now gives a $(\epsilon, \hat{\delta})$-DP guarantee by Remark 1, placing us in a position to compare the community level utilities of the shuffle and the central models of DP under the histogram query for a fixed level of privacy. In particular, we juxtapose $\mathcal{W}(\mathcal{M})$ with $\mathcal{W}(\mathfrak{N}_{\epsilon,\hat{\delta}})$, as seen in the experimental results with location data from San Francisco and Paris in Fig. 3.

References

1. Agrawal, R., Srikant, R., Thomas, D.: Privacy preserving olap. In: Proceedings of the 2005 ACM SIGMOD International Conference on Management of Data, pp. 251–262 (2005)
2. Balcer, V., Cheu, A.: Separating local & shuffled differential privacy via histograms. arXiv preprint arXiv:1911.06879 (2019)
3. Balle, B., Bell, J., Gascón, A., Nissim, K.: The privacy blanket of the shuffle model. In: Boldyreva, A., Micciancio, D. (eds.) CRYPTO 2019. LNCS, vol. 11693, pp. 638–667. Springer, Cham (2019). https://doi.org/10.1007/978-3-030-26951-7_22
4. Balle, B., Wang, Y.X.: Improving the gaussian mechanism for differential privacy: analytical calibration and optimal denoising. In: International Conference on Machine Learning, pp. 394–403. PMLR (2018)
5. Bittau, A., et al.: Prochlo: strong privacy for analytics in the crowd. In: Proceedings of the 26th Symposium on Operating Systems Principles, pp. 441–459 (2017)
6. Cheu, A.: Differential privacy in the shuffle model: a survey of separations. arXiv preprint arXiv:2107.11839 (2021)
7. Cheu, A., Smith, A., Ullman, J., Zeber, D., Zhilyaev, M.: Distributed differential privacy via shuffling. In: Ishai, Y., Rijmen, V. (eds.) EUROCRYPT 2019. LNCS, vol. 11476, pp. 375–403. Springer, Cham (2019). https://doi.org/10.1007/978-3-030-17653-2_13
8. Duchi, J.C., Jordan, M.I., Wainwright, M.J.: Local privacy and statistical minimax rates. In: 2013 IEEE 54th Annual Symposium on Foundations of Computer Science, pp. 429–438. IEEE (2013)
9. Dwork, C., McSherry, F., Nissim, K., Smith, A.: Calibrating noise to sensitivity in private data analysis. In: Halevi, S., Rabin, T. (eds.) TCC 2006. LNCS, vol. 3876, pp. 265–284. Springer, Heidelberg (2006). https://doi.org/10.1007/11681878_14
10. Erlingsson, Ú., Feldman, V., Mironov, I., Raghunathan, A., Talwar, K., Thakurta, A.: Amplification by shuffling: From local to central differential privacy via anonymity. In: Proceedings of the Thirtieth Annual ACM-SIAM Symposium on Discrete Algorithms, pp. 2468–2479. SIAM (2019)
11. Feldman, V., McMillan, A., Talwar, K.: Hiding among the clones: A simple and nearly optimal analysis of privacy amplification by shuffling. arXiv preprint arXiv:2012.12803 (2020)

12. The gowalla dataset. [online]. https://snap.stanford.edu/data/loc-gowalla.html (2011), (Accessed 10 Aug 2021)
13. Kairouz, P., Bonawitz, K., Ramage, D.: Discrete distribution estimation under local privacy. In: International Conference on Machine Learning, pp. 2436–2444. PMLR (2016)
14. Koskela, A., Heikkilä, M.A., Honkela, A.: Tight accounting in the shuffle model of differential privacy. arXiv preprint arXiv:2106.00477 (2021)
15. Sommer, D.M., Meiser, S., Mohammadi, E.: Privacy loss classes: the central limit theorem in differential privacy. Proc. Priv. Enhancing Technol. **2019**(2), 245–269 (2019)

Author Index

M. Mosbah et al. (Eds.): FPS 2023, LNCS 14551, pp. 459–460, 2024.
https://doi.org/10.1007/978-3-031-57537-2

Printed in the United States
by Baker & Taylor Publisher Services

Printed in the United States
by Baker & Taylor Publisher Services